Examining Lister

Research and practice in assessing second language listening

For a complete list of titles please visit: http://www.cambridge.org/elt/silt

Also in this series:

Experimenting with Uncertainty: Essays in honour of Alan Davies
Edited by C. Elder, A. Brown, E. Grove, K. Hill, N. Iwashita, T. Lumley, T. McNamara, K. O'Loughlin

An Empirical Investigation of the Componentiality of L2 Reading in English for Academic Purposes
Edited by Cyril J. Weir, Yang Huizhong, Jin Yan

The Equivalence of Direct and Semi-direct Speaking Tests
Kieran O'Loughlin

A Qualitative Approach to the Validation of Oral Language Tests
Anne Lazaraton

Continuity and Innovation: Revising the Cambridge Proficiency in English Examination 1913–2002
Edited by Cyril J. Weir and Michael Milanovic

A Modular Approach to Testing English Language Skills: The development of the Certificates in English Language Skills (CELS) examination
Roger Hawkey

Issues in Testing Business English: The revision of the Cambridge Business English Certificates
Barry O'Sullivan

European Language Testing in a Global Context: Proceedings of the ALTE Barcelona Conference, July 2001
Edited by Cyril J. Weir and Michael Milanovic

IELTS Collected Papers: Research in speaking and writing assessment
Edited by Lynda Taylor and Peter Falvey

Testing the Spoken English of Young Norwegians: A study of testing validity and the role of 'smallwords' in contributing to pupils' fluency
Angela Hasselgreen

Changing Language Teaching through Language Testing: A washback study
Liying Cheng

The Impact of High-stakes Examinations on Classroom Teaching: A case study using insights from testing and innovation theory
Dianne Wall

Assessing Academic English: Testing English proficiency 1950–1989 – the IELTS solution
Alan Davies

Impact Theory and Practice: Studies of the IELTS test and *Progetto Lingue 2000*
Roger Hawkey

IELTS Washback in Context: Preparation for academic writing in higher education
Anthony Green

Examining Writing: Research and practice in assessing second language writing
Stuart D. Shaw and Cyril J. Weir

Multilingualism and Assessment: Achieving transparency, assuring quality, sustaining diversity – Proceedings of the ALTE Berlin Conference, May 2005
Edited by Lynda Taylor and Cyril J. Weir

Examining FCE and CAE: Key issues and recurring themes in developing the First Certificate in English and Certificate in Advanced English exams
Roger Hawkey

Language Testing Matters: Investigating the wider social and educational impact of assessment – Proceedings of the ALTE Cambridge Conference, April 2008
Edited by Lynda Taylor and Cyril J. Weir

Components of L2 Reading: Linguistic and processing factors in the reading test performances of Japanese EFL Learners
Toshihiko Shiotsu

Aligning Tests with the CEFR: Reflections on using the Council of Europe's draft Manual
Edited by Waldemar Martyniuk

Examining Reading: Research and practice in assessing second language reading
Hanan Khalifa and Cyril J. Weir

Examining Speaking: Research and practice in assessing second language speaking
Edited by Lynda Taylor

IELTS Collected Papers 2: Research in reading and listening assessment
Edited by Lynda Taylor and Cyril J. Weir

Examining Listening

Research and practice in assessing second language listening

Edited by

Ardeshir Geranpayeh

Head of Psychometrics and Data Services, Cambridge English Language
Assessment

and

Lynda Taylor

Consultant, Cambridge English Language Assessment
and
Senior Lecturer in Language Assessment, Centre for Research in English
Language Learning and Assessment (CRELLA), University of Bedfordshire

CAMBRIDGE
UNIVERSITY PRESS

CAMBRIDGE UNIVERSITY PRESS
Cambridge, New York, Melbourne, Madrid, Cape Town,
Singapore, São Paulo, Delhi, Mexico City

Cambridge University Press
The Edinburgh Building, Cambridge CB2 8RU, UK

www.cambridge.org
Information on this title: www.cambridge.org/9781107602632

First published 2013

Printed and bound in the United Kingdom by the MPG Books Group

A catalogue record for this publication is available from the British Library

Library of Congress Cataloging-in-Publication Data
Examining listening : research and practice in assessing second language listening
/ Edited by Ardeshir Geranpayeh, Head of Psychometrics and Data Services,
Cambridge English Language Assessment and Lynda Taylor, Consultant,
Cambridge English Language Assessment and Senior Lecturer in Language
Assessment, Centre for Research in English Language Learning and Assessment
(CRELLA), University of Bedfordshire.
    pages cm. -- (Studies in Language Testing; 35)
  Includes bibliographical references and index.
  ISBN 978-1-107-60263-2 (pbk.)
    1. Listening--Ability testing. 2. Listening comprehension. 3. Language and
languages--Ability testing. 4. Second language acquisition. I. Geranpayeh,
Ardeshir, editor of compilation. II. Taylor, Lynda B., editor of compilation.

PE1128.A2E93 2013
418.0028'7--dc23
2012046199

ISBN 978-1-107-60263-2

Contents

Abbreviations   vi
Series Editors' note   ix
Acknowledgements   xvii
Notes on contributors   xx

1   Introduction   1
    Lynda Taylor
2   Test taker characteristics   36
    Mark Elliott
3   Cognitive validity   77
    John Field
4   Context validity   152
    Mark Elliott and Judith Wilson
5   Scoring validity   242
    Ardeshir Geranpayeh
6   Consequential validity   273
    Roger Hawkey
7   Criterion-related validity   303
    Gad S Lim and Hanan Khalifa
8   Conclusions and recommendations   322
    Lynda Taylor and Ardeshir Geranpayeh

Appendices
Appendix A: Sample Listening tasks at five levels   342
Appendix B: Candidate Information Sheet (CIS)   393
Appendix C: Standard procedures for the production of Listening
             test materials   395
Appendix D: Administrative setting and management of
             Listening tests   402
Appendix E: Cambridge ESOL staff induction worksheet on
             the CEFR   411

References   413
Author index   441
Subject index   448

Abbreviations

ACTFL	American Council for the Teaching of Foreign Languages
ADHD	Attention Deficit Hyperactivity Disorder
AERA	American Educational Research Association
ALTE	Association of Language Testers in Europe
AOG	Assessment and Operations Group
APA	American Psychological Association
AUA	Assessment Use Argument
AWL	Academic Word List
BBC	British Broadcasting Corporation
BEC	Business English Certificates
BNC	British National Corpus
BSL	British Sign Language
BULATS	Business Language Testing Service
CAE	Certificate in Advanced English (Cambridge English: Advanced)
CAT	Computer Adaptive Testing
CB	Computer Based
CBT	Computer Based Testing
CEFR	Common European Framework of Reference for languages
CELS	Certificates in English Language Skills
CELTA	Certificate in English Language Teaching to Adults
CIC	Cambridge International Corpus
CIS	Candidate Information Sheet
CLC	Cambridge Learner Corpus
CLIL	Content and Language Integrated Learning
CoE	Council of Europe
CPE	Certificate of Proficiency in English (Cambridge English: Proficiency)
CRELLA	Centre for Research in English Language Learning and Assessment
CSEM	Conditional Standard Error of Measurement
CTT	Classical Test Theory
CUP	Cambridge University Press
Delta	Diploma in teaching English to speakers of other languages
DIF	Differential Item Functioning
DSI	Designated Subgroup of Interest

EALTA	European Association of Language Testing and Assessment
EAP	English for Academic Purposes
EAQUALS	Evaluation and Accreditation of Quality in Language Services
ECD	Evidence-Centered Design
EFL	English as a Foreign Language
EIL	English as an International Language
ELF	English as a Lingua Franca
ELL	English Language Learner
ELT	English Language Teaching
ESL	English as a Second Language
ESOL	English for Speakers of Other Languages
ESP	English for Special Purposes
ETS	Educational Testing Service
EVP	English Vocabulary Profile
FACETS	Multi-faceted Rasch Measurement analysis program
FCE	First Certificate in English (Cambridge English: First)
FCEfS	First Certificate in English for Schools (Cambridge English: First for Schools)
GMYL	General Marking and Young Learners
iBTOEFL	Internet Based Test of English as a Foreign Language
ICFE	International Certificate in Financial English
IDP	International Development Program
IELTS	International English Language Testing System
IIS	IELTS Impact Study
ILEC	International Legal English Certificate
ILR	Interagency Language Roundtable
ILTA	International Language Testing Association
IRR	Inter Rater Reliability
IRT	Item Response Theory
ISO	International Standards Organisation
IU	Idea Unit
IWG	Item Writer Guidelines
JCQ	Joint Council for Qualifications
JLTA	Japan Language Testing Association
KET	Key English Test (Cambridge English: Key)
L1	First Language
L2	Second Language
LCE	Lower Certificate in English
LIBS	Local Item Banking System
LMS	Lower Main Suite (i.e. KET and PET)
LSP	Language for Specific Purposes
MCQ	Multiple Choice Question
MLP	Modified Large Print

MM	Multiple Matching
MS	Main Suite
NCLB	No Child Left Behind Act
NCME	National Council on Measurement in Education
OMR	Optical Mark Reader
PA	Public Address (system)
PB	Paper Based
PBT	Paper Based Testing
PDF	Portable Document File
PET	Preliminary English Test (Cambridge English: Preliminary)
PL2000	Progetto Lingue 2000
QPP	Question Paper Production
R&V	Research and Validation
RLK	Reading and Language Knowledge Test
RNIB	Royal National Institute for Blind People
RNID	Royal National Institute for Deaf People
RP	Received Pronunciation
SD	Standard Deviation
SEM	Standard Error of Measurement
SEM	Structural Equation Modelling
SFL	Systemic Functional Linguistics
SiLT	Studies in Language Testing
SLA	Second Language Acquisition
SR	Special Requirements
SVO	Subject-Verb-Object
TESOL	Teaching English to Speakers of Other Languages
TKT	Teaching Knowledge Test
TL	Target Language
TLU	Target Language Use
TOEFL	Test of English as a Foreign Language
TTCs	Test Taker Characteristics
UCLES	University of Cambridge Local Examinations Syndicate
UMS	Upper Main Suite (i.e. FCE, CAE and CPE)
VI	Visually Impaired
VPA	Verbal Protocol Analysis
VRIP	Validity, Reliability, Impact, Practicality
VRIPQ	Validity, Reliability, Impact, Practicality and Quality
WIDA	World-Class Instructional Design and Assessment
WM	Working Memory
XHTML	Extensible HyperText Markup Language
YLE	Young Learners English Tests

Series Editors' note

In the final chapter of *Studies in Language Testing* (SiLT) volume 15 (Weir and Milanovic (Eds) 2003), which focused on the CPE 2002 revision, the authors emphasised the need for Cambridge ESOL to continue to keep abreast of and initiate research into the cognitive processes, strategies and performance conditions involved in the four macro-skills tested by its English language examinations. This was to be one of the core aims of the 'constructs' volumes in the SiLT series, the idea for which was already being discussed by the editorial team back in 2002.

Examining Listening is the fourth volume in the SiLT series to directly address the approach used by Cambridge ESOL in its assessment of the four main language skills, the first being SiLT 26, *Examining Writing* by Shaw and Weir (2007), the second SiLT 29, *Examining Reading* by Khalifa and Weir (2009), and the third SiLT 30, *Examining Speaking* edited by Taylor (2011). *Examining Listening* completes the set of 'construct' volumes on the four macro-skills; together these four volumes constitute a significant endeavour in academic and publishing terms, representing more than 10 years of dedicated work among academics and practitioners working in the field of language test validation with and within Cambridge ESOL.

The extensive authorial collaboration between academics at Cambridge ESOL and the University of Bedfordshire which brought these volumes into being was facilitated by the strong endorsement and support of Dr Michael Milanovic as Chief Executive of Cambridge ESOL and Dr Nick Saville, the Director of Research and Validation; this innovative initiative has resulted in a tangible and permanent resource which could have immediate and lasting value for both the academic language testing community worldwide and the world of commercial language testing at the local, national, regional and international level.

The volumes are testimony to the academic rigour, experience, scholarship, and enormous expertise that resides within Cambridge ESOL and among its external consultants, as well as to the organisation's continuing commitment generating validity evidence on how language constructs are measured by their language examinations.

They represent a significant contribution in the field to our theoretical understanding of the nature of the language abilities we are seeking to measure and to the practical approaches that test providers can adopt to achieve that goal with integrity, building a systematic, transparent and defensible body of validity argumentation in the process. Similar to the Educational Testing Service's efforts in the late 1990s to develop the TOEFL 2000 Framework documents, the significant impact of these construct volumes on a wide variety of fronts should not be underestimated.

The perceived benefits of a clearly articulated theoretical and practical position for assessing listening/writing/reading/speaking skills in the context of the Cambridge ESOL examinations are essentially twofold:

- Within Cambridge ESOL – this articulated position deepens understanding of the current theoretical basis upon which Cambridge ESOL assesses different levels of language proficiency across its range of products, and informs current and future test development projects in the light of this analysis. It thereby enhances the development of equivalent test forms and tasks.

- Beyond Cambridge ESOL – it communicates in the public domain the theoretical basis for the tests and provides a more transparent rationale for the way in which Cambridge ESOL operationalises this in its tests. In addition, it provides a suitable framework for others interested in validating their own examinations, offering a principled basis and a practical methodology for comparing language examinations across the proficiency range. It therefore adds to the range of frameworks and models now available to test developers for analysing and describing the qualities of their tests and for guiding their research and validation activity.

Examining Listening sets out to describe and evaluate how Cambridge ESOL tests different levels of listening ability in English as a second language, across the range of examinations it offers covering the Reference Levels of the CEFR from A2 to C2, principally through a careful analysis of the five examinations in the Cambridge ESOL Main Suite (KET, PET, FCE, CAE, CPE). As with the earlier *Examining Writing, Examining Reading* and *Examining Speaking* volumes, this is achieved by presenting an explicit framework that structures the approach to validation according to a number of dimensions or parameters. This volume utilises the same theoretical framework which was originally proposed by Weir (2005a) and which seeks to take account of both the aspects of cognition, related to the mental processes the individual needs to engage in order to address a task, and the features of language use in context that affect the ways in which a task is addressed. The authors also look at the practical assessment issues related to the marking and scoring of listening tests. Like its companion volumes therefore, *Examining Listening* explores the triangular relationship between three critical internal dimensions of language testing tasks – the test takers' *cognitive abilities*, the *context* in which the task is performed and the *scoring process*. Set alongside these are the twin external dimensions of consequential validity and criterion-related validity.

Cambridge ESOL has been involved in the assessment of listening skills ever since it launched its first English language examination in 1913, albeit initially receptively through an integrative dictation test and interactionally in the conversation part of the oral test. Since that time we have seen a significant development in our understanding of the listening construct, from its early conceptualisation as an integrated skill (assessed by dictation and conversation) through to the approaches focusing more specifically on the listening construct from the 1970s. In 1970, a Listening comprehension test was introduced to LCE, and then to CPE, after which it spread to other UCLES EFL examinations that were launched throughout the 1980s and 1990s. They all consisted of non-interactive, or rather non-participatory, Listening tasks where candidates were required to listen and respond to written questions instead of answering orally or participating in a conversation.

Ever since the MCQ Listening comprehension test was introduced to LCE in 1970 and to other examinations from 1975 onwards, measurement of the listening construct has experienced a steady evolution. From literary passages read out loud in the examinations, requiring not much more than comprehension of factual detail and utterance-level processing, through to the more communicatively oriented tests from 1984 onwards, the measurement of listening has steadily developed. Context and cognitive validity have improved, with tasks becoming more situationally and interactionally authentic.

When the CPE was introduced in 1913, listening in the form of dictation was part of the separate oral paper. The history of CPE, including its most recent revision, is well documented in SiLT volume 15, *Continuity and Innovation: Revising the Cambridge Proficiency in English Examination 1913–2002* (Weir and Milanovic (Eds) 2003). The volume explains how the approach to the original design of CPE in 1913 related closely to *The Practical Study of Languages* (Sweet 1899) and how candidates spent over 12 hours on a demanding set of activities that included translation to and from English, an essay on a topic such as Elizabethan travel and discovery, an English literature paper, English phonetics, dictation, reading aloud and conversation. Reading aloud, dictation and conversation formed a separate oral paper in the 1913 examination and there was an additional written paper in phonetics.

Figure 1 1913 CPE examination

(i) Written:	(a)	Translation from English into French or German 2 hours
	(b)	Translation from French or German into English, and questions on English Grammar 2 ½ hours
	(c)	English Essay 2 hours
	(d)	English Literature (The paper on English Language and Literature [Group A, Subject 1] in the Higher Local Examination) 3 hours
	(e)	English Phonetics 1 ½ hours
(ii) Oral:		Dictation ½ hour
		Reading and Conversation ½ hour

A century ago, therefore, language learners wishing to certificate their command of English as a foreign or second language faced 'an extremely demanding test of their abilities' (Weir 2003:2), in which the testing of aural as well as oral language ability, both directly and indirectly, was integral to assessing their overall English language proficiency.

Since 1913, most new Cambridge ESOL examinations have followed the model originally set by CPE and they have included an oral paper as an integral component of the language test battery, alongside tests of reading, writing, grammar and vocabulary; and later, in the 1970s, listening was to be tested in its own right. (For more details see accounts of other Cambridge tests in Hawkey 2004, 2009, and O'Sullivan 2006).

The work of the Council of Europe in its Modern Languages programme, the emergence of the Threshold level, and the rise of the communicative language teaching movement all occurred in the 1970s and 1980s and impacted on the Cambridge approach to language testing. The 1975 revisions saw CPE taking a shape that in its broad outline is familiar to the candidate of today. The Listening and Speaking tests in particular represented major developments on the 1966 revision and echoed the burgeoning interest in communicative language teaching in the 1970s. This era saw a change from teaching language as a system to teaching it as a means of communication, as detailed in Widdowson's *Teaching Language as Communication* (1978).

In addition, an important study carried out in the late 1980s at Cambridge was to have a powerful influence on the shape of things to come. Bachman, Davidson, Ryan and Choi (1995) conducted a Cambridge-sponsored study entitled *An Investigation into the Comparability of Two Tests of English as a Foreign Language* (published in SiLT volume 1). While ostensibly looking at the comparison between FCE and TOEFL in order to establish an empirical link between the level systems of each examination, this study actually ended up providing an in-depth critique of the Cambridge approach with specific reference to the then well developed and documented psychometrically oriented approach as instantiated by the TOEFL. Significant issues in relation to reliability and validity emerged from the comparability study, which were addressed vigorously with the 1996 release of the FCE and subsequent release of CPE in 2002.

Bachman et al's study (1995) helped to drive a much sharper focus on test construct definition and validation. Where test construct had had to be pieced together *post hoc* from test specifications in earlier versions of FCE and CPE, explicit statements on test construct now appeared. Measures were put in place not only to develop test content with systematic reference to an underlying construct but also to validate the nature of that construct. Additionally the resulting work on standardising the test format was of major importance and instrumental in improving the reliability of the tests across the Main Suite.

More recently, we have also seen the emergence of the *Common European Framework of Reference for Languages: Learning, Teaching and Assessment* (Council of Europe 2001), which encourages examination providers to map their certification to the Framework. This volume examines how Cambridge has approached this task in significant depth when exploring criterion-related validity. The approach taken by Cambridge seeks not only to establish the relationship with the Framework as a one-off study, but to deploy a methodology that ensures a long-term and continually verifiable relationship which is surely in the overall best interests of test users.

Skills assessment at Cambridge is now underpinned more formally than ever by a validation framework which builds on the work of Canale and Swain (1980), Bachman (1990) and more recently Weir (2005a), amongst others. This is in addition to the validity, reliability, impact and practicality approach developed by Cambridge in the early 1990s, which evolved to include the feature of quality and became known as the VRIPQ approach. (This is outlined in the organisation's *Principles of Good Practice: Quality Management and Validation in Language Assessment*, first published in 2010 and regularly revised, most recently in January 2013.) The approach outlined in this volume not only allows Cambridge ESOL to determine where current examinations are performing satisfactorily in relation to a range of relevant validity parameters, but also provides the basis for a programme of quality assurance, continuous improvement and for the construction of an ongoing research agenda. It provides an important benchmark against which test developers can evaluate the effectiveness of their respective approaches and it offers test users a model of what to expect from responsible examination providers.

The structure of the volume

Examining Listening follows a similar structure to that which was success-fully adopted for its sister publications, *Examining Writing* (Shaw and Weir 2007), *Examining Reading* (Khalifa and Weir 2009) and *Examining Speaking* (Taylor (Ed) 2011). The outline shape closely follows their organisation with separate chapters on *test taker characteristics; cognitive validity; context validity; scoring validity; consequential validity;* and *criterion-related validity*. Apart from the opening and closing chapters, each of the other six chapters takes one component of the socio-cognitive validation framework to examine it in detail with reference to the Cambridge ESOL Listening tests, i.e. discussion of issues arising in the *research* literature on each component part is followed by consideration of Cambridge ESOL *practice* in the area.

Examining Listening is an edited collection of chapters from a team of contributors. All the chapter authors are acknowledged specialists in language teaching, learning and assessment, many in the specific field of listening testing and assessment. In addition, they have direct experience of working with the Cambridge Listening tests from a number of differ-ent perspectives (test design and development, test writing and adminis-tration, exam preparation and materials development, oral examining, test validation and research). As a result, they are able to combine their extensive theoretical knowledge with practical application and expertise in these areas, and so provide valuable insights into the complex endeavour or ecology that constitutes the assessment of listening proficiency. In doing this they draw on input from other informants as explained in the opening chapter.

Chapter 1, by Lynda Taylor, offers an introduction that sets the scene for what follows in the rest of the volume. It explicates the audience for the volume, its intended purpose and the ground that will be covered. It also details a short historical perspective on the tradition of assessing listening at Cambridge. The methodological appropriacy in the volume is explained and the multiple voices appearing in the volume are discussed.

In Chapter 2 on *test taker characteristics*, Mark Elliott discusses the test taker, who stands at the heart of any assessment event. He reviews the general research literature in this area and reports on research undertaken into Cambridge ESOL tests to demonstrate how the tests take account of key test taker characteristics. This covers not only general features of the candi-dature cohort that need to be reflected in tests at different proficiency levels (e.g. age), but also the ways in which test taker characteristics arising from special needs or disabilities on the part of individual candidates are catered for through test accommodations or modifications.

Chapter 3 on *cognitive validity*, by John Field, reviews what the theo-retical and empirical research to date tells us about the nature of listening, particularly the cognitive processing involved, both in a first and second language. He examines the processing involved in the Cambridge ESOL Listening test tasks across different proficiency levels and evaluates the extent to which this can be claimed to replicate or reflect 'real-world' processing when listening in the world beyond the test.

In Chapter 4, Mark Elliott and Judith Wilson examine in detail the many *context validity* parameters, or contextual variables, that have been recognised in the research literature to impact on listening performance in terms of their cognitive load. They go on to analyse the contextual variables that characterise content and tasks used in the Cambridge Listening tests in order to understand how these are differentiated across proficiency levels. Aspects of the physical conditions surrounding the delivery of the Listening tests are considered in Appendix D on *Administrative setting and management of the Listening tests*.

Chapter 5, by Ardeshir Geranpayeh, focuses on *scoring validity*, exploring the many factors associated with the reliable and valid scoring of listening tests, including the use of item analysis in test construction and evaluation, and the importance of meaningful score reporting and interpretation. The available research literature in these areas is reviewed, and some of the research undertaken by Cambridge ESOL over the past 20 years is highlighted. The policy and procedures which have emerged as a result of this ongoing research and validation programme in relation to undertaking large-scale standardised listening assessment are presented (see also Appendix C which describes *Standard procedures for the production of Listening test material*).

Chapter 6, by Roger Hawkey, considers the *consequential validity* of listening tests, exploring issues of test washback and impact to establish where and how these play out within the complex process of validating high-stakes international examinations. He surveys Cambridge ESOL's research initiatives and studies undertaken designed to help the institution understand the consequential validity of its exams, especially as it relates to testing listening ability.

Chapter 7, by Gad S Lim and Hanan Khalifa, examines issues of *criterion-related validity*, in particular the need to establish comparability across different tests and between different forms of the same test, as well as with external standards and reference frameworks. They describe and discuss how Cambridge ESOL has addressed this for its own tests, and how the board has linked, or maintained a pre-existing link, between its examinations and the reference levels of external internationally accepted frameworks such as the CEFR and the ALTE frameworks.

Finally, in Chapter 8 Lynda Taylor and Ardeshir Geranpayeh draw together the threads of the volume, summarising the findings from applying the validity framework to a set of Cambridge Listening tests. They reflect upon how far the tests in their current incarnation operationalise contemporary thinking, research evidence about the listening ability construct, and consider where refinements might be appropriate in future revision projects. They also make recommendations for further research and development which would benefit not only Cambridge ESOL but also the wider testing community.

Michael Milanovic
Cyril J Weir
Cambridge – August 2012

Acknowledgements

This book is the fourth in a series of academic volumes published at two-yearly intervals since 2007 and focusing on the testing of the four main language skills. *Examining Listening* finally joins its sister publications on the bookshelf – *Examining Writing*, *Examining Reading* and *Examining Speaking* – thus completing the set and representing more than 10 years of dedicated work among academics and practitioners working in the field of language assessment.

As was true for its older siblings, there exists a long list of friends and colleagues to whom we are indebted for their contribution in bringing this fourth volume to publication. At the top of the list must be the individual chapter contributors and our co-authors: Mark Elliott, John Field, Roger Hawkey, Hanan Khalifa, Gad S Lim and Judith Wilson. Without their professional expertise, clarity of expression and sheer perseverance this volume could never have made it into print.

Special thanks must go to Dr Gary Buck (President, Lidget Green, Inc.) and Dr John Field (Senior Lecturer at CRELLA, University of Bedfordshire), both of whom are acknowledged experts in listening having successfully published their own contributions on the teaching and assessment of listening ability. They kindly agreed to serve as external readers and reviewers once the complete manuscript had been assembled. Their insightful comments and constructive criticism enabled us to revise and refine the final version before it went into production. Thus their expertise, sound advice and collaboration have contributed significantly to the quality of this volume.

We are also extremely grateful to the large number of people from both academic and practitioner communities within and beyond Cambridge ESOL who provided valuable input to or feedback on the individual chapters. Colleagues in AOG provided input to the overview tables in Chapter 1: Andrew Balch, Rod Boroughs and Hugh Moss (Assessment Group Managers), Terence Bradley and Bronagh Rolph (Senior Assessment Managers). For Chapter 2, Laurence Calver (Research and Validation Analyst, R&V) provided the CIS data; Amanda Chisholm and Kate Ingham (Senior Assessment Managers, AOG) supplied input for text selection, while Anthony King (Senior Assessment Manager, AOG) provided guidelines for text selection for the for Schools candidates; Trevor Forster (Operations Administrator, AOG) provided data on special requirements entries and

Mike Gutteridge (Cambridge ESOL Special Circumstances Consultant) supplied information on Special Arrangements policy; in addition, Dr John Field provided information and insights from a cognitive perspective on aspects of Special Arrangements provision. For Chapter 3, many different AOG colleagues reviewed and provided feedback on various drafts, including Michael Abberton, Amanda Chisholm, Chris Cullen, Kate Ingham, Hugh Moss, Diane Reeve, Bronagh Rolph, Paul Wade and Ron Zeronis. In addition, Dr Katy Salisbury kindly provided access to her PhD findings on item writer practices. For Chapter 4, our sincere thanks are due to Dr Norbert Schmitt (University of Nottingham) for his analysis of lexical resources in the Listening tests and for his review of this section of the manuscript draft; Nick Kenny (Cambridge ESOL Consultant) and Dr Spiros Papageorgiou (then a Language Assessment Specialist at the University of Michigan) both provided a critical review of an early draft of the overall chapter content. Amanda Chisholm and Kate Ingham (Senior Assessment Managers, AOG) reviewed a chapter draft and provided key information; Hugh Moss and Ron Zeronis (Assessment Group Managers, AOG), Chris Hubbard (Senior Assessment Manager, AOG) and Chris Cullen (Assessment Manager, AOG) supplied sample papers for Dr Schmitt's analysis; Paul Wade (Assessment Manager, AOG) provided information and guidelines on the use of the LIBS Dictionary; Dr Szilvia Papp (Senior Research and Validation Manager, R&V) supplied comments and suggestions on aspects relating to young learners; and Dr John Field provided information and insights relating to speech rate. For Chapter 5, Dr Neil Jones (Assistant Director, R&V) contributed to forming the argument for the relationship between reliability and communicative language tests; Chris Bell (Research and Validation Analyst, R&V) provided score data for listening tests and reliability estimates (also for Chapter 7); Judith Davis (Operations Manager, GMYL) provided data and documentation concerning clerical marking procedures and accuracy. For Chapter 6, Dr Jay Banerjee (University of Michigan) provided feedback on an early draft and Dr Evelina Galaczi (Principal Research and Validation Manager, R&V) informed discussion of the status of the socio-cognitive framework. In Chapter 8, Dr Andrew Somers (Principal Research and Validation Manager, R&V) contributed to the proposal on future score reporting. Finally, thanks must go to Amanda Chisholm who checked Appendix C on organisational policy and procedures and to Claire McCauley (Centre Quality Assurance Manager, Customer Services) who did the same for Appendix D, as well as to Mark Elliott who reviewed and co-ordinated feedback on both these appendices. This volume could not have been completed without the co-operation of all those mentioned above. Their expertise and the time they have given from their busy schedules are greatly appreciated.

As ever, Professor Cyril Weir (University of Bedfordshire) maintained a

close involvement in the development of the entire volume, carefully reviewing each draft chapter in turn and offering constructive criticism. As one
of the Series Editors for SiLT and as co-author of *Examining Writing* and
Examining Reading, his editorial guidance and advisory feedback have been
invaluable and a constant source of encouragement at every stage. We also
acknowledge the support and encouragement of Dr Michael Milanovic
(Cambridge ESOL Chief Executive and lead Series Editor for SiLT). It is his
vision which made the publication of this and of the other construct-focused
volumes in the SiLT series a reality, and his willingness to support future
research into issues raised in this volume makes this publication especially
worthwhile.

To all of the above, and to any others we have failed to mention, we extend
our sincere thanks and appreciation.

Ardeshir Geranpayeh and Lynda Taylor
August 2012

Notes on contributors

Mark Elliott is a Research and Validation Manager at Cambridge English Language Assessment. He holds an MA in Mathematics from the University of Cambridge (UK) and an MA in ELT and Applied Linguistics from King's College London (UK). He is responsible for providing validation, data analysis and research support for a range of Cambridge examinations and for conducting research related to the assessment of listening. Mark previously worked as an Assessment Manager at Cambridge English Language Assessment, and has extensive EFL experience as an English teacher, teacher trainer, director of studies, examiner and materials developer in the Czech Republic, the UK and China.

John Field is Senior Lecturer in cognitive approaches to language learning at the Centre for Research in English Language Learning and Assessment (CRELLA) at the University of Bedfordshire, UK. He also teaches at the Faculty of Education, Cambridge University. His main area of expertise is second language listening, on which he has researched and written widely. His recent book *Listening in the Language Classroom* (2009a) won the Ben Warren Prize for its contribution to the field. He has a background in psycholinguistics, which he taught for several years at undergraduate and postgraduate level. He has written a reference book on the subject and is currently engaged in projects that apply psycholinguistic principles to the notion of cognitive validity in language testing. Before becoming an academic, he worked in many parts of the world as an ELT advisor, materials writer, curriculum designer and teacher trainer.

Ardeshir Geranpayeh is the Head of Psychometrics and Data Services at the Research and Validation Group, Cambridge English Language Assessment. He leads a large team of research managers and analysts who carry out the statistical analysis of Cambridge English exams, run the computer-based testing engines and develop the associated IT systems. He holds a PhD in Applied Linguistics from the University of Edinburgh on the comparability of language proficiency testing. He has 22 years' experience of test validation and has contributed to the design, development, validation, revision and evaluation of many internationally recognised language proficiency tests. He is a regular presenter and workshop leader in several international conferences such as: *National Council on Measurement in Education, Association of Test Publishers, Language Testing Research Colloquium, Language Testing*

Forum and *International Test Commission*, and has published extensively on language proficiency testing.

Roger Hawkey has many years of experience in English language teaching, teacher education, course design, and assessment projects in Africa, Asia and Europe. He is now a consultant on language assessment with Cambridge English Language Assessment, with particular reference to the impact of high-stakes tests. He is also a Visiting Professor at the Centre for Research in English Language Learning and Assessment (CRELLA) at the University of Bedfordshire (UK). Roger Hawkey has published widely in applied linguistics, language teaching and assessment, including three volumes in Cambridge's *Studies in Language Testing* series – *A Modular Approach to Testing English Language Skills* (2004), *Impact Theory and Practice* (2006) and *Examining FCE and CAE* (2009).

Hanan Khalifa, PhD, is Head of Research and International Development at the Research and Validation Group, Cambridge English Language Assessment. She leads a team of research experts on language testing validation issues, assessing K-12, CEFR matters and impact assessment. She has extensive assessment and evaluation experience working with universities, ministries of education and international development and donor agencies in the Middle East and North Africa region. Her expertise lies in the fields of assessing reading, educational evaluation, strategic planning, and issues related to the CEFR and impact assessment. She has led educational reform projects, built institutional capacity in the area of educational assessment and conducted numerous programme evaluation and impact studies. Hanan's 2009 published work was a runner-up for the prestigious Sage/ILTA Award for Best Book on Language Testing and is used as course material for the Association of Language Testers in Europe (ALTE) professional development programmes and on certain MA/MPhil for Master's programmes in UK universities.

Gad S Lim is Senior Research and Validation Manager at the Research and Validation Group, Cambridge English Language Assessment, where he leads research on the assessment of writing and on IELTS. Before joining Cambridge ESOL, he worked for the University of Michigan English Language Institute, where he conducted test-related research and managed the development of speaking tests. He has taught in higher education and trained language teachers in Asia, North America, and Europe. He has also published numerous refereed articles and chapters. His research interests at present focus on raters and rating scales in language performance assessments.

Lynda Taylor is a Consultant to Cambridge English Language Assessment and formerly Assistant Director of their Research and Validation Group. She holds an MPhil and PhD in Applied Linguistics and Language Assessment from the University of Cambridge (UK). She has over 25 years' experience of the theoretical and practical issues involved in L2 testing and assessment and has provided expert assistance for test development projects worldwide. She regularly teaches, writes and presents on language testing matters and has edited and contributed to several of the volumes in Cambridge ESOL's *Studies in Language Testing* series, including *IELTS Collected Papers 1* and *2* (2007, 2012), *Multilingualism and Assessment* (2008), *Language Testing Matters* (2009), *Aligning Tests with the CEFR* (2010) and *Examining Speaking* (2011). She is also a part-time Senior Lecturer at the Centre for Research in English Language Learning and Assessment (CRELLA) at the University of Bedfordshire (UK).

Judith Wilson has worked extensively over many years as a teacher, ESP lecturer and teacher trainer in schools and universities in England, Europe, Africa and the Middle East. She is an experienced item writer for a wide variety of Cambridge ESOL exams, particularly in the area of Listening, and chairs various teams of item writers. She has written textbooks and other materials for several Cambridge ESOL examinations including FCE, CPE and IELTS.

1 Introduction

Lynda Taylor
Consultant to Cambridge English Language Assessment

The context for the volume

Examining Listening stands as the fourth in a series of volumes designed to explore the ability constructs underpinning the testing and assessment of English language skills. The specific focus in this volume is on the testing of second language listening ability. The title is a companion to three earlier construct-focused volumes in the *Studies in Language Testing* series: *Examining Writing* by Shaw and Weir (2007), *Examining Reading* by Khalifa and Weir (2009), and *Examining Speaking* edited by Taylor (2011). Publication of this latest volume on listening completes the set of four volumes focusing on the four skills as they have been traditionally conceptualised and operationalised by the language testing and assessment community over many years.

This fourfold categorisation of language proficiency (i.e. according to the skills of reading, writing, listening and speaking) has been adopted as the organising principle behind the four-volume series because it continues to occupy a central role in the activities of examination boards and other language test providers. However, some consideration is given to integrated skills testing, for example, reading into writing in summary tasks in the reading volume, and reading as input into writing tasks in the writing volume. Some descriptive frameworks choose to compartmentalise overall language proficiency according to dimensions or skill-sets other than the traditional quartet, e.g. enabling knowledge (such as lexis and grammar), or they focus instead on integrated skills (Listening and Speaking, Reading into Writing). Interestingly, the *Common European Framework of Reference for Languages: Learning, teaching, assessment* (Council of Europe 2001) proposes several different ways of categorising language proficiency: one approach sub-divides overall proficiency into Speaking/Writing/Understanding (with Understanding being used to cover both Reading and Listening); an alternative approach conceptualises language proficiency according to Receptive/Productive/Interactive dimensions (in this case Speaking can be either Productive or Interactive); and a third approach adds a further dimension of Mediation. In light of this, the four volumes, each with their dominant focus on a single language skill, are not intended to offer the definitive or final word on approaches to describing language proficiency for the purposes of assessment. As the language testing profession continues to reconceptualise and expand its understanding of the complex interaction of the skills that make up language proficiency, it is always possible that additional construct-oriented volumes will be added to the *Studies in Language Testing* series in the future.

Given its function as part of a coherent set of skills-focused volumes, *Examining Listening* not surprisingly covers some of the ground already mapped out by its predecessors, *Examining Writing, Examining Reading* and *Examining Speaking*. A strong family resemblance will be discernible between the volumes, in terms of both format and approach. The theoretical framework for validating language examinations first outlined in Weir (2005a) remains the springboard for reflecting upon our understanding and conceptualisation of the listening ability construct for assessment purposes. The Cambridge ESOL examinations are once again taken as the practical context for undertaking a critical evaluation of listening tests ranging across different proficiency levels, enabling us to examine how the theoretical framework for validation can be operationalised in practice and with what outcomes. As in previous volumes, each chapter closely scrutinises Cambridge practice in terms of the particular component of the framework under review. Although each volume replicates the approach of its predecessors to some degree, it also seeks to build upon and extend the earlier work reported in the series, bringing fresh and novel insights into the process of construct definition and operationalisation for the particular skill of interest. It thus allows Weir's original (2005a) theoretical framework to be continually developed and refined in light of the ongoing experience of applying it in practice. It also has an obvious synergy with the volume by Weir, Vidaković and Galaczi (forthcoming 2013) which traces the prevailing conceptualisations of language constructs in language assessment over more than century, particularly as these have been operationalised through the Cambridge English language examinations.

It is only appropriate at this point to acknowledge the existence of other important frameworks and models that are available to language testers and examination boards. These include Evidence-Centered Design (ECD) as proposed by Mislevy, Steinberg and Almond (2002, 2003; see also Mislevy, Almond and Lukas 2003), and Assessment Use Argument (AUA), as set out by Bachman (2005) and Bachman and Palmer (2010). Other test providers have found these to be accessible and fruitful ways of guiding their practical test design and validation, as demonstrated by Chapelle, Enwright and Jamieson (2008). However, Cambridge ESOL has found the socio-cognitive framework, first offered in Weir (2005a) and subsequently refined through the experience of applying it to operational tests, to match well with the kinds of tests the examination board produces, addressing the validation questions that arise and providing at least some of the answers that are needed. The framework has proved to be both theoretically sound and practically useful over a number of years in relation to a variety of different examinations produced by Cambridge ESOL, and for this reason it is adopted as the framework for description and analysis in this and in the companion volumes.

The intended audience for the volume

The intended audience for the volume is primarily the constituency of professional language testers who are directly involved in the practical assessment of second language listening ability. This growing constituency around the world typically includes staff working for examination boards and testing agencies at regional, national and international level, as well as those working within education ministries whose remit is to advise on the development of assessment policy or the implementation of examination reform programmes. In an age where public institutions such as examination boards and related organisations are increasingly called to account for how and why they design and administer their tests in the way they do, issues of openness and transparency are of growing importance. The approach outlined and exemplified in this volume offers one way of placing in the public domain the rationale and evidence in support of the testing policy and practice of one large and influential testing organisation. The sharing of one examination board's expertise and experience in this way will hopefully encourage and enable other institutions and test providers to review and reflect upon their own testing theory and practice, and thus engage in a similar exercise in public accountability for their own assessment products.

The volume is also directly relevant to the academic language testing and assessment community, i.e. researchers, lecturers and graduate students, especially those with a specific interest in assessing (second language) L2 listening ability. While the overview of the theoretical and empirical research should be of obvious and immediate value to them, members of this community will hopefully find the detailed description and discussion of operational language testing practices just as useful. The complex practical constraints facing an examination board can sometimes mean that experimental research findings are not immediately or readily applicable to large-scale testing activities. Operational testing, as opposed to language testing research, often has to concern itself with far more than just the issues of construct definition and operationalisation, assessment criteria and rating scale development. Large-scale commercial tests conducted on an industrial scale, such as those offered by Cambridge ESOL and similar agencies, are usually located within a complex ecology comprising multiple, interacting factors, many of which are simply not present or relevant in more academically oriented language testing research endeavours. Such factors include sustainability issues to do with test production, delivery and processing systems; practical issues concerning test timing, security, cost, accessibility; organisational issues relating to personnel (e.g. developing and sustaining the rater cadre) or management (e.g. the revision of an existing test or development of its replacement). Hopefully, the explication of theory *and* practice presented in this volume will lead to a broader and deeper understanding of the issues and will serve to strengthen the relationship between the academic and practitioner communities.

There will undoubtedly be other readers for whom certain sections, if not the whole of this volume, will be of direct interest and relevance, perhaps because they are involved in teaching and assessing L2 listening ability, or because they are preparing learners to take one or more of the Cambridge ESOL examinations. Listening is, of all the skills, the one where the methods used in teaching tend to correspond most closely to those used in testing. Any investigation into testing methods must therefore be of value to materials writers and classroom teachers, who themselves have to find ways of designing comprehension questions that are valid in representing the construct and indicative of the proficiency of their students. Thus, interested readers are likely to include English language teachers, teacher trainers, curriculum developers, textbook writers and other materials developers. Although the primary focus of this volume is on the testing of English as a second language, some of the theory, principles and practice explored and explained in the volume will hopefully prove helpful to teachers and learners of other languages, especially of those less commonly taught languages for which assessment theory and testing practice are still in the early stages of development and remain relatively under-resourced.

In addition to the audiences highlighted above, this volume should be of direct interest to the vast community of English language professionals who, in one way or another, are directly involved with the Cambridge ESOL Listening tests. They include the hundreds of test materials writers who draft and edit Listening test tasks and rubrics for the multiple language proficiency levels. The Cambridge ESOL examinations could not function as successfully as they do without the expertise and dedication of this professional cadre. Indeed, the item writer community has made its own contribution to the development of this volume, as this will become clear.

Finally, in a globalised world where the testing and assessment of second, third or additional language skills are steadily moving centre stage within education and society, this volume is offered as a contribution towards the promotion of assessment literacy. Language tests, and the scores they generate, are increasingly used across contemporary society worldwide: within education, from primary age to higher education; in employment contexts, from the registration and licensing of health professionals, to health and safety issues in the catering or construction industry; and, more controversially, in migration and citizenship policy and practice around the world.

Such trends mean that there are not just more people taking language tests. Growing numbers of people are directly involved in selecting or developing tests and in using test scores for decision-making purposes. In practice, they often find themselves doing this without much background or training in assessment to equip them for this role. They include classroom teachers tasked with designing or delivering standardised tests to evaluate their pupils' progress, tests that are sometimes then used to hold teachers and schools accountable for that progress, or the apparent lack of it. A similar burden of expectation is laid on staff in university admissions, in professional registration bodies and in immigration agencies to know *what tests measure* and *what test scores mean*, and to understand how to integrate them into their complex, usually high-stakes decision-making processes. The language testing community is in a position, indeed it arguably has a moral obligation, to encourage the sharing of the core knowledge, skills and understanding that underpin good quality assessment as widely and accessibly for the benefit of all. (For a fuller discussion of the importance of assessment literacy and approaches to its development, see Taylor 2009a).

In summary, then, this volume is offered as a rich source of information for a wide variety of audiences on multiple aspects of examining L2 listening ability.

The purpose of the volume

As explained above, *Examining Listening* is one of a series of construct-oriented volumes focusing upon the four language skills of writing, reading, speaking and listening. The genesis of the series lies partly in a close collaboration that developed in the early 2000s between, on the one hand, applied linguistics and language testing specialists at Cambridge ESOL and, on the other, Professors Cyril J Weir and Barry O'Sullivan, both of whom were at that time working at the University of Roehampton, Surrey. Together they identified a shared interest in, and enthusiasm for, finding ways to explore more systematically the nature of construct validity in language testing and assessment and to bridge the gap between research and practice, between theoretical construct definition and applied construct operationalisation in relation to real-world language testing, particularly the sort of large-scale language testing undertaken by examination boards and agencies such as Cambridge. Initial discussions led to the conceptualisation of a long-term project to research and to produce a draft of a series of documents (e.g. internal position papers, research reports and published monographs) which would describe and reflect upon the theory and practice of assessment and how this is operationalised in the Cambridge ESOL examinations, with particular reference to the five proficiency levels of the General English suite of tests traditionally referred to as the Cambridge Main Suite (MS). It was envisaged this project might include publication of a set of academic volumes in the *Studies in Language Testing* series and this vision became a reality over the period 2007–13.

A major motivation for embarking on such a project was the growing expectation in the public domain, both nationally and globally, for examination boards and other test providers to be transparent and accountable in what they do, especially in terms of the standards to which they adhere, the quality and validity claims they make for their products, and the provision of theoretical and empirical evidence in support of these claims. This external, public expectation that emerged within wider society was paralleled by a growing sense within the language testing and assessment profession itself of the need to develop its own professional ethic. It is in the light of this awareness that the field of language testing and assessment has undergone a process of increasing professionalisation over recent years. A raft of quality standards, ethical codes and guidelines for good testing practice has been embraced or generated by language testers, in many cases touching upon matters that extend well beyond a test's purely technical qualities. Examples include the *Code of Fair Testing Practices in Education* (Joint Committee on Testing Practices 2004) and the AERA/APA/NCME *Standards* (1999), both of which concern assessment in general. There also exist language testing specific codes such as the ALTE *Code of Practice* (1994), the ILTA *Code of Ethics* (2000), the EALTA *Guidelines for Good Practice* (2006) and the ILTA *Guidelines for Practice* (2007). Various professional associations of language testers and testing organisations were established during the 1990s at national, regional and international level, including the Japan Language Testing Association (JLTA), the Association of Language Testers in Europe (ALTE), the International Language Testing Association (ILTA), and the European Association of Language Testing and Assessment (EALTA). Kunnan (2004, 2008) reflects on the ethical milieu that emerged for language testers, prompted by various factors in the professional field such as: demands for accountability and responsiveness to clients; increased use of language tests and types of delivery method; use of new measurement and other analytical techniques; and expanded concepts of validity (i.e. Messick 1989, 1996). Kunnan suggests the language testing community responded to these factors by developing explicit standards and codes for its community and practice, and that its professional ethic continues to evolve, informed by the wider literature in ethics and moral philosophy.

An ethic that embraces openness, transparency and accountability is essential given that examination boards and other test institutions offer assessment tools whose use has both direct and indirect consequences for education and wider society. Such consequences may be high stakes, influencing an individual's life chances, the formulation of public policy or the shaping of attitudes in society. Messick's re-conceptualisation of validity, which brought together traditional validity concerns but also added value implications and social consequences as essential facets, undoubtedly contributed to growing awareness of the consequences of testing, whether intended or unintended, whether positive or negative. This trend is clearly illustrated in the wealth of research literature published over recent years on the theory and practice of language testing washback and impact (see, among others, Alderson and Wall 1996, Cheng 2005, Cheng, Watanabe and Curtis 2004, Green 2007, Hawkey 2006, Kunnan 2000, Wall 2005, Wall and Horak 2006, 2008), as well as other publications discussing the wider role of testing in education and society (see, for example, McNamara and Roever 2006, Shohamy 2008, Spolsky 2008).

Transparency and accountability are particularly important for testing organisations that offer multiple tests targeted at different proficiency levels, different domains of language use or different groups of language users. In this context, examination providers need recourse to an explicit and appropriate methodology for describing, analysing and comparing their tests in a systematic and comprehensive manner so that test users can clearly understand the features of each testing option available to them and can decide appropriately on their selection and use.

Cambridge ESOL has never subscribed to a philosophy of 'one size fits all' where English language assessment is concerned. Over time, and in response to market demands and opportunities, the examination board has developed a wide range of assessment products that include: tests at *different proficiency levels* (e.g. KET, PET, FCE, CAE, CPE); tests involving a *multi-skills package* (IELTS) and tests which are *modular* (e.g. CELS, ESOL Skills for Life); tests across *different language domains* (e.g. General English, Academic English, Business English); tests for *adult teachers* of English (CELTA, Delta) and tests for *young learners* of English (YLE); tests in *pencil and paper mode* (Standard BULATS) and tests in *computer mode* (CB BULATS); tests for general *certificated* use and others for *institutional* use.

The development and promotion of a variety of testing instruments places an obligation upon the test producer to be able to clearly demonstrate how they are seeking to meet the demands of validity in each product and, more specifically, how they actually operationalise criterial distinctions, not only between tests offered at different *levels*, i.e. on the *vertical* proficiency continuum, but also between alternative testing *domains, formats* and *modes*, i.e. along a *horizontal* axis.

To be able to do this requires some sort of methodology for analysing and describing the component validity features of any test, as well as for constructing an interpretative framework of reference within which multiple tests and their respective validity features can be explicitly presented and co-located. The use of such a methodology has the potential to achieve two significant and beneficial outcomes for the language testing world. First, it should enable test *producers* to assemble and present, with some degree of transparency and coherence, the validation evidence and arguments in support of quality claims made for each of their tests so that these can be scrutinised and evaluated. Secondly, it should serve as a means of communication, assisting test *users* to understand better the nature of the testing tools available to them and aiding them in decisions about which test (or tests) best suit a given purpose and context of use.

Transparency and coherence are stated aims underpinning the development of the Common European Framework of Reference for languages (CEFR), originally released by the Council of Europe in draft form for consultation in 1996, and formally published in 2001 (North 2008). North also expressed the hope that the CEFR would 'establish a metalanguage common across educational sectors, national and linguistic boundaries that could be used to talk about objectives and language levels', as well as 'providing encouragement to practitioners in the language field to reflect on their current practice' (2008:22). Cambridge ESOL's construct volumes project embody similar aspirations and can thus be seen within a broader historical frame, especially, though not exclusively, within the European language education context, where there has been an increasing focus on the importance of analysing and describing language proficiency for the purposes of learning, teaching, and assessment.

The theoretical framework for validating language examinations first outlined in Weir's *Language Testing and Validation: An evidence-based approach* (2005a) offered Cambridge ESOL a potential approach and methodology for undertaking such an enterprise in relation to its own examinations. Drawing upon theoretical and empirical research in the field, it provided a useful conceptual heuristic for identifying core features in the process of improved construct definition for the tests. More importantly, perhaps, it also offered the hope that it could be proactively applied to operational tests, i.e. to the *test-in-practice* rather than just the *test-in-theory*. It was anticipated that a socio-cognitive framework for validating examinations, as expounded by Weir (2005a), would permit a systematic and comprehensive critical evaluation of construct definition *and* operationalisation, and ideally furnish explicit evidence, both theoretical and empirical, to support claims about the usefulness of the Cambridge ESOL tests. The socio-cognitive approach to test validation resonated strongly with the thinking and practice on test development and validation which had been emerging in Cambridge ESOL during the 1990s, namely the VRIP approach where the concern is with Validity (the conventional sources of validity evidence: construct, content, criterion), Reliability, Impact and Practicality. The early work of Bachman (1990) and Bachman and Palmer (1996) underpinned the adoption of the VRIP approach, as set out in Weir and Milanovic (Eds) (2003), and found in various Cambridge ESOL internal documents on validity (e.g. Milanovic and Saville 1996).

Weir's approach covers much of the same ground as the original VRIP framework but it attempts to reconfigure validity to show how its constituent parts (context, cognitive processing and scoring) might interact with each other. Listening, the construct of interest in this volume, is viewed as not just the underlying latent trait of listening ability but as the result of the constructed triangle of trait, context and score (including score interpretation). The approach adopted in this volume is therefore effectively an *interactionalist* position, which sees the listening construct as residing in the interactions between the underlying cognitive ability, the context of use and the process of scoring, as discussed by Weir (2005a). In addition, O'Sullivan (2011) notes a shift of emphasis over recent years towards the role of the individual test taker, leading to an interest in test taker characteristics, cognitive validity and contextual parameters in any assessment event.

Like its predecessors *Examining Writing, Examining Reading* and *Examining Speaking*, this volume develops a theoretical framework for validating tests, a framework which then informs an attempt to articulate and evaluate the Cambridge ESOL approach to assessing L2 listening skills. The perceived benefits of a clearly articulated theoretical and practical position for assessing listening skills in the context of the Cambridge ESOL examinations are essentially twofold:

- *Within Cambridge ESOL* – this articulated position will deepen understanding of the current theoretical basis upon which Cambridge ESOL assesses different levels of language proficiency across its range of products, and will inform current and future test development projects in the light of this analysis. It will thereby enhance the development of equivalent test forms and tasks.

- *Beyond Cambridge ESOL* – it will communicate in the public domain the theoretical basis for the tests and hopefully provide a more transparent rationale for the way in which Cambridge ESOL operationalises this in its examinations. In addition, it may provide a suitable framework for others interested in validating their own examinations, offering a principled basis and a practical methodology for comparing language examinations across the proficiency range. It therefore adds to the range of frameworks and models now available to test developers for analysing and describing the qualities of their tests and for guiding their research and validation activity.

The focus of the volume

The intention, then, in this volume is to apply a theoretical framework for validating tests of second language listening ability in order to examine, articulate and evaluate the approach to assessing L2 listening skills adopted by

Cambridge ESOL. The board's suite of examinations in General English (the Main Suite) offers a useful picture of how listening ability is measured across a broad language proficiency continuum, i.e. from beginner to advanced level. Its five levels correspond to equivalent levels of the ALTE and of the CEFR. The levels reflect the levels of language ability familiar to English language teachers around the world. They have thus been described as 'natural levels' (North 2006:8), not in the sense that they are themselves naturally occurring phenomena in either language acquisition or learning, but rather in the sense that language teachers and educators, especially in the English language teaching industry, gradually came to perceive them as *useful* curriculum and examination levels over a number of years. The relationship between Cambridge ESOL levels, ALTE levels and the CEFR levels is discussed in Chapter 7. However, for initial orientation the reader is referred to Table 1.1 for an overview of ALTE Can Do statements for Listening/ Speaking and to Tables 1.2 and 1.3 on pages 13–14 which provide CEFR A2 to C2 overall level descriptors for listening comprehension. In their development, the ALTE Can Do statements were originally organised into three general areas: Social and Tourist, Work, and Study. Each of these areas included up to three scales, for the skills of Reading, Writing and Interaction; hence in Table 1.1 Listening and Speaking are combined into a single scale for Interaction. (For more details of this project see Appendix D in Council of Europe 2001:244–257.)

In relation to Listening, or aural reception, the CEFR (Council of Europe 2001) offers several different illustrative scales for the six levels of the Framework, i.e. overall listening comprehension, understanding conversation between native speakers, listening as a member of a live audience, listening to announcements and instructions, and listening to audio media and recordings; a sixth illustrative scale is provided for audio-visual reception in which the language user simultaneously receives an auditory and a visual input, e.g. watching TV, film or other types of multimedia. To help orientate the reader to the levels, the CEFR's overall listening comprehension scale is presented in Table 1.2, together with the set of descriptors from the CEFR self-assessment grid in Table 1.3. (See Jones 2002b for further information of a Cambridge ESOL project that linked the ALTE levels to the CEFR).

When considering the ALTE Table (1.1) and the CEFR Tables (1.2 and 1.3), the reader may feel that the distinctions between adjacent levels are not always clear and the characterisations on occasion imprecise. A key aim of this volume is to improve on these descriptions by clarifying the underlying theoretical construct of Listening at CEFR Levels A2 to C2, combined with a close examination of Cambridge ESOL practice, to specify more precisely, where possible, the differences that exist between adjacent levels in terms of a range of contextual and cognitive parameters. A current reservation expressed in Chapter 3, for example, is the low prominence given to listening

Table 1.1 ALTE Listening/Speaking Can Do statements

CEFR levels (ALTE levels)	Listening/Speaking Can Do statement			
	Overall general ability	Social and Tourist typical abilities	Work typical abilities	Study typical abilities
C2: Mastery (ALTE Level 5: Good User)	CAN advise on or talk about complex or sensitive issues, understanding colloquial references and dealing confidently with hostile questions.	CAN talk about complex or sensitive issues without awkwardness.	CAN advise on/handle complex delicate or contentious issues, such as legal or financial matters, to the extent that he/she has the necessary specialist knowledge.	CAN understand jokes, colloquial asides and cultural allusions.
C1: Effective Operational Proficiency (ALTE Level 4: Competent User)	CAN contribute effectively to meetings and seminars within own area of work or keep up a casual conversation with a good degree of fluency, coping with abstract expressions.	CAN keep up conversations of a casual nature for an extended period of time and discuss abstract/cultural topics with a good degree of fluency and range of expression.	CAN contribute effectively to meetings and seminars within own area of work and argue for or against a case.	CAN follow abstract argumentation, for example the balancing of alternatives and the drawing of a conclusion.
B2: Vantage (ALTE Level 3: Independent User)	CAN follow or give a talk on a familiar topic or keep up a conversation on a fairly wide range of topics.	CAN keep up a conversation on a fairly wide range of topics, such as personal and professional experiences, events currently in the news.	CAN take and pass on most messages that are likely to require attention during a normal working day.	CAN give a clear presentation on a familiar topic, and answer predictable or factual questions.
B1: Threshold (ALTE Level 2: Threshold User)	CAN express opinions on abstract/cultural matters in a limited way or offer advice within a known area, and understand instructions or public announcements.	CAN express opinions on abstract/cultural matters in a limited way and pick up nuances of meaning/opinion.	CAN offer advice to clients within own job area on simple matters.	CAN understand instructions on classes and assignments given by a teacher or lecturer.

Table 1.1 Continued

CEFR Levels (ALTE Levels)	Listening/Speaking Can Do Statement			
	Overall General Ability	Social and Tourist typical abilities	Work typical abilities	Study typical abilities
A2: Waystage (ALTE Level 1: Waystage User)	CAN express simple opinions or requirements in a familiar context.	CAN express likes and dislikes in familiar contexts using simple language such as 'I (don't) like . . .'	CAN state simple requirements within own job area, such as 'I want to order 25 of . . .'	CAN express simple opinions using expressions such as 'I don't agree'.
A1: Breakthrough (ALTE Breakthrough Level)	CAN understand basic instructions or take part in a basic factual conversation on a predictable topic.	CAN ask simple questions of a factual nature and understand answers expressed in simple language.	CAN take and pass on simple messages of a routine kind, such as 'Friday meeting 10am.'	CAN understand basic instructions on class times, dates and room numbers, and on assignments to be carried out.

Source: Council of Europe (2001:249–257)

in the ALTE Can Do statements. Another reservation is the fact that the CEFR criteria are based quite heavily upon the *input* to the listener rather than the operations (especially the cognitive operations) that the listener has to perform in relation to the input. Even the criteria of examination boards tend to be loosely based upon conventional 'listening for' categories utilised by materials writers (listening for gist, listening for detail, listening for main point).

Although the General English tests (KET to CPE) form a major source of reference in this volume for illustrating how the listening construct differs from level to level in Cambridge ESOL examinations, the volume will also make reference to other Listening tests from examinations in the Cambridge ESOL family, such as the Business English Certificates (BEC) and the International English Language Testing System (IELTS) examination which cater for more specific English for Special Purposes (ESP) and English for Academic Purposes (EAP) populations. This is intended to provide further clarification of how various performance parameters help establish distinctions between different levels of listening proficiency on the vertical axis, and it may begin to provide some insights into the criterial features across domains and modes on the horizontal axis too. It will also demonstrate

Table 1.2 CEFR Common Reference Levels: Overall listening comprehension

	OVERALL LISTENING COMPREHENSION
C2	Has no difficulty in understanding any kind of spoken language, whether live or broadcast, delivered at fast native speed.
C1	Can understand enough to follow extended speech on abstract and complex topics beyond his/her own field, though he/she may need to confirm occasional details especially if the accent is unfamiliar. Can recognise a wide range of idiomatic expressions and colloquialisms, appreciating register shifts. Can follow extended speech even when it is not clearly structured and when relationships are only implied and not signalled explicitly.
B2	Can understand standard spoken language, live or broadcast, on both familiar and unfamiliar topics normally encountered in personal, social, academic or vocational life. Only extreme background noise, inadequate discourse structure and/or idiomatic usage influence the ability to understand. Can understand the main topics of propositionally and linguistically complex speech on both concrete and abstract topics delivered in a standard dialect, including technical discussions in his/her field of specialisation. Can follow extended speech and complex lines of argument provided the topic is reasonably familiar, and the direction of the talk is sign-posted by explicit markers.
B1	Can understand straightforward factual information about common everyday or job-related topics, identifying both general messages and specific details, provided speech is clearly articulated in a generally familiar accent. Can understand the main points of clear standard speech on familiar matters regularly encountered in work, school, leisure etc., including short narratives.
A2	Can understand enough to be able to meet needs of a concrete type provided speech is clearly and slowly articulated. Can understand phrases and expressions related to areas of most immediate priority (e.g. very basic personal and family information, shopping, local geography, employment) provided speech is clearly and slowly articulated.
A1	Can follow speech which is very slow and clearly articulated, with long pauses for him/her to assimilate meaning.

Source: Common European Framework of Reference (Council of Europe 2001:66)

how research conducted in relation to these more specific examinations has had wider effects throughout the full range of examinations offered by the board, for example in helping improve task design or scoring validity. These more specialist English examinations are well documented in their own right in other volumes in the *Studies in Language Testing* series and the reader is referred to these for comprehensive coverage of their history, operationalisation and quality assurance. The BEC examinations are taken by those wishing to gain a qualification in Business English as a result of the growing internationalisation of business and the need for employees to interact in more than just a single language (see O'Sullivan 2006 for full details of this test). IELTS is principally used for admissions purposes into tertiary-level institutions throughout the world (see Davies 2008 for a detailed history of the developments in EAP testing leading up to the current IELTS). Overviews

Table 1.3 CEFR Common Reference Levels: Self-assessment grid for Listening

	A1	A2	B1	B2	C1	C2
U N D E R S T A N D I N G Listening	I can recognise familiar words and very basic phrases concerning myself, my family and immediate concrete surroundings when people speak slowly and clearly.	I can understand phrases and the highest frequency vocabulary related to areas of most immediate personal relevance (e.g. very basic personal and family information, shopping, local area, employment). I can catch the main point in short, clear, simple messages and announcements.	I can understand the main points of clear, standard speech on familiar matters regularly encountered in work, school, leisure, etc. I can understand the main point of many radio or TV programmes on current affairs or topics of personal or professional interest when the delivery is relatively slow and clear.	I can understand extended speech and lectures and follow even complex lines of argument provided the topic is reasonably familiar. I can understand most TV news and current affairs programmes. I can understand the majority of films in standard dialect.	I can understand extended speech even when it is not clearly structured and when relationships are only implied and not signalled explicitly. I can understand television programmes and films without too much effort.	I have no difficulty in understanding any kind of spoken language, whether live or broadcast, even when delivered at fast native speed, provided I have some time to get familiar with the accent.

Source: Common European Framework of Reference (Council of Europe 2001:26–27)

Table 1.4 A description of Main Suite levels in terms of what materials candidates can handle and what they are expected to be able to do in Listening

CPE (C2)	Candidates need to be able to handle dialogues in a variety of contexts including conversations, interviews and discussions, and monologues including talks, broadcasts and podcasts. Texts will be delivered at a natural pace. Candidates are expected to be able to show understanding of general gist, detail, explicit and implicit opinion, function, attitude, feeling, purpose, intention, topic, course of action, agreement/disagreement, identity of speaker/addressee, genre, place, situation, specific information and inference.
CAE (C1)	Candidates need to be able to handle dialogues in a variety of contexts including conversations, interviews and discussions, and monologues including talks, broadcasts, podcasts and multiple *vox-pop* style extracts. Texts will be delivered at a natural pace. Candidates are expected to be able to show understanding of agreement, attitude, course of action, detail, feeling, function, gist, interpreting context, main points, opinion, speaker purpose and specific information.
FCE (B2)	Candidates need to be able to handle dialogues in a variety of contexts including conversations, interviews and discussions, and monologues including talks, broadcasts, podcasts and multiple *vox-pop* style extracts. Texts will be delivered at a natural pace. Candidates are expected to be able to show understanding of feeling, opinion, attitude, detail, specific information, function, genre, gist, main idea, opinion, place, purpose, place/situation, relationship, topic, agreement, identity of speaker/addressee, relationship between speaker and addressee.
PET (B1)	Candidates need to be able to handle dialogues including interviews and conversations between friends, family and strangers of an interactional or transactional nature, and monologues including talks, broadcasts, podcasts, recorded messages and announcements. Texts will contain redundancies and language outside the defined limits of PET and will be delivered at a natural pace. Candidates are expected to extract information of a factual nature (times, dates, etc.), be able to show understanding of the sense of a dialogue and show appreciation of the attitudes and intentions of the speakers.
KET (A2)	Candidates need to be able to handle dialogues and monologues, including: conversations between friends, relatives and strangers; telephone conversations, and recorded messages, in both informal and neutral settings on a range of everyday topics. The texts will be delivered at a pace which is slow but not unnaturally so. Candidates are expected to be able to extract relevant factual information from what they hear.

Source: Extracted from University of Cambridge ESOL Examinations Item Writer Guidelines (2006a, 2007d, 2008d, 2009e) and Handbooks for Teachers (2007b, 2008c, 2009c)

of the listening elements of these examinations are shown in Tables 1.5 and 1.6 below for information and comparative purposes.

Further comment may be helpful here on the twin issues of test purpose and test specificity and how these issues relate to the listening tests which are

Table 1.5 A description of BEC levels in terms of what materials candidates are expected to be able to handle and what they are expected to be able to do in Listening

BEC Higher (C1)	Candidates need to be able to handle dialogues including meetings, discussions, interviews and telephone conversations, and monologues including presentations, lectures, announcements and briefings. Texts will be delivered at a natural pace.
	Candidates are expected to be able to extract specific information, understand gist, attitude, opinion, topic, context and function and identify main points and detail.
BEC Vantage (B2)	Candidates need to be able to handle dialogues including meetings, discussions, interviews and telephone conversations, and monologues including presentations, lectures, announcements, briefings and telephone messages. Texts will be delivered at a natural pace.
	Candidates are expected to be able to extract specific information, match information to speakers, understand and interpret feeling and opinion.
BEC Preliminary (B1)	Candidates need to be able to handle dialogues including telephone conversations, face-to-face conversations, interviews and discussions, and monologues including presentations, lectures, announcements and briefings. Texts will be delivered at a natural pace.
	Candidates are expected to be able to extract specific information, distinguish between main and secondary points and recognise attitude.

Source: Extracted from University of Cambridge ESOL Examinations Item Writer Guidelines (2006a, 2010) and Handbooks for Teachers (2009c)

Table 1.6 A description of IELTS in terms of what materials candidates are expected to be able to handle and what they are expected to be able to do in Listening

Candidates need to be able to handle dialogues including conversations, discussions and interviews (face-to-face or over the telephone), and monologues including speeches, public talks and announcements, recorded messages, broadcasts, podcasts, lectures and presentations. Texts are delivered at a natural speed.

IELTS is a multi-level test, and candidates' band scores are determined by their ability to show understanding of: main ideas and details, distinguishing between the two and understanding their relationship; a linked series of events; opinion; attitude; purpose; inference; gist; description and detail, and location and direction.

Source: Extracted from University of Cambridge ESOL Examinations Item Writer Guidelines (2007d) and IELTS Information for Candidates (http://www.ielts.org/PDF/ Information_for_Candidates_2007.pdf)

scrutinised or referred to in this volume. Test purpose is sometimes defined in terms of type of test and its function, i.e. whether it is designed for selection, certification or diagnostic purposes (Davies, Brown, Elder, Hill, Lumley and McNamara 1999). McNamara (1996:92) writes of the 'rationale' for a test in terms of '*who* wants to know *what* about *whom* and for what *purpose*'? Definition of test purpose or rationale will naturally guide decisions about test content and format, approaches to scoring and test administration procedures. The 1999 *Standards for Educational and Psychological Testing* stress the importance of defining 'the purposes of the test and the domain represented by the test', so that it is clear 'what dimensions of knowledge, skill, processes, attitude, values, emotions, or behavior are included and excluded' (AERA/APA/NCME 1999:43–44; see also Fulcher and Davidson 2007). This last reference touches upon the complex inter-relationship between the test (and the scores it generates) and the world beyond the test (in which the test scores are used for some practical outcome). In the world beyond the test, scores from the test need to be interpretable in a valid and meaningful way since they are likely to be used for decision-making purposes with individuals and institutions, sometimes with significant or high-stakes consequences. Kane (1992) explains how inferences can be used to construct an interpretive argument in support of test validity claims, building on notions of 'generalisation' and 'extrapolation' from the test and its scores to the world beyond the test. (See also the Assessment Use Argument proposed by Bachman and Palmer (2010), which is based on Toulmin's (2003) approach to practical reasoning, using inferential links to build an argument structure.)

Questions of test purpose and of the validity of inferences that can be drawn from scores on a test lead us on to questions of the nature of test specificity. Both Douglas (2000) and O'Sullivan (2006) provide a comprehensive discussion of this area and its challenges, including the difficulty of determining exactly how far a test can be considered general or specific in its focus and purpose. This volume, like the previous construct volumes, focuses primarily on the General English examinations offered by Cambridge ESOL (KET–CPE). These tests were primarily developed to meet the educational needs of particular age groups and ability levels, for the most part within school or college-based language learning contexts worldwide. Their purpose or function can therefore be seen as supporting English language teaching and learning in such contexts, whether that teaching and learning takes place formally (e.g. in a classroom) or more informally (e.g. through a home-stay or self-study programme). The Cambridge Main Suite tests (KET–CPE) are 'general' tests in the sense that, unlike IELTS, BEC or BULATS (the Business Language Testing Service), they are not intentionally linked to a specified domain of language use but rather to a general purpose context within education. Unlike specific purpose tests, they are therefore not designed to reflect domain-specific language in terms of its 'precise' or 'context-appropriate' characteristics (e.g. its vocabulary, syntax, rhetorical organisation).

Despite the *Standards'* emphasis on defining test purpose and domain (i.e. the dimensions of knowledge, skill, processes, attitude, values, emotions or behaviour to be included or excluded), a definition of general language

proficiency is understandably difficult to pin down since it invariably constitutes a broad construct without clear boundaries. Specific purpose domains
and language may appear easier to define, though some suggest that defining
the boundaries of specific context areas can be equally problematic (Davies
2001, Elder 2001). O'Sullivan appears to treat this traditional 'general versus
specific' distinction more lightly, suggesting that all language tests are to
some degree 'specific' and can be 'placed somewhere on a continuum of specificity from the broad general purpose test . . . to the highly specific test . . .'
(2006:14). He further proposes that specific purpose language may actually
sit within general language, located at its core: 'Business language, like scientific or medical language, is situated within and interacts with the *general
language domain*, a domain that cannot, by its very nature be rigidly defined'
(2006:7). For language test developers, therefore, the general–specific
purpose distinction may not be as straightforward as we might hope.

This has interesting implications regarding the take-up and use of listening (and other skill-based) tests for purposes or in contexts for which they
may not have been originally or explicitly designed, raising understandable
concerns about the valid use of tests and their scores. The *Standards* readily
acknowledge that tests can be designed or used to serve multiple purposes,
but they also caution that such tests are unlikely to serve all purposes equally
well (AERA/APA/NCME 1999:145). It is sometimes argued that 'General
English' tests cannot be suitable for workplace recruitment because they
were not originally designed for specific occupational purposes. In some
cases this is undoubtedly true. It is highly unlikely that a general purpose
listening test will be appropriate for certificating the specialised, often technical language competence required in certain professional contexts, e.g.
the occupation-specific language of oil rig workers, air traffic controllers or
hospital radiographers. Clearly, examinations should not be used for purposes for which they are not intended and no claim is made in this volume
that Cambridge ESOL's General English tests, such as FCE or CAE, are
suitable for certificating the sort of occupation-specific language described
above. Certification of this type of linguistic ability is likely to demand a different and highly specific listening test, and such a test may need to be developed internally by the profession or by an employer, with expert assistance
from testing specialists. Such a test is also likely to involve the assessment of
occupation-specific knowledge and skills beyond the purely linguistic (e.g.
the technical legal knowledge needed for a courtroom exchange, or the clinical skills needed for doctor–patient interaction).

However, it is not unreasonable to assume that General English tests, such
as FCE or CAE, can potentially serve a useful function in evaluating a language user's proficiency level for some employment or educational contexts,
perhaps acting as an initial filter before the candidate embarks on more specialised language training and assessment that is specific to the occupational

context. In both employment and educational contexts, not all language use lies at the 'highly specific' end of the specificity continuum; much of it is general in nature, e.g. in the everyday exchanges of the office environment or in the social interaction that takes place on the university campus. This is consistent with O'Sullivan's notions of 'core and general language use domains' (O'Sullivan 2006:177). It is possible, therefore, to see how a General English listening test, such as those offered by Cambridge, *may* be perceived as useful by a range of test users because it fulfils a necessary function, while not being sufficient on its own to meet every aspect of the assessment need.

Test developers and providers bear the primary responsibility for ensuring that all test users fully understand the intended design purposes of any test and test users need to be made fully aware of any limitations that should be placed upon generalisation and extrapolation from listening test scores. Responsible test providers aim to achieve this through their publicly available documentation and their ongoing interaction with their stakeholder constituencies. Nonetheless, the ALTE *Code of Practice* (1994), the *Standards* (AERA/APA/NCME 1999) and most other recent professional guidelines for language testing also stress that the appropriate and ethical use of tests must be a *shared* responsibility between test providers and test users.

The tradition of listening assessment at Cambridge

In this introductory chapter it may be helpful to provide readers with a brief historical background on the tradition and experience of Cambridge ESOL in assessing L2 listening ability. This will hopefully explain the examination board's historical legacy as far as the testing of listening is concerned, as well as highlight the changes to assessment approaches that have resulted from technological and other advances over the past 50 years.

The introduction of CPE in 1913

Cambridge ESOL examinations have a long tradition of testing L2 listening skills dating back a century to the introduction in 1913 of the Certificate of Proficiency in English (CPE), a high-level test designed for 'foreign students who sought proof of their practical knowledge of the language with a view to teaching it in foreign schools' (Roach 1944:35, cited in Weir 2003:5). The CPE was a 12-hour examination consisting of several 'Written' papers, including a Translation paper into/from English, an Essay paper and an English Literature paper. It also included a 90-minute written paper on English Phonetics (testing knowledge of what words sounded like and how they were produced) as well as a compulsory Oral component that adopted a direct, face-to-face approach. Test takers faced half an hour of reading aloud and spontaneous conversation with an Oral Examiner, plus half an hour of oral dictation. The result was thus a Speaking and Listening test lasting a full hour.

Spolsky suggests the new CPE test in 1913 reflected 'the growing interest in direct method teaching', which 'required of teachers "reliable command of the language for active classroom use" rather than academic or descriptive ability' (Spolsky 1995:63). This may explain the prominence given to assessing aspects of oral and aural ability within the test battery. A century ago, therefore, language learners wishing to certificate their command of English as a foreign or second language faced 'an extremely demanding test of their abilities' (Weir 2003:2) in which testing of their listening ability was integral to assessing their overall English language proficiency.

Interestingly, the original design and development of CPE highlights for us the challenge discussed in the previous section of determining how far a language test is actually 'general' or 'specific' in terms of its 'test purpose'. From one perspective, the new CPE in 1913 could be regarded as a 'General English' test of overall language proficiency, since it covered both receptive and productive skills quite comprehensively, though apparently with no particular emphasis on relating these to a specific domain. From another perspective, and according to both Roach (1944) and Spolsky (1995), CPE was a high-level test designed to provide proof of a knowledge of the English language needed for the specific purpose of being able to teach it in the classroom in schools overseas. McNamara (1996:28) suggests that it was the early 1960s that saw *test purpose* as beginning to determine the form of tests as much as any linguistic theory of the knowledge or skills being tested. The comments of both Roach and Spolsky, however, suggest that test purpose and test specificity may have been a significant consideration in test development long before that.

Was CPE in 1913 a general purpose test or a domain-specific test? Or was it a blend of the two? Did the inclusion of Translation and English Literature papers make the test *more* specific, or were these components simply considered an integral part of the overall language proficiency construct as it was understood at that time? After all, the content and structure of CPE mirrored high-level Certificates in Proficiency for other modern European languages at that time, e.g. French and German. We cannot be definitive about what was in the minds of the original CPE test developers and it is probably unlikely that the test developers of a century ago worked with the terms and concepts that are familiar to us as 21st century language testers today. For example, CPE in 1913 contained no Listening test designated as such; but it did include a Phonetics paper, a Dictation component and a Conversation – all of which, it could be argued, point to some evidence of the testing of listening skills. It might also be argued that the Phonetics paper gave CPE a domain-specific quality, since some specialist training in phonetics and phonology (e.g. knowledge of terminology, the skill of phonetic transcription) was presumably needed by candidates for them to answer the test questions (a facsimile of the 1913 Phonetics paper can be found in Weir and Milanovic (Eds) 2003:483–484). This is perhaps not surprising given that qualified foreign language teachers at that time were probably expected to have some level of competence in phonetics and phonology, i.e. it was perceived as part of the construct to be assessed. Weir, Vidaković and Galaczi (forthcoming 2013) provide an extended discussion of the central role played by Phonetics in the teaching and learning of modern languages during the late 19th and early 20th centuries and how this impacted on developments in language assessment.

The example of the original CPE illustrates quite well the dilemma and questions that language testers face when designing and developing a new test, or when re-engineering an existing test. What does it mean in theory for a test to be 'general' or 'specific'? Is the distinction always as clear-cut as we believe or wish it to be? How is a theory of the inter-relationship of content and language operationalised in practice, whether in a listening or any other test? And what happens when a test takes on something of a life of its own in the world beyond the constraints and controls of the original test developers?

The history of CPE also helpfully illustrates for us how examinations evolve over time, sometimes changing their purpose in the process. In 1913 CPE was introduced 'to meet the needs of foreign students who wished to furnish evidence of their knowledge of English with a view to teaching it in foreign schools' (Wyatt and Roach 1947:126). This purpose is made explicit in the examination board's 1913 Regulations. By 1933, however, this purpose had disappeared from the printed Regulations, and by 1947 the Regulations state that CPE was 'open to all candidates whose mother tongue is not English and it is designed not only for prospective teachers but also for other students with a wide range of interest within the field of English studies.' It would appear that both the test purpose and the test taker constituency for CPE 'generalised' somewhat over this period. Nevertheless, the test, which included some focus on listening skills even though it had no named Listening component as such, still retained its relevance for L2 teachers of English presumably because it was perceived to be relevant and useful to broader pedagogical needs. (See Weir 2003, in Weir and Milanovic (Eds) 2003, for a full account of CPE's evolution throughout the 20th century.)

Fulcher and Davidson (2009) offer us an interesting conceptual analysis of changes in test use over time, drawing upon the field of architecture as a metaphor for language test development. Their discussion of 'test retrofit' (which can be applied to the development of a listening or any other test) provides the language testing community with a valuable framework for exploring this important area of the changing use of tests, though their analysis may risk oversimplifying what is in fact a more complex reality in education and wider society. For example, the theoretical distinction they draw between 'upgrade retrofit' and 'change retrofit' may not always be clear-cut in practice. The development of CPE and its legacy with regard to subsequent Cambridge tests testify to the complexities surrounding rigid notions of test purpose and specificity and how these can evolve over time within a wider and constantly changing ecology. It is essential that the take-up and use of a language test, along with the nature of its test taker constituency, are carefully monitored over time, and that the test itself is adapted accordingly to take account of changing purposes or trends, some of which may be beyond the control of the test provider. For example, if test candidates become younger because more English language teaching and learning worldwide takes place lower down the age range, in the primary as opposed to the secondary curriculum (Graddol 2006), then the topics in a listening test may need to change, as in the case of the PET and KET for Schools examinations developed in recent years (see Chapter 2). Similarly, if CAE is to be widely adopted as an English language proficiency requirement for university entrance purposes, then the test may need to become more academically oriented in the Listening (and any other) component with regard to features of cognitive and context validity.

The role of dictation

Though the English Phonetics paper was dropped from the Cambridge Proficiency examination in 1932, the oral dictation section survived the 1934, 1938, 1945, 1953, and 1966 revisions of CPE (Weir 2003:2–24). A dictation section also formed part of the first specification of the Lower Certificate in English (LCE) when it was introduced in 1939. The inclusion of a dictation component in both tests undoubtedly reflected contemporary approaches to foreign language teaching and learning. The 'grammar-translation' method was widely practised at that time, and dictation skills, which combined listening, writing and knowledge of lexis and syntax, formed part of this paradigm. However, under the influence of advances in linguistics and language pedagogy during the 1960s, a dedicated (and explicitly named) Listening Comprehension Paper was introduced in LCE in 1970, replacing the earlier dictation section. The first LCE listening comprehension test was approximately 40 minutes long. Candidates listened to an examiner reading aloud a set of passages at the front of the examination room. Passages were read aloud twice, the second time with some pausing, and candidates wrote down their answers to printed comprehension questions, including a number of items in multiple-choice format. A similar reading aloud listening comprehension paper found its way into the revised CPE in 1975. At around the same time LCE was revised and renamed the First Certificate in English (FCE) (see Hawkey 2009 for a detailed account of the history of FCE).

The impact of technology on listening assessment

The nature and quality of acoustic input in listening tests is an aspect that changed considerably in line with developments in technology over the past 50 years. Until the 1970s the acoustic input for the Cambridge tests could only be delivered, as we have seen, by a human speaker reading aloud a passage to a group of test takers in the examination room. By 1984, however, the growing availability of tape recorders had led to the introduction of recorded listening material when FCE and CPE were revised. The revised Listening tests used simulated (rather than authentic) recordings of radio news, situational dialogues and announcements, and at the same time incorporated charts, diagrams and picture prompts as the basis for test items. By the 1990s, advances in audio technology were providing better facilities for the administration of the listening comprehension tests. Cumbersome reel-to-reel tapes were replaced by smaller, more convenient tape cassettes and some years later Compact Discs (CDs) were introduced, significantly improving the quality of the speech signal in listening tests.

Such technological advances have direct implications for issues of test validity and fairness in the context of listening assessment. Use of recorded listening input on cassette or CD aids standardisation of test administration and removes the variability (and thus potential threat to reliability) often associated with a live reader, which is an important consideration in large-scale testing. Of course even if the recorded material is standardised in this way, the acoustic suitability of the room in which the listening comprehension test takes place may impact on the performance of test takers. The nature and quality of the play-back equipment (i.e. cassette recorder, PA system, language laboratory) is clearly important. A candidate who listens to the recorded material via headphones may experience the test and perform differently from one who listens to the same prompt via loudspeakers in a large hall. The recent advent of wireless headphones has the potential to affect candidate performance on the listening tests. All these issues require investigation to establish the impact of variability in aspects of the administrative setting for listening tests and they are more fully discussed in Chapters 3, 4 and 5 of this volume.

The use of technology, particularly in computer-based testing, also allows language test producers to explore and develop new item types. This may in turn prompt us to review and expand our understanding of the listening construct, or it may enable us to test aspects of the listening construct that were not previously possible, e.g. the inclusion of more interactive/integrative tasks. In his review of available resources for ESP testing, for example, Douglas (2007) advocated incorporating podcasts into tests, arguing that these have become increasingly popular among US students in campuses as a means of social interaction and academic study, and are thus worthy of consideration.

Changing assessment needs in education and society, together with the advent of new and innovative technologies, mean that examination providers such as Cambridge ESOL need to keep a range of testing methods under review and to investigate these as appropriate. In recent years, for example, this has included exploring the opportunities afforded by computer-mediated and internet-based options for listening assessment.

Defining the nature of L2 listening ability

Questions of what constitutes an 'authentic' or 'valid' approach to testing second language listening comprehension ability have long been debated and different historical periods have taken different stances, often shaped by the prevailing approach to describing language and the nature of language proficiency. The use of dictation tests in CPE and LCE referred to above, for example, reflects one view of the nature and importance of listening ability. The inclusion in CPE from 1913 to 1932 of a 90-minute paper on English Phonetics suggests that knowledge of what words sounded like and how they were produced was at one time considered an important component of language proficiency. From the late 1960s onwards, however, English language teaching, learning and testing saw a marked shift away from a focus on *knowledge about how the language system works* towards an emphasis on *the ability to use language*. The communicative language teaching paradigm of the 1970s aimed to teach language as a *means for communication* rather than as a *system for study*, and this view was increasingly reflected in approaches to the assessment of L2 listening. Changes in testing method over the decades, combined with a growing commitment to undertaking research, reflect Cambridge ESOL's longstanding concern for authenticity in testing, i.e. the attempt to develop tests that approximate to the 'reality' of non-test language use (real-life performance), a concern that was taken up vigorously during the communicative testing movement of the 1970s and 1980s (see Alderson 2000, Hawkey 2004, Morrow 1979, Weir 1983, 1990, 1993, 2005a). During the 1990s, Cambridge ESOL found it helpful to conceptualise authenticity according to Bachman and Palmer's (1996) two-way categorisation: *interactional authenticity*, which is a feature of the cognitive activities of the test taker when performing the test task (see Chapter 3 on cognitive validity below), and *situational authenticity*, which attempts to take into account the contextual requirements of the tasks being performed (see Chapter 4 on context validity). Widdowson (1978) had also employed the notions of *situational* and *interactional* in his discussion of what makes for authenticity in the classroom, distinguishing authenticity of content and context from authenticity of the learner's interaction with that content and context. The Cambridge ESOL approach to listening assessment acknowledges the importance of both these perspectives, and though full authenticity may be unattainable in the testing situation, it recognises that, as far as is possible, attempts should be made to use situations and tasks which are likely to be familiar and relevant to the intended test taker, bearing a demonstrable correspondence to language use in the world beyond the test, i.e. the target language use domain.

Today, we generally understand L2 listening proficiency to involve the ability to process acoustic-phonetic input (possibly accompanied by visual input) and to construct from this input some sort of mental representation which can be drawn upon for a variety of purposes. Taking a socio-cognitive perspective, Weir (2005a:45) places acoustic/phonetic processing (sometimes accompanied by visual processing too, e.g. in the case of video input) as one of several activities which the current research literature suggests are essential if we wish to develop a theoretically grounded and empirically oriented *cognitive processing* framework for L2 listening. Other processes, including imposing a syntactic structure, drawing inferences and self-monitoring, combine with resources such as language and content knowledge. This internal mental processing dimension of listening is also shaped by a broad set of external *contextual factors* covering elements of the *setting* for the listening task (e.g. task characteristics, time constraints, conditions for test delivery) and the *demands* the listening task makes on the language user in terms of linguistic stored knowledge (e.g. lexis, grammar, functions) as well as other variables associated with the acoustic input (e.g. speech rate, variety of accent). The *individual characteristics* of the listener – physical, psychological and experiential – will also help to shape the nature and outcomes of the listening experience. These three dimensions – internal cognitive processing, external contextual factors and individual characteristics – constitute three components of a socio-cognitive framework for developing and validating tests of L2 listening. They provide us with a helpful way of analysing and understanding different aspects of listening tests in terms of their cognitive and context validity.

The interplay of cognitive and contextual factors

As discussed above, the socio-cognitive perspective expressed in the framework proposed by Weir (2005a) distinguishes between internal mental processes and external contextual features. In a language test, of course, there exists a close relationship between these two, as well as with how performance on the test is marked or scored (scoring validity). Weir describes this interplay in the following way:

> There is a symbiotic relationship between context – and theory-based validity and both are influenced by, and in turn influence, the criteria used for marking which are dealt with as part of scoring validity . . . (Weir 2005a:20).

[N.B. In later versions of the socio-cognitive framework Weir replaced the term 'theory-based validity' with 'cognitive validity' and this is the preferred term used in this and in the previous volumes.]

One of the places where matters of cognitive and context validity overlap in listening tests is in the issue of how many times the listening input is heard by test candidates. Should the recording be played only once – in an attempt at 'authenticity', i.e. replicating listening as we tend to experience it in the non-test context where it is ephemeral and we rarely get a 'second chance'? Or should it be played twice (or more) – given that the listening test context has an inherent artificiality to it, i.e. it lacks many of the visual and other support features that typically accompany the listening experience outside the test context? Interestingly, 'second chances' may be more common than we think. For example, in interactive dialogic talk there is usually the chance to ask an interlocutor to repeat something; moreover, 21st century technology in the home, education and society makes it increasingly possible nowadays to 'listen/watch again' (see, for example, the BBC Radio digital audiofiles and iPlayer on the BBC website). Chapter 3 contains an in-depth discussion of this particular issue.

Aside from the issue of single or double play, there are clearly other factors that impact on the interplay of cognitive and context validity in listening tests. These include factors such as speech rate, variety of accents, number of speakers and gender of the interlocutor, all of which can have implications for the design and format of listening tests. Over recent years, for example, there has been a gradual shift in thinking about the variety of accents in listening tests. A generation ago the accents found in listening tests were predominantly British RP (Received Pronunciation), or Standard American English in the case of the Test of English as a Foreign Language (TOEFL). Nowadays, with the widespread use of English around the globe and increased exposure to local, regional and international varieties, there is greater willingness to include different accents in the same test. Some listening tests use a variety of native speaker accents i.e., British English, Australian and North American English. Even within one national variety there may be arguments for the inclusion of regional native speaker varieties such as Welsh, Scottish, Cornish, Birmingham, or Liverpool accents. This debate is ongoing (see for example the exchange between Jenkins and Taylor in the *ELT Journal*, January 2006) and Chapters 3 and 4 explore this issue further. It is an issue that touches directly upon the areas of *scoring, consequential* and *criterion-related* validity, as well as on *context* and *cognitive* validity. Inclusion of more heavily accented varieties on context, cognitive and consequential validity grounds has to be carefully balanced against the risk of introducing test bias, which is well recognised as a threat to test validity. This is where the bias studies become so important and relevant in the continuous validation of language tests. Chapter 5 in this volume reports on some recent work investigating differential item functioning (DIF) conducted in relation to the Cambridge ESOL Listening tests.

The methodological approach in the volume

As previously indicated, the methodological approach adopted in this volume builds directly upon that originally laid out in Weir (2005a), and subsequently applied and refined in Shaw and Weir (2007), Khalifa and Weir (2009) and Taylor (Ed.) (2011).

The validation process is conceptualised in a *temporal frame* to identify the various types of validity evidence that need to be collected at each stage in the test development, monitoring and evaluation cycle. This is represented graphically in Figure 1.1 on page 28.

The framework is described as *socio-cognitive* in that the abilities to be tested are conceptualised in terms of the *mental processes* of the candidate (the cognitive dimension). At the same time, the use of language in performing tasks is viewed as a *social* rather than a purely linguistic phenomenon, resonating with the CEFR's perspective on language for a social purpose which sees the learner (and presumably the test taker) as 'a social agent who needs to be able to perform certain actions in the language' (North 2009:359). The framework represents a unified approach to conceptualising and assembling validation evidence for a test. Figure 1.1 is intended to depict how the various validity components (the different types of validity evidence) fit together both temporally and conceptually. Weir explains that 'The arrows indicate the principal direction(s) of any hypothesised relationships: what has an effect on what, and the timeline runs from top to bottom: before the test is finalised, then administered and finally what happens after the test event' (2005a:43). Conceptualising validity in terms of temporal sequencing is of potential value as it offers test developers a plan of what should be happening in relation to validation and when it should be happening. The framework represented in Figure 1.1 comprises both *a priori* (before-the-test event) validation components of context and cognitive validity and *a posteriori* (after-the-test event) components of scoring validity, consequential validity and criterion-related validity.

A number of critical questions will be addressed through applying this socio-cognitive validation framework to Cambridge ESOL Listening tests across the proficiency spectrum:

- How are the physical/physiological, psychological and experiential characteristics of candidates catered for by this test? (Focus on the *test taker* in Chapter 2.)
- Are the cognitive processes required to complete the test tasks appropriate and sufficiently comprehensive to be treated as

Figure 1.1 A framework for conceptualising and investigating listening test validity (adapted from Weir 2005a)

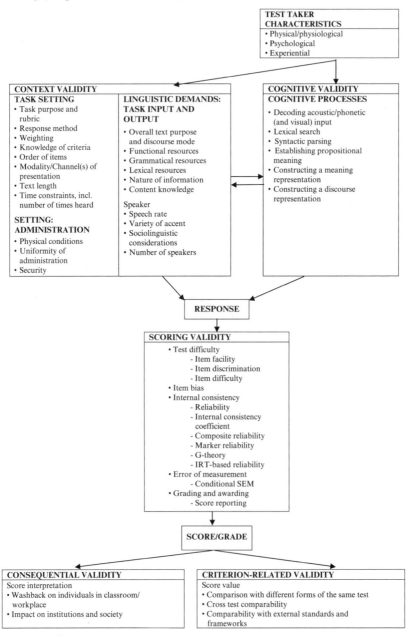

representative of the construct? (Focus on *cognitive validity* in Chapter 3.)

- Are the characteristics of the test tasks and their administration appropriate and fair to the candidates who are taking them? (Focus on *context validity* in Chapter 4.)
- How far can we depend on the scores which result from the test? (Focus on *scoring validity* in Chapter 5.)
- What effects do the test and test scores have on various stakeholders? (Focus on *consequential validity* in Chapter 6.)
- What external evidence is there that the test is measuring the construct of interest? (Focus on *criterion-related validity* in Chapter 7.)

These are the types of critical question that anyone intending to take a particular test or to use scores from that test would be advised to ask of the test developers in order to be confident that the nature and quality of the test matches their requirements.

The *test taker characteristics* box in Figure 1.1 connects directly to the cognitive and context validity boxes. As Weir points out, 'these individual characteristics will directly impact on the way the individuals process the test task set up by the *context validity* box. Obviously, the tasks themselves will also be constructed with the overall test population and the target use situation clearly in mind as well as with concern for their cognitive validity' (2005a:51). Individual test taker characteristics can be sub-divided into three main categories:

- *physical/physiological characteristics* – e.g. individuals may have special needs that must be accommodated, such as visual impairment or a speech impediment
- *psychological characteristics* – e.g. a test taker's personal interest or motivation may affect the way a task is managed, or other factors such as preferred learning styles or personality type may have an influence on performance; this concerns generic personal traits as well as those individual characteristics which may pertain to the immediate test situation, e.g. anxiety
- *experiential characteristics* – e.g. a test taker's educational and cultural background, experience in preparing and taking examinations as well as familiarity with a particular test may affect the way the task is managed; not surprisingly, this also embraces the test taker's experience of listening and their prior exposure to the L2.

All three types of characteristics have the potential to affect test performance (see Chapter 2 for more detail on this).

Cognitive validity is established by *a priori* evidence obtained before the live testing event as to the cognitive processing activated by the test task (e.g. through verbal reports from test takers), as well as through the more traditional *a posteriori* evidence on constructs as measured by the statistical analysis of scores following test administration. Language test constructors need to be aware of the empirically supported theory relating to the cognitive processing that underpins equivalent operations in language use beyond the world of the test (see Chapter 3 for a full discussion of this area).

The term content validity was traditionally used to refer to the content coverage of the task. *Context validity* is preferred here as the more inclusive superordinate which signals the need to consider not just linguistic content parameters, but also the social and cultural contexts in which the task is performed (see Chapter 4 for detail). Context validity for a listening task thus addresses the particular performance conditions, the setting under which it is to be performed (such as response method, time constraint, order of tasks as well as the linguistic demands inherent in the successful performance of the task) together with the actual examination conditions resulting from the *administrative setting* (Weir 2005a).

Scoring validity is linked directly to both context and cognitive validity and is employed as a superordinate term for all aspects of reliability (see Weir 2005a:Chapter 9, and Chapter 5 in this volume for detail). Scoring validity accounts for the extent to which objectively scored tasks are constructed and marked to produce reliable results as well as the extent to which scores on constructed response tasks are arrived at through the application of appropriate criteria, exhibit agreement, are as free as possible from measurement error, stable over time, appropriate in terms of their content sampling and engender confidence as reliable decision-making indicators.

Messick (1989) argued the case for also considering *consequential validity* in judging the validity of scores on a test. From this point of view it is necessary in validity studies to ascertain whether the social consequences of test interpretation support the intended testing purpose(s) and are consistent with other social values (see Chapter 6 for detail). There is also a concern here with the washback of any test on the learning and teaching that precedes it as well as with its impact on institutions and society more broadly. Weir's original 2005 framework included a third element within the *consequential validity* component relating to *avoidance of test bias*. Data collected on test takers and their scores should be checked to investigate the potential for unfair bias. Since bias is often (though not always) associated with differential item functioning, and as listening tests are item-based in format, this volume locates the discussion of bias (and measures to check for and avoid bias) within Chapter 5 on scoring validity, rather than in Chapter 6. This allows Chapter 6 to restrict its focus to matters of impact and washback; more importantly, it also reflects changes in Weir's own thinking in this area since 2005.

Criterion-related validity is a predominantly quantitative and *a posteriori* concept, concerned with the extent to which test scores correlate with a suitable external criterion of performance with established properties (see Anastasi 1988, Messick 1989, and Chapter 7 in this volume for detail). As Khalifa and Weir (2009) point out, evidence of criterion-related validity can come in several forms. A relationship can be demonstrated between test scores and an external criterion which is believed to be a measure of the same ability. Another source of evidence is demonstration of the qualitative and quantitative equivalence of different forms of the same test, by means of validation studies involving verbal report with test takers (retrospectively, of course for listening tests) or generalisability analyses comparing performance across listening tasks. A third source of evidence results from linking a test to an established external standard, or to an interpretative framework of reference such as the Common European Framework of Reference (CEFR) through comprehensive and rigorous procedures of familiarisation, specification, standardisation and empirical validation (Council of Europe 2003, 2009). Linking tests to an external standard or framework is not straightforward, however, and the use of the CEFR in this way remains somewhat contentious. Even if the recommended linking procedures have been followed, claims about CEFR alignment for a given test may need to be considered with some caution and careful attention paid to other essential quality aspects of the test in question. For a fuller discussion of the challenges and risks of CEFR linking, see Milanovic and Weir (2010).

Although for descriptive purposes the various elements of the framework in Figure 1.1 are presented as being separate from each other, a close relationship undoubtedly exists between these elements, for example between context validity and cognitive validity. Decisions taken with regard to parameters in terms of task context will impact on the processing that takes place in task completion. Within the specific context of practical language testing, there exists a third dimension which cannot be ignored: the process of scoring. In other words, at the heart of any language testing activity we can conceive of a triangular relationship between three critical components:

- the test taker's cognitive abilities (including their procedural knowledge, linguistic knowledge and world knowledge)
- the task and context, and
- the scoring process.

These three dimensions, which are reflected in the *cognitive validity*, *context validity* and *scoring validity* boxes of Figure 1.1, offer a perspective on the notion of construct validity which has both sound theoretical and direct practical relevance for test developers and producers. By maintaining a strong focus on these three components and by undertaking a careful analysis of their tests in relation to these three dimensions, test providers should be able to provide theoretical, logical and empirical evidence to support validity claims and arguments about the quality and usefulness of their exams.

In addition, the interactions between, and especially within, these aspects of validity may well eventually offer further insights into a closer definition of different levels of task difficulty. For the purposes of the present volume, however, the separability of the various aspects of validity will be maintained since they offer the reader a helpful descriptive route through the socio-cognitive validation framework and, more importantly, a clear and systematic perspective on the literature which informs it.

The structure of the volume

Examining Listening follows a similar structure to that which was successfully adopted for its sister publications *Examining Writing*, *Examining Reading* and *Examining Speaking*. The underlying shape closely follows the organisation of the framework described in Figure 1.1 with its six component parts as explained above. Apart from the opening and closing chapters, each of the other six chapters takes one component of the socio-cognitive validation framework to examine it in detail with reference to the Cambridge ESOL Listening tests, i.e. discussion of issues arising in the *research* literature on each component part is followed by consideration of Cambridge ESOL *practice* in the area.

While *Examining Writing* and *Examining Reading* were primarily co-authored publications, *Examining Speaking* was an edited collection of chapters written by a team of contributors and *Examining Listening* follows a similar approach. All the chapter authors are acknowledged specialists in language learning, teaching and assessment, many in the specific field of listening testing and assessment. In addition, they have direct experience of working with the Cambridge Listening tests from a number of different perspectives (test design and development, test writing and administration, exam preparation and materials development, test validation and research). As a result, they are able to combine their extensive theoretical knowledge with practical application and expertise in these areas, and so provide valuable insights into the complex endeavour or ecology that constitutes the assessment of L2 listening proficiency. In doing this they draw on other informants as explained below.

This opening chapter aims to set the scene for what follows in the rest of the volume. In Chapter 2 on *Test taker characteristics* Mark Elliott discusses the person of the test taker who stands at the heart of any assessment event. Chapter 3 on *cognitive validity*, by John Field, reviews what the theoretical and empirical research to date tells us about the nature of listening in a first and second language, particularly the cognitive processing involved. In Chapter 4 Mark Elliott and Judith Wilson examine in detail the many *context validity* parameters, or contextual variables, that have been acknowledged in the research literature to impact on listening ability.

Chapter 5 by Ardeshir Geranpayeh focuses on *scoring validity*, exploring the factors associated with the marking and scoring of listening tests. Chapter 6 by Roger Hawkey considers the *consequential validity* of listening tests, exploring issues of test washback and impact to establish where and how these play out within the complex process of validating high-stakes international examinations. Chapter 7 by Gad S Lim and Hanan Khalifa examines issues of *criterion-related validity*, in particular the need to establish comparability across different tests and between different forms of the same listening test, as well as with external standards. In the final chapter, Lynda Taylor and Ardeshir Geranpayeh draw together the threads of the volume, summarising the findings from applying the validity framework to a set of Cambridge Listening tests and making recommendations for further research and development.

The multiple 'voices' in the volume

In the three previous construct volumes, the opening chapters drew attention to the fact that, as the volume progresses, readers will become aware of different *voices* in the book together with varying styles of expression. This notion of multiple voices will also be apparent in *Examining Listening*, given that this is an edited volume with chapter contributions from a variety of authors each of whom writes in their own style and, to some degree, from their own perspective. Beyond this, however, the voices of a range of other contributors will hopefully be detected and appreciated, all of whom make a unique and lasting contribution to our understanding of the issues under discussion.

The presence of multiple voices can be regarded as a strength of the four published volumes since it allows the many and varied participants in any large-scale language testing enterprise to be brought together so that their perspectives can be shared and their contributions duly acknowledged. Amongst them are voices from the wider academic community of theorists and researchers in the fields of Applied Linguistics and Language Testing who provide essential theoretical foundations and guiding principles, and thus help to shape thinking and practice. Other voices offering key insights on Cambridge ESOL policy and practice in listening assessment come from the community of language testing practitioners within Cambridge ESOL, i.e. Assessment Managers, Research and Validation staff, Systems and Production personnel, as well as many other internal Cambridge ESOL staff who are directly responsible for developing, administering and validating the board's examinations. In addition to this internal practitioner community, there exists a vast cadre of external professionals upon whom the Cambridge ESOL examinations depend. They include item writers, test centre administrators, clerical markers, trainers and seminar presenters, and their important contributions are reflected in the extensive use of quotations from or references to examination handbooks, item writer guidelines, examination reports, centre documentation and training materials.

As was the case for *Examining Writing, Examining Reading* and *Examining Speaking*, this volume places into the public domain a wealth of information relating to the operational activities of Cambridge ESOL examinations. Some of this updates material which has previously been available. Other documentation has up to now been internal and confidential, usually for proprietary reasons, and appears in the public domain for the first time. Some reference will also be made to internal working reports and other documentation not currently available in the public domain. Like any large institution, Cambridge ESOL undertakes a large number of investigations and routine analyses relating to its examinations on a day-by-day basis. These typically take the form of internal working papers and reports which cannot easily be released into the public domain without considerable extra time and effort to write them up for external publication, e.g. on the board's website or in print media. Occasionally, documents include proprietary or commercial information which makes them unsuitable for public release. In recent years Cambridge ESOL has sought to channel much more of its research into the public domain via peer-review journals and other academic publications in the field of language assessment and educational measurement. While this strategy has proved fairly successful, the editorial resources available in-house to achieve this remain limited when set alongside daily operational demands. References in this volume to internal reports and working documents that are not in the public domain are included because they are relevant to the discussion in hand and because they help to illuminate the workings of a large examination board.

Conclusion

Chapter 1 of *Examining Listening* has argued that the credibility of language tests depends to a large extent upon a coherent understanding and articulation of the underlying latent abilities or construct(s) which they seek to represent. If these are not well defined or understood, then it becomes difficult to support claims test producers may wish to make about the usefulness of their tests, including claims that a test does not suffer from factors such as construct under-representation or construct-irrelevant variance. Examination providers need to be able to demonstrate transparently and coherently, to both internal and external audiences, how they conceptualise language ability and how they operationalise it for assessment purposes, especially with regard to satisfactory differentiation of levels across the proficiency continuum.

The characterisation of overall language proficiency, and of its component skills, remains an ongoing process among applied linguists and language testers even though some progress has been made since the late 1980s when Spolsky commented as follows: 'Communicative competence theories have not yet clarified the relationship between function and structure, nor provided a theoretical basis for exhaustively describing the components of language proficiency or delimiting the boundaries between them' (1989:144). Applied linguists and language testers (Bachman 1990, Bachman and Palmer 1996, McNamara 1996, and others) sought to address this through their theoretical work during the 1990s, offering the wider language testing community valuable frameworks for its thinking and practice concerning the nature of language ability and its assessment. More recently, work by Mislevy, Steinberg and Almond (2002, 2003), Weir (2005a) and Bachman and Palmer (2010) has helped to advance understanding of the complex nature of language test design, development and validation in theory and practice.

This volume aims to demonstrate how Cambridge ESOL has found the Weir approach to fit particularly well with its way of thinking about the validation questions that arise for the kinds of tests that the board offers. The socio-cognitive framework for test validation outlined in this chapter offers a promising methodology for attempting such an enterprise. It seeks a sound foundation in underlying theory and conceptualises validity as a unitary concept, while at the same time allowing a systematic analysis of six core components that reflect the practical nature and quality of an actual testing event. Drawing upon multiple professional perspectives, combined with a wide variety of documentary and other sources, the following chapters now address each of these six components in greater detail, beginning with test taker characteristics in Chapter 2.

2 Test taker characteristics

Mark Elliott
Cambridge English Language Assessment

Introduction

As well as considering *what* is being tested when a test is taken, the question of *who* is taking the test is one of primary importance. The target candidature needs to be borne in mind at the level of individuals and subgroups and during all stages of test development and administration, since a test is otherwise at risk of exhibiting bias towards or against certain groups or individuals. This chapter examines questions surrounding test takers and their unique characteristics which can, if left unaddressed, lead to threats to validity. The first part of the chapter presents an overview of different categories of test taker characteristics, then explores how Cambridge ESOL seeks to take account of some of these factors when designing its Listening tests through a routine demographic analysis of test candidatures for its different tests, helping to build a detailed understanding of the nature of the test-taking population. There follows a section focusing on the Special Arrangements that can be required when a candidate has some temporary or permanent condition affecting their ability to take a standard Listening test. The chapter concludes with a discussion of procedures that may be needed in the case of exceptional circumstances associated with a Listening test.

Before undertaking an analysis of test taker characteristics, it is necessary to establish a theoretical framework within which to base such an analysis. In the companion volume *Examining Speaking*, O'Sullivan and Green (2011) discuss the development of theoretical classifications of test taker characteristics in depth. Following O'Sullivan and Green, this analysis is based upon O'Sullivan's (2000) framework, which is a more comprehensive refinement of Brown's (1996) earlier work. O'Sullivan's framework identifies three categories of test taker characteristics: *physical/physiological*, *psychological* and *experiential*. The three categories are subdivided into various characteristics which are of relevance to listening tests, outlined in Table 2.1 and discussed below.

Though the characteristics outlined in the Table are helpful in providing a general framework for analysis, it is important to recognise that they do not constitute a comprehensive list of test taker attributes. Nor are they discrete, since they naturally interact with, and in some cases are partially dependent upon, one another. Nonetheless, each characteristic needs to be considered and addressed during *a priori* test validation in an attempt to reduce the risk of bias. However, it is important to be aware that it is not possible to 'factor out' all effects of test taker characteristics on performance entirely; the best that test developers can do is to consider the context of the test and the target candidature and identify those factors which may result in unfair effects in this context.

On the interaction between test taker characteristics and test performance, Geranpayeh and Kunnan (2007:1) note:

> It is essential for test developers to continuously monitor their tests in terms of whether all test takers are receiving a fair test . . . One approach to this problem has been to examine test scores from a pilot group or, if the test has already been launched, to examine test scores from a large sample of test takers and detect items that function differently for different test taking groups and to investigate the source of this difference.

This approach, known as *Differential Item Functioning* (DIF) analysis, can provide an empirical basis upon which to form judgements as to the appropriacy of different formats and types of test content and therefore a principled basis for test construction to minimise test bias. (See Chapter 5 for a fuller discussion of DIF analysis.)

Table 2.1 Test taker characteristics (adapted from O'Sullivan 2000:71–72)

Physical/Physiological	Psychological	Experiential
Age	**Cognitive**	Education
Gender	Working memory	Examination preparedness
Short-term ailments	Cognitive style	Examination experience
Longer-term disabilities	Cognitive development	Target Language (TL)-country
	Attention span	residence
		Topic knowledge
	Affective	Knowledge of the world
	Personality	
	Affective schemata	
	Emotional state	

Physical/physiological characteristics

This category firstly covers obvious biological features which all candidates share, most notably candidates' age and gender. The category also includes other physical characteristics which not all candidates share, and which may render the test in its standard format and under standard administrative arrangements unfair for candidates with those characteristics: short-term ailments, such as a heavy cold or a broken arm – these are by their nature unpredictable – and longer term disabilities, such as visual or hearing impairment, motor problems and special educational needs. Candidates with such *special requirements* form a particular sub-group of the candidature for whom it is often necessary to provide *Special Arrangements* in order to provide access to tests. Provisions for candidates with special requirements are treated separately later in this chapter.

Psychological characteristics

The term *psychological characteristics* refers to a range of attributes which can be further subdivided into *cognitive* characteristics, e.g. memory, cognitive style, cognitive development and concentration, and *affective* characteristics, e.g. personality, affective schemata, motivation and emotional state. Cognitive characteristics are likely to affect test performance directly, while affective characteristics are likely to do so indirectly by influencing or interfering with cognitive processes. It is also likely that the effects of cognitive characteristics can be determined more accurately, since there is a stronger empirical basis from the psychological literature upon which to draw when investigating such effects. A distinction is being drawn here between, on the one hand, those cognitive characteristics which are specific to the individual and can affect their performance, and, on the other hand, those cognitive processes which are acknowledged to form part of expert behaviour in a given skill.

Cognitive characteristics

Working memory

The relationship between working memory and listening is a complex one. A listener needs to hold a group of words in his or her head until they can be parsed syntactically (see Chapter 3 for a discussion of parsing); the number of words that can be held in working memory depends on word duration, with syllable duration important as well as the number of syllables (Baddeley 1986:78–81), the efficiency of processing (1986:194) and the listener's working memory capacity. Working memory also plays a role in the cumulative construction of meaning when listening to extended texts, since the listener needs to hold a discourse representation of the text up to the present at the level of propositional representations and a situational model, which represents 'the state of affairs that a text refers to' (Carroll 1994:169). In interactive listening, memory enables appropriate topic development and the emergence of a coherent thread of discourse. These points inevitably mean that some people will naturally be better listeners than others due to differences in working memory (this applies to first language (L1) as well as second language (L2)). See Chapter 3 for a more detailed discussion of memory and the cognitive processes underlying listening, and Chapter 4 for discussions of how test format can interact with memory in ways which may pose a threat to validity if not controlled carefully.

Cognitive style

Cognitive style refers to 'individual differences in preferred ways of organising, processing, and representing information' (Sadler-Smith 2011:263); these differences are 'partly fixed, relatively stable and possibly innate preferences' (Peterson, Rayner and Armstrong 2009:520). Cognitive style can be broken down into three dimensions correlating to organising, processing and representing information respectively: the *global–local* (a tendency to organise information in whole or in parts); the *intuitive–rational* (a tendency to process information intuitively or analytically), and the *verbal–visual* (a tendency to represent information verbally or in images) (Sadler-Smith 2011:265). They are both separate from intelligence and independent of personality (Riding 1997). Since cognitive style does not equate to cognitive ability, i.e. *what* an individual can do, but rather to modes of cognition, i.e. *how* the individual does it, it is a factor to consider in test development in order to avoid bias. There is evidence that the effectiveness of instructional materials improves when the input is matched to an individual's cognitive style (Thomas and McKay 2010); similarly, test performance can be affected by cognitive style when the task type favours one style over another, particularly if the task involves a degree of problem solving. This indicates that a balanced range of listening task types should ideally be provided to ensure that no particular cognitive style is favoured overall.

Cognitive development

Cognitive development refers to the 'changes in cognitive structures and processes that occur with age' (Small 1990:2), many of which concern the cognitive characteristics under discussion in this chapter. Of relevance are the changes typical of middle childhood and adolescence relating to attention, memory (including working memory), content knowledge, the automation of memory processes, inferencing, schemata, reasoning and formal operations. These cognitive abilities may not be fully developed in younger candidates, a fact which needs to be considered when constructing tests so as to avoid introducing cognitive demands beyond those directly relating to the listening process which may result in bias against younger test takers. (See Papp and Rixon (forthcoming) for a fuller discussion.)

Cognitive development is therefore an important issue for young learners taking language tests, and in particular listening tests, which present particularly high cognitive demands. Firstly, there are problems of attention span, with younger candidates less able to direct attentional focus (Small 1990) and able to sustain it for shorter periods than more mature candidates. In addition, certain functions associated with testing listening at higher proficiency levels can be problematic for younger learners. As Little (2007:651) notes of the Common European Framework of Reference for languages (CEFR) (Council of Europe 2001):

> The descriptors for B2 and more especially C1 and C2 levels assume a high degree of cognitive maturity, educational achievement, and professional experience. B2, which introduces a focus on effective argument (Council of Europe, 2001), can be adapted to the requirements of CLIL programs by expanding descriptors to embrace specific content; but C1 and C2 levels describe tasks that lie beyond the cognitive and experiential range of children and the great majority of adolescents.

Little's argument suggests that tests at high levels of proficiency, as conceptualised by the CEFR, may not be suitable for the majority of learners below a certain age. This may be due to cognitive development, the rate of which varies between individuals, or to differences between candidates' experiential ranges (see Papp and Rixon forthcoming, for a full discussion of these issues). It should be noted, however, that there are young learners who do manage to perform well in tests at C1 or C2 level, although they are the exception rather than the rule.

Attention span

Attention span does not only vary as a product of cognitive development: there are also variations between cognitively mature individuals. Attention span can become a factor affecting performance when heavy attentional demands are placed on candidates for extended periods; since listening is particularly cognitively demanding (see Chapter 3), care needs to be taken not to place unnecessary additional burdens on candidates' attentional resources. This may be a particular issue in the case of younger learners, implying the likelihood of an upper limit in the reasonable length of listening tests.

Affective characteristics

Personality

Personality is of less relevance in listening tests than in tests of speaking, for example, where it may have a direct bearing on the interaction being assessed. It may still, however, interact with certain aspects of the test and influence scores, for example, in relation to the inclination to take risks. Risk takers are more likely to guess and consequently tend to perform better on multiple-choice based tests; here it is worth noting that there is evidence that male test takers tend to be more inclined to take risks than female test takers (Ben-Shakhar and Sinai 1991), and are thus potentially favoured by multiple-choice formats which are commonly used in listening tests. This suggests that a listening test should contain a balance of task types to reduce bias. Furthermore, in terms of interactive listening, personality becomes a factor in that different individuals might approach the task of listening during a conversation in different ways according to their personality (see Galaczi and ffrench (2011) for a discussion of interactive listening and how it is addressed in Cambridge ESOL Main Suite Speaking tests).

Affective schemata

Affective schemata 'provide the basis on which language users assess, consciously or unconsciously, the characteristics of the language use task and its settings in terms of past emotional experiences in similar contexts' (Bachman and Palmer 1996:65). As such, test takers need to ensure that the affective schemata activated by a listening task do not adversely influence a candidate's performance. This is of particular concern with regard to the selection of topics for a listening test. Bachman and Palmer further note on this theme that '[i]f we ask test takers to deal with an emotionally charged topic, such as abortion, gun control, or national sovereignty, their affective responses to this topic may limit their ability to utilize the full range of language knowledge and metacognitive strategies available to them' (1996:66), which constitutes an unfair disadvantage for the candidate.

Emotional state

The emotional state of the test taker during a test is transient and potentially volatile, and can be heightened or aggravated by the level of anxiety associated with the test event itself. For this reason it is the responsibility of the test provider to ensure that the format of the listening test and, equally importantly, the administrative setting and procedures are familiar to the test takers and do not cause an exaggerated level of anxiety which could potentially impair performance. Performance can also be affected if the test taker is upset by the emotional effects of events external to the test, for example by a family problem or bereavement. Some Special Arrangements described towards the end of this chapter are designed to try and take account of such eventualities.

Experiential characteristics

The life experience a test taker brings to a listening test can influence his or her performance in several ways. While there will certainly be cases where the testing objectives are related to a candidate's life experience, such as their background and level of education, this will not always be the case. It is the test developer's duty to identify features of the listening test which may create unfair bias against candidates who do not fit a particular profile of life experience, particularly in terms of their educational experience, experience of taking examinations, knowledge of the word or particular topics, or experience of target language speaking countries (excepting cases where such experience may be relevant to the testing context), and to take steps to ensure fairness to all candidates, as far as is possible. The key experiential characteristics from O'Sullivan's (2000) framework will now be examined in turn.

Educational experience

Educational experience is one experiential factor, covering not only formal instruction in the target language but also the broader experience of educational practices and norms. The target language use (TLU) domain is of importance here; listening tests are tests of language proficiency and, in order to avoid introducing bias, should not necessarily assume that candidates have reached a level of educational experience beyond that which would be typical of their TLU domain. In the case of an English for Academic Purposes (EAP) listening test, for example, certain assumptions regarding educational level would be appropriate, whereas in the case of a test of day-to-day survival language for non-L1 immigrants, such assumptions may be unfounded and lead to unfair bias against sections of the candidature. At higher proficiency levels (particularly the C levels of the CEFR), the type of language in terms of lexical, grammatical and textual features and the level of abstraction associated with language functions at these levels as defined by the CEFR mean that there may necessarily be an assumption of a certain level of education. This is also implicit in the assumption that learners at the C levels are familiar with and can handle a broad range of topics.

Examination experience

Candidates' broader examination experience also has the potential to affect their performance, both in terms of language tests and examinations in general. Examination experience can affect candidates in two ways. Firstly, familiarity with a formal testing environment and the consequent knowledge of what to expect can help a candidate to cope with the pressure of the situation (although candidates with negative experiences of examinations may develop greater anxiety as a result) and plan their approach to the timing of the test and their use of metacognitive planning. Secondly, candidates with more examination experience will have received more exposure to typical testing formats and be more accustomed to answering examination questions in general.

Examination preparedness

While it is reasonable to expect that candidates prepare for a test, especially when the stakes are high, test developers should none the less avoid making too many assumptions about the level of candidates' preparedness; personal circumstances vary and it is always possible that some test takers will not be familiar with certain formats used in a test, perhaps because these are different from what they have been used to in a classroom context. It is therefore incumbent on test developers to facilitate candidates' preparation by providing an appropriate amount of information and sample test material for prospective test takers. This will help test takers to become familiar with the task formats they will encounter during the test and enable them to perform to their best. However, it is also the case that examination preparation can involve developing *test-wiseness* regarding the test in question among candidates who have had wide exposure to sample papers and other practice material. Candidates may prepare by developing specific test-wise strategies relating to different task types and response formats in an attempt to exploit loopholes in the testing format, such as guessing strategies for multiple-choice strategies. While it may not be possible to 'proof' a test entirely against such strategies, the aim of which is to enable candidates to bypass the testing objectives to a certain extent, well-crafted items and a range of response formats can minimise the effect. Ideally, the design of a listening test should encourage test preparation practice that relates directly to the construct being tested rather than to mastery of an artificial test method. (See Chapter 3 for a fuller discussion of the issues around such strategies and their relation to aspects of cognitive validity).

Residence in the target language (TL) country

TL-country residence is likely to lead to a high level of exposure to the TL and experience in listening to it. Since this is likely (although not certain) to help develop the language user's listening skills, it may be considered relevant to the testing objectives and therefore not strictly a matter of fairness or bias. However, the issue is slightly different when it comes to exposure to different non-standard accents; this is often serendipitous, especially where accents vary considerably in different parts of the country, and care needs to be taken not to unfairly advantage some candidates on this basis (for a fuller discussion of the issues surrounding accents in listening tests see Chapter 3 and Chapter 4).

Topic knowledge

Topic knowledge is largely the product of individual experience and educational background, and it can potentially advantage a candidate. Whether this is an unfair advantage depends on the nature of the test. In general listening tests such as those of Cambridge's Main Suite it is important to avoid topics where certain candidates may have specialist knowledge while others may not. This will be the case for both the familiarity of ideas to certain candidates and the familiarity of terminology that is used. In a language for specific purposes (LSP) test such as a Business English test, however, it is not unreasonable to expect that candidates should possess a certain degree of knowledge of a given topic, although the depth and specificity of such assumed knowledge should not be too great. In practice, it appears that ESP texts should be either *highly* specific to a particular field or fairly generalised, since a position in-between risks falling between two stools: it may not offer the possibility of drawing inferences specific to the field in question, whilst simultaneously being inaccessible to those outside the field (Clapham 1996). In less specific listening tests, assumptions of content knowledge become a matter of chance and texts should be selected to avoid creating a potential advantage for candidates with such knowledge and with correspondingly better-developed schemata (for further discussion of this theme see Chapter 4).

Knowledge of the world

Knowledge of the world naturally varies from candidate to candidate in terms of age and cultural background, and care should be taken to avoid making assumptions about the type of world knowledge candidates have, such as awareness of different countries, cultures and cultural practices. Since all texts assume certain underlying general knowledge to some degree, they need to be carefully scrutinised for such assumptions as this will help to avoid the introduction of bias due to age or cultural background. Underlying assumptions of world knowledge can be less obvious than assumptions of specific topic knowledge.

The framework outlined in Table 2.1 includes both topic knowledge and knowledge of the world. The former can perhaps be conceived in terms of *content* knowledge, linked to domains and ideas, while the latter is more concerned with *experiential* knowledge, linked to background and culture. In a more fully developed version of Table 2.1 it might be desirable to separate out the role of culture in its own right, since this may be an important factor in tests taken by an international (i.e. multi-lingual and multi-cultural) candidature. In listening tests taken by such a candidature, issues of cross-cultural awareness, including cross-linguistic pragmatics, will undoubtedly need to be taken into consideration.

Test taker characteristics: Cambridge ESOL practice

This section first explains how Cambridge ESOL seeks to build a detailed profile of its Main Suite test candidates, particularly with regard to some of the test taker characteristics discussed above. It goes on to consider how the examination board uses this demographic analysis to build a broad understanding of the candidature which can be used to inform the design of its Listening tests.

Knowing the candidature

For small-scale tests with well-defined candidatures, knowing the character-istics of the test taker population is relatively straightforward. For large-scale international tests with an open entry, however, it is necessary to implement standardised procedures to gather data on the candidature on a regular basis. Candidates entering Cambridge ESOL examinations are asked to com-plete a (non-compulsory) Candidate Information Sheet (CIS) (included as Appendix B). The CIS provides Cambridge ESOL with data on the gender, age, nationality, L1, educational level, degree of test preparation, reason(s) for taking the examination and previous examination experience, together with the country in which the examination was taken. This data is collated and anonymised to provide Cambridge ESOL with as detailed a profile of the demographics of the test candidature as possible, for two purposes:

1. To allow for the profiling over time of examination cohorts defined by different parameters according to the CIS data, and the monitoring of those cohorts' performances to ensure that the test is free of bias.
2. To ensure that the typical test taker characteristics of the candidature are taken into account in examination revisions. These characteristics can change over time, and Cambridge ESOL uses the CIS data to ensure that examinations remain fit for purpose for the candidature (Cambridge ESOL 2011a:7–9).

To illustrate the detailed nature of the CIS data that is routinely gathered and analysed by Cambridge ESOL, Table 2.2 provides an overview of the candidature for the Main Suite examinations in the 12-month period from June 2010 to May 2011. A brief commentary immediately follows Table 2.2 discussing the breakdown of test takers' L1 across the different examination levels. Discussion of the analyses relating to age, gender, etc. is integrated within later sections of the chapter exploring Cambridge ESOL practice with regard to the physical/physiological and experiential characteristics of test takers.

It is worth noting that the period 2010–11 saw some significant changes in Main Suite examinations with the introduction of FCE for Schools and with the growing establishment of KET for Schools and PET for Schools as alternative forms; in light of this, the figures for these examinations are included as separate entries in Table 2.2. It should also be noted that the figures for FCE for Schools are drawn from only two sessions – March 2011 (the inaugural session) and May 2011 – so may not prove representative of the make-up of the FCE for Schools candidature over the whole annual cycle, especially since new examinations tend to take time to establish settled candidature patterns.

Table 2.2 Test takers' profile for Main Suite examinations, June 2010 to May 2011*

Exam	L1 Top 10	Age	Gender	Educational level	Test preparation by attending classes	Reasons for taking Main Suite examination*	Examination experience*
CPE (C2)	• Greek: 21.5% • Spanish: 19.6% • Portuguese: 8.7% • German: 5.4% • Polish: 5.2% • Swiss–Ger.: 5.0% • Dutch: 4.8% • Italian: 3.4% • French: 3.4% • Catalan: 2.0% • Blank: 7.5% • Other: 13.4%	• 15 or less: 5.8% • 16–18: 30.3% • 19–22: 21.1% • 23–30: 23.7% • 31 or more: 18.3% • Blank: 0.8%	• Female: 55.3% • Male: 36.0% • Blank: 8.7%	• College/University: 32.8% • Secondary school: 22.4% • Primary school: 0.1% • Blank: 44.7%	• Attended: 71.3% • Didn't attend: 27.8% • Blank: 0.9%	• For personal interest: 25.0% • For further study of English: 21.8% • For further study of other subjects: 13.8% • For university recognition: 7.9% • To help career: 55.8% • Employer organised: 1.3%	• Same exam: 25.1% • Other exams: 97.3% • Blank: 1.3%
CAE (C1)	• Spanish: 21.1% • German: 11.0% • Romanian: 7.1% • Polish: 6.7% • Portuguese: 5.9% • Swiss–Ger.: 5.2% • Dutch: 4.6% • Italian: 4.3% • French: 4.2% • Swedish: 3.5% • Blank: 10.0% • Other: 16.5%	• 15 or less: 3.1% • 16–18: 43.0% • 19–22: 22.9% • 23–30: 19.7% • 31 or more: 10.4% • Blank: 0.9%	• Female: 59.5% • Male: 37.6% • Blank: 2.9%	• College/University: 33.8% • Secondary school: 41.7% • Primary school: 0.2% • Blank: 24.2%	• Attended: 82.4% • Didn't attend: 16.5% • Blank: 1.1%	• For personal interest: 23.8% • For further study of English: 31.4% • For further study of other subjects: 16.0% • For university recognition: 11.2% • To help career: 63.2% • Employer organised: 1.0%	• Same exam: 8.8% • Other exams: 66.3% • Blank: 1.5%

	First language	Age	Gender	Education level	Exam preparation course	Reasons for taking exam	Other Cambridge exams
FCE (B2)	Spanish: 28.1% Italian: 11.0% French: 5.9% German: 5.5% Portuguese: 5.4% Polish: 3.7% Swiss-Ger.: 3.7% Greek: 2.9% Catalan: 2.5% Czech: 2.0% Blank: 16.5% Other: 12.9%	15 or less: 17.6% 16–18: 44.8% 19–22: 15.8% 23–30: 14.3% 31 or more: 6.5% Blank: 1.0%	Female: 56.9% Male: 39.3% Blank: 3.8%	College/University: 27.8% Secondary school: 48.8% Primary school: 0.8% Blank: 22.6%	Attended: 86.7% Didn't attend: 11.6% Blank: 1.6%	For personal interest: 20.1% For further study of English: 32.1% For further study of other subjects: 10.7% For university recognition: 12.0% To help career: 56.3% Employer organised: 0.8%	Same exam: 10.1% Other exams: 39.9% Blank: 2.0%
FCE for Schools (B2)	Greek: 65.7% Italian: 13.4% Spanish: 6.3% French: 3.0% Russian: 2.0% Swiss-Ger.: 1.2% Albanian: 0.8% Polish: 0.6% Catalan: 0.5% German: 0.5% Blank: 4.3% Other: 1.8%	15 or less: 60.8% 16–18: 33.4% 19–22: 4.1% 23–30: 1.0% 31 or more: 0.4% Blank: 0.3%	Female: 46.7% Male: 36.6% Blank: 16.7%	College/University: 4.6% Secondary school: 93.1% Primary school: 1.1% Blank: 1.2%	Attended: 84.6% Didn't attend: 15.0% Blank: 0.5%	For personal interest: 10.1% For further study of English: 21.9% For further study of other subjects: 6.6% For university recognition: 8.0% To help career: 30.3% Employer organised: 0.1%	Same exam†: 1.95% Other exams: 33.5% Blank: 0.9%

Table 2.2 Continued

Exam	L1 Top 10	Age	Gender	Educational level	Test preparation by attending classes	Reasons for taking Main Suite examination*	Examination experience*
PET (B1)	• Italian: 33.1% • Spanish: 18.5% • German: 8.9% • French: 3.8% • Portuguese: 3.4% • Chinese: 3.1% • Russian: 2.2% • Arabic: 1.8% • Catalan: 1.4% • Turkish: 1.4% • Blank: 11.7% • Other: 10.6%	• 12 or less: 5.4% • 13–14: 18.3% • 15–18: 56.6% • 19–22: 6.9% • 23 or more: 11.7% • Blank 1.1%:	• Female: 56.4% • Male: 40.3% • Blank: 3.3%	• College/University: 12.8% • Secondary school: 5.3% • Primary school: 72.7% • Blank: 9.1%	• Attended: 86.8% • Didn't attend: 11.3% • Blank: 1.9%	• For personal interest: 21.9% • For further study of English: 34.7% • For further study of other subjects: 11.0% • For university recognition: 12.6% • To help career: 49.6% • Employer organised: 1.3%	• Same exam: 7.6% • Other exams: 34.9% • Blank: 2.1%
PET for Schools (B1)	• Spanish: 31.5% • Italian: 14.6% • Turkish: 7.1% • Chinese: 6.8% • Greek: 5.3% • Russian: 2.8% • French: 2.6% • Catalan: 2.2% • German: 1.9% • Portuguese: 1.7% • Blank: 13.5% • Other: 10.1%	• 12 or less: 16.8% • 13–14: 41.1% • 15–18: 39.1% • 19–22: 1.0% • 23 or more: 0.6% • Blank: 1.3%	• Female: 52.8% • Male: 42.3% • Blank: 5.0%	• College/University: 3.1% • Secondary school: 72.2% • Primary school: 18.7% • Blank: 6.0%	• Attended: 86.8% • Didn't attend: 11.1% • Blank: 2.1%	• For personal interest: 17.5% • For further study of English: 47.4% • For further study of other subjects: 13.7% • For university recognition: 10.4% • To help career: 36.7% • Employer organised: 0.5%	• Same exam: 12.9% • Other exams: 27.4% • Blank: 2.4%

	Languages	Age	Gender	Institution	Attendance	Reasons	Other exams
KET (A2)	• Italian: 24.0% • Spanish: 18.4% • Chinese: 7.1% • Portuguese: 4.9% • French: 4.0% • Turkish: 3.9% • Russian: 3.3% • Singhalese: 2.3% • Arabic: 2.0% • Catalan: 1.5% • Blank: 11.6% • Other: 17.0%	• 12 or less: 24.4% • 13–14: 44.0% • 15–18: 17.4% • 19–22: 4.0% • 23 or more: 9.1% • Blank: 1.1%	• Female: 53.3% • Male: 42.8% • Blank: 3.9%	• College/University: 8.6% • Secondary school: 78.4% • Primary school: 63.9% • Blank: 19.2%	• Attended: 85.8% • Didn't attend: 11.4% • Blank: 2.8%	• For personal interest: 21.5% • For further study of English: 44.7% • For further study of other subjects: 16.6% • For university recognition: 6.7% • To help career: 34.3% • Employer organised: 1.7%	• Same exam: 16.2% • Other exams: 26.5% • Blank: 3.0%
KET for Schools (A2)	• Spanish: 23.3% • Italian: 22.8% • Turkish: 9.7% • Chinese: 8.7% • Greek: 3.5% • Vietnamese: 2.6% • Russian: 2.5% • Catalan: 1.8% • French: 1.7% • German: 1.7% • Blank: 12.7% • Other: 9.1%	• 12 or less: 36.4% • 13–14: 52.7% • 15–18: 9.5% • 19–22: 0.2% • 23 or more: 0.3% • Blank: 0.9%	• Female: 52.3% • Male: 43.5% • Blank: 4.2%	• College/University: 1.5% • Secondary school: 62.8% • Primary school: 31.5% • Blank: 4.2%	• Attended: 86.6% • Didn't attend: 11.0% • Blank: 2.5%	• For personal interest: 17.3% • For further study of English: 51.4% • For further study of other subjects: 16.9% • For university recognition: 7.3% • To help career: 27.6% • Employer organised: 0.4%	• Same exam: 16.7% • Other exams: 28.8% • Blank: 2.7%

Source: Output data generated using CIS data from paper-based sessions between June 2010 and May 2011

* Figures may add up to more than 100% since candidates may select more than one option.
† In the case of for Schools examinations, 'same exam' includes standard versions, e.g. for KET for Schools, both KET and KET for Schools are included.

First language

The candidature for Main Suite examinations for the period June 2010 to May 2011 was drawn from all around the world, with Europe and South America forming the majority. The breakdown differs for FCE, CAE and CPE compared to KET and PET (in all cases including for Schools versions):

- For FCE, CAE and CPE all top 10 L1s were Indo-European and almost all were Romance, Germanic or Slavic. The two exceptions were Greek, which was notably the largest cohort for FCE for Schools, and Albanian, which featured for FCE for Schools (although only 0.8% of the candidature on two sessions – note the earlier caveat on the representativeness of the FCE for Schools CIS data).
- For KET and PET the candidature was more mixed. Romance and Germanic languages were again predominant, but Russian was the only Slavic language to feature in the top 10, and there were several other languages and language groups among major cohorts, all spoken predominantly in Asia. Turkish (Turkic), Chinese (Sino-Tibetan) and Arabic all featured consistently, while Singhalese (Indo-European) also featured for KET.

As a major international language test provider, it is clearly important for Cambridge ESOL to monitor the L1 breakdown of its candidature given the potential effects of a test taker's L1 on their L2 listening practices (e.g. in terms of the presence of cognates and the role of rhythm). While it may be unrealistic, and possibly inappropriate, to think in terms of trying to shape listening test input in light of L1 considerations, it is nonetheless helpful to know the dominant language backgrounds of the test taker cohort and thus to be able to understand some of the factors which may affect their test scores, including aspects which make the target language especially challenging for them. Such insights can feed into post-examination reports which in turn can provide valuable diagnostic guidance for teachers.

Physical/physiological characteristics: Cambridge ESOL practice

Age

Constant monitoring of CIS data enables Cambridge ESOL to detect trends in the age profile of the Main Suite candidature and ensure that the content of the tests remains relevant to the interests and life experience of candidates. The age profile of Cambridge ESOL's Main Suite candidature has changed significantly over recent years as the general level of English has increased among school-age candidates around the world, which has led directly to the creation of the for Schools versions of KET, PET and FCE. While the specifications of these newly developed Listening tests are identical to the older, standard tests in terms of format (bar cosmetic changes to the type-setting), construct coverage and difficulty, the range of topics selected for inclusion in the Listening tests is tailored to the target age group. This has had the simultaneous effect of allowing the 'standard' versions of the tests to cater more appropriately for a more mature candidature by no longer needing to consider younger candidates to the same extent. For example, recordings on the topic of work in a day-to-day sense would be more appropriate for the standard versions, particularly if they reflected assumptions that the listener had experience of a working environment, since recordings on this topic might prove less accessible to candidates still at school. The converse might be true for recordings discussing topics and activities of interest to young teenagers, such as teenage fashion or pop music, since mature candidates may not be familiar with these. An additional consideration beyond accessibility is that of perceived relevance to the candidates, who may regard topics of no relevance to them as 'dull' (in the case of work-related topics for young teenagers) or 'childish' (in the case of teenage fashion for mature candidates), and therefore demotivating. Feedback from pretesting centres – from both candidates and teachers – provides a valuable source of data as to which types of topics are appropriate or potentially problematic.

Figures 2.1 and 2.2 show a steady progression in age through the five Cambridge levels, with KET having the youngest candidature and CPE the oldest. KET for Schools, PET for Schools and FCE for Schools all attracted

Figure 2.1 Age profiles of test takers taking KET, KET for Schools, PET and PET for Schools, June 2010 to May 2011

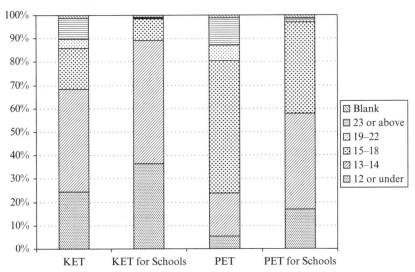

Figure 2.2 Age profiles of test takers taking FCE, FCE for Schools, CAE and CPE, June 2010 to May 2011

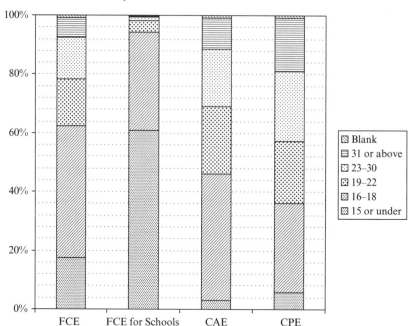

younger candidatures than the 'standard' versions, largely matching their target age groups and showing an increasing age profile from KET for Schools to FCE for Schools. The age profiles of the candidatures for KET, PET and FCE differ from those of their for Schools equivalents in a way which broadly reflects the intended candidature.

Gender

Figure 2.3 shows the gender profile of the candidature of all Main Suite examinations, including both 'standard' and for Schools versions. All eight examinations under scrutiny featured more female candidates than males.

Monitoring the gender profile of the Main Suite candidature is important for a number of reasons. Firstly, it can help to inform decisions about the balance and treatment of topics included in a listening test. Although traditional gender stereotypes concerning tastes and interests no longer hold in many parts of the world (e.g. traditionally 'male' interests are now also enjoyed by females in many countries), there are none the less some topics, such as certain sports, which may tend to interest and motivate more candidates of one gender than the other, thus creating the possibility of bias. The treatment of topics is equally important: a listening passage describing

Figure 2.3 Gender profiles of test takers taking Main Suite examinations June 2010 to May 2011

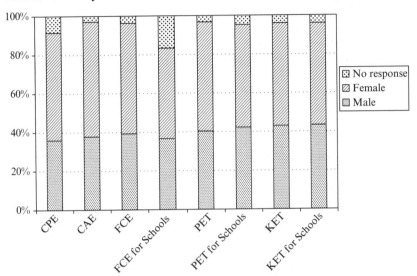

a sportsperson's approach to their sport which assumes an interest in that sport may risk alienating some candidates, while material describing the life of the sportsperson which does not focus heavily on the sport itself is likely to be more broadly accessible, and thus suitable for testing purposes. It is Cambridge ESOL policy to avoid the selection of material which may exhibit gender bias, specified in the *Item Writer Guidelines: Information Common to All Papers* for all examinations (Cambridge ESOL 2006a:8):

> Texts should be chosen to be accessible, and of interest, to the broad range of the candidature [and] should not exclude any large group in terms of its standpoint or assumptions. It is obviously impossible to interest everybody, but subjects which appeal only to a minority should be avoided.

Judgements of suitability are therefore made with both the topic and its treatment in mind.

Monitoring the gender profile for tests is clearly also important to highlight where or when it may be advisable to conduct non-routine investigations into the potential for test bias on grounds of gender. Such studies can form an important part of the argument to support validation claims for listening and other tests.

Psychological characteristics: Cambridge ESOL practice

Personality

Main Suite Listening tests contain a range of Listening task types in an attempt to achieve a balanced content and approach. They seek to ensure that no one task type predominates in order to minimise the possible effects of personality type in relation to different task types; for example, a test entirely comprised of multiple-choice items potentially favours risk-takers (Ben-Shakhar and Sinai 1991).

Memory

Candidates taking Cambridge ESOL Main Suite Listening tests are given time to read the rubric and items for a task before Listening to facilitate understanding of the task, but they may refer to the written items as they listen in order not to force them to hold several items in their working memory as they listen (see Chapter 3 for a discussion of memory in terms of cognitive validity). The dual channel format (spoken and written) does, however, have a negative effect here in terms of split attention in line with Wickens' (1984) multiple resource theory. See Chapter 3 and Chapter 4 for discussion of the effects of the dual channels of writing and speaking.

Cognitive style

The tasks in Cambridge ESOL Main Suite Listening tests employ a range of response formats in order not to favour a particular cognitive style, as may be the case where only one response format is used. See Chapter 4 for a full discussion of response formats used in Main Suite Listening tests.

Cognitive development

The typical ages from which the Main Suite examinations are suitable in terms of cognitive development, i.e. the age by which test takers should have developed the cognitive processes required to process both the language and the concepts presented within the tests, are the lower stated ages for which the for Schools versions have been developed: age 11 for both KET for Schools and PET for Schools, and age 12 for FCE for Schools (Papp and Rixon forthcoming). For younger learners, Cambridge ESOL provides a suite of examinations specifically designed for young learners aged 7–12, *Cambridge English Young Learners: Starters, Movers* and *Flyers* (also discussed in Papp and Rixon, forthcoming). Due to the more abstract nature of the content of CAE and CPE, these examinations are not typically suitable for candidates who have not developed fully in cognitive terms and who may struggle conceptually as a result.

Affective schemata

In order to avoid disadvantaging candidates by potentially distressing them, Cambridge ESOL maintains a list of 'taboo' topics which may cause an adverse affective reaction and this list is included in the item writer guidelines for all papers, including for listening recordings. Some topics on the list are included for reasons of cultural sensitivity, although they cannot be entirely separated from affective schemata since what is relevant here is that they are likely to induce a negative affective reaction; this again highlights the overlap and occasional interdependence between the categories in the O'Sullivan test taker characteristics framework. This policy is summarised in the *Item Writer Guidelines: Information Common to All Papers, FCE, CAE and CPE* as follows:

> Material must not contain anything that might upset or distract candidates as this will affect their performance. Candidates who are angered, upset or mystified by a text are unlikely to provide a genuine sample of their language skills in an examination situation.
> (Cambridge ESOL 2006b:8)

The following is the full list of taboo topics for Cambridge ESOL Main Suite examinations, covering topics which may be unsuitable for either personal or cultural reasons (Cambridge ESOL 2006a):

- alcohol
- cigarettes (where smoking is the focus of a text, picture or task)
- drugs
- examinations, passing and failing
- gambling
- historical subjects or references likely to offend certain nations or groups
- national standpoints (in particular those where the practices of one country may be perceived negatively by others)
- politics
- potentially distressing topics (e.g. death, terminal illness, severe family/ social problems, natural disasters and the objects of common phobias)
- religion (including related topics such as those which are not acceptable to certain religions)
- sex, sexuality and bodily functions
- stereotypes (including racism, sexism, cultural clichés and attitudes which could be interpreted as patronising towards other countries, cultures, beliefs or individuals)
- war.

The use of the list may be open to a degree of interpretation, as outlined in the Upper Main Suite *Item Writer Guidelines: Information Common to All Papers* (Cambridge ESOL 2006a:9):

> Common sense is essential in interpreting these unsuitable topics. Some topics are not suitable as the main focus of material although they may be mentioned. A text on British drinking habits might offend some candidates, but a mention of a glass of wine may be acceptable in texts (not in visuals). The Second World War can be mentioned as a historical period, but specific events in it should not be.
>
> When considering the suitability of any topic, it is necessary to remember that it is not always the topic itself which could render it inappropriate as much as the treatment of it in any given text, and judgement may need to be the deciding factor here.

Emotional state

While taking any examination is likely to be a stressful experience for some candidates, particularly when the test is a high-stakes one, Cambridge ESOL policies on test format and administration are designed not to impose any unnecessary additional anxiety on candidates. Instructions are designed to be simple and delivered on the recording at an appropriate (i.e. slower than usual) pace and in an unthreatening manner. Texts are carefully chosen so as not to cause any potential discomfort to candidates (see the section on affective schemata, this chapter). The fixed format of each test provides a familiar framework for candidates who have undertaken appropriate preparation (see the section on examination preparedness, this chapter); this familiarity should help reduce stress levels. Similarly, the twice-played format of Main Suite Listening tasks can help make the experience less stressful since candidates are less at the mercy of distractions such as external noises at critical moments due to the second chance to hear the recording (see Chapter 3, page 127, and Chapter 4, pages 197–203, for a full discussion of single and double play).

Experiential characteristics: Cambridge ESOL practice

Education

The CIS data collected on the Main Suite candidature (see Table 2.2 above) enables Cambridge ESOL to monitor the educational experience of the general cohort taking each Listening test and to ensure that texts and task types do not assume unrealistic levels of education. Given the effects of educational background and current level of education upon areas such as topic knowledge, world knowledge and cultural awareness, this information can help to shape the choice of topics in a listening test.

Figures 2.4 and 2.5 illustrate a clear upward trend in the educational level

Figure 2.4 Educational level profiles of test takers taking KET, PET, FCE, CAE and CPE June 2010 to May 2011

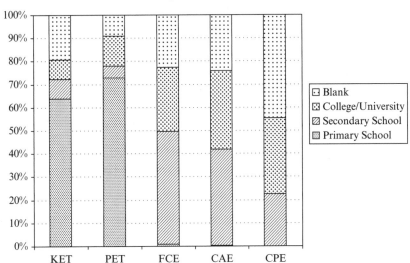

Figure 2.5 Educational level profiles of test takers taking KET for Schools, PET for Schools and FCE for Schools June 2010 to May 2011

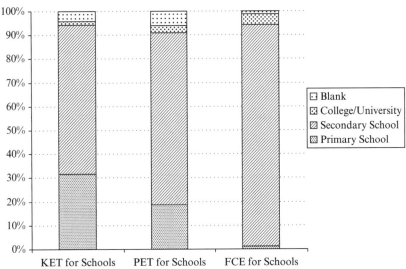

of candidates as the suite progresses from KET to CPE, which is unsurprising in view of the increasing age profile. Given the targeted nature of the for Schools versions, at KET and PET level a majority of the candidature (63.9% and 70.2% respectively) reported primary school as their educational level. At FCE level and above, the primary-level candidature virtually disappears (around 1%), and the candidature is comprised of secondary-level and college-level educated candidates instead.[1]

The educational levels for all three for Schools examinations reflect their target age groups. A majority of the candidature at all three levels reported secondary level education, with the proportion rising from 62.8% (KET for Schools) to 93.1% (FCE for Schools); conversely, the proportion reporting primary school education fell from 31.5% (KET for Schools) to 1.1% (FCE for Schools). The proportion of college/university level candidates was low (maximum 4.6%).

As discussed earlier, the types of function outlined in the CEFR descriptors for high proficiency levels, particularly the C levels, do seem to imply a fairly high level of education; for example, the CEFR illustrative scale for understanding conversation between native speakers at C1/C2 states that a C-level listener 'Can easily follow complex interactions between third parties in group discussion and debate, even on abstract, complex unfamiliar topics' (Council of Europe 2001:66). In some cases, this could even be desirable since tests designed to be relevant to academic and professional domains, especially EAP tests, are naturally aimed at an educated candidature. The *Item Writer Guidelines: CPE Listening* (Cambridge ESOL 2009d:5) reflect the CEFR descriptors, stating that candidates 'are expected to comprehend spoken language that is both linguistically and conceptually complex', indicating an assumption of education which might be inappropriate at lower proficiency levels.

Examination preparedness

Familiarity with the specifics of a listening test may be important in two key respects. Firstly, the tasks in any test require a certain degree of familiarisation for test takers to demonstrate their true level of ability. This may be more so in the case of listening tests where the tasks involve a degree of reading and/or writing and test takers need to adjust their metacognitive strategies to the task at hand, which is never entirely authentic (see Chapters 3 and 4 for a fuller discussion of different task types). Although the standard test formats used in listening tests such as those offered by Cambridge ESOL are somewhat artificial, they have the strong advantage of being familiar to candidates because they are used in other domains (e.g. in classroom practice) or because they are easily downloadable as practice materials. Secondly, Cambridge ESOL's policy of using of standardised task rubrics, i.e. the instructions to test takers, is designed to help engender test familiarity. The lexico-grammar of task rubrics is constrained to a level with which candidates can reasonably be expected to be familiar, particularly at lower proficiency levels; the only changes in wording relate to a brief description and contextualisation of the text to be heard. This allows candidates to familiarise themselves with the test rubrics as part of their exam preparation and to ensure that they will not be surprised by any unknown lexis in the test rubrics (see Chapter 4, pages 00–00 for a full discussion of rubrics and associated issues).

As Table 2.2 shows, an overwhelming majority of candidates for Main Suite examinations up to CAE – between 82.4% (CAE) and 86.8% (PET and PET for Schools) – have attended examination preparation classes, which will typically include preparation for the Listening test. The figure is lower for CPE at 71.3%, but still represents a strong majority. Candidates who do not attend specific preparation classes can none the less prepare for the Listening test via the available sample tests, past paper packs and preparation and practice materials, much of which is available free of charge, to ensure they are familiar with the nature and format of the Listening test in its entirety.

The question arises of how to minimise the effects of the particular form of test-wiseness which consists of format-specific guessing strategies discussed earlier and which can be seen as a way of playing the system rather than demonstrating ability in the construct being assessed. It is questionable whether it is possible to produce a listening test which is absolutely proofed against this type of test-wiseness, although as noted it is possible to minimise its effect by ensuring that items are well crafted, for example by avoiding any possibility of direct lexical matching, i.e. 'wordspotting' – which is particularly important in relation to the skill of listening; ensuring a balance of listening test response formats also helps. The item writer guidelines for all examinations stipulate a strict set of criteria for the writing of items using different response formats which, as well as outlining best practice in the writing of well-crafted items generally, are designed in part specifically to reduce the possibilities of employing gaming strategies and thus minimise their effect. The following bullet points, drawn from the *Item Writer Guidelines: CAE Listening* (Cambridge ESOL 2007d:14), represent a (far from comprehensive) sample of principles that help avoid test-wise strategies; in this case they relate to the writing of three-option multiple-choice questions:

- the options should avoid words such as 'always'/'never' (often incorrect) or 'sometimes'/'usually' (often correct)
- the key should not repeat, or be a simple paraphrase of, the words found in the text
- the key should not be the only option to contain a word heard in the text (or be the only one not to)
- the key should not stand out from the other options, e.g. be longer, shorter or have a different form.

It is also important to note the link between test preparation and wash-back. If assumptions are to be made that candidates prepare for a listening test, and indeed are encouraged to do so, then a responsibility is placed on the test developer to ensure that, as far as possible, the effects of test preparation are positive and support effective learning. Cambridge ESOL has always placed strong emphasis on ensuring that its examinations foster positive washback, a subject which forms part of Cambridge ESOL's principle of *impact by design,* explored in depth in Chapter 6.

Examination experience

Since it should not be assumed that candidates have a high level of prior experience of taking high-stakes tests of language, it is Cambridge ESOL policy to ensure that the procedures and expectations for each examination are made as explicit as possible to candidates, both via clear and unambiguous test rubrics and via the information which is made publicly available on the Cambridge ESOL website, including test handbooks and sample papers (accessible at www.cambridgeenglish.org). For most Main Suite examinations, the CIS data for those *re*-taking an examination suggests a relatively low figure, between 7.6% and 16.7%. The figure was somewhat higher for CPE, at 25.1%.

TL-country residence

The issues relating to TL-country residence, and in particular those relating to serendipitous exposure to specific accents, are accounted for in Cambridge ESOL Main Suite Listening tests by avoiding accents markedly different from those with which candidates in a global context can be reasonably expected to be familiar (see Chapter 3 and Chapter 4 for fuller discussion of issues surrounding the use of different accents in listening tests). This is of importance for international examinations such as the Cambridge ESOL Main Suite, where it cannot be assumed that candidates either have been, or intend to go, to specific regions of native English-speaking countries. There is also the question of exposure to non-native varieties. The ability to understand these varieties, as with regional varieties of L1 English, may be equally serendipitous and heavily dependent upon the experience and contacts of the individual test taker.

Topic knowledge

Since Cambridge ESOL Main Suite examinations are not tied closely to a specific target language use domain, it would be inappropriate to assume specific topic knowledge of the candidature (see Chapter 4 for a full discussion of the effect of topic knowledge on performance). The *Item Writer Guidelines: Information Common to All Papers* for FCE, CAE and CPE give specific guidance on this point (Cambridge ESOL 2006b:9–10):

Material should not favour candidates with specialised knowledge of a particular subject, or contain content that would be too specialised or technical for the majority of candidates. For example, material about sport may be acceptable as long as it is accessible to those who know nothing about a particular sport, but will be rejected if it would favour those with knowledge of that particular sport. Texts on science and technology are acceptable if expressed in terms readily comprehensible to the lay reader. Thus, a text discussing the environmental consequences of using herbicides in general terms may be acceptable; a text about the chemical composition of a herbicide would not be. Similarly, texts about the arts must be accessible to readers who may not have knowledge of or any particular interest in, for example, literature or painting.

Knowledge of the world and cultural background

The material in Cambridge ESOL Main Suite Listening tests is selected according to reasonable expectations about the world knowledge of the candidature based on the CIS data. As discussed earlier, this has led to the creation of the for Schools versions of KET, PET and FCE in order that the content of the Listening tests be appropriate for the target candidature, whether younger or older. Topics in the for Schools versions are chosen to reflect the target candidature's likely level of world knowledge; texts which focus on experiences at work, for example, would not be suitable. This has simultaneously made it possible for the 'standard' versions to focus on more typically adult-oriented topics, such as the workplace, without needing to accommodate to the world knowledge of the for Schools candidate, making both versions more suitable for their target candidatures.

Cultural background is also a primary consideration in assessing the appropriacy of material for inclusion in Main Suite Listening tests. The *Item Writer Guidelines: Information Common to All Papers, FCE, CAE and CPE* document provides the following guidance on this point (Cambridge ESOL 2006a:9):

> The candidature is worldwide and as English continues to develop as an international language, so the range of people who become English learners is ever more diverse. Many learners may use English as a kind of lingua franca and may never visit Britain or any other English-speaking country. They may, therefore, find it difficult to access, or may indeed be alienated by, learning or testing materials that assume an interest or involvement in the culture of one particular English-speaking region. What's more, increasingly, learners in certain cultures are alienated by materials that assume a common cultural heritage, or that seem to impose the concerns and interests of people in western cultures on them.

The above considerations are taken into account during test development when determining the format and content of Cambridge ESOL Listening tests. They are also monitored on an ongoing basis during the annual Exam Review and Evaluation process, which includes an in-depth analysis of CIS data over time to ascertain whether tests remain appropriate for the target and to determine whether test revisions are needed. In some cases, more radical developments may be appropriate; the recent creation of the for Schools examinations is an example of such a development.

Candidates with special requirements

Perhaps the most obvious case of a test taker's characteristics leading to the risk of their being disadvantaged in a test is where the candidate has a disability or short-term ailment that makes it difficult for them to demonstrate their true level of ability on the standard version of that test. In cases where the candidate has special requirements (SR), their test performance can be negatively affected due to their physical condition rather than due to any factors related to the ability being measured. It is the responsibility of the test provider to find a means of providing the SR candidate with *fair access* (i.e. the opportunity for the candidate to be neither unfairly disadvantaged nor unfairly advantaged when taking a test); this is both a legal and an ethical duty for the test provider, who should make explicit and public precisely what provisions they offer. These provisions take the form of *Special Arrangements* (often referred to as *accommodations*) based on the principle of offering reasonable adjustments to the testing materials – *modified material* – and/or special *administrative arrangements* as appropriate in order to provide test access for the candidate without compromising the testing objectives.

General considerations

The question of how to accommodate candidates with special requirements is a complex one, not least because the circumstances of such candidates can differ widely. Partly for this reason, and partly because it is difficult to find a large enough sample of participants to produce statistically significant findings, there is a relative lack of research into the effects of different provisions on the performance of candidates with SR. Policy therefore tends to be determined by the use of expert judgement based on a set of guiding principles; several codes of practice exist, some designed specifically for language tests (AERA/APA/NCME 1999, ALTE 1994, EALTA 2006, ILTA 2000, 2007). The UK's Joint Council for Qualifications (JCQ) summarises the basic principle behind special requirements provisions as follows (Joint Council for Qualifications 2011:vii):

> The intention behind many access arrangements is to meet the particular needs of the disabled candidate without affecting the integrity of the assessment. In this way awarding bodies will comply with the duty of the Equality Act 2010 to make 'reasonable adjustments'.

The term 'reasonable adjustments' here covers modifications to the examination material itself and changes to the administrative arrangements for the examination. Critical to interpretation of the policy is the phrase 'without affecting the integrity of the assessment', which should be interpreted as meaning that candidates with special requirements should be provided the opportunity to demonstrate their true level of ability – removing any unfair *disadvantage* due to their circumstances – without being marked more leniently than other candidates or otherwise put at an unfair advantage, and without changing the construct being tested. This is explicated by the JCQ, who notes that '[a]n adjustment may not be considered reasonable if it involves unreasonable costs, timeframes or affects the security *or integrity of the assessment*' (2011:vii, emphasis added). Under UK law, as in many other countries, all test providers have a legal duty to offer such reasonable adjustments to candidates with SR.

In order to decide whether Special Arrangements are appropriate for a given case, the awarding body needs to determine whether a candidate's SR will cause him or her to be unfairly disadvantaged by the standard testing method – the format and administrative arrangements – rather than the items themselves. Testing formats are predicated upon certain, normally reasonable, assumptions relating to candidates' ability in skills other than those relevant to the testing objectives; in the case of candidates with special requirements, however, the assumptions are often not valid and become the cause of systematic error. As Kane (2011:27) puts it, '[t]he argument for accommodations on standardized tests for students with disabilities is essentially an argument for removing a source of systematic error'. In other words, the standard testing format contains elements which do not cause systematic error for test takers without special requirements – and which may well make the test more practical and efficient – but which interact with the circumstances of candidates with special requirements in a manner which introduces a source of systematic error for those candidates, and those candidates only. The provision of Special Arrangements is therefore a means of addressing this systematic error where it is believed to exist by changing the format and/or administrative arrangements. However, as Taylor (2012a:308) notes: 'It is still the case that relatively little is known or understood about how different accommodations benefit (or fail to benefit) particular students, or about how they affect the nature of the test itself and the meaning of the scores generated'. This means that there are two critical aspects of the provision of Special Arrangements about which little is known:

1. Whether Special Arrangements actually do reduce unfair disadvantage – or indeed avoid giving the candidate an unfair advantage.
2. The extent to which efforts made to keep the construct being tested the same are successful.

It is sometimes the case for language tests with different components covering different skills that Special Arrangements may be appropriate for certain components but not others.

Special requirements for listening tests

SR for listening tests can be classified into various groups, each of which requires different Special Arrangements. These fall into the following categories:

• visual impairment and blindness
• hearing impairment and deafness
• motor problems
• special educational needs such as dyslexia, autism and Attention Deficit Hyperactivity Disorder.

While it is easy to see why a listening test presents a major challenge for test takers who are deaf or partially hearing, it is of course also the case that hearing candidates with disabilities (e.g. visual impairment, motor problems or special education needs) may want or need to take a listening test but that the standard test format or administrative conditions are inappropriate or inaccessible due to their disability. Thus alternative provision will need to be made for them to access the listening test in an appropriate way. The following scenarios may help to illustrate the problems faced by candidates with differing disabilities when taking a listening test:

A. a candidate with motor problems which cause her to write slowly
B. a candidate who is blind
C. a candidate who is deaf.

Candidate A (candidate with motor problems)

Special arrangements would be appropriate wherever a listening test includes, for example, a gap filling task that requires written responses, or wherever answers have to be transferred to an answer sheet. Extra time to allow the candidate to record their answers in written form is an appropriate provision for a listening test, since the testing objectives relate to the cognitive processes underpinning the candidate's comprehension, which are distinct from the mechanics of recording written answers. How this extra time is implemented needs to be interpreted in relation to the format of the test, since there is the additional question of how recording answers interacts with listening to the recording.

Candidate B (candidate who is blind)

This candidate represents a clear case where the candidate will be unfairly disadvantaged by the standard presentation of the test; thus the listening test question paper will need to be provided in a more accessible format such as Braille. Since reading and writing in Braille is typically significantly slower than sighted reading and writing, extra time is an additional standard provision in such cases. As with Candidate A, this needs to be interpreted in relation to the format of the test and specifically the relationship between listening and producing responses while a recording is playing.

Candidate C (candidate who is deaf)

This candidate is a case of particular relevance to listening tests given that a deaf (or hearing-impaired) candidate clearly cannot listen to an audio recording and achieve satisfactory comprehension. This raises the question of what alternative channels of presentation are appropriate. The two options available would be *sign language* and *lip-reading*, which will be considered briefly in turn.

Sign language

A sign language, such as British Sign Language (BSL), is a distinct language in its own right, fully formed and with its own rich vocabulary, grammatical rules and regional dialects; accordingly, the inferences drawn from scores on a test of an English-based sign language such as BSL cannot easily be extrapolated to correspond to those derived from a conventional test of oral/aural proficiency in English. In addition, combining the scores from a test of listening/speaking in sign language with scores from conventional tests of reading and writing in English would become problematic in terms of score meaning and interpretation. Given the potentially differing constructs of the two languages, competence in signing is best evaluated and certificated in a separate test, in its own right, rather than within the context of a conventional oral/aural test.

Lip-reading

Unlike sign language, lip-reading involves understanding conventional spoken language, albeit utilising different means through the visual channel. Lip-reading language users can take part in face-to-face communication in the target language, and a lip-reading version of a listening test assesses their ability to do so using lip-reading. This is exemplified in the case of listening tests delivered by video, where a lip-reading deaf candidate could potentially take a standard form of the test (see Chapter 4 for a full discussion of the use of video in listening tests). However, since candidates cannot lip-read and read a question paper simultaneously, Special Arrangements may be needed to facilitate reading and responding to items when these are presented in written form and to allow candidates to alternate their attention between the question paper and the video or interlocutor's face.

Candidates with special requirements: Cambridge ESOL practice

Cambridge ESOL makes every effort to ensure that its tests are accessible to all candidates with special requirements. The examination board liaises closely with relevant organisations in the UK, particularly the Royal National Institute for Blind People (RNIB) and Action on Hearing Loss (formerly the Royal National Institute for Deaf People (RNID)), on an ongoing basis to ensure that the format and content of modified test versions reflect current practice in their respective fields.

Cambridge ESOL also adheres to internationally recognised standards for the assessment of candidates with special requirements, along with broader concerns of access, fairness and ethics. The *Special Circumstances Booklet* for Cambridge's test centres outlines the principles underlying the examination board's policy. The provisions are intended:

- To remove, as far as possible, the effects of the disability on the candidate's ability to demonstrate his or her true level of attainment in relation to the assessment objectives. Cambridge ESOL cannot compensate candidates for lack of attainment caused by their disabilities.
- To ensure that the Special Arrangements do not give disabled candidates an unfair advantage over other candidates. Disabled candidates will not usually be permitted provisions which would enable them to circumvent the assessment objectives.
- To avoid misleading the user of the certificate about the candidate's attainment.

(Cambridge ESOL 2010c:5)

Special arrangements for Cambridge ESOL Listening tests

Special arrangements available for Cambridge ESOL Listening tests include the provision of *modified materials*, *special administrative arrangements* and the use of *access technology*. Some of the Special Arrangements for Listening tests discussed below are specifically devised for test takers who are deaf or hard of hearing, for whom taking the standard Listening test raises obvious difficulties. Other arrangements are more general in nature, relevant for test takers with other types of physical or cognitive disability for whom the visual form in which a language test is presented (whether a test of listening or another skill) causes significant problems.

Modified materials for Listening tests

The production of modified materials is highly resource-intensive, both in terms of time and money, so while modified materials are prepared on a routine basis for all the most common types of special requirements (see Table 2.3 below for a contextualisation of 'common' here), it is not feasible to cover every eventuality on a routine basis given the variety of possible special requirements in terms of both type and severity. Where routinely produced modified materials do not meet a candidate's needs, Cambridge ESOL is committed to producing bespoke modified material on a case-by-case basis. In such cases, applications must be submitted at least three months prior to the test date in order for the materials to be produced to the board's quality assurance standards, which are applied as rigorously to modified materials as they are to standard test versions. Table 2.3 shows the number of candidates taking each type of modified material during the period from 2006 to 2010.

Table 2.3 Cambridge ESOL Special Arrangements for Main Suite Listening tests involving modified material, 2006–10

	2006	2007	2008	2009	2010
Test S	51	10	32	17	67
Braille Test S	38	46	15	25	20
Test H	46	50	42	21	31
MLP (A4-enlarged) Test S	39	46	21	20	19
A3-enlarged standard test	43	56	47	75	113

Test S (listening version for candidates with special requirements)

The Listening paper suitable for candidates with SR, known as *Test S*, is routinely produced to meet a range of different special requirements.

Candidates who require extra time for the other written papers, whether due to motor problems, special educational needs such as dyslexia, or injuries such as a broken arm, can apply for this version of the Listening paper. Candidates who are blind or visually impaired can apply for *Test S* in Braille or Modified Large Print (MLP) versions. The paper is constructed to identical standards as the standard version and contains items drawn from standard versions, but differs in that the recording is paused at pre-determined points throughout the second hearing of each passage in order to allow the candidate time to read the items and write and check answers. For candidates with motor problems or dyslexia, these pauses provide them with time to produce their responses, which will typically take them longer than other candidates (candidates with dyslexia may also require more time to read the items); without the pauses, such candidates would be unfairly disadvantaged by the test format. As well as generally requiring more time to record their answers, candidates who are blind or have visual impairment cannot be expected to internalise large numbers of items (and options in the case of multiple-choice items) and would be placed at a further unfair disadvantage without pauses due to the test format.

Test S has modified rubrics to reflect the differences in procedure, and a separate CD is supplied to reflect these changes in rubrics; the listening passages themselves, however, are unchanged from the standard version to ensure the candidate receives the same input. A *Supervisor's Booklet* is also supplied, containing detailed instructions on how to administer the test, which requires separate invigilation. The locations of the pauses are indicated on a transcript of the recording. The invigilator is required to follow the recording on the transcript and pause the recording manually each time a pause is indicated. The length of each pause is left to the supervisor's discretion, since they will naturally vary according to different candidates' individual circumstances; the supervisor is in the room with the candidate and able to observe the candidate's progress and so judge the appropriate length of each pause. Pause locations are determined to ensure that they do not break up the flow of the recording more than necessary, and it is policy that they do not always correspond with test items in order to avoid the 'flagging up' of key information in the text. Since visually impaired and blind candidates typically have better than average recall of the form of words used and of informational content, the fracturing effect of pausing the recording is unlikely have much effect (John Field, personal communication); this does not, however apply to candidates with motor difficulties, although it is difficult to propose alternatives which represent an improvement.

Braille *Test S*

The Braille version of *Test S* presents the same content as the print version but in Braille form, with the same rubrics, *Supervisor's Booklet* and CD, and it can be supplied in either contracted or uncontracted Braille. Administrative procedures are essentially the same as for the print version, a copy of which is supplied to the supervisor for reference.

Blind candidates, particularly those who have been blind since birth, could potentially be disadvantaged by listening passages which assume visual knowledge in the same way that texts assuming certain topic knowledge could disadvantage candidates who are unfamiliar with the topic. For this reason, the content of each *Test S* is carefully vetted to avoid such bias and to ensure that blind candidates are not disadvantaged indirectly as well as directly by their blindness.

As with the standard-format *Test S*, the CD is paused at prescribed points throughout the second hearing of each passage to allow the candidate sufficient time to read the test items and write and check their answers.

Modified Large Print (MLP) *Test S*

The MLP version of *Test S* is appropriate for test takers with visual impairment. It has the same content as the standard format *Test S*, with the same rubrics, *Supervisor's Booklet* and CD. Cambridge ESOL MLP versions conform to the guidelines laid out by the RNIB, and feature, among others, the following key formatting conventions to facilitate reading, which are used for all Cambridge ESOL MLP test materials:

- standardised easy-to-read font (18 point Arial bold) throughout
- no columns, frames, tables or visuals to distract or confuse
- single column, left-aligned ('ragged right') text
- page numbering centred 1.5 cm from the bottom of the page
- no italics or underlining – emphasis is marked throughout by capitalisation, with an exception where underlining is used for extra emphasis to highlight item numbers and option letters in rubrics
- the insertion of blank pages where appropriate to ensure that tasks appear on a single two-page spread where possible.

Again, as with the standard-format and Braille versions of *Test S*, the CD is paused at prescribed points throughout the second hearing of each passage to allow the candidate sufficient time to read items and write and check answers.

Test H **(listening version for hearing-impaired candidates)**

The Listening paper suitable for hearing-impaired candidates, known as *Test H*, is routinely produced for deaf and hearing-impaired candidates. Any hearing-impaired candidate can opt to take *Test H* rather than the standard Listening test.

There is no CD with Test H. Instead, the script is read out 'live' by either one or two interlocutors. Candidates use either lip-reading (for deaf candidates) or a combination of listening and lip-reading (for hearing-impaired candidates) to follow the interlocutor. Since lip-reading candidates cannot simultaneously follow the interlocutor and read the items on the question paper, the script has built-in pauses during the second reading for candidates to read items and write and check answers, in the same manner as *Test S*. Due to the additional demands caused by such switching of attention and the fact that reading and answering cannot be accomplished simultaneously with lip-reading – an issue generated by the testing context and unique to candidates taking *Test H* – candidates are given a third reading of the script (without any pauses). Gutteridge (2010:2) outlines the rationale behind this policy:

... to compensate for the fragmented nature of the second reading, in that some candidates lose the thread of the argument or topic while struggling to understand the reader and at the same time find answers to the items. The third reading allows the candidate to review the whole text and, particularly, check their answers to global questions.

The issue of the number of interlocutors within a listening passage is one that has led to certain practical decisions. For KET and PET, where the exchanges are straightforward, there may be two interlocutors where appropriate. For FCE, CAE and CPE, however, this has proved to be too problematic due to the relative complexity of the exchanges, so all passages are delivered by a single interlocutor. To achieve this, dialogues are converted into monologues by means of minimal changes. For interview-type tasks where the interviewer has limited input, the interviewer's turns may be absorbed into a monologue by making minimal changes to the script; in particular, care is taken to ensure that parts containing the key information, which always occurs in the interviewee's turn, are unedited. None the less, it should still be recognised that there will likely be some effect on the text in terms of its overall coherence, if not the informational content. For 'genuine' dialogues, especially those where two speakers disagree, it is often not possible to convert passages into reasonable monologues, so these are not included. This has the consequence of rendering CAE Part 3 and CPE Part 4[2] (testing agreement between two speakers) unsuitable for inclusion in *Test H*. These two parts are therefore omitted and scores on the remaining three parts converted to an equivalent score over four parts, taking into account the relative difficulties of the truncated and full tests using Item Response Theory (IRT) analysis (see Chapter 5 for a discussion of IRT). Whilst there will naturally be questions over the absolute comparability of the edited passages and the loss of construct coverage in CAE and CPE due to the omission of one part of the test, this has proved to be the only workable compromise within the context of reasonable adjustments to provide access for deaf and hearing-impaired candidates, whilst retaining as far as possible the format and integrity of the original test.

The 'live' delivery of *Test H* inevitably leads to a certain degree of non-standardisation. Although the content of the script is the same for all candidates taking the same form of *Test H*, different interlocutors will naturally deliver the script with different rhythms, speeds and emphasis, and with different clarity of lip movements. Interlocutors are provided with guidelines and instructions in the *Supervisor's Booklet*, but it is of course impossible to remove the variation in delivery outlined above. This reflects the situation in the past with standard Listening tests. Until 1975, FCE and CPE (then the only tests available) were read out live routinely; standardised recordings on audio cassettes (now CDs) were introduced precisely to address the issue of non-standard delivery. A similar move in future towards standardised delivery of *Test H*, involving the production of video recordings of interlocutors, would be desirable to bring *Test H* into line with the standard Listening test.

A3 enlarged version

The A3 enlarged version is simply the standard Listening paper enlarged to A3 size, i.e. 141% of the original size, and is taken with the standard CD. It does not require special administrative arrangements such as separate invigilation.

The A3 enlarged version is suitable for candidates with mild visual impairment who find normal size print difficult to read but do not require additional time to read or write their answers. It should be noted that although the font size of the A3 enlarged version is larger than the standard version, it does not contain any of the VI-friendly formatting found in the MLP version of *Test S*.

Listening test question papers printed on coloured paper

Some candidates with special requirements, particularly those with dyslexia or dyspraxia, benefit from taking the test on coloured paper of the candidate's choice. This typically involves black text on green, buff or blue paper, but may include other colour combinations such as white text on black paper. Alternatively, candidates may bring their own coloured overlay to place over a Listening question paper.

Bespoke modifications for Listening tests

Cambridge ESOL will accept any reasonable requests for modified Listening test materials in accordance with the needs of candidates with special requirements. These often include text enlarged beyond the standard MLP font size of 18 points; MLP papers with 25.5 point text (printed on A3 paper) or 36 points (printed on A2 paper) are typical here, although Listening question papers with a font size as large as 72 points (printed on A0 paper, with dimensions of 841mm x 1189mm) have even been supplied. MLP papers with additional spacing in the text have also been provided.

Special administrative arrangements for Listening tests

Separate invigilation

Where appropriate, candidates can take the Listening test in a separate room, supervised on a one-to-one basis. This is the case with all candidates taking *Test S* (including MLP and Braille versions) and *Test H*.

Use of headphones (in those test centres where they are not the norm)

For candidates with mild hearing impairment, in centres which do not use headphones as a matter of course, it may be appropriate for the candidate to use headphones for the purposes of volume and sound quality, and to exclude background noise. This is best administered with separate invigilation to avoid the candidate being exposed to the recording from the speaker, which can cause problems, especially if the sound through the headphones is not perfectly synchronised.

Use of coloured overlays

As discussed above in the section on Listening question papers printed on coloured paper, allowing candidates with dyslexia and dyspraxia to use coloured overlays on their Listening question papers can often mitigate against their condition.

Use of an amanuensis

Candidates who are physically unable to write their answers in a Listening test can apply for the use of an amanuensis, who will transcribe their answers exactly as dictated to them, including the candidate's spelling. This accommodation will naturally require the provision of *Test S*, since such candidates will not be able to complete the Listening test under standard administration. Note that this arrangement is not allowed for candidates with dyslexia or dyspraxia since their writing issues are not due to a physical inability to write; instead, a scribe is the appropriate provision (see below).

Use of a scribe

A scribe differs from an amanuensis in that an amanuensis takes dictation without the candidate writing while a scribe is used when the candidate is able to write but there are issues of legibility. Candidates who have serious handwriting problems, including candidates with dyslexia and dyspraxia, can apply for the use of a scribe in a Listening test. Candidates complete the test themselves, whether *Test S* or the standard version, then the scribe copies the candidate's answers clearly, *exactly* as written by the candidate, onto the Listening answer sheet after the test. This takes place in the presence of the candidate, who can provide clarification where necessary.

Exemption from the Listening paper

Unfortunately, there will always be some cases where it is not possible to make reasonable adjustments in order to provide access for the candidate to the Listening paper, for instance in the case of a deaf candidate who cannot lip-read. In such cases, the candidate may apply for an exemption from taking the Listening component of a test. Certificates for candidates with exemptions receive an endorsement stating: 'The candidate was exempted from satisfying the full range of assessment objectives in the examination'. Note, however, that for Cambridge ESOL Main Suite examinations, candidates may apply for an exemption from only *one* test paper, either the Listening or the Speaking component.

The list of administrative arrangements above is not exhaustive, and other administrative arrangements for a Listening test may be offered as appropriate on a case-by-case basis.

Access technology

Use of keyboards to record answers

Candidates who have problems writing their answers, for example those with problems with fine motor skills (the co-ordination of small muscle movements), can opt to record their answers using a keyboard. This provision applies to candidates with dysgraphia (a condition causing difficulty in writing by hand which is manifested in poor handwriting and a tendency to transpose letters and write them in mirror image). For many such candidates the use of a keyboard helps to alleviate their writing problems. Visually impaired candidates can use large print keyboards, although they need to supply these themselves.

Use of Braille keyboards to record answers

Similarly to the use of a keyboard for some sighted candidates, blind candidates can opt to record their answers using a Braille keyboard. Candidates typically supply their own equipment in such cases.

Magnifiers

Visually impaired candidates may use magnifiers – either magnifying glasses or electronic magnifiers – if they are accustomed to using them for reading. These may be used in conjunction with either the standard or MLP version of *Test S*. As with Braille keyboards, candidates typically supply their own equipment in such cases.

Screen readers

Blind candidates, especially those who do not read Braille, may opt to take a paper-based (PB) test on-screen using screen-reading software. In such cases, Cambridge ESOL supplies a pdf of the test paper which has been specially modified to make it more screenreader-friendly and which the candidate accesses via a computer. Since blind candidates typically have their computers carefully set up in a manner with which they are familiar, candidates may be permitted to use their own laptops in such cases. Note that for security and quality assurance reasons, Cambridge ESOL will under no circumstances supply an editable version of a question paper (for example in Microsoft Word format); this is in order to protect the integrity of the paper, and the pdf files must be securely shredded after use to maintain test security (Cambridge ESOL supplies guidelines on how to accomplish this).

Computer-based (CB) access arrangements

The Flash-based delivery system currently used for CB versions of Cambridge ESOL tests does not allow for the requisite modifications necessary for candidates with SR. Candidates with special requirements are instead offered the PB provisions outlined above. However, Cambridge ESOL is in the process of developing a new XHTML-based delivery engine for CB tests, which will contain the following built-in accessibility features of relevance to Listening tests for candidates with special requirements:

- user-definable font sizes
- user-definable background and font colours
- a facility for supervisors to pause recordings
- compatibility with refreshable Braille displays
- compatibility with embedded video recordings
- compatibility with screen readers.

These features will allow for the administration of CB versions of *Test S* Listening papers under the same conditions as PB versions, and the replication of the full range of access arrangements as outlined for PB tests, accommodating blind and visually impaired candidates as well as those with motor difficulties and special educational needs. The system's compatibility with embedded videos will also provide the facility to administer CB *Test H* versions of Listening papers when the tests are moved to video format.

Sign language

Cambridge ESOL does not provide a sign language version for any of its Listening tests for the reasons explained earlier. Cambridge ESOL's examinations are tests of *English language* proficiency, and the candidate's ability to communicate within an English-language environment. Deaf or hearing-impaired candidates who are unable to lip-read should therefore apply for an exemption from the Listening paper. The position taken by Cambridge ESOL should not be taken as an indication of any judgement regarding the relative statuses of English and English-based sign languages, but as a reflection of their independent status and the consequent testing concerns outlined above.

Special Consideration

Whatever procedures and systems are put in place for the administration of a test, there are inevitably occasions when events go awry due to unforeseen incidents, leaving candidates disadvantaged through no fault of their own. Disturbances, sudden illness and human error in administration can conspire to thwart a candidate's careful preparation and affect their performance negatively. This is especially true of listening tests, where the recording is typically played through from start to finish with no possibility of rewinding and replaying. Even a passing jet plane or a sudden noise outside can easily cause candidates to miss key information, and technical problems with the audio equipment can naturally have a major effect on candidates. Such incidents can affect candidates in two ways:

1. The immediate effect of missing key information, which becomes an issue of scoring validity (see Chapter 5), since the affected candidates' scores on the item(s) in question can no longer be considered reliable.
2. The effect on the candidate's psychological state, which can be said to alter the test taker's characteristics, albeit temporarily, and can often have a greater impact on the candidate's performance than the initial incident.

In such cases, the test provider needs to assess the extent of the effect, if any, on the candidate's performance and, where appropriate, put into place measures to mitigate against this, which usually take the form of the awarding of extra marks according to a pre-determined set of criteria.

Special Consideration: Cambridge ESOL practice

Where an incident has taken place in a Listening test which may merit Special Consideration, the test centre manager must submit a Special Consideration form to Cambridge ESOL after the session but before results have been issued (see Appendix D for more details on this). On the form the centre manager is required to describe the nature, duration and severity of the problem, plus any other relevant details. The case is scrutinised by a Special Consideration panel, which attempts to ascertain to what extent, if any, the candidates involved were disadvantaged and which recommends appropriate action in the light of this. Special Consideration may also be applicable in cases where a candidate is absent from a component with good reason, for instance when he or she falls ill on the day of the Listening test.

Special Consideration is not appropriate for candidates with special requirements; the appropriate course of action in such cases is to provide Special Arrangements to facilitate access, as outlined above in the section on candidates with special requirements. Only in cases where the Special Arrangements provided can be shown to be inappropriate or inadequate is Special Consideration applicable.

Conclusion

This chapter has discussed the extensive variety of individual characteristics of a physiological, psychological (both cognitive and affective) and experiential nature which can affect a test taker's performance on a listening test. While some of these characteristics may be relevant to the construct being tested, others may not be relevant; in the latter case, where a test taker's performance is affected, this can be seen as representing unfair bias (positive or negative). In light of this, test taker characteristics must be taken into account in all facets of listening test design to ensure a balanced test which avoids as far as possible the risk of bias towards or against test takers possessing certain characteristics.

A particular case where test taker characteristics can have a major effect on performance in a listening test is where a test taker has special requirements. In some instances, there may be no effect, or the effect may be relevant to the testing objectives; in these cases, no specific measures are necessary. However, in other instances certain assumptions built into the test format which may be reasonable for the majority of test takers, such as the ability to record answers while listening to the recording, may unfairly disadvantage test takers with special requirements; in these cases, wherever possible, test developers need to make appropriate provisions to allow candidates to demonstrate their true level of attainment without compromising the testing objectives.

This concludes an investigation of test taker characteristics, motivated by the effect that such characteristics can have on a test taker's performance in a listening test, and in particular on the test taker's cognitive processing. Attention now turns in Chapter 3, on cognitive validity, to a study of the cognitive processes involved in listening comprehension and the validation of these aspects of listening tests.

Endnotes

1. The large number of blank responses means that it is difficult to interpret some differences between levels and may, for instance, explain why more PET candidates reported a primary education than at KET level (the figures are virtually identical as a proportion of completed responses). It almost certainly explains why more CAE candidates reported college/university level education than at CPE (the CPE figure was actually considerably higher as a proportion of completed responses, but there were 44.7% blank responses).
2. The revised CPE listening format (from 2013) will, however, no longer require the removal of Part 4 from *Test H*.

3 Cognitive validity

John Field
CRELLA, University of Bedfordshire

Introduction

This chapter considers the cognitive validity of the Listening tests which form part of the Cambridge ESOL suite. By 'cognitive validity' is to be understood the extent to which the tasks employed succeed in eliciting from candidates a set of processes which resemble those employed by a proficient listener in a real-world listening event. A second consideration is how finely the relevant processes are graded across the levels of the suite in terms of the cognitive demands that they impose upon the candidate.

This volume is the fourth of a series proposing principles for establishing the validity of tests of proficiency in second language skills. The present chapter can therefore draw upon approaches to cognitive validity already established in Chapters 3 of Shaw and Weir (2007) on writing, Khalifa and Weir (2009) on reading and Taylor (Ed.) (2011) on speaking. As with the previous analyses, a major goal is to outline a process model of the construct under consideration, which can serve as a framework for judging the cognitive validity of any test of skilled performance.

A secondary goal, again following earlier precedents, is to identify aspects of test design which impose additional cognitive demands upon the candidate and have the potential to divert the candidate from the processes which might normally be employed during a real-life listening situation. The features to be considered would appear to be more numerous in the case of listening. Because it is a receptive skill, they include the techniques which have to be employed by a tester in order to obtain a reliable external quantification of what is essentially a process internal to the listener. They also include (following Khalifa and Weir 2009) the type of text and the use to which the test taker is required to put it; and (following Field 2011a) the cognitive demands imposed upon test takers by the formats used. In considering listening, one additionally needs to take account of features of the input which are subject to considerable variation from one speaker or context to another, in contrast to the relatively standardised form in which a reading text appears.

The chapter falls into three parts. Firstly, there is an explanation of the general notion of cognitive validity, which retraces and extends some of the points made in earlier volumes but does so with specific reference to the present exercise and its focus on listening. Next, there is a brief overview of research findings on the nature of listening. This leads on to a process account of the skill, drawing upon models provided by various researchers and commentators. The models are adapted to provide a five-level framework for an examination of the cognitive validity of the tests in the Cambridge ESOL suite.

Finally, the discussion moves on to consider a number of characteristics of the Cambridge ESOL Listening tests which potentially enhance or compromise cognitive validity or which determine the cognitive load upon the listener. There will be consideration of each of the three main components of a listening test: the recorded material, the task and the items. This line of enquiry recognises the symbiotic relationship between cognitive and context validity, where decisions taken on contextual parameters potentially affect the way in which the input is processed. In this chapter, the three components will specifically be considered from the perspective of a) the likely cognitive demands which they impose upon the candidate as compared to those that a real-life listening event imposes; and b) how finely the facets of task design are calibrated in terms of gradations of cognitive difficulty across the Cambridge ESOL suite.

The cognitive validation exercise

Cognitive validity

The concept of cognitive validity came to prominence in the 1990s (Glaser 1991). A strand of construct validity, it addresses the extent to which a test requires a candidate to engage in cognitive processes that resemble or parallel those that would be employed in non-test circumstances. This consideration is particularly relevant to educational and professional contexts. Does an achievement test in a philosophy course demonstrate that its students have come to think like philosophers or simply that they can reproduce theories? Does a medical qualification indicate that a graduate can make professional judgements or simply that he/she has acquired the body of knowledge on which those judgements are based?

Cognitive validity has had a considerable impact upon recent thinking in educational measurement in the USA. It has been applied to tests of scientific and logical reasoning (Baxter and Glaser 1998, Ruiz-Primo and Shavelson 1996, Thelk and Hoole 2006) and to the measurement of other forms of higher order reasoning (Linn, Baker and Dunbar 1991). It has been used to evaluate concept mapping (Ruiz-Primo, Schultz, Li and Shavelson 2001) and self-report instruments for assessing mastery of lesson content (Koskey, Karabenick, Woolley, Bonney and Dever 2010). Researchers have also investigated the cognitive processes that underlie tests of clinical diagnosis

(Gagnon, Charlin, Roy, St-Martin, Sauvé, Boshuizen and van der Vleuten 2008), and aids to decision-making (Larichev 1992). More generally, Snow, Corno and Jackson (1996) have proposed a framework to enable the validation of aptitude tests.

The criterion of cognitive validity was applied to second language assessment by Weir (2005a) as part of his socio-cognitive framework, where it was originally termed *theory-based validity*. Weir not only draws attention to the importance of achieving a better understanding of the construct being tested; he also relates cognitive validity to concerns over traditional *post hoc* approaches to investigating construct validity, where statistical methods such as factor analysis are applied to test results in order to establish the nature of what has been tested. He raises the question of whether the data under examination might be compromised by the form and content of the test and by assumptions underlying its design. To put it in simple cognitive terms, he identifies the dangers of relying exclusively on an approach that attempts to track back from a product or outcome to the process that gave rise to it. Instead, he argues for an additional strand of construct validation where testers take account, from the outset, of empirical evidence about the nature of the expertise that the test aims to assess.

Cognitive validity is of particular concern in the case of tests whose scores are employed predictively to indicate the test taker's suitability for a future university place, for a job in a domain such as business, medicine, teaching or tourism or for acceptance under an immigration programme. It is not enough for such tests to demonstrate that a test taker has reached a criterial level of language knowledge; they must also be capable of demonstrating that the test taker is capable of linguistic behaviour that meets the requirements of the target context. If there is a significant qualitative difference between the processes elicited by the test and those demanded by the context, then the ability of the test to predict performance is open to question.

Tests such as those of the Cambridge ESOL suite aim to assess competence in the four language skills across a proficiency continuum. Their value to a language teacher, employer or academic recruiter lies in their ability to indicate how competently a candidate might be expected to perform in actual L2 contexts. Thus it becomes important for test designers to know, and to be able to demonstrate, how far what happens in the testing situation replicates cognitive processing in the world beyond the test, so that test users can have confidence in the meaningfulness and usefulness of the score outcomes from the test.

What is at issue here is not a simple matter of ecological validity. Clearly, it is not possible for the conditions under which a language test is administered to approximate closely to those of an actual listening or speaking event. The goal is to establish whether the tasks proposed by the test designer elicit *mental processes* adequately representative of those which a language user would employ in a target real-world context. The processes in question might relate to the way in which the user assembles or interprets input; or they might reflect the types of response required of the user by facets of the task. As the concept of cognitive validation in language testing has evolved, the term 'representative' in the characterisation above has in effect come to cover three main questions.

a. *Similarity of processing.* Are the processes adopted during a test sufficiently similar to those which would be employed in the target context? Or do candidates adopt additional processes that are a product of facets of the test (procedure, test method, item) rather than part of the normal operations associated with the construct being tested? (Field 2012). In other words, is there what Messick (1989) terms *construct irrelevance*?

b. *Comprehensiveness.* Do the items in the test elicit only a small sub-set of the cognitive processes that a language user would employ in a natural context? Or do they tap into a sufficiently broad range of such processes for the test to be deemed representative of real-world behaviour? This might be a reflection of the method employed; but it might equally be a question of how diverse the test items are. Do the majority operate at a single level of processing or do they operate at various levels? This would seem to relate to Messick's (1989) concern over possible construct *under-representation*.

c. *Calibration.* Across a suite of tests graded by reference to a scale, are the cognitive demands imposed upon test takers at each level appropriately calibrated in relation to the performance features that might be expected of a listener at these levels?

These three considerations will guide the cognitive validation exercise conducted later in this chapter.

Why cognitive validation?

At this point, it is not unreasonable to ask why we have need of the kind of external evidence just discussed. Surely the content and goals of language skills testing have already been elaborated in some detail by experts working within the field? We possess a number of widely recognised sets of criteria, including the Common European Framework of Reference (CEFR) (Council of Europe 2001), the ALTE Can Do statements and Cambridge's own set of handbook specifications (see Chapter 1 of this volume).

While these documents have proved invaluable guides to those designing tests or seeking to standardise scales, they suffer from certain limitations. They are intuitive: based upon the perceptions of experts accrued over time, not upon empirical evidence or a framework of well-substantiated theory. In addition, they have not taken on board a recent shift in thinking that accords a much more central place in test design and validation to the role of the test taker (Kunnan 1995, O'Sullivan 2011). They focus upon the *what* rather than the *how*: they are concerned with the products of skilled performance but do not characterise the skill that underlies it. In attempting to specify levels of competence, they place emphasis less upon the behaviour of those who are being tested than upon the content which the successful candidate is capable of producing or understanding.

This is particularly evident in the case of listening, which is probably the most thinly profiled of the four skills (it does not even feature in 14 of the 24 ALTE Can Do categories for oral skills (see page 11 in Chapter 1)). In the CEFR Scales (see pages 13–14), the criteria are almost exclusively based upon the input that a listener can comprehend: covering topical content (familiarity, complexity and abstractness), linguistic content (idiom and register, syntactic complexity) and discourse structure, and also referring to speaker characteristics (variety and speech rate). This certainly assists test designers in selecting appropriate recorded material; but it provides no insight into *listener* characteristics and into how test takers might be expected to respond to the material selected. Buck (2001:102) seems to have this distinction in mind when he identifies two ways of defining a construct: in terms of the tasks which a test taker is capable of accomplishing or in terms of test taker competence.

Something similar can be said about the specifications provided by the Cambridge ESOL handbooks under the heading 'test focus' (see Table 3.1 below). At lower levels, they propose a few conventional 'listening for' categories. At higher levels, they list the language functions that the test taker can be expected to understand, though the areas covered seem to vary little across levels. There is nothing equivalent to the notions of fluency or automaticity in speaking and writing or to the processing parameters (local/global and expeditious/careful) proposed by Urquhart and Weir (1998) for reading.

Table 3.1 'Test focus' criteria cited in Cambridge ESOL handbooks

Test	'Test focus'
KET	Listening to identify key information; listening and writing down information
PET	Listening to identify key information from short exchanges, listening to identify specific information and detailed meaning; listening to identify, understand and interpret information; listening for detailed meaning and to identify the attitudes and opinions of the speakers
FCE	General gist, detail, function, purpose, attitude, opinion, relationship, topic, place, situation, genre, agreement etc.
CAE	Feeling, attitude, opinion, purpose, function, agreement, course of action, gist, detail etc.
CPE	Gist, detail, function, purpose, topic, speaker, addressee, feeling, attitude, opinion etc.

Source: Cambridge ESOL 2008c, 2012c:31, 2012d:35,50)

Cognitive validation can add an additional dimension to these criteria. Using research methods such as retrospective verbal report (Field 2012), it can shed light on how test takers manipulate the material of a test and how closely their behaviour under these circumstances can be said to correspond to that of a real-world language user. Through exercises such as the present one, it can examine the extent to which existing test material does or does not tap into underlying cognitive processes specific to the construct and attested in empirical findings. It also, as Weir (2005:18) intimates, provides test designers with criteria based on candidate behaviour, thus equipping them to design future test materials *ab initio* on the basis of an informed view of the construct they wish to measure.

The cognitive perspective

The framework outlined here relies chiefly upon theory and evidence taken not from testing studies or from general linguistics but from psycholinguistics, speech science, phonetics and discourse analysis. Within those fields, two areas of enquiry are particularly relevant to the present exercise. The first consists of research on *speech processing*: specifically, on how speech is perceived, matched to stored representations in the mind, assembled into propositions and enriched by the use of external knowledge. The second concerns *the nature of expertise*; the assumption here being that the ability to decode speech with a high degree of automaticity and to construct wider meanings from what has been heard is a type of *expert* behaviour (Ericsson and Simon 1993, Feltovich, Prietula and Ericsson 2006) which has elements in common with playing chess or driving a car.

The notion of expertise can be quite simply explained. Human working memory resources are limited (Baddeley 1986, Gathercole and Baddeley 1993), which obliges us to direct attention to those aspects of a mental operation that are most fundamental to its success. A novice in any skill has to lend considerable attention to low-level processes (examples might be putting a car into motion or assessing the relative positions of chess pieces). Over time and practice, two important developments occur (Anderson 1983). The basic processes become increasingly **automatised**, demanding less and less attention. In addition, small-scale processes become combined into larger operations. The result is to considerably reduce the demands made upon an individual's working memory when employing the skill, leaving them with spare memory capacity to give to the wider picture. The notion of expertise has been much applied to second language speech production (Johnson 2005, Kormos 2006). It is equally relevant to listening, where the fundamental process of deriving words from connected speech becomes increasingly automatic with experience, thus enabling the listener to lend attention instead to larger and more abstract judgements about a speaker or recording, including inferences and the evaluation of ideas.

There are implications here for mapping listener development across a suite of tests.

Second language acquisition (SLA) commentators occasionally misunderstand what cognitive approaches to language skills entail. It is mistaken to suggest that, in examining language processing, cognitive scientists ignore issues of context or deny their relevance. On the contrary, in the case of listening, they concern themselves quite closely with the types of inference which occur when a listener has to take account of speaker factors such as illocutionary intent or knowledge that is assumed to be shared. They also allow for the possible impact upon a listener's attentional resources of affective factors such as tiredness or anxiety. However, their principal focus is on the mental operations which are engaged by language users (in our case, listeners) under normal circumstances and the way in which situation-specific information of various kinds is integrated into those operations.

Nor do cognitive psychologists rely upon the assumption that all language users behave identically. While certain processing routines may provide the easiest and most efficient routes to language production and reception, some users (including L2 learners) achieve the same goals by less direct means. It is evident that individuals, whether listening in L1 or L2, vary enormously in the range of vocabulary they command and in their experience of certain listening contexts and types of speaker. It is also evident that L2 listeners respond in very individual ways to the challenges posed by an inadequate lexical or grammatical repertoire, with some more inclined to strategy use than others. Nevertheless, the premise is adopted that the four language skills are dependent upon certain established and shared routines which can be identified by examining the performance of expert language users. These routines are determined by the nature of the skill (to give a simple example, all readers, of whatever script, have to move their eyes across a page or screen and decipher marks on it). They also seem to reflect certain biases and constraints in the way the human brain operates.

In the case of listening, one needs additionally to consider the constraints upon performance imposed by the nature of the signal. Listeners have to make sense of input that is subject to enormous variation from one speaker to another and from one speech event to another. They have to do so under extreme pressures of time and usually without being able to refer to any permanent record of the transaction. These circumstances apply in all listening encounters – and must inevitably determine the way in which listeners behave.

In specifying the processes which enable human beings to perceive and understand spoken language, the discussion that follows will in the main exclude consideration of situation-specific social and affective factors (motivation, tiredness, anxiety, personal feelings about the speaker) which might influence the level of attention accorded by the listener to the speaker's words, determine the degree of empathy exhibited by the listener and affect the interpretations that the listener derives. These features are the concern of social rather than cognitive psychology and fall more appropriately under the test taker characteristics covered in Chapter 2.

Similarly, most issues relating to text type and content are dealt with in Chapter 4. To the extent that the present chapter considers linguistic difficulty, it does so purely in terms of the cognitive effort which the retrieval of a piece of vocabulary or the assembly of a syntactic structure might require. The phonological and phonetic features of the recorded input are analysed only in terms of the processing demands which they impose upon the test taker and in terms of whether they require the type of listening process that might occur in a real-life context.

The approach to cognitive validation

The direction taken by the chapter conforms quite closely to the approach to validation developed in earlier volumes in this series (Shaw and Weir 2007:34–62, Khalifa and Weir 2009:34–80, Field 2011a: 65–111). It entails constructing an empirically attested model of the target skill as employed by expert users under non-test conditions; then relating the processes which feature in the model to the specifications of the test under scrutiny. The models presented in the previous accounts of writing, reading and speaking were based upon information-processing principles, thus enabling the researcher to identify specific phases through which a language user normally proceeds (though Shaw and Weir (2007) make the point that the phases are not necessarily sequential and that not all of them are obligatory). These phases provide a framework for determining in a systematic way how the various processes which make up performance in a given skill are represented, explicitly or implicitly, in the types of response required of the test taker.

While adhering closely to this line of attack, Khalifa and Weir (2009) extended the scope of cognitive validation by considering not simply the processes involved in employing the language skill in question, but also the varying cognitive demands placed upon the candidate by the tasks mentioned in the test specifications. Thinking along similar lines, Field (2011a) argued that cognitive validity should include the consideration of certain other task parameters over which test designers exercise control. In particular, he identified, in relation to speaking, the question of degree of interaction and the question of time allowed, or not allowed, for pre-planning. These, he claimed, affected the type of speaking that test takers were required to produce. They carried implications in terms both of the cognitive demands imposed upon the test taker and of the extent to which processing under test conditions could be said to replicate or resemble that of real life.

Listening is arguably the most complex of the four language skills to test. A comparison between the variables to be discussed here and those identified by Khalifa and Weir (2009: Chapter 1) in relation to reading demonstrates how much more multi-faceted the construct is. Additional components requiring consideration include the characteristics of the recording; the types of task that serve to quantify what is essentially a process internal to the listener; and the form of the items, which, significantly, are in a different modality from the construct being tested. All three potentially add to the cognitive demands imposed upon the test taker and all have the potential to lead the test taker away from processes which would normally be employed in a real-life listening event.

The discussion will adopt a strictly cognitive perspective, to avoid overlap with the more extensive examination of task design in Chapter 4; the criteria identified will then be related to characteristics of the Listening tests in the Cambridge ESOL General English suite.

In sum, the scope of this chapter is:

1. To consider the nature of cognitive processing involved in first and second language listening by reviewing the relevant academic literature, both theoretical and empirical.

2. To propose a model or framework against which listening tests, including those produced by Cambridge ESOL, could be analysed, described and evaluated for the purposes of cognitive validation.

3. To apply the model to a specific set of Cambridge ESOL Listening tests at the different General English proficiency levels in order to generate an analysis of the cognitive processes underlying the test takers' performance which might serve, *a priori*, to guide future test design (Weir 2005a:18).

4. To consider cognitive factors which might determine the relative difficulty of tests at different levels in the Cambridge ESOL suite. These relate mainly to task variables, which can be seen as adding to or alleviating the cognitive demands made upon the candidate; but there will also be consideration of the recorded materials used.

Psycholinguistic accounts of speech processing

Listening has tended to be accorded low priority in second language research. By contrast, it is often said in first language speech science and psycholinguistics that the receptive skills have received far more attention than the productive ones and that there has been a particular focus on the processing of speech. In point of fact, the bulk of this very extensive research has focused on speech *perception;* there has not been comparable interest in how a listener goes on to deal with the message that is derived from the signal. In discussing the construction of meaning, a commentator therefore has to draw quite heavily upon research and theory within discourse analysis – though work in that field is often strongly underpinned by an understanding of general psychological concepts relating to memory limitations and to how world knowledge is stored and used.

From whatever sources, the body of research is very large, and it is impossible to do it justice in a brief overview. We will therefore concentrate on aspects that draw attention to some of the principal characteristics of the listening skill. They are the variability of the input; word recognition; and analysis at clause and discourse level. The discussion will be rather more extensive than in other volumes in this series, since it is assumed that the basic principles of listening research may be less familiar to the reader.

Variability of input

Phoneme level

Much early psycholinguistic research into speech perception focused on the phoneme. It has long been known from spectrographic evidence that in natural speech phonemes vary widely. Researchers in the 1960s at Haskins Laboratories and elsewhere strove to find an explanation for the way in which the listener is able to match acoustic cues in the speech signal to the sounds of a phonological system. However, they were unable to find any one-to-one relationships between particular clusters of cues and the phoneme categories that listeners perceived. Two basic tenets became established (Nygaard and Pisoni 1995):

- **non-invariance**: the recognition of consonants depends upon the acoustic context within which they occur and the recognition of vowels is relative to the fundamental frequency of the speaker's voice
- **non-linearity**: phonemes do not have clear boundaries but blend into adjoining phonemes.

A number of hypotheses were explored as to how the perceptual system operated at segmental level. They included proposals that the principal unit of analysis for a listener was larger than a phoneme (a demi-syllable or syllable) or that the listener mapped directly from cues in the signal to words without any intervening categorisation into phonemes. An even more radical solution to the 'non-invariance' problem proposes that listeners do not package the signal into linguistic units at all but divide it up into equal sections determined by time. This is the approach adopted by the most well-known computer simulation of listening. TRACE, a connectionist model (McClelland and Elman 1986), processes the signal in small **time-slices** which are independent of phoneme, syllable and word boundaries. Each time-slice is connected to those that immediately precede it, so the processor can combine evidence from current input with evidence from what has immediately gone before.

Lexical

There is often considerable difference between the citation form of a word and the way it is realised in connected speech. Three major factors are in play. The first is the relative importance of the word within the intonation group. Intonation in English assists the listener by foregrounding the most critical word in an utterance by means of focal stress. However, this carries a price, in that the surrounding words may become considerably reduced in prominence (in particular, shorter in duration). Function words are very likely to occur in their reduced forms. The second factor is the articulatory demands placed upon a speaker when producing a complex consonant sequence in a word (*twelfth*) or two words in conjunction (*next spring*). The third is the level of formality of the utterance, and thus the precision of articulation that the speaker chooses to employ. In all these circumstances, words may be subject to assimilation, elision and resyllabification, all processes well documented by phoneticians. See Brown (1990) for an excellent overview, and Field (2009a: Chapter 9) on the implications for second language learning.

Speaker variation

Less frequently considered are the differences between individual speakers. There is obviously wide variation in the fundamental frequency of voices, relating to gender and age. There are differences of voice quality due to the size and position of the speaker's articulators. In addition, speech rate and pitch range vary considerably between individuals and even within the speech of one individual, depending on context (Brown 1990). Then there are variations due to regional and social accents, of which much is often made in tests of second language listening.

A listener must process features of the speaker's voice at the same time as processing the information content that the speaker is transmitting. Speech rate and fundamental frequency are factors that contribute to phoneme recognition, while other features, such as a sudden shift in pitch, can be rhetorical devices supporting meaning or an understanding of the speaker's state of mind. For psycholinguists, this raises the question of how the listener manages to suppress the **indexical** features which have just been described in order to leave only the linguistic content that has to be analysed for meaning. The traditional solution is that a process of **normalisation** takes place (Pisoni 1997) in which features specific to the speaker are edited out, leaving a version of the signal that is in some kind of standardised phonological form. However, there is some evidence (Goldinger 1997) suggesting that indexical information is held in working memory alongside linguistic, thus explaining why listeners can recognise voices so accurately on the telephone.

The issue of normalisation is little discussed in second language contexts. But it is clear that the candidate's need to adjust to unfamiliar voices (including their speech rate and fundamental frequency) is an important consideration for the language tester. It should certainly inform decisions on aspects of the recording such as the number of voices to be adjusted to and their potential confusability, not to mention factors such as accent and speech rate which add to the cognitive load associated with normalisation.

A possible solution to variation

A radical but persuasive solution to these problems of variation has recently received much serious consideration. For a long while, psychological studies assumed that the human brain was a poor storage device but was strong in processing information extracted from memory. Recent evidence, however, has demonstrated that the brain has much greater storage capacity than was ever assumed (see Dąbrowska (2003) for a summary). This has given credibility to the view that we store far more information when listening to a speaker than had been assumed. In terms of phonemes, it is suggested (Bybee 2001) that the speaker does not store a template of an ideal phoneme in the mind but instead stores multiple versions of it that have been heard in everyday speech. This permits a direct match to be made between an example of a phoneme in a piece of incoming speech and a similar previously encountered example. It can also apply at the level of lexis, enabling the listener to recognise many variants of a given word on the basis of previous experience of them. Similarly, when we normalise to indexical features of a speaker's voice such as speech rate or pitch, we may well be drawing upon experience of many other similar speakers we have previously encountered.

One strength of this **exemplar** (or **multiple-trace**) hypothesis is that it dovetails neatly with growing evidence of the important part played by **formulaic chunks** in the production and processing of both written and spoken language. With greater storage capacity, multiple chunks and collocations can be assumed to be stored as separate entries in the lexicon alongside single-word items and compounds (Wray 2001). A gradual development of this resource would be a mark of growing lexical proficiency in a second language learner.

Even more importantly, the model provides a convincing account of the way in which listeners, whether in L1 or L2, adjust to unfamiliar accents. On this analysis, adding a new variety to one's repertoire of intelligible accents is a matter of exposure. As a listener encounters more and more speakers of a given variety, he/she is able to build up a set of traces in long-term memory which provide points of reference for future encounters. This would appear to account for the holistic aspect of accent recognition – the way in which, for example, a rhotic /r/ triggers an expectation in the listener of certain other features associated with a known variety such as Standard American or Scottish English. But it also suggests that the development of the ability to decode non-standard varieties is serendipitous, and dependent upon the extent to which a listener has been exposed to them over time. This has implications for the policy adopted towards accents in the tests of the Cambridge ESOL suite, and will merit further discussion.

Lexical search

A second important area of enquiry concerns the recognition of spoken words. Here, thinking was influenced by an early finding by Marslen-Wilson (1973) that listening is an **online** activity. Instead of waiting until an utterance is complete, the listener attempts to decode what the speaker is saying at a delay of as little as a syllable. Largely on the basis of this premise, Marslen-Wilson devised his **Cohort Theory** (1989), which postulates that the lexical recognition process opens up a cohort of possible matches on the basis of early evidence of a word (perhaps its first syllable) and that the cohort is narrowed down as more evidence becomes available.

There are many loopholes in Cohort Theory – amongst them the difficulty of determining when a word is complete, given that many items contain others embedded within them (the word *activity* contains *act, active, it* and *tea*). The theory also seems to run counter to an early finding (Pollack and Pickett 1963) that it is impossible to recognise many short words (especially function words) if they are spliced out of natural running speech. This has been confirmed by experiments (Grosjean 1985) using a method known as **gating** in which listeners are exposed to progressively larger chunks of an utterance and report what they think they hear. It seems that much listening is *retroactive*, with many words not accurately identified until as late as three words after their offset. Grosjean comments that 'word recognition is not a word-by-word, left-to-right process. Rather, . . . the process is very much a feed-forward, feed-back operation, where there are constant adjustments being made to early and/or partial analyses . . .' (1985:309).

A further factor contributing to the gating findings is the absence in natural speech of consistent pauses between words corresponding to the white spaces in written text – which means that it is the listener who has to determine where words begin and end. This is not as easy as might be supposed, as the 'activity' example just given demonstrates. Many years' work by Cutler and associates has uncovered a number of different cues to word boundary position that are used by listeners, which vary according to language. They exploit features such as lexical stress, syllabicity and vowel harmony (Cutler 1997), and a constraint against dividing up the speech signal in a way that leaves a stranded non-word (Norris, McQueen, Cutler and Butterfield 1997). Evidence suggests that English listeners make use of a **Metrical Segmentation Strategy** (Cutler 1990), based upon the likelihood that a syllable bearing lexical stress marks the onset of a content word. It has been claimed, somewhat controversially (Cutler 1997:97), that speakers of languages with different segmentation systems do not succeed in acquiring the English one; Field (2001) provides evidence that this may not be the case.

The high variability of words in connected speech and the need to determine boundary locations pose considerable problems when accounting for how listeners manage to recognise words in connected speech. Most current accounts of spoken word recognition adopt the premise that words in the listener's lexicon are **in competition** as possible matches for short sections of the speech signal (McQueen 2007). They receive varying degrees of *activation* (effectively, listener confidence) depending upon how close a fit they provide, until the activation of one of them reaches such a high level that recognition occurs. Multiple cues contribute to the activation of a word candidate – knowledge of the word's various possible phonological forms, its relative frequency (and thus the likelihood of it occurring), the extent to which its boundaries conform to segmentation preferences, the word's association with other words heard earlier and – as more and more co-text becomes available – the extent to which the word accords with those around it.

The significance of this is that small misarticulations by the speaker or mishearings by the listener at phoneme level can be cancelled out. If a listener hears the word *veshtable*, he/she will not be fazed by it because knowledge of the existence of the word 'vegetable' will deal with any uncertainties – over-ruling the irregular / ʃ / in a 'top-down' fashion. If one accepts this highly **interactive** view of lexical retrieval, it raises questions about the value of items in listening tests which are based narrowly on phoneme-level distinctions. It also reinforces the doubtful validity of some of the earliest tests of listening, which relied heavily upon phoneme discrimination tasks (Weir forthcoming 2013b).

The notion that multiple sources of evidence participate in the word recognition process led to discussion as to whether information from the input has priority (in the sense of being processed first) or whether all sources are available from the outset. Findings such as those of Swinney (1979) and Ganong (1980) have been both challenged and replicated, and the issue remains unresolved. Its relevance for studies of second language listening is that this and similar controversies seem to have given rise to a mistaken notion that there are separate models for listening, described loosely as 'bottom up' (by which is often meant drawing on input), 'top down' (drawing on context) and interactive (drawing on both). It is self-evident that it is meaningless to think of either input or context as operating independently of the other. Amongst L1 listening specialists, the issue of concern has been whether the information is drawn upon sequentially or in parallel. For a clarification of the terms 'bottom up' and 'top down', see Field (1999a).

Syntactic parsing

What emerges from the description outlined so far – from input variation, from the use of multiple cues in word recognition, from segmentation strategies based upon probability and from the gating findings – is that listening is a highly tentative operation. If one accepts that processing is online, then a listener must be constantly creating hypotheses as to what a speaker is saying and retaining them in the mind until such time as they are confirmed or replaced. These hypotheses might be at the level of the phoneme, the word or the whole utterance; but it is at the level of syntax that there is a particular tension between the way in which the information is delivered and the linguistic forms that have to be derived from it. The listener has to impose a syntactic pattern on the utterance – but can only do so in a piecemeal fashion, since the input is received in real time, syllable by syllable.

There has been considerable interest in the process of **syntactic parsing** in both reading and listening. In the early days of psycholinguistics, research focused on the way in which readers (and occasionally listeners) chose to attach constituents when they were presented with cases of ambiguity in the form of '**garden path**' sentences such as *The lawyer questioned . . . by the judge admitted lying*. Researchers sought evidence that language users were constrained by a canonical word order (subject/verb/object (SVO) in the case of English) and/or by principles such as building the simplest syntactic structure or attaching a new constituent to the nearest possible preceding one. Other theories were based on verb valency and upon semantic criteria (a lawyer is more likely to question than be questioned). For a review, see van Gompel and Pickering (2007). The evidence was not entirely conclusive; in addition, there are also quite serious problems in applying this garden path approach to the investigation of listening since sentences that are ambiguous in writing are often disambiguated by prosody when they are spoken.

However, research into ambiguity has raised some interesting questions which continue to be discussed. One concerns the process of forming and holding hypotheses. Does a listener form a primary conjecture and keep alternatives in reserve; or does he/she hold all possible interpretations in the mind until the ambiguity is clarified? Research in reading seems to lend support to the first view; readers hesitate and backtrack not where the ambiguity occurs but at the point where it is resolved (Frazier and Rayner 1982). The relevance to second language listening – where additional ambiguities may be caused by uncertain lexical and grammatical knowledge – will be obvious.

This interesting area of study has been extended to the effects of metaphor, and more generally of idiom, upon the way language is processed. There is evidence (Gibbs 1994, Gibbs and Colston 2004) that figurative language of this kind imposes additional cognitive demands. One view is that a listener first accesses a literal interpretation of a string of words like *we painted the town red* before arriving at the intended one. An alternative is that the listener simply needs to inhibit normal online parsing until the chunk is complete. Knowledge of second language idiom, like much vocabulary knowledge, tends to be highly individual. Given this and the evidence that it increases cognitive load, testers should clearly be circumspect about targeting it when it occurs in listening passages.

The construction of meaning

An early account of memory and the nature of knowledge (Bartlett 1932) gave rise to the notion of the **schema**, which is still widely employed. A schema is best defined as a knowledge structure containing all that an individual knows about and associates with a particular concept. A schema for APPLE includes the fruit, the computer manufacturer and the association with New York, enabling a listener to make sense of disparate sentences such as: *He ate the apple, She uses an Apple* and *They live in the Big Apple*. Studies of reading such as Bransford and Johnson (1973) showed the extent to which the title of a text (or its immediate context of occurrence) enables the reader to use schematic information to create presuppositions in advance of reading; the same is clearly true of a listener.

There was considerable interest in how the listener or reader added inferential information to the bare proposition contained in a literal interpretation of an utterance (Singer 2007). One assumption (Sanford and Garrod 1981) is that a default interpretation is often set up, based upon schematic knowledge, but that it can quickly be reversed if there is subsequent counter-evidence (hearing the phrase *a lorry driver* might suggest a male but the pronoun *she* at a later stage in the discourse is sufficient to overturn the default). Other studies of inference (Bransford, Barclay and Franks 1972, Johnson, Bransford and Solomon 1973) indicated that listeners find it difficult to say with confidence whether a point they report hearing has been made explicitly by a speaker or results from an inference on their own part. This finding, supported by long-established thinking in semantics, led to the fundamental notion (Johnson-Laird 1983) that an utterance affords two levels of meaning: a **propositional** one based upon a literal interpretation, and a more complex one (with contextual information, schematic information and inferences added) which is referred to variously as a **mental model** or **meaning representation**.

It then becomes important to distinguish a further level of meaning, under-represented in many psycholinguistic accounts but much discussed by discourse analysts. It is referred to here as a **discourse representation** (Brown and Yule 1983a:206). As pieces of information accrue during a speech event, they are progressively integrated into the listener's overall recall of what has been said, which includes not just the points made but the line of argument that links them. A much-cited theory of discourse processing (Kintsch and van Dijk 1983) highlighted the reader/listener's need to establish the relative importance of incoming information and to differentiate between **macro-** and **micro-propositions**. The construction of a discourse representation was also addressed by Gernsbacher (1990), who argued on the basis of empirical evidence that the difference between a skilled and an unskilled comprehender lies partly in the latter's inability to recognise a new strand in an argument and to initiate a new conceptual structure. Weak comprehenders tend to build linear rather than hierarchical structures.

Summary

This brief overview has identified a number of components of listening which need to be borne in mind when attempting a cognitive validation. They are:

a. the highly variable nature of the input

b. the need for the listener to allocate word boundaries

c. the need for the listener to process words in real time, which entails holding a string of words in the mind to enable parsing and disambiguation to take place

d. consequent upon a, b and c, the highly tentative nature of the listening process, which requires listeners to form and revise hypotheses as to what has been heard

e. three levels of representation when constructing the meaning of an utterance: a proposition, an enriched meaning representation relating to the current utterance and a structured discourse representation relating to the wider speech event.

Two current theories of how listening is made possible will inform later discussion:

a. an interactive account of the way in which word forms are recognised by drawing upon multiple cues

b. an exemplar model as an account of how listeners deal successfully with variation at phoneme, lexis or speaker level.

A cognitive processing framework for listening

Levels of analysis

Following information processing principles, cognitive models of language use generally take the form of flow charts. In the case of listening, the point of departure has to be a set of disturbances of the air caused by the operation of a speaker's vocal apparatus; the end-product has to be an idea in the mind that embraces not just the incoming message but all that has been said on the topic so far. As a matter of convenience, the stages in a model of this kind are often represented as sequential; but the point should be made that one stage does not necessarily wait upon another. Current thinking (see above) is that, in the performance of a skill such as listening, language users are capable of processing information at more than one level. The 'stages' are therefore more correctly referred to as **levels of analysis** or **levels of representation**[1].

An information processing approach indicates three types of operation within listening, corresponding to differences in the form of the information being analysed. The first is *perceptual*, with acoustic-phonetic input being matched to the phonological system and vocabulary repertoire of the language being spoken. The second is *linguistic*, with groups of words that have been identified being matched to syntactic structures. The third is *conceptual*, consisting of an interaction between the meaning that has been derived from an utterance and external knowledge possessed by the listener. These three operations correspond to what Anderson (2000), who has been much quoted in the L2 literature, refers to as *decoding, parsing* and *utilisation*. The last term, originally from Clark and Clark (1977), is somewhat misleading; the terms *meaning construction* and *discourse construction* will be preferred here.

Fully elaborated models of the complete listening process are relatively rare in the literature – perhaps a reflection of the direction of much research in cognitive psychology, which (as already noted) tends to focus primarily upon speech perception rather than the whole listening operation and often restricts itself to a single level of representation (phoneme recognition, word recognition, sentence processing etc.). The models that are most quoted focus solely or mainly upon processing at word level. Examples are the Distributed Cohort Model of Gaskell and Marslen-Wilson (1995); the Ellis and Young (1988) model of spoken word processing; and computer programs such as TRACE (McClelland and Elman 1986).

A rare example of a more comprehensive model features in a 1999 paper by two leading L1 listening researchers, Cutler and Clifton. It consists of not three but four levels, which the authors refer to as:

- *decode:* transforming an input consisting of patterns of signal variation over time into an abstract representation
- *segment:* comprising a) segmental and suprasegmental analysis of the input; b) the use of segmentation cues indicating where word boundaries fall;
- *recognise:* comprising a) activation of lexical candidates that form potential matches to the input and competition between them; b) utterance level processing
- *integrate:* adding the derived message to the discourse model.

There are a number of difficulties with the Cutler and Clifton (1999) account as a framework for the discussion that follows. Perhaps the greatest concern is that (reflecting the main locus of research) it focuses heavily upon speech perception and analysis, with processing at the level of meaning construction very little represented. A second concern is that the full rationale behind the model has yet to be presented; the commentary that accompanies it reviews various aspects of auditory processing but there is only a brief discussion of the architecture of the listening skill (1999:151–155), which does not defend the model's four levels or explain the interactions between its different parts.

In addition, the unidirectional structure of the model does not entirely reflect the fact that listening must necessarily be a tentative process, in which provisional hypotheses at word, phrase and clause level constantly have to be updated and revised as acoustic input continues to come in.

The framework employed here incorporates some of the features of the Cutler and Clifton model. In particular, it follows their precedent of dividing the perceptual level into two (one relating to phonological operations and one to lexical). This usefully distinguishes two levels of processing, each with its own goal and each linked to a separate knowledge source. However, the framework also draws upon levels proposed by Field (2009a) with reference to second language listening. The Field model is more evenly distributed between perception and understanding; and it takes greater account of decisions made at the higher (meaning building) levels, which are obviously critical to performance in any approach to L2 listening based on comprehension. By subdividing the level at which meaning is explored, we can mark a distinction between processes which aim to contextualise and extend the bare meaning of an incoming utterance and those which are examples of 'utilisation' (taken literally) in that they concern what the listener does with information once it is extracted from a piece of speech.

The outcome is a model which conforms to the three traditional Anderson (2000) operations but sub-divides two of them. The five levels of processing are as follows:

- *input decoding*: when the listener transforms acoustic cues into groups of syllables, some marked for stress and others not (effectively, Cutler and Clifton's (1999) 'decode')
- *lexical search*: when the listener identifies the best word-level matches for what has been heard, based on a combination of perceptual information and word boundary cues (equivalent to Cutler and Clifton's (1999) 'segment' and the lexical part of 'recognise')
- *parsing*: when the lexical material is related to the co-text in which it occurs in order to a) specify lexical sense more precisely; b) impose a syntactic pattern (the syntactic part of Cutler and Clifton's (1999) 'recognise')
- *meaning construction*: when world knowledge and inference are employed to add to the bare meaning of the message

- *discourse construction*: when the listener makes decisions on the relevance of the new information and how congruent it is with what has gone before; and, if appropriate, integrates it into a representation of the larger listening event (Cutler and Clifton's (1999) 'integrate').

Lower-level processes

Figure 3.1 is a graphic representation of lower-level listening processes, incorporating the first three of the five levels. (The term *lower-level* is widely used in psycholinguistic contexts to refer to the listening processes that take place when a message is being encoded into language. *Higher-level processes* are those associated with building meaning). The oval panels on the left represent the linguistic knowledge sources which support these three levels. Note the changing form of the message, which develops from acoustic input to a phonological string, to a set of word meanings and finally to an abstract proposition. An early view of listening might have represented this progression in linear fashion, with each form dependent upon the one that preceded it.

acoustic cues	→	phonological forms
phonological forms	→	syllables
syllables	→	words
words	→	chunks/clauses

However, as already noted, recent researchers have concluded that the human mind is capable of operating simultaneously at more than one level of representation. A listener assessing the likelihood that the sequence [ʤəs'mɪnɪt] represents the expression *Just a minute* might judge the evidence *in parallel* at phoneme, syllable, word and chunk level to establish how closely it fits the target. Familiarity with the expression as a whole can overrule the fact that two important phonemes have been omitted by the speaker. In other words, positive information from a higher level (the chunk) can overrule negative information at a lower level (the phoneme) – hence the upwards pointing arrows in Figure 3.1.

The figure features the principal processes implicated at each of the three levels.

- *Input decoding*. Perceptual organisation gives the listener access to a sequence of speech-like sounds; the sounds then have to be converted into representations that conform to the phonological system of the language being spoken. Analysis at this level is difficult to account for because of the large amount of variation in the way in which any phoneme is realised. Figure 3.1 includes phoneme decoding for the sake of completeness; but some commentators have argued that the most important unit of analysis is not the phoneme but the syllable or the word.

Figure 3.1 Model of lower-level processes in listening, drawing upon Cutler and Clifton 1999 and Field 2009a

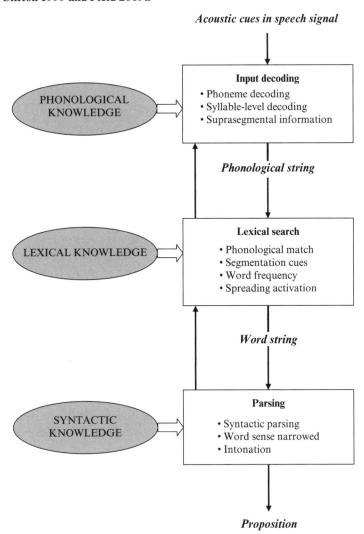

There are obvious implications here for the way in which teachers and testers view the decoding task faced by an L2 listener.

Sometimes overlooked in cognitive accounts is the need for phonological analysis to include prosody. If the target language features lexical stress (or indeed distinctive tones), listeners need to identify which syllables carry the feature. This contributes to word recognition; indeed some commentators (e.g. Grosjean and Gee 1987) have suggested that it serves as an important cue to the presence of a word – with /næʃ/ providing the cue for *interNATional* and /tɒg/ the cue for *phoTOGraphy*. Listeners also have to direct their attention to syllables that bear focal stress since this provides a cue to the most important (and most perceptually reliable) word in the intonation group. The output of decoding is thus not just a string of phonemes, but a string divided into syllables that are marked, where appropriate, for relative stress.[2]

- *Lexical search.* The next level requires a listener to map from sequences of sounds to spoken word forms in their lexicon. The process is generally assumed to involve the identification of a number of likely matches for a given stretch of the signal, some of them more probable than others. The number of these *candidates* is gradually reduced as more evidence becomes available. Phonological-level information about which syllables bear stress or tone assists the listener when the target language makes use of those features to distinguish similar but unrelated words.

One of the major problems faced by a listener at this level is *lexical segmentation*. Because there are no regular between-word pauses in connected speech, the listener has to determine where word boundaries fall. In some languages, segmentation is relatively straightforward since it is supported by fixed stress that falls on the first, last or penultimate syllable of each lexical word. In others, it is more complicated; and the strategy used appears to draw quite often upon features of prosody specific to the language in question (Cutler 1994). In many languages, prosodic cues based on syllable prominence and duration also help the listener to distinguish likely content words bearing lexical meaning from likely function words that perform a syntactic role.

So far, this account of lexical search has mainly concerned the process of mapping from cues in the input to information in memory about a word's spoken form. Listeners also draw upon other types of lexical knowledge, of which two are represented in Figure 3.1. Firstly, an awareness of the relative *frequency* of words in natural speech assists listeners to give added weight to the most likely match for a group of sounds. Leaving aside considerations of context, a listener hearing the sequence [hɜːd] would lend greater support to the candidate *heard* than to the equally precise match *herd*. In an utterance such as *We never found . . .* (encountered out of context), there would be a preference for interpreting the verb as the past simple form of *find* rather than the present simple form of *found* (='establish').

The other process, known as *spreading activation*, exploits the way in which words are linked in the mind by intricate lexical networks. When a listener hears the word *doctor*, it triggers an association with words like *nurse, hospital,* and *patient* – and the result is that the listener recognises those words more rapidly if they occur in the discourse that follows.

A lexical search requires the listener not simply to form perceptual matches but also to access the meanings of the words that are identified. The output of this level is thus a string of content and function words, the former with a sense attached – or (more likely) a range of possible senses pending decisions that can only be made when the intonation group or syntactic structure is complete.

- *Parsing.* Parsing takes place online, while the utterance is still being produced. As 'garden path' examples show, it often has to be provisional, with the listener anticipating what the grammatical structure will be and then checking against subsequent evidence. An understanding of a language's standard word order can assist parsing, as can features that disrupt the order, such as (in English) inversion or the use of *do* auxiliaries that signal an interrogative early on in an utterance.

But there comes a point at which the speaker reaches the end of an intonation group (indicators might be a pause, a drop in pitch or the placing of focal stress, which often occurs late in the group). Here, listeners are assisted by the fact that an intonation group boundary often corresponds with that of a syntactic element such as a clause. Alternatively, it might be apparent that the speaker has completed a syntactic structure that was anticipated by the listener as the utterance was evolving. When this point is reached, the listener has to make a final decision as to what has been said at clause level, and from it has to construct an abstract idea, a *proposition.* This proposition replaces the linguistic form in which the message has been held up to now, and represents the output of parsing.

The term *parsing* has been chosen for this operation because it is so widely used, but the analysis of co-text entails more than simply imposing a syntactic structure upon a group of words. It also offers the listener the opportunity to decide which of several possible senses of a word is appropriate when due account is taken of its setting. In addition, it is at this point that a full intonation contour becomes available, which not only foregrounds the most important element of the message but also provides indications of the speaker's attitude and intentions.

It is also worth noting that successful parsing is greatly assisted by limitations on the complexity of the syntactic structure that a speaker can pre-assemble in his/her mind. The unit of production is very often at the level of the clause (Levelt 1989), and utterances are often loosely linked by co-ordinators (*and, so, but, or*). These characteristics of natural speech assist listening, since they limit the amount of language that the listener has to carry forward in working memory before parsing it. By contrast, the reading aloud of a literary text, with reduced pausing at syntactic boundaries and complex subordination, can lead to a cognitive over-load where the listener finds it difficult to retain the words necessary for achieving the parse. Hence the importance of using input in L2 teaching and testing that is as close as possible to natural speech.

Higher-level processes

Meaning construction

The proposition produced by a speaker as a result of decoding and parsing is abstract (i.e. no longer in the form of language) and is taken to be context-independent (Lyons 1977) – in effect, to represent a literal interpretation of the speaker's words. It is the task of the listener to relate the proposition to the circumstances in which it was produced in order to grasp its full rele-vance. This is one of the principal functions of what we have termed 'meaning construction'.

A second consideration is that much human communication, whether in speech or writing, is highly abbreviated in form. The reason it can be so is because the speaker takes it for granted that a large quantity of knowledge is shared with the listener; and the listener co-operates in this presupposition (Schank and Abelson 1977). Thus, there is an unspoken agreement between speaker and listener that if the former says *I caught a train to Cambridge*, the latter will supply 'I went to the railway station – I bought a ticket – The train came – The announcement said it was for Cambridge – I got on – I sat on the train for a while – I got off at Cambridge'.

A similar phenomenon occurs between sentences, where connections between two facts are often left unexpressed by a speaker and have to be inferred by a listener. If a radio newsreader says *A body was found in the house. There were no signs of a struggle.*, it is the listener who has to draw the immediate inference that the potential struggle involves the owner of the body and the secondary inference that a crime may not have been committed.

The point at issue, then, is that the raw meaning of the speaker's words is insufficient to convey the significance of what is being said or why it has been said. The listener is therefore responsible for supplying information that enriches what is said in a number of ways. These might be:

* *Pragmatic.* The listener interprets the speaker's illocutionary intentions, using knowledge of the pragmatic forms of the language. Interpretation may go beyond the forms of language used and take account of context, speaker knowledge etc.
* *Contextual.* The listener relates the proposition to the context in which it occurs by making use of a) world knowledge, knowledge of the speaker

and knowledge of the situation; and b) recall of what has been said so far.

- *Semantic.* The listener draws upon world knowledge of entities and ideas that have been mentioned by the speaker. If the speaker refers to somebody as *like a tiger*, the listener will know enough about tigers to recognise the qualities that are being referred to.
- *Inferential.* The listener supplies details that the speaker has not felt it necessary to include (cf the *signs of a struggle* example just given).

One further operation that the listener has to perform is to link anaphors such as *she, him, that, what I just said* to their antecedents. This function is not always easy to perform in listening, where anaphors are often used quite loosely and at some distance from the mention of the person, thing or concept they refer to (Brown and Yule 1983a:214–222). Here, as already noted, the listener is reliant upon an awareness, regularly updated, of what the current topic of discourse is.

The processes that have been described in this section are illustrated in graphic form in Figure 3.2. It is important to note again that they are not necessarily sequential. They may also operate in close conjunction – for example, an understanding of the general context may be closely linked to recognising the speaker's pragmatic intentions.

Figure 3.2 Model of meaning construction in listening

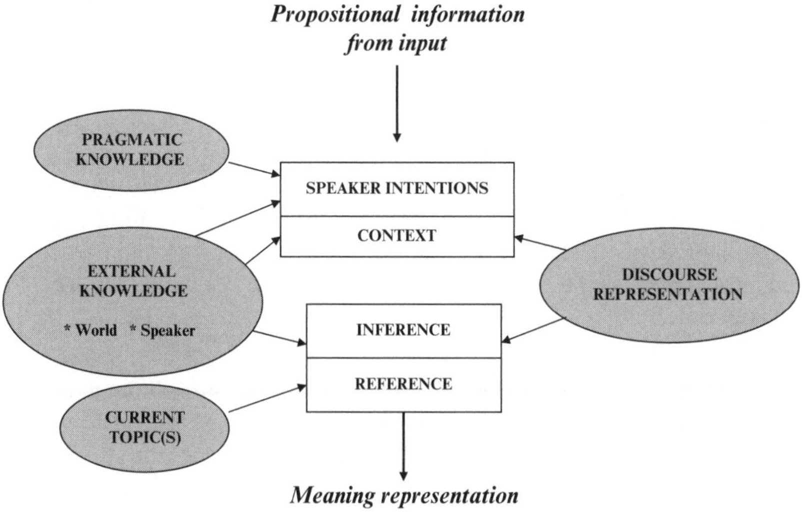

Propositional information from input

PRAGMATIC KNOWLEDGE

SPEAKER INTENTIONS

CONTEXT

EXTERNAL KNOWLEDGE

* World * Speaker

DISCOURSE REPRESENTATION

INFERENCE

REFERENCE

CURRENT TOPIC(S)

Meaning representation

The knowledge sources that support the various processes are shown in the oval panels. Broadly, they are of three types:

- *pragmatic knowledge*: knowledge of the relationship between linguistic form and speaker intentions

- *external knowledge*: including world knowledge, speaker knowledge and knowledge of the situation

- *discourse representation*: the listener's recall of the listening event so far and (possibly associated or possibly separate) the listener's awareness of the current topic.

All of them function as 'meaning construction' in that they add to the literal meaning of the words uttered by the speaker. At the risk of labouring the point, it is important to stress again that they are all the responsibility of the listener, who has to apply knowledge, often individual to him/her, to what has been gleaned from the words that were decoded. The elaborated output of this level of listening is here termed a *meaning representation*, though some commentators refer to a *mental model* (following Johnson-Laird 1983).

Discourse construction

That is not the end of the operation. The listener now has to make important judgements about the information that has been obtained and to relate it to what has occurred in the listening event so far. Here, it is important to make a clear terminological distinction (sometimes missing in accounts of comprehension) between the meaning representation derived from a particular utterance and the ongoing *discourse representation* (Brown and Yule 1983a:206) relating to the whole of the conversation, lecture, broadcast, film etc. that is being attended to. We should not lose sight of the fact that a discourse representation is not a complete and well-defined record of what has been said so far; but *the listener's recall of what has occurred*. This is especially important when considering the performance of a second language listener.

Drawing loosely on Van Dijk and Kintsch (1983) and Gernsbacher (1990) as well as Oakhill and Garnham's (1988) authoritative account of comprehension processes in children's reading, one can identify four main processes that are applied as the listener constructs a larger-scale comprehension of a spoken text.

- *Selection*. The listener needs to decide upon the relevance of a new piece of information to the discourse as a whole. It might be redundant (phatic or a repetition of a point made earlier); or it might be central or peripheral to the topic being developed. The listener also judges the information in relation to what are perceived to be the goals of the speaker – and in relation to the listener's own goals, which may be rather different. On the basis of these considerations, the listener has the options of letting the piece of information decay from memory, storing it in some detail, or retaining it in an indeterminate form.

- *Integration.* The listener needs to add the new item of meaning to the developing discourse representation. The process entails recognising conceptual links between an incoming piece of information and the information that immediately preceded it; those links might be explicitly marked by formulations such as *On the other hand, The result was . . .*; but they are quite often implicit.
- *Self-monitoring.* Part of integration entails comparing a new piece of information with what has gone before, to ensure that it is consistent. If it is not, then the listener must decide whether to reserve judgement about the accuracy of the new item or whether to question his/her understanding and recall of what was said before.
- *Structure building.* As more and more information is acquired, the listener has to take account of the relative importance of each item. On this basis, he/she constructs a hierarchical pattern of what has been said, consisting of a set of major points with subordinate points attached to them. A skilled listener is capable of storing quite complex information structures of this kind; a less skilled one may produce little more than a linear sequence in which equal importance is accorded to each point (Gernsbacher 1990). In certain circumstances, the operation is assisted by the listener's knowledge of certain discourse conventions (for example, the fact that a lecture often follows a problem–solution format or introduces main points followed by exemplification).

The processes described in this section are illustrated in graphic form in Figure 3.3. Similar knowledge sources are engaged to those in Figure 3.2, though it is worth noting that the interaction with the stored discourse representation is very much a two-way one here. In addition, the listener draws upon previous experience of different types of speech event, which enables him/her to recognise certain patterns of discourse that recur regularly. Obvious examples would be the tendency for lecturers to preface their talk with an outline of what they are going to cover; or the tradition on radio or TV of giving headlines before a more detailed news bulletin.

Again, it should be noted that the processes are not necessarily sequential. The listener may be constructing a hierarchical representation of the discourse at the same time as integrating a new piece of information.

Listening processes and the second language listener

The complex operations just outlined are those employed by an expert listener; they are often modified or absent in the performance of listeners who are less skilled. In the case of those listening to a second language, two general factors constrain performance: one being level of knowledge (linguistic or

Figure 3.3 Model of discourse construction in listening

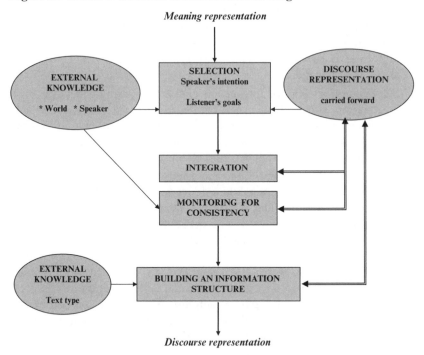

Meaning representation

Discourse representation

cultural) and the other, level of expertise. The result is that the L2 listening experience differs markedly from the L1 listening one for most listeners, with a much greater reliance upon remedial strategy use. A cognitive perspective must thus qualify Buck's assertion (2001:148) that 'the evidence to date gives no reason to suppose that second language listening is in any fundamental way different from first language listening'.

Language-related knowledge

Inadequacies of knowledge can affect many of the information sources shown in ovals in Figure 3.1.

In terms of *phonological knowledge*, many learners taking tests at lower levels of the Cambridge suite will have an imprecise or incomplete set of phoneme values. In cognitive terms, the effect upon input decoding is to reduce a test taker's confidence in their ability to match acoustic-phonetic input to phonemes and syllables. One outcome may be that learners rely more heavily upon co-textual cues or upon non-perceptual sources such as world knowledge. Recent research (Field forthcoming) has suggested another possible scenario: namely, that L2 listeners attach added weight to word-level matches, in effect extending the process for resolving L1 phonological ambiguity mentioned in the *veshtable* example above. This might lead them to accept an approximate lexical match for a group of sounds on the grounds that the phonological evidence is less than reliable.

The incompleteness of the listener's *lexical knowledge* complicates lexical search in other ways. It is important to recognise that 'knowing' a word does not consist simply of the ability to recognise a word's citation form and to match that form to a sense or range of senses. It also entails the ability to recognise the word in a number of variant forms, determined very much by the co-text within which the word is embedded and by how precise the articulation of the speaker is. The kind of exemplar model described above would suggest that we achieve this by dint of extended exposure, whether to a first or a second language. In addition, as Meara (1997) points out, knowing a word is not simply a matter of mastering its form and range of senses; the word also has to be integrated into a network of associated items.

Spreading activation of the kind employed by an expert listener to anticipate upcoming lexis is not available to an L2 listener until networks of this kind have been built up. A further advance in lexical knowledge which appears to play an important part in listening development is the listener's increasing familiarity with high-frequency formulaic chunks. Ability to recognise a chunk often serves to resolve ambiguities at word level resulting from the need to process input as it is received. Again, this is the product of extended exposure to the second language.

Self-evidently, *parsing* also draws upon stored knowledge, this time syntactic. Knowing that a default interpretation of the sequence *was + -ing* represents pastness plus continuity is clearly a prerequisite to recognising the pattern when it occurs and to interpreting it appropriately. Because a sentence reaches the listener's ears a syllable at a time, successful parsing also depends upon an implicit understanding of how strong are the target language's constraints upon word order. When allocating roles (subject, object etc.) to the various elements within an utterance, listeners need to know whether to rely upon a canonical word order, inflection, thematisation or animacy. Evidence suggests that they are often bound by the priorities of their L1: native English speakers, for example, rely too heavily upon word order when parsing speech in Italian or Japanese (MacWhinney and Bates 1989).

Cultural knowledge

Linguistic knowledge affects L2 listening performance at a perceptual level; but once the signal has been converted into a proposition, other factors come into play. Here, the most important constraint lies in what can broadly be termed *cultural knowledge*. This might be language-related in that it concerns the learner's knowledge of the pragmatics of L2, and hence his/her ability to attribute speaker intentions to a particular form of words. But it might also concern the kind of world knowledge that the learner brings to a listening encounter, which may be very much shaped by his/her own cultural background and an incomplete understanding of the background of the speaker. Knowledge of this kind affects the ability to understand allusions that the speaker takes for granted; it also affects the types of schema that an L2 listener holds, and thus the ability to apply default information to a word or phrase. Consider, for example, how certain superordinate concepts such as *FRUIT, FURNITURE* or even *FAMILY* would be subject to different interpretations across cultures.

Expertise

Linguistic and cultural knowledge may be necessary components of skilled listening; but they are by no means sufficient ones. The effectiveness with which stored information is deployed depends critically upon how accessible the information is to the user and how automatic is the connection made between perceptual or contextual cues and the corresponding linguistic units.

A good example is provided by the grammatical knowledge that enables parsing. Because of the time pressures under which listening takes place and because of the way the signal is delivered (the need to construct a syntactic structure syllable by syllable), generalised declarative knowledge in the form of rules is of little assistance to the listener unless it is supported by a mastery of the processes for applying the rules to incoming speech. These processes entail mapping automatically from a grammatical form to the concepts that it represents. For the second language listener, the ability to apply syntactic knowledge is thus heavily dependent upon acquired patterns of behaviour – in other words, upon the listener's level of expertise.

Likewise, a critical component of lexical search is the ability to form an automatic link between the form of a word as uttered by a speaker and its range of senses, without the need for an intentional meaning search. Something similar can be said about phonological representation, where the key to skilled L2 listening lies in the ability to form immediate matches between acoustic-phonetic information reaching the ear and the sound system of the target language. Here the situation is more complex, given the extent to which the input varies in relation to the vocal characteristics of the speaker. It is safe to assume that, without exposure to a large range of L2 speakers, the learner will be slower to normalise to unfamiliar voices.

The importance of automaticity in all these processes cannot be overstated; see the explanation of expertise above. If a basic operation like matching a set of speech sounds to a word requires an effort of attention, it imposes demands upon a listener's working memory that can preclude other operations. By contrast, when the mapping from word form to word sense is highly automatic, working memory resources are freed for higher-level processes such as making inferences, interpreting the speaker's intentions, recognising a line of argument and so on. This criterion would appear to mark an important distinction between lower and higher levels of listening proficiency, and will be used in this way in the analysis that follows.

Also important in a competent listener is a degree of flexibility when decoding an utterance as it unfolds. The point has been made that auditory processing is necessarily approximate given the way in which the signal reaches the listener in real time. What this entails is that (at the levels of word and sentence structure) a competent listener must be prepared to exchange one hypothesis for another if early expectations are not met. Field (2008) demonstrated that mid-range L2 listeners are much slower and less likely to revise a wrong lexical-level hypothesis than expert listeners. One reason may be their reduced confidence in the accuracy of what they have decoded.

Listening strategies[3]

Faced with limitations in their linguistic knowledge and expertise, second language listeners have recourse to **strategies** in order to compensate for sections of the recording that have not been successfully processed. There has been considerable research interest in listening strategies over the past 20 years (Cohen 1998, Goh 1998, Graham, Santos and Vanderplank 2008, Vandergrift 2003). There have been proposals for taxonomies of the strategies employed by learners (Field 2008a:286–303, Lynch 2009:80, Rost 1990:177, Vandergrift 1997). Attempts have also been made to determine which strategies appear to be characteristic of a successful L2 listener. For a perceptive review of the strengths and weaknesses of these studies, see Macaro, Graham and Vanderplank (2007). There has been relatively little focus on the effects of strategy instruction (perhaps because of methodological difficulties) – and virtually none at all on the role of strategies in testing.

Field (2012) points out that a test taker undertaking a test of listening might engage in three different types of cognitive activity:

- *processes* which form a part of skilled L1 listening
- *communication strategies* which compensate for gaps in understanding
- *test-wise strategies* which exploit potential loopholes in the test method.

In terms of cognitive validation, evidence of the first of these provides a positive indication that a test is indeed eliciting processes which form part of the target construct. By contrast, evidence of the third provides an indication of possible flaws of test design which permit the test taker to sidetrack normal processes; it thus constitutes a challenge to cognitive validity. But what of the second? A narrow characterisation would suggest that strategies do not form part of expert listening, except perhaps in conditions of noise or topic unfamiliarity. On the other hand, the effective use of strategies is an intrinsic part of an L2 listener's struggle after meaning in a real-world setting context. It can extend the comprehension of a listener well beyond what his/ her knowledge and expertise might otherwise permit. Strategic competence is therefore to be seen as an important part of L2 listening proficiency; and evidence of strategic behaviour in a test should not be taken as compromising cognitive validity.

That said, it is important to extend the notion of strategy use some way beyond the areas generally identified by commentators. Strategies represent more than the use of contextual and co-textual 'top-down' information in order to resolve local difficulties of comprehension. They also take place at word level, where uncertainty about the reliability of what has been perceived might lead a listener to adopt approximate word matches regardless of context and sometimes of co-text (Field 2004).

Cognitive validation of tests in the Cambridge ESOL suite

We will now go on to analyse the tests of the Cambridge General English suite in relation to the five levels of listening identified in the cognitive model. A validation exercise of this kind needs to take account of the effect upon cognitive processing of three essential components of a listening test: namely, *the recording, the test method* and *the test items*. The characteristics of these components and the way they vary across the proficiency levels of the suite will be matched against the listening framework outlined earlier in this chapter. The goal is to determine how representative they are of the types of input and processing which are implicated in general listening events, how comprehensive they are in representing the range of processes and how well graded is the cognitive load placed upon test takers in relation to the levels of the suite. Here, reference will be made to a number of Cambridge ESOL documents including the *Handbooks for Teachers*, the Cambridge ESOL Research Reports and the item writer guidelines (IWGs) issued to the test writers for the various examinations. Illustrations will be drawn from the sample tests for KET, PET, FCE, CAE and CPE which appear in Appendix A.

Intuitively, each of the three components to be considered would seem to be important at some levels of processing but not at others. However, this is not strictly the case. To give an example, the nature of the recording would appear to have important implications for input decoding but to be peripheral elsewhere; whereas, in fact, features such as speech rate or propositional complexity also impact upon processing at other levels. Similarly, it might appear that the content and form of the items chiefly influence processing at the meaning construction level; whereas there are also implications for lexical processing. The discussion will therefore need to move between different levels of processing when examining the three components.

We will consider the cognitive validity of the recorded material and the task formats from three main angles. The first two will be dealt with together under a single heading.

How representative?

a. How closely do the processes elicited by the tests resemble those that would be employed by the test taker in a real-world context?

b. Do the cognitive processes elicited by the tests in the Cambridge suite cover a sufficiently large and representative range of the processes contained in the listening framework?

How well graded?

c. How well graded are the tests of the suite in terms of the cognitive demands imposed upon test takers at different proficiency levels of the suite?

There will then be discussion of the items in terms of the level of information they target and of their length and ease of interpretation.

Recorded material

How representative?

Origin

The first and most obvious issue to be addressed in relation to the choice of recording is whether the input to which candidates are exposed can be said to resemble normal everyday speech; and thus to demand decoding processes resembling those of a real-world listening event. Self-evidently, there are different types of 'normal everyday speech' ranging from informal conversation to more formal transactional dialogue, from the informal presentational style of a popular broadcaster to the formal monologue of a public lecture. But all of them (with the possible exception of the last-mentioned) possess certain linguistic characteristics which are the inevitable result of the way in which most speech is delivered under pressures of time and with minimal preplanning. In addition, natural spoken input entails a transformation of citation forms that does not apply in the case of written texts. There is an enormous difference between a string of words uttered one by one and the same words embedded in a stretch of connected speech. Other important phonological variables are voice quality, precision of delivery and speech rate.

In choosing recordings for the teaching or testing of L2 listening, materials designers have a number of options (Field 2009a:272–3). In terms of recording origin, they can employ *scripted* material, *improvised* material where studio actors follow general situational cues, fully *authentic* material recorded live or authentic material that has been transcribed and *re-recorded*. When one examines the scripts in Appendix A and listens to the recordings, it becomes clear that those at the lower levels of the Suite are entirely or almost entirely scripted. This seems a necessary expedient at these levels, given the need to control for linguistic content and for clarity of delivery. From FCE upwards, it would seem that the tests employ a mixture of scripted material and of authentic material re-recorded under studio conditions, sometimes after quite extensive revision by item writers. The instructions given in the IWGs confirm that this is the case, and that wholly authentic material taken direct from source is not used.

So what are the implications of using this type of material? From a cognitive perspective, the concern here is not with 'authenticity' for its own sake, but with the extent to which the nature of the recorded material makes decoding easier or more difficult than it would be in real-world conditions. Clearly, read-aloud speech, even when delivered by experienced actors, differs from natural speech. One consideration is that actors working from a studio script mark punctuation and sentence boundaries much more clearly than they would in natural speech. This has implications at the level of *parsing*, in that it demarcates clauses and other syntactic groups more precisely than would normally be the case. Another characteristic is that read-aloud material has a greater tendency to rhythmicity, with focal stress more consistently marked. This provides additional support at the level of *lexical search*, since it assists the test taker in identifying the most critical word of the intonation group and thus in building a set of hypotheses as to the main points which the speaker is making.

The effect of using a script is also heard in the omission of the kind of planning pauses, hesitations, false starts and speaker overlaps that characterise the types of speech that candidates at higher proficiency levels should be capable of handling. Arguably, the ability to deal with these features of spontaneous speech is a skill which should be tested. Their absence has a levelling effect, with the result that distinctions between different genres of spoken discourse become less salient.

While these features of studio-recorded speech detract from cognitive validity, test designers would no doubt argue that the use of re-recorded material brings important benefits in the ability to minimise background noise, redundancy and speaker overlap and to exercise greater control over delivery and informational content. Not all of these hold up to close scrutiny. Background noise is not an obstacle if broadcast material is used, while speaker overlap is surely an important part of dialogic interaction. The main motive for favouring re-recording would appear to be that it enables item writers to manipulate text content: adding definitions for low-frequency terms, reducing or increasing the level of redundancy and inserting possible distractors. This is reflected in the IWGs, which provide reasons for adaptation that include 'ensure the piece has a clear introduction', 'ensure that items are spaced evenly throughout text' and 'add distraction to a text' (Cambridge ESOL 2006b). Here, the task rather than the integrity of the text, appears to be the priority.

The comments so far have focused on perceptual features of the input. As mentioned above, speech also commonly has lexical and syntactic characteristics which are a consequence of the way in which it is planned and delivered under pressures of time. They include: imprecise lexis, shorter sentences broken into clause-length utterances, and a preference for co-ordination over subordination (i.e. fewer embedded clauses than would occur in written prose). For the expert listener, these features form an important part of the parsing process, which has to allow not only for the editing out of hesitation markers and false starts, but also for more approximate lexis and syntax, fewer clear connectives and a vaguer use of reference. The reliance on simple clause-length utterances rather than complex sentence units is particularly important: here, the working memory limitations on how much language a spontaneous speaker can plan at any one time dovetail with similar limitations on how much a listener can retain in the mind during a parsing operation.

Clearly, there are exceptions to this type of spoken discourse. There are certain high-attention situations – for example, academic lectures, job interviews or arts programmes – where the speaker aims for precision in lexis and might employ more complex sentences in order to make transparent the relationships between ideas. The linguistic characteristics of spoken discourse can thus be thought of as forming a cline, but one that is heavily weighted, in terms of frequency of occurrence, towards the more spontaneous and less controlled end.

Examination of the tapescripts in Appendix A suggests that the item writers at KET and PET levels succeed quite well in replicating some of the basic linguistic features of speech. Ironically, this may be because the material is scripted and subject to frequency and complexity constraints, so that care has been expended on making it natural. However, at higher proficiency levels, there are a number of speaker turns which resemble written discourse more closely than spoken. In a situation like a radio interview, it could be argued that an interviewee can be expected to produce more complex and more lexically precise utterances because of the need to put across ideas transparently. But even allowing for this, there are passages in the sample transcripts that are unconvincing as samples of speech.

> Any coach will tell you that being psychologically motivated is crucial to being the best in sport. Not everyone experiences the same kind of motivation, and I think there are at least two main kinds. There is ego orientation – playing sport because you want to be the winner; or task

orientation – continually trying to improve your own personal best performances.
(Cambridge ESOL 2012a:376)
You can stroll along tree-shaded paths, over bridges, and for those interested in the project, there are, in keeping with the natural feel of the area, stones, with useful information displayed on them. Did you know, for example, that 99% of all chemical transformations on earth require water?
(Cambridge ESOL 2012a:390)

One can sympathise with the difficulty of designing listening material that is demanding enough for these higher levels. It may simply be that the original has been over-edited to make it more complex. However, there is another possible explanation. Verbal reports collected for a research study of item writer expertise (Salisbury 2005) indicated that item writers showed considerable variation in the procedures followed during the construction of a listening test. One surprising finding (Chapter 7) was that, of 10 experienced writers studied, only one regularly used oral material as his point of departure. Most of the others used articles taken from *written* sources such as magazines. Their material was thus only authentic in the sense that its content derived from written texts not designed for language teaching. It had to be converted into a simulation of spoken language – a process that might entail devising interview-style exchanges and that faced obvious dangers in the influence of the wording of the original. Issues of cognitive and construct validity are certainly raised if candidates are required to process a piece of input that has so little claim to verisimilitude; as noted above, natural speech is usually delivered in the form of loosely co-ordinated clause-length utterances.

Salisbury's data was collected between 2002 and 2004; and she makes the point that, since then, authentic spoken material has become more widely available via the internet. When item writers select texts today, they have many more opportunities of drawing upon sources in the appropriate modality. However, extracts like those quoted above suggest that they may not always do so. The examples also illustrate the difficulty of emulating natural spoken discourse without the support of an original model.

While the general precepts for item writers strongly support the use of authentic sources, there is considerable ambivalence in instructions specific to the listening tests. This is particularly noticeable at FCE level (Cambridge ESOL 2012b) where the following guidance is offered:

As far as possible, all FCE 4 material should come from authentic sources, *although the material will need to be adapted.* Every effort should be made to ensure that the final script sounds like natural speech *if the original source is a written one.* [italics added]

One cannot deny that test setters may need to adapt authentic recordings for the purposes of testing; but it seems unfortunate that this is signalled as an unavoidable necessity rather than an expedient. Similarly, foregrounding the use of written sources ('written material such as newspaper and magazine articles, extracts from books, leaflets, brochures, advertisements') seems to endorse a procedure that should, in an ideal world, be avoided. Only a brief warning indicates that 'care is required' with this kind of material.

The Guideline specifications at A2 and B1 level strike a more positive note:

> KET: 'ensure that *if* material is scripted it sounds as authentic as possible' (p.6) [italics added]
> PET: 'wherever possible, tapescripts should be based on original spoken source material and retain as many examples of natural spoken language as possible'. (p.5).

But here, if anything, the requirements seem rather idealistic, given the need to employ largely scripted material at these lower proficiency levels.

One would expect greater insistence on authentic spoken sources at the higher levels of the suite. In fact, no advice is given on authenticity in CPE other than the comment that 'The constraints of the examination preclude the use of fully authentic material in the tests . . .' (p.5). By contrast, the CAE Guidelines recommend sources for each of the four parts of the test:

Part 1: 'should be based on real examples of spoken language, gathered from a range of sources' (p.12)

Part 2: 'Real-world texts of this type are likely to have been prepared or semi-scripted and therefore have a clear logical structure' (p.16)

Part 3: 'should be based on authentic sources' (p.19)

Part 4: 'will generally be either scripted by the item writer or heavily reworked from an authentic source'. (p.23)

This constitutes a welcome attempt to highlight authenticity as a criterion. However, it is striking that, in both CAE and CPE, the option of drawing upon written originals is left open. They are a possible source at CAE 'for most parts of the test' (p.6); and at CPE 'for some parts of the test' (p.6). The guidelines for both tests also specify scripted materials as appropriate for the Part 4 multiple-matching task.

It would seem, then, that the IWGs do not sustain an entirely consistent position on authenticity in listening. While the general precepts show a commitment to using authentic language, instructions for designing the listening papers sound a different note. In addition, written sources are endorsed when, with construct validity in mind, they should perhaps be treated as a last resort rather than a desirable alternative. These factors may account for differences of practice among item writers, and for the occasional use of texts like the extracts above, which are undoubtedly closer to written than to spoken discourse.

Generalising somewhat, it seems fair to say that the test development procedure outlined in the IWGs emphasises the fine-tuning of tasks and items, with rather less prominence given to the recorded material. Indeed, the commissioning process provides for the development, scrutiny and acceptance of items before the recording has actually been made. There are obvious practical and financial reasons for this procedure; but it is prudent not to sign off a version of a test until the recordings have undergone a final check to confirm that they fully support the items that have been pre-written. There is a small but not negligible danger that the way in which a script is realised by an actor may run counter to the interpretation placed upon it by the item writer.

With this in mind, a final check on features of the recording forms part of standard procedure at Cambridge ESOL. The internal *Work Instructions for Routine Test Production* (4.4.1, p.28) require two members of the Listening team to 'monitor the recording in terms of the speed of delivery, the clarity etc, and make relevant changes to the scripts (and question papers, as appropriate) . . .'. The precaution makes good sense, though it would carry more impact if the instructions specified concretely some of the mismatches between recording, script and items that can occur – not least, the possibility that variations in speech rate or in an actor's interpretation of the script can downgrade the perceptibility of an information point targeted by the item writer. It might also be desirable to submit the recording to the original item writer for a final review. These measures would counterbalance the degree of attention accorded to task and item in the present test development process. Test provider guidelines should so far as possible encourage setters and administrators to see the *raison d'être* of a listening test as the recording, with the task no more than an artefactual and often approximate device for gaining access to the mind of the listener in order to assess the level of understanding achieved.

Visual input

A second consideration when discussing the input authenticity of an audio-based test is the absence of the visual support that would be available in a real-life context. This includes not simply a visible setting or situation in which the listening event occurs but also the paralinguistic signals provided by the speaker.

The lack of visual cues is not entirely un-ecological: for certain types of recording, particularly those that draw upon radio broadcasts, an absence of visual input is entirely appropriate and compensated for in the text. In addition, two features of the Cambridge ESOL suite serve to counterbalance the disadvantages of audio-only material. One is the brief context-setting rubric at the beginning of each section, though its main purpose is usually to specify participants, topic and type of interaction rather than to create a visual context. The other is the convention of allowing the test taker to hear the recording twice. These two features of the Cambridge ESOL Listening tests undoubtedly compensate for the lack of visual support. However, from a cognitive perspective, the nature and importance of that support within a real-world listening experience still merits discussion.

The part played by multi-modal cues has been the subject of enquiry in second language listening research (Baltova 1994, Gruba 1999). In addition, recent research (Green 1998) has demonstrated that visual information from lip-reading is integrated into the listening process at a very early stage. In other words, visual information is not additional or supplementary to auditory; it forms an intrinsic part of a listening event. As technology improves (and in particular as test takers themselves become more accustomed to audio-visual contact with the target language through internet sources), it would seem to be inevitable that examination boards will need to give careful consideration to the practicality of video-based testing of listening. Still images cannot, it seems, fulfil the same purpose (Ockey 2007).

Monologue versus interaction

Over the years, there has been some discussion about the relative merits of monologue and dialogue material. It has sometimes been suggested (e.g. by Brown and Yule 1983b) that 'eavesdropping' on a two-way conversation is an unlikely event – in effect, that it lacks cognitive validity. However, eavesdropping is not as uncommon as is sometimes suggested. A learner might be part of a conversation involving three or more people, in which case he/she will be a passive partner for at least some of the time.[4] There are also multiple opportunities for listening to conversation in the form of film and broadcast drama. There is therefore every reason for including both monologue and dialogue recordings in a test of listening.

The approach of Cambridge ESOL to these two types of recorded material seems to be even-handed. Each level of the suite achieves a balance between monologue and dialogue material, though with an understandable bias towards dialogues in the longer recordings, where it serves to break up the input. The one exception in the sample materials in Appendix A is KET, where there is a much higher use of dialogues in the short Part 1 recordings than elsewhere. The thinking behind this would appear to be that simple question and answer patterns serve to instantiate a topic much more unambiguously for a low-level listener than a monologue would, thus assisting the *meaning construction* process at an early stage. However, it seems (personal communication, Assessment Group) that there is no explicit policy on the proportion of dialogue to monologue material at lower levels of the suite.

It might be worthwhile incorporating guidance on this issue into the IWGs rather than leaving it to the instinct of the test writer.

Auditory input

Speaker voice

Variation at speaker level (associated with voice setting, pitch range etc.) is an important consideration when recording for testing purposes. A contributory factor in *input decoding* is the ability to adjust to differences between speakers and speaking styles. In processing terms, this entails allowing a listener sufficient time in each section of a test to normalise to the characteristics of voice and delivery. While normalisation by first language listeners is very rapid, it would seem likely that listeners are slower to adjust to a voice in a second language. This is especially a matter of concern in those sections of the tests that make use of multiple short recordings.

One way of allowing for normalisation is to ensure that no question is asked that targets the first 10 seconds or so of a recording. This is not easy to achieve where the passages are short. However, an examination of the sample materials in Appendix A indicates that item writers do indeed show sensitivity on this score. Taking the FCE materials as an example, no item targets the first utterance produced by a given speaker; with one exception (Recording 4 of Item 1), where the information in question is indicative of the speaker's general goals rather than conveying a point of detail. Normalisation at KET level is also assisted by an item writer requirement (IWG: KET, p.11) that only one speaker in the dialogue conveys information essential to answering the items.

The cognitive demands associated with normalisation are increased by the number of voices in a recording (a factor that, according to Brown and Yule 1983b, makes a major contribution to listening difficulty). IWGs, especially at lower proficiency levels, ensure the distinctiveness of the two voices in a dialogue by specifying a mix of genders. Care also appears to be taken to ensure that, where same-gender voices are used in three-speaker recordings, they are distinctive in fundamental frequency.

Accent

A further aspect of speaker variation that merits comment is the range of accents featured. Over recent years, there has been considerable pressure on testing boards from certain individuals who argue that content validity in the testing of listening demands a wide range of accents in the recorded material used. For a flavour of the discussion, see the exchange of views between Jenkins and Taylor (2006) and Taylor's conclusions (2008, 2009b) on the implications of language varieties for testing and assessment.

Those advocating this approach to recording content do not base their arguments on any established theoretical model of the way in which accent variety is integrated into the phonological repertoire of a language learner. At best, their assumption seems to be that adjusting to a new variety entails somehow stretching the tolerances of the variety that the listener has initially acquired. There is no empirical evidence in the psycholinguistic literature to support such an interpretation. The multiple-trace hypothesis outlined above is perhaps the most plausible model that we currently have to account for accent acquisition. If one accepts it in whole or in part, one has to embrace a view that the ability to recognise speakers of a given variety is serendipitous and dependent upon the extent to which, by chance, a listener has been exposed to the variety in question. The conclusion must be that to feature a wide range of accents in a test may be to discriminate unfairly against those who lack the funds or resources to travel internationally and therefore have limited access to L2 speakers from different regional and social backgrounds (Taylor 2006; see also recent research by Harding 2011).

Another issue that is often overlooked is that the major differences between the main varieties of English lie in the vowels (see Wells (1982) for a description of the main varieties). By contrast, in Spanish it is the consonants that vary. Listeners rely more on vowels as cues to words because of their greater duration and steady-state form. Encountering an unfamiliar variety of English can therefore obstruct *lexical search* to a greater degree than with some other languages.

Perhaps with these considerations in mind, Cambridge ESOL takes a commendably moderate approach to the use of varieties[5]. In the recordings accompanying the sample tests in Appendix A, standard southern British English features quite extensively, especially at the lower levels, where it is important to ensure that test takers are spared apprehension about what they are likely to hear. In the KET recordings, all the speakers employ this variety; while the PET recordings feature one speaker of standard American and two of northern British. A gradual growth in non-British varieties occurs at FCE and CPE levels – reflecting the recognition that these candidates are likely to have had greater exposure to the L2. In the sample materials, the level that appears inconsistent with this gradualist approach is CAE, where a large range of accents is featured and there is even quite extensive mixing of accents within recordings. What is curious is that some of the accents in these recordings are not entirely representative of the varieties targeted, but are diluted variants of them – which surely defeats the object of the exercise. In a review of FCE Part 1, Fried-Booth (2007:24) refers to these as 'mild accents': suggesting a policy of getting studio actors to modify their natural speech. There is also some evidence in the sample recordings that actors may have been asked to adopt accents not their own. Clearly, some actors are more capable of this than others; and there is always the problem of inconsistency if attention slips.

It would appear that asking actors to simulate accents is no longer common practice. A member of the Assessment and Operations Group

(AOG) at Cambridge ESOL affirms in respect of one test of the suite that: '[In] Dec 2008 we did encourage actors to use a range of accents at recording. Since late 2009 however, we tend to keep to the actor's natural accent'. Another AOG member describes policy as follows: 'We tend to try to include a few examples of different varieties at most recording sessions . . ., despite the majority of them being southern British English. However, this is fairly arbitrary and dependent on the abilities of the actors on the day'. Here, the term *abilities* suggests that some simulation does indeed still take place. More generally, the comment seems to indicate that the number of accents featured in any version of a test is random. Some standardisation would surely help, especially at the lower levels, where variations in the number of accents used may result in inconsistencies between the processing demands made by different versions of the same test.

Speech rate

Speech rate is a further aspect of speaker variation which has implications for cognitive validity. The general descriptions of KET and PET in the handbooks do not mention this factor; however, it is evident from the recordings accompanying the sample tests that Cambridge ESOL expects a slow rate of delivery at these levels.

Slowing down speech delivery serves to counter a major cause of listening anxiety at lower proficiency levels – the impression that L2 speakers speak unreasonably fast. In fact, this impression is not entirely correct. It has long been demonstrated in phonetics (Goldman-Eisler 1968:24) that slow speech is much more closely associated with the extent to which a speaker pauses and to precision of setting than it is to the speed with which words are articulated. Its effect is to assist lexical segmentation since the pauses mark word boundaries more frequently than might be the case in more naturally paced speech. In addition, the absence of assimilatory features ensures that words resemble their citation forms more closely. So, contrary to what is generally assumed, slow speech has an impact at the level of *lexical search* rather than at that of input decoding.

For the purposes of this exercise, questions raised by the use of slower speech are: To what extent does slowed input distort the cadences of natural speech and thus the naturalness of the listening experience? How carefully are speech rates graded across the lower levels of the suite from KET to PET to FCE? On quality, the speaking style in KET and PET is sometimes a little laboured, but the actors are relatively successful at maintaining natural prosodic and intonational features. On the fine-tuning of speech rate, Table 3.2 below shows mean rates across the three lower proficiency levels in the sample tests. Each section of the test is reported separately, to allow for variations in rate according to recording length and type (monologue vs dialogue). Means are indicated for sections where there are multiple short recordings. As a benchmark, a mean

Table 3.2 Mean speech rates across three levels of the Cambridge ESOL suite (words per second)

Test	Part 1	Part 2	Part 3	Part 4	Part 5	Overall
KET	2.69 (0.19)	2.62	2.65	2.30	2.05	2.51 (0.34)
PET	3.17 (0.37)	2.67	2.66	3.03		2.79 (0.17)
FCE	3.54 (0.37)	3.16	3.38 (0.21)	3.26		3.46 (0.34)

rate of around 200 wpm or 3.3 wps can be regarded as typical of medium-paced conversational speech (Calvert 1986:178, Griffiths 1992), though clearly much depends upon the context and the speaker's goals (the rate of a monologue speaker in particular can vary widely in the course of an extended presentation). The table shows a well graduated increase towards this level. At FCE level, the speakers in the recordings reach what can be regarded as a natural conversational rate (IWG: FCE, p.4); this rate is sustained consistently (with some exceptions reflecting situation type) at higher levels of the suite.

The use of slow speech certainly makes lexical processing easier than it might be in many listening events (Blau 1990). However, the slowing of speech at lower levels seems unexceptionable. Though slow, the rates at KET and PET levels do not fall outside what might conceivably be encountered in real-world contexts (especially where a native speaker is making concessions towards a non-native speaker with limited English). Ramsaran (1978, cited in Gimson 1989:308) puts the lowest level for spontaneous RP speech at 3.1 syllables per second (equivalent to about 2.25 words per second) and the highest at 5.4 syllables per second.

How well graded?

Discussion of the gradual increase in speech rate has anticipated the second line of enquiry. How well does the difficulty of processing the recordings correspond to the various levels of the suite? The issue here is no longer the differences between test input and real-world input; but the relationship between features of the test and the cognitive demands placed upon the learner. The areas to be discussed are recording length and linguistic and semantic features of the recording-as-text.

Recording length

Listening to an audio recording in a second language imposes quite heavy working memory demands upon a test taker who has had limited exposure to the target language. For less skilled listeners, word identification is a process that is *controlled* (in the sense of not being automatic) and not entirely confident. Considerable attentional resources thus have to be focused on lower level processing, particularly *input decoding* and *lexical search*. Recording length

Table 3.3 Actual recording times in seconds across sections of tests (Appendix A)

	Part 1	Part 2	Part 3	Part 4	Part 5	Total
KET	91 (18)	59	72	77	92	391
PET	197 (28)	147	105	103		552
FCE	245 (31)	196	206*	147* (29)		794
CAE	183 (61)	235	223	164 (33)		805
CPE	232 (58)	254	204	203		893

* Figures for Parts 3 and 4 at FCE are reversed to enable comparison with the item matching task (No. 4) at CAE level

also has an impact at higher levels of processing (*meaning construction* and *discourse construction*). The longer the recording, the more complex the discourse representation that the listener has to carry forward in his/her mind at the same time as paying heed to the speech signal. Furthermore, the more pieces of information there are in the text, the less confident the test taker may be of matching a test item against the part of the recording that bears the answer.

The information in the handbooks on target length of recording possesses some gaps: no guidelines are indicated for KET and PET or (curiously) for Part 1 of CAE. Table 3.3 therefore shows the actual timings in seconds for the recorded input accompanying the sample tests at the end of this volume. It illustrates the way in which recording length (and with it cognitive load) gradually increases across the levels of the suite. Figures in brackets indicate mean lengths of recording in sections where there are multiple short passages.

The figures in Table 3.3 do not take into account the contribution made by the number of items per recording. The effects upon a test taker of the interaction between recording length and item frequency can increase cognitive load in two ways.

a. A combination of a *short recording* and *multiple items* increases the load upon the test taker because of the need to assemble answers under pressure of time.

Table 3.4 Ratio of timings (secs.) to items, across sample tests (Appendix A)

	Part 1	Part 2	Part 3	Part 4	Part 5	Mean
KET	18.2	11.8	14.4	15.4	18.4	15.64
PET	28.14	24.50	17.50	17.17		21.83
FCE	30.63	19.60	29.43*	29.40*		27.26
CAE	30.50	29.38	37.17	16.40		28.36
CPE	29.00	28.22	40.80	33.83		32.96

* Figures for Parts 3 and 4 at FCE are reversed to enable comparison with the matching task (No. 4) at CAE level

b. A combination of a *longer recording* and relatively *few items* also increases the demands upon the test taker since the recording provides many more points of information that offer possible matches for the items, making it more difficult to determine where the correct answer lies.

To represent the effects of item density, the timings for each section were divided by the number of items to be answered.

The last column shows a steady progression in the mean amount of recorded material to be processed per item answered (in effect, scenario b); KET and PET are sharply distinguished from the higher proficiency levels. But there are also other interesting indications in relation to gradation of cognitive difficulty. In Part 1, the figures for FCE, CAE and CPE are closely similar. But that is because there is an increase in CAE and CPE not just of recording length but also of number of items (from one to two per recording). A similar interpretation applies to the low figure for CAE Part 4, where recording length remains standard but the number of items is doubled from 5 to 10 (in effect, scenario a), thus providing a very marked hike in the cognitive demands of the matching task.

Idea units

In designing L2 listening materials, the difficulty of a piece of recorded material is conventionally associated with linguistic features of the recording-as-text, such as lexical range and frequency or syntactic complexity. They relate to the test taker's knowledge of the target language rather than to the cognitive processes in which the test taker engages, and are the concern of Chapter 4. The text features that would appear to contribute most to the cognitive demands upon the listener are semantic rather than linguistic in nature. Prominent amongst them is what Bachman (1990:130) refers to as propositional content. This aspect of text difficulty has been relatively little explored in the literature – even less so in relation to listening than to reading.

The choice of the term *propositional* is unfortunate: strictly speaking, a proposition is context-independent, whereas a major consideration here is the contribution made by a piece of information to the overall discourse representation that a listener builds. The term *idea unit* (IU) proposed by Chafe (1979) will therefore be used instead. The assumption is that an idea unit serves two distinct purposes in a test of listening.

a. It forms part of the discourse representation which a listener builds up accretionally in the course of hearing the recording.

b. It forms a potential match to an item in the test – either as an answer or as a distractor to be eliminated.

The sample tests at three levels of the Cambridge ESOL suite (PET, FCE and CPE) were examined in order to establish whether there was a graded increase in the density of idea units, and thus in the cognitive demands associated with *meaning building* and *discourse building*. Part 1 of each test was chosen for analysis since this section with multiple short recordings is common to all levels of the suite. In addition, it allowed a mixture of mono- logues and dialogues to be covered, and a variety of topics and situations. Idea units within the text were conceptualised quite strictly in terms of points of information; phatic language and uninformative content such as greetings or back channelling were ignored.

Table 3.5 Density and embeddedness of idea units in Part 1 recordings of three tests

	Mean IUs	*Mean words per IU*	*Mean secs. per IU*	*Mean IUs per main verb*
PET	11.71 (10–13)	6.92	2.40	1.63 (0.49) / 1.49 (0.34)
FCE	14.25 (12–16)	7.36	2.14	1.74 (0.30)
CPE	22.00 (18–26)	8.70	2.64	1.84 (0.24)

Column 1 of Table 3.5 indicates the mean number of idea units (IUs) in each of the Part 1 tests, and (in brackets) the range in the number of units. There is an evident staged increase between PET and FCE levels, where the timing of the recordings is roughly the same. The number of idea units at CPE level (18–26) is about twice those at PET level; but the position here is less clear, since the recordings at this level are twice as long. The second and third columns of the table shed some additional light: the mean number of words expressing an idea unit rises by degrees from PET to CPE. In addi- tion, the average time taken by an idea unit rises from 2.14 at FCE level to 2.64 at CPE. [The figure for PET might seem anomalous, but is no doubt a reflection of the slow speech rate.]

The significance of these figures is that the increase in difficulty would seem to lie in the *parsing* of the idea units rather than in their density. The clause that has to be parsed in order to extract an idea unit becomes longer in both time and number of words as the proficiency level increases. Bearing in mind that a string of words has to be held in the mind until parsing is complete and a syntactic structure can be assigned, this represents a ratch- eting up of cognitive load that complements any conventional increases in linguistic difficulty. [Note that this relates strictly to the form in which the idea unit is expressed; it is distinct from Bachman's compact/diffuse distinc- tion (1990:134–5), which refers to how widely the necessary information is distributed. A distribution criterion of this kind might merit investigation in relation to the longer passages used in the tests of the suite.]

Attention was also given to the syntactic relationships between idea units. Discourse construction requires the listener to trace a link between an incoming proposition and others previously identified, in order to build an information structure. This process becomes more demanding if the linking takes the form of embedded clauses. The number of idea units per main verb (final column in Table 3.5) was taken to be an indication of the degree of embedding. (Here, allowance was made for elided verbs; and resultative *so* was treated as co-ordination since it was often used as a loose connective.) The figures show signs of a staged increase in this measure; the staging is even more marked if an outlier text in PET (a formal monologue introduction to a TV science programme) is omitted; this reduces the PET figure to 1.49.

While informational density does not emerge as a major determinant of processing difficulty in the shorter passages, it seems to be so in one of the longer CAE ones. The sheepdog trials recording (p.377) contains a total of 56 information units in 482 words (words per IU: 8.61) and 162 seconds (secs. per IU: 2.91). This level of information processing is comparable to that demanded by the shorter texts (see the figures for CPE in Table 3.5), yet the test taker is expected to sustain it for three times longer. To require a listener to process such large amounts of information in a relatively short space of time places a heavy strain upon the process of constructing and integrating meaning into a wider discourse representation. It also runs the risk of biasing the test in favour of candidates who possess greater powers of mental storage and retrieval. This is not to deny that working memory serves an important function by supporting the temporary storage of chunks of language while parsing is taking place. What is at issue here is the ability to *retain and recall* multiple discrete points of information, an area in which candidates are likely to vary widely, regardless of their listening skills.

To be fair, the other recordings in the sample CAE and CPE papers do not share this informational density; and a brief survey of retired papers suggested that it is not a commonly used method of stepping up text difficulty (a possible exception is found in Test 2 Part 2 of Cambridge CAE 2 (2008a)). However, the examples mentioned suggest that there may be limits to the extent to which density of information can reasonably be increased.

Amongst Bachman's criteria for determining propositional complexity (1990:135–6) is the relative abstractness of the information to be processed. This suggests a gradation from the representation of unambiguous facts at the levels of KET and PET to less concrete lines of reasoning at CAE and CPE levels. The progression appears to work well in the sample materials included as Appendix A, though, just occasionally, the quest for demanding material gives rise to a level of abstraction that would prove challenging even to a native listener. A case in point is the 'Memory and Imagination' passage from Part 1 of the CPE sample test, where processing difficulty is further compounded by a high level of metaphorical analogy:

S: As a writer, I find it very exciting that *memory and imagination are part of the same process*. When we imagine, we *create the future* out of

fragments from the past. And when we remember, we construct *path-ways* in our brains to *remake* the *experience* and, at a certain moment, it's as if the *jigsaw comes together*, and we'll accept that as *the truth*. But then if your memories are *acts of creativity*, it does cast a terrible doubt on . . .
L: . . . on all *decision-making*.

This text illustrates the dangers facing item writers when attempting to provide demanding material for higher-level listening tests. It conveys abstract information in the kind of densely packed form that is much more likely to be found in writing, where the reader can backtrack to support understanding, than it is in speech. It lacks the redundancy or exemplification that an experienced real-world speaker (even a lecturer) would introduce in order to lighten the processing load.

The processing problem lies not in the abstract terms used but in the difficulty of establishing a line of argument that links them. Abstract constructs are indeed more difficult to process than concrete ones because of their lack of imageability – a finding that has been widely demonstrated in relation to both lexical search (e.g. Paivio, Walsh and Bons 1994) and sentence comprehension (e.g. Haberlandt and Graesser 1985). But this is certainly not an argument for avoiding abstraction in a test for high-proficiency candidates. What makes the passage in question problematic is its lack of contextualisation for the abstract terms used. A 'context availability' view of lexical search, supported by research findings (Schwanenflugel and Stowe 1989), indicates that the relevance of abstract words becomes much harder to grasp when they do not occur in a transparent context. The study just cited focuses on sentence-level reading by expert L1 readers; but its conclusions apply even more aptly to L2 listening.

The difficulty is compounded by the use made here of figurative language. It was noted earlier that metaphor imposes additional processing demands upon a listener, who potentially has to instantiate both a literal and a figurative interpretation. Here, that ambivalence serves to further obscure the logical links between the abstract terms.

The CAE passage thus provides an illustration of the skill-specific limitations that apply when attempting to upgrade the difficulty of a higher-level listening text. Uncontextualised abstractions and extensive use of figurative language impose processing demands upon the candidate which might just be manageable in reading but take us some way beyond what is normally required of even the most accomplished listener.

To sum up this section: the evidence that has been examined suggests that content across the levels of the Cambridge ESOL suite is indeed finely graded in terms of the parsing of information units and the syntactic complexity of the links between units. However, two texts have exemplified the dangers of an over-reliance on information density and on loosely contextualised abstractions as the means of raising the level of difficulty of a test. There is a wider issue here of measuring candidate characteristics (memory capacity and the ability to impose patterns on abstractions) which are not central to the listening construct.

Methods

Methods: How representative?

This section of the validation exercise first considers three general characteristics of the methods employed in the Cambridge ESOL Listening tests – namely, the use of rubrics, the pre-presentation of items and the convention of playing the recorded material twice. It then goes on to examine, from a cognitive perspective, the five formats used in the suite. There are some final comments on the general effects of choice of format on cognitive validity.

Text conventions
Rubric

Instructions for the tasks are included in the recording, and are repeated in written form on the test paper. This ensures that the test taker is exposed to them both in an ecologically appropriate spoken form and in a more permanent one which can be referred back to.

Introductory information about the recording is also given. The most generally cited justification for this provision is that it compensates for the lack of visual input in an audio-based test. However, a careful look at the sample tests in Appendix A reveals that the information supplied rarely relates to the physical context. Instead, the rubric furnishes the listener with advance details of the topic of the recording, the situation and the relationship of the speakers. Its chief function thus seems to be to activate the type of schematic information described above as part of *meaning construction* and to create listener expectations akin to those that might occur in a real-world listening event.

Pre-presentation of items

The questions to be answered are presented before the recording is heard and test takers are allowed a brief period to read them. There is a sound cognitive rationale behind this procedure. Pre-presented questions provide test takers with a set of goals, without which the listening operation would lack direction and focus. In addition, post-set questions run the risk of memory effects, favouring those with the ability to recall multiple pieces of information regardless of relevance.

However, the pre-setting of test questions carries costs to cognitive validity as well as benefits. The availability of question items in advance of listening provides the test taker with a great deal of information about the recording which would not normally be available in a non-test context. This is particularly of concern in a test of listening because the information is expressed in a different modality from the one that is the target of the assessment. Written forms carry particular power for any literate individual. They are the forms in which we choose to store language in order to assist recall. They are not transitory like speech; they are also forms which, at word level, are much less subject to variability than spoken ones. Small wonder if language users, especially second language users, have greater confidence in information in written form than in spoken. The consequence is that processing in a test of listening often takes the written form rather than the spoken as its point of departure. It is also likely to embrace test-wise strategies which exploit the weakness of the format: they include predicting the content of the recording or seeking out what appear to be key words from the test items. Such strategies pose a serious challenge to cognitive validity, since they would not be available in a comparable real-world listening event[6]. See Field (2012) for evidence of strategy use in relation to the IELTS test and Field (forthcoming) for such evidence in relation to CAE.

The implications may extend even further. Field (1993) found evidence of what he termed a 'schema effect', whereby L2 listeners used the relative probability of true/false items to construct a preliminary mental representation of what they would hear. In certain cases, the content of a false item prevails with test takers despite contrary evidence in the recording. The power of such pre-constructed schemas has been demonstrated recently by what is known as *auditory priming*: it has been shown, for example, that a jury's processing of the words that are used in an audio recording can be biased by prior assumptions about the guilt of a defendant (Fraser, Stevenson and Marks 2011). Further investigation is needed into the extent to which expectations raised by pre-set items in a listening test can prove stronger than information provided by auditory input that is evanescent and (for L2 learners) less reliable. Sherman (1997:185) puts the issue very well: 'question preview may affect comprehension positively by focusing the attention or supplying information about the text, or negatively by interfering with subjective comprehension processes, increasing the burden on the attention or imposing shallower processing'.

With these considerations in mind, some test providers (an example is the revised TOEFL iBT test) have reverted to post-set questions. This decision is not without its own threats to cognitive validity: as already noted, setting questions after a recorded passage of (say) more than a minute is likely to lead to unfocused listening and to introduce variables related to powers of recall. But the post-setting of items for the short passages is an option that might perhaps be considered in future by Cambridge ESOL. It is especially easy to implement in the case of computer-delivered tests, where items can remain concealed until the test designer wishes to reveal them. Another solution is to make the items available between the two hearings of the recording (Sherman 1997), which would appear to reduce both the cognitive demands associated with reading the items out of context and the danger of predictive guessing. Again, this is a solution well suited to computer presentation but less easy to implement with a paper-based test.

Double play

A further characteristic of the tests in the suite is that, across all sections, listeners are permitted to hear the recorded material twice. The double-play policy is not uncontroversial: it is sometimes argued, on cognitive grounds, that real-life listening does not permit the listener to hear the same piece of speech more than once. Part of the logic behind this convention has already been discussed; it compensates to some extent for the lack of the visual and paralinguistic cues which would normally be available to an L2 listener in a real-world context. It also compensates for the fact that there is no opportunity to employ repair strategies and to ask the speaker to repeat or to clarify what has been said – as there would be in a normal conversational context. For a thoughtful review of the issues, see Geranpayeh and Taylor (2008).

Less often cited in favour of double play is the nature of the listening task that the test taker is asked to perform. Conventional test formats such as those employed in the Cambridge TESOL suite require the candidate to undertake a process of *checking or matching information*. This type of activity is an artefact of the testing situation rather than a characteristic of much real-world listening; it is therefore surely fair to allow the test taker the means of accomplishing the task as efficiently as possible. The limited research that has considered the effects of double play (Buck 1990, Field 2009b) suggests that different types of checking process are involved in the two hearings. The test taker makes use of the first play to establish the location of information in the recording and to make a preliminary match against the items in the paper. Processing is thus very much at the level of *lexical search* and *parsing*. On a second hearing, the test taker is able to locate the relevant information more confidently and to confirm or revise provisional answers. In addition, he/she moves on to construct a higher-level *discourse representation*. While this may not mirror real-world listening, the processes involved seem entirely appropriate to the artificial nature of the task that has been set.

The CAE test formerly included a gap-filling task in which only one play was permitted. When it was revised in the 2008 revision, a further argument for double play was put: namely that 'the concept of the once-heard task could become less relevant in the CAE context, given changes in technology, which mean that people can generally listen to on-line materials e.g. radio programmes, as often as they wish' (Murray 2007:21).

Test formats

Tests of the Cambridge ESOL suite make use of five different formats.

- multiple choice
- visual multiple choice
- gap filling
- multiple matching
- true/false.

Their distribution and number of items are shown in Table 3.6 on page 134. There are persuasive reasons for employing these standard formats: the most important being their reliability and the ease of marking which they permit. An additional consideration is familiarity. Washback has ensured that the formats feature in most standard listening coursebooks and are well understood by teachers. It is thus fairly safe to assume that all candidates taking a test in the suite will have been exposed to them at some point. Cambridge ESOL has recently made a further concession to familiarity by standardising the types of format to be used in each of the four sections of any of its tests (Hawkey 2007:7).

Familiarity, however, has its disadvantages. The multiple-choice and gap-filling formats have proved a goldmine for crammers in various parts of the world, which train potential candidates not to become better listeners or readers but to exploit loopholes in the test methods they will encounter. The loopholes in question are easily identified, and part of the cognitive argument must be that they result in the adoption of test-wise strategies which would not be present in normal listening circumstances (Field 2012). Another concern is that, as already suggested, the standard methods of testing entail a very specific type of listening, involving the checking of information and the matching of information against input – one that cannot be said to occur very widely outside tests or certain academic contexts.

Let us briefly consider the cognitive impact of the formats of the Cambridge ESOL suite.

- *Multiple-choice questions.* Perhaps the greatest advantage of the MCQ format from a cognitive perspective is that it allows the use of items that tap into the various levels of processing identified in the listening model above. Thus, it can focus on input decoding through options that are minimally different phonologically; on lexical search through items that target word-level information; on parsing through items that target discrete sentence-level information units; on meaning construction through items that demand inference, anaphor resolution, pragmatic interpretation etc.; and on discourse construction through items that require an understanding of the main point of the recording or the goals of the speaker.

But a price is paid for this flexibility. The task imposes quite heavy cognitive demands which go well beyond those that would apply in a non-test context. The test taker first has to discriminate, often finely, between the three or four options that are presented; and then has to carry forward these multiple concepts in the mind while listening to the recording. There are issues of *dual task interference* here (Pashler and Johnston 1998), heightened by the fact that the two information sources are in different modalities. Working memory limitations (Miller 1956) dictate that, at any one time, there is likely to be a limit of two items (six or eight options) foregrounded in the mind for possible matching against the recording. As a consequence, the test taker is quite heavily dependent upon the convention that the items will follow the order of the recording. This raises the possibility (evidenced by verbal reports such as those quoted in Field 2012) that failure to make a successful item-recording match will lead the candidate to continue listening for an answer when it is long past and thus to run the risk of missing the answers to succeeding items. Geranpayeh and Kunnan (2007:199–201) cite a similar effect when an item of high difficulty in a DIF study appeared to lower the level of successful responses to the apparently easy item that succeeded it.

It was remarked above that conventional listening test formats require the test taker to engage in a very specific type of listening, involving the cross-matching of facts from two sources, one auditory and one visual. In the MCQ format, an extra dimension is added by the presence of distractor options. All options need to be processed in depth well ahead of the location in the listening passage where they are likely to occur. But more than that: identifying the correct option does not necessarily entail the immediate abandonment of the others. Test takers do not simply listen out for positive evidence in an MCQ test; they also seek evidence that might *disconfirm* any of the options. In other words, at any given point in the test, the test taker is striving to match three or more propositions against two possible outcomes (confirmation or elimination). In cognitive terms, this is a complex operation and, importantly, one that is a by-product of the test method rather than of the construct being targeted. It certainly needs the support of the second play, which enables the test taker to check provisional decisions.

Of the test methods discussed here, the MCQ format is the one that has been most investigated in relation to listening tests. This is partly because of concern (Farr, Prichard and Smitten 1990) over the extent to which difficulty in a test loads on to the item rather than on to the input. The most detailed study to date has been that of Freedle and Kostin (1999), who used factor analysis to identify the extent to which variables relating to item and listening passage content correlated with difficulty in TOEFL mini-talks. The authors are careful about the claims they make in respect of content validity – with reason, since their study exemplifies what Weir (2005:18) characterises as a 'post-hoc' approach to the issue of test method variables. Like other similar investigations, it seeks correlations with test difficulty, but does not directly address the question of the extent to which the method constrains the behaviour of the candidate.

Freedle and Kostin conclude that item variables do not play a major role in test difficulty. However, they define 'item variables' narrowly, limiting the category to surface features. A separate category, which they term 'text/item overlap' (variables relating to semantic and lexical parallels between items and recording) is treated as contributing to the part played by the recording, whereas it is precisely these factors and the extent to which candidate behaviour is determined by them which form the greatest potential threat to cognitive validity. In the Freedle and Kostin categorisation, they include: shared lexis, position of item in relation to information in the recording, attractiveness of correct option and types of processing elicited by the item.

There have been relatively few attempts (e.g. Buck 1990, Wu 1998) to use verbal report to investigate taker takers' cognitive behaviour in response to the MCQ format. Contrary to Freedle and Kostin's conclusions, Wu found that pre-viewing a set of options assisted one advanced participant; but that it stimulated much uninformed guessing in others. She also found that, in some cases, it was misinterpretation of the options rather than the recording that led to subjects choosing incorrect answers.

- *Visual multiple choice.* The first sections of KET and PET require test takers to match short recordings against three visual options. The use of visuals is confined to these tests, presumably on the assumption that options in written form are more vulnerable to being misunderstood by lower-level test takers. The format sidesteps some of the general reservations expressed above about the role of written forms in MCQ testing and the dangers of divided attention. However, it is a method with limitations in terms of the levels of processing which it can elicit. Visual representations can illustrate distinctions of lexis. They can also represent distinctions between a course of action or state of affairs that is referred to in the recordings and others that are explicitly excluded. They thus permit a test to tap into processing at the levels of input decoding, lexical search and parsing, but not into higher-level processes.

While most of the visuals in the sample materials in Appendix A succeed well in terms of transparency, occasional items such as PET 1.3 take us close to the point where the item loads excessively on the test taker's visuo-spatial capacity. In this case, the chief cognitive burden lies not in interpreting the recording but in decoding and differentiating the visual options. The IWGs provide useful advice on avoiding detail

(KET, p.9) and on aiming to ensure that a set of visuals forms a coherent and easily differentiated group (PET, p.10)

- *Gap filling.* Intuitively, the gap-filling format would appear to be the one which resembles most closely the kind of task that a listener might have to perform in a real-life context (e.g. taking notes during a lecture or meeting). In reality, of course, the notes are not the test takers' own and they therefore require careful reading, both before and during the playing of the recording. In addition to reading and listening simultaneously, the test taker also has to enter provisional answers during the first recording and to check these answers during the second. This therefore is a task which divides the test taker's attention (Pashler and Johnston 1998) between three types of processing: listening, reading and writing. It is consequently very cognitively demanding – much more so than most real-life listening events. Testimony to this is found in some of the verbal reports obtained by Field (2012) in relation to the IELTS Listening test.

  Some general remarks were made earlier about the way in which test takers use written information to predict what occurs in the recording. They particularly apply to gap-filling, since the notes with which students are presented represent an accurate if incomplete version of events, in the way that the majority of MCQ options do not. This encourages test-wise strategies based upon predicting how the slots might be filled.

  However, a curious feature of many of the answers submitted by less able candidates is that they do not fit the sentence frame syntactically or semantically (Field forthcoming). Instead, they seem to reflect the perceptual prominence of a particular word or words in the text. This is suggestive of a form of processing that is heavily based upon lexical search. The phenomenon is unsurprising, given that gap-filling items tend to target this particular level of processing. The sentence frame may well paraphrase information from the text, but the words to be inserted are often to be taken verbatim from the recording and rarely form a larger unit than a lexical chunk. See the recommended answers in the sample materials for Section 2 at FCE, CAE and CPE. Buck (2001:82) suggests that integrative tests (in which he includes gap filling) have limited scope for tapping in to higher-level processes.

- *Multiple matching.* A major advantage of the multiple-matching task is that it is not constrained, like other methods, to follow the order in which information units occur in the recording (though, curiously, the matching exercise in the CPE sample materials does so). What is more, it can greatly reduce the amount of written material that a listener has to process and avoids the propositional overload of MCQ. It also provides the opportunity of testing comprehension across a range of levels of detail, from local information to general topic to interpretation of speaker intent, in a way that gap filling does not.

However – and it is a big however – it achieves this at the cost of a task which extends beyond the listening construct itself and implicates the test taker's ability to manipulate information. This function is quite distinct from the types of discourse construction that were described earlier as forming part of the core listening process. The test taker is not required to link propositions, to build an argument structure or to integrate idea units into a larger discourse representation. Instead, he/she has to hold a series of propositions in the mind which can occur at any point in the recording (or even not occur at all); and to match them as and when supporting evidence becomes available. Again, a strong case can be made for the use of second play in order to enable the checking of initial decisions.

- *True/false.* The true/false format is employed in only one section of the suite: Part 4 of PET. Reluctance to use the method more widely no doubt reflects a history of scepticism about its reliability, given the 50% likelihood of a correct response. Here, the method is adapted to make it more ecological (Yes/No replace True/False) and to include a 'Both' option (rather than the more usual 'not mentioned').

The method runs some risk of creating incorrect schematic expectations based upon the false items. The risk is greater than with MCQ, since only one version of events is offered. An early piece of research (Ebel 1972:180) provided evidence of a response style biased towards True responses, suggesting a tendency for test takers to accept rather than challenge an item.

It may well be that there is little current alternative to the use of these five formats because of their value in terms of reliability, ease of marking and familiarity. They are standardly used worldwide by test providers other than Cambridge ESOL, and even by researchers; but we should not lose sight of the fact that they must be regarded as less than ideal when cognitive validity is the issue. For the moment, the best that validation can do is to seek evidence that a test provider has been sensitive to some of their drawbacks by giving careful attention to the types of item that are set and to the levels of processing at which test takers can be expected to perform. These considerations will be explored when considering items.

Some additional comments

At various points, the discussion in this section has touched upon the levels of processing which the methods employed in the suite elicit from test takers. One of the virtues of MCQ, it was noted, is that its items can range widely in terms of the assessment focus. They can target possible misinterpretations at lexical level or at the level of parsing; they can tackle discrete idea units, global summation and meanings that require inference or interpretation. They can even target input decoding (requiring test takers to show that they can discriminate between *The train's at seven-fifteen* and *The train's at seven-fifty*) – though in practice they do not appear to be used in this way. The pictorial MCQ format was viewed as less flexible. It is best adapted to testing processing at the levels of decoding, lexical search and parsing. Similarly, gap filling is quite restricted in its scope, as it is mainly reliant on successful lexical search and even potentially inclines test takers to focus attention at that level. Finally, multiple matching is well suited to testing the candidate's ability to identify the main point of a short passage or to contrast the views of speakers. It could thus be argued that the different formats complement each other and that the use of several formats in each test ensures that a range of levels of processing are covered.

There is, however, one level of processing that is under-represented. These conventional formats provide little opportunity to test *discourse construction*. The reader will recall that, as outlined in the listening model, this covers: identifying the relative importance of utterances that have been processed, linking idea units, integrating incoming idea units into a developing discourse representation and building a hierarchical structure representing the speaker's line of argument. To be sure, the present formats do allow testing that requires the test taker to foreground the main idea (especially in a short recording) and sideline secondary ones. But the ability to target the highest levels of decision making is limited by their design. With longer recordings in particular, formats such as MCQ or gap filling mainly target discrete points of information. There is no requirement upon the candidate to recognise the logical links that connect these points, or to build them into a discourse-level information structure. In addition, it is the tester who decides which points to focus on. Listeners do not have to make the judgements they would make in a real-world listening event (especially a monologue one) as to the relative importance of every new proposition and whether it should be retained, retained in generalised form or allowed to decay. For a more extended discussion of this lack of representation, see Field, 2011c.

Here, then, is a major gap in the way in which conventional test methods can claim to represent the listening skill in its entirety. There are also side-effects connected with memory load. The MCQ and gap-filling formats require the listener to hold propositional information in the mind and to match it against what is heard in the recording. Clearly, it would impose a very heavy burden on memory to mentally store eight or 10 items in this way. There is therefore an implicit assumption that the test taker will seek one match at a time. The consequence is seen in two conventions that are widely recognised – and indeed exploited – by test takers: that the *order* of the items should follow the order of the recording; and that the items should be relatively *evenly spaced* to allow the test taker time to move on to a new item

Examining Listening

(Brindley 1998, Buck 2001:138). Instructions to this effect occur in the IWGs at all levels. Even if one assumes the rare scenario of a listener approaching a non-test listening event with a set of questions in mind, neither of these conditions would be likely to apply.

Test formats can further compromise cognitive validity if they are accorded too much importance by item writers. While it seems not unreasonable to consider the suitability of a recording for a particular format (IWGs Information Common to all Papers: FCE/CAE/CPE, p.10), it would be unfortunate if this consideration were allowed to outweigh other factors such as the extent to which the recording is representative of a given genre of discourse or likely to give rise to a particular type of listening. There is always a danger that, in the minds of some item writers, the format (usually of somewhat doubtful cognitive validity for the reasons given above) will drive the agenda, rather than the nature of the construct to be tested. This might lead, for example, to excessive adaptation of original sources in order to fit them to a particular format.

Methods: How well graded?

Table 3.6 below shows how the various formats discussed above are distributed across the five levels of the Cambridge ESOL suite, as exemplified in the sample materials in Appendix A.

Table 3.6 Formats used across five levels (see Appendix A)*

Test	Part 1	Part 2	Part 3	Part 4	Part 5
KET	5 Visual MCQ (3)	5 Match	5 MCQ (3)	5 Gap fill	5 Gap fill
PET	7 Visual MCQ (3)	6 MCQ (3)	6 Gap fill	6 True/false	
FCE	8 MCQ (3)	10 Gap fill	5 Match (6)	7 MCQ (3)	
CAE	6 MCQ (3)	8 Gap fill	6 MCQ (4)	10 Match (16)	
CPE	8 MCQ (3)	9 Gap fill	5 MCQ (4)	6 Match (3)	

* *No. of items followed by format and (brackets) no. of options*

Examining the relevance of these formats to different levels is principally the concern of Chapter 4. However, in line with Chapter 3 of Taylor (Ed.) (2011), there will be a brief consideration of the extent to which cognitive task demands have been calibrated across levels.

The *visual MCQ format* is only used at the two lowest levels (KET and PET). This takes account of the fact that, at these levels, a candidate's reading skills may not be sophisticated enough to decode and interpret MCQ options. An important consideration here is that many candidates are from L1 contexts which do not employ the Western European alphabet; one can therefore expect that, at these early levels, their reading might be slow and cognitively demanding.

The *gap filling* format is used at all levels. This may seem curious, given what has already been said about the complexity of the task, which imposes divided attention demands upon the candidate in that listening has to be combined with reading and writing. However, paradoxically, the task particularly loads on low-level processing in the form of lexical search. It is no doubt for this reason that it has been included at KET and PET levels, since it is at these levels that basic problems of word recognition are likely to be most salient.

Attempts have clearly been made to calibrate the cognitive demands of processing the *MCQ options*. The number of options is restricted to three up to Level B2, and only rises to four with CAE and CPE. This shows sensitivity to the demands entailed in holding a number of propositions in the mind while at the same time listening to a recording. More open to question is the way in which the length and conceptual complexity of some of the MCQ options are controlled until FCE but then increased steeply at CAE level; this aspect of task difficulty is discussed under 'items'.

The complex cognitive demands made by the *multiple-matching* format have been noted above. The format is used at four of the five levels: the exception being PET, where a less challenging *True/False* alternative is used. Multiple matching might appear excessively demanding at KET level; however, as the sample materials show, the task has been carefully restricted to processing at the level of lexical search – precisely the level at which KET candidates principally operate. From a set of eight options, test takers have to choose five which are associated with five listed terms (in the sample materials, clothing to wear has to be matched to five different days).

The FCE task as exemplified in the sample materials appears to work well and to be appropriate for the level in terms of task demands. From six relatively transparent statements of teaching policy, the candidate has to match five against five monologues. By contrast, at CAE level, the task becomes hugely complex: the test taker is required to choose five items from a total of eight and to do so *for two different lists* at the same time as listening, as shown in this extract from the task rubric:

> For questions 21 – 25 choose from the list (A – H) the difficulties each speaker has had to overcome. For questions 26 to 30 choose from the [second] list (A – H) what each speaker enjoys most about the process of creating art. *While you listen, you must complete both tasks.* [italics added]

The aim is presumably to put distance between CAE and FCE. However, once again, this is achieved by loading difficulty onto the task rather than onto the recording. The task is not only very cognitively demanding in terms of the manipulation of 16 pieces of information (listed in no particular order), but also bears very little resemblance to any kind of operation that a real-world listener would ever have to perform.

To its credit, Cambridge ESOL recognised the heavy working memory demands imposed by the task; and in the 2008 revision, the possibility was mooted of reducing the choices from eight per column to six (Murray 2007:21–23). A research study was conducted using a small focus group, together with a larger population who took a six-option x 2 version of the test and an eight-option x 2 one and completed a questionnaire. The focus group commented that they were 'under too much pressure processing the options at the same time as they were listening to the extracts' (p.22). The experimental group's responses (Khalifa 2005) reveal that the majority felt that the six-option format allowed them time to prepare in a way that the eight-option format did not.

Despite this compelling evidence of heavy cognitive load originating in the task rather than the text, the eight-option format was finally retained. The decision was made partly on statistical grounds; but it was also asserted that the six-option version might have 'the potential to focus the task more firmly on detailed listening' (Murray 2007:23). This seems a curious line of argument, given the point made earlier about the ability of this particular format to target a range of levels of processing – and its special aptness for requesting global and gist information.

By contrast, the parallel task at CPE level is much simpler, with relative difficulty linked instead to the way in which the test taker handles the input. The specifications in the CPE Handbook refer to the identification of 'stated and non-stated opinion, agreement and disagreement'. Processing of the input thus takes place at an advanced conceptual level, and provision is made for inference as well as explicitly expressed ideas. Focusing on the type of high-level processing associated with meaning construction and discourse construction is very appropriate at this top level of the suite.

To summarise: In general, the use made of the five formats across the five levels of the suite is sensitive to the cognitive load imposed by the various tasks. There are exceptions at CAE level, where some of the sections do not seem to be aligned with the gradation of difficulty across the suite and rely heavily upon the nature of the task to create difficulty rather than upon the interaction between test taker and recording.

Items

Processes targeted

A cognitive framework was outlined earlier, based on five major levels of listening. Any test claiming to be representative of the construct as a whole clearly needs to elicit processes that cover as many as possible of these levels. However, an important proviso is that there may be limitations on what it is possible for a test taker to achieve at a particular stage of proficiency. Very broadly, one might expect a test taker at Levels A2 and B1 to need to focus a great deal of attention at the more local levels of processing (input decoding, lexical search and parsing) and to have little spare attentional capacity to give to the wider areas of meaning construction and discourse construction. As test takers progress through the tests of the Suite, one can expect increasing automaticity in local-level perceptual processing and hence an increasing capacity for handling complex meaning-related processes such as inference, interpreting speakers' intentions or building a wider discourse structure.

It is chiefly the items written by the setter which determine the levels of processing elicited in a test. Do they demand processing chiefly at lexical level or does the candidate have to parse complete sentences or interpret the speaker's intentions? Is the candidate only expected to reproduce facts or does he/she have to extrapolate information that is not explicitly mentioned? Here, an additional factor is the test format. As already noted, some formats (e.g. gap filling) are heavily oriented towards lexical search, while others (e.g. MCQ and multiple matching) allow different items to target different levels of processing.

Clearly, it is incorrect to imply that an item is constructed in such a way as to tap into a single level of processing. Listening is a very complex operation, in which a range of processes interact closely. It may well be that an item requires the listener to obtain a piece of information by means of inference; but the listener is only able to make that inference thanks to successful processing at other levels, including input decoding, lexical search and parsing. So if, here and elsewhere, an item is referred to as 'targeting' a given level of processing, it should not be taken as implying that only one level is involved. What is of interest is the *highest level of processing* at which an item requires a test taker to engage – a criterion that can be conceptualised concretely in terms of the level and complexity of the information that the listener is required to extract from the recording.

Several types of information can be distinguished, corresponding loosely to the five levels of the listening framework.

- minimal phonological distinctions between words (input decoding)
- meaning at the level of the word or lexical chunk (lexical search)
- factual meaning at the level of the utterance (parsing)
- interpretive meaning at the level of the utterance (meaning construction)
- meaning at discourse level (discourse construction).

These categories cannot be more than loosely indicative. When assessing the complexity of processing associated with an item, one also has to take account of the role of any distractors – not simply in the item itself, but also in the recording. Alongside the complexity of the information demanded, one therefore has to allow also for the relative difficulty of excluding other possibilities indicated by the item. In some cases, a test taker might need to process at a higher level (across a speaker's complete turn or across several turns) in order to determine which of three or four options is the most probable or most precise.

With this proviso, level of information focus still enables a very rough comparison of how widely the items in the tests of the Cambridge ESOL suite range in terms of the processing demands which they make of the test taker. Answers to the items in all sections of the sample Listening tests in Appendix A were classified according to the five levels identified above. The results appear in Figure 3.4 below.

Figure 3.4 Information focus at five levels: number of items per test

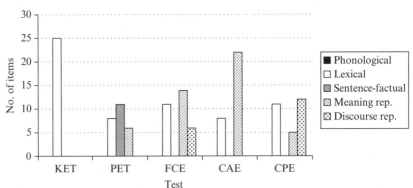

In general, it would appear that the processing demands upon the test taker are sufficiently varied and well graded. The absence at KET level of items based upon fine phonological distinctions (*the eight-thirty train* versus *the eight-thirteen train*) is unsurprising, given the reaction in present-day communicative listening tests against early methods based upon minimal pair discrimination (Weir forthcoming 2013b). Rather more unexpected is the lack of focus beyond PET upon strictly factual information at sentence level. Already at FCE, inference and interpretation of speaker intentions play an important part. Lexical level information features throughout, mainly due to the fact that each of the tests includes a gap-filling task. Of course, what becomes more complex at higher levels is the frame in which the word or chunk has to be embedded. Slightly anomalous, at least in the sample materials, is the fact that Part 4 at FCE features MCQ items of some conceptual complexity, which oblige the test taker to differentiate quite finely between points of information within an entire speaker's turn (i.e. to operate at discourse level). The same level of informational complexity is not demanded at CAE. At CPE, discourse-level processes are well represented by a task (Section 4) which requires test takers to match opinions against speakers.

So far as the lower proficiency tests (KET and PET) are concerned,

Figure 3.4 shows a strong focus upon perceptual level processing. The items set at those levels are thus sensitive to the limitations upon higher-level operations that occur when learners have to commit heavy attentional resources to decoding.

However, it should now be admitted that the account given previously was incomplete in one important respect. Although they bring greater resources of attention to bear on decoding, lower-proficiency listeners are likely in practice to be less successful in matching sounds to words – partly because of their limited linguistic knowledge, partly because of their inability to employ that knowledge under pressures of time and partly because of their lack of listening experience. The consequence is that the performance of these listeners, whether in test conditions or in the real world, depends critically upon their ability to make successful use of *compensatory strategies* which enable them to infer general meaning from input that has not been completely mastered. It would thus seem appropriate to include at lower levels of the suite a number of items that require test takers to demonstrate that they are capable of reporting the main point made by a speaker, even if they have not grasped the full detail of the content. In short, alongside perceptual processing, some provision should arguably be made for items that demand gist. A careful examination of the items in the sample KET test suggests that relatively few of them fit into this category, though, to be fair, the T/F items in Part 4 of PET do serve a function that is not entirely dissimilar.

Item length and processability

A second means of grading difficulty takes the form of a progressive increase in item length and complexity. Table 3.7 below shows the mean number of words per item across five tests of the suite, with the various parts of each test reorganised according to format. The figure of 0 for KET and PET Part 1 reflects the use of visuals. It has been included in the overall means quoted; but, even when it is not taken into account, it is clear that there is a sharp increase in reading load from FCE level upwards. The high SDs at CAE and CPE reflect the extent to which at higher levels, the parts of the tests diverge considerably in amount of reading according to the format employed.

Table 3.7 Mean number of words per item across four test formats

	Short MCQ	Gap	MCQ	Match*	Mean	SD
KET	0	4 / 4.6	11.4	3	4.6	4.19
PET	0	6.8	18.5	10	8.825	7.68
FCE	38.1	11.7	34.3	10.7	23.7	14.52
CAE	28	12	48.4	7.4	22.6	22.46
CPE	41.7	13.9	41.2	8.3	26.275	17.67

* *True/False at PET level*

The figures indicate a gradual increment in the number of words per item, especially so far as gap filling and standard MCQ formats are concerned. One or two apparent anomalies stand out. Particularly striking is the disparity in the reading load of the CAE MCQ items. A brief look at this section of the test (see p.373) reveals that the items are not only long, but also in some cases conceptually and/or syntactically quite complex. Here is an example.

> 17. According to Peter, when he took on the role of Prospero, he was
>   A. relieved to be playing a challenging character for a change.
>   B. apprehensive at having to portray so much anger on stage.
>   C. amused by the audience's reaction to his performance.
>   D. doubtful as to whether he would enjoy the experience.

The information that the test taker has to bring to listening is quite intricate. These options are not in mutual contrast or minimally different: each has a separate detailed proposition attached to it and each relates to a different affective stance on the part of the speaker. It should be borne in mind that at this level of the suite the cognitive demands of the task have already been ratcheted up sharply by increasing the number of MCQ options from three to four[7].

Item difficulty here appears, if anything, to be greater than at CPE level. Compare the item just cited with the longest item in the equivalent MCQ task at CPE level (p.384), where the propositions are simpler and more easily conceptualised:

> 22. What does Ray's fictional hero have in common with Sayers' hero?
>   A. They both prefer not to talk about their private lives.
>   B. They both have a complex family tree, created by the author.
>   C. They are both easily irritated, and have no time for fools.
>   D. They are both in tune with contemporary trends.

One has to conclude that (at least in this particular version of the test) CAE Part 3 falls out of line with the gradation of the suite. It could be argued that the length and complexity of the items are the inevitable outcome of the more complex questions that have to be set at a higher proficiency level. However, in Part 1 of this same CAE test, the mean words per item average only 28.

To be fair, the IWGs show considerable sensitivity to the problems raised by item length and complexity. Cautionary notes are sounded on the demands imposed by the written form of the items ('No item should represent too great a reading load', FCE p.15). There are only general guidelines on the complexity of individual items; but item writers at CAE level are advised (p.20) that 'options should appear parallel with each other in form and structure' – a precept which, if more closely observed, would considerably reduce the heavy propositional processing load associated with the MCQ format. (As it is, only one item out of six in the CAE Part 3 sample exhibits this kind of pattern.) It would also be helpful to have more prominently displayed limits on option length and conceptual complexity in MCQs, to prevent the type of overload exemplified above.

Another apparent anomaly in Table 3.7 is the high number of words per item in Part 1 of FCE (MCQs on short passages). This is more easily explained. Here, the additional reading load is counterbalanced by the fact that the questions and MCQ options feature in the recording as well as on the page. Reading aloud is much slower than silent reading, so this form of delivery grants the test taker more time to master content[8].

To summarise, there is evidence that the cognitive demands imposed upon the test taker at the various levels of the suite are to some degree determined by the length and complexity of the items used, particularly in the extended MCQ task. This might seem a conventional way of controlling difficulty across the suite. However, in relation to cognitive validity it raises quite serious concerns. It loads difficulty onto the test format rather than onto the construct being tested. The practice might be partly defensible in a test of reading, where the cognitively challenging component is in the same modality as the target construct; but the same argument cannot apply to a test of listening. The fact is that difficulty is being manipulated by means of the written input that the test taker has to master rather than by means of the demands of the auditory input which is the object of the exercise. This appears to be further evidence of test format driving the thinking of test designers and item writers rather than the nature of the construct to be tested.

Some conclusions

Let us now bring together the main points that have arisen in order to address the three validation questions that were raised at the beginning.

Real-world processing

How closely do the processes elicited by the tests resemble those that would be employed by the test taker in a real-world context?

Various features of the tests were noted, which align their content and the behaviour they elicit with what we know about the nature of spoken input and the way a listener handles it.

The recorded material:

- Combines monologue and dialogue texts, on the grounds that listening to non-participatory dialogue is an important listener function. There is no provision for interactive listening; but this is a component of the Speaking tests, even if it is not separately assessed.
- Is sensitive to the difficulty of normalising to unfamiliar L2 voices. Where there is a dialogue, speakers are of mixed gender and, where there are

three speakers, distinctive voices are used. The question of normalisation is also catered for by ensuring that the first item in any task does not depend critically on the opening words of the speaker.

- Reflects a measured approach to the proportion and range of non-standard varieties featured. This is in tune with what multiple-trace theory would suggest is the random and highly individual way in which accent familiarity develops. Some inconsistency was apparent in the IWGs at PET level, which refer (p.7) to a much wider range of varieties than elsewhere: 'Standard English in a variety of accents . . . as spoken by native speakers and non-native speakers'.
- Employs slowed speech at KET and PET levels that remains within the lower limits of conversational style. Steps are taken to ensure that, where slowed speech is used, the speakers retain natural speech rhythms.

The test tasks:

- Feature a combination of formats. Some allow item writers to target information at several different levels of processing, while one focuses on a single level. Some employ quite a lot of written text, while others require few words. Some are constrained to follow the order of the recording, while one is not. One (gap filling) is well adapted to local processing; another (multiple matching) is well adapted to global processing and to eliciting opinions.
- Feature rubrics which enable candidates to activate schematic information in advance of listening.
- Make use of double play. The test designers have not subscribed to the much-quoted argument that real-world listening never permits of a double play (in point of fact, it quite often does). Instead, they permit two plays of the recorded material throughout all parts of the suite: presumably on the grounds that it compensates for the lack of visual cues when audio recordings are in use and for the inability of a test candidate to use repair techniques when understanding breaks down. An additional suggestion was made here: that the double play mitigates the heavy cognitive demands of the checking and matching operations that conventional test methods require, with the first play allowing candidates to locate information and the second to check it.

Four relatively intractable issues emerged, all of which raise questions of cognitive validity in that they create circumstances and goals for the test taker which differ from those that would apply in a non-test context. It should be stressed that these considerations pose headaches for any kind of listening test and not just for those of the Cambridge ESOL Suite. They are:

- the desirability of the *auditory input* resembling natural everyday speech as closely as possible

- the necessity of *presenting items in written form*, thus implicating reading processes in the construct being tested
- the convention of *pre-presenting items* to enable test takers to listen in a focused way and to avoid memory effects
- the use of *conventional test formats.*

Auditory input. If a test is to adequately predict how test takers will perform in normal circumstances, it is clearly desirable that the spoken input should closely resemble that of real-life conversational or broadcast sources. This indicates a reliance, where possible, upon authentic materials that have been minimally edited (exceptions can reasonably be made at lower levels from A1 to B1, where the use of scripted material may be unavoidable). In principle, the practice of re-recording materials combines the linguistic and discoursal features of authentic speech with the benefits of studio-quality recording. In practice, as noted above, an actor reading aloud from a script is likely to articulate more rhythmically and to faithfully mark punctuation.

More importantly, conversational features and speaker overlaps will be absent. It is worth sensitising item writers and studio managers to these issues. It might also be advisable to revise the present informal script conventions (IWG: CAE, p.8) and to adopt a transcription system that more adequately represents important features of the original spoken language such as hesitation and planning pauses and false starts. Long term, it would be beneficial to make increased use of authentic materials taken directly from broadcast sources. Finding and selecting material of this kind has become much easier with the growth of the internet.

The other marked difference from natural speech is the absence of visual cues in the form of physical context, facial expressions and speaker gestures. As speech scientists discover more about the role that visual cues play in interactional listening or viewing films, testers may be under pressure to consider a move to video material. There are no doubt concerns about the availability of equipment in some of the countries where the Cambridge ESOL tests are administered. However, as the internet becomes more and more widely available, as broadband connections improve and as the transmission of recorded material becomes ever easier, this should cease to be an obstacle.

The role of the written word. The designer of any listening test faces an unenviable choice between requiring a candidate to write extended answers, and thus implicating the writing skill in the construct being tested, or presenting a set of relatively detailed questions in written form, and thus implicating the reading skill. In common with other major test providers, Cambridge ESOL adopts the latter course. It is important not to lose sight of the consequences for cognitive validity. In point of fact, the Cambridge ESOL tests make good use of certain formats to reduce the candidate's exposure to the written word. Visual MCQs are used at KET and PET level, though serious limitations on the fineness of the information that can be tested preclude their use at higher levels. In addition, skilful use is made of the multiple-matching format to keep written input brief and succinct. However, item writers always face a temptation, particularly at higher levels, to load difficulty onto the item rather than onto the recording. They face the conflicting demands of wishing to target more abstract and complex ideas but needing to keep the written text as transparent and as short as possible. The sample materials indicated they were relatively successful in balancing these priorities at both FCE and CPE levels, but some of the items at CAE level illustrate the dangers that can be faced.

Pre-presentation of items. In line with current practice by most test providers, Cambridge ESOL pre-presents items. This enables the test taker to listen in a directed way and avoids the memory effects which occur with post setting. However, the convention carries important consequences in terms of how the test taker handles the task. It promotes the use of test-wise strategies, where test takers seek to identify forms which they hope will sustain easy, lexical-level matches with the listening passage. In addition, it was noted that reading is, in a sense, privileged as compared with listening. It is both less transitory and (thanks to standardised spelling) less subject to variation. Candidates therefore place faith in it and use the written input as a point of departure when approaching the listening text – even to the point where they hear what they expect to hear.

There are a number of ways of mitigating the effects of pre-presentation. Computer-delivered tests might withhold written items until after the first play; conventional tests might in the fullness of time deliver items on a Powerpoint screen, linked to recorded material on CD. At higher proficiency levels, the view that gap-filling items need to provide a coherent account of the listening passage should not be encouraged; items should instead do no more than identify main points in paraphrased form.

The use of conventional formats. The suite makes use of a variety of well-established formats across the four or five parts of a test. Each has its advantages but also its disadvantages; hence the benefits of using a mixture. All the formats entail certain processes that are specific to a testing context and fall outside what would be required of a listener in a real-world listening event. Generally, they require the listener to master a set of propositions and then to check them against a piece of spoken input. In the case of MCQ and multiple matching, a test taker might also feel the need to *disconfirm* the options that will not be chosen. This type of operation imposes quite considerable cognitive demands upon the listener in relation to the manipulation of information – demands which go beyond the set of processes that are strictly associated with the listening construct. To be sure, Cambridge ESOL has sound reasons for choosing these formats: their reliability, ease of marking and familiarity. However, given concerns about the impact of test method upon test taker performance (Brindley and Slatyer 2002, Farr et al 1990, Freedle and Kostin 1999, In'nami and Koizumi 2009), it may be time to re-evaluate some of these tried and trusted procedures, to see if others can be devised which will achieve great construct validity.

This validation exercise identified two particular areas of concern in respect of the current test formats. Firstly, there are divided attention effects resulting from the need to investigate listening by means of other skills. While some involvement of other skills is impossible to avoid, steps can be taken to minimise their effects. The extent to which the tests of the suite draw upon the written word could be reduced by limiting the present heavy dependence upon the MCQ format. The reading load at FCE level might be alleviated by the use of a visual labelling task instead of gap filling. In addition, greater attention could be given to ensuring that item writer limits on the length and complexity of items are adhered to. This particularly applies to MCQ options, which often impose heavy processing demands unrelated to the construct. It would be good practice for those commissioning tests to ensure that candidates are assisted in their overall processing of MCQ items by syntactic or semantic parallels between the options.

Secondly, some of the formats entail complex cognitive operations which derive from the nature of the task rather than the listening construct. A number of less compromised tasks are possible, including gapped summaries which paraphrase the recording; true/false/not mentioned; short option choices describing the speaker's stance on issues identified from the recording; and even (at lower levels) transcription to test perceptual processing or single-sentence auditory cues with a written choice of possible responses. A higher-level version of the multiple-matching task might be one where candidates compare and contrast the information contained in two middle-length listening passages. This would serve a valuable function in marking out CPE from CAE by virtue of processing demands that derive from the listening texts rather than from the test format (see similar proposals in Field 1999b).

Comprehensiveness

Do the cognitive processes elicited by the tests in the Cambridge suite cover a sufficiently large and representative range of the processes contained in the listening framework?

The question was partly answered by comparing information focus across the suite (see Figure 3.4 above). In extracting information at a given level of processing, a test taker necessarily draws upon all the levels below it: for example, constructing a meaning representation is also dependent upon input decoding, lexical search and parsing. The data from Figure 3.4 can thus be reconfigured as shown in Table 3.8 below. Following Khalifa and Weir (2009:70), it shows all the levels of processing associated with items across the suite.

Table 3.8 Levels of processing elicited by the tests of the suite

	KET	PET	FCE	CAE	CPE
Input decoding	✓	✓	✓	✓	✓
Lexical search	✓	✓	✓	✓	✓
Parsing		✓	✓	✓	✓
Meaning construction			✓	✓	✓
Discourse construction			✓		✓

The table illustrates that the tests comprehensively cover the levels of processing specified in the framework. At KET and PET, the tasks set are limited to perceptual processing. This accords with the notion that, at these levels, large reserves of working memory have to be allocated to basic decoding and lexical recognition processes, leaving only limited scope for higher-level processes like inference.

As Table 3.8 shows, the sample materials feature discourse representations at both FCE and CPE levels. However, the coverage of this level of processing is quite limited. The Cambridge ESOL tests suffer from the disadvantages of all assessment instruments using conventional test formats in that certain important discourse construction processes are under-represented or not represented at all. The reason, as briefly discussed, is that the formats mainly focus upon discrete idea units without requiring test takers to trace links between the units or to assemble them into an overall conceptual structure. In addition, it is the item writer who selects which information units in the recording to focus on, thus depriving the listener of the decisions that normally have to be made as to whether an incoming proposition is important, largely irrelevant or worth preserving at an indeterminate level.

It is by no means impossible to devise techniques and tasks that target higher-level discourse construction processes. More extensive use could be made of the multiple-matching format as a means of targeting candidates' ability to identify the main point of a short passage. An alternative to the present gap-filling format is a skeleton outline of the information in a listening passage, in which headings and subheadings are represented with partially completed phrases. Summary is neglected as a test method because of issues of reliability and ease of marking; however, a controlled task could take the form of a summative version of the listening passage (perhaps with changes to the order of the points) in which candidates fill gaps. Another possibility is to provide test takers with a list of paraphrases of points made (or not made) in the recording and to ask them to identify and list in order those that actually occur.

Calibration of cognitive demands

How well graded are the tests of the suite in terms of the cognitive demands imposed upon test takers at different proficiency levels of the suite?

In terms of levels of analysis, the restriction of KET and PET to perceptual processing was noted in the previous section and deemed appropriate. It is only at FCE level that higher-level processes such as inference are first engaged and that external knowledge has to be invoked in order to build a meaning representation. The FCE and CPE samples both include items that require information to be assembled into a discourse representation; but engage the process in different ways.

A number of other features mentioned in this validation exercise suggest that considerable care has been given to calibrating cognitive demands at different levels of the suite. The sample tests display sensitivity to the processing limitations of lower proficiency test takers, notably in KET and PET. Particular attention has been given to the characteristics of the recorded material, both phonologically and as a set of idea units.

- *Speech rate.* Slowed speech in KET and PET recordings assists lexical search, a level of processing which is critical for test takers at these proficiency levels.
- *Visual items.* Visual MCQ items are used at KET and PET levels. This is appropriate, given that reading skills may be at a rudimentary stage (especially where an unfamiliar writing system has to be mastered). Visual items are not employed at any higher levels of the suite, given limitations on to what can be shown in a small graphic. Nevertheless, there surely remains scope for (e.g.) map and plan annotation tasks at FCE level, which would reduce the dependence upon written input.
- *Recording length.* Text running time is limited at KET and PET, where listening is a demanding operation, given the considerable resources of attention that need to be given to low-level processing. Text length is progressively increased from FCE to CPE.

- *Items per recording*. The ratio of items to running time is gradually *reduced* across the suite. This reflects the increasing linguistic complexity of the information points that are targeted. It also has the effect of making more propositions available for potential matching against each item.
- *Complexity of idea units*. The mean number of words constituting each idea unit and the complexity of the syntactic structures that link them gradually increase across the tests in the suite.
- *Abstractness*. In general, test content becomes increasingly dependent upon abstract concepts and patterns of logic as one advances from FCE to CPE. This feature is a valid determinant of upper-level difficulty when its source is the recording; its validity is questionable when abstractness and conceptual complexity originate from the items.

In general, the grading of difficulty between levels appears to take full account of the relative cognitive demands entailed. It would seem that FCE represents quite a major step up from PET in terms of content and task difficulty; but this is consistent with what has been observed in relation to the other three skills (Field 2011a:105, Khalifa and Weir 2009:72, Shaw and Weir 2007:62). It was also noted that, in at least two sections, CAE appeared to impose greater processing demands than CPE. This suggests that the distinction between the two levels (at least in the minds of item writers) is not as sharply defined as it might be. More detailed specifications might be helpful.

Some final comments

This validation exercise has indicated that the specifications for the tests of the Cambridge ESOL suite, together with the sample materials provided in Appendix A, are broadly in line with criteria suggested by cognitive psychology and auditory phonetics. To be sure, the recordings do not entirely resemble natural real-world speech. However, they retain many of its features and include a range of voices and varieties of English. The tasks engage several levels of processing, and are generally well calibrated with respect to proficiency.

Certain reservations have been expressed about the extent to which the processes elicited by the tests can be said to be representative of those that occur in non-test domains. These concerns relate almost exclusively to the impact of the test formats that are employed. Perhaps the most important is the problem of divided attention, where candidates have to engage one and even two other skills while engaging in listening. Another is the fact that the conventional targeting of discrete idea units excludes the possibility of tapping into certain higher-level processes associated with building a discourse representation. A third is the manipulation of information across modalities, with tasks requiring candidates to 'check and match' in a way that rarely occurs outside academic contexts. Cambridge ESOL's motives in choosing these formats are entirely sound from a testing point of view: the formats offer reliability and ease of marking, and are familiar to most test takers. It is no coincidence that these same formats (with the exception of multiple matching) are employed in other high-stakes tests of English, as well as in language teaching materials. What has been pinpointed here is thus not an issue peculiar to the tests of the suite; it is a long-standing and intractable problem which affects all teaching and testing of second language listening. Testing boards need more information about the precise effects of test formats upon learner behaviour in order to extend the existing research of Buck (1990), Freedle and Kostin (1999), Wu (1998) and a few others. And the profession as a whole needs input from listening specialists which will assist teachers and testers alike to represent the target construct more faithfully in the tasks which they employ.

One or two further issues that have been referred to in passing are specific to Cambridge ESOL, and form the basis for the brief recommendations that follow. The first is the rather general nature of the specifications laid down in the Cambridge ESOL 2008 handbooks. It would be helpful to teachers and item writers alike if the construct were more precisely and consistently characterised (e.g. in terms of functional content, listener goals, listening type and/or processes), and the gradations in test focus more sharply marked. Even a simple mention of listening types using 'listening for' categories or the parameters *local / global* and *high attention / low attention* (Field 2009a:64–68, Urquhart and Weir 1998) might provide useful indicators.

A less concrete point concerns cognitive load that is external to the construct being tested.

It was suggested that the sample materials very occasionally display a disproportionate reliance upon the working memory (WM) of the test taker. On one occasion it was the consequence of a heavy information load in a recording; in another it resulted from a complex task which required the retention and manipulation of multiple pieces of information. It is important for item writers to bear in mind that WM capacity varies from one individual to another. To load recording difficulty or task difficulty too heavily onto memory is to skew a test in favour of a trait which, while it supports listening, also has functions (i.e. retention and recall) that fall outside.

A different case of heavy cognitive load was observed in a few MCQ items which were hard to process. In principle, one can ratchet up the difficulty of an MCQ item by increasing the length or abstractness or propositional density of the options. One can also increase the fineness of the distinctions between options or the prevalence of distractors that are hard to disconfirm. However, a combination of several of these factors can make it difficult for the test taker to master the necessary detail and, again, loads onto a trait (namely the candidate's powers of logical reasoning) that largely falls outside the construct being tested.

The examples just quoted provide a good illustration of the challenges faced by item writers when designing listening tests at higher levels. The writers have to target idea units in the recorded text which are more linguistically demanding, more complex, more abstract and more propositionally dense than those at lower levels. It is quite hard to do so without also significantly increasing the processing demands of the items that are set. However, with construct and cognitive validity at stake, it is vitally important to limit the extent to which difficulty is loaded onto items – particularly given that those items are in a different modality from the target construct. The sample materials at CPE level seem to have managed this complicated balancing act quite well; but a few items at CAE level are a reminder of the dangers that lie in wait.

The issue of items which are as or more complicated than the propositions which they target is perhaps part of a larger picture. During the validation exercise, there were occasional indications that the test format rather than the recorded material had become the leading factor in the decisions made. Sight was briefly lost of the construct being tested – and of the fact that the methods in question are not strong on construct validity. The criteria for choosing a recording should surely foreground genre, topic, linguistic level and propositional density, with suitability for testing by a particular method a secondary issue. By the same token, the editing of an authentic text should surely be light of touch, keeping as closely as possible to the original, rather than guided by a desire to insert distractors to challenge the unwary. It is also important that the physical recording rather than the script alone should form the basis for the items that are set, enabling due account to be taken of the relative saliency of idea units within the text and of aspects of the speaker's style of delivery that may cause difficulty in accessing information. We need to place centre stage what is the most critical component of any listening test – the acoustic-phonetic signal.

Endnotes

1. The term *level* is problematic as it is used in this account to refer both to *level of processing* and to the candidate's *level of proficiency* – and indeed to *levels of the Cambridge ESOL suite*. Attempts have been made to carefully distinguish the three.
2. Unless, of course, we assume, with (e.g.) Klatt 1979, that the listener maps directly from input to word.
3. The term *strategy* is often very loosely defined in the literature. It is used here strictly in this compensatory sense. Strategies are thus held to be distinct from the *processes* which constitute normal listening. There will be no discussion of the types of strategy that assist learning; simply of those that support communication (what Cohen (1998) terms 'strategies of use').

4. This is not, of course, to deny the very valid point (Anderson and Lynch 1988, Brown and Yule 1983b, Lynch 2009) that what we conventionally ask students to do with this conversational material is very far from the way it would be handled in a real-world setting.
5. An exception can be found in the IWGs for PET which (p.7) suggest the unrealistic target of 'Standard English in a variety of accents . . . as spoken by native speakers and non-native speakers'.
6. The Item Writer Guidelines seem relatively impervious to this issue. Indeed, at CPE level, they call for coherent gap-filling items so that 'candidates are guided through the listening test by the items' (p.14).
7. A review of recently published past CAE papers suggests that the reading load and complexity of items in Part 3 of the sample test in Appendix A is not unrepresentative. See items in (e.g.) CAE 2 (2008a):29, 104; CAE 3 (2009a):29, 81, 107; CAE 4 (2010a):29, 55, 81, 107.
8. The provisions for Part 1 (short recording MCQ) vary considerably from level to level. At KET and PET levels, candidates are allowed 5 seconds to look at the visual MCQs; at FCE level, candidates have as long as it takes to read aloud the item; at CAE level, candidates have 15 seconds after hearing the rubric for the extract; at CPE level, candidates have around 12 seconds before the extract is announced.

4 Context validity

Mark Elliott
Cambridge English Language Assessment

Judith Wilson
Consultant to Cambridge English Language Assessment

Introduction

Chapter 3 discussed the cognitive processes involved in the listening process, and how these processes can be engaged and/or interfered with by the tasks undertaken by a candidate during an examination. This chapter switches the focus to *context validity*, by which is understood 'the appropriateness of both the linguistic and content demands of the text to be processed, and the features of the task setting that impact on task completion' (Khalifa and Weir 2009:81). In his earlier writing, Weir (2005a:19) conceptualised context validity in terms of the tasks in a test:

> Context validity is concerned with the extent to which the choice of tasks in a test is representative of the larger universe of tasks of which the test is assumed to be a sample. This coverage relates to linguistic and interlocutor demands made by the task(s) as well as the conditions under which the task is performed arising from both the task itself and its administrative setting.

With this in mind, the operationalisation of the critical criterial parameters which define listening tasks will be examined, and the five Cambridge ESOL Main Suite tests (KET, PET, FCE, CAE and CPE) will be scrutinised within this framework.

Context validity exists in a triangular relationship with cognitive validity (Chapter 3) and scoring validity (Chapter 5) with each of them influencing, and being influenced by, the other two. Reference will be made therefore to both cognitive and scoring validity throughout this chapter when relevant to the contextual parameters under discussion.

Different tests are designed for different purposes, and critical to this is the consideration of what kind of language the candidate is likely to use or be exposed to in the real world, and in what kinds of situations of use. These situations represent the *target language use domain* (*TLU domain*) of a test, which can be defined as 'a set of specific language use tasks that the test taker is likely to encounter outside of the test itself, and to which we want our inferences about language ability to generalize' (Bachman and Palmer 1996:44). All questions of context validity need to be viewed in terms of the specific contextual features of the TLU domain as well as the target proficiency level, since this is the universe of listening tasks from which the test attempts to draw a representative sample.

Following the format established by the previous SiLT construct volumes, this chapter draws on the contextual parameters suggested by Weir (2005a) and identified by Taylor and Geranpayeh (2011) as being most likely to have an impact on listening test performance (Figure 4.1). This framework will be the basis for a systematic exploration of task parameters relating to context validity in terms of *Task Setting, Linguistic Demands (Task Input and Output)* and *Speakers*. Close examination of each contextual parameter from the perspective of current theoretical and empirical research is followed by analysis and evaluation of Cambridge ESOL practice in its Main Suite Listening tests. It is important to note that the socio-cognitive framework properly includes the administrative setting of any test as a key dimension of context validity (see Figure 1.1 on p.28). However, because this chapter is already lengthy, the wider context of the conditions surrounding the delivery of the Cambridge Listening tests is considered in Appendix D, *Administrative setting*; hopefully, this may also make it easier to reference.

Figure 4.1 Aspects of context validity for listening (adapted from Weir 2005a:45)

CONTEXT VALIDITY	
Task setting ■ Task purpose and rubric ■ Response method ■ Weighting ■ Knowledge of criteria ■ Order of items ■ Channel of presentation ■ Text length ■ Time constraints, including number of times heard	**Linguistic demands: Task input & output** ■ Overall text purpose and discourse mode ■ Functional resources ■ Grammatical resources ■ Lexical resources ■ Nature of information ■ Content knowledge **Speakers** ■ Speech rate ■ Variety of accent ■ Sociolinguistic considerations ■ Number of speakers

Task setting

Task purpose and rubric

Authenticity

The *authenticity* of a test is an issue which pervades all considerations of validity. Spolsky (1985:31) notes that '[l]ack of authenticity in the material or method used in a test weakens the generalizability of results'. Authenticity is therefore a critical parameter to be considered by test developers.

It is first important to define what we understand by authenticity in terms of a language test. Authenticity must necessarily be seen as a relative, rather than an absolute, quality, since the context of a testing situation differs greatly from that of typical real-life situations, and '[a]ny language test is by its very nature inauthentic, abnormal behaviour, for the test taker is being asked not to answer a question by providing information but to display knowledge or skill' (Spolsky 1985:39). Lewkowicz (2007) disputes the notion that authenticity can be defined with scientific accuracy, arguing that it is 'a nebulous concept, perhaps unattainable in any objective way in practice' (2007:6). None the less, it is possible to define certain parameters within which to measure authenticity, and within which it is the task of test developers to maximise test authenticity. Authenticity can be a function of both the input (the text) and the output (the task) (Lewkowicz 2000) and it is possible for a test to possess a high level of authenticity in one but not the other. Tasks and texts, the relationship between which is discussed below under Task purpose, are therefore closely bound up. Bachman proposed the notion of *situational authenticity*, 'the perceived relevance of the test method characteristics to the features of a specific target language use situation' (1991:690). He further defined the notion of *interactional authenticity*, 'the interaction between the test taker and the test task' (1991:691), which is a measure of the level of engagement of the candidate's language skills and strategies in undertaking the task, i.e. aspects relevant to the cognitive validity of a test.

Bachman and Palmer (1996) recast interactional authenticity as *interactiveness*, separating it from notions of authenticity and instead considering it a measure of how 'the test taker's areas of knowledge, metacognitive strategies, topical knowledge, and affective schemata are engaged by the test task' (1996:25), which again can be seen as primarily relating to cognitive validity. In terms of context validity, however, we are primarily concerned in this chapter with situational authenticity, since situational authenticity relates more closely to the basic concern of context validity – to what exent the tasks in a test are representative of real-life listening activities.

One of the most fundamental considerations in terms of context validity is the purpose of the tasks which the candidate is required to undertake.

Context validity is in part a question of the generalisability of tasks in the test to real-life listening situations, so tasks must be selected which form a representative sample of the types of listening the candidate would be exposed to within the TLU domain. Test developers therefore need to determine firstly what those real-life listening tasks are before designing the test to cover a representative sample.

Task type

Task purpose does not exist in isolation; rather, it is inextricably bound up with text type. For example, someone listening to a news broadcast on the radio will naturally have a different purpose for listening from someone engaged in conversation with an old friend over a cup of coffee. However, the text type does not entirely determine the listening purpose – the listener to the news broadcast may wish to get a rough overview of what has been happening in the world on that day, or they may just want to find out the score in their team's football match that afternoon, and these two different aims would entail different types of listening. Similarly, the listener meeting an old friend may want to find out the details of a recent incident he or she has heard about, or may simply be engaged in phatic communication for the interpersonal (Halliday 1994) purpose of maintaining and strengthening their relationship, and thus be focused instead on empathising and establishing common ground. Both of these aspects – the likely real-life text types and the likely real-life listening goals – need to be considered in terms of the TLU domain in order to establish suitable task purposes for the test.

The most commonly used classification of task types for reading comprehension, proposed by Urquhart and Weir (1998), breaks task types down according to two dimensions: (i) global or local focus in terms of extent; and (ii) expeditious – 'process[ing] texts quickly and selectively' (1998:101) – or careful reading in terms of level of attention that needs to be allocated. While this classification is also useful for listening, the situations are not entirely analogous due to the different nature of the input, especially in terms of the linear nature of listening; a listener cannot navigate around the text at will as a reader can, but is instead 'locked in' to the sequence of the input. Furthermore, the message extracted by a listener tends to be more generalised and less precise than that of a reader, even in careful listening (Lund 1991). Field (2009a) proposes a modified model of task purpose for listening, replacing the expeditious/careful dichotomy with a four-step gradation of attention levels which more closely reflects the way listeners allocate their attention whilst listening (see Table 4.1). This is an important consideration given the online nature of listening and the extent to which L2 listening can be tiring due to the considerable demands it makes on limited attentional resources, especially at lower proficiency levels where listeners' processing is inefficient; conversely, as well as being able to process input more efficiently,

Table 4.1 Types of listening as determined by listener's goals (from Field 2009a:66)

	Global	Local
Shallow attentional focus	Skimming *e.g. TV channel hopping, TV advertisements, eavesdropping* Phatic communication *e.g. greetings*	Unfocused scanning *e.g. news headlines*
Medium attentional focus	Listening for the plot; listening to commentary *e.g. film/TV drama, TV/radio interview* Conversational listening *e.g. everyday chat* Information exchange *e.g. tour guide*	Focused scanning *e.g. airport announcement, weather forecast* Search listening *e.g. hotel/travel information* Message listening *e.g. answerphone*
Deep attentional focus	Close listening *e.g. lecture listening*	Close listening *e.g. negotiation*
Very deep attentional focus	Listening to check critical facts *e.g. witness evidence*	Listening to vital instructions *e.g. street directions* Listening to the form of words *e.g. listening to quote somebody*

more proficient listeners are better able to determine the appropriate (i.e. minimal) attention level for the successful completion of a given task.

Such a taxonomy of types of listening can enable test producers to create balanced tests which seek to reflect the range of types of listening that the candidate might be expected to perform in the TLU domain. Furthermore, it becomes a key consideration for the selection of appropriate response methods. Ideally, a response method will be in harmony with the type of listening being tested. Sometimes, the type of listening we wish to target is associated with a particular response format; sometimes a response format can give rise to two or more different types of listening, in which case we need to design the items accordingly. The effects of format and item on listening type are to some extent already covered in Chapter 3.

Rubrics

Bound up closely with task purpose are rubrics (here defined in the sense understood in the United Kingdom, i.e. the instructions for the test taker), which play an important role in any type of test by clarifying the procedure for the candidate. Weir (2005a:58) points out that in order to help the meta-cognitive strategies of goal-setting and monitoring, 'test takers should be given a clear unequivocal idea in the rubric of what the requirements of the test are so that they can choose the most appropriate strategies and determine what information they are to target in the text in comprehension activities'. Unclear rubrics might have a direct detrimental effect on candidate performance, and rubrics which are over-long or complex can divert attentional resources which the candidate needs to allocate to the task, again potentially affecting performance. These considerations are especially important in the case of language tests, where the language used in the rubric needs to be carefully graded so as to avoid causing the candidate linguistic problems, especially at lower proficiency levels. Furthermore, in the specific case of listening tests, rubrics are usually presented in written form as well as aurally.

Bearing the above in mind, it is important to establish a set of criteria for the writing of listening test rubrics in such a way that they:

- provide all the information the candidate needs in order to complete the task as expected
- are short and simple enough so as not to cause a significant processing load
- do not contain language which is likely to cause problems for the candidate at the proficiency level being tested
- are clear so as not to cause any confusion.

An additional consideration in terms of listening tests is the extent to which a text and task are contextualised prior to or at the start of listening. In a testing situation, candidates typically encounter listening texts and tasks without the contextual information they would normally have access to in real-life listening situations. It is imperative that rubrics provide at least the basic context of the text in order to aid the activation of appropriate schematic information. There is therefore a fine balance to be struck between providing maximum contextual information and keeping rubrics sufficiently brief to minimise both the additional linguistic and time demands incurred by the rubrics.

Task purpose and rubric: Cambridge ESOL practice

Information on text type and task purpose is available to test takers from various sources. The Cambridge ESOL website provides information for candidates about the structure of the five Main Suite exams together with the response format and the focus (or purpose) for each task. For example, from *KET Information for Candidates*, Listening Part 1 (Cambridge ESOL 2006b:8):

> In this part you will hear five separate short conversations. The conversations are either between friends or relatives, or between a member of the public and a shop assistant, booking office clerk, etc. You have to

listen for information like prices, numbers, times, dates, locations, directions, shapes, sizes, weather, descriptions of people and current actions.

From *CPE Information for Candidates*, Listening Part 1:

In Part 1 of the Listening test, you have to listen to four separate recordings ... The four recordings will each be different and may be monologues, prompted monologues (introduced by, for example, an interviewer) or conversations. Each question focuses on a different aspect of the text, for example:
• What is the speaker's attitude to people who complain?
• In the speaker's opinion, what explains the team's recent lack of success?
• What is the programme going to be about?
• What should you do if you want to enter the competition?
(Cambridge ESOL 2007a:14)

Information about text types and task focus is also provided in the handbook for each exam. Table 4.2 summarises the information on text type and task focus provided there. At lower levels (KET and PET), tasks focus mainly on the identification of key information, although clearly stated opinions and attitudes do also appear as testing foci. At FCE level a wider variety of attitudinal responses is tested, reflecting the greater variety of listening text genres and purposes that candidates will meet at this level. This reflects the CEFR descriptor for B2 in Listening to Audio Media and Recordings: 'Can ... identify speaker viewpoints and attitudes as well as the information content' (Council of Europe 2001:68). By CPE level, there is greater focus on the testing of attitude, opinion and inference, and less on specific information and detail.

In practice, these task foci may overlap, so that a single item may, for example, demand understanding of both inference and attitude, and experts may sometimes disagree over the focus of individual items. Furthermore, it may be the case that different test takers adopt differentiated strategies to answer the same test item (Taylor and Geranpayeh 2011). However, specification of task focus can aid comparison within and between tests and help to ensure that each listening test includes a variety of task purposes.

Rubrics may need to include contextual features such as the speakers and their location, the name of the speaker or speakers and the channel of communication (e.g. radio, podcast, face to face), as well as the topic and purpose of the talk and instructions for completion of the task. However, at the same time they have to remain accessible to the candidates and not impose a heavy additional reading or listening load. In Cambridge ESOL Listening examinations the weight given to each of these two potentially conflicting sets of requirements varies both with the level of the examination and the nature of the task. Rubrics for each paper are standardised and the difficulty of

Table 4.2 Listening text type and task focus: Cambridge ESOL Main Suite

Test	Part	Text type	Task focus
KET	1	Short neutral or informal dialogues	Listening to identify key information (times, prices, days of week, numbers etc.)
	2	Longer informal dialogue	Listening to identify key information
	3	Longer informal or neutral dialogue	Taking the 'role' of one of the speakers and listening to identify key information
	4	Longer neutral or informal dialogue	Listening and writing down specific information (including spelling of names, places etc. as dictated on recording)
	5	Longer neutral or informal monologue	As KET Part 4
PET	1	Short neutral or informal monologues or dialogues	Listening to identify key information from short exchanges or clearly stated attitude/opinion
	2	Longer monologue or interview	Listening to identify specific information, detailed meaning and clearly stated attitudes/opinions
	3	Longer monologue	Listening to identify, understand and interpret information
	4	Longer informal dialogue	Listening for detailed meaning and to identify the attitudes and opinions of the speakers
FCE	1	Short monologues or exchanges between interacting speakers	General gist, detail, function, purpose, attitude, opinion, relationship, topic, place, situation, genre, agreement etc.
	2	A monologue or text involving interacting speakers	Detail, specific information, stated opinion
	3	Five short related monologues	As FCE Part 1
	4	A monologue or text involving interacting speakers	Opinion, attitude, gist, main idea, specific information
CAE	1	Short extracts from exchanges between interacting speakers	Feeling, attitude, opinion, purpose, function, agreement, course of action, gist, detail etc.
	2	Monologue or prompted monologue	Specific information, stated opinion
	3	Conversation	Attitude and opinion
	4	Five short themed monologues	Gist, attitude, main points, interpreting context
CPE	1	Short monologues or exchanges between interacting speakers	Gist, detail, function, purpose, topic, speaker, addressee, feeling, attitude, opinion, etc.
	2	Monologue or prompted monologue	Specific information, stated opinion
	3	A text involving interacting speakers	Opinion, gist, detail, inference
	4	A text with interacting speakers	Stated and non-stated opinion, agreement and disagreement

Source: KET, PET, FCE, CAE and CPE Handbooks for Teachers (Cambridge ESOL 2008b, 2012a, 2012b, 2012c, 2012d)

vocabulary controlled; they are also presented in both spoken form in the recording and in written form on the question paper to provide additional support to candidates.

Note or sentence-completion tasks generally focus on the identification and recording of specific information, detail and (at higher levels) stated opinion. For such tasks, rubrics focus on establishing the general setting and channel, and the topic of the conversation or talk. Example rubrics for such tasks are:

> **KET Listening Part 4**
> You will hear a man telephoning the Tourist Information Centre in Windfield.
> Listen and complete questions **16 – 20**.
> You will hear the conversation twice.
> (Cambridge ESOL 2012c:26)
> **FCE Listening Part 2**
> You will hear an interview with a woman called Helen Hunter who runs a summer camp for teenagers.
> For questions **9 – 18**, complete the sentences
> (Cambridge ESOL 2012b:43)
> **CPE Listening Part 2**
> You will hear part of a lecture on soap and its role in society.
> For questions **9 – 17**, complete the sentences with a word or short phrase.
> (Cambridge ESOL 2008c:54)

In matching tasks, the individual items will all have a common focus, and so this can be provided by the rubric – for example, from FCE Listening Part 3:

> You will hear five different people talking about a mistake they recently made. For questions **19 – 23**, choose from the list (**A – F**) the type of mistake that each person made. Use the letters only once. There is one extra letter which you do not need to use.
> (Cambridge ESOL 2012b:43)

Here the task requires identification of different types of mistake and focuses on understanding of general gist. One matching task at CAE level asks candidates to identify 'the aspect of their new job that each speaker appreciates most' and the task therefore focuses on attitude.

For multiple-choice tasks the testing focus of each item can vary. The rubric therefore provides information about the setting and topic, and gives instructions for how the task is to be completed, but the testing focus for each item is provided by the stem – either a question or an incomplete sentence – of each item. For example, an FCE Listening Part 4 task featuring a recording about a cable car project has the following rubric:

You will hear an interview with a conservationist who has built a cable car in the rainforest. For questions **24 – 30**, choose the best answer (**A**, **B**, or **C**).
(Cambridge ESOL 2012b:44)

This provides the general context, but the focus for each item is different; for example, the item stems for the given task (omitting the options) include the following:

25 What is the main aim of the cable car project?
26 What is the advantage of the project for the local people?
30 Donald thinks the future survival of the rainforest will depend on . . .
(Cambridge ESOL 2012b:44)

Understanding the purpose of the task and the type of information required is therefore helped by reading the task on the question paper.

Response method

There are many different techniques used in the testing of listening, which vary in their suitability for testing different assessment focuses (Alderson, Clapham and Wall 1995, Brown and Hudson 1998), and also in terms of considerations of the cognitive validity of the processes they elicit (Field 2011c, 2012) and the construct-irrelevant variance they entail through, among other elements, the reading and writing loads imposed on the candidate. For these reasons, it is generally desirable to employ a variety of response methods to ensure fairness by avoiding over-reliance on one response method with its concomitant features (Alderson et al 1995). Additionally, different response methods may be appropriate for tests at different levels of language proficiency (Khalifa and Weir 2009), and may be sensitive to different aspects of the text they are based on, such as complexity and rhetorical structure (Kintsch and Yarborough 1982). They can also influence the strategies employed by candidates in answering the items (Nevo 1989).

All response methods have their drawbacks as well as their advantages as a consequence of method effect (Shohamy 1997), by which the method used to test can affect the results obtained (this is not restricted to response method, but is also caused by other factors such as text genre). All response methods introduce elements of reading, writing or speaking, which are by definition outside the construct of listening. Furthermore, a given response method can only test part of the listening construct, so over-reliance on a single response method is likely to lead to construct under-representation. The task of the test developer is to use a blend of response methods which permits broad construct coverage. In this way, the validity of the composite test will not be overly threatened by the drawbacks of any individual response method.

Different response methods testing the same assessment focuses may also exhibit bias towards or against different groups of candidates (Hambleton and Kanjee 1995). For these reasons, the choice of response format for a given testing objective is an important one.

There now follows a discussion of response methods typically used in the testing of listening. The list presented here does not pretend to be a complete taxonomy, but covers some of the main response methods used in tests of listening that have been shown to be both practical and of defensible validity, in particular those used in the Cambridge ESOL Main Suite examinations. As in *Examining Reading* (Khalifa and Weir 2009), response methods are classified as either selected response formats or constructed response formats, according to whether the candidate selects a response from a list of options (words, phrases, sentences or paragraphs) or produces the answer by writing a word, phrase, sentence or short paragraph on the answer sheet. This classification is not an exhaustive one; there are also other more visual response formats such as colouring pictures and identifying people or objects within pictures by drawing lines, which are particularly suited to younger learners. These lie outside the scope of this volume, however, but will be covered in detail in the forthcoming volume *Assessing Younger Language Learners* (Papp and Rixon forthcoming).

Certain considerations are shared by all response formats. These include the need for clarity in rubrics and, at item level, the need for the key to be unambiguous and for there to be no correct answers beyond the key (including distractors for selected response questions). Anther important item-level factor to be borne in mind for all formats is that the use of challenging lexis in the item stem (the question/incomplete sentence before the options) can cause construct-irrelevant variance due to the candidate not understanding the item; for this reason, it is generally desirable to frame the item using lexis below the proficiency level being tested and that used in the text (Brindley 1998).

Another question is whether to allow candidates to take notes as they listen. Some studies have shown that note-taking has no significant effect on performance on short texts (Hale and Courtney 1994), while actively urging candidates to take notes has been shown to have a significant detrimental effect (Chaudron, Loschky and Cook 1994, Hale and Courtney 1994). Carrell, Dunkell and Molhaun (2004) found contrasting results depending on the length of the lectures involved: for shorter lectures performance was better when note taking was allowed and worse when it was not allowed, while for longer lectures performance was about the same whether note taking was allowed or not. Of note is Carrell's (2007) finding of a moderate relation between note-taking and performance on short lectures, varying according to the note-taking strategy employed. This variance due to note-taking strategies suggests that the TLU domain may be an important consideration here; while allowing note-taking may increase authenticity for TLU domains where note-taking is likely, such as an EAP lecture context, there is the possibility of introducing an element of construct-irrelevant variance relating to candidates' note-taking skills for TLU domains where note-taking is not likely.

The memory load placed on candidates by the response method is another consideration, although as Henning (1991) notes, short-term memory must of necessity be an element of any listening construct, since the cumulative construction of meaning, particularly with longer texts, requires holding concepts and propositions in the listener's mind, within the context of which to interpret further utterances. This latter point raises certain questions about whether multiple items on a single text can be truly independent; while each item may be carefully constructed so as not to overlap, the cumulative construction of meaning means that 'interpretations and inferences made in answering one item will influence the comprehension of later sections of text' (Buck 1994:160), suggesting that where such interpretations and inferences are incorrect, they have the potential to affect the candidate's responses on later items. As well as the 'knock-on' effect described above, item independence is important since it is a prerequisite for some psychometric methods (see Chapter 5).

Following the format established in the previous volume in this series, *Examining Reading* (Khalifa and Weir 2009), those response formats which involve a selected response will now be discussed in turn, then those which involve a constructed response, as this offers a clear organising principle. Selected response formats involve choosing an option from a closed set, usually either by shading a lozenge on an electronically scannable mark sheet for paper-based tests or by clicking on the option for computer-based tests. Constructed response formats are more open, and involve the candidate writing or typing the response on the answer sheet or screen, with no options presented.

Selected response formats

Multiple-choice questions/items (MCQs)

Multiple-choice questions have long been a mainstay of language tests, particularly tests of receptive skills, for a number of reasons. MCQs can be manipulated by the item writer to ensure that the items are of the appropriate difficulty and discriminate well; this can be done by modifying the stem and/or the options, e.g. by making a distractor more or less attractive. This feature is particularly useful in cases where the text cannot be edited, for example when the items are written after the text has been recorded (whether scripted, semi-scripted or authentic). Furthermore, since candidates do not need to write anything when answering MCQs, one possible source of construct-irrelevant variance is removed, though the additional reading involved in answering MCQs could of course be seen as a different source of variance.

Candidates attempting a multiple-choice item where the item stem and options are previewed may arrive at the answer at least in part by a process of elimination of distractors which they identify as being incorrect as by identifying the correct option. This involves different skills from the positive identification of the correct answer (Weir 2005a), and candidates are indeed often trained to approach MCQ tasks in this fashion as part of their test preparation in class and in published test preparation materials (see, for example, Gude and Duckworth 2002). This process mirrors that identified in reading tests, where candidates undertake 'a reading task that [is] directed by the test questions' (Farr, Prichard and Smitten 1990:222), rather than processing the text and constructing meaning models in a natural way (Khalifa and Weir 2009). Verbal protocol analysis has suggested that MCQ items 'promote a process of checking information against pre-established cues rather than the more ecological one of receiving, interpreting and organising it' (Field 2012:417). The additional written input tends to favour more advanced learners, who, unlike less advanced learners, are able to use the input to form expectations and to focus their listening (Wu 1998). More generally, construct-irrelevant variance may occur if the results of a listening test are affected by the candidates' reading ability; when the written multiple-choice options are more difficult to interpret than the recording, '[i]f the learner fails to get the right answer, it is as likely to be due to inadequate reading ability in handling the questions as to inadequate listening ability in handling the recording' (Field 2009a:28).

Rupp, Ferne and Choi suggest that MCQ leads candidates to 'segment a text into chunks that are aligned with individual questions and focus predominantly on the micro-structure representation of a text base rather than the macrostructure of a situational model' (2006:469) – or, viewed in terms of listening type, even ostensibly global questions become a matter of listening for specific information.

Another issue surrounding multiple-choice questions is that of guessability. In a four-option multiple-choice item, for example, a candidate has a 25% chance of guessing correctly at random, and it is impossible to ascertain the precise extent for any given candidate (Hughes 2003). Buck (2001), however, argues that the effect of guessing may not be so pernicious, as candidates are often not guessing at random, but on the basis of partial comprehension, which will be reflected in their score (unlike in constructed response items, where partial comprehension is much less likely to result in any credit). Conversely, distractors can sometimes cause candidates to consider interpretations of a text that they might not have done without their presence, 'tricking' them into giving an incorrect answer (Alderson et al 1995).

Research has suggested (Rodriguez 2005) that three options may be optimal for MCQ in general, with only minor effects on item difficulty and discrimination compared to four-option or five-option items, and in fact with a generally positive effect on reliability. Viewed in the context of tests of listening, where additional options incur an additional reading load, this would suggest that three-option items may generally be the most suitable (see also Moreno, Martínez and Muñiz 2004). In a study based on the expert judgement of measurement professionals, however (Moreno, Martínez and Muñiz 2006), it was felt that four or more options were sometimes appropriate, and a review of the four-option MCQ task in Part 3 from live administration analysis of the Cambridge CPE Listening paper (at CEFR Level C2), undertaken for the 2002 revision project, showed that the task consistently performed at an appropriate difficulty level and with high levels of discrimination (Boroughs 2003). These findings suggest that, although the merits of three options have been established in general, a case-by-case approach based on the unique features of an individual testing situation may be more appropriate, taking into account parameters such as the level of the test.

A variation on the standard format of multiple-choice testing made possible by computer-based testing technology is *confidence-based* multiple-choice testing (Adeboye and Culwin 2003, Davies 2002), with candidates selecting not only an answer, but also a degree of confidence in the answer; in addition, a modified scoring system awards more marks for more 'certain' correct answers, but corresponding penalties for incorrect answers so as to discourage guessing. Adeboye and Culwin found that the modified scoring system produced a lower mean score with a higher standard deviation, suggesting that this method may discriminate better. However, the added cognitive complexity of the response method, requiring candidates to select both the correct answer and the degree of confidence, suggests further investigation is called for, particularly in the context of a listening test with its time demands. Furthermore, questions surrounding the fairness of the complex scoring system, and its relation to candidates of different temperament in terms of their inclination towards guessing (and mathematical ability in terms of calculating the odds when guessing) are also raised, since these are potential sources of test bias. Other alternatives include schemes where candidates may choose more than one answer if they are unsure, gaining partial credit (Bush 2001), or eliminate incorrect answers rather than select the correct one, again giving partial credit where not all distractors are eliminated (Jennings and Bush 2006). The appropriateness of these MCQ variants for assessing listening comprehension remains to be established, however, and their reliability needs to be determined (Ng and Chan 2009).

True/false items

True/false items are essentially a sub-class of MCQ with two options. They have the drawback of high guessability – there is a 50% chance of guessing correctly – so work best when there is a large number of items to reduce the significance of the guessing factor and thus produce higher reliability (Brindley 1998, Khalifa and Weir 2009). For these reasons, their appropriacy for use in formal tests has been questioned (Alderson et al 1995, Hughes 2003). An interesting psychological feature of true/false items is that, when guessing, some candidates are more likely to guess 'true' than 'false' due to a tendency towards acquiescence, meaning that false items tend to be more valid and reliable than true ones (Cronbach 1942:402).

Despite the fact that true/false items clearly lend themselves to guessing, there are some who argue in their favour on the grounds that they provide 'simple and direct indications of whether a particular point has been understood' (Brown and Hudson 1998:658), thus lending themselves to the testing of specific, factual information in a text, particularly at lower proficiency levels where testing points are more likely to be of such a concrete nature. For example, the CEFR illustrative scale for listening at B1 includes the descriptor 'can understand straightforward factual information about common everyday or job related topics, *identifying both general messages and specific details*' (Council of Europe 2001:66, emphasis added), whereas mention of understanding 'specific details' is not present at higher proficiency levels since learners are assumed to be able to do this.

In tests of reading, a third option, 'not given' or 'don't know', is often added to reduce guessability. This is likely to be overly demanding on a listening candidate's memory, however, especially if there is more than one item per passage. Candidates need to hold all the 'not given' items in their head whilst simultaneously answering subsequent items before they can determine the answers since they cannot determine whether they are 'not given' until the end of the recording; this potentially leads to confusion (Alderson et al 1995). In a practical test (Burger and Doherty 1992), such items were indeed found not to work well, a fact which Burger and Doherty attributed to candidates' focusing on 'what is said and not what is not said' (1992:315).

Multiple matching

Multiple-matching tasks can be viewed as further variants of MCQ in which several items share the same options – the task could be recast as MCQ with the same options for each item. There are two types of multiple-matching task: those where each option may be chosen once only, and those where each option may be chosen on more than one occasion. It is important for the rubric to clarify this in order to avoid confusion.

Compared to standard MCQ, multiple matching has the advantage that the probability of guessing the correct answer to an item is reduced by the number of options (Brown and Hudson 1998). Additionally, the format is more compact in terms of space on the page and has a correspondingly lower reading load (Brindley 1998), thus reducing the cognitive load due to the dual channels (Wickens 1984), especially since candidates do not need to read a new set of options for each item (Wilson 2009). Conversely, however, it should be noted that there can be a large number of options for candidates to master.

In cases where each option can only be chosen once, however, a degree of interdependence between items is introduced, since incorrectly choosing the key for another item naturally has an effect when the candidate attempts the second item. Introducing distractors to this type of multiple-matching task by having more options than the number of answers required reduces this effect (Alderson et al 1995), although it cannot be eliminated entirely.

Multiple-matching tasks are often used to test elements of global listening such as identifying main ideas, identifying contexts and identifying attitudes. At C1 level, such global multiple-matching tasks (with two tasks to be completed over two hearings of the text – see Appendix A, page 373) have been shown to work consistently well in terms of an appropriate level of difficulty and a high level of discrimination in live administrations of the Cambridge CAE Listening Part 4 (Murray 2007). Interestingly, structural equation modelling of this task has indicated that the task can have a tendency to load strongly on the reading factor. This suggests that this particular 'two-task' multiple-matching format, where the candidate has two separate lists to match to options, is in fact an integrated skills task of both listening and reading (Geranpayeh 2007). Further SEM analysis would be required to establish whether this is also the case for 'one-task' multiple matching where the candidate has only one list to match to options (for example, FCE Part 3 – see Appendix A, page 364).

Constructed response formats

In constructed response format items, candidates respond by completing gaps on the question paper with short answers. These are typically of a specified length, for example one word or up to three words. Compared to MCQ and other selected response formats, they have the advantage that they do not 'feed' the candidate with options, and hence do not have as much effect on the cognitive processes involved in listening – the candidate has to construct meaning in a manner closer to real-life listening, rather than seek evidence to confirm or reject hypotheses. Furthermore, the guessing factor present in selected response formats is greatly reduced, although contextual and linguistic cues such as parts of collocations can sometimes make guessing possible (Field 2000).

Perhaps the main drawback of constructed response formats is that the element of writing they introduce presents a risk of construct-irrelevant variance. This is most prominently manifested in the area of spelling, and the question of what, if any, incorrect spellings to accept in candidates' answers. There are essentially three policies which may be adopted regarding spelling:

1. Accepting all plausible phonetic misspellings of a word.
2. Accepting a limited, prescribed range of misspellings of a word and no others.
3. Accepting only the correct spelling of a word.

Where correct spelling is required, this should include all acceptable regional variations, such as the British English and US English variants *colour* and *color*, since it would be difficult in the extreme to defend the exclusion of such variants as being relevant to the listening construct. It should firstly be noted that spelling does not form part of a narrowly defined construct of listening, on which grounds variance in marks due to misspelling could be considered an element of construct-irrelevant variance. However, Taylor and Geranpayeh (2011:97) argue that 'it is perfectly reasonable to expect accuracy in sound-symbol correspondence at advanced proficiency levels and that integrated tasks involving multiple skills (e.g. listening-into-writing) better reflect academic literacy skills'. In terms of practical test administration, Hackett, Geranpayeh and Somers (2006:1) also note the following:

> [A]llowing a wide range of misspellings in productive listening tasks does raise a number of issues. The acceptance of any spelling that appears to resemble the key phonetically is open to interpretation by different markers. Some misspellings deemed to be phonetically correct may spell another word, so there could be doubt as to whether the candidate actually selected the right answer. It is also difficult to tell from a misspelling whether a candidate has genuinely understood the key or is merely reproducing one of a number of sounds they have heard. To maintain objectivity between markers, all misspellings deemed acceptable need listing and the longer this list is, the more complicated the marking instructions become, which can itself introduce error, especially when using non-specialist markers.

In other words, different spelling policies involve a potential trade-off between validity in terms of the listening construct on the one hand and fairness and reliability of marking on the other, especially in light of the practical issue of co-ordinating the marking of large-scale testing where flexibility is introduced.

Depending on the marking policy, certain constraints on the spelling difficulty of keys need to be applied in order to avoid items testing spelling ability as much as listening ability. Unless a liberal marking policy is adopted, it would seem unreasonable to select lexical items for keys which are likely to cause spelling problems, either due to non-transparent spellings or features such as irregular plural forms. Secondly, if a strict policy is to be adopted, it seems reasonable to stipulate that the word be one which learners at a lower proficiency level than that being tested could be expected to use productively, and one which is unlikely to present any spelling issues due to the orthographic idiosyncrasies of non-phonetic languages such as English, in order to minimise the effect of spelling. This does, however, naturally reduce the potential range of lexis from which to select keys.

The question arises of whether the same policy should be adopted at all proficiency levels, or whether spelling policy should be stricter at higher proficiency levels. Bound up with this is the question of what are reasonable assumptions in terms of what all candidates at a given proficiency level should be able to produce accurately within the context of a listening test. The CEFR scales on orthographic competence state the following in terms of spelling accuracy:

Table 4.3 Spelling competence at different CEFR levels (adapted from Council of Europe 2001:118)

CEFR level	Spelling competence
C2	Writing is orthographically free of error.
C1	Spelling is accurate, apart from occasional slips of the pen.
B2	Spelling is reasonably accurate but may show signs of mother tongue influence.
B1	Spelling is accurate enough to be followed most of the time.
A2	Can write with reasonable phonetic accuracy (but not necessarily fully standard spelling) short words that are in his/her oral vocabulary.
A1	Can spell his/her address, nationality and other personal details.

These criteria seem to support the adoption of stricter spelling policies at higher proficiency levels in conjunction with the constraints on lexical selection discussed above, providing that it is reasonable to assume a relatively flat ability profile across different skills. This question can only be addressed in terms of the test purpose and target candidature, in order not to disadvantage some candidates unfairly. In the case of a test with a target candidature including a significant proportion with limited literacy skills, for example, such an assumption may not be reasonable. In any case, there is always a risk that some candidates will be disadvantaged by a strict spelling policy. Furthermore, it should be noted that the above table does not take into account the particular circumstances of writing during a listening test, with its heavy cognitive load, stress and time pressure; to compensate for this, the timing of the test should make allowances for candidates to check and review their spelling while they are not simultaneously listening and/or reading.

Adopting different spelling policies for the same item is naturally bound to affect its performance in psychometric terms in terms of difficulty and discrimination. Hackett, Geranpayeh and Somers (2006) found that adopting a liberal marking policy generally resulted in minor decreases in item difficulty and minor increases in item discrimination when compared to a restricted range of misspellings, although one item examined showed a sharp decline in difficulty and a similarly sharp increase in discrimination. It should be noted that higher item discrimination is linked to higher test reliability, which suggests that the inevitable reduction in inter-marker reliability resulting from a liberal policy would be mitigated by the accompanying increase in theoretical item reliability due to the increased discrimination levels (the lower reliability of stricter policies is due to the introduction of the spelling trait as a partial determiner of performance).

The specification of a word limit, and how long that word limit should be, is an important consideration. Longer keys allow a greater variety of possible correct answers, which can often result in unwieldy keys that cause practical problems in marking, and potentially lead to inconsistent marking, particularly if a variety of possible spellings is accepted. Furthermore, the more candidates have to write, the greater the effect of the writing trait on the item.

Three widely used types of constructed response format and their particular features will be highlighted and discussed here: sentence/summary completion; table/chart completion; and note completion.

Sentence/summary completion

In sentence-completion items, candidates fill in gaps to complete sentences. This allows for the testing of main ideas and details, for example by presenting a paraphrasing of key information, requiring candidates to process the propositions in the text and match them to the framework presented in the item. Since an item requires the completion of a sentence, the candidate's response needs to fit the sentence grammatically. While this is usually accomplished by means of identifying a word or phrase in the text and writing it verbatim, it does raise questions in terms of marking policy regarding grammaticality and its relevance to the testing construct similar to the issues surrounding spelling. Should a response be accepted, for example, if it contains mistakes in subject–verb agreement, or if the wrong part of speech is used? Determining what constitutes an acceptable response can be problematic (Field 2000), and the answers to these questions may well be different at different proficiency levels. In some contexts, for example EAP tests, summary completion tasks could lay claim to greater situational authenticity on the grounds that they replicate the real-life listening task of lecture listening to a greater extent, where the listener would be creating an overview of the lecture and noting key information. It is worth noting in this respect that the writing element of the task would form part of the real-life TLU domain listening activity on which the test task is predicated, where listeners would be making notes as they listen; as such, the writing element of the task should no longer be considered

construct-irrelevant since the simultaneous use of different skills and concomitant division of attention reflect real-life listening within the TLU domain.

Table/chart completion

Table/chart-completion tasks are similar to sentence Completion except that
the information is presented in a different format, for example a table, which
is not comprised of grammatical sentences. This avoids the issue of grammaticality, making the response method potentially more suitable at lower
proficiency levels where this may be more of an issue. In some contexts, table/
chart completion tasks may benefit from a high degree of situational authenticity in terms of the TLU domain, for example those TLU domains where
completing tabulated data would be a typical task.

Note completion

Note-taking tasks can lay claim to representing a situationally authentic task
for TLU domains where the candidate would be faced with real-life listening
situations involving the noting down of key information; a wide range of, if
not most, TLU domains are likely to involve such listening tasks to a certain
extent. Since a natural feature of such real-life listening tasks is writing, the
test demands of juggling skills and dividing attention accordingly can be seen
as construct-relevant here. Note completion differs from 'pure' note-taking
in that the framework provided in the task guides the candidate's selection of
information. As Field (2012) observes, such structured tasks exempt the candidate from certain high-level information-handling decisions about what
information is important enough to note down, as well as providing certain
cues. The advantage of the structured note-completion format, however,
resides in marking, which is far easier to conduct consistently and accurately
due to the objective nature of the task (no decisions need to be taken by the
test developers about what information is appropriate to note, which can be
subjective); furthermore, the constraints that the structure imposes on the
potential range of acceptable keys can lead to greater inter-rater reliability.

Response method: Cambridge ESOL practice

Since the 2008 FCE and CAE revisions, the formats of all Main Suite
Listening papers are now fixed in terms of tasks; the format for each examination is described in its handbook and also on the Cambridge ESOL website.
Candidates and teachers can therefore know what to expect at each stage in
the Listening paper (see Table 4.4), in terms of the response format as well
as the testing focus and the text type (or range of possible text types) that
will be heard (for example, whether short or long, and the number of speakers). The emphasis of Cambridge ESOL examinations on assessing language
users' overall communicative ability means that in all cases the focus is on

Table 4.4 Listening test response format: Cambridge ESOL Main Suite Listening papers

Test	Part	Task type	Items/ weighting	Text format
KET	1	3-option visual MCQ	5	5 texts (25–60 words) Neutral or informal dialogues
	2	Matching 6:8 (inc eg)	5	1 text (150–170 words) Informal dialogue
	3	3-option MCQ	5	1 text (160–180 words) Neutral or informal dialogue
	4	Note completion	5	1 text (150–170 words) Neutral or informal dialogue
	5	Note completion	5	1 text (150–170 words) Neutral or informal monologue
	Total		25	
PET	1	3-option visual MCQ	7	7 texts (60–90 words) Dialogues or monologues
	2	3-option MCQ	6	1 text (390–420 words) Monologue or interview
	3	Note/sentence completion	6	1 text (270–300 words) Monologue
	4	True/False	6	1 text (290–320 words) Informal dialogue
	Total		25	
FCE	1	3-option MCQ	8	8 extracts (80–110 words) Monologues or exchanges between interacting speakers
	2	Sentence completion	10	1 text (600–675 words) A monologue or text involving interacting speakers
	3	Multiple matching (5:6)	5	Five related monologues (90–110 words)
	4	3-option MCQ	7	1 text (600–675 words) Monologue or text involving interacting speakers
	Total		30	
CAE	1	3-option MCQ	6	3 extracts (170-190 words) Two speakers each
	2	Sentence completion	8	1 text (450-500 words) Monologue
	3	4-option MCQ	6	1 text (650-750 words) Interacting speakers (e.g. interview or discussion)
	4	Multiple matching Two tasks each (5:8)	10	5 monologues (maximum 112) on a theme
	Total		30	
CPE	1	3-option MCQ	8	4 extracts (140-190 words) Monologues, prompted monologues or texts involving interacting speakers
	2	Sentence completion	9	1 text (600-700 words) Monologue or prompted monologue

Table 4.4 Continued

Test	Part	Task type	Items/ weighting	Text format
	3	4-option MCQ	5	I text (600–750 words) Text involving interacting speakers (e.g. interview)
	4	3-way matching (statements matched to either or both of two speakers)	6	1 text (600–650 words) Text involving interacting speakers
	Total		28	

Source: KET, PET, FCE, CAE and CPE Handbooks for Teachers (Cambridge ESOL 2008b, 2012a, 2012b, 2012c, 2012d)

processing of meaning. Tasks do not involve simple dictation or completing gaps in a text which is a transcript of the recording.

To avoid construct under-representation, each Listening paper contains a range of task types, including a mixture of selected and constructed response tasks. The use of a variety of task types helps to ensure that a range of testing focuses can be covered (see Table 4.2). Thus the focus of a constructed response format such as note or sentence completion is likely to be identification of detail and stated opinion, while a selected response task, such as multiple choice or multiple matching, can focus on testing candidates' understanding of other aspects of the text such as speaker's attitude, opinion and purpose. The avoidance of an over-reliance on one testing method also means that individual candidates who may be less comfortable with one particular response method are not disadvantaged.

While it is impossible to avoid the need for reading and writing entirely in Listening tests, the effect of these factors must be reduced as far as is practical. The vocabulary in the Listening tasks is generally at a rather lower level than the vocabulary of the text, and items are kept as short as possible to reduce the reading load for candidates. To take PET as an example: the stems (questions or incomplete sentences) for MCQ items in Parts 1 and 2 are no longer than 10 words, with written options for Part 2 no longer than 8 words; the whole text for the note-completion task in Part 3 is 50–75 words, and the true/false items in Part 4 are no longer than 12 words. These points will be further discussed below with relation to particular response methods.

Selected response formats

Three types of selected response items are used in Cambridge ESOL Main Suite Listening papers and will be discussed here: multiple-choice questions; true/false items; and multiple-matching items. Since the most common type is MCQs, which occur in all Main Suite Listening papers, these will be discussed at some length. Some of the issues discussed are equally relevant to the other two types.

Multiple-choice questions (MCQs)

This response method allows objective marking and therefore supports a high degree of marking reliability. Ideally, MCQ options in Listening, as in Reading, should mirror the way in which a listener may interpret the text, offering keys which reflect meaning accurately and distractors which reflect some of the types of misunderstanding a learner might plausibly make, such as 'reading more into a text than is actually there, stated or implied' or 'failing to see the grammatical relationship between words, or groups of words' (Munby 1968, quoted in Alderson 2000:205). This can be illustrated by the following FCE Listening item, from the sample test in Appendix A:

> Recording transcript:
> Interviewer: But what attracts those gymnasts to the pole vault?
> Sandra: Well, as I say, their training is relevant and, of course, women gymnasts do tend to reach their best at a pretty early age. But I don't feel those are the main reasons. I reckon they just feel that this is a sport where you can make the same sort of money, but it's not so stressful on your body and it has a pretty fun and carefree atmosphere by comparison.
> Item:
> **29** According to Sandra, why have so many good gymnasts taken up pole vaulting?
> **A** It is not as physically demanding.
> **B** It is better paid than many other sports.
> **C** It is an easier sport to do as you get older.

The correct answer to Item 29 is Option A, reflecting the exchange between the interviewer and Sandra. Option B is designed to attract a candidate who fails to recognise the grammatical relationships (in the discussion of money) that indicate pole vaulters are paid the same as gymnasts, not more. This option proved to be the more commonly chosen distractor. Option C is intended to attract a candidate who overinterprets what they hear; the speaker states that gymnastics gets harder as gymnasts get older, and that pole vaulting is relatively easier in this regard, but not that pole vaulting gets objectively easier. This is also designed to test a candidate's recognition of the anaphoric link in the following statement 'I don't feel those are the main reasons'; this second, perhaps clearer cue may be why the distractor attracted fewer candidates when used in a live administration.

As pointed out in the preceding section, to avoid construct-irrelevant variance the language in the options should where possible be less challenging than that of the text. However, at lower levels where the language of the recording is already at quite a simple level, and where texts are short, it may be hard to construct written options on this basis. This can be exacerbated by the fact that at lower levels, the testing focus is often a concrete fact such as a number or an everyday object, for which it may be difficult to find synonyms at an appropriate level. The problem can be addressed in two ways: by having non-verbal options or by constructing items which are expressed using actual words from the text.

In KET Part 1 (see pages 342–343), candidates listen to five short texts which are all neutral or informal dialogues. The testing focus is the identification of key information. The candidates have to listen to each dialogue and choose the picture which provides the correct answer, from a choice of three. Since the options are non-verbal and the candidates hear the question as well as reading it, the reading load is very low and the language used can be tightly controlled. There are certain constraints on visual complexity in such items: visuals need to overlap but the key needs to be clearly distinct, and there cannot be too much peripheral distraction obscuring the focus of the visuals.

In KET Part 3 (see page 344), three-option MCQs are again used but here the options are written, and a longer text is used, supporting five items plus an example. Questions and options at this level are very short, with options being single words or short phrases. At this level the options tend to include key words from the text, rather than synonyms. For example, (Appendix A, KET sample test):

> Recording transcript:
> F: Was the hotel nice?
> M: Beautiful. We were high up in the mountains. We looked down on the lake where we swam every morning, and across the town to the other side.
> Test item:
> 11 Duncan stayed in a hotel   A   in a town.
>   B   near the sea.
>   C   in the mountains.

Here Options A and C are both heard in the recording, and Option B is supported by the reference to swimming. The listening task involves identifying which of these options correctly identifies the location of the hotel.

PET (see pages 351–354) follows the same format, with Part 1 being 3-option MCQs with visual options, and Part 2 being 3-option MCQs with verbal options. Here the options may be at phrase or (short) sentence level, and the focus is on the identification of specific information or detailed meaning. As in KET, vocabulary from the recording may appear in each option, but the options tend to be slightly longer. For example (Appendix A, PET sample test):

Recording transcript:
M: Today we have with us in the studio Lucy Rainbow, who earns her living as a painter. Good morning Lucy. Can you tell us about your job?
F: Well, I don't paint pretty pictures you can hang on your walls at home. Mainly, I work in a theatre, painting the background scenery for plays. I've also done a couple of CD covers. That was great, because I got to meet my favourite pop stars.

Test item:
8   What does Lucy usually paint?   A   scenery for stage plays
                                    B   pictures of pop stars
                                    C   the walls in people's homes

MCQs continue to be used in Main Suite Listening papers at higher levels. Part 1 in FCE, CAE and CPE (as in KET and PET) focuses on shorter, discrete texts with 3-option MCQs. The use of a set of short texts means that a range of topics and genres can be covered and that the candidate has a fresh start each time. It also means that candidates have to show understanding of a range of voices, and allows for items testing global comprehension, which is often difficult when longer texts are used since gist questions may overlap with other items. However, whereas the options are visual at KET and PET, at FCE, CAE and CPE level they are written. A second MCQ task (see Table 4.4 above) involves items based on a longer text. At FCE level this is a 3-option MCQ task on a text which may have one or two speakers. For CAE and CPE there is a 4-option MCQ task on a text involving interacting speakers. For the 2008 revision of CAE, the possibility of a 3-option MCQ task based on a longer text to replace the existing 4-option MCQ task was investigated, but trials suggested that this variant did not appear statistically to be meeting the target difficulty level of the exam, and that it discriminated less well. It was suggested that the apparent contradiction compared to the use of 3-option MCQs in Part 1, where they performed well, might be due partly to the fact that Part 1 texts tend to be interactive dialogues (as opposed to monologues or interviews with one speaker restricted to supplying prompt questions) and partly due to the fact that they cover a broader range of testing focuses in Part 1, including targeting interactive features such as speaker agreement (Murray 2007:22).

At lower levels, items can be used with longer stretches of text to target gist understanding, i.e. the ability to recognise the main point of a text despite limited knowledge of syntax and vocabulary, which is a mark of competent listening. At higher levels, items may also test understanding of the gist of an utterance or of the discourse rather than of detail, and they also avoid repeating the wording of the text as far as possible so that the extent to which the text has to be processed increases. In many cases, the candidate may be processing features of speech such as fixed phrases or idiomatic language and matching them to a shorter, more stylistically neutral paraphrase in the option. The following example is from CPE Part 3 (Appendix A). While neither the key nor the distractor uses lexis from the text, the distractors are all based on an aspect of the text and are plausible, but incorrect, reflections of what is said:

Recording transcript:
Interviewer: What about the character of Sayers herself? What do you most admire?
Ray: She had in many ways an unhappy life – for various reasons, she was largely separated from her only child, and she never came to terms with that. I admire her hugely, both for achieving so much, which I think she was justifiably proud of, and the fact that she was so industrious. Having a streak of indolence in me, I'm in awe of that. It was extraordinary – people would write to her about some obscure point, and they'd get pages back, telling them what they ought to think and do, when most of us would just shrug and say, 'Oh dear, another boring letter from so-and-so'. She saw it as part and parcel of the job.

Test item:
18 What does Ray most admire about Sayers as a person?
    A her self-confidence when giving advice to other people
    B her modesty when talking about her achievements
    C her pragmatic attitude towards her relationships
    D her conscientious approach to her commitments

For all MCQs at FCE to CPE level there is a wider range of test foci including general gist, detail, function, purpose, attitude, opinion, relationship, topic, place, situation, genre and agreement.

True/false items

True/false items appear only in PET Part 4 (see page 354). As pointed out in the previous section, these items have been regarded as appropriate for the testing of straightforward factual information. In fact the task focus here is the testing of attitude and opinion, and some of the items may involve the identification of agreement/disagreement between the speakers. It seems that in addition to testing understanding of factual information, this task type does appear to be suitable for less concrete situations where the candidate is being asked to identify the correct option from two polar opposites, for example, a positive versus a negative attitude, or agreement versus disagreement. True/false items therefore appear appropriate for the testing of attitude and opinion at lower levels, where the candidates are not expected to recognise fine distinctions. However, given the limitations of the response format discussed earlier, this may be an area for future targeted research.

Multiple matching

Multiple-matching tasks appear in FCE and CAE (and will appear in CPE from 2013), and can be seen as another variant of multiple choice. In both FCE and CAE, candidates listen to five short monologues with a linked theme or topic, and they have to match an option or options from a set to each speaker. Each option is used once only. In FCE, candidates match one option to each speaker, while at CAE (and CPE from 2013) candidates do two parallel tasks, each with a different focus. For example, in the sample CAE test (Appendix A), the linking theme was students on art courses talking about their experiences, and the first set of options were all related to the difficulties each speaker had to overcome, while the second set focused on what each speaker enjoyed most about the process of creating art. A particular feature of the parallel task format in CAE, as discussed earlier, is the number of distractors candidates have to master across the two tasks.

During the 2008 revision of CAE, a research group was set up to investigate how this task was perceived by candidates. This was partly to decide whether or not to reduce the number of distractors for each task, resulting in a reduction of the options from eight to six for each task. It was thought that this might be necessary as the task may involve candidates in scanning the lists of options for both tasks simultaneously as they listen, although candidates can choose whether or not they wish to do this. Candidates at one stage of the trial observed that 'it was not the number of options in the task that worried them, but that options longer than a phrase sometimes posed a challenge to read and keep in mind at the same time as listening' (Murray 2007:22). A Structural Equation Modelling analysis of CAE Listening papers showed that Part 4 (multiple matching) was 'an integrative task testing both Reading and Listening, more strongly the latter' (Geranpayeh 2007:8). A recommendation was made that attention should be paid to the number of words used in the distractors; this recommendation was subsequently implemented to reduce the level of reading and conflicting attentional demands in line with Wickens' (1984) multiple resource theory.

The use of five separate texts on a common topic has the advantage of allowing a number of 'fresh starts' without the need to establish the theme each time, although the basic situation in which the monologues are being delivered is not specified. The short length of the texts allows the testing of gist as well as understanding of detail, purpose, attitude and opinion. For CAE, where there are two items for each text, candidates are told that they may be answered in either order. The format of this task, with the two sets of questions laid out in parallel, supports the possibility of this choice and reinforces the fact that the keys for the two items in each text may not follow in the same order as the items on the test paper. However, it is important for candidates to be familiarised with this layout before taking the examination.

Constructed response items

All Cambridge ESOL Main Suite Listening papers contain one or more constructed response tasks. For these, the candidate completes gaps in sentences or notes, using a word or short phrase from the text, while listening to the recording.

One of the main challenges in using constructed response tasks is to avoid open keys, which can lead to problems of reliability. In Cambridge ESOL Listening papers, all words and phrases which the candidates have to write as their answers will be heard in the listening text. Since the objective is to test understanding rather than memory, synonyms of these words and phrases are also accepted. However, in cases where there are a large number of synonyms or partial synonyms, a key may become too open. This is often the case with high-frequency adjectives and verbs, and so nouns tend to be used more often as keys. In addition, keys which involve processing or manipulation of grammatical structures are avoided; candidates never have to make any grammatical changes to a word in order to make it fit the context of the sentence or notes, since this is not the focus of the Listening paper.

The general trend to use nouns as keys is supported by the findings of an analysis of candidate performance in two IELTS tasks (Proudfoot 2010) which provided tentative support for the claim that nouns are easier for candidates to identify than other word forms. Out of 24 cases in which candidates made errors involving changing word classes, only two were transformations from noun to adjective, the remainder being in the opposite direction. Furthermore, the focus of the task is to locate specific, concrete information, which is most likely to be communicated via nouns and noun phrases.

Since constructed response items focus on the understanding of specific information and detail, they are based on informative, factual texts such as radio talks, podcasts or, at higher levels, lectures. Items require the identification of relevant information and key ideas from the text, which are central to its overall argument.

The layout of the task on the question paper makes it clear that only a limited amount of information is required; this is clearly stated in the exam handbooks. For FCE, the *Handbook for Teachers* states that '[a]nswers will not exceed three words in length' (Cambridge ESOL 2012b:40). For other Main Suite papers, it is stated that a word or short phrase is required.

The point has already been made in the general discussion of constructed response formats that a requirement for correct spelling may lead to construct-irrelevant variance, since control of the written form of the word is not involved in the listening skill. However, if there were no constraints on spelling at all, this might make it difficult to identify whether or not the key information has been understood, as in the example of candidates who wrote 'pat', 'peat' or 'bat' when the key was 'pet'. A compromise has therefore to be made. In the case of KET and PET the requirement is for *recognisable* spelling, except in the case of spelled-out items and very high-frequency words such as days of the week, for which accurate spelling is required. For FCE, the *Handbook for Teachers* (2012b) states that '[m]inor spelling errors are not penalised, but the candidate's intention must be clear and unambiguous. Candidates will not be asked to spell words which are above FCE level', a criterion determined in the first place by the expert judgement of the item writing team and in the second place through pretesting, where quantitative data on item performance and qualitative feedback from pretesting candidates and their teachers provide an empirical basis for testing the experts' judgement and making adjustments where necessary. Further work on the English Profile could help to clarify this (see page 217 in this volume). Correct spelling (either British or American) is required for CAE and CPE (Cambridge ESOL 2008b:50, 2012a:44). In addition, item writer guidelines instruct writers that keys for constructed response tasks should not pose significant spelling problems. At all levels, there is careful scrutiny of wrong answers given by candidates at pretesting (see Appendix C). These wrong answers, which provide concrete evidence of the items being misspelled and the frequencies of different misspellings, allow for identification of items which may be causing spelling problems and of misspellings which are acceptable at lower levels. If an item shows itself as causing major problems due to misspelling at the pretesting stage, it will not be used in a live test.

Cambridge ESOL has adopted a marking policy for lower proficiency levels (KET and PET for Main Suite) of allowing a prescribed range of acceptable misspellings of a given word. Acceptable variants of a given word are determined and recorded in the LIBS dictionary, which is then used as the reference point for all future tests requiring productive use of the word. The broad criteria for acceptance or rejection of a given misspelling are outlined in the *LIBS dictionary – guidelines for accepting misspellings*:

> The overriding criterion for accepted misspellings is that the word is unambiguous and it is clear to a non EFL professional that the candidate has understood the meaning of the text and words. This means that it is not acceptable for a candidate in a Listening test to merely transcribe phonetically a word from the recording, i.e. *skullpcha* for *sculpture* would not be acceptable, as the word does not clearly resemble the key word.
> (Cambridge ESOL 2010b:2)

The requirement that misspellings be recognisable precludes misspellings which create different words or lead to ambiguity, for example *meat* for *meet*, or *badroom* for *bedroom* (ambiguous due to similarity with *bathroom*). The requirement for correct spelling of high-frequency words applies to basic single-syllable words such as *red*, *car* and *bus*. For high-frequency lexical sets, such as days of the week, allowances are made where particular items are problematic, for example *Wednesday*, although correct spelling is expected for more straightforward items such as *Sunday*. Correct punctuation, including capitalisation, is not required.

Various specific considerations are also taken into account when determining whether a misspelling is acceptable, such as accepting the omission of silent letters, the elision of silent syllables in words like *secretary* [sekrətri:] and contravention of certain spelling conventions such as doubling letters when forming participles. Allowances are also made for word-specific common misspellings, using data drawn from the Cambridge Learner Corpus; expert judgement is then applied to determine which misspellings to allow.

The use of the LIBS dictionary ensures consistency of marking not only across the candidature for a particular form of a test but also across different forms, since whenever the same word is used as a key in different tests it is subject to identical spelling criteria. This second point is a considerable advantage, since although a monitor can ensure a good degree of consistency of marking (if not 100%) as different possible misspellings are raised during marking, it is not possible to guarantee this consistency across different sessions or different tests.

Various studies (e.g. Brindley and Slatyer 2002, Buck and Tatsuoka 1998, Freedle and Kostin 1996) have pointed out the impact of lexical overlap on the difficulty of constructed response tasks. If a candidate can 'lift' the correct answer without processing the surrounding text, this tells us only that they can identify word boundaries and recognise individual words, but not that they can understand the speaker's meaning. The text on the question paper therefore usually reformulates the language of the recording, rather than presenting it as a gapped dictation. For example (FCE sample test, Appendix A):

> Recording transcript:
> Charlie: Well, the main characters only came on for the last take. They looked very glamorous. But we weren't allowed to talk to the stars or take photos or anything like that as we'd signed a contract to that effect. Pity, because my family and friends would've loved a photo.
>
> Test item:
> **17** Charlie's . . . . didn't permit him to talk to or to photograph the stars of the film.

One issue with both sentence and note-completion tasks is the extent to which candidates may be able to guess answers from the linguistic context or from their general knowledge. In analysis of two IELTS tasks, Proudfoot (2010:35) found that candidates were sometimes predicting answers to note-completion tasks by using their knowledge of high-frequency collocations – e.g. *population density* – a strategy which may misfire if the candidate does not subsequently check their prediction against what is said in the text (in this case, the key was *traffic density*). Main Suite policy involves avoiding the testing of half compounds or strong collocations, but it is inevitable that weak collocations may activate collocational associations, as in the given IELTS example. Knowledge of syntactic structure, indicating word class, and contextual cues may also increase the possibility of correct guessing. Interestingly, these three aids to guessing – collocations, syntax and context – which constitute drawbacks of the response format, are all also important factors in assisting successful listening comprehension through the spreading of lexical activation (collocations), syntactic parsing (knowledge of syntax) and meaning enrichment (contextual cues) – see Chapter 3 for a discussion of these cognitive processes.

Constructed response tasks may involve the completion of notes, sentences, forms, tables, or a summary. They can also involve the labelling of diagrams, maps or plans. However, in Cambridge Main Suite Listening examinations only the first three types are used. Note or form-completion tasks are used in KET and PET. It is important to point out, however, that the candidate is not involved in constructing their own notes, but in completing an outline of the text by identifying key points from the text. The notes may have subheadings and bullet points to indicate the number and relationship of key ideas, and some key information may already be provided. The focus of the task is on understanding practical information in everyday settings – for example, information about leisure activities. Note completion is also a common task in IELTS Listening, particularly in Section 4, where the focus is on testing listening skills in an academic context, and the input is part of a lecture. Here the enforcement of a stated word limit helps to constrain keys. This task was also analysed for CPE for the 2002 revision, but at this level it was found to be too difficult to constrain the keys without a word limit and it was also found that the task tended to focus on 'lists of hard factual information which did not always test to the level' (Boroughs 2003:326); for these reasons, sentence completion, which permitted a wider range of testing focuses, was preferred.

Weighting

Weighting of items – the allocation of a different number of marks to an item or task compared to others in the test – is sometimes employed to reflect the perceived greater importance or more time-consuming nature of particular items or tasks within a test. In the case of listening, this could hold for, for example, items testing global understanding, of which it may not be possible to generate as many for a given length of text, in order to keep the overall test length down. Such a policy should be based on sound criteria.

Weir (2005a) emphasises the importance of informing candidates of any weighting applied to items or tasks within a test so that they may allocate their time and attention accordingly. In the case of listening, the issue of time allocation does not arise where the recording is played through without stopping, since it is out of the candidate's control. However, should a (computer-based) test include a task where candidates have a fixed time to answer questions on a recording which they may pause and rewind, for example to simulate listening to a podcast, such considerations would come into play.

Ebel (1972) outlines how differential item weighting is sometimes applied to tests on the grounds that some items are more important in terms of their technical quality, complexity, difficulty or the time they consume. However, he goes on to note that '[r]easonable as such differential weights seem to be on the surface, they seldom make the test to which they are applied a more reliable or valid measure' (1972:219). Ebel's position is echoed by Alderson et al (1995) and is supported by Jones' (2000b) findings in a study based on live administration data that differentially weighting items in different parts of a test can actually reduce reliability. Jones describes the findings as expected, attributing them to the fact that weighted items 'take on a larger part of the burden of measurement: the unweighted items contribute less to the measurement of the candidates. Effectively the test is made shorter' (2000b:6). Jones reflects Ebel's (1972:199) contention that '[i]f an achievement test covers two areas, one of which is judged to be twice as important as the other, then twice as many items should be written in relation to the more important area', arguing that the resulting test will be more valid and reliable than one with fewer, weighted, items. Indeed, construct coverage is certain to be higher in a test with more items, increasing construct validity. All the above would seem to suggest that unless there is a particularly good reason to apply differential weighting, equal item weighting should be the default position.

Weighting: Cambridge ESOL practice

Information on the weighting of different parts of the Listening paper (where each item always carries one mark), and on the weighting of the Listening paper to the exam as a whole is available online and in the handbooks for teachers as well as on the question papers themselves.

On the cover page of the Listening question papers at each level candidates are told that each question carries one mark, and this is also specified in the handbooks. Questions are numbered within the Listening test. There are

25 questions for KET and PET, 30 for FCE and CAE and 28 for CPE. For FCE, CAE and CPE the total number of marks is then converted to a mark out of 40, which forms 20% of the final result for the exam as a whole. The handbooks also specify how grades are calculated from the total percentage. (See also Chapter 5 for more detailed information on score processing, score reporting and grade allocation.)

Candidates are therefore aware both of the weighting of individual parts of the paper, and of how these marks translate to the final score and to the grade they are given. However, unlike in Reading or Writing papers, information on weighting is unlikely to affect decisions made by candidates on how much time to spend on an individual item, since they are 'locked in' to the timing of the Listening test, responding to items as the recording plays and unable to navigate around the test at will as, for instance, in a Reading test.

Knowledge of criteria

This aspect of context validity can be simply stated: candidates should be aware of the criteria by which their responses are to be marked. Candidates who are unsure of how they are being assessed cannot reasonably be expected to produce a performance which reflects their true ability, and are likely to be further impeded by the anxiety caused by this uncertainty. The ETS *Standards for Quality and Fairness* (ETS 2002:62) states that candidates should be informed 'whether there are scoring procedures that may affect their results (e.g. if there is a correction for guessing), unless providing such information is inconsistent with the purpose for testing'.

In addition to these considerations of fairness, there are theoretical grounds for insisting that marking criteria are transparent. As Weir (2005a) points out, candidates are likely to employ different strategies according to the marking criteria employed for a given test – for example, if correct spelling is necessary for the award of a mark, this will form part of their strategies, affecting the cognitive processes employed compared with a test where there is tolerance of incorrect spelling. This is especially true of listening tests, where candidates are processing texts online and need to allocate scarce working memory resources appropriately and efficiently. This applies equally to grammar and punctuation (Taylor and Geranpayeh 2011).

Knowledge of criteria: Cambridge ESOL practice

Candidates and their teachers need to know what criteria they are expected to fulfil in order to gain a pass grade. This might include information on the language and skills required and the text types and discourse structure that they are expected to be able to handle, as well as information on areas such as spelling requirements for constructed responses. This is available from various sources.

The Cambridge ESOL website (http://www.cambridgeesol.org/exams/exams-info/faqs/index.html) provides information on the relation of Main Suite exams to the CEFR levels and to the ALTE Can Do statements (see also Chapter 7). The handbooks for teachers (KET and PET) provide the same information as described above together with details of the precise standardised scores required for each grade. In addition, they contain information on text types, skills and language specifications, and there are links to the online vocabulary lists for each examination. The KET and PET handbooks provide language specifications, and there are links to the online vocabulary lists for each of these examinations. Published support materials and past papers show candidates and teachers how these criteria are applied to actual examinations.

Order of items

A listener constructs the meaning of a listening text in a cumulative fashion (see Chapter 3), with each new utterance processed and interpreted in the light of the preceding utterances as well as the surrounding contexts. For this reason alone, it makes sense for items to be presented in the order they appear in the text so as not to interfere with the cognitive processing involved in the process of constructing meaning. However, unlike reading, the online nature of listening and the fact that the candidate is usually unable to navigate backwards and forward in the text at will makes the sequencing of items of higher importance. Presenting items out of their chronological order within the text can place an unnecessary extra cognitive burden on the candidate, who needs to identify the item to be responded to from the list of items whilst simultaneously processing the text and answering the items. This can lead to confusion (Buck 2001) and prevent the candidate from demonstrating his or her true level of performance; furthermore, having items 'out of order' can disrupt candidates' metacognitive processes, particularly planning, since they are expecting a certain flow of information (Chi 2011). It would seem that there needs to be sound justification for presenting items in any order other than that of the text.

According to Kintsch's (1998) construction-integration model of comprehension, the constructed meaning of a text is under a constant process of revision as the text progresses, meaning that the listener's understanding of what is said at one point in a text may be modified in the light of subsequent utterances. For this reason, a task with multiple items should present those testing local understanding first in the order they appear in the text, without later contradictory information after the candidates have moved on to later items, and those testing global understanding afterwrds.

As well as presenting items in the order they appear in the text, it is essential that items are spaced out enough to allow candidates time to answer one item and prepare themselves for the next before the relevant part of the text is heard (Hughes 2003), in order to avoid missing an item, with a potential 'domino effect' on subsequent items. There should also be a sufficient amount of untested text at the start to allow candidates adequate time to orient themselves to the text and normalise to the speaker's speech rate, loudness and pitch (Field 2009a) before they are required to respond to items. This process allows candidates to establish a 'baseline' (Field 2009a) according to which to interpret shifts in speech rate, volume and pitch, as well as normalising to the speaker's accent. Where there is more than one speaker, this process takes longer, so requires a correspondingly longer normalisation period at the beginning of the text. This process of normalisation applies to L1 listeners also (Brown 1990) but must be more demanding for L2 listeners.

In terms of item difficulty, it can be argued that there should be some kind of gradation from easier to more difficult, at least in terms of the first few items of the test to allow candidates to warm up. Taylor and Geranpayeh (2011), however, argue that there may be cases, such as EAP tests, for which it might more accurately reflect the TLU domain demands of rapid acclimatisation to the speaker if no such considerations took place.

Order of items: Cambridge ESOL practice

In Cambridge ESOL Listening papers, the items in a task generally follow the order of information in the text. The only exceptions to this are CAE and CPE Part 1 and CAE (and CPE from 2013) Part 4. In the case of CAE and CPE Part 1, there are two items targeting a single short text; the keys may occur in either order or may be spread across the whole text, especially when gist is being tested. In the case of CAE Part 4 (and CPE Part 4 from 2013), there are two tasks to be completed in parallel, with two sets of items corresponding to the order of the recordings. Here, the format may have an effect in that the candidates may need to switch their attention between the tasks; there are effectively two items per recording, the keys to which may occur at any point within the recording or, more typically, be spread throughout.

In terms of the order of the tasks in a test, some general patterns can be observed, with the underlying principle being a progression from what candidates may see as easier tasks to more difficult ones. In all cases, the test begins with an MCQ task based on short texts, meaning that the candidate does not have to consider the written form of their response. Where a paper has multiple-choice items with both visual and verbal options, as in KET and PET, the visual options come first in the paper, so that initially the candidate can focus on understanding the text and does not have to relate this to a written option. Where a paper has both 3-option MCQs and 4-option MCQs (as in CAE and CPE) the 4-option tasks come later in the paper.

The focus of the task may also affect its position in the test as a whole. The point has already been made that constructed response tasks focus on identification of specific information and detail. In KET, where the test as a whole targets key/specific information, these tasks come at the end of the test, since they involve writing as well as listening. At higher levels, these tasks occur earlier in the test – Part 3 in PET and Part 2 in FCE, CAE and CPE – and are followed by selected response tasks involving the identification of attitude, feeling and opinion (see Table 4.4). This reflects the relative cognitive demands of the tasks, since constructed response formats inevitably focus to some extent on lexical-level processing, in other words the lower-level stages of the listening process.

Channel of presentation

A characteristic of tests of listening is that they generally feature at least two different channels of presentation – audio for the listening input and written for the test items. They may feature other presentation modes, in the case of input presented in video format or with visuals supporting the text, or where test items are presented with visuals such as tasks involving labelling diagrams.

Means of transmission

Research suggests that there is little difference between cassettes and CDs in terms of effect on candidate performance, providing the recording is of sufficient quality (Jones 2002a). However, there is evidence that candidates using headphones perform better than those listening through loudspeakers (Somers 2007) – this is perhaps unsurprising, given that headphones cut out much interference from background noise and eliminate issues related to the acoustics of large rooms. One implication of this difference is that it is desirable for the delivery system of the audio to be standardised to avoid unwanted external noise or acoustic effects. It is worth noting, however, that simply providing any set of headphones is not in itself sufficient to improve the quality of delivery; the headphones must be of a suitable quality in order to realise any advantage over good-quality loudspeakers, preferably covering the candidate's ears (Buck 2001).

Visual input and use of video

At lower proficiency levels, where the effect of an additional reading load for listening test items is likely to be more significant than at higher levels (Wickens 1984), visual images are often used in place of written text for some items to avoid this problem. This is not to suggest that the visual channel has no place at higher proficiency levels; diagrammatic representations can be a more efficient way of presenting information (Larkin and Simon 1987), helping to reduce the non-listening processing burden for candidates.

The multimedia capacity of computer-based testing (CBT) allows for the inclusion of still images (single or multiple) and video in listening tests much more straightforwardly than in paper-based testing (PBT) – the video or still images and items can appear alongside each other on screen, rather than necessitating looking up and down from question paper to screen. Ockey found evidence that candidates have 'little or no engagement with still images' (2007:533), suggesting that there is likely to be little effect on the construct. Buck notes that a still image can be useful and have a positive cognitive effect in that it 'activates relevant knowledge schemata and provides a focus of attention' (2001:173); Suvurov (2011), however, found that the inclusion of a single still image had no significant effect on test scores (Suvurov's study did not encompass the use of multiple images). In a study of the effect of still images on candidate performance in TOEFL listening, Ginther found that providing content visuals which 'bear information that complements the audio portion of the stimulus' (2002:133) helped candidate performance, but that providing merely context visuals was detrimental to candidate performance. Commenting on Ginther's findings, Vandergrift notes that, compared to content visuals, context visuals 'still require processing themselves, thereby consuming attentional resources and limiting the amount of working memory available to the listener for attending to the required information' (2004:5–6).

Real-life situations can be classified into three groups: those in which the listener has no visual reference to the speaker, for example a telephone conversation; those in which the listener has visual reference, but is a passive participant, for example watching a television programme or listening to a lecture; and those in which the listener is an active participant with visual reference, i.e. a face-to-face conversation. The relevance of video and the resultant access to non-verbal signals to the listening construct can perhaps best be determined by considering the TLU domain and the inferences to be drawn from the test result (Douglas and Hegelheimer 2007). It seems clear that video adds little to situations in which the listener would have no visual reference to the speaker in a real-life situation. However, where the listener would be a passive participant with visual reference to the speaker or, to a lesser extent, where the listener would be an active participant with visual reference, there is a strong argument that it is desirable to strive for authenticity by including video (Field 2012); this is particularly the case where the TLU domain is more narrowly defined and would typically include visual input, for example EAP tests claiming predictive validity for lecture listening. Buck (2001) acknowledges that video (and still images) can be useful in activating candidates' schemata, but draws a clear distinction between language and visual cues in construct terms:

> We are usually interested in the test takers' language ability, rather than
> the ability to understand subtle visual information . . . There are good
> reasons to keep the emphasis on the audio information (2001:172).

In face-to-face communication on the other hand, the meaning is carried in part by non-verbal signals and, critically, this is intentional; it can be argued that they form an integral part of the information on which a listener draws. Burgoon (1994:270–271) notes regarding non-verbal signals that 'rather than being mere auxiliaries to the verbal stream, they carry a significant, and often dominant, portion of the social meaning in face-to-face exchanges'. In this regard, the visual channel must be seen as an important facet of context, particularly in primarily interpersonal interaction.

Studies of the effect of video on candidates' attitudes and performance have produced mixed results. Progosh (1996) found that candidates generally preferred a video listening test to an audio-only one, while another study (Wagner 2007) showed that most candidates tended to watch the video most of the time, but that there was wide variance among candidates. Londe (2009) found that displaying either a close-up of the speaker's head or the speaker's full body had no effect on candidate scores compared to taking the test without video. However, another study by Wagner (2010) comparing candidate performance on a listening test with and without video showed that candidates achieved higher scores, at a statistically significant level, when the text was mediated by video, suggesting that visual cues do indeed provide support for candidates. Wagner also noted that the variance due to the use of video was not consistent across the sample, implying that candidates' ability to use such input varied. There are construct implications here, since Wagner's findings would suggest that the trait of listening ability when accompanied by video is not unidimensional (this view is, however, disputed by, *inter alia*, Buck (1994)). In another study, however, it was found that video had a detrimental effect on candidates' scores for lecture-based tasks, although not for dialogues (Suvorov 2011), a finding which supports both Buck's (2001) contention that visual information has greater importance for interactional than transactional language use and Burgoon's (1994) observations regarding the importance of non-verbal signals in carrying social meaning, discussed above.

Rost (2002) considers visual signals to be co-text and categorises them as either *exophoric* signals, such as 'a speaker holding up a photograph or writing on a blackboard' (2002:37), or *kinesic*, meaning 'the body movements, including eye and head movements, the speaker makes while delivering the text' (2002:37), going on to make further sub-distinctions and identify the communicative functions of the categories. The visual and audio signals are known to interact, with the visual signal having the potential to modify the listener's interpretation of the audio signal they hear, even at the level of phonemic discrimination (McGurk and MacDonald 1976). In short, the visual channel has an effect on the listening process, a fact which is not generally recognised in construct definitions of the listening skill (Gruba 1999).

As well as visual input, there may be other relevant potential channels of input related to specific TLU domains. In the case of EAP tests, Field (2012) points out that there are cases where showing PowerPoint slides or providing candidates with handouts outlining the text to be heard may be relevant, as they would reflect the real-life listening situation of a lecture, while Lynch argues that EAP listening tests should incorporate multimodality in order to 'exploit the sort of integrated video/audio output that university students will encounter in real academic life' (2011:86). These questions of additional channels of presentation, which may or may not be appropriate for listening tests with different purposes, lead us to conclude that since listening is rarely a 'pure' skill which exists in isolation, not all of the non-aural input present in tests of listening is necessarily a cause of construct-irrelevant variance *per se*; indeed, there are often strong grounds for consciously adding more of such input. The listening construct could be said to vary across different TLU domains in terms of the relevance of non-aural input, which should ideally be reflected in listening test design.

Computer-based testing (CBT)

CBT is an increasingly popular medium for language tests. In terms of listening tests, the primary differences compared to paper-based tests (PBT) are that rubrics and items are presented on screen rather than on paper, the answer mode is different (responses are entered on the computer with the mouse and keyboard), and there is scope for additional multimedia resources such as video. CBT permits more flexibility in the way a test is presented, for example previewing items between two listenings (see *Response method*, this chapter), which would be administratively impractical in PBT.

A key question related to CBT is whether scores on versions of the same test delivered via different media are comparable to PBT scores, and consequently whether the two formats could be used interchangeably, with the same inferences drawn from the results in each format. Various studies (e.g. Blackhurst 2005, Choi, Kim and Boo 2003, Green and Maycock 2004, Maycock 2005, Maycock and Green 2004, 2005, Thighe, Jones and Geranpayeh 2001) have suggested that such comparability does indeed hold, although Hackett (2008:24) notes:

> Though the task formats for Cambridge ESOL exams . . . is the same for both [paper-based] and [computer-based] versions, it would be difficult to claim direct equivalence, i.e. that a candidate would score the same on both formats. As with a candidate taking two [paper-based] forms of a test, there will inevitably be some minor variation in performance and result.

This echoes Jones and Maycock's (2007:11) observation that the most likely scenario of comparability between PB and CB tests is one where 'they differ to some extent for practical reasons inherent in the formats'. The different orientation of most PB tests (portrait) versus CB tests (landscape) affects the layout, and the amount of space on screen can be an issue if scrolling is necessary, but this is less likely to be an issue for listening tests, which are not text-heavy (Hackett 2005). The answer mode for CBT generally involves clicking on radio buttons for MCQ items and for matching items (although matching items may involve drag-and-drop), and typing for constructed response format items. Typing responses to constructed response items raises the interesting question of whether candidates are as comfortable typing while listening as they are writing, although allowing candidates to take notes and then transfer their answers is one solution (Hackett 2008), while some candidates may indeed be more comfortable using the keyboard in this situation than a pen and paper.

The question arises of the effect of computer literacy levels on candidate performance (Huff and Sireci 2005). Providing tutorials is one possible solution to this issue, although it will always be an issue when considering the comparability of CB and PB tests. In a Cambridge ESOL CB versus PB equivalence study for PET which otherwise found no significant differences between CB and PB performance, Maycock (2005:3) did find 'some evidence to suggest that the younger candidates (aged 20 or under) performed better on the CB test than the older candidates (aged 21 or over), relative to their PB performance'; this may be a reflection of intergenerational differences in IT skills. Offering candidates the choice of CB and PB versions is another natural solution, since candidates are likely to opt for PB versions where they believe their computer skills are likely to adversely affect their performance, making it reasonable to assume that candidates opting to take CB versions possess the level of computer familiarity necessary for PB and CB tests to be comparable (Dooey 2008).

Computer-adaptive testing (CAT) is a form of CBT whereby the test does not have a fixed, linear format but is instead tailored to a candidate's level by selecting tasks/items from a pool on the basis of a combination of item/task difficulty and the candidate's previous responses (Chalhoub-Deville and Deville 1999, Linacre 2000, Wainer, Dorans, Eignor, Flaugher, Green, Mislevy, Steinberg and Thissen 2000). CAT has certain advantages over linear tests: CAT produces shorter tests than linear tests for a given level of precision due to the closer match between item difficulty and candidate (which also has a positive effect on the candidate, who is faced with fewer over-easy or over-difficult items); in addition, security is enhanced since no two tests will be identical (Meunier 1994). The format does have its drawbacks, however. The format best lends itself to discrete items, so that the algorithm can adapt more quickly to the candidate's level, and consequently CAT listening tends to involve short texts, such as that in Coniam's (2006) study of CAT/PBT comparability, which involved a test consisting of texts no longer than 60–70 seconds. This tendency is difficult to reconcile with the need for longer listening texts to test the full range of assessment focuses, in particular at higher levels of proficiency. It is also complex and expensive to develop due to the requirement to develop an extremely large bank of items/tasks – potentially thousands of items – each with its testing focus determined, to avoid the risk of construct under-representation by ensuring that there are enough items/tasks to test all aspects of the construct at all levels of difficulty (Chalhoub-Deville and Deville 1999, Dunkel 1999, Ockey 2009), and a high level of statistical expertise is required (Ockey 2009).

Channel of presentation: Cambridge ESOL practice

Means of transmission

The Listening paper in all paper-based Main Suite Cambridge ESOL examinations is now presented on audio CD. This is recorded with rubrics and pauses built in so that input is standardised for all candidates. Centres may use either headphones or loudspeakers at present since insisting on the use of headphones would not be realistic in all parts of the world for cost reasons; in the context of a global test, this is naturally an important consideration when maximising access to the test. Clear regulations for the administration of listening tests are laid out in the *Handbook for Centres* (Cambridge ESOL 2012e) to ensure that sound quality is good. These include: checking the quality of the equipment used (whether headphones or loudspeakers); where loudspeakers are used, ensuring that the room is suitable in terms of acoustics (in particular when the room is full); ensuring that the number, position and direction of the loudspeakers provides good sound quality to all candidates, and ensuring that the room is not one which is subject to excessive outside noise (2012e:23).

Candidates receive a question paper and a separate answer sheet. After the initial introduction to the test, the CD is paused briefly so that candidates can ask if they are unsure about any aspect of the procedure. Candidates write their answers on the question paper as they listen, then transfer their answers to an answer sheet at the end of the test. Sometimes information is provided through multiple channels, for example, candidates hear the rubrics for tasks as well as being able to read them on the question paper.

Visual input and use of video

In KET and PET Part 1 the questions for MCQs are recorded as well as being printed on the question paper. Since the options for the answers to these tasks are in visual form, candidates are able to answer these questions without having to process any written text. At FCE, the questions for Part 1 (stem and options) are currently delivered aurally as well as being printed on the question paper. Candidates are not otherwise expected to process non-verbal information in Main Suite exams, and pictures are not used to establish the context. IELTS Listening may also include other tasks with visual input such as matching labels to a plan, map or diagram. As previously mentioned, in all paper-based tests, candidates have time at the end of the test to transfer their answers to a separate answer sheet, meaning that they do not have to shift their attention from the question paper during the test.

Video-based listening tasks have been used in the past by Cambridge ESOL in tests for specific purposes, starting in 1998 in one part of the *Linguaskills* listening test (now discontinued). *Linguaskills* was delivered in CB-only format, which negated any issues over comparability with PB versions. However, video-based listening tasks are not used in Main Suite examinations. The first reason for this is the lack of feasibility of delivering video in PB tests. Since Main Suite is delivered in both PB and CB format, with the same tasks in both formats, it is not possible to introduce video; introducing video to the CB version without also doing so in the PB version would introduce serious comparability issues. The second reason relates to the history of the Main Suite tests, as discussed in Chapter 1. Furthermore, as was suggested in the preceding general discussion on channel of communication, there is not yet an established consensus from research into the use of video, which makes its introduction in large-scale CB tests of General English problematic in any case.

Computer-based delivery

In addition to the paper-based tests, computer-based tests are now available for all Main Suite Listening tests except CPE, using Cambridge Assessment's specially developed computer-based test delivery system *Cambridge Connect*. Test materials are downloaded directly by the centre to candidate workstations. After the candidates have finished the exams, their responses are uploaded directly to Cambridge ESOL for assessment. In all cases, candidates can choose whether or not to take a CB version of a test.

These tests retain the same exam format as the paper-based tests, with identical task types and results being reported on the same scale. However, the conversion of paper-based materials to on-screen delivery required some adaptations to be made. For example, a feasibility study carried out for CB PET (Hackett 2005) identified the Part 3 gap-fill task as being potentially problematic, since for this task candidates would have to type in their answers as they listened, rather than just clicking on answers. In trialling, candidates generally gave positive feedback to the tasks. Some candidates said they would find it helpful to make hand-written notes while listening, and this is now allowed.

In addition to adapting and trialling task types, navigation systems had to be designed and trialled. These were based on standard navigation practices used on websites. A brief tutorial in the navigation techniques required was also designed for candidates to take before beginning the test. Trialling showed the new format was very popular for Listening, with '87% expressing a preference for listening individually on computer to listening as a group from a CD or cassette player' (Hackett 2005:13). These principles of task adaptation, navigation practices and introductory tutorials showing the main item types and required techniques such as scrolling are now used in all Main Suite CB tests, as well as in other tests such as CB Business English Certificate (BEC) Preliminary, Vantage and Higher levels. The Listening papers are all automarked, with acceptable misspellings for constructed response tasks determined by the Dictionary for Automarking, which stores all such agreed acceptable misspellings. Online practice tests are also available for all CB tests.

Computer Adaptive Tests (CATs) are not used in Main Suite exams but are used in the computer-based version of the Cambridge ESOL Business Language Testing Service (CB BULATS). Candidates have the option of taking the Reading and Language Knowledge (RLK) test and the Listening test either in their standard paper-based form or in a computer-adaptive CB test. In a study of the reliability of the CB BULATS test, Cope (2009) found that the test scores produced were highly reliable and that this reliability was not affected by the length of the test (an important finding since in a CAT test candidates may not all answer the same number of questions).

Text length

Research, interestingly, has generally not supported the intuitive position that longer texts imply more difficult items. Bloomfield, Wayland, Blodgett and Linck (2011) note that the relationship between text length and task difficulty can be complex and confounded with other factors: 'a faster speech rate (which results in a shorter length) should make listening more difficult; more redundancy of information, which should increase length, should decrease listening comprehension difficulty' (2011:2318); they further question the invariability of other factors within previous studies and suggest that this area requires further research with other factors more tightly controlled.

The target proficiency level of the task often determines the length of the text in terms of time, and in particular the maximum appropriate length of a text for the level. At Level B1 of the CEFR and below, the length of texts is important since more effortful decoding (see Chapter 3) means that candidates cannot reasonably be expected to maintain their attention at a sufficient level for extended periods of time. There is a natural progression through the levels from A1 to B1 in terms of how much candidates can cope with as processing becomes more efficient (see Chapter 3). At B2 level the picture changes, however; the CEFR descriptors for Overall listening comprehension contain their first mention of candidates' being able to 'follow extended speech' (Council of Europe 2001:66), although what length of text constitutes 'extended' is not specified. This reflects a degree of automaticity in processing which learners at Level B2 and above have developed and which allows them to devote sufficient attentional resources to construct an extended discourse representation. The element of difficulty at higher proficiency levels is provided much less by the length of the text than by other textual features such as the lexical and grammatical content employed in the text, as well as the rate of speech and accents of the interlocutors and the complexity, familiarity and abstraction of the concepts contained in the text. Text length still contributes to difficulty in terms of the cumulative effect of meaning construction and the holding in the listener's mind of a growing discourse representation, but practical considerations of the overall length of a test mean that it is not possible to include texts above a certain length while still providing the range of text and task types to ensure adequate construct coverage and context validity in terms of generalisability to the range of TLU domain listening situations.

The appropriate relationship between the length of a text and the number of items allocated to it is generally determined by the need for candidates to have sufficient time between items to respond to one and prepare for the next before the relevant part of the text is heard, plus the need for a period of normalisation to the speaker(s) at the beginning of the recording.

In terms of task/item type, it is worth noting that longer texts require different skills from shorter ones; in particular, they 'tend to require discourse skills, whereas shorter texts tend to focus more on localized grammatical characteristics' (Buck 2001:123). Tasks focusing on discoursal elements will therefore typically require longer texts.

Text length: Cambridge ESOL practice

All Main Suite Listening papers begin with a set of unrelated short texts with 3-option MCQs. These allow candidates a fresh start for each text and also increase the range of voices that they are exposed to. However, it could also be argued that the constant shifting of topic and voice with each fresh start constitutes a cognitive load in its own right. This is a question that could be more fully explored in the future.

From KET to FCE the overall text length of the Listening paper increases as the level rises. For KET, individual texts will not be longer than about 180 words, with a maximum of just over 1,000 words for the paper as a whole. By FCE this may rise to a maximum of about 675 words for an individual task, or about 2,780 for the paper as a whole. Above FCE, this increase levels off, so that CAE and CPE are not significantly longer (see Table 4.5 below).

Table 4.5 Total text length in Main Suite Listening papers

Exam	Minimum test length (words)	Maximum test length (words)	Sample test length* (words)
KET	735	990	947
PET	1,370	1,670	1,561
FCE	2,290	2,780	2,689
CAE	2,110	2,380	2,287
CPE	2,360	2,860	2,554

* *See Appendix A for sample tests*

As already noted, the challenge for the listener at the C levels is less in the length of the text than in the type of information that he or she can process and the extent to which information can be processed without explicit sign-posting. As well as being more abstract and complex in nature, information in texts at the C levels is likely to be denser, with less repetition and refor-mulation, and with less glossing or circumlocution. These differences can be illustrated by comparing two extracts on similar topics from the sample FCE and CPE tests (Appendix A):

Extract 1 (FCE Part 4)
Interviewer: What made you take it [the pole vault] up personally?
Sandra: Well, I'd always regarded it as one of those sports that women just didn't do. I was a heptathlete, doing a range of track and field sports – and my coach came to me and said, 'Hey, why don't you try the pole vault?' and I just looked at him in amazement and said, 'What me?' and he just said, 'Well why not?'
              [71 words]

Extract 2 (CPE Part 1)
Presenter: Helen, why did you decide to take up fencing a couple of years ago?
Helen: Well, after my son was born I thought it would be good to learn something new and complex, prove to myself that I could, and particularly something that'd be extremely taxing both physically and mentally – you know, like playing chess with your whole body – in split seconds.
              [61 words]

Much of the later part of the first extract is a step-by-step description of a conversation in which the speaker uses direct speech and repetition for dramatic effect. The answer that Sandra gives to the interviewer's question is 'My coach suggested it'. However, the item relating to this extract goes beyond the basic propositional content and targets Sandra's reaction when pole vaulting was suggested to her, reflecting the ability of candidates at B2 level to 'identify speaker viewpoints and attitudes as well as the information content' (Council of Europe 2001:68).

The second extract is shorter but the information is both more abstract in nature and more densely packed. It includes ellipsis ('prove to myself that I could') and moves quickly from one proposition to another, with little repetition or signposting. The item relating to this extract targets Helen's intention in using the chess simile, testing candidates' ability to understand meaning 'when relationships are only implied and not signalled explicitly' (Council of Europe 2001:66).

Time constraints, including number of times heard

Listening tests typically comprise a recording which is played through from the start of the test to the end without stopping or pausing. Within this context, two issues arise regarding timing: how much time to allow candidates between recordings to read rubrics and items and to write and check their answers (or transfer to them to an answer sheet where appropriate); and whether each recording should be heard once or twice.

Task timing

A listening test should include sufficient time for candidates to read all necessary instructions and rubrics, plus time to read the tasks and write and check answers, otherwise construct-irrelevant variance will result as candidates have insufficient time to complete the non-listening elements of the test. This should all be made clear to the candidates in order to avoid anxiety on the candidates' parts and allow them to plan their approach to the test.

Single play or double play

While the above considerations border on the obvious, the issue of whether texts should be heard once or twice is a controversial one, with arguments on both sides. As Geranpayeh and Taylor (2008:2) note:

> A convincing case can be made for both approaches, depending upon factors such as test purpose, cognitive demand, task consistency, sampling and practicality, all of which reflect the need to balance competing considerations in test design, construction and delivery.

With respect to many real-life listening situations, for example lectures, once-heard texts could be said to have a greater situational authenticity in that second hearings are often not possible in the real-life TLU domain. Indeed, even in other listening situations where there is repetition of ideas, the listener never hears an identical text again; prosodic features such as intonation are bound to be different even when the words are exactly the same (Buck 2011). However, this situational authenticity comes at the price of cognitive validity, since listening tests require far greater precision of comprehension than most real-life once-heard situations, where comprehension 'is normally much more approximate than we realise (Buck 2001:171). In favour of the situational authenticity of twice-heard listening, 'second chances' are actually fairly common in everyday life – face-to-face dialogues allow for repetition (although this is more typically in the form of reformulations than exact repetitions), and modern multimedia formats such as podcasts, BBC Radio digital audio files and iPlayer on the BBC website allow listeners to rewind and listen again as they wish (Geranpayeh and Taylor 2008, Taylor and Geranpayeh 2011). In the latter case, listeners do indeed hear precisely the same text again, and although face-to-face repititions do inevitably involve differences between the two texts as Buck argues, it is difficult to argue that not hearing any of the text again therefore results in greater situational authenticity than hearing a similar, if not identical, paraphrasing; furthermore, as Berne (1995:326) argues, 'repetition, restatement and paraphrasing are all important factors in the negotiation of meaning', going on to contend that tests should 'incorporate opportunities for additional exposure to the passage and negotiation of meaning' (1995:326).

Questions of situational authenticity naturally depend on the unique features of the TLU domain. In some contexts, for example EAP, once-heard texts could 'mirror the sorts of skills and tasks test takers would encounter in the fairly narrowly-focused Target Language Use (TLU) domain' (Geranpayeh and Taylor 2008:4), given that there are no second chances in a live lecture, in contrast with the considerations related to other TLU domains such as face-to-face conversation discussed earlier. However, it is worth noting that many universities now provide downloadable recordings of lectures for students, and that some students make their own recordings by taking MP3 players to lectures. In these cases, the students concerned can listen as many times to all or part of a lecture as is needed.

Even where the situational authenticity of a once-heard text has been established, the level of authenticity of the texts used in listening tests should lead us to raise further questions. Taking the EAP context as an example, fully authentic EAP lectures have been shown to be unsuitable for use in listening tests even where they do not violate guidelines on appropriacy of content (e.g. taboo topics and topics where content knowledge would advantage some candidates) due to, among other things, the amount of referencing to visual elements present in the 'live' lecture and references to previous lectures in the series, the content of which would be necessary in order to understand the lecture (Douglas and Nissan 2001). Listening test texts therefore have an inherent artificiality and lack visual and other support features that typically accompany the listening experience outside the test context' (Geranpayeh and Taylor 2008:2); listening twice can be seen as compensating for this. In the case of podcasts, rather than playing the whole text through once or twice, an alternative might be to allow candidates to control the text and pause, rewind and fast forward as required, perhaps within an overall time limit. This would, however, be controversial in that it risks eliminating natural online processing and would potentially undermine or challenge the traditional listening construct on which many tests are premised. Further research would be necessary to establish the consequences of such a policy.

Buck (2011) raises two questions concerning the construct validity of twice-heard texts. Firstly, he notes that automaticity of processing, particularly in bottom-up terms, is a key listening skill, indeed perhaps the single most important variable in second language performance testing, and that hearing the text twice means that this part of the construct may be lost. Secondly, listening twice reduces the effect of inferencing (when the listener fails to catch part of the text) since candidates can hear the part they failed to catch again, meaning that another part of the construct is potentially lost.

Buck (2011) notes that the construct involved in listening may be different on first and second hearings since we do not know whether listening to a text for a second time involves the same cognitive processes and suggests that this represents grounds for a once-heard policy since texts are generally heard once in the real world. The first part of this hypothesis is supported by Buck's (1990) findings that listeners engage with the text differently on the first and second hearing – at a local level during the first hearing and on a global level on the second hearing. Field (2012), however, relates this difference to the heavy cognitive load of test conditions, typically involving listening, reading, and writing simultaneously. Such a cognitive load does not reflect a typical listening situation and is exacerbated by the extreme time pressure of a once-heard testing context (see Chapter 3), a view reflected in the ACTFL and ILR guidelines (American Council for the Teaching of Foreign Languages 1985; Interagency Language Roundtable 1985); this suggests that repetition may be necessary at lower proficiency levels (reported in Berne 1995). This may be linked to Sherman's (1997) findings that previewing questions between two hearings leads to their being significantly easier than presenting them either before the first hearing or after the second. In this scenario, candidates are able to engage fully with the text in cognitive terms, particularly since there is no method effect interfering with cognitive processes during the first listening. Berne's (1995) study found that all candidates' performance improved after repeated hearing, but candidates who performed a vocabulary preview activity before listening improved nearly twice as much, possibly suggesting that 'previewing vocabulary items distracts listeners from attending to the content of the passage' (1995:326) on the first hearing. Perhaps as a consequence of the heavy cognitive demands imposed by once-heard listening, the format has a tendency to foster test-wise strategies (Field 2012), which can have a negative effect on validity. In terms of item discrimination, however, Fortune's (2004) study of performance on once-heard versus twice-heard FCE tasks suggests that once-heard items may demonstrate better discrimination than the twice-heard version in the majority of, although not in all, cases.

There are other factors which call into question the cognitive validity of once-heard listening. Real-life listening has more redundancy than the brief recordings used out of necessity in a test in order to keep the overall text length within reasonable limits (Field 2012). There are also broad differences between taking a listening test with a recorded text and listening in typical real-life situations, relevant factors of which include the fact that the recording does not have the paralinguistic features and contextual information found in real-life listening situations (Field 2000), including the broader input of background reading and experience of previous lectures and seminars. Candidates cannot interrupt the speaker for clarification, which is far removed from real-life interaction (2000), and need time to normalise to the speaker (Boroughs 2003 – see *Order of items*, this chapter).

In trials undertaken for CPE, it was found that 'the difficulty levels of [constructed response] tasks increased dramatically when heard once only' (Boroughs 2003:335), but that the difficulty for selected response tasks only increased slightly. This suggests that task type is a factor to be considered when considering the appropriacy of once-heard or twice-heard listening, perhaps due to the different cognitive demands that the task places on the candidate, especially with respect to the various channels of presentation involved in the task (*Channel of presentation*, this chapter). It is worth noting here, though, that the texts in the Boroughs study feature very little in the way of redundancy; further research would be necessary to determine the effect on difficulty of once-heard or twice-heard texts with constructed response tasks where there is more redundancy in the text.

A strong practical argument in favour of once-heard texts is that they are more efficient. Twice-heard texts increase the length of the test without increasing the number of items; listening once means that it is possible to have more items, and hence more construct coverage and higher reliability (Buck 2011). This argument has particular force in the case of multi-level tests, which by their nature need to cover a greater construct range than those focusing on one particular level since they need to reflect the listening construct across all the levels they test (Geranpayeh and Taylor 2008).

Since listening tests involve a process of matching the written text to the spoken text, candidates 'tend to process one item at a time' (Field 2000:3), meaning that the candidate will continue to listen for the key information for an item if they miss it, potentially missing the key for the next item (Field 2012). As well as being problematic in its own right, undermining the independence of the items to a certain extent, this can create tension and anxiety in candidates, due to the realisation that there is only one chance to catch each key (Field 2009a), which can impair performance unfairy. Buck (2011) acknowledges this, although he notes that tension can also sometimes enhance performance.

Given that administrative conditions for large-scale international tests are not always identical, twice-heard texts can be seen to reflect 'concern for fairness in a large international market where the ability to conduct listening tests in optimum quality conditions may vary due to local constraints' (Geranpayeh and Taylor 2008:3). In live administrations, there may be background noise and disturbances such as coughing and passing cars or aeroplanes which can affect candidate performance, and playing the text twice helps to mitigate this.

The question of whether texts should be once-heard or twice-heard appears far from straightforward. A case-by-case approach seems to be indicated; test developers need to take into account all of the considerations discussed above and how they relate to the specific testing context and TLU domain before making a decision.

Time constraints, including number of times heard: Cambridge ESOL practice

Task timing

The overall time for the Listening test increases from approximately 30 minutes (including transfer time) in KET and PET to approximately 40 minutes (including transfer time) for FCE, CAE and CPE. This includes time at the end of the test for candidates to transfer their answers to the answer sheet. While the lengths of the individual recordings for each task increases from KET to FCE, from which level it remains relatively stable (see *Text length*, this chapter), there is thus not a great difference in terms of overall timing including rubrics and pauses between levels.

All Cambridge ESOL Listening tests are recorded as one self-contained CD. Apart from one pause at the beginning, when candidates have the chance to ask any necessary questions, the CD is played without stopping. Pauses are built into the recording before each task, to allow candidates time to read the task, and time is allowed at the end of the test for candidates to transfer their answers to the answer sheet. The appropriate lengths of these pauses have been determined via the accumulated experience gained through a combination of trialling and feedback from both pretesting and live test administrations.

In selected response formats, candidates mark the answers as they listen. Items are constructed so that candidates have time to process the information and mark the answer to one item before they hear information relevant to the next item. In constructed response tasks, key information is spaced throughout the text so that candidates have time to write their answers. Answers to these tasks are generally just one or two words, meaning that extensive writing time is not needed.

Single play or double play

Texts for all Main Suite Listening papers are now heard twice. Geranpayeh and Taylor (2008:2) outline the principles behind this policy:

> A twice listening format is used in most Cambridge ESOL examinations for a variety of reasons. One reason relates to the fact that listening to a recorded text in the context of an examination is clearly different from the listening experience that typically takes place in the world beyond the test. Relevant factors in the testing context include the absence of paralinguistic and contextual information, the time needed to normalise to speaker accents and speech patterns, and the sequential nature of the listening test task (see Boroughs 2003:336, for further discussion). Another reason concerns the need to ensure consistency across test tasks and levels (see below for an example of this with CAE). Playing the listening input twice also helps to minimise the impact of noise disturbances during live test administrations.

As discussed, fairness is another consideration behind the policy due to variations in testing conditions – another reminder of the practical issues of large-scale test administration which test developers need to attend to as much as theoretical considerations. Before the 2008 revision of CAE, a once-heard task was included, in which redundancy was introduced to ensure that key information was heard more than once, allowing candidates a second chance if they missed it the first time. When revising CPE, the inclusion of a similar once-heard task was considered, but it was felt that this recycling might make the task too easy. It was also felt that two hearings were necessary to compensate for the lack of contextual information in the Listening test situation and to give them the chance to make up for missed answers if they lost their way in a test (Boroughs 2003:336). Following consultation the once-heard task in CAE was subsequently dropped in the 2008 revision, 'in the interests of standardisation' (Hawkey 2009:187).

The double-play format of Main Suite contrasts with the single-play format of IELTS, which stems from 'the desire for an assessment instrument that would mirror the sorts of skills and tasks test takers would encounter in the fairly narrowly-focused Target Language Use (TLU) domain of study/training' (Geranpayeh and Taylor 2008:3). Another consideration with IELTS compared to the Main Suite is its multi-level nature, which indicates a test with more items to ensure acceptable levels of construct coverage and reliability (IELTS Listening has 40 items, while Main Suite examinations have no more than 30); as discussed above, a single-play format helps to facilitate this whilst keeping the length of the test within reasonable limits.

Linguistic demands: task input and output

Overall text purpose and discourse mode

When selecting appropriate texts for use in listening tests, it is important that the texts be of a type which are broadly representative of those the listener is likely to encounter in the TLU domain. Taking a high-level view, a primary consideration is the overall purpose of the text, particularly when the test is referenced to a functionally based framework such as the CEFR. Kinneavy (1969:297) defines text purpose (using the term 'aim of discourse') as 'the effect that the discourse is oriented to achieve in the average listener or reader for whom it is intended'. This definition grounds purpose in the intention of the speaker or writer when producing a text. Kinneavy provides examples of discourse modes which are typically associated with each purpose (Table 4.6), and which are closely related to Jakobson's (1960) model of functions based on the orientation of the text.

Table 4.6 A system of text purposes (adapted from Kinneavy 1969:299, 302)

Referential	Informative	e.g. news articles, reports, summaries
	Scientific	e.g. proving a point by arguing from accepted premises, proving a point by generalising from particulars, a combination of both
	Exploratory	e.g. dialogues, seminars, a tentative definition of . . . , proposing a solution to problems, diagnosis
Persuasive		e.g. advertising, political speeches, religious sermons, legal oratory, editorials
Literary		e.g. short story, lyric, short narrative, limerick, ballad, folk song, drama, TV show, movie, joke
Expressive	of individual	e.g. conversation, journals, diaries, gripe sessions, prayer
	of society	e.g. minority protests, manifestoes, declarations of independence, contracts, constitutions of clubs, myth, utopia plans, religious credos

The discourse modes of the texts in a listening test are of considerable importance. In order for the inferences drawn from the test scores to be generalisable across the TLU domain, a test should cover a representative sample of the relevant discourse modes within the TLU domain, coupled with appropriate tasks (see *Task purpose*, this chapter). It is important to distinguish between discourse modes and genres, since one type of discourse mode can encompass a variety of genres; lectures, for example, can range from conversational to highly formal and from spontaneous to entirely scripted, as well as varying levels of interaction with the audience (Jensen and Hansen 1995). Vähäpassi (1982:279) classifies written discourse modes according to two dimensions: the function of the text as the first dimension and the cognitive processing involved (reproducing another text, organising/reorganising another text or inventing/generating a new text from 'scratch') as the second dimension. An analogous exercise could be undertaken for spoken discourse modes, although it is not obvious how Vähäpassi's cognitive processing categories map onto spoken texts.

Discourse modes vary greatly in their lexical, grammatical, phonological and discoursal features. Different discourse modes, both spoken and written, exist at different points along an oral/literate continuum (Chafe and Tannen 1986, Tannen 1982a, 1982b), with unplanned informal conversation at one end and formal written language at the other.

The particular linguistic features of different discourse modes make some easier to process than others-for example, unplanned conversation contains more irregular stress patterns and has a narrower pitch range than a formal speech (Field 2000), which makes it more difficult to process. The *gestural magnitude* – the magnitude of the physical movements of the jaw, lips and tongue – is also reduced in casual speech compared to more formal speech (Browman and Goldstein 1991) since the focus of the speaker is on efficiency in terms of making gestures sufficient for the speech to be identifiable but no more (Brown 1990:57). Conversely, more literate text types tend to have a higher propositional density than more oral types (Shohamy and Inbar 1991), which can have an effect on difficulty. These considerations are relevant when considering the appropriacy of particular discourse modes for different proficiency levels, although as Alderson, Figueras, Kuijper, Nold, Takala and Tardieu (2006) note, identifying appropriate discourse modes in terms of proficiency levels can be problematic.

The ways listeners interact with different discourse modes also vary, since the listener will have different purposes for listening—Field (2009a:62) gives the example of listening to airport announcements, where the listener's attention will vary from low level (as they monitor for their destination) to high (as they listen for their flight details, such as the gate number) to none (as they tune out for the rest of the announcement). This suggests that different discourse modes should be accompanied by task types which require candidates to engage in the type of listening they would be likely to encounter in a real-life situation, and that the purposes for listening should be clear. Brown and Yule (1983b) differentiate between a *transactional* and an *interactional* purpose for communication. Communication which has a transactional purpose aims primarily to transfer information and so is more *message-oriented*, for example news broadcasts and lectures. Transactional listening is often used in situations which require accurate comprehension of a message and where there may be no opportunity for clarification with the speaker, as in the case of public announcements. Communication which is interactional in purpose, on the other hand, exists largely to satisfy the social needs of the participants, for example small talk and casual conversations. Interactional listening is therefore *socially oriented* and highly contextualised. The conversation may include references to features in the immediate environment or to facts which are apparent to both speakers; the primary aim is not to convey information about these but to establish peer solidarity or to negotiate role relationships.

The discourse *mode* in listening is affected by the nature of the setting, or discourse *domain*. This may vary according to the number of speakers, their relationship(s) with one another, their locations (face to face or distant), and also their relationships with the listener or listeners. The CEFR identifies four main domains – *educational, occupational, public* and *personal* (Council of Europe 2001:10); the different discourse modes may be realised within different discourse domains, although there will naturally be some modes which are likely to be more common within certain domains (for example, referential *scientific* within the *educational* domain); conversely, some modes may be unlikely in particular domains (for example, *expressive (of society)* within the *occupational* domain).

Overall text purpose and discourse mode: Cambridge ESOL practice

Since interactional purposes for listening would be extremely hard to embody in a listening test, the purpose for listening in Cambridge ESOL Listening tests is primarily transactional, although the paired nature of the Main Suite Speaking tests allows for interactional listening (Galaczi and ffrench 2011); there is empirical evidence that such interactive speaking tasks measure listening-into-speaking abilities (Nakatsuhara 2011).

Using Kinneavy's (1969) system of text purposes, the primary purposes of most Main Suite Listening texts appear to be informative and expressive (of individual) (see Table 4.7). At lower levels the purpose is almost purely informational, while higher levels are distinguished by an increasing proportion of texts which include an expressive purpose. CPE is the only exam to have a part which could be classified as exploratory in its construct (Part 4). However, although a text may have been classified as having a primarily informational purpose, it is likely to have a number of secondary functions within it. For example, an informative talk in PET Part 3 may also sometimes have a secondary persuasive function, such as giving recommendations, and an interview with an informative/expressive purpose in CPE Part 3 may also include scientific, exploratory or literary functions. In addition, the short texts in Part 1 in CAE and CPE may sometimes have different functions as their primary purpose. The only purpose which appears to be unlikely to appear in a Cambridge ESOL examination is *Expressive (of society)*, which would be likely to be too polemical or culture-specific in its content for an international examination.

Table 4.7 Text purpose and discourse mode: Cambridge ESOL Main Suite Listening tests

Test	Part	Purpose
KET	1	Informative
	2	Informative
	3	Informative
	4	Informative
	5	Informative
PET	1	Informative / expressive (of individual)
	2	Informative / expressive (of individual)
	3	Informative
	4	Expressive (of individual)
FCE	1	Informative / expressive (of individual)
	2	Informative / expressive (of individual)
	3	Informative / expressive (of individual)
	4	Informative / expressive (of individual)
CAE	1	Informative / expressive (of individual)
	2	Informative
	3	Informative / expressive (of individual)
	4	Informative / expressive (of individual)
CPE	1	Informative / expressive (of individual)
	2	Informative
	3	Expressive (of individual)
	4	Exploratory

Source: KET, PET, FCE, CAE and CPE Handbooks for Teachers (Cambridge ESOL 2008b, 2012a, 2012b, 2012c, 2012d).

The four main domains identified in the CEFR – *educational*, *occupational*, *public* and *personal* (Council of Europe 2001:10) – are also represented in the Cambridge Main Suite Listening examinations, where listening texts may be conversations between native speakers, talks in which the speaker is assumed to be face to face with a live audience, announcements or instructions, and radio or podcast recordings. A single speaker will usually be addressing an audience, either face to face (as in a lecture) or at a distance (as in a TV or radio programme). The audience may be known or unknown to the speaker.

The genre and channel of communication will both affect the type of discourse mode used by the speaker. However, as has been pointed out in the previous section, there is not a one-to-one match between genre and discourse mode. Instead, one genre may be realised in a number of different modes according to the individual speaker, the assumed audience and their purpose.

The setting which is most likely to lie at the oral end of the oral–literate continuum is an informal face-to-face conversation between two friends. Here both speakers share a common setting and common knowledge, and the conversation may be accompanied by non-verbal paralinguistic signalling. As a result the conversation may be highly referential, with a great deal of ellipsis. The propositional density may be low, with inclusion of a lot of repetition or word-play, and the language is likely to be at the 'spoken' end of the spoken-written continuum. Many authentic conversations of this type would be extremely difficult to test even through a video recording, and even more so with an audio recording. Futhermore, however authentic the recording itself, the candidate would be in an inauthentic situation as a listener who did not share the speakers' knowledge of the situation. At the other end of the continuum, the language in a formal talk such as a politician's speech read from an autocue is likely to be much more explicit and more overtly structured, with a higher propositional density and with many more features of written language.

Most texts used for testing listening in Cambridge ESOL examinations fall somewhere between these two extremes of formal and informal talk. Texts are edited to remove or gloss deictic or cultural references which could put the candidate at a disadvantage, and also for reasons connected with item construction. This may involve fewer changes to a text from the 'literate' end of the spectrum than to a text from the spoken end. In a comparative analysis of the features in transcriptions of Parts 1 and 2 of PET Listening and CPE Listening using Streaming Speech, Cauldwell (2003:4) notes that 'To the extent that CPE and PET recordings try to mimic scripted genres (radio reports; thoughts for the day; travel news) they are closer to natural. To the extent that they try to mimic social interaction of a domestic nature they are less close to natural.' To support this, Cauldwell identifies among other factors the low occurrence of strategic repetition (see *Grammatical resources: Cambridge ESOL practice*, this chapter) and the discarding and correcting of lexical items.

The above concerns would appear to suggest that the use of semi-scripted texts (Buck 2001:163–165) may be an alternative, since they naturally incorporate more features of spoken language such as more natural pro-nunciation and hesitations, although as Buck (2001:163, 164) observes, can sometimes lead to a certain degree of artificiality. It is also more difficult to ensure that there are sufficient testable points in the text to sustain the desired task length with reasonable spacing between items, and to manipulate the text where necessary to ensure that items perform satisfactorily. Whether such an approach is suitable for at least some tasks may be an area for future research.

Functional resources

The functional description of language presented in the CEFR is mainly pred-icated on illocutionary acts, or the illocutionary *force* of utterances (Green 2011), building on the foundations laid by Wilkins (1976) and the *Threshold* series (van Ek and Trim 1998a, 1998b, 2001). By illocutionary force is meant the question of 'whether certain words . . . *had the force of* a question, or *ought to have been taken as* an estimate and so on' (Austin 1975:99, original emphasis). This is distinct from the literal semantic meaning of the utterance, and may be more or less explicitly present in the propositional form, as in the following three utterances:

1. *Close the window.*
2. *Would you mind closing the window?*
3. *It's rather cold in here.*

The illocutionary forces of the three utterances are the same – requests for someone to close a window – but the utterances are realised as a *direct request*, a *conventionally indirect request* and an *indirect request* (Breuer and Geluykens 2007), according to considerations of appropriacy and the speaker's intended level of force. While the illocutionary force of the direct and conventionally indirect requests can be interpreted from the form of the utterances, the situation is different with the indirect request (or hint), which requires *pragmatic inferencing* (Levinson 1983). The ability to identify and correctly interpret illocutionary acts, realised at different levels of explicit-ness, is a criterial feature of listening proficiency.

To establish context validity in functional terms, listening test developers need to consider both the *types* of function, i.e. the range of speech acts, in terms of their complexity and the *explicitness* with which they are realised, i.e. the range of their manifestations, weighed against the target proficiency level of the test and the typical functions encountered in the TLU domain, when selecting texts and items focusing on the functional dimension of those texts.

The *Threshold* series (Van Ek and Trim 1998a, 1998b, 2001) identify six broad categories of language function. These are, following the terminology preferred in *Vantage* (Van Ek and Trim 2001):

- imparting and seeking factual information
- expressing and finding out attitudes
- deciding on and managing courses of action: suasion
- socialising
- structuring discourse
- assuring and repairing communication repair.

Each of these broad categories contains a wide range of specific functions which are categorised according to whether they are classified as Waystage (A2), Threshold (B1) or Vantage (B2) level.

Functional resources: Cambridge ESOL practice

At KET level, functions exhibited by speakers in listening recordings are mainly in the category of imparting factual information. At this level, functions may be most clearly differentiated by topic, for example talking about the weather, asking for and giving travel information. The grammatical and lexical constraints for this level mean that these functions are realised in the simplest possible ways.

The main functions candidates will meet in PET Listening are drawn from *Threshold* (van Ek and Trim 1998), which also informed the development of the CEFR, and are listed in the *Handbook for Teachers* (Cambridge ESOL 2012d:4). Functional exponents are still limited by grammar and vocabulary restrictions but listening papers at this level tend to include more functions related to expressing and finding out about attitudes. In spite of this, the testing focus at this level is still primarily on factual information, although Part 4 explicitly targets attitude and opinion, as does Part 2 to a lesser extent.

There is no inventory of functions for FCE, CAE or CPE listed in their respective *Handbooks for Teachers*. Functions for FCE are similar to those at lower levels but exponents are more finely subcategorised and complex (Van Ek and Trim 2001:27–28). At CAE and CPE level, in the Listening papers examined there did not appear to be any significant additions to the functional exponents described for Reading, where hypothesising, prioritising and summarising appeared for the first time at this level (Khalifa and Weir 2009:114–5), apart from one instance of hypothesising at CPE level. This may be because the treatment of content in listening texts tends to be at a less abstract level than in reading texts.

Table 4.8 outlines the functional areas from the Threshold series which are targeted by the sample Main Suite tests in Appendix A – a progression can be traced, with some functions targeted at all levels, while some feature only at higher levels:

- *Imparting and seeking factual information* is targeted at all levels. All KET items target this function; the information targeted is naturally simple and includes, for example, numerical information such as times, sums of money and telephone numbers (see items 3, 5, 17, 20, 21, 23 and 25 in the KET sample test, Appendix A). As the levels progress, however, there is an increasing sophistication in both the type of information expressed and the way it is expressed: for example, see Parts 1 and 3, PET sample test, and Part 2 in the FCE, CAE and CPE sample tests (all in Appendix A).
- *Expressing and finding out attitudes* is not targeted in KET, but at all other levels, for example, see item 20, PET sample test; item 26, FCE sample test; item 19, CAE sample test; item 2, CPE sample test (all in Appendix A). The nature of the opinions and the level of directness with which they are expressed provide the progression in difficulty.
- *Deciding on and managing courses of action: suasion* is targeted in all levels from PET upwards, although it is of primary importance for the B level tests (PET and FCE): for example, see item 25, PET sample test; item 1, FCE sample test; item 2, CPE sample test (all in Appendix A). The sample CAE test does not feature this function, although it can appear as a testing focus.
- *Socialising* is not targeted in any Main Suite Listening tests since it is of primary relevance to interactive listening.
- *Structuring discourse* is only explicitly targeted at CPE, where Part 4 focuses on whether opinions are shared by two speakers across turns (see the CPE sample test, Appendix A); as discussed in Chapter 3, this taps into highest levels of cognitive processing, which are appropriate to the C levels.
- *Communication repair* is not targeted in any Main Suite Listening test since the focus is not on interactive listening; it is, however, tested in Main Suite Speaking tests in the collaborative tasks which each level contains (see Galaczi and ffrench 2011).

Table 4.8 Functions targeted in Cambridge ESOL Main Suite Listening sample tests

Language functions	KET	PET	FCE	CAE	CPE
Imparting and seeking factual information	✓	✓	✓	✓	✓
Expressing and finding out attitudes		✓	✓	✓	✓
Deciding on and managing courses of action: suasion		✓	✓		✓
Socialising					
Structuring discourse					✓
Communication repair					

Source: KET, PET, FCE, CAE and CPE Item Writer Guidelines (Cambridge ESOL 2008b, 2012a, 2012b, 2012c, 2012d), sample KET, PET, FCE, CAE and CPE tests (Appendix A)

Grammatical resources

Grammatical features are naturally important in determining the complexity of a test and in contributing to its difficulty, although the complexity of grammar is not the only determinant of difficulty: in listening as with reading, Khalifa and Weir's (2009:118) observation that '[a]lthough longer complex sentences will often be harder than shorter simple ones, if the language used is very elliptical and the lexis used is highly colloquial, short simple sentences may actually be harder to understand than longer sentences' holds true. Moreover, ellipsis and colloquial language are typical features of informal spoken language.

It should, however, be noted that 'grammaticality' is a problematic concept when related to spoken language, since 'spoken transcripts often have frequent occurrences of items and structures considered incorrect according to the norms of standard written English' (Carter and McCarthy 2006:167). The neat parcelling of language into grammatical *sentences* with full clauses which typically characterises writing gives way to a more flexible spoken grammar comprised instead of *utterances* which 'may consist of single words, phrases, clauses and clause combinations spoken in context' (Carter and McCarthy 2006:177). An utterance may not be fully formed or 'correct' when judged against written grammar criteria, so the notion of an *adequately formed* spoken utterance rather than a *well formed* utterance may be more appropriate (McCarthy and Carter 2001). Indeed, the notion that utterances should be well formed in this sense does not stand up to close scrutiny but stems from a relative downgrading of spoken norms due to the historical privileging of written language (McCarthy and Carter 1995). Recursive structures are often replaced by paratactic strings which are more easily processed online by both speaker and listener, distinctive (and, importantly, standardised) grammatical features such as 'heads' and 'tails' (Carter and McCarthy 2006:192–196) are common, and prosodic features such as marked intonation and emphatic stress are often used to delineate and disambiguate utterances which might be ambiguous when written down.

Although listening tests do not face the issue of having to develop grammatical criteria in the way speaking tests do, they do need to take account of the nature of spoken, rather than written, grammar. Spoken grammar differs from written grammar in two broad areas:

1. *Non-systematic differences:* Spoken texts contain grammatical inconsistencies and false starts. These are due to the online nature of the construction of utterances, with speakers often revising their utterances as they are produced, often in accordance with competing internal plans (Baars 1980).

2. *Systematic differences:* Certain grammatical structures which do not generally appear in written English but are common in spoken English,

for example: 'heads' and 'tails'; paratactic linking of ideas rather than embedding of clauses; more flexible word order, and structures spanning turns (Carter and McCarthy 2006). These structures may facilitate online processing of the input, but can also serve specific, often affective, purposes (McCarthy and Carter 1997).

The degree to which a given spoken text will feature both systematic and non-systematic features of spoken grammar will depend on the context and degree of planning, with spontaneous, unplanned conversation containing more non-systematic features than prepared speeches; informal conversations will contain more systematic differences than more formal texts.

Grammar also serves a further function in listening – syntactic parsing is one of the stages of listening comprehension (see Chapter 3 for a full discussion). Listeners make use of their knowledge of syntactic patterns to help them decode the incoming signal. The more predictable the text in grammatical terms, therefore, the easier it is to process. Parsing is a highly sophisticated, probabilistic process among L1 listeners facilitated by chunks and verb patterns (Field 2009a) in which listeners 'can form expectations about the shape a sentence will take; but they may have to revise them as they hear more and more' (2009a:188), although there is evidence that the effect of syntax on word recognition is very limited. None the less, meaning enrichment cannot take place until the input has been parsed at utterance level, meaning that the extent to which the text conforms to a listener's syntactic expectations can influence their level of comprehension (Rost 1990). The grammatical content of a text therefore needs to reflect the reality of the TLU domain for performance on the test to be generalisable to performance in the TLU domain.

In terms of the CEFR, Keddle (2004:49) notes that, as a function-based framework, there is 'not a consistent approach to grammar, or reference to commonly accepted concept areas such as the future, in the CEF descriptors', although concept areas such as 'describe past activities' (A2) and 'narrating' (B1) are inevitably bound up with the grammatical forms necessary to fulfil the functions. The *English Profile* project has begun to identify criterial features of grammar at different proficiency levels in productive terms from a corpus of written learner English (Hawkins and Buttery 2010, Hawkins and Filipović 2012), although criterial features for receptive comprehension, which typically occurs at lower proficiency levels, remain as yet undefined. Furthermore, work needs to be done in terms of spoken, rather than written, grammar for the results to be fully applicable to listening; this needs to be done in relation to the way speech is parsed online by the listener in order to determine criterial grammatical features for listening.

It seems natural to assume that comprehension will ultimately be affected by the relationship between the complexity of the grammatical structures within a text and the listener's familiarity with those structures, and that this will be a greater issue at lower proficiency levels where listeners will neither have been exposed to as wide a range of structures nor have the depth of familiarity with those structures as listeners of a higher proficiency level. This is also likely to be exacerbated by the fact that listeners at lower proficiency levels appear to rely more on syntactic cues than those of higher proficiency levels (and L1 listeners), who rely more on semantic cues (Conrad 1985). Such lower-level listeners will not yet have developed automaticity in processing syntactic structures, which impedes their comprehension by diverting attentional resources. Therefore, the grammatical complexity of a recording needs to be considered carefully, especially when choosing the section of a recording to target with an item – the grammatical complexity should be appropriate for the level of processing targeted by the item.

Grammatical resources: Cambridge ESOL practice

For KET and PET, the range of structures that candidates may be exposed to in Cambridge ESOL tests (including Listening tests) is based on the inventory provided in the *Handbook for Teachers* for each exam, and these in turn are based on Waystage and Threshold levels. Above these levels, candidates are expected to be familiar with the main structures of the language. Levels may here be distinguished in terms of the range of structures used, and the complexity of the sentence structure.

The KET *Handbook for Teachers* (Cambridge ESOL 2012c) specifies the grammatical areas which may be covered. These include sentences containing a main clause only, co-ordinate clauses and a limited range of subordinate clauses – e.g. following certain verbs, relative clauses with who/whose/which and following if/where/where/because. The inventory is not an exhaustive list; candidates may meet other forms but these will not be directly tested. The inventory of grammatical areas covered at PET includes a wider range of subordinate clauses and more complex noun, verb and adverbial phrases. No inventory of grammar items is given for FCE level or above, but according to the FCE *Handbook for Teachers* (2012b:4), at FCE level candidates should 'be able to handle the main structures of the language with some confidence'.

Alderson et al (2006:49) provide four categories of grammatical complexity and it has been suggested that these can be mapped onto Cambridge ESOL Main Suite examinations as follows (Khalifa and Weir 2009:119):

- only simple sentences   KET
- mostly simple sentences   PET
- frequent compound sentences   FCE
- many complex sentences   CAE and CPE

These categories do not map quite so well for listening as they may do for reading due to the differences between spoken and written grammar discussed above.

Similarly, the descriptions given in the handbooks apply to the examinations as a whole, rather than specifically to the Listening papers, and are based on models of written rather than spoken language. In Listening, grammatical complexity of this nature may not always relate directly to variation in difficulty between the levels. Even at KET level, listening texts may include frequent compound sentences, although the individual clauses are short and the links between them transparent, as in the following example from the sample KET test (Appendix A):

> He's worked here in England for ages but he was born in Canada so he speaks French and English.

In addition, even though listening texts at C2 level may be dealing with abstract ideas, this does not mean they always use long, complex sentences with a high degree of subordination to express these ideas, as would be typical in written texts with this type of content. Instead, they may combine chains of clauses with co-ordinators such as 'and' and 'but' rather than using subordination or nominalisation. This helps the listener since co-ordination is more transparent than subordination, and also helps the speaker, who is constructing the chain of propositions clause by clause while speaking. For example, from the FCE sample test (Appendix A):

> Well, a few weeks later, my commanding officer summoned me **and** told me to get changed **and** prepare for a rather unusual photoshoot. **And** you know what?

From the CPE sample test (Appendix A):

> **And** when we remember, we construct pathways in our brains to remake the experience **and**, at a certain moment, it's as if the jigsaw comes together, **and** we'll accept that as the truth.

At high proficiency levels, it has already been observed that difficulty is not necessarily likely to arise from complex grammatical structures, since these tend to be less prominent in spoken language. However, candidates are expected to process stretches of text which reflect rhetorical structures, for example strategic repetition and the use of cleft and pseudo-cleft structures for emphasis as in the following extract from the CPE sample test (Appendix A):

> Naturally, there are all sorts of people working on the project – **some** are passionate about the environment, **some** are into the arts, **some** want to get the schools involved, **but the thing that inspires them all** is a sense of community and wanting to do their very best for it.

Texts may also display other features of speech such as hesitation, or alternatively 'latching', in which there is no gap between participants' (non-overlapping) turns (Liddicoat 2007:113), as in the CPE sample test (Appendix A):

> Simone: But then, if your memories are acts of creativity, it does cast a terrible doubt **on . . .**
> Leo: **. . . on all decision-making.**
> Simone: Exactly.

The grammatical progression across Cambridge ESOL Main Suite Listening tests can be seen in two dimensions. The first dimension represents a move from simple, predictable grammatical structures to more complex structures featuring greater subordination and more sophisticated textual features including focusing structures such as cleft sentences. The second dimension, which partly mitigates increased grammatical complexity, is that candidates can deal with grammatical features specific to spoken language, which do not necessarily conform to neat packaging in terms of standard 'written' grammar.

Since recordings are scripted, however, there is inevitably an inherent degree of artificiality in the linguistic features designed to correspond to natural spoken language. This suggests that from the standpoint of better reflecting natural spoken language, a mixture of scripted, semi-scripted and authentic texts, depending on the context and practicability, may be appropriate, with semi-scripted or authentic texts used where more spoken grammatical features are appropriate – i.e. unplanned, spontaneous speech – and scripted texts for planned/scripted contexts (see Chapter 3 for a further discussion of authentic versus scripted texts).

Lexical resources

One of the main barriers to successful comprehension is a lack of *lexical coverage* of a text, in terms of the proportion of lexis in the running text known by the listener. Although vocabulary size has been found to correlate considerably less well with listening comprehension than it does with reading comprehension (Stæhr 2008), it is still statistically significant and substantial. Stæhr (2009) found that 39% of variance in listening scores among low-level listeners was correlated with vocabulary size, with a figure of 49% at C2 level.

The intrinsic difficulty of a lexical item in a text (Laufer 1997) is not the only factor when considering the difficulty of identifying and understanding the item while listening. Compared to reading, there is a greater likelihood of not understanding a known word which is encountered in a spoken text, for example where the listener knows a word but does not recognise it in connected speech due to mis-segmentation (Field 2003). The connection between knowing a word and identifying it as a known word is therefore more complex than it is in reading, and familiarity interacts with other, non-lexical, factors to determine whether the listener is able to discriminate a word in connected speech. In particular, two issues make this difficult:

1. Spoken language mostly lacks distinct pauses representing word boundaries, in contrast to spaces in written language.
2. There are no standard word forms in connected speech as there are in writing due both to differences in pronunciation of a word as a result of different accents or sentence stress (*have*, for example, can be rendered as [hæv], [həv], [əv] or [v]), and to word-linking features such as assimilation, catenation and elision.

Research on L2 reading comprehension has indicated that 98% lexical coverage provides adequate comprehension of written text (Laufer and Ravenhorst-Kalovski 2010). This figure has been transferred to listening comprehension, and has been used to set vocabulary size targets for L2 learners. However, recent research (van Zeeland and Schmitt 2011) demonstrates that listening to everyday narratives does not appear to require 98% coverage, but rather a coverage between 90% and 95%. Much, however, depends on the goals of the listener and the depth of listening that a task requires. In order to achieve a lexical coverage of 95% coverage of spoken language, a listener needs to know around 2,000 word families (Bauer and Nation 1993) for informal conversation (Nation 2001) and transactional language (Adolphs and Schmitt 2003). The same 2,000 word families, however, provide only 90% lexical coverage of broader unscripted spoken discourse (Nation 2001, Stæhr 2008); here, a vocabulary of 5,000 word families has been shown to give slightly over 96% coverage (Adolphs and Schmitt 2003). In a different context, around 3,000 word families has been shown to give 95% coverage for watching films (Webb and Rodgers 2009). In criterial terms for learners at different levels, the 2,000 word families necessary for 95% coverage appears to be a 'crucial learning goal for low-level EFL learners' (Stæhr 2008:149), at which point an adequate level of listening comprehension is typically reached. In terms of more advanced learners, at C2 level a vocabulary of 5,000 word families appears to be the minimum for adequate performance on the CPE Listening test (Stæhr 2009).

When selecting appropriate texts for listening tests, the frequency of the lexis in the texts must therefore be a primary consideration; the frequency of lexis must be such that a candidate with a typical vocabulary for the level of proficiency targeted by the test will have a sufficient lexical coverage of the text in relation to the listener's goals and the task accompanying the text. Considerations of lexical coverage also strongly suggest the notion of a core vocabulary, or rather core vocabularies, which may vary across modes and spoken/written TLU domains both in terms of size and content (Lee 2001, Nation 2001). There have been attempts to define core vocabularies, such as the *Cambridge English Lexicon* (Hindmarsh 1980) and the *Academic Word List* (Coxhead 1998, 2000) based on frequency of use in authentic texts in specified TLU domains, in order to define the vocabulary needed to achieve adequate text coverage. These lists are based on written, rather than spoken, data, however; in terms of listening, similar exercises based on spoken data would be more relevant. A different approach has been taken in the *English Profile Wordlists* project, which developed word lists typical of learners across the different levels of the CEFR from corpus data obtained from live administrations of Cambridge ESOL examinations, the *Cambridge Learner Corpus*, a corpus of over 42 million words of learner English calibrated to CEFR levels according to usage in productive texts (Capel 2010) and further informed by the 1.2-billion-word *Cambridge International Corpus* of spoken and written L1 English. The English Profile is also primarily based on written data, although in this case there is a spoken element. Such wordlists, provided it can be demonstrated that they are relevant to the mode and TLU domain – and in particular whether written or spoken – can form the basis of principled decisions regarding the lexical content of tests, with the wordlist selected according to the test's purpose to ensure an appropriate level of lexical coverage for the target candidature. The likelihood of comprehension problems arising from lexical factors in the text can be assessed, although the possibility of circularity needs to be borne in mind given that both the source and the application of the data are examination English.

In an EAP context, the notion of academic word lists is not a straightforward one, however. Questions have been raised as to whether the wide variation in use of language across different TLU domains and academic disciplines makes the use of a single, generalised wordlist such as the Academic Word List relevant, or whether different, discipline – and domain-specific wordlists are instead indicated (Hyland and Tse 2007). Whether such a plethora of word lists would be practical for use in large-scale international testing, however, is questionable.

Other considerations not taken into account by text coverage statistics are those of polysemy and, of particular relevance to listening, homyphony. Word frequency counts cover all senses of a word, which may result in a word being classified as high-frequency when in fact the sense used in a text is of a much lower frequency. This is particularly the case at higher proficiency levels, where texts are more likely to contain such less frequent meanings since the understanding of different senses of the same token is a criterial feature of different proficiency levels, for example the verb *keep*, with different senses being typically acquired from CEFR Level A2 (the senses 'to have something permanently' and 'to stay') through CEFR Level B1 ('to continue doing something') up to CEFR Level B2 (12 phrasal verbs) (Capel 2010). The issue is clouded further in terms of homyphony, since word frequency counts do not take account of homyphonous words.

Simply knowing enough words in isolation is not in itself a guarantee of successful comprehension. In listening, an important cue to lexical recognition is when the words occur in a recurrent chunk, so knowledge of chunks is particularly important. As Khalifa and Weir (2009) note, at lower proficiency levels, where the CEFR is defined in primarily functional terms, it is the recognition of patterns of words and their relation to linguistic functions which is necessary. Similarly, particularly at higher proficiency levels the recognition of collocations and multi-word phrases (fixed or semi-fixed) and their attendant composite meanings are of critical importance, as is the recognition of multi-word lexical items such as phrasal verbs at all levels (Moon 1997). Simpson-Vlach and Ellis (2010) identified a core of 'academic formulae', which represent a multi-word complement to the *Academic Word List*; to obtain a true measure of lexical coverage, knowledge of the composite meaning of such phrases as well as individual words should be considered. Further research here would be appropriate in order to determine which of the formulae identified by Simpson-Vlach and Ellis are truly characteristic of academic texts in order to delineate a core of academic-specific items. Martinez and Schmitt (2011) term a multi-word lexical item a *phrasal expression*, defined as a 'fixed or semi-fixed sequence of two or more co-occurring but not necessarily contiguous words with a cohesive meaning or function that is not easily discernible by decoding the individual words alone' (2011:14).

It should further be noted that knowing additional infrequent vocabulary, while making a negligible contribution to text coverage statistics, also contributes to comprehension (Laufer and Ravenhorst-Kalovski 2010). In particular, knowledge of difficult lexis specific to a text has, perhaps unsurprisingly, been shown to have a highly significant effect on comprehension (Mehrpour and Rahimi 2010), which suggests that simple measures of vocabulary frequency can be too crude to determine how comprehension might be facilitated.

It should further be noted that as well as *breadth* of vocabulary knowledge, *depth* of knowledge is an important contribution to comprehension, in particular making a significant contribution to listeners' ability to make lexical inferences (Nassaji 2006). Nation (1990) provides the following multidimensional taxonomy of depth of knowledge of a word:

1. Spoken form of the word.
2. Written form of the word.
3. Grammatical behaviour of the word.
4. Collocational behaviour of the word.

5. Frequency of the word.

6. Stylistic register constraints of the word.

7. Conceptual meaning of the word.

8. Associations the word has with other related words.

This relationship between depth of knowledge and comprehension may well reflect notions of *grammar* versus *lexis* versus *lexico-grammar* in that depth of vocabulary knowledge is linked to knowledge of features such as syntactic patterns and preferred structures associated with lexical items.

As well as the lexical resources required for successful comprehension of the text, lexical resources are also relevant for the written element of the task and, in the case of constructed response items, the response; these issues are discussed in detail in *Response method* (this chapter), so it is sufficient here to mention only that, in a test of listening, incorrect responses due to insufficient lexical resources for reading or writing would constitute construct-irrelevant variance, and therefore the language in both the reading and writing elements should be as simple as possible.

Lexical resources: Cambridge ESOL practice

The CEFR defines lexical competence as knowledge of, and ability to use, the vocabulary of a language (Council of Europe 2001:110). This includes lexical elements such as single word forms and fixed expressions, and also grammatical elements belonging to closed word classes.

The descriptions of vocabulary range in the CEFR differentiate between levels in terms of learner needs and familiarity of topics at A and B levels, with reference to command of idiomatic, colloquial and connotative use of lexis at B level. However, the descriptors tend to focus on productive rather than receptive use. For example, for B1 (Council of Europe 2001:112):

> Has a sufficient vocabulary to express him/herself with some circumlocutions on most topics pertinent to his/her everyday life such as family, hobbies and interests, work, travel, and current events.
> Has sufficient vocabulary to conduct routine, everyday transactions involving familiar situations and topics.

In the CEFR overall listening comprehension descriptors (Council of Europe 2001:66), lexical difficulty is also described as relating to the type of information being processed. The descriptors describe this information in terms of the familiarity of the topic to the candidate, the frequency of the topic, and whether it is concrete or abstract in nature (e.g. 'very basic personal and familiar' at Level A2, 'common everyday or job-related topics' at B1, 'concrete and abstract topics' at B2, and 'abstract and complex topics' at C1). These descriptors are reflected in the topics in Cambridge ESOL

Main Suite tests, which are guided by lists provided in item writer guidelines and handbooks. Personal and everyday topics such as *Clothes,* or *House and Home* appear at KET and PET levels, while more general or abstract topics such as *Language and Communication* or *Psychology* are included at FCE level and above. However, many topics such as *Health*, and *the Natural World* appear at all levels but will involve a broader range of vocabulary and concepts at higher levels. There is naturally a link between some topics and lexical complexity, since it is difficult to discuss topics such as psychology in any meaningful way without introducing more complex, lower frequency lexis. Topics such as health, however, can involve a wide range of lexical complexity depending on the sub-topic and, equally importantly, its treatment.

In addition, the CEFR descriptors specify features of style and register. For example, at C1 level the candidate can 'recognise a wide range of idiomatic expressions and colloquialisms'. At CAE and CPE level this may include a range of phrasal verbs or fixed phrases, although texts are rarely highly colloquial. It is rare to find authentic texts of this nature which are culturally appropriate and of a sufficiently high conceptual level for CAE and CPE and often these do not survive pretesting. The figurative or metaphorical use of language may be part of the key at CAE level, and particularly at CPE level, but only with common expressions which candidates may be expected to know; furthermore, there will be additional information or a glossing of the figurative or metaphorical expression elsewhere in the recording, so a correct response will not depend solely on understanding the expression. This policy is designed to mitigate the additional processing demands imposed by figurative and metaphorical language and possible literal interpretations.

In addition to using the CEFR, Cambridge ESOL Listening tests for KET and PET make use of vocabulary lists which are available to the public on the Cambridge ESOL website *www.CambridgeESOL.org*. These were developed in consultation with external consultants and include vocabulary from the Council of Europe's Waystage (Van Ek and Trim 1998b) specification for KET, and from Threshold (Van Ek and Trim 1998a) for PET, as well as other vocabulary which has been shown by corpus evidence to be high frequency. As well as an alphabetical vocabulary list, they also include lists of word sets (e.g. days of the week), affixes and topics. The lists are updated annually, using the Cambridge Learner Corpus and the British National Corpus. However, they are not exhaustive lists of all words which may occur in a Listening Paper; they represent cores of basic lexis appropriate to the two levels. The proportion of lexis outside the word lists is controlled in line with accepted lexical coverage measures.

At FCE level and above, there are no vocabulary lists. Test takers at higher levels are expected to know the core lexis outlined in the PET word list plus a further range of lexis covering typical contexts, which cannot be exhaustively specified in list form. Professional decisions on vocabulary level are made by Cambridge ESOL staff and by item writers, supported by corpora (in particular the *English Vocabulary Profile* (EVP), which is graded by level). Pretesting also plays an important role here, providing an indication of the lexical suitability of texts both qualitatively (through the written feedback supplied by participating candidates and teachers) and quantitatively (through item statistics). At CPE level, some listening texts may also contain a higher proportion of academic vocabulary as defined by the Academic Word List (Coxhead 2000).

The EVP is growing in importance, providing information at both word and sense level and presenting the level of each meaning of a word with reference to the CEFR. While not providing an exhaustive list of vocabulary in papers at the different levels, the EVP provides support to expert decisions on lexical difficulty on an objective, empirical basis. For the C levels, the Academic Word List (Coxhead 2000) and the Academic Formulas List (Simpson-Vlach and Ellis 2010), plus frequency data on idioms have also been used to inform the content of the EVP.

Lexical resources: analysis of Main Suite Listening papers

In order to gain a better understanding of lexical progression across the five Main Suite Listening papers, a lexical analysis of the listening question papers and tapescript input was commissioned from Norbert Schmitt, an acknowledged expert in the field of second language vocabulary and assessment at the University of Nottingham (UK). Schmitt's findings are reported below; they represent an empirical basis upon which to evaluate the appropriacy of the lexical resources across the five Main Suite examinations in terms of the theoretical considerations and principles of Cambridge ESOL practice described above.

The recordings from five tests were analysed for each of KET, FCE, CAE and CPE, and four for PET (including the sample tests in Appendix A), using *Lextutor* (both Classic and BNC-20) analysis, and tabulated for comparison. An analysis was also conducted of the written lexis used in question papers, the key findings of which are discussed at the end of this section. Table 4.9 below shows the results of the analysis of the listening tapescripts. A number of points can be noted from these results, related to both frequency analysis and type-token ratio.

Using the 95% lexical coverage requirement as a general benchmark for comprehension, we can check whether the level of vocabulary at each Main Suite level is appropriate. At KET level, close to 94% of the vocabulary is from the K1 frequency band, therefore candidates who only have knowledge of this vocabulary should have a reasonable chance of comprehending the KET tapescripts, at least from the lexical standpoint. In lexical terms,

Table 4.9 Results of listening tapescript lexical analysis

Frequency level	KET[a]	PET[b]	FCE[a]	CAE[a]	CPE[a]
K1	93.72%[c]	92.38%	90.23%	87.43%	86.94%
K2	3.53%	4.64%	5.60%	6.05%	5.36%
K3	0.74%	1.16%	1.53%	2.36%	2.50%
K4	0.20%	0.43%	0.68%	1.30%	1.16%
K5	0.29%	0.36%	0.39%	0.63%	0.79%
K6–10	0.22%	0.22%	0.53%	0.92%	1.48%
K11–15	0.03%	0.04%	0.13%	0.22%	0.39%
K16–20	0%	0%	0.08%	0.17%	0.13%
Off-list[c]	1.28%	0.78%	0.83%	0.93%	1.24%
Words	6,890	9,081	17,289	14,937	16,240
Types	902	1,354	2,399	2,612	2,913
Tokens per type	7.64	6.71	7.21	5.72	5.58
Lexical density[d]	0.49	0.47	0.46	0.48	0.47
AWL %	0.13%	0.90%	1.96%	3.05%	3.54%

a. combined analysis of five tests
b. figures from four tests – extrapolating up to five tests would give a Words figure of 11,785
c. percentages for tokens
d. content words divided by total words

candidates at PET level need to know close to 1,500 word families in order to comprehend the PET tapescripts. By FCE level, knowledge of the first 2,000 word families is necessary, but this seems a reasonable expectation at this level. At CAE and CPE levels, it seems reasonable to expect examinees to know a minimum of the first 3,000 word families; this would easily achieve 95% coverage at CAE (95.84%) and is just on the boundary for the CPE (94.80%). However, this is the minimum, and at these two levels, examinees would be expected to know more than 3,000 word families, which should easily surpass 95% coverage. In short, it seems that the frequency distributions of the five level tapescripts are in line with increasing lexical expectations for the Listening papers from KET to CPE level. Here we should note again that simply knowing enough words is a necessary but not sufficient condition for comprehension; the listener also needs to be able to recognise those words in connected speech. It is also worth reiterating that the percentages should not be interpreted rigidly in light of the caveats discussed on page 216 relating to listener's goals and the particular task.

The number of words in the listening tapescripts generally increases with proficiency level, which is to be expected as part of the increasing lexical progression of the Listening papers. As has already been noted in the discussion of text length in this chapter, the exception is FCE. In the papers analysed, this has the longest listening passages of any level. Although difficulty is obviously not synonymous with length, this seems somewhat incongruous, as a normal expectation might be for CPE level to have the longest extended listening input (see *Text length: Cambridge ESOL practice*, this chapter for further discussion of the relationship between text length and difficulty). From an internal Cambridge ESOL perspective, it should be noted that the greater length of FCE tests stems from the eight Part 1 texts (as opposed to three in CAE and four in CPE) and the considerably longer rubrics – all items and options are read in Part 1, for example, whereas this is not the case for CAE or CPE. The actual tested recording passages are longer for CAE (805 seconds) and CPE (893 seconds) than for FCE (794 seconds) (see Chapter 3 for a detailed discussion of recording length).

The number of types required increases systematically as the proficiency levels increase. As with the listening question paper input, this is appropriate for increasing proficiency levels. The 'Tokens per Type' figures do not vary a great deal between the various levels. Likewise, there is no systematic pattern in lexical density across the levels.

The percentage of academic vocabulary (AWL) in the listening passages steadily increases with proficiency level, although in absolute terms it remains at fairly low levels. This is not surprising as the tapescripts contain spoken discourse, which is typically less dense and formal than written discourse, and focus on discourse which is not academic in nature. Nevertheless, AWL vocabulary is not only found in academic discourse but is also a feature of more intellectually demanding discourse generally, and so the increasing levels of academic vocabulary is one indication of the increase in intellectually challenging content at CAE and CPE levels. From an internal Cambridge ESOL perspective, this reflects the purpose of CAE and CPE as tests suitable for academic and professional purposes, and for higher education entry purposes in particular.

The tapescript passages from KET and PET, and to some extent FCE, should focus on General English and should therefore contain low levels of academic vocabulary; this is the case (less than 2%). Conversely, given that CAE and CPE examinees might probably wish to operate in academic and professional contexts, it is worth considering whether these listening passages should include more academic and/or professional contexts, with a corresponding increase in the percentage of academic vocabulary.

The majority of the off-list words (i.e. frequency levels beyond the first 20,000 level) are proper names of locations or speakers mentioned in the listening passages. The location names probably should not pose a problem for examinees, since questions will not assume that candidates have geographical information about these locations beyond what is provided in the tapescript. The issue of names for speakers is perhaps a more interesting case. While these are not tested directly, it is possible that the use of less common names, (e.g. in PET: *Jemma*, *Rolf*) may insert an unnecessary level of difficulty in the exams. It might therefore be worth considering using only common speaker names at all levels.

Question papers

Laufer and Ravenhorst-Kalovski (2010) suggest that 98% coverage is necessary for independent comprehension from reading, while 95% coverage is adequate for comprehension with some guidance and help. Analysis reveals that none of the Main Suite levels meet the 98% requirement. KET approaches the 95% 'with help' coverage figure, but the other tests fall short of this as well. Given that reading the question paper is part of the listening examination, clearly independent comprehension is desirable. From this perspective, it would be desirable to control the frequency of the written prompt material to a greater extent (i.e. 95% or above from K1+K2), particularly in the context of a listening test where incorrect responses due to reading comprehension failure would represent construct-irrelevant variance. However, it is important to note that much of the less frequent (beyond K2) lexis is formulaic language specific to the tests' instructions and rubrics, which enables the writing of brief, precise rubrics (see *Task purpose and rubric*, this chapter). This formulaic language is standardised across all forms of the tests, so well-prepared candidates should be familiar with the lexis through the publically available materials such as sample materials, handbooks and the published vocabulary lists, even when they have not undertaken preparation courses (see Chapter 2 for a discussion of *Examination preparedness*).

Nature of information

Nature of information primarily refers to the level of abstraction in the text. There is evidence that concrete words are accessed more quickly than abstract ones (Kounios and Holcomb 1994), and that this is because they are processed differently by the brain, with both hemispheres of the brain processing concrete words but only the left hemisphere processing abstract words (Binder, Westbury, McKiernan, Possing and Medler 2005); the quicker processing is due to the extra input from the brain's visual system (Kounios and Holcomb 1994). This appears to be reflected in Anderson's (1974) finding that the addition of concrete modifiers to nouns, for example *the huge earth-moving vehicle* rather than *the vehicle*, aid sentence recall (1974).

In a related vein, Hansen and Jensen (1994) found that in the case of EAP lectures, the distinction between *technical* and *non-technical* subject matter has a significant effect on the comprehension of higher level listeners, whose comprehension was lower on the technical subject, but had no effect on the comprehension of lower level listeners.

The CEFR contains criterial features relating to *Overall listening comprehension* in terms of the concrete/abstract nature of texts. For example, the CEFR states that at C1 level, a listener can follow 'abstract and complex topics beyond his/her own field' (Council of Europe 2001:66), while at B2 level they can follow 'propositionally and linguistically complex speech on both concrete and abstract topics' (2001:66). At B1 there is no mention of following abstract topics, while at A2 it is explicitly stated that the user's understanding is limited to meeting 'needs of a concrete type' (2001:66).

Nature of information: Cambridge ESOL practice

At lower levels the nature of information in Cambridge ESOL examinations is certainly predominantly factual. Texts for KET are based on activities common in daily life and involve the communication of simple factual information. At PET level, the texts are still mainly factual, apart from Parts 2 and 4, which include elements of opinion and attitude. However, these elements are still related to a factual topic such as a holiday or a public event. For FCE, a higher proportion of texts may reflect the opinion or attitude of the speaker, but these remain linked to factual or personal topics. At CAE level, the *Item Writer Guidelines* make explicit the link to the ALTE Level 4 (CEFR C1 level) descriptor for listening that candidates can 'cop[e] with abstract *expressions*' (Cambridge ESOL 2006a:5, emphasis added); for CPE, the *Item Writer Guidelines* refer to the fact that C2-level learners 'are expected to comprehend spoken language that is *linguistically and conceptually complex*' (Cambridge ESOL 2009d:5, emphasis added). The *Handbook for Teachers* (Cambridge ESOL 2008b) and *Item Writer Guidelines* (Cambridge ESOL 2009d) distinguish between texts which are primarily factual in nature (used in Part 2) and texts which are more attitudinal (used elsewhere). Examination of the sample CPE Listening test (Appendix A) shows that at this level, although many texts are predominantly factual, there is some inclusion of more abstract material, both in terms of abstract reasoning and abstract nouns: a discussion of the principles of design; a discussion of how memory functions, and evaluation of TV watching habits. The discussion of memory, from the CPE sample test Part 1 (Appendix A) is discussed in Chapter 3 (pages 123–124), while extracts from the other two recordings are presented below:

From CPE sample test Part 1 (Appendix A):

> From the 1960s, which saw groundbreaking design brought to everyday objects like that car, the Mini, and the Trimphone, manufacturers have constantly tried to tempt us with more imaginative designs. But does this emphasis on design bring real benefits, or does a basic product, which does the job at a basic price, serve just as well? In other words, is something like the humble paperclip the ultimate in design?

From CPE sample test Part 4 (Appendix A):

> Claire: [Laughing] It just goes past your eyes like animated wallpaper, doesn't it? But I don't subscribe to this idea that relaxation has to be passive. What strikes me about this kind of TV is that it

> isn't at all stimulating. It just tempts people to take the easy
> way out, slump in front of it and indulge in complete idleness!

The following example from the CAE sample test Part 1 (Appendix A)
shows abstract language, but with the more abstract concepts glossed in less
abstract language:

> At least you recognise the need to get motivated, Alex. That's a good
> start. Any coach will tell you that being psychologically motivated is
> crucial to being the best in sport. Not everyone experiences the same
> kind of motivation and I think there are at least two main kinds. There's
> ego orientation – playing sport because you want to be the winner; or
> task orientation – continually trying to improve your own personal best
> performances.

Content knowledge

There are two types of content knowledge which are salient in terms of
comprehension: *background knowledge* and *subject knowledge*. Variance in
test scores due to differences in either type of knowledge can be considered
construct-irrelevant variance except in cases where it is a reasonable assumption that all candidates should possess the knowledge in question, which may
be the case in tests of English for Specific Purposes, where the test targets
'an interaction between the test taker's language ability and specific purpose
content knowledge . . . and the test tasks' (Douglas 2000:75). Here, the
assumption of subject knowledge is a necessity to draw appropriate inferences regarding listening within the specific TLU domain, where the knowledge would be a pre-requisite and is highly salient.

In an EAP context, prior knowledge of the subject seems to have a greater
effect on comprehension in technical subjects than non-technical ones (Jensen
and Hansen 1995); Chi (2011) found that in the case of EAP lecture listening tasks, topic familiarity not only had a significant effect on comprehension, but that it was a more significant factor than impeding factors within
the recording such as unfamiliar accents and background noise. Schmidt-
Rinehart (1994) found that there is no differential effect of content knowledge
on comprehension at different proficiency levels, meaning that the construct-
irrelevant effect caused by the inclusion of texts with unfamiliar topic content
holds as true at high proficiency levels as it does at low levels. This position
is supported by Tyler (2001) who, in a study comparing comprehension rates
of L1 and experienced L2 listeners with and without topic knowledge, found
that L2 listeners appear to rely more on topic knowledge for comprehension
than L1 listeners do, in that they consume a significantly greater proportion
of available attentional resources without topic knowledge (unlike L1 listeners, for whom there was little difference).

The considerations above indicate that test developers need to consider the issue of topic knowledge carefully in order not to place candidates who do not benefit from such knowledge at a disadvantage compared to those who do, even at high proficiency levels. It is interesting to note, however, that research indicates that repeated listening to a passage may have more effect on comprehension than prior content knowledge (Berne 1995, Long 1990), which suggests that having twice-heard texts may be one way of mitigating the effects of content knowledge (see *Time constraints*, this chapter, for a fuller discussion of once-heard versus twice-heard texts).

One specific problem related to background knowledge is that of tests which display *cultural bias* due to the content of their texts. Behind any text is a presupposed world (Marsen 2006) of facts, concepts and cultural norms, since speakers presuppose a certain degree of shared knowledge and leave unstated certain, often salient, information which it is assumed that the listener knows. Often, it is not possible to fully interpret the speaker's message without recourse to this knowledge. In the context of a listening text, this means that candidates from a different cultural background may be disadvantaged, sometimes significantly, compared to those who share the cultural background knowledge presupposed by the text.

Content knowledge: Cambridge ESOL practice

The CEFR distinguishes between 'areas of most immediate priority' (Council of Europe 2001:66) at A2 and 'familiar matters regularly encountered in work, leisure etc./common everyday or job related topics' (2001:66) at B1. At B2 level the descriptors refer to 'reasonably familiar' (2001:66) topics, or those related to the listener's field of specialisation, while C1 refers to the ability to follow speech on topics 'beyond his/her own field' (2001:66).

Care has to be taken that material does not favour candidates with specialised knowledge of a particular subject, or have content that is too specialised or technical. In addition, care is taken to avoid the use of topics that could become out of date during the test production process (e.g. communications technology). At the same time, the world experience and cognitive level of the target age group must be taken into account, particularly in tests designed especially for school-age test takers (see Chapter 2 for a discussion of issues related to age and cognitive development). In addition, the cultural accessibility of the examination materials must be ensured – candidates may not necessarily be wishing to work or study in the United Kingdom and thus may have no common need to engage with the culture from which their English-language test originated.

Unfamiliar topics which candidates are unlikely to have encountered before are avoided as the candidate has insufficient chance in a listening activity to draw upon a schema associated with a completely unknown topic. The majority of candidates taking Main Suite exams also follow a preparatory course, and will have become familiar with the issues relating to particular topics through texts and activities in coursebooks. At KET and PET levels, content is mainly related to everyday needs, or to situations and topics which a candidate is likely to have direct experience of (see list of topics below). Above these levels, topics become broader and may cover issues that candidates have experienced only indirectly, through discussion or the media. The KET and PET *Handbooks for Teachers* provide lists of topic areas found in each test (Cambridge ESOL 2012c:5–6, 2012d:6), which reflect the limited range of functions and lexis available to lower-level learners outlined in the CEFR descriptors for Overall Listening Comprehension for A2 – 'Can understand phrases and expressions related to areas of most immediate priority (e.g. very basic personal and family information, shopping, local geography, employment)' (Council of Europe 2001:66) – and B1 – 'Can understand straightforward factual information about common everyday or job related topics' (2001:66). For FCE, CAE and CPE, candidates are expected to be able to cope with a wider range of topics. *The Item Writer Guidelines: Information Common to All Papers, FCE, CAE and CPE* (Cambridge ESOL 2006a:8) contains a list of suggested topics which have proved suitable over time, but this list is provided as an aid to item writers (especially new item writers) and is not intended to be exhaustive; for this reason, the list is not made public. Advice accompanying the list includes noting that '[w]hen considering whether a text on a certain topic is suitable for any particular level, the treatment and the language used will need to be taken into consideration' (Cambridge ESOL 2006b:8). For all examinations, feedback on the suitability of the topics covered by recordings is collected from candidates and teachers during the pretesting process, which provides a further check on the suitability of a topic and may prompt re-evaluation or even rejection of material.

The cultural perspective presented in a recording is not only a matter of topic, however, but also of the treatment of this topic; this includes assumptions made by the speaker about the knowledge, attitudes and experience of the listener or listeners. The topics employed are therefore only appropriate if their treatment makes them accessible to the target candidature. A conversation on video games or sport, for example, might appear suitable for a candidature consisting of teenagers and young adults, but could be inappropriate if the speakers shared knowledge, attitudes or experience that the candidates might not have. If the same topic was covered in a talk addressed at a wider audience who were likely to know less about the topic, more information would naturally be glossed or explained by the speaker, making the text more suitable for testing the candidate's listening skills. This is reflected in the *Item Writer Guidelines*; in the case of CAE Listening, for example, it is stipulated that texts should be amended for the purposes of 'glossing/paraphrasing cultural references if they are to be retained' and 'making the content more accessible . . . to the target candidature' (Cambridge ESOL 2007c:24). Differentiation between levels is thus mainly achieved through treatment of topic rather than through the topic itself.

Speakers

Speech rate

Given the online nature of listening, with the listener having to process input as it arrives, it is natural that a faster speech rate will have a detrimental effect on comprehension, since the same cognitive processes need to be completed in less time. Buck and Tatsuoka (1998:132) point out that the ability to process faster text is 'not one simple ability, but more a result of all the other abilities being more efficient, or more automatized'. Research has shown that there is a gradual decline in comprehension until a threshold rate is reached, at which point there is a dramatic fall in comprehension (Foulke 1968, Griffiths 1992). This threshold is naturally lower for L2 listeners than for L1 listeners, although it increases with proficiency.

Typical speech rates naturally vary across discourse modes, with (informal) conversations the fastest at a mean speech rate of around 210 words per minute (260 syllables per minute) (Tauroza and Allison 1990:97). Tauroza and Allison also analysed some lectures delivered to predominantly non-native speaker audiences, which had a mean rate of around 140 words per minute (190 syllables per minute) (1990:7). Since the lecturers had the opportunity to identify through experience an optimal speech rate for the delivery of lecturers to non-native speakers, this may be of significance, although further empirical research would be necessary to confirm this.

Mean speech rates represent a fairly crude figure, of course, with speakers often changing their rate of speech for various communicative purposes, such as slowing down for emphasis or to allow listeners to process important or complex information. In general, speech rate is a function of the communicative purpose of the speaker, the context and the content that the speaker is putting across – they can vary to as high as 400 syllables per minute, 54% faster than the typical conversational mean – for common phrases and clichés (Goldman-Eisler 1954). None the less, over a reasonable stretch of speech, 200 words per minute appears to be the benchmark figure for natural speech, as discussed in Chapter 3.

Variations in speech rate can be caused by either changes in the rate of articulation of speech, but are more often due to an increase in hesitations and pause time – in fact, in practice nearly all variation is due to the latter; Goldman-Eisler (1961:171) found that articulation rate is 'a personality constant of remarkable invariance', with the range of pause time in relation to speech time varying being five times as much as the range of mean articulation rate; this also holds in the case of interaction between L1 and L2 speakers where L1 speakers are modifying their speech rate to aid comprehension (Derwing 1990). As well as allowing the listener more time to process the input, pauses and hesitations also assist the listener to identify word boundaries more easily (see Chapter 3).

The question arises of whether speech rates in listening tests should be modified according to the target proficiency level of a test. The comprehension threshold rates discussed above are for L1 listeners; further research on whether and to what extent the threshold varies as a criterial feature of L2 listening proficiency across different levels may prove instructive, particularly at low levels where the threshold is probably lower than that of natural speech (Griffiths 1992). This is reflected in the CEFR *Overall listening comprehension* descriptors (Council of Europe 2001) at the A1 and A2 levels, which state that listeners can follow speech which is 'very slow and carefully articulated' (A1) or 'clearly and slowly articulated' (A2). Speech rates may therefore have to be reduced at such low proficiency levels, preferably primarily in the form of increased length and frequency of pauses to reflect how natural speech rates vary. At higher proficiency levels, however, speech rates should reflect natural rates since it is a reasonable expectation that candidates can follow natural speech rates, if not necessarily with perfect comprehension; this is reflected by the absence of any mention of speech rate at Level B1 and above in the CEFR *Overall listening comprehension* descriptors (2001:66), which further specify the contexts and types of texts of which the listener would be expected to achieve adequate comprehension at different levels. The *Listening to audio and media recordings* descriptor for B1, however, does mention understanding recorded material 'delivered relatively slowly and clearly' (2001:68), which may reflect the lack of visual support when listening to, for example, radio programmes or podcasts delivered solely through the audio channel. It is precisely this interaction between speech rate, content and channel which defines performance at different proficiency levels.

Ultimately, questions of speech rate need to be determined in relation to the purpose of the test, even at low proficiency levels. It may be the case that a test at a low proficiency level is developed for a TLU domain in which the candidates will not have the luxury of listening to the slow, clear speech described in the CEFR and discussed above; the question for the test developer then becomes one of defining precisely what level of comprehension can be expected of candidates when exposed to speech at a full, natural rate in the TLU domain, and design tasks accordingly. This may involve a more approximate level of comprehension than would be expected from slower, clearer speech, but would lead to more meaningful inferences from test scores than those based on slower speech rates which do not reflect the reality of the TLU domain.

Speech rate: Cambridge ESOL practice

Field's analysis (Table 3.2, Chapter 3) of the five sample Main Suite tests (Appendix A) showed that KET and PET featured slow speech rates, but not outside the range that may be encountered in the TLU domain, while FCE, CAE and CPE featured 'what can be regarded as a natural conversational rate' (page 119). This represents Cambridge ESOL policy, which is in line with the CEFR illustrative scales; in the case of PET it is important to note that the test listening conditions are linked to the criteria for understanding recorded material, where speech rate does form part of the criteria. This perhaps highlights one compromise necessary in standardised large-scale testing using recorded material: the tests are limited in their ability to test listening ability under interactive conditions, where the greater support available to the listener through visual and paralinguistic features, and typically a sympathetic interlocutor, may assist in following faster speech rates. Unfortunately, it is not possible to test interactive listening of this type without introducing considerable threats to validity through non-standardisation of delivery and test content. It is worth noting here that interactive listening does form part of the Cambridge ESOL Speaking tests, specifically in the collaborative tasks they contain (see Galaczi and ffrench 2011 for a discussion of interactive listening in Cambridge ESOL Speaking tests).

Although the recording speeds are comparable to those of natural speech, pretesting feedback from candidates suggests that speed is often seen as a source of difficulty. This could be because they are used to hearing classroom language which may be delivered at a slower speed. However it is also possible that this is due to differences in pause length in unscripted speech and in scripted recordings, as discussed in the previous section. It is also possible that the positioning of pauses is different in texts which have been recorded from a script, where they tend to reflect sense group boundaries, than in unscripted speech, where they may occur within sense groups where the speaker is, for example searching for a word. Both pause length and the positioning of pauses within speech would be interesting areas to investigate further. An initial impression is that speech rate may be no faster than PET, but such pauses are shorter. In addition, Brindley and Slatyer (2002) point out that calculations of average speech rates may fail to reflect variations within these rates at different parts of the text, or variations between rates of different speakers in a text with two speakers.

Variety of accent

A basic consideration of the content of a listening test is the types of accent used in the test delivery. Accents can vary both inter- and intra-nationally, with established 'standard' varieties existing in different countries and a range of regional dialects within those countries. In the case of English, international varieties include, alongside native speaker varieties such as British, American and Australian English, 'new Englishes' such as Hong Kong, Singapore and European Union English (Taylor 2009b). Intranational variation can also vary significantly; in the case of British English, regional accents from London, Liverpool, Cornwall, Glasgow, Cardiff and the Shetland Islands are all different, and all of them differ from 'received pronunciation' (RP). Such variety is the case not only for English and other widely spoken languages such as German, Spanish and Portuguese, but also for languages such as Welsh and Basque, both of which are spoken by fewer than one million people (Taylor 2008).

On the matter of linguistic variation generally, Taylor (2002:19) notes that '[t]he guiding principles . . . must be to do with the test purpose and the underlying construct, including the need to sample content widely but appropriately without significantly disadvantaging any candidate group'. When we relate Taylor's principles to the practice of accents in standardised recorded tests, the question is one of what range of accents to include. There are three broad policies here:

1. To include only 'standard' native-speaker accents (either from one NS country or from a variety of NS countries).
2. To include non-standard regional native-speaker accents.
3. To include non-native-speaker accents.

The answer as to which policy is preferable for a test will be determined by its compatibility with Taylor's criteria of construct, sampling and avoidance of bias.

In terms of the relevance of accents to the listening construct, Field (2000:7) notes:

> It is reasonable to assume, particularly at [high proficiency levels], that an attribute of a competent L2 listener is the ability to process information delivered in a range of native accents; I would extend this to include varieties such as Indian or African English and some of the more frequent non-native accents.

However, Field goes on to caution against the over-ready adoption of too wide a variety of accents. According to *exemplar theory* (Field 2009a:165–167), over time listeners build up a store of records of different words as spoken by different speakers (and hence different accents). Thus, where an accent which candidates are less likely to have been exposed to is featured in a text, and is significantly different from 'standard' accents, those candidates who have had more exposure to the accent will be at an advantage compared to those who have not. Since this is effectively a matter of random chance – the selection of a different accent would result in a different subgroup of candidates being advantaged – rather than a function of the candidates' core language proficiency, it can be considered to be introducing an element of construct-irrelevant variance and should therefore be avoided. This highlights a tension at the heart of the issue of accents within a test – the question of whether candidates' being able to normalise to different accents is part of the construct being tested, particularly for those accents they are likely to encounter within the TLU domain, or whether tests should avoid the potential construct-irrelevant variance outlined above by restricting accents to those they have been exposed to in the past (Taylor 2009b), which are most likely to be standard accents.

The considerations outlined above need to be interpreted in terms of the TLU domain – it could be the case that certain non-standard accents will feature prominently for some tests – but in the case of large-scale international tests without such a specific TLU domain, a narrower range of accents which do not deviate markedly from 'standard' accents would seem preferable. For certain testing contexts, it can be argued that L2 accents are as appropriate as L1 accents, if they are representative of the accents which the candidates are likely to encounter in real-life listening situations in the TLU domain; such contexts might include, for example, tests for air traffic controllers. Taylor (2006) cites the example of IELTS as a case where the TLU domain has evolved, but remained well defined; the original ELTS was designed for study and training in the UK, so contained only British English, while IELTS now includes British, Australian, New Zealand, Canadian and American varieties to reflect its current, broader TLU domain.

In a broader sense, Graddol (2006) notes that L2 English speakers are becoming increasingly common, citing the example of Indian and Singaporean teachers being reclassified as native speakers in many Asian countries (2006:115). This pattern of English as a Second Language (ESL) and English as an International Language (EIL) speakers being the norm to which learners are exposed raises broader questions about the norms against which L2 speakers' – and listeners' – proficiency should be judged, even in tests with less specific TLU domains. There are interesting and potentially significant differences between some ESL/EIL varieties and 'inner circle' (Kachru 1992:38) varieties such as British or American English; Singapore English, for example, is syllable-timed rather than stress-timed (Grabe and Low 2002).

One possible response to the changing nature of English around the world is to adopt the norms of EIL as an alternative approach to modelling accents on a standard L1 accent, a position advocated by (among others) Jenkins (2006) and Leung and Lewkowicz (2006). EIL norms consist of a common core of features among primarily L2 speakers, which may include pronunciations which would be considered to be 'errors' compared with native speaker norms but are commonly used in an EIL context without affecting intelligibility; Jenkins (2006) cites the examples of /d/ and /z/ substituted for /ð/ in *this*, while Jenkins (2002:99) provides a more detailed analysis of the relation between some native-speaker and EIL norms. However, there are considerable problems in defining precisely what this core is, making operationalising such principles problematic at best; Jenkins notes that the EIL core is both limited in scope and 'not alone sufficient to achieve the goal of preventing pronunciation from impeding communication' (2000:96) while Seidelhofer, Breiteneder and Pitzl (2006:22) note that 'more descriptive work on ELF is urgently needed, as this is bound to affect in very significant ways just *what* is, or can be, tested'. Taylor (2008) concurs, going on to note that a description of EIL is some way off and that in any case, reflecting such linguistic diversity 'may be difficult to achieve in large-scale formal, standardised assessment practice' (2008:290). These considerations may not apply directly to listening tests which, unlike speaking tests, do not require an assessment of the input, but none the less remain constraints when the listening test forms a component of a test battery.

Whatever TLU domain a test is targeted at, the constantly changing landscape of English and other languages, often reflecting broader global changes, means that test developers constantly need to reassess the appropriateness of their practice regarding varieties of accent in listening tests. As Taylor (2009b:149) contends, '[p]olicy and practice on test content and the contextual features of test tasks may need to change over time as the surrounding linguistic landscape itself evolves'.

Variety of accent: Cambridge ESOL practice

Taylor (2006:56) outlines the principles which guide Cambridge ESOL policy towards language varieties, which includes considerations of accents:

> For testers, especially providers of large-scale, high-stakes English proficiency tests, issues of quality and fairness must be paramount. Quality and fairness therefore provide the background against which to consider policy and practice relating to varieties of English.

In light of the discussion above about the serendipitous nature of exposure to less frequently encountered accents, this indicates a cautious policy towards the range of accents used in Cambridge ESOL tests. For example, the PET Listening *Item Writer Guidelines* (Cambridge ESOL 2008e: state that:

> Candidates can expect to listen to Standard English in a variety of accents (i.e. not dialectal variations) as spoken by native speakers and non-native speakers approximating to the norms of native speaker

accents. Varieties of English, e.g. US, Australian, etc are used as appropriate to the context. The speech is at a relatively natural speed appropriate to the context.

In other words, there may be a variety in terms of national accents since, as Taylor (2006:57) notes:

> Cambridge ESOL tests are designed to provide globally recognized certification of English language proficiency. It is therefore reasonable that the type of language represented in our tests and anticipated from our candidates should reflect varieties of English that enable them to function in the widest range of international contexts rather than a single, more restricted local context.

However, regional accents which may potentially cause problems and bias due to their unfamiliarity to many candidates are not used. In practice, this means that listening tests may contain some recordings with 'light' regional accents but 'strong' regional accents (and dialectal variations) are not used, nor are non-native speaker accents; 'light' and 'strong' here are to be interpreted as meaning that they are similar enough to 'standard' accents to be accessible to candidates with little or no previous exposure to them. The inclusion of an untested stretch of text at the beginning of a recording is designed to assist candidates in normalising or 'tuning in' to the new voice or voices as well as setting the scene and introducing the topic. At the time of recording, the suitability of an accent is determined by expert judgement on the basis of experience of which accents are appropriate for a given level. Whilst this does leave room for interpretation and non-standardisation of accents, the suitability of the accent is ultimately determined by the statistics and feedback from candidates and teachers gathered during the pretesting process.

Sociolinguistic considerations

There are a variety of social factors which exert influence on the register of language used on a given occasion. These factors can be broadly classified under three headings:

1. *Individual speaker characteristics*, including gender, age, cultural background and socio-economic status (Anderson, Brown, Shillcock and Yule 1984, Hudson 1996).
2. *Relationship between speaker(s) and listener(s)*, including considerations such as acquaintanceship and power relations.
3. *Contextual features of the speech event*, including formality, degree of rituality, the potential for conflict, etc.

These features interact to determine the variety of language (e.g. standard or dialect, restricted code or elaborated code) (Anderson, Brown, Shillcock and Yule 1984), the degree of directness and recourse to politeness strategies, particularly in the case of face-threatening acts (Breuer and Geluykens 2007, Geluykens and Kraft 2007, O'Donnell 1990, Ogiermann 2007), discourse management, such as turn-taking (Gallois and Markel 1975), and how attitudes are encoded and interpreted (Elliott 2008). In terms of observable variables for testing purposes, these factors manifest themselves in the actual realisation of language functions (*Functional resources*, this chapter), and consequently have implications for the proficiency levels at which candidates can be expected to identify and interpret those functions. This *sociolinguistic competence* (Hymes 1972) is a key element of language proficiency.

In testing terms, this means that the range of variation in language in the test due to sociolinguistic factors will often need to be restricted at lower levels, especially when functions are targeted, which entails a certain artificiality in the language. The CEFR suggests that at proficiency levels up to B1, 'a relatively neutral register is appropriate, unless there are compelling reasons otherwise' (Council of Europe 2001:120). As proficiency levels increase, candidates are able to interpret more natural texts, and the targeting of the candidate's awareness of differing degrees of sociolinguistic variance becomes a criterial feature at Level B2 and higher. Table 4.10 outlines the progression of sociolinguistic appropriateness across the six CEFR levels. As well as the ability to cope with different registers, other criterial features include the ability to handle politeness conventions, which is first mentioned at B1 level (although formulaic polite forms are mentioned at A1 level); at higher levels, the ability to deal with idiomatic expressions, colloquialisms and slang is of importance, and is first mentioned at C1 level. There is a certain amount of conflation of receptive and productive criteria in Table 4.10, such as 'mediate effectively between . . .' for C2, while the vast majority of the lower level descriptors refer to production; these points suggest that further work needs to be done to identify receptive sociolinguistic criteria for listening.

It should also be noted that 'most of the descriptors [of the CEFR descriptive scale for sociolinguistic appropriateness] lack an empirical basis' North (2008:51), suggesting that they need to be interpreted with caution and that this is an area for further research. While the descriptors for A1 and A2 are reasonably well defined in terms of the simple, typically formulaic acts they refer to, there appears to be increasing looseness as proficiency increases; descriptors such as 'appreciates fully the sociolinguistic and sociocultural implications of language used by native speakers and can react accordingly' (C2) and 'can sustain relationships with native speakers without unintentionally amusing or irritating them or requiring them to behave other than they

Table 4.10 Sociolinguistic appropriateness and the CEFR

	Sociolinguistic appropriateness
C2	Has a good command of idiomatic expressions and colloquialisms with awareness of connotative levels of meaning. Appreciates fully the sociolinguistic and sociocultural implications of language used by native speakers and can react accordingly. Can mediate effectively between speakers of the target language and that of his/her community of origin taking account of sociocultural and sociolinguistic differences.
C1	Can recognise a wide range of idiomatic expressions and colloquialisms, appreciating register shifts; may, however, need to confirm occasional details, especially if the accent is unfamiliar. Can follow films employing a considerable degree of slang and idiomatic usage. Can use language flexibly and effectively for social purposes, including emotional, allusive and joking usage.
B2	Can express him or herself confidently, clearly and politely in a formal or informal register, appropriate to the situation and person(s) concerned. Can with some effort keep up with and contribute to group discussions even when speech is fast and colloquial. Can sustain relationships with native speakers without unintentionally amusing or irritating them or requiring them to behave other than they would with a native speaker. Can express him or herself appropriately in situations and avoid crass errors of formulation.
B1	Can perform and respond to a wide range of language functions, using their most common exponents in a neutral register. Is aware of the salient politeness conventions and acts appropriately. Is aware of, and looks out for signs of, the most significant differences between the customs, usages, attitudes, values and beliefs prevalent in the community concerned and those of his or her own.
A2	Can perform and respond to basic language functions, such as information exchange and requests and express opinions and attitudes in a simple way. Can socialise simply but effectively using the simplest common expressions and following basic routines. Can handle very short social exchanges, using everyday polite forms of greeting and address. Can make and respond to invitations, suggestions, apologies, etc.
A1	Can establish basic social contact by using the simplest everyday polite forms of: greetings and farewells; introductions; saying please, thank you, sorry, etc.

Source: Council of Europe (2001:122)

would with a native speaker' (B2) seem somewhat less than rigorously defined and would be highly problematic to operationalise for testing purposes. Furthermore, the conflation of being able to both 'perform' and 'respond to' functions in a defined manner at the same level without acknowledging any likely developmental lag between reception and production certainly merits close further research.

Sociolinguistic considerations: Cambridge ESOL practice

It has already been established that social factors may include individual speaker characteristics, relationships between speakers and listeners, and contextual features of the speech event. Cambridge ESOL Listening test items are unlikely to focus on sociolinguistic or sociocultural implications of language. Recordings for Main Suite Listening exams include a mixture of monologues and interactive texts. Candidates are informed in the rubric at the beginning of each task whether the task involves one or more speakers. In most cases, interactive texts have two speakers, one male and one female, to allow clear distinction between speakers' voices.

Relationships may include the relationships between the speakers in interactive texts, or the relationship between the speaker(s) and the assumed listener(s). These are also linked to contextual features of the speech event. The rubric usually establishes who the speakers are, and often also establishes the relationship between them, as well as the basic context. For example, from the PET sample test (Appendix A):

> You will hear a man called Karl, and his wife Jenny, talking about a holiday they have just had.

From the CAE sample test (Appendix A):

> You overhear a sportsman called Alec talking to his coach.
> You hear part of a radio programme in which a reporter called Tony Beesley is talking about a museum located in a castle.

From the CPE sample test (Appendix A):

> You hear part of a talk in which a scientist, Dr Engle, is describing a project designed to improve water quality.

The listening may be presented as an actual recording – for example, part of a radio programme, a podcast, or a recorded telephone message, in which case the candidate is in the position of the assumed listener. The same is true for talks which as assumed to be given to a live audience – for example, in a lecture theatre.

Number of speakers

The number of speakers is thought to affect the difficulty of a text (Bejar, Douglas, Jamieson, Nissan and Turner 2000). This could be due to several reasons. Firstly, as noted in *Order of items* (this chapter), candidates need more time to normalise to the different speakers' voices; there are also the questions of distinguishing between speakers and switching focus from one to another. Furthermore, very little is known about how listeners normalise to voices in a foreign language, and tasks with multiple speakers may penalise certain linguistic groups or individuals who find it difficult to distinguish between English voices in terms of pitch, loudness or speech rate (Field 2000), so test developers need to ensure that it is as easy as possible for candidates to distinguish between speakers. Since it is easier to distinguish between a male and a female speaker (Weir 2005a), it makes sense for dialogues to feature one speaker of each gender, although this naturally has a certain limiting effect on the possible range of content of the text. Where there are more than two speakers, it is important to ensure that they are clearly identifiable to prevent confusion of a sort which would not be present in a typical real-life listening situation, except perhaps for a conference telephone call (should this be part of the TLU domain, a different policy might be in order). For tests presented via a video format, however, distinguishing between speakers naturally becomes less of a concern, since candidates are able to use the visual channel as well as the audio channel to assist them.

Ultimately, the appropriate number of speakers for a text is a question to be determined primarily by the TLU domain, although the considerations outlined above represent practical constraints where a large number of speakers might otherwise be desirable. A business TLU domain, for instance, might imply the desirability of a meeting-type listening task with several speakers putting over ideas and opinions, as might an EAP test in the context of a seminar. But without the visual element to assist the listener in following proceedings this may well simply prove too confusing in practice, once again reminding us of the practical limitations of language testing.

Number of speakers: Cambridge ESOL practice

Interactive texts are likely to identify more features of spoken language and candidates may have to listen to identify features such as agreement, disagreement and how meaning is negotiated between speakers. These are listening skills which candidates will need to follow conversations in the real world. However, difficulty may also arise in listening to audio recordings with several speakers if a candidate is unable to identify who is speaking, particularly if performance of a task involves identification of speaker(s). The use of speakers of different genders in interactive texts to overcome this problem has already been mentioned. Candidates will hear a range of voices during the exam, but this range is achieved through including a number of different recordings rather than through multiple voices in one recording.

The number of speakers in each test part is summarised in Table 4.11. The only part of any test which may feature more than two speakers is CAE Part 3, which may constitute an interviewer with two interviewees. When there are two speakers, a male and female speaker are chosen to assist the candidate in identifying speakers; where there are three speakers in CAE Part 3, the two speakers of the same gender are voiced by actors with easily distinguishable voices. The pretesting process helps to ensure that multiple speakers do not cause the candidates difficulty, both through objective statistical analysis of the difficulty of the items in the task and through feedback gathered from candidates and teachers participating in pretesting.

Table 4.11 Number of speakers in each test part for Main Suite Listening tests

Test	Part 1	Part 2	Part 3	Part 4	Part 5
KET	2	2	2	2	1
PET	1 or 2	1 or 2	1	2	n/a
FCE	1 or 2	1 or 2	1	1 or 2	n/a
CAE	2	1*	2 or 3	1	n/a
CPE	1 or 2	1*	2	2	n/a

* May feature a second speaker providing a short introductory prompt but otherwise not contributing to the discussion

Source: KET, PET, FCE, CAE and CPE Handbooks for Teachers (Cambridge ESOL 2008b, 2012a, 2012b, 2012c, 2012d)

Conclusion

In this chapter we have discussed multiple aspects of listening test texts and tasks which affect context validity as laid out in Weir's (2005a) socio-cognitive framework for test development and validation, and we have analysed the elements of Weir's taxonomy of contextual task parameters for listening tests. The 2005 taxonomy has been subjected to detailed scrutiny in the light of more recent theoretical and empirical research and, as a result, minor refinements have been made: we have broadened the scope of the aspects of *acquaintanceship* and *gender* to cover the more general, and highly interrelated, *sociolinguistic considerations*. We have seen how the identification of suitable criteria for a listening test depends on various factors, of particular importance being the target proficiency level and the TLU domain. Within these parameters, we have identified criterial features appropriate to different proficiency levels and TLU domains; we have catalogued Cambridge ESOL practice with regard to these parameters and described the manner in which Cambridge ESOL treats them in the development of its tests in general and the Main Suite tests in particular.

In terms of criterial features at different proficiency levels, the need for features of both text and task to vary across levels has been discussed. Texts need to be selected in light of the demands they make of the candidate and whether those demands are appropriate at the proficiency level in question; tasks need to be representative of typical TLU-domain tasks and reflect the Can Do statements of the CEFR for the appropriate level and be presented in a manner which reflects what the candidate can reasonably be expected to cope with in terms of the secondary channels (i.e. reading and writing) at the target proficiency level.

At Cambridge ESOL, detailed Item Writer Guidelines are produced for each test in order to ensure that texts and tasks conform to appropriate parameters of context validity and meet the criterial features for the test's proficiency level and TLU domain. During the question paper production cycle, texts and tasks are subjected to scrutiny by expert judgement against the criteria laid out in the item writer guidelines, before undergoing pretesting and statistical analysis at item level to ensure their performance is acceptable. After appropriate revisions (and repeated pretesting where necessary), tasks are submitted for test construction and inclusion in live tests. This process is detailed in Appendix D.

This concludes the discussion of aspects of *a priori* validation – considerations of cognitive and context validity. Attention will now turn to *a posteriori* validation – post-administration analysis based upon live administration data – beginning with scoring validity in Chapter 5. Certain elements of scoring validity, specifically reliability, have already been touched upon in the discussions of *Response format*, *Weighting* and *Time constraints*; these will now be examined in depth along with other relevant aspects of scoring validity in relation to tests of listening in general and the Cambridge English Listening tests in particular.

5 Scoring validity

Ardeshir Geranpayeh
Cambridge English Language Assessment

Introduction

Previous chapters have considered test takers' characteristics, cognitive validity and contextual validity of the Cambridge ESOL examinations with reference to a socio-cognitive framework.

This chapter concentrates on the scoring process itself although its inter-connectedness to other aspects of validity within the socio-cognitive framework is acknowledged. Khalifa and Weir (2009) have already argued that although the various elements of the socio-cognitive model are presented separately, there is a 'symbiotic' relationship between cognitive validity, context validity and scoring validity which in turn constitute what is frequently referred to as construct validity:

> Scoring validity is concerned with all aspects of the testing process that can impact on the reliability of test scores. It accounts for the extent to which test scores are based on appropriate criteria, exhibit consensual agreement in marking, are as free as possible from measurement error and bias towards any cohort, are stable over time, and engender confidence as reliable decision-making indicators (2009:143).

Scoring validity is important because it indicates the replicability of the test scores under various conditions; if it is not possible to depend on the consistent reporting of student scores, it matters little that the tasks developed are potentially valid in terms of both cognitive and contextual parameters. The more reliable the scores are, the more confidence score users can have in using those scores for making important decisions about test takers. Inconsistent test scores and unsystematic or ill-conceived procedures for grading and awarding can all lead to a reduction in scoring validity and increase the risk of construct-irrelevant variance. That is why examination boards must devote considerable attention and resources to all aspects of scoring validity.

This chapter will focus not only on factors that influence the suitability of test material for listening tests from a scoring validity perspective, such as *test difficulty* and *internal consistency,* but also on statistical procedures which would help mitigate any potentially negative effects resulting from the influence of unwanted variables such as *item bias* on test scores. The discussion begins with test difficulty in the context of Classical Test Theory (CTT) where attention is given to item facility and discrimination, which will be explained shortly. This is followed by consideration of the use of Item Response Theory (IRT) in addressing test difficulty, together with an explanation of item bias by means of differentiating item functioning techniques and of how to control its impact on scoring validity within listening tests. The notion of *reliability* as one aspect of test quality will be examined in terms of its definition, its importance in listening tests, different types of reliability and how they are measured, as well as ways of reporting test reliability to users in conjunction with reporting Error of Measurement. The relationship between scoring validity and communicative language tests will be explored and the mechanism for setting cut scores for listening (and other skill-based) components to contribute to an overall language test grade will be discussed. Figure 5.1 summarises all the key parameters which influence scoring validity.

Figure 5.1 Scoring validity parameters

SCORING VALIDITY
• Test difficulty
o   Item facility
o   Item discrimination
o   Item difficulty
• Item bias
• Internal consistency
o   Reliability
o   Internal consistency coefficients
o   Composite reliability
o   Marker reliability
o   G-theory
o   IRT based reliability
• Error of Measurement
o   Conditional SEM
• Grading and awarding
o   Score Reporting

Test difficulty

One of the most important issues in test construction is the determination of test difficulty for a given audience. Item writers usually think of an intended test taker level when they construct their items but they can never be sure how difficult their tasks are until they are taken by real candidates. Test difficulty is usually determined by means of some statistical analysis of candidates' response data using a test theory. Allen and Yen (1979:56) describe a test theory 'as a symbolic representation of the factors influencing observed test scores which is described by its assumptions'. In essence, a test theory, as

McDonald (1999:9) puts it, 'is a collection of mathematical concepts that formalise and clarify certain questions about constructing and using tests, and then provide methods for answering them'.

There are two widely used test theories in language assessment which complement each other: CTT and IRT. CTT is a theory of measurement error which describes how errors of measurement can influence the observed scores of a test, including a listening test. It is customary to consider Spearman (1904) as the originator of CTT. Gulliksen (1950) standardised the approach in more detail but, as Haertel (2006) reports, the most comprehensive treatment of this theory remains that offered by Lord and Novick (1968) in their publication *Statistical Theories of Mental Test Scores*. According to CTT, the *observed score* (i.e. the score that a candidate gets if we add up the number of correct answers they give to the items on a test) is comprised of two elements: the *true score* and the *error score*.

The first element is the *true score* – that is, the score the candidate would get if the listening test was a perfect reflection of the ability to be measured. Unfortunately this is far from the reality. Inevitably, part of the score for each individual will reflect something other than what the test is intended to measure. There are a number of reasons why a very able candidate may get a listening test item wrong even when they know the right answer. Perhaps they misunderstood the instructions or inadvertently clicked on the wrong option in a computer-based test, or perhaps the marker made a mistake. It is probable for a low ability candidate to make a lucky guess and get an item right, even when they do not know the answer. Any factor that causes a difference between the observed score and the true score is considered to be *error*, which constitutes the second element in the observed score. This relationship can be shown in Equation 1 where X is the observed score, T is the true score and E is the error:

Equation 1: $X = T + E$

In more technical terms, the observed score variance consists of both true score variance and error variance. The tester's objective is to maximise the true score element and minimise the error. It is assumed that the variability of the observed score, X, is the additive combination of the variability of the true score and the error as seen in Equation 2:

Equation 2: $\text{variance}(X) = \text{variance}(T) + \text{variance}(E)$

CTT is a simple yet powerful model for measurement. It has three basic assumptions. Assumption One states that an observed score in a test is the sum of two parts known as (i) the true score and (ii) the error score or error of measurement as shown in Equation 1. Assumption Two states that the expected value (ξ) or population mean of an observed score is the true score as expressed in Equation 3. The true score is defined as the mean observed score if the test was administered to the same population multiple times.

Equation 3: $\xi(X) = T$

This implies that the errors are evenly distributed, i.e. that they cancel out over repeat measurement. Hence, the observed score is expected to be the same as the true score. Assumption Three states that the error scores and the true scores obtained by a population of examinees on one listening test are uncorrelated as expressed in Equation 4, where ρ(Greek Rho) is correlation.

Equation 4: $\rho ET = 0$

This assumption is quite important. It assumes that the error in CTT should have no meaningful relationship with the true score. The error, according to CTT, happens independently in the test at random. If, however, there was a systematic error in the test correlation other than zero between the error and the true score in a listening test then the causes of the error need to be identified. Since this condition is hypothetical, it cannot be objectively evaluated. What one has to do in constructing a listening test is to avoid errors. This will be followed up in the discussion of *item bias* later in this chapter.

CTT is commonly used for the analysis of listening test items. Item analysis provides a way of measuring the quality of test questions, i.e. seeing how appropriate they were for the test takers. Item analysis also enables a means of quality assurance of materials prior to live use in different listening test instruments with prior knowledge of how they are going to perform.

To see whether the candidates and a set of listening test items are well matched, the candidates' performance on the test needs to be investigated. By analysing their responses using CTT, it is possible to build up a picture of how well the listening test worked for that population: which parts of the test are contributing to overall test information and which parts are not providing useful information because they are too easy, too difficult or posing the wrong kind of question. The most commonly used statistics in CTT are *item facility* and *item discrimination*.

Item facility, otherwise known as the p-value, is simply the proportion of candidates who get an item correct, as shown in Equation 5; the higher this value is, the easier the item.

Equation 5: $p = \dfrac{N_{correct}}{N_{total}}$

Item facility is a useful piece of information which enables test constructors to gauge their listening test at the right ability level. Item writers generally expect 50–60% of their target candidates to get the item correct, as this is where maximum information may be available to provide an estimate of candidates' listening ability. According to Thompson and Levitov (1985:164–165) 'items tend to improve test reliability when the percentage of students who correctly answer the item is halfway between the percentage expected to correctly answer if pure guessing governed responses and the percentage (100%) who would correctly answer if everyone knew the answer'. Items that are too easy or too difficult provide little information to the overall listening test as either the majority of candidates will get them right or wrong, respectively. As a general rule, item facility values between 0.35 and 0.85 are deemed to be acceptable for listening test construction purposes.

A second important piece of information provided in CTT is item discrimination. Measures of item discrimination show how successfully a listening test item distinguishes between higher and lower ability candidates. Item discrimination is usually defined in one of two ways: by explicitly dividing the candidates into high-scoring and low-scoring groups and comparing their relative performance, or by correlating scores on an individual listening item with total scores on the listening test. The former approach produces a discrimination index which is simply calculated by subtracting the facility value of the lowest scoring group of candidates from that of the highest scoring group: $p_{high} - p_{low}$. However, looking at the correlation between a candidate's performance on a single listening item and their performance on all items in the listening test is a better measure of discrimination. This is often achieved by calculating the point-biserial correlation, i.e. establishing whether those people who answer the item correctly also score highly on the rest of the test. Discrimination values between 0.30 and 0.85 typically indicate a good level of item discrimination.

One of the major shortcomings of any CTT analysis is that it is purely descriptive and sample dependent. It only relates to how well a candidate or group of candidates has performed on a particular listening test on a particular occasion. Using CTT means that it is not possible therefore to predict with any degree of accuracy how well a candidate who has taken one listening test will perform on another. A different test theory, IRT, can offer a way round this problem by providing a mathematical model that places the performance of candidates and the difficulty of items on the same probabilistic scale. In an IRT model the probability of giving a correct response to an item is defined as shown in Equation 6:

$$\textbf{Equation 6: } p = c + \frac{1 - c}{1 + \exp(- a(\theta - b))}$$

In this equation a represents the 'discrimination', b represents the 'difficulty' of the item, c models the effects of 'guessing' and θ is the ability of the candidate. If one decides to believe that a test is not prone to guessing parameters due to the kind of productive item types used in the test, the above formula can be reduced to the version shown in Equation 7.

$$\textbf{Equation 7: } p = \frac{1}{1 + \exp(- a(\theta - b))}$$

Equation 7 is the one-parameter logistic model (Rasch) for estimating item difficulty which is often used in a large scale item banking approach to test construction. α in this case is a scale constant determining the units of θ and b is the location parameter of the difficulty of item. Items with larger values of b are more difficult; those with smaller values are easier. Later in this chapter Rasch difficulty is used as a synonym for 'item difficulty'. There are many advantages in using a Rasch model in test construction, some of which are beyond the scope of this chapter.

A word of caution is appropriate here. All statistical discussions around item difficulty in this chapter are relevant to the analysis of candidates' actual responses to listening items; that is, how difficult listening items were found by candidates relative to other listening items in the test. The item difficulty hence calculated is a reflection of the ranking of listening items in terms of their statistical difficulty. Such difficulty may not necessarily relate to the conceptual difficulty, cognitive or contextual, of the listening items. It may be possible that two listening items of the same cognitive demand or contextual clues might be ranked differently in terms of their statistical difficulty due to variations in test prompts, ambiguous rubric, bad recording or poor administration. Similarly, there can be very easy (statistically) listening items of a cognitively difficult task and hard (statistically) items of a cognitively easy task. See the discussion of item difficulty of recorded material in Chapter 3 for examples of such tasks. The outcome of test difficulty analysis is to allow item writers to review their listening items and improve their quality if various statistical parameters of listening tests do not conform to expectations of the item writers. The next section brings practical examples of how to interpret the outcome of test difficulty analysis.

Test difficulty: Cambridge ESOL practice

Cambridge ESOL uses a Local Item Banking System (LIBS) for Listening test construction where all test items are calibrated to a common scale of difficulty linked to the Common European Framework of Reference for Languages (CEFR) (Council of Europe 2001). See Beeston (2001) and Marshall (2006) for descriptions of LIBS and its development. Figure 5.2 shows a typical Listening test production cycle of test items in Cambridge ESOL using LIBS (see also Appendix C). As can be seen from the test production cycle, all proposed listening items are first reviewed in pre-editing meetings to ensure that they comply with test specifications for a particular Listening test. The amended items are then captured in LIBS and turned into pretest listening tasks. The tasks will subsequently be turned into pretest bundles which resemble the format of a live Listening test. The Listening pretest bundles, together with other objective skills pretests such as Reading

Figure 5.2 Listening test construction cycle

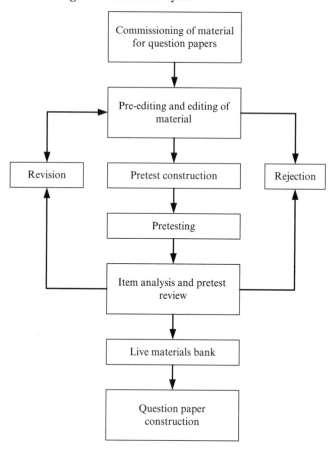

and Use of English, will be sent to a representative sample of test takers for trialling. Once the listening answer sheets have been returned to Cambridge ESOL and processed by markers, several statistical analyses will be carried out on the candidate response data. Both CCT and IRT statistical characteristics for the pretested items will be loaded into LIBS. Content experts will then examine the suitability of the pretested items using the statistical information attached to them. If the values are within the acceptable range for a given test, the calibrated items will be assigned as ready for use in a live Listening test. If, however, the statistical values of the pretested items fall outside the acceptable range, then the items may either be sent back for further exposure in another pretest or they may be rewritten for a new trial. This section will report on various statistical characteristics which measure the difficulty of Listening test items prior to their live use.

To determine the test difficulty, the Listening pretest is analysed as a whole to explore the relationship between the test material and the candidates. This is done to find the answers to two key questions:

- Is the difficulty of the Listening test appropriate to the level of the candidates?
- Does the test discriminate between lower- and higher-ability candidates?

With regard to the first question, item facility is estimated by counting the number of correct responses in relation to the total responses for an item. For a Listening test as whole, an overall item facility of 0.60–0.70 is desirable. Of course the items within a Listening test will vary in range in terms of their individual item facility. Values above 0.90 indicate items that are too easy and those below 0.10 suggest items that are too difficult for the target candidates. Such items will be avoided in live tests as they will add little information about the candidates' ability level.

Using a Rasch model the difficulty of listening items is also estimated in logits and converted to a scale of 0–100, referred to in Cambridge ESOL as Rasch difficulty within the Common Scale of difficulty. This is achieved by the use of anchoring techniques that link the pretest items of unknown difficulty to the common scale by using anchor items of known difficulty administered at the same time.

Point biserial correlation is also used as a means of estimating the item discrimination. A discrimination value of 0.35 to 0.85 is typically deemed to be acceptable for test construction. In practice, however, lower or higher values may sometimes be tolerated for some Listening test items if a particular item is part of a multi-item task where the statistical parameters for the other task items in the set fall within the acceptable range. It is often the case that revising a single listening item within a complex Listening test task may actually have a negative impact on the difficulty of other items. Content experts will carefully scrutinise the set of test items and their statistical characteristics to judge the advantage of retaining an out-of-range item within a task as opposed to revising it with some potential impact on the difficulty of other items.

In practice a minimum of 250 candidates is generally used for determining test difficulty parameters using a Rasch model. Table 5.1 illustrates a set of summary statistics for a live Listening paper of 30 items.

In this table, the second column indicates the number of test responses used in the analysis, the third column shows the number of candidates who answered the item correctly, the fourth column demonstrates the percentage of candidates getting the item right (Facility), the fifth column represents the item difficulty on the Cambridge ESOL Rasch scale and the sixth column shows the point biserial correlation (discrimination) for each item

Table 5.1 CTT and IRT analysis showing item statistics of a typical Listening test

Item	# Tried	# Right	Facility % Right	Difficulty Rasch	Item* test correlation Point biserial correlation
1	13,822	10,802	78	63	0.37
2	13,822	11,152	81	61	0.32
3	13,822	9,896	72	67	0.18
4	13,822	10,568	77	64	0.38
5	13,822	11,044	80	62	0.22
6	13,822	8,875	64	71	0.30
7	13,822	5,831	42	82	0.31
..	. ...	.. ... .	.. ..	.. ..	..... .
24	13,822	12,742	92	49	0.32
25	13,822	12,580	91	51	0.32
26	13,822	10,261	74	65	0.36
27	13,822	10,514	76	64	0.43
28	13,822	10,044	73	66	0.33
29	13,822	7,774	56	75	0.34
30	13,822	12,653	92	50	0.30

The fourth, fifth and sixth columns are the most useful statistics that are used for test construction and interpretation. The Facility column shows a range of item facilities between 42 and 92, with an average test facility of 73 for the whole Listening test. The Difficulty column shows a range of item difficulties between 49 and 82 with an average test difficulty of 65 on the Rasch scale. The Point biserial column ranges between 0.09 and 0.55 with an average discrimination of 0.35 for the whole listening paper. Although the overall point biserial correlation is appropriate for test construction, some of the individual figures reported above are not, which as was discussed earlier can be tolerated in a real Listening test if the items in question are part of an acceptable task. All other statistics (facility and difficulty) are within acceptable range for Listening test construction purposes. Since it is easier to understand how such statistics should be interpreted with reference to an actual detailed example, this will be presented after a brief discussion about target difficulty for the Listening papers.

In general, each Listening paper is constructed to an overall mean target difficulty where items can vary in difficulty by approximately10 Rasch scaled marks in either direction on the scale. This is to ensure that a wide range of items can be included in the test to cover a broad range of ability levels, e.g. not just items narrowly focusing at the passing grade level. For example, for the Cambridge English: First (FCE) a target difficulty of 62 Rasch is set and the individual items in the test can thus vary in difficulty between 52 and 72. Table 5.2 shows the target difficulty values on the Common Scale for the Cambridge English suite of Listening tests across the five levels.

Table 5.2 Approximate target difficulty values for Cambridge ESOL Listening tests

Tests	Target difficulty
KET	41
PET	56
FCE	62
CAE	71
CPE	77

See Tables 7.1 and 7.2 in Chapter 7 for the actual test difficulties of the Listening components of the Cambridge English suite in 2009 and 2010.

The two examples below, taken from a PET Listening test, help to illustrate how item statistics are used in the process of test construction.

Example 1:
Question 9: You will hear a woman called Lucy talking on the radio about a trip in a balloon. For each question, put a tick (✓) in the correct box.

9   How did Lucy feel when she got into the balloon basket?   A   afraid

B   excited

C   proud

When Question 9 was pretested, it produced a Rasch difficulty value of 56 along with the two sets of CTT statistics shown below.

```
      Item Statistics                    Alternative Statistics
- - - - - - - - - - - - - - - - - -    - - - - - - - - - - - - - - - - - - - -
Seq. Scale Prop.  Disc.  Point            Prop. Endorsing Point
No.  -Item Correct Index Biser.    Alt.  Total Low  High Biser. Key
09   1-13  .80     .43    .47       A      .05  .12  .01  -.22
                                    B      .80  .55  .98   .47    *
                                    C      .14  .33  .02  -.39
                                    Other  .00  .00  .00  -.02
```

The *item statistics* on the left show a facility and point biserial correlation for Question 9, while the *alternative statistics* on the right show the statistical performance of the three multiple-choice options which make up Question 9. Seq.No. on the far left-hand side indicates the sequence of the item within the test, i.e. item 9. The facility value (Prop. Correct) is 0.80 and the point biserial (Point Biser.) is 0.47, both of which fall within the acceptable range for Listening test construction. The alternative statistics show that 80% of candidates (Prop. Total) chose the correct answer – Option B (the answer key is indicated with a star). In addition, the columns give a detailed breakdown of the number of people in the low and high ability groups who successfully chose the correct option: 98% of the candidates in the high ability group chose Option B against only 55% of the low ability group. This is an indication of good discrimination between these two groups reflected in a 0.47 point biserial correlation. Similar statistics are presented for Options A and C (the item distractors); these show that Option C attracted more candidates than Option A, and in both cases it was the low ability candidates who chose these incorrect answers. This detailed information allows item writers to check the effectiveness of the distractors for this particular item.

Example 2:
Question 8: You will hear an interview with David Silver, who is talking about a train journey. For each question, put a tick (✓) in the correct box.

8   The train leaves at   **A**   5.15.

                                                           B   6.00.

                                                           C   7.00.

When Question 8 was pretested, it produced a Rasch difficulty value of 45 along with the item and alternative statistics shown below.

Item Statistics					Alternative Statistics				
Seq. No.	Scale -Item	Prop. Correct	Disc. Index	Point Biser.	Alt.	Prop. Total	Endorsing Low	Point High	Biser. Key
8	1-8	.91	.21	.35	A	.06	.13	.01	-.25
					B	.03	.03	.00	-.23 *
					C	**.91**	**.78**	**.99**	**.35**
					Other	.00	.00	.00	-.04

Question 8 is clearly easier than Question 9 in Example 1 and this is reflected in both the Rasch difficulty of 45 and the facility value of 0.91. Although this item is on the borderline of acceptability in terms of its facility, its point biserial value of 0.35 suggests that it still discriminates well between stronger and weaker candidates. Both distractors (Options A and B) are still drawing some attention, albeit marginally. The use of high facility items in a Listening test raises a practical issue. Since most of the candidates will get the item right, the distractors will attract relatively few candidates. None the less, in this particular case the two distractors have attracted some attention, particularly from the low ability group.

To summarise, Question 9 in Example 1 fulfils all the acceptability criteria for test construction concerning difficulty and can easily be selected for a test at PET level; however, the PET test constructors may only decide to select Question 8 in Example 2 if there are no other similar easy items in the same test.

Finally, this discussion of test difficulty cannot be concluded without a reference to the potential for guessing responses in multiple-choice listening tests. The use of a parameter to model guessing was briefly touched upon at the beginning of the section on test difficulty when discussing the use of IRT models. As a one-parameter model, the Rasch model does not take account of the effect of guessing. Since most of Cambridge ESOL's Listening tests include productive test items (for which test takers must generate a constructed response), guessing will not have a significant impact on the overall difficulty of the items in the same way as it does for selected response items, such as pure multiple-choice listening tests. However, there are circumstances where a listening test might not have many productive items and the test may have multiple cut scores, in which case guessing may impact on the accuracy of cut scores, particularly at a low level. In such cases a guessing correction factor can be introduced to adjust the cut scores at the low levels, i.e. A1/A2 levels. This is often referred to in the Rasch literature (Linacre 2000) as the standard correction for guessing and it ensures that candidates are not unfairly awarded lower level certificates by simply randomly guessing the items. The standard correction for guessing adjusts only for truly random guessing among the possible answers. Cambridge ESOL implements the standard correction for guessing in tests such as the BULATS paper-based test.

Item bias

A test may be considered biased when it produces *systematic* differential performance among test takers from the same ability group but from different subgroups of interest (e.g. in terms of age, gender, race and ethnicity, nationality, academic major, native language, religion, and test takers with disability). Such systematic differential performance can be due to the presence of construct-irrelevant test characteristics in a test or in test items or relevant secondary item characteristics. Irrelevant item characteristics may be found in different components of a test: language variety, test instructions, content, response process and administration. Thus, differences in test performance for a *designated subgroup of interest* (DSI) could result in differences in the meaning of test scores such that the validity of the test scores can be in doubt. This definition also implies that test bias is not a result of random differential performance for a DSI when compared to another DSI as such comparisons would include ability levels. Therefore, a difference in performance mean for a DSI does not automatically imply that the test in question is biased.

Item bias procedures have received attention since the 1970s because they were considered as a convenient approach when no external criteria were available for such analysis. From the early stages, the focus was on the concept of relative item difficulty for different test-taking groups. The idea was to match test takers with similar ability (as measured by the total score) from different subgroups. The expectation is that there would be comparable individual item difficulty for the subgroups because the test takers are matched in terms of overall ability. In cases where items performed or functioned differently for specific subgroups, such items were to be flagged and examined for potential bias. This procedure came to be known as Differential Item Functioning (DIF) (Holland and Thayer 1988) and a considerable literature (see, for example, Holland and Wainer (Eds) 1993) has developed around this concept and accompanying procedures. Some of the most common approaches for investigating DIF are listed below:

- the Mantel-Haenszel statistic – Holland and Thayer (1988)
- the Standardisation procedures – Dorans and Kulick (1986)
- the Logistic Regression methods – Rogers and Swaminathan (1989), Zumbo (1999)
- the Logistic Discriminant function analysis
- Lord's Chi-Square – Lord (1977)
- Raju's Area measures – Raju (1988)
- the Likelihood Ratio test – Thissen, Steinberg and Wainer (1993).

The major benefit from these procedures, as Camilli and Shepard (1994:16) put it, has been to help 'clarify what a test is measuring and highlight the influence of irrelevant factors'. They cited the example of a study by Shepard, Camilli and Williams (1984) in which the researchers found that verbal maths problems were systematically more difficult for black examinees; that is, differences between black and white students were greater on this type of problem than on straight computation problems. Are verbal maths problems biased against black students? Not necessarily – solving verbal maths problems is an important goal in its own right. However, once such results are known, they force re-examination and justification of the content framework of a test. In the case of the mathematics test with a heavy verbal component, findings from the bias screening would prompt a more conscious appraisal of what proportion of the test items should be word problems and an effort to control the reading level required (Camilli and Shepard 1994:17).

Geranpayeh and Kunnan (2007) list a number of empirical studies which have been carried out in language testing focusing on test bias.

Item bias: Cambridge ESOL practice

Cambridge ESOL follows the AERA/APA/NCME Standard 7.3 (1999:81) which states that:

When credible research reports that differential item functioning exists across age, gender, racial/ethnic, cultural, disability, and/or linguistic groups in the population of test takers in the content domain measured by the test, test developers should conduct appropriate studies when feasible. Such research should seek to detect and eliminate aspects of test design, content, and format that might bias test scores for particular groups.

Much of Cambridge ESOL's attention is devoted at the Listening test construction level to avoiding test bias in the first place. As already reported in Chapters 2 and 4, there are a number of design considerations outlined in the item writer guidelines which address item bias. There is a list of topics and content words to be avoided for each exam level which will take into account not only the avoidance of taboo words (which can be culturally biased as well as give offence) but also the appropriacy of texts for gender, age and a variety of cultures. Cambridge ESOL always pretests its items on a broad-based and multilingual sample of candidates to avoid calibration being biased against any particular cohort. For example, a number of sampling procedures are in place to ensure that no single test taker cohort will comprise more than 30 percent of the candidature at the pretesting stage. There is also a balance of gender in the cohort and a proper representation of the target candidate age group.

Cambridge ESOL also carries out empirical *post hoc* test analysis to detect DIF. For example, Geranpayeh and Kunnan (2007) report on an empirical DIF study relating to age in the Cambridge English: Advanced (CAE) Listening paper. A two-step approach was used: first, the test items were examined for the presence of DIF and second, the items that were flagged were subjected to content analysis by expert judges. Following careful examination, the judges did not consider that the flagged items were biased against specific age groups. No clear pattern emerged in terms of why the items were identified as exhibiting DIF and the expert judges were unable to identify the causes of DIF for the items.

Geranpayeh and Kunnan hypothesised that the source of the invariance in performance on one of the Listening test items (item 4) was related to test takers' difficulty in responding to item 3 – the immediate preceding item. They did not, however, offer an explanation of why the rest of the items exhibited DIF. In the absence of any further empirical evidence, they concluded that one possible explanation might lie in the different cognitive processes which test takers may have employed in attempting to answer the listening questions. It is possible that the ability to recall information or ability to use memory strategies may be critical in the items that exhibited DIF and different age groups might use these processes differently. This is difficult to investigate as the study did not collect data on test-taking strategies.

They also conjectured that it was quite possible that the DIF exhibited could relate to the multidimensional nature of CAE Listening items. Geranpayeh (2005a, 2005b, 2007) has shown that the CAE Listening items have moderate to high correlations with items that test reading, writing and speaking skills in addition to having high correlation with items that test grammatical ability. In other words, the CAE Listening items measure multiple dimensions to some extent. Each listening item has a primary function of measuring some aspect(s) of listening comprehension. However, since there is some reading material associated with the listening tasks (e.g. prompt questions on the Listening question paper, or a set of written notes for completion), the candidates are also required to process this reading input in order to respond to the listening items. The processing of the reading input is a secondary dimension which the Listening items test. The large DIF values observed on some of the items are probably due to measuring the secondary dimension of the items differently across the reference and the focal groups.

Internal consistency

Reliability

In non-academic contexts the word 'reliable' is commonly understood to mean 'a consistent dependability of judgement, character, performance, or result' (Braham 1996:168). For applied measurement specialists, 'reliability is typically thought of as a desired property of tests, which should be dependable measurement instruments of the constructs that they are supposed to measure' (Zumbo and Rupp 2004:75).

Anastasi (1988) defines reliability as the consistency of scores obtained by the same persons when re-examined with the same test on different occasions, or with different sets of equivalent items, or under other variable conditions. Bachman (1990) represents reliability and validity as 'complementary aspects of a common concern in measurement – identifying, estimating, and controlling the effects of factors that affect test scores' (1990:160). To paraphrase Bachman, reliability is concerned with minimising the effects of measurement error, while validity is concerned with maximising the effects of the language abilities we want to measure.

To summarise the scope of reliability one can say that reliability is concerned only with 'the replicability of measurements, not with the constellation of attributes those measurements reflect' (Haertel 2006:66). There are, of course, candidate features such as test wiseness, motivation, health, stress, first language and speed of working that may influence an examinee's scores across replications of a measurement procedure but such issues are largely related to 'test score validity, not reliability' (Haertel 2006:66).

Reliability is generally accepted to be an important aspect of test quality. On the one hand, reliability is a statistic – a number which looks more impressive the closer it gets to 1. The common statement that reliability refers to the results obtained with an evaluation instrument, not to the instrument itself, is a statement about reliability as a statistic. At the same time, reliability clearly relates to the tendency of a set of test items to define a single, internally consistent, uni-dimensional trait. In this sense, reliability is actually akin to construct validity; at least, if the trait it defines is the same as the one the test claims to measure.

Types of reliability

Within language testing, much of the literature on the reliability of language test scores has been based on work in educational and psychological testing more generally, e.g. the American Psychological Association Standards between 1954 and 1985. In the most recent volume of *Standards* (AERA/APA/NCME 1999) the updated chapter on Reliability and Errors of Measurement (Part 1, Section 2) still identifies the broad categories of reliability which have traditionally been recognised in the field:

- test–retest reliability
- parallel forms reliability
- internal consistency coefficients
- inter-rater reliability
- composite reliability
- generalisability theory (G theory)
- standard error of measurement (SEM)
- IRT-based reliability.

Test–retest and parallel forms reliability are hardly used in language testing for practical reasons; hence they will not be discussed here. See Haertel (2006:70) for a further discussion of such forms. The remaining six methods will be discussed individually in the sections that follow. Some of these methods are based on CTT, which assumes that an observed score on a listening test is a composite of a true score reflecting an individual's level of ability, and an error score that is due to factors other than the ability being measured. The lower the error score is, the closer the observed score will be to the true score, hence the more reliable measurement tool. However, the error in a test comes from a number of different sources. The contribution of each source of error may vary from administration to administration, but there is no way to take account of this in classical test theory. This is where the G theory can help to account for multiple sources of error.

Internal consistency coefficients

Because of the problems associated with parallel forms and test–retest reliability other measures may be more practical. The internal consistency form of reliability focuses on the consistency of a test's internal elements with one another, i.e. the homogeneity of its test items. It estimates test-score reliability from a single administration using information from the relationship among the test items. There are three forms of internal consistency coefficient: *Split-half, Kuder-Richardson 20* and *Cronbach's α (alpha)*.

Split-half reliability can be seen as a logical development from parallel forms reliability. Instead of correlating performance on two separate tests, it simulates this approach by correlating performance on different halves of the same test. This is possible where the test consists of a number of dichotomous items, all of which are intended to test the same ability. As the items are all intended to test the same ability, both halves of the test should, in theory, rank the students in the same way. A flaw in the split-half reliability method is that there may be many ways to split the test into two halves, each of which could give a different result.

The solution to this problem is to determine the mean of all possible split-half correlations. In this way the biases of any individual split-halves are substantially ironed out. A simple formula for estimating the mean of all possible split halves is known as Kuder-Richardson 20, or simply KR20. An equivalent formula is known as Cronbach's alpha. Whereas KR20 may be used where items are scored 1 or 0, Cronbach's alpha may be used where items are awarded scores on a range, e.g. 0, 1, or 2. In practice, Cronbach's alpha is the internal consistency reliability coefficient most often quoted, and indeed the most common way of estimating and reporting reliability.

Marker reliability (Intra-rater and inter-rater reliability)

The AERA/APA/NCME *Standards* (1999) make it clear that when the scoring of any test involves judgement by examiners or raters, it is important to consider reliability in terms of the *accuracy and consistency* of the judgements or ratings which are made. Tests of speaking and writing fall into this category because the assessments are typically (though not always) made by human examiners or markers using rating scales with criterion-related rating descriptors. However, marker reliability can also extend to a listening test if it contains constructed response items, i.e. short written responses comprising one or more words. (See Chapter 4 for a full discussion of the use of constructed response items in listening tests.)

Markers of listening test items involving constructed responses need to be consistent in two ways. Each marker needs to be internally consistent, i.e. given a particular quality of performance, a marker needs to award the same mark whenever this quality appears (*intra-rater reliability*). There also needs to be consistency of marking between markers, i.e. one marker will award the same mark to a constructed response as another when confronted with a performance of the same quality (*inter-rater reliability*).

Composite reliability

The overall reliability of an examination comprising several component papers (e.g. reading, listening, grammar) is known as its composite reliability. Just as the reliability of individual components, at least when using internal consistency estimates, depends on the homogeneity of the test items, so the composite reliability reflects the inter-correlation of the components. The stronger the inter-correlation is, the higher the composite reliability.

Feldt and Brennan (1989) provided the basic statistical theorems about composites that are composed of linear combinations of weighted components, which can be used to study the reliability of composite scores within the CTT framework.

Generalisability theory (G theory)

There is an alternative model of classical test theory, namely, generalisability theory (G theory), which is grounded in the framework of factorial design and analysis of variance. According to G theory reliability is a function of the circumstances under which the listening test is developed, administered and interpreted. Reliability in this model is a matter of generalisability. G theory simultaneously considers all possible main effect sources of measurement error and all possible interactions of these measurement errors. Thompson and Vacha-Haase (2000:183) argue that G theory is important:

> a) analytically in that the theory allows the estimation of score reliability in a manner 'that reflects the impact of **all** sources of measurement error' (Feldt and Brennan 1989:109), and b) conceptually in that the theory allows us to understand that measurement error influences cumulate and may interact to produce even more error variance.

These models allow test developers to investigate the relative effects of different sources of variance in the listening test scores and to decide on how to deal with them in order to minimise measurement error under operational conditions. Despite the powerful investigative nature of G-theory, this approach is not commonly used operationally for determining the reliability of listening tests.

Standard error of measurement (SEM)

Listening tests, like other measurement events, are subject to the influence of many factors that are not relevant to the ability being measured such as poor test administration, fatigue and candidate anxiety. Such irrelevant factors contribute to what is called 'measurement error'. The SEM is related to reliability in terms of test scores. While reliability refers to a group of test takers, the SEM shows the impact of reliability on the likely score of an individual; it indicates how close a test taker's observed score is likely to be to their 'true score', to within some stated probability. For example, where a candidate receives a score of 67 on a listening test with an SEM of 3, there is a high probability that their true score is between 64 and 70. This is a very useful piece of information that test users can accordingly utilise in their decision making.

The reliability coefficient is related to the error of measurement. The SEM is not a separate approach to estimating reliability, but rather a different way of reporting it. It is computed from the reliability coefficient:

$$\textbf{Equation 8: } SEM = \sigma_x \sqrt{1 - r_{xx}}$$

where σ_x is the standard deviation of the score, r_{xx} is the reliability coefficient.

Nitko (1996:71) comments on the size of the SEM value as follows: 'For a fixed value for the reliability coefficient, SEM becomes larger as standard deviation increases. For a fixed value for the standard deviation, SEM becomes smaller as the reliability coefficient becomes larger.'

Measurement error cannot be directly compared from test to test. Anastasi (1990) suggests that error of measurement is useful when the interest lies in interpreting individual scores. However, the reliability coefficient is the better measure for comparing the reliability of different tests.

IRT-based reliability

Lord (1980) proposes a different estimation of reliability using IRT. Generally speaking, there are two steps in producing IRT-based reliability estimates for an objective test such as a test of listening comprehension where the items are scored dichotomously, i.e. there is either a right or a wrong answer. The first step estimates the SEM for each scaled score point, and an SEM specific to each score point is called a conditional SEM or a Conditional Standard Error of Measurement (CSEM). Item parameters and person ability estimates from an IRT model are used in calculating the CSEM values. In the second step, the CSEM values across all the scaled score points are averaged, and this averaged CSEM value is used in the calculation of the reliability estimate for the overall test of listening by substituting this overall SEM (averaged CSEM) for the SEM in formula. The CSEM provides an estimate of reliability, conditional on the proficiency estimate. In other words, it provides a reliability estimate, or error estimate, at each score point. Because there is typically more information about students with scores in the middle of the score distribution, the CSEM is usually smallest in this range, and scores are more reliable there.

Reliability and communicatively oriented listening tests

There are two particular features of communicatively oriented listening tests that are important to a discussion of reliability in the context of a socio-cognitive framework: multidimensionality and truncated samples.

The multidimensionality of listening tests has already been referred to in the discussion of DIF earlier in this chapter. Chapters 2, 3 and 4 discussed the importance of individual test taker characteristics, of cognitive and of contextual factors that influence the design of communicative listening tests. This showed how multiple aspects of the listening construct can be explained and accounted for according to a socio-cognitive framework. The inclusion of a variety of tasks into listening tests will to some extent compromise the effort to maximise internal consistency estimates. Other things being equal, a listening test which focuses on a narrow range of tasks will provide more information about candidates' listening ability in that range than will a similar length test with a wide focus.

Task-based exercises have steadily been replacing discrete point multiple-choice items in communicatively oriented listening tests, in order to provide greater context and authenticity, both situational and transactional but not interactional as the latter is hard to establish in listening tests. (See Chapter 4 for detailed discussion on Cambridge ESOL practice concerning overall text purpose and discourse mode.) In consequence, task-based exercises may tap a broader range of language skills than a narrowly conceived, psychometric listening test that includes only discrete monologue single items. Introduction of heterogeneity (variety of longer task-based items) into listening tests may have an additional consequence that items take longer to respond to as there is more demand on candidate's memory load due to the length of the input task, and so fewer items can be accommodated within practical time constraints. This may bring about a small reduction in the estimated reliability using an internal consistency estimate when compared with listening tests using a greater number of discrete point items.

Depending on purpose, a listening test may cover an entire system of ability levels (e.g. all CEFR levels for placement purposes) or focus on one particular level such as Cambridge Proficiency (CPE). Where listening tests cover language proficiency at a single ability level (CPE), within a comprehensive system of levels (i.e. CEFR levels), they can be expected to provide more efficient, focused, relevant and in-depth measurement of ability. However, candidates of widely ranging ability are easier to rank reliably, and so it is not uncommon for short placement listening tests to show reliability indices as high as or higher than extended, multi-component listening exams at a single level such as CPE.

Summary

Reliability, as the internal consistency of a listening test, may conflict with the heterogeneous, inclusive conception of communicative language ability. Within a socio-cognitive framework reliability and validity are interconnected and both reflect different aspects of test qualities: reliability has to do with *data quality* whereas validity has to do with *inferential quality* (Zumbo and Rupp 2004). It seems necessary, therefore, to maintain a balance between the demands of reliability and validity. Listening sub-constructs *should* be uni-dimensional, to be of practical use, because otherwise they cannot be measured, and if they cannot be measured then it is difficult to argue for their usefulness in a theory of language ability. Reliability, in the sense of internal consistency, is essential evidence for the construct validity of tests. The pursuit of reliability becomes pathological if it leads to a perverse distortion of the construct by narrowing the focus in terms of content and method, or by focusing on testing what is most measurable. Equally, the pursuit of validity could be considered pathological if it leads to the inclusion of aspects of listening which are too heterogeneous to measure properly. A pragmatic balance between reliability and validity is thus the best that can be aimed at. It is clearly sensible to attempt to measure distinct listening sub-constructs separately, to the extent that this is practical.

Internal consistency: Cambridge ESOL practice

Cambridge ESOL takes the view that reliability is an integral component of validity; there can be no validity without reliability. Hence any approach to estimating reliability must reflect potential sources of evidence for the construct validity of the tests.

Reliability

There are various ways to estimate the reliability of a Cambridge ESOL exam. Most Cambridge ESOL exams have two main types of component: objectively scored papers and performance-rated papers. Objectively scored papers are those that do not require human judgement for the scoring of the majority of their items i.e. tests of Reading Comprehension, Listening Comprehension and Use of English (although constructed response items in any of these components clearly require an element of judgement, as discussed earlier).

The scores achieved in Cambridge ESOL's Listening tests are simply calculated by adding up the total number of correct responses to each section; no section weighting is involved. The reliability estimates for the Listening papers are calculated using Cronbach's alpha. The closer the alpha is to 1, the more reliable the Listening test is. Table 5.3 shows average reliability and standard error of measurement figures for the Cambridge ESOL Listening Comprehension tests in 2010.

Table 5.3 illustrates respectable alpha coefficients for all Cambridge Listening components. It demonstrates that an exam such as IELTS, which covers a wider range of candidate ability across multiple levels, is likely to have a higher reliability coefficient than exams such as CPE which covers a

Table 5.3 Internal consistency (Cronbach's alpha) and SEM figures for Cambridge ESOL Listening Comprehension papers in 2010

Examination	Average alpha	Average SEM
KET	0.82	1.84
PET	0.76	2.02
FCE	0.80	2.24
CAE	0.80	2.28
CPE	0.74	2.17
BEC Preliminary	0.82	2.21
BEC Vantage	0.83	2.08
BEC Higher	0.83	2.32
ILEC	0.87	2.03
ICFE	0.88	2.19
IELTS	0.91	0.389*

Source: Cambridge Local Item Banking System 2010

* *SEM in IELTS refers to band score levels whereas in the other Cambridge exams it refers to raw scores.*

single ability level, despite the latter providing a much more efficient, focused, relevant and in-depth measurement of the ability being measured. The lower reliability coefficient for CPE is also partly due to the fact that the ability range of candidates who sit CPE Listening tests is limited, i.e. the sample is truncated. Listening exams that cover more than one ability level and hence a wider candidate ability range are also expected to have higher reliability coefficients, e.g. ILEC and ICFE.

Standard error of measurement

The SEM values in Table 5.3 are all around 2 raw marks. The fact that most Cambridge ESOL Listening tests have more than 30 items engenders confidence that individual candidate Listening scores are close to their 'true score'. In the case of IELTS, the SEM shown is the average across all bands and is estimated at less than half a band. The conditional SEM for IELTS Bands 5–7, where the most precision is targeted, is even lower at around one third of a band.

Composite reliability

For Cambridge ESOL exams the decision to pass or fail a candidate is almost always taken at the syllabus level. That means the overall score on the test is the composite of all the scores in a test's subcomponents. It is this score which is reported to candidates. The score is reported in the range of 0 to 100 by scaling raw scores to standardised scores. While it is worth having a measure of the reliability of each test component, what typically matters most to candidates and test score users is the overall reliability of the whole syllabus, the composite reliability. This is especially true for the Cambridge English exams where no single component (i.e. listening) score is reported to candidates. The test score users, accordingly, rely on the overall score (a standardised score) for their decision making, hence the reason why the composite score is important. The composite reliability of all the exams reported in Table 5.3 is above 0.90. This figure suggests a high level of confidence can be placed in the reliability of the overall test scores.

Inter-rater reliability

One of the characteristic features of Cambridge ESOL Listening tests is the inclusion of productive tasks as a measure of communicative language ability. These typically take the form of constructed response items which require test takers to write a single word, letter or number, or possibly a phrase of two or three words (see Chapter 4 for examples and further discussion). Such tasks introduce additional scoring demands for which human markers (known as 'clerical markers') are needed. In the marking of such productive tasks used to test listening comprehension ability, Cambridge ESOL expects its clerical markers to behave like a rating machine so as to ensure that the scores derived from such tasks are as accurate as the objective marks obtained from scanning the selected responses to other listening tasks which are auto-marked by a machine. The purpose for the agreement between Cambridge's clerical markers is to find out: 'Do pairs of raters agree on the same rating?' Raters are expected to achieve an agreement of 90%+. Cambridge ESOL's Listening markers are always trained with this outcome in mind.

The clerical markers for ESOL Listening papers work in groups on a number of different papers. Each set of candidate constructed response data is marked by one marker. Random selections of allocated marks are marked by a second marker on a daily basis and the difference in agreement is recorded; if necessary, the original mark will be amended. At the end of each marking day the accuracy rate of all clerical markers is monitored to ensure that the marking is as accurate as possible. If the error rate of a particular clerical marker is outside of the required accuracy, all their ratings will be checked, and if necessary they will undergo further training. Table 5.4 demonstrates that the average accuracy rate for clerical markers rating the productive listening tasks is 99.74%, which is well above the 90% confidence target one would expect for such marking.

Chapter 4 notes that one major issue in designing constructed response tasks is how to treat spelling. It explained various issues that are important in relation to accounting for spelling mistakes and highlighted Cambridge ESOL policy with regard to marking spelling for different listening tasks in the exams. Situations when misspelling is acceptable were listed, such as accepting the omission of silent letters, the elision of silent syllables in certain

Table 5.4 Inter-rater agreement for Listening clerical markers – Spring 2011

Paper	Accuracy rate %	Error rate %
ILEC February Listening	100.00	0.00
ICFE May Listening	100.00	0.00
BEC March – Listening	99.70	0.30
KET February – Listening	99.70	0.30
KET March – Listening	99.77	0.23
KETS March – Listening	99.88	0.12
PET February – Listening	99.68	0.32
PET March (P) – Listening	99.43	0.57
PET March – Listening	99.71	0.29
PETS March – Listening	99.68	0.32
PET May A – Listening	99.78	0.22
FCE Listening	99.74	0.26
CAE Listening	99.42	0.58
CPE Listening	99.91	0.09
Average	99.74	0.25

words and contravention of certain spelling conventions such as double letters when forming participles. The chapter reported that a long list of acceptable misspellings has been incorporated into a tool called the LIBS dictionary. It is this dictionary that is used to create an item response key for accounting for all the different kinds of acceptable misspelling in constructed response listening tasks.

The use of the LIBS dictionary allows the marking of acceptable misspelling in all listening tests to be standardised with great consistency, not only across different forms of a test but across different sessions and different tests. The figures reported in Table 5.4 are testament to the consistency with which the LIBS dictionary has been applied to all the Cambridge Listening tests.

IRT-based reliability

Cambridge ESOL uses IRT-based estimates when reporting the reliability of the computer-adaptive tests (CAT) such as CB BULATS. These reliability estimates are mainly used in a CAT context where every test taker will see a different set of test items, which means that there are as many unique test versions as the number of candidates taking the test. In other words, each test will only have one set of response data which makes the use of the commonly reported Cronbach's alpha inappropriate in a CAT environment. A typical CB BULATS Listening test section has 25 Listening items. The IRT-based reliability that Cambridge ESOL uses is a Rasch reliability estimate. Cope (2009) reports a Rasch reliability of 0.92 for the Listening section of CB BULATS with a mean SEM of 0.45. Both these figures are much higher than any reliability estimates reported so far for the conventional paper-based Listening tests. The higher precision is due to the inherent nature of an adaptive test whereby the selection of test items, and thus the overall difficulty of the test, is determined on the basis of a candidate's emerging ability as they complete each test item.

Grading and awarding

Grading is the process of setting cut scores for various points on a *scale* of achievement test data. It is helpful here to explain the relationship between a scale and a test. In describing how the Rasch model is used to scale achievement test data, Wright (1977) notes that:

> When a person tries to answer a test item the situation is potentially complicated. Many forces might influence the outcome – too many to be named in a workable theory of the person's response. To arrive at a workable position, we must invent a simple conception of what we are willing to suppose happens, do our best to write items and test persons so that their interaction is governed by this conception, and then impose its statistical consequences upon the data to see if the invention can be made useful (Wright 1977:47).

The above statement underpins the Rasch model used to scale achievement test data. The implication is that such a scale can be used to predict the behaviour of test takers and to facilitate the interpretation of the scale scores. Kolen and Brennan (2004:331) explain that 'the scaling process is used to associate numbers to appropriately reflect levels of the attribute'. Since no level of the attribute can ever be well enough defined by any psychometric theory, it is very difficult to relate test scores to levels of achievement without certain assumptions. Numbers alone (i.e. the listening test scores) will have no meaning unless they are accompanied by some informed expert judgement about what the numbers actually mean given a typical population and bearing on different aspects of the testing process. This is usually achieved by *setting performance standards.*

Hambleton and Pitoniak (2006) argue that 'when educational assessments are used to categorise individuals, performance standards must be established along the score range' (2006:433). Setting performance standards is in sharp contrast to traditional methods of norm-referencing where a fixed percentage of test takers will pass or fail an exam. Members of the public are generally more familiar with norm-referenced approaches to standards, particularly in the school education system. In contrast to norm-referenced approaches, setting performance standards is based on a criterion-referenced approach which is very common in high-stakes assessments and in credentialing or licensing examinations, e.g. for the health professions or for the teaching profession. The criterion is usually the set of content standards outlining the knowledge, skills and abilities that are judged to be necessary for the achievement of the standard. For example, it may be judged that in order for a candidate to pass a listening test at a B2 level, they need to get a minimum of 60% of the items right. In a listening test of 40 items that means a minimum score of 24 if only raw scores were reported to candidates. The latter becomes the cut score for achieving a B2 level in that listening test.

In short, grading, whether norm-referenced or criterion-referenced, sets cut scores on an achievement scale with meaning attached to each point on the scale.

Grading and awarding: Cambridge ESOL practice

Grading of Cambridge English exams has evolved over many years. There is no documentation on how the CPE examination was originally graded in 1913 but Hawkey (2009) reports that the grading of awards for FCE (initially named LCE) involved both norm and criterion referencing standards in the early 1940s.

During the 1980s and 1990s several new tests (PET, CAE and KET) were added to the Cambridge English suite. All three reflected the evolving conceptualisation of what came to be known as the CEFR levels and they have similar Listening papers to FCE/CPE. (See Chapter 1 for a description of CEFR levels and see Chapter 4 for a content description of these tests.) The 1990s is the era when numerous psychometric procedures were introduced into the Cambridge English exams suite to ensure form equivalence and to improve the reliability of test scores. One of the outcomes of the application of psychometric theory to test construction was the creation of the LIBS. The approach to grading in the 1990s continued to be a combination of criterion and norm-referenced and results were reported in terms of each candidate's overall performance in the examination as a whole rather than their success in individual skill components. Saville (2003) describes the grading approach for Cambridge ESOL exams as passing or failing the whole exam with no hurdles in individual papers. That is, a candidate's success in one paper, e.g. the Listening paper, may not necessarily reflect their passing of the whole examination.

By way of example, the typical procedure for grading FCE is as follows. Each of the five test papers is equally weighted to 40 marks, and these are added up to make a total score of 200 for the whole exam (sometimes referred to as the syllabus). Each objectively scored paper (Reading, Listening, Use of English) is provisionally graded on the IRT ability-driven criterion where a cut score is determined for passing the paper. The ability criterion for the cut score is linked to the Cambridge Common Scale where there are fixed ability cut scores for each CEFR level. Table 5.5 shows the criterion ability cut scores for an FCE Listening paper.

Table 5.5 Ability cut scores for an FCE Listening paper

Grades	Criterion ability*	Weighted score
A (C1)**	84	35
B	77	31
C (B2)	69	25
(downward) (B1)	62	18

*   *No ability below 62 is reported here because FCE does not measure such levels accurately*
**   *C1, B2, B1 are CEFR levels*

These individual cut scores for Grade C for each objective paper are then combined with the criterion-referenced cut scores for Speaking and Writing. The total score of all papers hence determined is then compared to the average historical overall cut score for the FCE exam to determine the final cut score for Grade C (the passing grade). There will be lots of checks on individual cohort performances pre- and post-grading to ensure that no unintentional negative consequence impacts on test scores. For Listening papers, where several forms may be used for a test administration session, equating procedures are in place to adjust for any differences in difficulty that may exist between the different forms. The following section on score reporting discusses in detail how other grades and cut scores for the overall exam are arrived at and reported.

Score reporting

It has already been explained that Cambridge ESOL does not currently set the performance pass at the level of the Listening paper. Although the grading process starts with setting the cut scores at component level, the pass or fail decision is taken with regard to the candidate's overall performance on the whole syllabus. For example, currently in an FCE examination the cut score for a pass would be set on a total weighted score of 0–200. This weighted score is not, however, reported to candidates and neither are their scores in any of the individual papers, including the Listening paper. The total weighted score is linked to the criterion ability as shown in Table 5.5. Since the total weighted score for a candidate of a given ability can vary from one session to another depending on test difficulty, it is inappropriate to report the total weighted score to candidates. Instead, total weighted scores are converted to standardised scores on a scale of 0–100.

What candidates are given, therefore, is a score on a fixed scale linked to the criterion ability whose meaning remains constant over different sessions. For example, the passing grade (Grade C) in FCE is always represented by scores from 60 to 74 on a standardised score scale of 100. Grade B is always represented by scores of 75 to 79. Together both Grades C and B at FCE level relate to Level B2 on the CEFR. Exceptional candidates sometimes achieve a standardised score of 80 or more (an A grade), thus showing evidence of ability beyond the B2 level. If a candidate achieves a Grade A in their exam, they will receive the First Certificate in English certificate stating that they demonstrated ability at Level C1 of the CEFR. Likewise, if their performance is below Level B2, but falls within Level B1, i.e. a score between 45 and 59, this level of achievement is also recognised with a Cambridge English certificate stating that they demonstrated ability at B1 level. For a description of FCE listening ability level coverage see Chapter 4.

Table 5.6 demonstrates how various total weighted scores are linked to standardised scores.

Table 5.6 Link between standardised scores and criterion ability for an FCE session

Grades	Criterion ability*	Syllabus weighted score	Standardised score
A (C1)**	84	173	80
B	77	156	75
C (B2)	69	129	60
B1	62	94	45
F		0	0

*   No ability below 62 is reported here because FCE does not measure such levels accurately
** C1, B2, B1 are CEFR levels

Following the examination, all candidates receive a Statement of Results which, in the case of FCE, is based upon their performance across all five papers in the exam. The Statement of Results (shown in Figure 5.3) contains information about the candidate's standardised score (e.g. 67 out of 100) and their overall grade (e.g. Pass at Grade C). As demonstrated in Table 5.6, the standardised score has set values for each grade, allowing comparisons across sessions of the exam.

The Statement of Results also gives candidates additional information about their performance in each paper shown against the scale (Exceptional – Good – Borderline – Weak). To elaborate, based on the cut scores reported in Table 5.6, a candidate who scores 67 in the overall FCE exam with an overall Grade of C could have scored the following scores in each component; 31 in Reading, 26 in Writing, 29 in Use of English, 24 in Listening and 29 in Speaking. This adds up to a total score of 139 which is converted to 67 on the standardised score scale and reported as an overall Grade C.

Although candidates are not given a breakdown in their Statement of Results of their scores in individual test components, they do receive a graphical profile as shown in the middle part of Figure 5.3. Figure 5.3 shows that this particular candidate has the strongest performance in Reading

Figure 5.3 Sample Statement of Results for FCE

Statement of Results

	Session
	May (F2) 2011

Reference No.	Candidate Name
115122190001	A.N. EXAMPLE

To be quoted on all correspondence	Place of Entry
	LONDON

Qualification	Score	Result
FIRST CERTIFICATE IN ENGLISH	67/100	Pass at Grade C

Candidate Profile

Exceptional

Good   Reading   Use of English

    Writing   Speaking

Borderline

    Listening

Weak

The **First Certificate in English (FCE)** is a general proficiency examination at Level B2 in the Council of Europe's Common European Framework of Reference. It is at Level 1 in the UK National Qualifications Framework (NQF).

CEFR Level	NQF Level	Examination	Results	Score
C2	3	Certificate of Proficiency in English (CPE)	Pass at Grade A	80 to 100
C1	2	Certificate in Advanced English (CAE)	Pass at Grade B	75 to 79
B2	**1**	**First Certificate in English (FCE)**	Pass at Grade C	60 to 74
B1	Entry 3	Preliminary English Test (PET)	Level B1	45 to 59
A2	Entry 2	Key English Test (KET)	Fail	0 to 44
A1	Entry 1		Other	

X — the candidate was absent from part of the examination

Z — the candidate was absent from all parts of the examination

Interpretation of results
Grade C covers the range of ability from a borderline pass to good achievement at the level. Grade B indicates the range of good achievement up to Grade A, which demonstrates an ability at Council of Europe Level C1. Level B1 covers the range of ability between weak and borderline.

Pending — a result cannot be issued at present, but will follow in due course

Withheld — the candidate should contact their centre for information

The total number of marks available in the examination is 200. Marks out of 200 are converted to a standardised score out of 100.

THIS IS NOT A CERTIFICATE
Cambridge ESOL reserves the right to amend the information given before the issue of certificates to successful candidates.

UNIVERSITY *of* CAMBRIDGE
ESOL Examinations

15/11/11

and the weakest in Listening though the weighted score in each component might not have given them the same picture. This is due to different ways that weighted scores in each component are linked to the criterion ability which makes the reporting of weighted scores to candidates misleading. The graphical profile shows how the candidate performed compared to the standard related to the overall historical profile. Candidates are also reminded that their graphical profile does not correspond to their Grade as the latter is determined at the overall syllabus performance and not at the component level. The use of terminology (Weak, Borderline, Good, Exceptional) in graphical profiling is deliberate to avoid giving the wrong impression that these words relate to passing/failing the components. Graphical profiling is designed to provide a level of diagnostic feedback on test performance, helping to indicate relative strengths and weaknesses across the skills and to identify where further efforts at language improvement might be usefully targeted in the future.

Finally, candidates receive a formal examination certificate which displays their overall performance level in the test, linking this to the levels of the CEFR framework to aid meaningful and useful interpretation. This is illustrated in Figure 5.4, where the candidate has achieved a B2 certificate, passing the FCE exam with an overall grade of either B or C.

Figure 5.4 Candidate's graphical profile on overall test performance in FCE

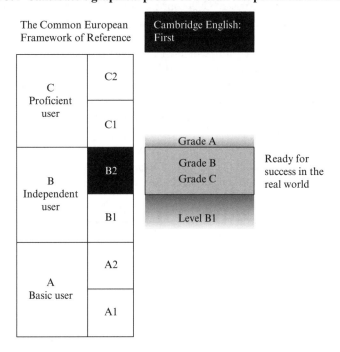

Conclusion

This chapter explored the various scoring validity parameters that influence the scoring validity of a listening test as identified in Figure 5.1.

Much of the discussion in this chapter has been around the suitability of listening test materials for test construction and how statistical analysis of pretested materials can help test constructors to build better listening tests. It is argued that to develop and build an appropriate listening test one needs to identify the most appropriate set of items from a calibrated listening item bank to ensure an effective measurement (Wright and Stone 1979). To achieve this, the first stage is to understand the intended target population, its location (average ability), dispersion (range of abilities represented) and distribution (the shape of the range of abilities – e.g. normally or uniformly distributed). In the case of all the Listening tests considered here, Cambridge ESOL has an established test taker population which takes the tests every year. At the very least, one needs to consider the suitability of the listening tests for their current populations and ensure appropriate coverage of each of the levels at which one would wish to certificate. It is also necessary to determine an appropriate level of precision for each test, which will depend upon its use and purpose and the number and nature of decisions it will be used for.

Using the Rasch model at Cambridge ESOL allows test constructors to define a listening test for any given purpose based on the average difficulty of the listening items, the range of item difficulties, and the total number of items. For each of the exams in question the total number of items is determined by the test specification, which seeks to take into account all aspects of the socio-cognitive framework; thus, this variable is constrained by choices associated with other parameters for test construction. In other words, one needs to define an appropriate target difficulty and range of items for a fixed number of items with a view to ensuring the best measurement possible across the levels of interest.

In Chapters 6 and 7 the focus shifts beyond matters of listening test design, development, production, processing and analysis to explore issues concerning the consequential and criterion-related validity of listening tests.

6 Consequential validity

Roger Hawkey
Consultant to Cambridge English Language
Assessment

Introduction

In Chapter 1 Taylor established the context, intended audience, purpose and focus of this fourth volume in a series, each volume with a main focus on the examining of one of the four language skills. This volume on the assessment of listening in Cambridge ESOL exams is structured around the socio-cognitive framework initiated in Weir (2005a) and since developed further by Cambridge ESOL in collaboration with him. Chapters 2 to 5 have covered in turn: test taker characteristics; cognitive validity; context validity, and scoring validity. This chapter deals with a further segment of the framework, labelled *consequential validity* by Weir, and which, as explained in Chapter 1 above, covers exam validation theory and practice on the washback and impact of tests, with particular reference to Cambridge ESOL exams.

The chapter begins with a recap of the meaning and status of consequential validity in test validation models, including the socio-cognitive framework. It suggests a modified interpretation of the Weir (2005a) consequential validity concept, offered in the light of Cambridge ESOL's theoretical and practical experience in the validation of its own exams over a number of years. The chapter then interprets test washback and impact and the role of both in test validation. The nature and use of impact studies, their structure and implementation are then discussed, highlighting the complexity of the variables involved. Finally, we survey impact-related research directly relevant to the Listening components of Cambridge ESOL exams, including examples of findings from impact studies. Throughout, the validation of tests of listening is a main focus.

Consequential validity

In Weir's framework, as shown in full in Chapter 1 and in abbreviated form in Figure 6.1, consequential validity concerns matters of score interpretation, covering washback on individuals in the classroom and the workplace, and impact on institutions and society.

The table is a refined version of Weir's (2005a) original validity framework

Table 6.1 Consequential validity (adapted from Weir 2005a)

CONSEQUENTIAL VALIDITY
Score interpretation • Washback on individuals in classroom/workplace • Impact on institutions and society

(2005a), which included a third element in the consequential validity box, namely avoidance *of test bias*. This element is omitted from the current discussion, however, just as it was in the equivalent chapter in the predecessor volume, *Examining Speaking* (Taylor (Ed.) 2011). In the second volume in the series, *Examining Reading*, Khalifa and Weir (2009:7) found it logical to include the main discussion of avoidance of test bias under *test taker characteristics*, positioned earlier in the Weir socio-cognitive model:

> The issue of test bias takes us back to the test taker characteristics box. The evidence collected on the test taker should be used to check that no unfair bias has occurred for individuals as a result of decisions taken earlier with regard to contextual features of the test.

Any discussion of test bias was therefore located in Chapter 2 in both *Examining Reading* and *Examining Speaking*. In this volume, however, the decision was made to relocate the discussion of listening test bias within Chapter 5 (in relation to statistical and other approaches for investigating bias as an aspect of scoring validity).

In the framework (see in bold in Figure 6.1, and in the full representation of the framework on page 28), it is worth noting that the consequential validity box appears in the final sector of the model, *after* a test has been developed and validated against test taker characteristics, the test context, internal learner processes and resources and cognitive processes, and after the scoring of the test. However, the discussion in this chapter, including the example of a *timeline* for test impact and washback studies in Figure 6.3 on page 284, will cover the consequences of tests as they apply *throughout* the process of preparing for, administering and scoring an exam. This is because those responsible for designing, developing and validating high-stakes exams need to take account of the effects that such exams may be having on test takers and other key stakeholders *before* as well as after the exam takes place. Exams may well wash back on exam preparation courses for future exams; the eventual scores on the exams will impact on test takers, stakeholders at the receiving institutions or organisations, and so on. With Cambridge ESOL, there is a clear interest in the consequences of exams *throughout* the exam development, validation, administration, scoring and results process.

According to the socio-cognitive framework, consequential validity is to

Figure 6.1 Consequential validity in the socio-cognitive test validation model (adapted from Weir 2005a:45)

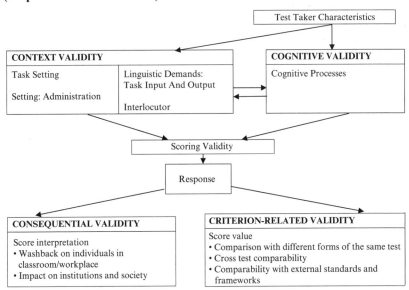

be ascertained at the same stage as criterion-related validity (cross-test and cross-version comparability, relationship to external standards, see Chapter 7). But, as noted by Weir and O'Sullivan (2011:23), 'an aspect of consequence that does not share this temporal sequence is the notion of consequence as ethical approach . . . an ethical approach to test development is a reflection of an understanding of the consequences of decisions made *during the process of development*' (italics added).

A brief exploration of the nature and status of test consequence in other validation models and frameworks should help clarify its status in the socio-cognitive framework. The work of Samuel Messick (e.g. 1989, 1996) remains a major influence on the definition and status of the consequential validity box in the socio-cognitive test validation framework referenced throughout this book and used significantly in the validation of Cambridge ESOL exams. As McNamara (2006:43) notes, Messick never actually used the term consequential validity, referring rather to 'the consequential aspect of construct validity' (1996:241). Nevertheless, Messick's concern for the 'consequences of test use' has been a key factor in 'the significant upsurge of interest over the last ten years' (McNamara 2006:43). Alderson (2004:ix), among others, notes the increasingly acknowledged importance of the consequences of exams and tests: 'Washback and the impact of tests more generally has become a major area of study within educational research'. The original diagram from Messick's (1989) work is shown here:

Table 6.2 Messick's 1989 conception of validity

	Test interpretation	Test use
Evidential basis	Construct validity	Construct validity + relevance/utility
Consequential basis	Value implications	Social consequences

Messick considers a model with three separate types of validity – content, criterion, and construct – inadequate because it fails to take into account 'both evidence of the value implications of score meaning as a basis for action and the social consequences of score use' (Messick 1995:74). Messick's unified view of validity inter-relates test interpretation and test use, 'score meaning and social values in test interpretation and test use' (Messick 1995:74). Clearly Messick's 'social consequences' connect with the consequential validity box in the Weir socio-cognitive framework.

Recent criticism of Messick's validity model is interesting. Cizek (2011) separates the validation (of test score inferences) from the justification (of test use), which is a departure from the unified theory of validity of Messick. But, like Cambridge ESOL, Cizek does acknowledge the significance of test consequences even though he assigns them to a separate category of justification of test use.

Alderson, in his introduction to *Washback in Language Testing: Research Contexts and Methods* (Cheng, Watanabe and Curtis 2004) questions the notion of consequence as a unique form of validity on practical grounds, because of 'all the myriad forces that can both enhance and hinder the implementation of . . . intended change' (2004:xi). The complexity of test consequences is discussed further below.

Consequential validity: Cambridge ESOL practice

However, neither issues of theoretical logic such as Cizek's (2011), nor reminders of practical difficulty such as Alderson's (2004) should significantly affect the framework of validation activities implemented by a major high-stakes language assessment organisation such as Cambridge ESOL. High-stakes test developers and users need to look at consequence in a number of ways. Awareness of consequence is crucial as it impacts on all elements of test validity and is a guiding principle for the test development process from the very beginning of the cycle.

The importance that Cambridge ESOL attaches to understanding the consequences of examinations in education and society is illustrated by the fact that, between 2005 and 2009, six new volumes focusing on major consequential validity related issues appeared in the *Studies in Language Testing* series (see Chapter 1, this volume). These volumes covered: the proceedings of the 2008 ALTE Cambridge Conference on the wider social and educational impact of assessment (2009); Liying Cheng's (2005) study of the impact of a high-stakes public examination on teaching and learning in Hong Kong secondary schools; Dianne Wall's (2005) case study of the impact of high-stakes testing on classroom teaching; Anthony Green's (2007) investigation of the washback of IELTS (the International English Language Testing System) in the preparation for academic writing in higher education; the Taylor and Falvey (Eds 2007) selected research studies on the IELTS test, a significant proportion of them impact-related; and Hawkey's (2006) studies of the impacts of the IELTS test and the Italian Ministry of Education *Progetto Lingue 2000*. Weir and Milanovic (Eds 2003) and Hawkey (2009) also cover significant recent Cambridge ESOL test impact research in the context of the review and updating of major exams, the former for the Certificate of Proficiency in English (CPE), the latter for the First Certificate in English (FCE) and the Certificate in Advanced English (CAE) exams.

This awareness of the importance of test impact is not a recent development. Cambridge ESOL (and previously UCLES EFL) have long claimed a concern for the effects of their own exams on their test takers and other stakeholders. A 1943 Cambridge Examinations in English for Foreign Students *Survey* asks: '. . . how far examinations of this kind may act as a stimulus and a focusing point for both teachers and taught, and thereby promote the expansion of the studies which they are designed to test'. In her review of the 1984 FCE exam, Hamp-Lyons (1987:19) appears to answer this question, encouraged by 'the Syndicate's [now Cambridge ESOL] attempts to bring it in line with pedagogic developments, particularly in communicative teaching/learning'.

Cambridge ESOL now investigates and reports on such matters routinely and transparently. As already illustrated in Chapters 1 to 5 of this volume, a concern with research into a test's consequential validity has grown into a systematic and evidence-seeking test validation framework. The socio-cognitive framework proposed in Weir (2005a) has been influential in focusing such Cambridge ESOL approaches, in combination with other developments, both internal and external (see below).

Principles of good practice

Despite long and growing acknowledgment of its responsibility for the various consequences of its exams both in ethical terms and in relation to claims about their validity and usefulness, Cambridge ESOL uses a variety of labels to describe its research in this area of validity. In an important recent publication *Principles of Good Practice: Quality Management and Validation in Language Assessment* (2011a), Cambridge ESOL does not actually use the term 'consequential validity' at all, though the phrase 'consequential aspects of validity' appears twice, wording which is closer to Messick's original phraseology 'consequential aspect of construct validity' above. Significantly, however, the word 'impact' appears no fewer than 25 times in the 35-page description of Cambridge ESOL's 'approach to language assessment' (2011a:5). The foundation statement at the beginning of the 2011 document reads as follows: 'To achieve fitness for purpose, we aim to maximise the appropriate balance of the following qualities: Validity, Reliability, Impact, Practicality and Quality or VRIPQ' (2011a:5). The VRIPQ model is shown in Figure 6.2 below.

Figure 6.2 The Cambridge ESOL VRIPQ model

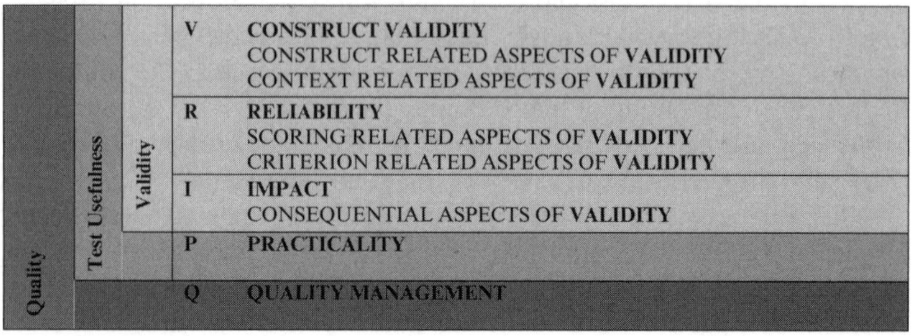

Quality	Test Usefulness	Validity	**V** CONSTRUCT VALIDITY CONSTRUCT RELATED ASPECTS OF **VALIDITY** CONTEXT RELATED ASPECTS OF **VALIDITY**
			R RELIABILITY SCORING RELATED ASPECTS OF **VALIDITY** CRITERION RELATED ASPECTS OF **VALIDITY**
			I IMPACT CONSEQUENTIAL ASPECTS OF **VALIDITY**
			P PRACTICALITY
			Q QUALITY MANAGEMENT

The 2011 VRIPQ document is explicit about the continuity with improvement of Cambridge ESOL's approach towards test validation. The diagram in Figure 6.2 'illustrates our approach to achieving fitness for purpose, and shows how developments in language testing theory and in quality management have been taken on board' (2011a:10). The Cambridge ESOL VRIPQ statement supports this broad approach, defining impact as follows:

> . . . the effects, beneficial or otherwise, which an examination has on the candidates and other users, whether these are educational, social, economic or political, or various combinations of these.

So, VRIPQ is actually seen as reflecting Messick's (1989) argument for a unitary approach to validity 'in which the interacting nature of different types of validity is stressed' (2011a:10), as represented by the validity 'side bar' in Figure 6.2. Bachman and Palmer's 1996 view is also reflected in this conceptualisation, consistent with their placing of practicality within their 'test usefulness' category. According to Bachman and Palmer (1996), test 'usefulness' entails six qualities: reliability, construct validity, authenticity, interactivity, impact and practicality. There is considerable overlap here with the validity, reliability, impact and practicality (VRIP) criteria that have long been used to guide UCLES EFL test validation procedures. Milanovic and Saville's 1996 internal Cambridge ESOL paper *Considering the impact of Cambridge EFL examinations – Principles of Good Practice*, specifies all four requirements for a test's 'balance of features'.

Impact and washback

The term impact is neutral in itself, as instanced in the literature (e.g. Hawkey 2006, Shohamy 2001). Impact is generally agreed to cover 'the total effect of a test on the educational process and on the wider community' (McNamara 2000:133). However, the impact construct in the VRIP set of targeted test characteristics (above) is normally characterised in the differentiated terms *impact* and *washback*. Some key definitions are examined here. In most cases their connection with Weir's term 'consequential validity' is quite clear.

Impact is concerned with wider influences, the broader social contexts of a test, and washback within the micro contexts of the classroom and the school (see Hamp-Lyons 2000, Hawkey 2006). When Bachman and Palmer (1996:29) envisage impact as operating on a 'macro' level, i.e. 'in terms of educational systems and society in general' and a 'micro' level, i.e. 'a local and personal level, in terms of the people who are directly affected by tests and their results', they appear to be making a distinction similar to that between impact and washback. Impact is the superordinate consequential validity construct, washback thus a part of impact (see Green 2007, Green and Hawkey 2004, Hamp-Lyons 1998, McNamara 1996, 2000, Shohamy 2001). The three earlier companion volumes in this series, *Examining Writing* (Shaw and Weir 2007), *Examining Reading* (Khalifa and Weir 2009) and *Examining Speaking* (Taylor (Ed.) 2011), agree that the consequential validation of Cambridge ESOL exams should cover both impact and washback.

Washback (Hughes 2003 and Green 2007 call the same phenomenon 'backwash') is generally taken to refer to an exam's influences on teaching, teachers, learning, curricula and materials (see, for example, Alderson and Wall 1993, Gates 1995, Hamp-Lyons 1998, Hawkey 2006, 2009, Shohamy, Donitsa-Schmidt and Ferman 1996). Messick refers to washback as 'the extent to which the introduction and use of a test influences language teachers and learners to do things they would not otherwise do that promote or inhibit language learning' (1996:241). Messick continues by suggesting that 'a test's validity should be appraised by the degree to which it manifests positive or negative washback, a notion akin to the proposal of "systemic validity" in the educational measurement literature'. Frederiksen and Collins (1989:189) consider systemic validity achieved 'if the activities employed to help students achieve an instructional objective do not merely increase test scores but increase performance on the construct cited in the objectives as well'. We are reminded of the 1943 Cambridge Examinations *Survey* statement cited above which suggested its English as a Foreign Language (EFL) exams even then should 'act as a stimulus' for teaching and learning as well as exam results.

Green's comprehensive (2007) review of the interpretations of washback in the language testing literature confirms it as a neutral term (as in Alderson and Wall 1993, 1996), which may refer to both positive effects (Bachman and Palmer 1996, Buck 1988, Davies, Brown, Elder, Hill, Lumley and McNamara 1999, Hughes 2003) and negative effects (Bachman and Palmer 1996, Buck 1988, Davies et al 1999, Hughes 2003).

Of the four skills, it is arguably listening where one can observe the closest parallels between the assumptions and methods employed in testing and those that are employed in instruction. A number of commentators have expressed reservations about the standard 'comprehension approach' (Field 2009a) adopted by teachers, in which a recording is played and answers sought to comprehension questions. Perhaps the most frequently aired criticism (Brown 1986, Sheerin 1987) is the view that the approach serves to test listening but does little or nothing to teach it.

Field (2009a:80) takes a different view, arguing that classroom practitioners have little choice but to adopt techniques which resemble those of a tester, since listening cannot be studied directly. On this analysis, the only evidence as to whether listeners are operating successfully has to take the form of responses to exercises, questions and tasks similar to those favoured by testers. However, we still cannot ignore the possible negative effects on pedagogy of washback from testing. For example, where practitioners adopt the comprehension approach (as in language teaching emphasising the understanding of the target language rather than its communicative use), one can question the way in which materials designed for the listening classroom rely so heavily upon the types of format that feature in international high-stakes tests. Considerations of reliability and ease of marking that constrain the methods used by large-scale tests do not really apply in the classroom or even in smaller-scale local tests (Field 2011b). It may be a cause for concern that so many models of listening instruction, published listening materials and local progress assessments employ formats such as multiple-choice items, which make heavy demands upon reading as well as listening.

But the effectiveness of the comprehension approach is also questioned because it is modelled upon a testing rather than a teaching/learning principle and tends to provide repeated practice without necessarily producing better listeners. Additional methods recently proposed involve training learners in constituent processes of the listening skill (Field 2008) or the acquisition of *compensatory strategies* which enable listeners to overcome their limitations of language or expertise. The effects of such approaches are to build listener confidence (Graham 2011) and to equip the listener to cope with the world outside the classroom (Vandergrift 1997) in a way that the standard approach does not.

Whatever the form of general instruction, a more conventional type of washback is seen in the excessive importance sometimes accorded to test practice when a group of learners is preparing for a listening exam. This partly reflects the intangible nature of the skill, and the uncertainty among some practitioners as to how to develop it through training. It also reflects the prevalence of the comprehension approach: if one is going to base one's lesson on asking questions, why not use questions devised by professional item writers?

Extended test practice becomes a particular problem when too much attention is directed towards the Achilles heel of the listening test – namely the information that can be derived from the written items that appear on the page. Reading provides a more reliable channel of information than listening because of the greater permanence of the text and its use of standard forms (see Chapter 3). Perhaps the most unfortunate feature of listening test washback is thus the extent to which teachers who are in fact 'cramming' learners for a test, focus learner attention on peripheral features of the test rather than developing the *construct* which the test aims to measure. With this aim, such teachers may train learners to listen out for 'key words' taken from the written items, to base judgements on the convention of evenly spaced keys in the recording and so on. This is an area that examining boards will need to address, since it would seem to challenge construct validity.

Test washback and test validation

In a personal communication to Alderson (Alderson 1995:3) Messick warns against too glib a view of the relationship between test washback and test validation:

> Washback is a consequence of testing that bears on validity only if it can be evidentially shown to have been an effect of the test and not of other forces operative on the educational scene. . . . Washback is not simply good or bad teaching or learning practice that might occur with or without the test, but rather good or bad practice that is evidentially linked to the introduction of the use of the test.

The complexity of the search for such evidence is seen below in this chapter where reference is made to actual listening test washback research in classrooms where a Cambridge ESOL exam is one of the eventual assessments. Considerations of the potentially construct-irrelevant nature of listening *test* approaches mentioned above (e.g. recordings followed by written questions to be answered; written multiple-choice items) may be raised again.

Significantly, Messick (1996) links positive washback to 'direct' assessments, which is what, in the main, Cambridge ESOL exams would claim to be. Messick stresses the need to minimise construct under-representation and construct-irrelevant difficulty in such tests, which would, presumably, harm test validity.

Bachman (2004:7) also recognises the complexity of the impact/ washback: validity relationship. He expresses concern that validity and test use are not always accepted as related in language assessment:

> Both the construct validity of our score-based inferences and the impact,
> or consequences, of test use need to be considered from the very begin-
> ning of test design, with the test developer and test users working
> together to prioritise the relative importance of these qualities.

If this is not the case, 'we are left with validity at one end and consequences
at the other, with no link between' (2004:7). Bachman's two-part assessment
argument (building on Kane, Crooks and Cohen 1999, Mislevy, Steinberg
and Almond 2002, 2003, Toulmin 2003) seeks to embrace the twin concerns
of validity and test use. The proposed logic combines the *assessment validity* argument linking assessment performance and interpretation, with the
assessment use argument, linking score-based interpretations with intended
uses or decisions (Bachman 2005:31). (See Bachman and Palmer (2010) for a
full discussion of the Assessment Use Argument (AUA).)

Impact by design

Bachman's insistence that test impact should be designed systematically
into test design and validation is certainly in line with current Cambridge
ESOL policy and practice on the validation of its exams, as seen in the socio-
cognitive and VRIPQ frameworks.

Given the acknowledged and apparently growing impact of tests of
English, it is hardly surprising that educational authorities and test developers
should consider how to ensure, as far as possible, that they optimise the positive impact of their tests and minimise any negative impact. In a recent study
to explore how test impact might be modelled theoretically for the purpose
of researching it in practice, Saville observes that 'the concept of impact by
design has emerged as a key feature of the impact model' (Saville 2009:254).
Saville explicitly acknowledges Messick's 1996 idea of achieving 'validity by
design as a basis for washback', though his account of some of Cambridge
ESOL's own exam impact studies also takes account of the complexities of
the variables involved in any teaching–learning–examining context.

Green (2007) and Hughes (2003) suggest the kind of conditions that need
to be in place for positive washback to be a reality. These include: emphasising the importance but attainability of the test tasks; making them direct,
appropriate for the test takers and criterion-referenced; ensuring the test
takers and teachers are familiar with the test, and providing optimal support
for teachers. Weir (2005a), Wall (2005) and Cheng (2005) also argue the cen-
trality of teacher support provision if beneficial washback is to occur. In this
connection, evidence of the major increase in Cambridge ESOL's support
to English teachers may be seen from the lesson plans and activities, seminars, conferences and other fora it offers, in addition to its comprehensive
set of teacher qualifications. One of the aims in this chapter is to explore how

conditions for impact by design may be optimised in relation to the testing of listening.

Though the concept of impact by design may be intended as benign, Chalhoub-Deville and Deville (2008) sound a note of caution. They indicate some of the dangers with reference to the No Child Left Behind (NCLB) Act, a recent US educational reform targeting the testing of all English language learners according to state-wide standards. Chalhoub-Deville and Deville show concerns redolent of the fears expressed by Shohamy in her 2001 book *The Power of Tests: A Critical Perspective on the Uses of Language Tests*. Problems may well arise when policymakers and bureaucrats grasp the power of assessment and take to implementing tests as a way of bringing about educational change, as policy tools which may not in actuality substitute for meaningful educational reform. Chalhoub-Deville and Deville note from past experience 'that test-driven educational reform had repeatedly fallen short in delivering the desired educational change' (2008:520). Both Shohamy and Chalhoub-Deville are close academic contacts of Cambridge ESOL and have, for some years, spoken regularly at fora sponsored by Cambridge ESOL, where their cautions are publicly voiced.

The 'impact by design' approach subscribed to by Cambridge ESOL, as an independent examinations board and not a state body, is characterised by efforts to achieve the beneficial consequential validity features discussed in this chapter and elsewhere in this book. With regard to listening tests, for example, a systematic attempt is made to ensure that the cognitive processes elicited by a listening comprehension task (e.g. identifying specific information) and the contextual features embodied in the task (e.g. a public announcement) reflect as faithfully and transparently as possible those processes and contexts that occur in the world beyond the test, bearing in mind of course that any task in a listening comprehension test unavoidably entails some degree of artificiality of format. Note here Cambridge ESOL's awareness of the problems of construct irrelevance mentioned above.

Fairness

Language testers should, says Kunnan (2003), locate their activities within a test fairness framework targeting five qualities: validity, absence of bias, access, administration and consequences. Kunnan (2008) sees the issue of fairness as the most important challenge in large-scale assessment. He defines fairness in terms of the use of fair content and test methods (see Weir's context and cognitive validities) and in assessing language ability through the fair use of the scores obtained from the test (Weir's consequential validity). These are clearly useful criteria for checks on fairness as an aspect of test validation although Bachman (2005:7) regrets the apparent absence here of any 'logical mechanism for relating these'.

So, test providers are concerned *a priori* with the washback of a test on curricula, course designs, materials, teachers, teaching/learning, learners, schools, parents and so on. They are equally concerned, *a posteriori*, with the impacts of test scores on, for example, candidates' further/higher studies, careers, attitudes, getting the right people into the right jobs or places; that is, with institutional, regional, national performances and ethos. In relation to the testing of listening, for example, it is clearly important that the tasks in a listening test should reflect the sorts of cognitive processing for the sorts of purposes and contexts that occur in educational and/or employment settings, e.g. listening to a lecture, participating in some realistic way in a discussion or understanding an answerphone message or mobile phone applications (Hawkey and Milanovic 2013).

Stakeholders

This chapter has already referred indirectly to various stakeholder groups associated with tests and the use of test scores, i.e. learners, teachers, employers, government agencies. The broader the community of stakeholders for whose interests the test developers are seeking to cater, the greater the ethical concerns. Figure 6.3 (Saville 2009:53 adapting Taylor 1999) reminds us of the range and diversity of stakeholders 'impacted by assessment or who contribute to assessment processes and mechanisms'.

Figure 6.3 Cambridge ESOL community of stakeholders

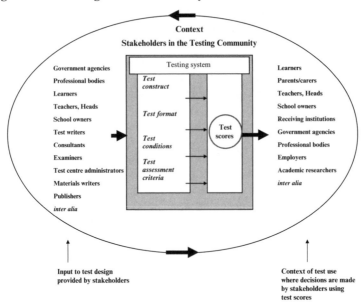

Taylor (2000:2) notes, with reference to the stakeholder community summarised here, the *a priori: a posteriori* distinction:

> Some of the stakeholders listed (e.g. examiners and materials writers) are likely to have more interest in the 'front end' of a test, i.e. the test assessment criteria or test format. Others may see their stake as being primarily concerned with the test scores. Some stakeholders, such as learners and teachers, will naturally have an interest in all aspects of the test.

It is to be expected in an era of the increasingly widespread use of high-stakes tests and such high-profile concern for their implications that the question of common standards and codes of practice should be advocated and developed. As Saville and Hawkey (2004:75) put it:

> [i]n tune with increasing individual and societal expectations of good value and accountability, testers are expected to adhere to codes of professionally and socially responsible practice.

This, they argue:

> . . . tends to increase the concern of high-stakes exam providers with the ethics of language testing. Such codes (for example, of the International Language Testing Association (ILTA), or the Association of Language Testers in Europe (ALTE)), were intended to improve test development rigour and probity.

Alan Davies, who chaired an ILTA Code of Practice Committee, considers that a Code of Ethics 'demonstrates to the members of an association or of a profession what its standards are' (2005:46). The ILTA Code of Ethics itself (adopted at the annual meeting of ILTA, March 2000), was 'to offer a benchmark of satisfactory ethical behaviour by all'. A Code of Practice, Davies adds, then 'instantiates that Code of Ethics' (2005:46–47). Cambridge ESOL now also routinely seeks ISO quality management certifications, intended to complement many other validity-seeking procedures. Such certifications underline the examination board's quest for good ethical standing for its exams.

The role and place of impact studies

The assumption is now that washback and impact must indeed be investigated as part of continuous test validation activity. The data collected on test washback and impact may inform changes designed to improve the test and its related systems. Cambridge ESOL's study of exam impact was characterised by Neil Jones and Nick Saville at the third Cambridge Assessment Conference in Beijing in October 2010 in the following terms:

- as accepting the Messick (1989:13) view that: 'Validity is an integrated evaluative judgment of the degree to which empirical evidence and theoretical rationales support the adequacy and appropriateness of inferences and actions based on test scores or other modes of assessment'
- as accepting the Bachman and Palmer (1996) algorithm:
  Test Usefulness = Validity + Reliability + Impact + Practicality
- as acknowledging that modern conceptions of validity encompass the *use and consequences* of test results i.e. tests can be valid for a purpose
- as seeing test consequences, impact at the macro-level and washback at the micro-level, as a crucial element of validity and recognising that an assessment may be valid if it has the intended positive impact and does not have unintended negative impacts.

The discussion of the nature of impact and washback so far has important implications for the timing and role of impact research within the test valida-tion process. Figure 6.4 below reminds us of where impact and washback studies may fit in the cycle of test impact study and validation.

Figure 6.4 Sequence of potential washback and impact study actions in rela-tion to a high-stakes test

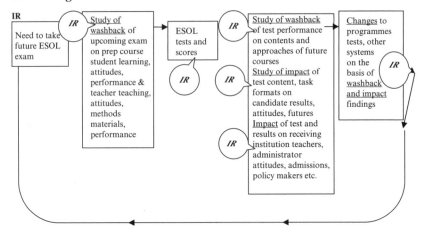

Figure 6.4 (from Hawkey 2006:12) indicates symbolically the points ((*IR*)) where potential test washback and impact may occur and be analysed. For example, the effects of an international gate-keeping language test such as IELTS on test preparation programmes (see, for example, Green 2007) or the effects of the test on candidates' futures at receiving institutions and the admissions policies of those institutions. As Figure 6.4 indicates, wash-back occurs throughout the implementation of a new language test prepa-ration course because a curriculum associated with the specifications of the

new exam is known in advance and this may shape the teaching and learning that occurs. Washback also takes place in subsequent preparation courses because of the experience of the previous course and because of the test performances and scores of learners on the tests at the end. Since it occurs before the test has been administered, the first occurrence of washback in Figure 6.4 is actually more like a 'bow wave' from the exam specifications and/or curriculum than washback from the exam itself. The second washback study occurrence is indeed from washback from the course and the test(s) that have already taken place.

The examples of 'impact' in Figure 6.4 also take account of the use of the term to include the effects of a programme or test *beyond* washback, that is on stakeholders, domains and systems in addition to language learners and teachers and their immediate context (see definition above). Notice also the final arrow and circle back, indicating continuing washback and impact and the iterative nature of its study. The data collected on test washback and impact should inform, in an iterative manner, subsequent cycles of change designed to improve the test and its related systems.

The range and complexity of the variables

As already intimated, the study of test washback and impact is complex in focus as well as timing. Though often defined as a hyponym of the superordinate concept of impact, washback is itself broad in its coverage, as indicated, for example, by Alderson (2004:ix), Bailey (1996), Cheng and Curtis (2004:12), Hawkey (2006:13), Spratt (2005:5) and Watanabe (2004:19). In the context of listening assessment, the study of the many sides of impact and washback is further complicated by the particular complexities of the listening construct itself.

Alderson and Wall (1993) identify no fewer than 15 washback hypotheses, including the potential influence of a test on the teacher and the learner, what and how teachers teach and learners learn, the rate and sequence of learning, and attitudes to teaching and learning methods. These hypotheses suggest that investigations of any aspect of test washback may be complicated by one or more intervening variables operating between the learning and the teaching and the target. For example, the format of a listening test and the kind of listening it invites may well, as exemplified above, shape the approach adopted by the classroom teacher and the nature of the learning experienced by the students. Even in teaching which follows a communicative approach, practice in listening often relies on the playing of recorded listening texts, followed by comprehension questions, an approach that closely mirrors the common listening test technique referred to above. The influences of test methods and teaching approaches are, of course, mutual, especially since testers and teachers are often the same people. In certain classes instruction relies heavily upon practising the use of *test* formats and in some parts of the world learners are specifically trained in test-wise strategies rather than in developing their listening skills. A second negative trend, referred to above, is the fact that because listening tests follow particular conventional formats, listening classes are quite often given over to test practice instead of fostering listening skills which could be applied in the real world.

In a recent issue of *Human Communication Research* (2006), Bostrom explores the listening construct, concluding that 'linear models of memory (first short-term memory, then intermediate storage, then long-term memory) do not describe listening' (2006:98). Bostrom's view is that 'like memory, listening has short-term and long-term elements, that listening research ought to examine short-term processing more carefully than before, and that any general definition of listening ought to include all elements, including long-term elements'. Other 'extremely important constructs in listening' are listener involvement and 'nonverbal indicators of listening' (2006:98). In Chapter 1 of this volume, Taylor refers to factors in listening tasks such as speech rate, variety of accent and acquaintanceship with the speaker as variables in any listening task.

So, as suggested above, we are dealing, in the assessment of listening, with a particularly complex skill, with its challenges for the tester and the impact studier correspondingly complex. Thus, the key role played by the washback of high-stakes test constructs and techniques. So, it is of interest, in a consideration of the construct of listening, the testing of listening skills and the relationship of this to both the impact and washback of such tests on stakeholders, to analyse the Listening test in a high-stakes global exam. We choose one of Cambridge ESOL's longest-standing and most widely taken assessments, the First Certificate in English (or Cambridge English: First) for its relationships with the skills, micro-skills (Munby 1978) or cognitive processes (Weir 2005a) involved in listening. We see the following task formats and target listening constructs (Cambridge ESOL 2012c):

Part 1 (Multiple choice): ability to *listen for gist, detail, function, purpose, attitude, opinion, relationship, topic, place, situation, genre, agreement, etc. in a series of unrelated short texts.*

Part 2 (Gapped sentences completion) ability to *listen for specific words or phrases from a single long text, focusing on detail, specific information and stated opinion. Candidates produce written answers by completing gapped sentences.*

Part 3 (Multiple matching (Candidates need to match an option to the correct speaker)) *listening for general gist, detail, function, purpose, attitude, opinion, relationship, topic, place, situation, genre, agreement, etc.*

Part 4 (Multiple choice) *ability to listen for opinion and attitude, expressed in gist, main idea, and specific information, and based on one long text.*

Much research and effort has clearly gone into the specification for assessment of a broad range of skills, abilities, strategies and techniques connected with the listening construct. With major exams such as the FCE to be taken, the washback is likely to be strong. But if teachers choose to offer communicative exercises and practice in the kind of listening experiences and tasks included in FCE (and similar exams), one can see the potential for positive washback in the classroom.

Care is needed, of course, in impact study observations, analyses and conclusions to avoid making washback assumptions that are over-simplified. Hamp-Lyons (1997:295–303) cautions against the over-simplification that exam washback necessarily leads to 'curriculum alignment', in the negative sense of teaching to the test. Green and Hawkey (2004:66) warn that washback should certainly not be assumed to be a 'harmful influence'. Alderson, while agreeing that 'test consequences are important and may relate to validity issues' (1995:3), has 'difficulty seeing washback and impact as central to construct validity' because of the 'myriad factors' impacting on a test, e.g. a teacher's linguistic ability, training, motivation, course hours, class size and extra lessons. For Alderson this 'is not, of course, to deny the value of studying test impact and washback in its own right, but it underscores the need to gather evidence for the relationship between a test and its impact on the one hand, and of the futility, given current understanding and data, of making direct and simplistic links between washback and validity' (Alderson 1995:3). Hawkey (2009:23) suggests that this inherent complexity means that the washback and impact of a preparation course in support of a high-stakes exam may need to be investigated not only directly, for example through participant responses to questions on how the course affected them, but also less directly, by probing what various other stakeholders think about the course in the contexts, narrow and broader, in which it is taking place. Green (2007:3) feels that washback 'is not generally considered to be a standard for judging the validity of a test', because it 'can only be related to a test indirectly, as effects are realised through the interactions between, *inter alia*, the test, teachers and learners'. Green cites Mehrens (1998:1–30) on the lack of agreed standards for the evaluation of washback and the problem of different stakeholders seeing the same effects differently.

There is interesting food for thought in Messick's 1996 advice, also cited by Green: 'rather than seeking backwash as a sign of test validity, seek validity by design as a likely basis for backwash' (1996:252). But Alderson and Wall (1993) and Wall (2005) are of the opinion that we should not take for granted that teachers actually use methods advised by exam syllabuses or teacher guides. Wall (2005) found empirical evidence suggesting that teachers may not be driven by the exam rather than the textbook or that they overfocus on skills in the textbook that are tested in the exam (see also Hawkey

2006). Nor should we assume that what teachers claim they teach necessarily coincides with their actual teaching (Wall 2005), or that teacher and student perceptions of exam-preparation lesson content are necessarily in tune (Hawkey 2006:138). Hawkey also reminds us that washback is not necessarily unidirectional, i.e. from exam to textbook and teaching, rather than bi-directional, i.e. also from textbook and teaching to exam (see also Wall 2005). Also of interest is the recent work of Wall and Horak, who report on a washback study for TOEFL on behalf of the Education Testing Service (ETS) (Wall and Horak 2006, 2008). Their study stresses the importance of gathering proper baseline data in washback studies. This helps to increase confidence that washback evidence can be attributed to the test in question and not to other factors.

So, a substantial research literature now exists that illustrates the range and complexity of potential variables associated with washback and impact. But the quest is still widely seen as worthwhile, as an important element in the larger quest for test validity.

Listening

The 'skill' of listening, as earlier chapters in this book have illustrated and as our own references and examples in this chapter above have confirmed, is in itself, of course, a complex matter. Buck (2001) combines elements of a competence and a task-based analysis to propose a construct of listening ability. For him, listening involves: processing extended samples of realistic spoken language, automatically and in real time; understanding the linguistic information that is included in the text; and making inferences that are 'unambiguously implicated by the content of the text' (2001:124).

In his book *Listening in the Language Classroom* (2009a), John Field (also see Chapter 3 above and in the listening test washback research examples below) questions the common focus on listening 'comprehension', the product rather than the *process* of listening. Field emphasises the psychological processes involved in the skill of listening, and the characteristics of the speech signal from which listeners attempt to construct a message. Field's suggested approaches to the teaching of listening involve learner practice in aspects of listening based on the perceptual or cognitive demands that listening makes on the learner. It is noted below that Field's research on the lecture-listening component of the IELTS Listening test below investigates the *cognitive* validity of the test. We are reminded of the cognitive processes box in the updated version of Weir's 2005 socio-cognitive framework shown in Figure 1.1 on page 28, with, for example, its 'decoding of acoustic input', 'establishing propositional meaning', 'building a discourse representation'.

Impact study research and the Cambridge exams

Whether impact is intended or unintended, it would seem to be a legitimate and crucial focus of test validation research to 'review and change' tests and programmes in the light of findings on, among other aspects, 'how the stakeholders use the exams and what they think about them' (Saville 2003:60).

In this section of Chapter 6, examples are cited of Cambridge ESOL impact research and related action with a focus on testing listening. The discussion below draws from:

- documentation of the routine processes and systems for exam development and revision
- reports in Cambridge ESOL's *Research Notes*, a quarterly publication on research, test development and validation within the organisation
- other accounts of project-specific exam impact and washback studies.

Cambridge ESOL validation studies related to the impact of its Listening tests

Regular reviews of its key exams (see, for example, Weir and Milanovic (Eds) 2003, Hawkey 2009) are a systematic part of Cambridge's approach to test validation. Taking a general exam-impact point of view, these reviews typically involve surveying a broad constituency of stakeholders (see page 284). In the case of the CPE exam, for example, Milanovic (2003:xviii–xix) describes 'an extensive consultation exercise on a scale not previously attempted by a British Examination Board', with questionnaires sent to 25,000 students, 5,000 teachers, 1,200 Oral Examiners, 800 Local Secretaries and 120 UK further education institutions. Boroughs (2003) explains the nature of the feedback received on the CPE Listening test from multiple stakeholder groups and how this assisted the test designers in rethinking the way in which the Listening test should be structured. Specific issues raised included: the overall format of the paper; the range of testing focuses; the range of task types, text types and register; perceptions concerning the authenticity of recordings; and the desirability (or otherwise) of a single-play listening section.

The FCE and CAE updating project (2004–08) administered a three-questionnaire survey (online and hard copy), eliciting responses from 1,900 candidates, 101 Centre Exams Managers across 20 countries, and from 625 other stakeholders including Directors of Studies, Examiners, teachers, teacher trainers and materials writers. The 2004–08 FCE and CAE review exercise also sought the views of key Cambridge ESOL management, administrative, research and business management staff, Principal Examiners, Senior Team Leaders, major Cambridge ESOL partners (e.g. the Evaluation and Accreditation of Quality in Language Services (EAQUALS)). As the review and updating of the exams reached firm decisions on the modifications to be implemented, communication was reported to thousands of stakeholders by means of face-to-face presentations and seminars around the world, hard copy and online hits in the thousands on the special exam update project Bulletins, and Specifications and Sample Papers for examinations from December 2008. Note the clear *consequential validity* intention in all these stakeholder communication efforts. Some of the key listening test-related impact matters emerging from the FCE and CAE review exercise are summarised here.

Of particular interest in the context of this volume is that the CAE/FCE (2004–08) revision project operationalised and implemented the socio-cognitive framework for data collection use according to the areas specified by Weir. The Cambridge ESOL internal report *FCE/CAE Modifications: Building the Validity Argument: Application of Weir's Socio-Cognitive framework to FCE & CAE* (ffrench and Gutch 2006) interpreted consequential validity categories as in Table 6.3 below.

Table 6.3 Grid for the application of Weir's socio-cognitive framework, consequential validation section

CONSEQUENTIAL VALIDITY		
Score interpretation		
Framework	Skills areas	Notes
Differential validity: Are the items free from bias towards candidates with different cultural backgrounds, background knowledge, cognitive characteristics, native languages, ethnicity, age and gender? Is there potential for unsuitable topics (e.g. religion, war) to be included? **Washback in classroom or workplace:** Does the test have beneficial impact on FCE/CAE classroom activities, FCE/CAE text books and teaching resources, and the attitudes and related practices of FCE/CAE stakeholders towards the exam? **Effect on individual within society:** Does the test have beneficial impact on the wider community?		

During the CAE review programme (see Hawkey 2007), and following consultation with stakeholders (including potential candidates) and pre-testing of versions of alternative listening tasks, the listening task types in Table 6.4 were approved, described here in terms of the activities, strategies or skills they are intended to assess within the listening construct. (Note the efforts clearly made to cover a wide range of listening purposes, strategies and (though these remain non-explicit) cognitive listening. On the impact-related question of the authenticity of test-task types, multiple choice and sentence completion continue to figure large.)

Table 6.4 Finalised CAE Listening (Paper 4) from December 2008

PART 1	Structure and tasks
Task type and focus	Listening for feeling, attitude, opinion, purpose, functions, agreement, course of action, gist, detail etc.
Format	Three short extracts from exchanges between interacting speakers with two multiple-choice questions for each extract.
PART 2	
Task type and focus	Listening for specific information, stated opinion.
Format	A 3-minute monologue (which may be introduced by a presenter); candidates required to use information heard to complete sentences.
PART 3	
Task type and focus	Listening for attitude and opinion.
Format	Long-text conversation between two or more speakers.
PART 4	
Task type and focus	Multiple matching (two parallel tasks); listening for gist, attitude, main points, interpreting context.
Format	Five short related monologues, of approximately 30 seconds each; candidates to select correct options from a list of eight.

There were still key additional steps to be taken in the complex process of test review and change: the creation of guidelines for item writers to draft tasks for pre-editing, editing, vetting and proofing; pretesting with 700 prospective CAE candidates; descriptive and inferential statistical analyses (see, in particular, Chapter 5 above); and analyses of qualitative feedback. These steps were followed by final discussions and recommendations for the updated CAE Listening test. The updated Listening test was agreed to have the desired range of tasks, text types and testing focuses as well as the advantage of saving 5 minutes of test time over its predecessor. In line with suggestions from participant feedback, the test would begin with the short extracts task: taking an impact-influenced view, Murray (2007:23) noted: 'Candidates might feel more comfortable listening initially to a series of short interactional extracts rather than a longer, extended monologue'.

The processes and examples cited above from the updating of the CAE Listening test following the 2004–08 review were similar to those in the simultaneous review of the FCE (see Hawkey 2007).

Cambridge ESOL *Research Notes* and Listening test impact and washback matters

A good measure of the increasing importance of the study of the consequential validity of Cambridge ESOL exams is the number of articles on impact and washback research which have appeared since 2000 in the *Research Notes* quarterly publication produced by the examination board. Articles in this journal, freely available via its website archive, report a wide range of studies, including some also published or presented elsewhere, for example in the *Studies in Language Testing* series volumes, in the *Language Assessment Quarterly* journal, at international conferences or seminars or as internal Cambridge ESOL documents.

No fewer than 23 *Research Notes* articles have impact and washback research matters as their main focus. These include six on impact constructs and approaches (using the term 'impact' here to include 'washback'); five on the study of impact in education systems overseas; four comparing the impact of Cambridge ESOL assessments with others; and seven on the impact of particular Cambridge ESOL exams (including four articles on IELTS impact). There are numerous other articles in *Research Notes* which also include reference to impact and washback though they may not be the primary focus.

The studies covered in *Research Notes* investigate both impact and washback, and have mainly *a priori* or, mainly *a posteriori* emphases, as differentiated in Figure 6.4 above. The frequency with which Cambridge ESOL's own quarterly publication presents washback and impact study research again underlines the significance of such studies in its thinking and action.

The assessment of listening is an important target of a fair proportion of this impact research, as indicated in Table 6.5. The table lists the main listening-related impact research covered in recent editions of *Research Notes*. The listening test research projects reported relate potentially to all sectors of the socio-cognitive framework, reflecting its unified approach to gathering validation evidence.

Table 6.5 *Research Notes* **studies related to listening tests**

Title	*Research Notes* No.	Author(s)
Redeveloping Part 1 of the CPE Listening paper	10, Nov 2002	Rod Boroughs
The effects on performance of computer familiarity and attitudes towards CB IELTS	20, May 2005	Louise Maycock and Tony Green
Listening, Reading and Writing on computer-based and paper-based versions of IELTS	21, Aug 2005	Andrew Blackhurst
Reviewing the CAE Listening test	30, Nov 2007	Steve Murray
Reviewing Part 1 of the FCE Listening test	30, Nov 2007	Diana Fried-Booth
Examining Listening: developments and issues in assessing second language listening	32, May 2008	Ardeshir Geranpayeh, Lynda Taylor
The Cambridge ESOL approach to item writer training: the case of ICFE Listening	32, May 2008	Kate Ingham
Vocabulary use in the FCE Listening test	32, May 2008	Dittany Rose
Using DIF to explore item difficulty in CAE Listening	32, May 2008	Ardeshir Geranpayeh
Adapting listening tests for on-screen use	32, May 2008	Ed Hackett

Looking at some of the listening test impact research listed here a little more closely, we recognise key impact and washback research issues. The articles by Boroughs (2002), Murray (2007) and Fried-Booth (2007) are all associated with a major review of a well-established examination and thus reflect a concern for washback, i.e. how the current listening test is perceived and what changes or improvements stakeholder constituencies might welcome as the test evolves over time, perhaps to reflect ongoing developments in language pedagogy or to suit classroom realities. Boroughs (2002:6) underlines the exam: teaching washback link, citing stakeholder comments that 'the task would have positive washback since teachers would find it more practical to replicate for classroom activities than tasks based on longer texts'. Maycock and Green (2005), Blackhurst (2005) and Hackett (2008) all explore the 'conversion' of an existing listening test to a computer-based (CB) format, which brings its own challenges in terms of impact not only on test takers but also on the test writers who produce the materials and on testing centres which make up the delivery network. Blackhurst (2005:17), for example, compares the impact of CB and paper-based (PB) IELTS test modules, including listening. He concludes that 'CB IELTS can be used interchangeably with PB IELTS, and that candidates, given adequate computer familiarity, will perform equally well on either version of the test' (2007:17). Blackhurst confirms the view of the IELTS partners that 'candidates should be able to take the test in the form with which they feel comfortable: the pen and paper test will continue to be available' (2007:7). Maycock and Green (2005:4), however, find that candidates were generally happier with the timing on the PB rather than the CB version of IELTS.

Geranpayeh and Taylor (2008) note the washback of the communicative approach to teaching on the CAE exam, which was first developed in the late 1980s. This saw the introduction of a single-play listening task in an attempt to add authenticity to the assessment. However, subsequent research for the review of FCE and CAE (above) resulted in Part 2 of CAE Listening being modified to double playing in the interests of consistency of testing method across exams in Cambridge's Main Suite. Boroughs (2002) and Weir and Milanovic (2003) have more on the research associated with single or double-play listening. Geranpayeh and Taylor suggest that 'CAE sought to mirror developments in English language teaching and to have a positive impact back into the ELT community – reflecting Cambridge's long established concern for fairness in a large international market where the ability to conduct listening tests in optimum quality conditions may vary due to local constraints (2008:3).

In his article on the use of Differential Item Functioning (DIF) to explore item difficulty in the CAE Listening test, Ardeshir Geranpayeh investigated the CAE exam for DIF in relation to test taker age, checking items for DIF and subjecting to expert content analysis those test items that had indicated, at least in statistical terms, a potential for bias. Interestingly, no clear pattern emerged to explain why the items should have demonstrated DIF.

In recent years, Cambridge ESOL has explored new and innovative methodologies for researching washback and impact issues associated with its examinations. For example, Hawkey, Thompson and Turner (2006:9) describe the development of a video database for the storing and analysis of Cambridge ESOL impact study data. The Cambridge ESOL Impact Video Database already serves its purpose in the analysis of data for three studies of IELTS (see below), the *Progetto Lingue* 2000 and of preparation courses for internal and external English language exams at a language centre in Florence. For the washback study of tests on classroom activity, as part of research into the impact and consequential validity of language tests, a video database can prove a practical and beneficial research tool. Its particular applicability to listening and speaking research is clear. Although listening comprehension is typically assessed within a dedicated listening test, listening can also be considered as part of communicative competence within a speaking test. Video recording provides very useful data which enables us to investigate speaker–listener interaction, back channelling by the listener, breakdowns of understanding and why such breakdowns occur (including whether they are the results of lack of clarity by the examiner).

Impact-related research on IELTS

The International English Language Testing System (IELTS), jointly owned by British Council, IDP: IELTS Australia and Cambridge ESOL, is widely used as an international assessment of English language for education, immigration and professional accreditation. From the mid 1990s the very high-stakes 'gatekeeping' nature of IELTS made it a natural subject for impact-related study and this also chimed with Cambridge ESOL's growing interest in matters of test washback and impact (Taylor 2012a). Of over 60 studies published in 12 volumes of research funded jointly by the IELTS partners since 1995, more than 30 are impact-focused studies of various kinds.

The IELTS Listening module is a regular focus of IELTS research (see Table 6.6 on page 297), sometimes in its own right and sometimes as part of a larger impact study covering all four skills components. Rea-Dickins, Kiely and Yu (2007) make interesting points regarding the listening construct. Reminding us of the 'non-essential correlations between English language abilities and academic achievements' (2007:34), Rea-Dickins et al find that more students in their case-study group 'expressed concerns with reading and writing than with listening and speaking skills for their subject learning'. Difficulties linked to understanding lectures were suggested as deriving from speakers' frequent use of academic terminology and speed. Listening in interactive contexts appeared to be 'more challenging in one-to-one tutorials than in peer group discussion, suggesting that interlocutor status and density of information are contributory factors' (2007:42). Useful consequential validity data here from this IELTS impact study.

Table 6.6 A selection of impact-related research reports (RR) studies receiving grants from the jointly funded IELTS research fund

Research title	Researchers	Published
Predictive validity of the IELTS Listening Test as an indicator of student coping ability in English-medium undergraduate courses in Spain	Ruth Breeze, Paul Miller	IELTS RR 12
An impact study into the use of IELTS by professional associations and registration entities: The United Kingdom, Ireland and Canada	Glenys Merrifield	IELTS RR 11 2011
The use of tactics and strategies by Chinese students in the Listening component of IELTS	Richard Badger, Xiaobiao Yan	IELTS RR 9 2009
A cognitive validation of the lecture-listening component of the IELTS Listening paper	John Field	IELTS RR 9 2009
Attitudes of tertiary key decision-makers towards English language tests in Aotearoa New Zealand: Report on the results of a national provider survey	Hilary Smith, Stephen Haslett	IELTS RR 7 2007
Student identity, learning and progression: The affective and academic impact of IELTS on 'successful' candidates	Pauline Rea-Dickins, Richard Kiely, Guoxing Yu	IELTS RR 7 2007
The attitudes of IELTS stakeholders: student and staff perceptions of IELTS in Australian, UK and Chinese universities	David Coleman, Sue Starfield, Anne Hagan	IELTS RR 5 2003
An impact study of two IELTS user groups: candidates who sit the test for immigration purposes and candidates who sit the test for secondary education purposes	Brent Merrylees	IELTS RR 4 2003
Survey of receiving institutions' use and attitude to IELTS	Clare McDowell, Brent Merrylees	IELTS RR 1 1998

Some Cambridge ESOL impact case studies

In the final sections of this chapter we select for closer analysis two studies intended to contribute to the validation argument for the positive consequences of Cambridge ESOL exams. The first is a major long-term programme of research by Cambridge ESOL into the impact of IELTS (see above). The second is the *Progetto Lingue 2000* (*PL2000*) Impact Study carried out by Cambridge ESOL with the support of the Italian Ministry of Education. This study sought to ascertain the effects of foreign language reform measures on the English language performance of language learners in state schools in Italy using Cambridge exams for their certification under the *PL2000* project.

The IELTS Impact Study: Findings on the Listening module

The IELTS Impact study (see Hawkey 2006, Saville 2009) looked for evidence of the washback and impact of the test on:

- the test-taking population
- classroom activity in IELTS-related classes
- teaching materials, including textbooks.

This case study was originally commissioned in the mid-1990s by the then UCLES EFL (now Cambridge ESOL), with Professor Charles Alderson and his research team at the University of Lancaster designing draft data collection instruments. The validated instruments were later used for the main data collection exercise with a case study sample of the IELTS candidate and teacher populations. Five hundred and seventy-two IELTS test takers, 83 preparation course teachers and 45 textbook evaluators responded through the questionnaires; 120 students, 21 teachers and 15 receiving institution administrators participated in face-to-face interviews and focus groups to enhance and triangulate questionnaire data.

Of relevance to the listening construct are the perceptions of IELTS preparation course students and teachers of levels of difficulty across the skills modules. The values in Table 6.7 indicate that candidates and IELTS preparation teachers have similar perceptions on the relative difficulties of the IELTS skills modules, the Listening test being the second least difficult in the view of both groups. The IELTS impact study pursued inter-relationships between perceived test module difficulty and other factors affecting candidates' performance.

Table 6.7 IELTS Impact Study student and teacher perceptions of IELTS module difficulty

Most difficult IELTS Module? (%)		
	Students	Teachers
Reading	49	45
Writing	24	26
Listening	18	20
Speaking	9	9

Table 6.7 emphasises the Reading test module as the most difficult according to the test takers and time pressure as the most prominent problem with the Reading test and, relatively, the Listening test. This kind of finding is clearly of relevance to test validation. It appears to agree with Rea-Dickins et al (2007), also studying IELTS impact and finding more test taker difficulty with reading and writing than with listening and speaking. But note, too, from Table 6.8 here, the complex factors affecting IELTS test taker

performance that may mitigate inferences on overall skill difficulty that are too clear-cut.

Table 6.8 Relationship between perceived skill difficulty and other factors perceived as affecting candidate test performance

| | Difficulty of: | | | | | | |
	language	questions	unfamiliar topics	time pressure	fear of tests	others	Total
Listening	4	7	6	16	4	1	38
Reading	13	20	28	51	14	2	128
Writing	10	10	19	26	8	0	73
Speaking	2	4	6	9	3	1	25

The study probed the perceived influence of the IELTS test on preparation courses. Clearly both participants' perception of content and the materials writer's or teacher's intended content are relevant to the analysis of test washback. Table 6.9 summarises the preparation course teaching/learning activities seen by high percentages of the teachers and the students as occurring most frequently on their IELTS preparation courses. The data analysis here suggests that listening and speaking communication skills were perceived as being given high priority in the courses concerned. The prominence of listening activities in Table 6.9 may suggest strong washback from the requirements and approaches of the IELTS listening module and the need for good skills in listening because of lectures, seminars, tutorial groups and the like on the courses in which IELTS candidates (at least the Academic Module takers) have to participate at their target institutions.

Table 6.9 Candidate and teacher perceptions of prominent IELTS-preparation course activities

Activities	Students %	Teachers %
Reading questions and predicting listening text and answer types	89	86
Listening to live, recorded talks and note-taking	83	63
Analysing text structure and organisation	74	90
Interpreting and describing statistics/graphs/diagrams	74	90
Learning quick and efficient ways of reading texts	73	93
Reading quickly to get main idea of text	77	96
Learning how to organise essays	82	99
Practising making a point and providing supporting examples	78	88
Group discussion/debates	83	76
Practising using words to organise a speech	74	83

In positive IELTS washback terms the prominent items here appear quite likely to make for interesting classroom lessons, including the use of a rather appropriate and engaging set of communicative activities, relevant to students' needs.

The *Progetto Lingue 2000* Impact Study

The Cambridge ESOL *Progetto Lingue 2000* (*PL2000*) Impact Study investigated the impact of government foreign language teaching reforms on English language learner performance and of external examinations, in particular the Cambridge ESOL Key English Test (KET) and the Preliminary English Test (PET), as used for the certification of *PL2000* student language levels. The *PL2000* aimed to provide foreign language education to better meet the communication and certification needs of students as defined by the Common European Framework of Reference for languages (CEFR) (Council of Europe 2001). The Italian Ministry of Education's reasoning was that external certification represents added value in 'transparent credit' in terms of negotiable certification in the professional world and across national borders (Ministry of Education (Italy) 1999).

Cambridge ESOL carried out the *PL2000* Impact Study with the encouragement of the Education Ministry, collecting data from stakeholders including students, teachers, parents, education managers and language testers. The study aimed to provide small-sample quantitative and qualitative impact information on teaching/learning module organisation, content, methodologies, media and learner success.

PL2000 teacher comments tended to express a positive view on the status and impact of external exams used for certification within a national education system.

Despite the intention that *Progetto* classes should provide good opportunity for spoken communication by the students, data from the *PL2000* impact study student questionnaires suggests quite a heavy proportion of teacher-to-whole-class talk, perhaps at the expense of learner individual or group listening and speaking opportunity.

It was noted, when comparing student responses with parallel data from the teachers in the impact study, that the students appeared to regard listening and speaking activities as somewhat *less* prominent in their *PL2000* classes than their teachers did. Note here the difference in perceptions between learners and teacher of the shape and elements of a classroom lesson. On the whole, though, the 161 case study students completing the *PL2000* Impact Study questionnaire felt that their English *speaking* skills were the most improved over the school year, their listening skills less so, as seen in Table 6.10.

Table 6.10 Student questionnaire responses on the most improved skill(s) over the 2001/02 school year

Reading	Listening	Writing	Speaking
29	25	51	56

Hawkey (2006:153) identifies a further exam consequential validity-related matter suggested by *PL2000* impact data:

> It was commonplace during the study to hear school Heads, teachers and students refer to 'the PET (FCE or CAE) course'; or to see curriculum specifications expressed in exam preparation terms. Making sure that students are prepared for the formats and conventions of external exams is, of course, an important and natural part of an examined course. School language courses that are simply exam cramming, however, would not have been in the spirit of the needs and task – based communicative approaches suggested by the *PL2000*.

What emerges here again is the responsibility of high-stakes exam providers to try to minimise the dangers of negative washback (and thus impact) by means of systematic processes, which are impact-by-design based, to encourage positive consequential validity. Typical of stakeholder feedback on this issue was the response of a CAE course student:

> *I think my English is better than the past year; probably because with the Cambridge course I can improve my vocabulary and my skills of listening and speaking.*

But the listening construct is a complex matter, of course (see above and the socio-cognitive framework itself, and Buck (2001) and Field (2009a)). This official Cambridge ESOL description of the CAE Listening test would seem to agree:

> Listening: 40 minutes
> The Listening test requires the candidate to be able to follow and understand a range of spoken materials such as lectures, speeches, interviews, discussions and anecdotes.
> Candidates must demonstrate understanding of gist and detail, feeling, attitude, opinion and purpose expressed.
> A variety of voices, styles of delivery and accents are heard in each paper to reflect the international contexts of the test takers.
> (Cambridge ESOL 2011c) (http://cambridge-english-advanced.cambridge esol.org/_guides/8182_1y10_ce_advanced_informationforcandidates _w.pdf)

There is thus, in the objectives, approaches and findings of an impact study such as that carried out for the *PL2000*, a fair amount to inform the consequential validity-related development of Cambridge ESOL Listening and other tests.

Conclusion

Chapter 6 has sought to build on the earlier chapters in this volume. The chapter has explored the constructs and implications of the consequential validity box in the socio-cognitive framework and other models for the analysis and validation of listening tests. It has re-visited definitions of test washback and impact and attempted to establish where they belong in the complex process of validating high-stakes exams. There is a growing concern with the consequences of English language tests for which the stakes grow ever higher. This leads to the expectation that responsible examination providers will meet the requirements of stricter and more critical international codes of practice, taking account of current assessment trends and values.

This chapter has surveyed and exemplified Cambridge ESOL and other research initiatives and studies to analyse and improve the consequential validity of its exams, particularly assessments of listening, taking account of the many complex variables involved.

Chapter 7 will examine the final set of parameters that examination boards need to consider in generating evidence on the validity of their tests, namely those involved in *criterion-related validity*.

7 Criterion-related validity

Gad S Lim and Hanan Khalifa
Cambridge English Language Assessment

Introduction

Language tests are given and taken so that inferences and generalisations can be made about people's language abilities. For this reason, they always bear some relationship to external realities. Further, for the results of the test to be meaningful, it is necessary that these relationships are consistently appropriate. Another way to put it would be that tests need to demonstrate criterion-related validity (Weir 2005a).

There are a number of relevant external realities. One is that language tests are seldom one-off affairs for examination boards. Examination boards test different people at different times on the same abilities, and it stands to reason that tests should behave in a consistent manner on multiple occasions. Second, apart from the same test measuring the same ability on different occasions, it is often also the case that there are different tests that attempt to measure the same constructs. If these tests are indeed measuring the same things, then, all other things being equal, the results of these different tests would need to be comparable to one other. Finally, the issue of comparability has become more important with the development of reference frameworks such as the Common European Framework of Reference for Languages (CEFR) (Council of Europe 2001). Now, test users want to know how tests are related to these external frameworks, and they also expect to see the evidence supporting any claims of alignment.

There are at least three kinds of comparisons to consider with regard to criterion-related validity (see Figure 7.1). This chapter will consider these three aspects of criterion-related validity with reference to the assessment of listening. It should be noted, though, that discussing the three aspects separately and consecutively is only for convenience in exposition. As will be seen, in Cambridge ESOL practice, the different aspects of criterion-related validity are very closely related to one another. The recent (post-1980s) history of Cambridge ESOL's Main Suite of exams (i.e. KET, PET, FCE, CAE, CPE), underpinned by standardised processes and a Rasch-based item banking approach, reflects a unified and coherent approach that seeks to ensure each exam's comparability across its different forms, in relation to other exams, and with reference to the levels of the CEFR.

Figure 7.1 Aspects of criterion-related validity for listening

Criterion-related validity
• comparison with different forms of the same test
• cross-test comparability
• comparability with external standards and frameworks

Source: Weir (2005a)

Comparison with different forms of the same test

While using the same test form repeatedly might be the easiest way to ensure comparable results, this is not an option in most testing contexts. In large-scale, high-stakes testing, the security of a single test form – and therefore, the integrity of the results – cannot be guaranteed over time. That being the case, the alternative is to create different or multiple forms of a test that are as similar to each other as possible.

In respect of the socio-cognitive framework (Weir 2005a), it should be evident that the first requirement in creating multiple forms is similarity with regard to cognitive and contextual parameters. Checklists, such as those produced by ALTE (n. d.) for the different skills, or forms for analysing examinations, such as those put forward in the Council of Europe's publication *Relating Language Examinations to the Common European Framework of Reference for Languages: A Manual* (2009) are particularly useful for this purpose, as they allow test producers to account for important features of test items and tasks relatively quickly. (For research using checklists, see O'Sullivan, Weir and Saville 2002, Weir and Wu 2006). When different forms are not comparable in respect of cognitive and contextual parameters, it is very difficult to argue that they are alternates for each other, even if they perform in similar ways statistically.

But in addition to different forms being comparable in content, it is also necessary that they perform similarly in statistical terms. The literature recognises degrees of similarity and difference. In the *Standards for Educational and Psychological Testing* (AERA/APA/NCME 1999), a distinction is made between parallel forms, equivalent forms and comparable forms. Parallel forms need to exhibit equivalence in resulting means, variances, and covariance for the same population. Equivalent forms are those where some method of score conversion is used to account for differences in raw scores. Comparable forms, for their part, are similar in content but their statistical relationship to each other is not verified.

As language assessment involves a complex, multi-faceted construct, it is perhaps impossible to come up with forms that are strictly parallel, and to do so on a regular and continuing basis (ALTE 1998). In recognition of that, it appears that most language test providers strive for the still difficult but at least possible task of creating equivalent forms. This is typically done using latent trait modelling to calibrate test items on a common underlying scale, collecting those calibrated items in a bank, and eventually drawing from that bank to construct test forms whose statistical properties are known, permitting the calculation of equivalent scores.

Comparison with different forms of the same test: Cambridge ESOL practice

Cambridge ESOL has long been concerned with the standardisation of exam forms and procedures. As early as 1945, for example, a report was issued with regard to the assessment of listening and in particular concerning the dictation test in the CPE and in what was then called the Lower Certificate in English (now FCE). At the time, the dictation test was read aloud by examiners to candidates, and it was understood that variations in this regard would affect comparability of outcomes. Thus, detailed guidelines to Oral Examiners were issued that same year, which stipulated how often, at what pace, and in what manner the dictation passage should be delivered. (For more on this, see Weir, Vidaković and Galaczi forthcoming 2013).

Procedures to ensure comparability of different exam forms have significantly increased since then, including both qualitative and quantitative approaches that account for the different socio-cognitive dimensions of language tests. The following sections discuss standard procedures in the production of examination materials for listening tests and, within them, the use of checklists and item writer guidelines, as well as the statistical procedures employed to ensure cross-form comparability. (Other contextual parameters such as administration procedures and marking reliability as they relate to listening tests are covered in Appendix D and Chapter 5 respectively and are thus not dealt with here.)

Standard procedures for the production of examination materials

Standard procedures for test development help to ensure production of comparable exam forms. All Cambridge ESOL Listening test tasks and items go through the process of commissioning, pre-editing, editing, pretesting, pretest review, test construction, and vetting and proofing (see Figure 1 in Appendix C).

First, external writers are commissioned to produce listening test material. Materials produced are then sifted during the pre-editing stage to see which ones progress to the editing stage, where materials are improved to an acceptable standard for inclusion in pretests. Pretesting involves participants that closely reflect the target population for a given test, usually those preparing to take the test involved. The result of pretesting is empirical information about the measurement characteristics and quality of the task. The results of pretesting inform the pretest review stage, and recommendations are made whether materials move on to the bank of items for use in paper construction. In paper construction, listening test tasks and items are put together in such a way that they meet the required standard in terms of construct coverage, content diversity, and test difficulty. The decisions made at this point are reviewed in the examination overview stage, and remedial action taken where necessary. After all this, question paper preparation is the stage where the constructed test paper, having been vetted and proofread, is prepared for printing, printed, and readied for use. (See Appendix C for a full description.)

Checklists

Throughout the standard test production process, checklists can be used at multiple points, e.g. during the commissioning stage, the editing stage, or the pretesting stage. Cambridge ESOL has, along with other ALTE members, developed skill-specific checklists for the purpose of facilitating exam construction, evaluation, and comparison (Stevens 2004). The listening content analysis checklist, available at http://www.alte.org/downloads/index.php, covers practical issues such as: number of pages; colour printing; guidance regarding instructions and rubrics; and several components that go into great detail regarding the contextual parameters of a listening test. These include descriptions of the input text (length, number, adapted/unadapted/specially written, text type, topics), task type, speakers (number, role of speakers, register used, whether speakers read from a script or not), quality of audio or video recording, the specific aspect of language ability being tested, the form of the expected response, and how responses are marked. (See Chapter 4 for a full discussion of contextual parameters for listening tests.)

It may be worth considering whether the checklists are as complete as they can be, as a host of variables may have an effect on the difficulty of listening items within and across levels, e.g. speech rate, discourse structure, which it would be wise to take account of. Furthermore, the checklists tend to focus more on contextual than on cognitive parameters. This is not surprising since the former are more easily observable whereas the latter are typically latent lending themselves less readily to systematic analysis, and more work in this area certainly is in order. Having said that, efforts have been made to develop cognitive processing questionnaires (see Weir, O'Sullivan and Horai 2006 for speaking, Weir, O'Sullivan, Yan and Bax 2007 for writing, and Weir, Hawkey, Green and Devi 2009 for reading). These studies have thus far involved experimental designs requiring significant resources which, for the moment, make them less than feasible for routine operational use.

Cambridge ESOL employs test taker questionnaires for post-test review and evaluation. For example, in terms of assessing listening, questionnaires would seek to find out the amount of time candidates have allocated to each test part or which test part candidates have found accessible or challenging, or explore with candidates whether the recording should be listened to more than once or investigate the types of cognitive processes a particular task has evoked. Findings from such investigations can then feed into revisions of exams within Cambridge ESOL's test development and review cycle (Saville 2003).

Item writer guidelines

Each Cambridge ESOL examination also has a set of detailed item writer guidelines (IWG). These provide item writers with guidance regarding the production of listening test materials. IWGs describe the features of an examination's listening paper – format, task type and focus, length of each task, recording information, overall timing, and mark scheme – as well as provide advice on the selection of materials, i.e. with regard to accessibility, fairness for different populations, and the like. Similarly, advice is given on the potential sources for a listening text, whether it is from a broadcast, real-life speech event, pre-recorded information or scripted material created by the item writer. Guidelines are also provided with respect to recordings and the input language. For example, the speakers' voices must be easily distinguishable; texts should be recorded by professional actors in a studio; lines should be delivered in a particular way; background sound effects should be avoided and a range of Standard English accents as well as other varieties such as 'mild' Australian, New Zealand, American, Canadian and Caribbean should be used. (For a discussion on the associated issues for using mild accents in listening tests from a Cambridge ESOL assessment perspective, see Taylor 2002, 2006, and also discussion in Chapter 3).

According to a Cambridge ESOL Assessment Manager (personal communication), IWG have proved to be essential and efficient given the high acceptance rate of items at the pre-editing stage (approximately 80%). It may therefore be useful if Cambridge ESOL would consider a similar document for professional actors even though they are highly experienced and familiar with Cambridge ESOL exams.

Statistical comparability: item banking

As mentioned earlier, a distinction is drawn in the literature between parallel forms, equivalent forms and comparable forms. This section discusses procedures followed by Cambridge ESOL to ensure equivalence between the Listening test forms used in different test administration sessions.

Cambridge ESOL follows an item banking approach to test paper construction. Its Local Item Banking System (LIBS) has been developed to handle the entire production process detailed above. LIBS is underpinned by a common measurement scale. Based on a Rasch model, the scale has been constructed with reference to objectively-scored Listening and Reading items, and has taken into account all Cambridge ESOL levels. (See also the discussion on Cambridge ESOL practice in Chapter 5.)

When listening test items are pretested, they are accompanied by anchor items with known difficulty parameters expressed in terms of the Common Scale, which makes it possible for the new items to similarly be calibrated onto the scale. It thus becomes possible to know the difficulty of any listening test form vis-à-vis any other Listening test form for the same proficiency level, as well as the relationship with other Cambridge ESOL Listening tests at other levels. This allows for the construction of comparable forms and exams at different levels, as illustrated in Figure 7.2.

Figure 7.2 Item banking approach to scale construction

Source: www.CambridgeESOL.org

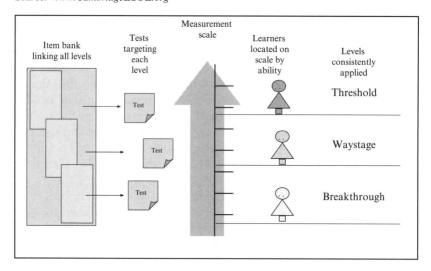

Over the years, Cambridge ESOL has used both *common person* linking, where a group of learners might, for example, take examination papers at two different levels, as well as *common item* linking, where different examinations share some items in common. The latter is the basic approach used in pretesting. These procedures have helped to verify and maintain the proper functioning of the common scale. In the case of listening, Table 7.1 shows that the predicted mean difficulty values of test papers at test construction are generally borne out in the live test, with no or only slight variation between the pairs of figures. This provides evidence that the Common Scale remains properly calibrated. It also provides evidence that following standard procedures during test construction would lead to comparable forms.

Table 7.1 Mean difficulty* of Main Suite Listening papers in 2009 and 2010 sessions

Exam	Exam session	2009		2010	
		At test construction	At live test/ grading	At test construction	At live test/ grading
KET (A2)	Dec	41*	40	41	40
PET (B1)	Dec	56	55	56	55
FCE (B2)	June	63	63	62	62
CAE (C1)	June	71	71	71	72
CPE (C2)	June	77	76	77	78

* Figures in the table represent difficulty values on the Cambridge ESOL Rasch-calibrated Common Scale.

The standard operating procedures for test construction also require listening papers to fall within specified ranges of difficulty, so as to achieve the targeted average for the test as a whole. The overall targeted difficulty values for Main Suite Listening papers on the Cambridge ESOL Common Scale are: 41 for KET, 56 for PET, 62 for FCE, 71 for CAE and 77 for CPE. Table 7.2

Table 7.2 Stability of Main Suite Listening papers across sessions in 2009 and 2010

Year	Exam	Administration sessions			
2009	KET (A2)	*Version A* 41	*Version B* 41	*Version C* 40	*Version D* 40
	PET (B1)	*Version A* 56	*Version B* 57	*Version C* 56	*Version D* 56
	FCE (B2)	*Version A* 63	*Version B* 63	*Version C* 64	*Version D* 64
	CAE (C1)	*Version A* 71	*Version B* 71	*Version C* 71	*Version D* 70
	CPE (C2)	*Version A* 76	*Version B* 76	*Version C* 77	*Version D* 76
2010	KET (A2)	*Version A* 39	*Version B* 40	*Version C* 40	*Version D* 40
	PET (B1)	*Version A* 56	*Version B* 55	*Version C* 57	*Version D* 55
	FCE (B2)	*Version A* 63	*Version B* 63	*Version C* 63	*Version D* 62
	CAE (C1)	*Version A* 72	*Version B* 72	*Version C* 70	*Version D* 70
	CPE (C2)	*Version A* 78	*Version B* 76	*Version C* 77	*Version D* 76

shows how different forms of these tests have stable difficulty values that are close to one another and within the specified ranges (i.e. 1 or 2 points above or below the specified figure).

Post-exam evaluation and review

After the administration of each exam, Cambridge ESOL conducts an evaluation and review, and reports based on these are provided annually. Among other things, these reports include information about:

- which tasks proved accessible or challenging as measured by candidates' performance
- the overall performance of candidates on each task per part
- advice that can be given to candidates and teachers when preparing for the Listening test paper
- the overall performance by candidates by session and by country
- the extent paper reliability has varied year on year since each paper comprises task-based activities rather than discrete items.

This information contributes to ongoing monitoring of the qualitative and quantitative equivalence of different test forms, ensuring comparability of test forms year on year.

Cross-test comparability

It is sometimes the desire of test score users (e.g. educational institutions or employers), even if they have only one test-use purpose, to recognise more than one test. For these users, cross-test comparability is of importance. As an example, English-medium universities enrol students from non-English first language backgrounds, and admissions personnel typically want to know what are 'equivalent' scores on various tests of Academic English (e.g. CAE, IELTS, TOEFL).

In this regard, it is important to emphasise that comparisons involve more than just scores. Indeed, in the measurement literature, equivalence (as a technical term) is possible only if exams are alike in virtually every respect (AERA/APA/NCME 1999). At the very least, before making any comparisons, users should consider whether two exams are measuring the same construct, whether the cognitive and contextual parameters of the tests are similar. If, for example, one exam of Academic English tested all four language skills whereas the other tested only two or three, then comparing overall scores on those exams might not be very meaningful or warranted.

Where tests have been determined to be similar enough in respect of cognitive and contextual parameters, then scores might be meaningfully compared. The best way to do this is presumably to get a group of people to take both tests and then to compare how they perform on the two. When this is done, it is important to ensure that the conditions are comparable, e.g. that the candidates were equally prepared for and equally motivated in taking the two exams. Where this is not possible, data collection should be appropriately counterbalanced so that order, preparation, and motivation effects are accounted for, or some other method employed to account for variables that may affect the validity of the comparison.

Cross-test comparability: Cambridge ESOL practice

Cambridge ESOL has historically been interested in cross-test comparisons, prompted not least by its desire to develop a range of different but also comparable fit-for-purpose exams. This interest can be seen as far back as 1987, when the examination board commissioned a three-year study to examine the comparability between one of its own exams – the First Certificate in English (FCE) – and the Educational Testing Service's (ETS) Test of English as a Foreign Language (TOEFL).

That study (Bachman, Davidson, Ryan and Choi 1995), published as the first volume in the SiLT series, is of interest today primarily for historical reasons, as both exams have since undergone substantial revisions. However, it remains an important precedent for cross-test comparability studies. It compared the two exams in terms of content and abilities measured, and in terms of reliability and of scores obtained in each. In so doing, the study emphasised that comparability is not merely an exercise in comparing scores, but that any such comparison should be founded upon a consideration of what each test is measuring. Score correspondences:

> . . . should not be taken as sufficient evidence that [the two tests] are arbitrarily interchangeable for any or all uses for which they are intended. Decisions regarding which test to take, or which scores to accept, for any given test-use situation should also be based on test content considerations (Bachman et al 1995:99).

The socio-cognitive validation framework (Weir 2005a) certainly supports this, as do other frameworks and principles of good practice.

Where the skill of listening is concerned, factor analysis in the Bachman et al (1995) study showed that the two tests' listening sections loaded onto the same first-order factor and were each largely uni-dimensional. The study also analysed the listening test passages and items, looking into the components of communicative language ability and into test method facets. The results showed that the FCE and TOEFL listening tests were more similar than different. For listening test items and passages at that time, both tests required lexical knowledge, ideational functions, and to a certain extent strategic competence; on the other hand, they generally did not require competence in manipulative, heuristic and imaginative functions, or in morphology. With regard to test methods, while the listening test items were largely similar across FCE and TOEFL in terms of item type and subskill focus, the listening passages differed somewhat, e.g. FCE passages were much longer; in addition, FCE passages contained largely British cultural content while the TOEFL passages reflected American culture, raising the interesting issue of how far each test might be biased against candidates with personal experience of the other culture. (An omission in the comparison of the tests is the delivery of the listening input, e.g. speech rate, and the potential effect of this on the difficulty of items in the respective tests.)

On the basis of substantial similarity, item-response theory (IRT) and multiple regression were used to come up with comparable scores on the two listening tests. However, as has been mentioned, specific comparisons between the tests no longer apply because, partly as a result of the study, significant changes were introduced to make specific improvements to Cambridge ESOL tests during the 1990s (Hawkey 2009). More recently, a study was conducted by ETS (2010) comparing performance on the new internet-based TOEFL test and IELTS, continuing comparisons across the Atlantic.

A more important focus for Cambridge ESOL has been the comparability of tests within its own suite of examinations. Holding to the principle that different contexts of use require different exams, Cambridge ESOL has an extensive number of exam products. In terms of the socio-cognitive framework, cognitive and contextual parameters are adjusted as appropriate, with other parameters held generally constant (see Chapters 4 and 5). Thus, as can be imagined, while their purposes might be different, Cambridge ESOL tests also share substantial similarities, e.g. in terms of task types and the cognitive processing the tasks intend to elicit. Some of them are also meant to measure at the same level horizontally, e.g. FCE and BEC Vantage are both targeted at Level B2 of the CEFR, as well as having specific relationships to each other vertically, i.e. in terms of how quality of performance on one exam at one level approximates to quality of performance on another exam at an adjacent level.

As mentioned earlier in this chapter, the relationship among the different Cambridge ESOL exams rests on common development procedures (attempting to minimise differences where relevant and appropriate) and on the calibration of test items onto a common scale within an item banking approach (and see also Appendix C). This approach makes it possible, in the case of exams at the same level, to construct exams that are comparable in difficulty, or in the case of exams at different levels, to know how performance on an exam at one level relates to performance on another exam at an adjacent level.

The validity of this item banking approach design has been verified in numerous ways. For example, in practice, there have always been a good number of candidates who take two Cambridge exams within days of each other; the similarity of the exams having been accounted for, candidates' performances on the two exams can thus be compared. Data covering 2009 and 2010 shows that for FCE and BEC Vantage candidates who took the two exams within days of each other, the classification consistency (at CEFR Level B2 or not at B2) for the Listening paper is a relatively high 84.9%.

Another study was conducted where IELTS Academic candidates were recruited to also sit the CAE, and vice versa, in order to confirm score relationships on the two exams (Lim, Geranpayeh, Khalifa and Buckendahl forthcoming). The candidates came from 24 different countries, covering important candidature populations for both exams. A counterbalanced design ensured that any preparation and motivation-related effects were cancelled out. The study showed a high correlation between overall scores on the two exams (0.87). The equipercentile approach (Kolen and Brennan 2004) was then used to obtain equivalent scores on the two exams. The study showed that a 'just passing' CAE Listening candidate – that is, a person whose score is identical to the C1 cut score on that paper – would obtain a score slightly higher than Band 7 if they also took IELTS Listening. Classification consistency for CAE and IELTS Listening across three CEFR levels (B2–C2) averaged 80%.

Together with earlier studies (e.g. Jones 2000a, 2001, Taylor 2004), these research analyses of examination data creates a picture of the coherent relationship between different Cambridge ESOL exams, as illustrated in Figure 7.3, thereby allowing a candidate's anticipated performance when taking another Cambridge ESOL exam to be determined. Thus, in addition to providing empirical confirmation of the soundness of Cambridge ESOL's item banking, investigations into cross-test comparability also allow

Figure 7.3 Relationship between Cambridge ESOL examinations

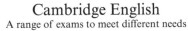

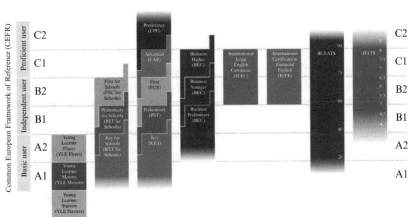

Cambridge ESOL to offer more information and guidance to prospective candidates. Future cross-test studies can confirm whether what candidates supposedly can do at a particular level on one exam matches what they can do at the same level on another exam.

Comparability with external standards and frameworks

Recent years have seen the rise to prominence of standards and frameworks. In the United States K-12 context, for example, there has been a drive towards standards-based curricula and assessment (McLaughlin and Shepard 1995, National Commission on Excellence in Education 1983). Because education is a responsibility devolved to individual states in the US federal system, each state has traditionally developed its own English language proficiency standards, creating a situation where it is more challenging to provide criterion-related evidence (e.g. how do students in one state compare to students in another state?). More recently, however, there have been moves towards adopting common standards (National Governors Association 2011) and to using common assessment tools (e.g. the WIDA (2004) Model which has now been adopted by 27 states).

Similarly, in the European context, the recent development of a reference framework – the Common European Framework of Reference for languages (CEFR) – has had a large impact in language assessment. The CEFR was created by the Council of Europe and generally divides language ability into six broad levels, so as to provide 'a common basis for the elaboration of language syllabuses, curriculum guidelines, examinations, textbooks, etc. across Europe' (2001:1). To support this endeavour, a number of resources for users have been made available. These include a manual and a reference supplement for relating exams to the CEFR (Council of Europe 2003, 2004, 2009), which contain suggested steps to take and procedures to follow. Other types of support include fora for practitioners to share experiences (see Martyniuk (Ed.) 2010), as well as sample materials illustrating the framework's different levels.

The CEFR's influence has been such that it is now used in prescriptive ways and for making exact comparisons, beyond what was originally intended. Language learning requirements throughout Europe are often now expressed in terms of CEFR levels (Eurydice 2008, Lim forthcoming), and this has spread beyond the continent and to other contexts as well (see Khalifa and Weir 2009 for a detailed account). For example, reference to CEFR levels is being used as one criterion for immigration purposes in the UK. The growing influence of the CEFR and the use of its levels for high-stakes decision making have created a political necessity for exam providers to demonstrate 'alignment' to the CEFR.

Doubt has been expressed, however, about the appropriateness and wisdom of aligning tests closely to the CEFR. As a reference framework, the CEFR is general and is 'deliberately underspecified and incomplete' (Milanovic 2009:3) so that it can function as a broad and accessible reference point; tests, on the other hand, are by their nature specific and well defined. Accordingly, it is a challenge to align exams to the CEFR without user intervention in order to at least make the illustrative scales useable for specific purposes (Fulcher 2004, Milanovic and Weir 2010, Weir 2005b). Contributing to these doubts are the results of various alignment studies produced by different examination providers which do not appear to match well with each other (Lim et al forthcoming).

It is important to remember that the CEFR is not intended to be used prescriptively and that there can be no single 'best' way to account for the alignment of an examination within its own context and purpose of use. As Jones and Saville (2009:54–5) point out:

> . . . some people speak of applying the CEFR to some context, as a hammer gets applied to a nail. We should speak rather of referring a context to the CEFR. The transitivity is the other way round. The argument for an alignment is to be constructed, the basis of comparison to be established. It is the specific context which determines the final meaning of the claim. By engaging with the process in this way we put the CEFR in its correct place as a point of reference, and also contribute to its future evolution.

Of course, the CEFR itself is a work in progress. Work continues apace to develop and elaborate on the framework, such as that being done by the English Profile Programme (e.g. Green 2012, Hawkins and Filipović 2012). As the CEFR is further refined, any alignment of exams to it will also need to be reviewed and refined.

It must also be recognised that alignment with any external standards is necessarily an ongoing process (Milanovic 2009). Alignment is something that needs maintaining and, beyond one-off studies, test development, quality assurance and administration procedures need to be in place to ensure that tests are aligned as claimed.

Comparability with external standards: Cambridge ESOL practice

The previous section provided a brief discussion of the role, status and limitations of the CEFR. Despite reservations made in the above section about alignment to the CEFR, real-world demands for statements about the nature of the relationship between a given test and the CEFR cannot be easily ignored and test providers such as Cambridge ESOL have to address public and governmental expectations in some meaningful and responsible way as the case studies below aim to illustrate. Before moving on to the case studies, a brief discussion of the relationship between Cambridge ESOL exams and the CEFR may be useful.

There is in fact a very close relationship between Cambridge ESOL exams and the CEFR which dates back to the early 1990s (Taylor and Jones 2006). Cambridge ESOL was among the stakeholders to provide input into the revision of the Waystage and Threshold level specifications (Van Ek and Trim 1998), representing the A2 and B1 levels of the CEFR, which became the basis for the specifications of the Key English Test (KET) and the Preliminary English Test (PET) in the Cambridge Main Suite. Conversely, the work to develop the Vantage/B2 level of the CEFR drew on Cambridge's FCE exam (Van Ek and Trim 2001). In the same way, the C2 level was defined against the Certificate of Proficiency in English (CPE) (North 2008). Of the CEFR, North (2004) writes:

> The levels have emerged in a gradual, collective recognition of what the late Peter Hargreaves of Cambridge ESOL described as "natural levels". This process has resulted in a set of levels shared by COE specifications (Waystage, Threshold, Vantage), the Cambridge ESOL suite, the main ELT publishers and many language schools. Over the past 10 years, Cambridge ESOL have in addition worked with other examination boards in Europe to begin to standardise on these levels through ALTE.
>
> The descriptors scales for these levels were developed in a four-step process: collecting and writing descriptors; identifying in workshops with some 250 teachers what kinds of categories and style of descriptors were clearest; mathematical scaling; checking the match of the resulting scale content to the levels represented by COE specifications and the Cambridge ESOL suite.

This relationship has continued, with Cambridge ESOL contributing to the development of the Council of Europe's manual for relating exams to the CEFR (Council of Europe 2009), the manual for test development (ALTE 2011), and the provision of learner samples from Cambridge ESOL exams illustrating the CEFR levels (Galaczi and Khalifa 2009a, 2009b).

While the historical, conceptual, and empirical relationship between Cambridge ESOL exams and the CEFR is well established, Cambridge ESOL nevertheless continues to maintain and develop this relationship. For example, Galaczi, ffrench, Hubbard and Green (2011) and Lim (2012) detail the development of test criteria that are explicitly pegged to the CEFR, while Khalifa and Weir (2009) discuss in depth how Cambridge ESOL has embedded the CEFR into its test development and validation practices. However, there remain differences, for example, between the formulation of Cambridge ESOL criteria for listening (which are often based upon goals in the form of 'listening for' descriptors) and the illustrative CEFR listening descriptors (which tend to relate more to listening context and the nature of listening input), which is a subject for future research to consider. The rest of the section now focuses on studies that engage with the suggested steps for alignment contained in the Manual (Council of Europe 2009).

Case Study 1: FCE and the CEFR

Khalifa, ffrench and Salamoura (2010) considered the first suggested steps in the Manual, i.e. familiarisation and specification, using these as a means of maintaining alignment to the CEFR and as a way of embedding the CEFR into test development procedures, thus extending the possible uses of the Manual. They report on a workshop where 14 participants engaged with a variety of Manual-prescribed and non-Manual-prescribed familiarisation activities. Manual-prescribed activities included descriptor sorting, self-assessment of foreign language ability using the CEFR, and rating of spoken and written performances. Non-Manual-prescribed activities included background readings, and juxtaposing a CEFR level with the levels adjacent to it. These activities also aimed at answering the question of 'how precisely do item writers and test developers interpret CEFR descriptors in terms of level assignment?' Although the workshop covered different language skill areas, the findings reported here related specifically to listening.

Workshop participants generally thought that the different activities were helpful, and in particular found putting a CEFR level in the context of adjacent levels to be the most effective activity in terms of becoming more familiar with the CEFR illustrative scales (Figure 7.4). Where the descriptor sorting activity was concerned, listening descriptors were placed at the

Figure 7.4 Participant evaluation of workshop activities

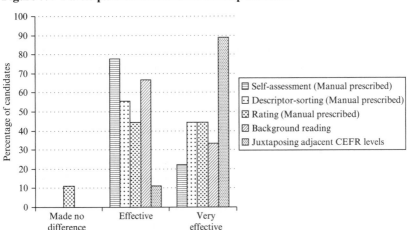

correct CEFR level 75% of the time. One explanation for the 75% agreement could be the selected scales used in the descriptor sorting activity. For example, some of the scales used did not have descriptors at the bottom and top end of the scale (see 'Listening to audio media and recordings') while in other scales the distinction between the adjacent levels is not very clear (see for example B1 and B2 descriptors in scale titled 'Listening as a member of live audience'). In the latter scale, the B1 descriptor states 'can follow a lecturer talk' and the B2 descriptor states 'can follow the essentials of lectures'. It is not clear what comprises essentials of lectures or why the use of 'essentials' would make it a B2 level. Similarly, in the former scale a B2 descriptor includes 'can understand most radio documentaries and other recorded or broadcast audio material' while a B1 descriptor states 'can understand the information content of the majority of recorded or broadcast audio material'. The use of 'most' and 'majority' in both levels could easily lead to confusion, and the focus on quantifying adverbs as a distinguishing factor rather than on type of information being processed or the speed of processing may have also led to the lower level of agreement among raters.

Overall, the workshop was seen to be successful, and the different activities seen to be helpful. Following on from the workshop, a number of self-access induction worksheets were developed for use in training Cambridge ESOL staff. All staff are required to complete at least two of the worksheets, the particular ones they do being dependent on their particular role within the organisation. As of 2009, the induction worksheets became a central component of the induction programme for new members of staff joining Cambridge ESOL or moving their jobs within the organisation. The induction worksheets were perceived as a way of introducing newcomers to the CEFR and to its applications and use by Cambridge ESOL. This represents one of a number of ways in which the CEFR has been embedded within Cambridge ESOL test development and validation procedures. More recently, Cambridge ESOL (2011b) produced a booklet entitled *Using the CEFR: Principles of Good Practice*, which has been circulated to the organisation's stakeholders. Verbal feedback received on these activities is encouraging and has led to the initiation of a more formal evaluation of in-house CEFR-related activities.

Case Study 2: IELTS and the CEFR

Cambridge ESOL has also carried out the latter steps contained in the Manual, i.e. standard setting and empirical validation, with relation to IELTS. A panel of 19 language testing experts familiar with the CEFR was convened for a two-day standard setting workshop to determine IELTS Academic scores that related to CEFR Levels B2, C1, and C2. The Listening element of this standard setting exercise used the Yes–No modification of the Angoff (1971) method. Empirical validation of the standard setting outcomes was achieved through the IELTS–CAE study described in an earlier part of this chapter. To recapitulate, that study involved candidates for each exam being invited to sit the other exam, and their results were then compared through equipercentile equating (Kolen and Brennan 2004). The CAE made for a suitable criterion measure given its established relationship to the CEFR, and also because there are scores on the test that correspond to CEFR Levels B2, C1, and C2. The cut scores obtained on the standard setting study and the empirical validation study could thus be compared.

As Lim et al (forthcoming) report, the cut scores obtained from the two studies were remarkably similar, and in those instances where the cut scores were not identical, rational explanations were available to account for them. For Listening, the cut scores obtained from the standard setting study and the empirical validation study were identical for B2 and C2. An IELTS Listening band score of 6.0 was determined to be at B2 level, and a band score of 9.0 was determined to be at C2. For C1, however, the two studies yielded different results. Empirical validation placed C1 between IELTS Bands 7.0 and 7.5, whereas the standard setting study indicated that the cut score should be 8.5.

Table 7.3 IELTS CEFR cut scores using two methods

Skill	Method	CEFR level		
		B1/B2	B2/C1	C1/C2
Listening	Standard setting	6.0	8.5	9.0
	Empirical validation (rounded up)	6.0	7.5	9.0
	Empirical validation (rounded)	6.0	7.0	9.0

The difference at C1 can be attributed to a method effect. It has been noted that the standard-setting method used – the Yes/No method – can under certain circumstances produce biased results. When the test is relatively easy, the Council of Europe (2009) notes that:

> . . . for all items, the borderline person has a probability of over 50% to give the correct response, so that a rational panel member should answer Yes for every item. But if he does so, his individual standard will be the maximum test score, while real borderline persons might obtain on average a score which is only slightly larger than half of the maximum score (2009:65).

Being a test that measures best between Bands 5 and 8, IELTS Listening does have relatively fewer items near the C1 cut point, which would explain why the cut score obtained for C1 is higher than it should be. As for the C2 level, it is true that IELTS Listening has even fewer items at that level. The agreement between standard setting and empirical cut scores at that level is probably best seen as a ceiling effect, as Band 9 is the maximum that a candidate can get on the test.

In sum, apart from discrepancies that can be attributed to method effects, the results of the standard setting study and the empirical validation study are identical, and this was true across the four skills tested in IELTS. The outcomes of these studies provide evidence that the claimed CEFR level cut scores for IELTS are sound and dependable.

Conclusion

The criterion-related validity of listening tests is an aspect that Cambridge ESOL has been exploring for a number of years and in an increasingly systematic way. Without knowing that different forms of an exam are comparable, there would be no basis for meaningful score interpretation, and whatever effort had been made to ensure validity in terms of test taker characteristics, cognitive and contextual parameters and scoring procedures would be undermined. Comparability between different exams and comparability with reference to external frameworks are important as well. In general, it is possible to agree on the nature of the language abilities being tested, and tests that purport to measure the same abilities should produce similar results. Otherwise, the validity of each measure would be thrown into doubt. Similarly, frameworks situate exams within larger contexts, helping to give them additional meaning.

The studies reported in this chapter provide evidence of the criterion-related validity of Cambridge ESOL Listening examinations in various ways; they show strong links between various Cambridge ESOL Listening tests, between different forms of the same listening test and with an external standard such as the CEFR. As was seen, in Cambridge ESOL practice the different aspects of criterion-related validity are very closely related to one another: the history of Cambridge ESOL's Main Suite Listening papers with their stable candidature; the rigid procedures followed in Listening test paper construction, production and review; the fact that the Listening papers are underpinned by standardised processes and a Rasch-based item banking approach; and the fact that Main Suite examinations were a basis for the CEFR levels. All these aspects testify to a unified and coherent approach that ensures criterion-related validity not only for the Listening papers but for other skill areas as well.

Chapter 7 is the last of the six chapters in this volume that have explored the socio-cognitive validation framework, seeking to examine it in detail with reference to Cambridge ESOL Listening tests. Chapter 8 will draw together the threads of the previous chapters, summarising the findings from the overall exercise and making recommendations for further research and development which would benefit not only Cambridge ESOL but also the wider testing community.

8 Conclusions and recommendations

Lynda Taylor
Consultant to Cambridge English Language
Assessment

Ardeshir Geranpayeh
Cambridge English Language Assessment

Chapter 1 of this volume asserted that nowadays public examination boards and commercial testing agencies are increasingly called to account for how and why they design and administer their tests in the way they do. As a result, openness and transparency on the part of test providers have become a priority. The approach outlined and exemplified in this volume on assessing listening, and in the previous companion volumes on the other skills, offers one way of placing in the public domain the rationale underpinning the testing policy and practice of a major international testing agency, together with the available theoretical and empirical evidence to support the board's claims made for the validity and usefulness of its language tests.

The theoretical framework for validating language examinations first outlined in Weir (2005a) was once more adopted as a tool for reflecting upon an understanding and conceptualisation of the listening construct for assessment purposes, as well as for reviewing the latest empirical research in the field. The Cambridge ESOL General English examinations were again taken as the practical context for undertaking a critical evaluation of widely used listening tests ranging across different proficiency levels. This enabled an examination of how the theoretical framework for validation can be operationalised in practice and with what outcomes. As in previous volumes, each chapter closely scrutinised Cambridge practice in terms of the particular component of the framework under review. Discussion of issues arising in the *research* literature on each component part was followed by consideration of Cambridge ESOL *practice* in the area. The analysis sought to build upon and extend the work reported in the earlier volumes, bringing fresh and novel insights to the process of construct definition and operationalisation for the particular skill of interest. Thus Weir's original (2005a) theoretical framework has been further developed and refined in light of the experience of applying it in practice.

This final chapter draws together the threads of the volume, summarising the findings from applying the socio-cognitive validity framework to a set of Cambridge Listening tests. It highlights some of the evidence supporting the claims and reasoning about the validity of the Listening tests, offering observations on their relative strengths and weaknesses, as well as recommendations on how the tests might evolve in future and on a potential research agenda associated with test revision. The following sections focus on each of the constituent parts of the socio-cognitive framework in turn, according to the order in which they were presented in the volume.

Test taker characteristics

Chapter 2 specified the many and complex test taker characteristics of a physiological, psychological (both cognitive and affective) and experiential nature that can affect a test taker's performance on a given test. It is important to acknowledge that the test taker is at the heart of any testing event and must therefore be considered at every stage of test development and continuously throughout live administrations of a test.

Cambridge ESOL constantly monitors the testing population and their interaction with the Listening test for each of its language examinations as described in Chapter 2. This is achieved on a routine, session-by-session basis through the collection of Candidate Information Sheet (CIS) data as well as by means of an ongoing programme of research into specific aspects of the relationship between test taker and test performance. The information gathered in this way also forms the basis for continual improvement and revision of the Cambridge ESOL Listening tests.

The long-established practice of collecting CIS data provides an invaluable source of information about test takers and this has for many years been routinely used by Cambridge ESOL for test development as well as grading decisions. Any change in candidate behaviour from a demographic perspective is carefully scrutinised during grading to ensure that test materials remain of suitable difficulty for the target population. When an age change in the test population has been observed over a period of a few years this has typically resulted in a formal review and revision of that test (or sections of it). Sometimes this process has led to the development of new, more age-appropriate tests, such as the recently developed PET and KET for Schools. Collection and analysis of CIS data for these newer exams will of course be especially important as they establish themselves, in order to monitor test performance for routine validation and to inform a programme of targeted research.

Given the volume of CIS data now routinely gathered by Cambridge ESOL for a wide range of English language tests across multiple proficiency levels and domains, it is becoming increasingly possible to analyse and interrogate the data collected in order to investigate the global state of English language learning and teaching. The widespread acceptance of English as a language for international communication serves as a powerful driver for initiatives to improve standards in the teaching and learning of English globally. Many countries and regions have embarked on educational reform programmes to improve English standards in their part of the world. Linking the available CIS information to test performance data can allow us to explore the impact of such educational initiatives and reforms, and may help provide some answers to complex questions such as the following:

- What contextual factors contribute most to improved language proficiency? (For example, socio-economic status; national policies such as life-long learning of foreign languages; a language-friendly living environment and language-friendly schools; initial/in-service teacher training and ongoing professional teacher development).
- How do socio-economic factors currently influence the demand for English proficiency around the world?
- How does the restructuring of the local economy change the profile of English needs in the workforce?
- What is the wider demographic, social and educational context within which English is learned and used?
- How have standards of English improved within a specific cohort (e.g. learners aged 12–17) over a specific period of time (e.g. last 10 years) within specific countries/regions?
- Do learners/children (e.g. in China, India, Brazil) start learning English earlier than was previously the case, i.e. five or 10 years ago?

New approaches to interrogating the extensive corpus of CIS data which is now routinely gathered by Cambridge ESOL should enable the board to offer its stakeholders an increasingly well described and informative global overview of trends in English learning, teaching and assessment. It is clear that there is considerable scope for future applied research in this area.

Another area meriting additional research is that of language testing accommodations, i.e. tests which are modified to meet the special requirements of certain test taker populations. There exists relatively little research in the area of accommodations for testing second language listening that is directly relevant to the testing of English as a Foreign Language (EFL) in the international context. Most of the published research relating to accommodations in language assessment has been conducted in the US with English language learners (ELLs), who are typically immigrants and indigenous groups in US school-based learning and assessment contexts. Such research tends to focus on the language of instruction, and while some studies have investigated the effectiveness and validity of accommodations for language learners with disabilities, it remains the case that relatively little is known about the effect of Special Arrangements on test takers whose listening ability is tested under the different conditions discussed in Chapter 2. The very small numbers of test takers and the diversity of the disabilities involved mean that conducting research into the effects of Special Arrangements is extremely challenging. None the less, it is clearly essential that the relevant issues are investigated in the interests of ensuring fair access to assessment opportunities, which is the fundamental principle underlying the provision of Special Arrangements.

From a validation perspective, it is also important that test score users can place confidence in the meaningfulness of scores from tests involving Special Arrangements and test providers therefore need to be able to bring forward evidence in support of any claims they make about the usefulness of scores from their modified tests. Given that examination boards are often in direct contact with test candidates and testing centres requesting Special Arrangements, a large and experienced organisation such as Cambridge ESOL may be well placed and well equipped to undertake some of this much needed research, in the form of small-scale but well-designed case studies (see, for example, the multi-faceted case study that investigated provision for candidates with dyslexia in writing assessment, reported in Shaw and Weir 2007:20–27).

Despite the growing range of provision for candidates with disabilities offered in recent years by the examination board, it is striking that the number of candidates requesting accommodations remains extremely small as a proportion of the overall candidature. The fact that the number of requests for accommodated tests seems not to reflect the likely distribution of EFL learners with disabilities in the wider population constitutes some cause for concern and it is possible to speculate on potential reasons for this. There may be a genuine lack of awareness among teachers and candidates, and even testing centres, concerning the wide range of test accommodations now available, despite the provision of information in published documentation and on the examination board's website. Alternatively, it may be that the administrative procedures associated with requesting modified tests discourage some from applying because it can involve a longer lead-time as well as additional paperwork. Furthermore, not all cultures have similar attitudes towards disability, both in terms of defining what constitutes a disability and of how disabilities should be dealt with, so this may well affect the take-up of language learning as well as assessment opportunities. This touches upon matters of test washback and impact, and Cambridge ESOL may wish to consider how to promote its accommodations more widely so that students with disabilities are encouraged to learn English and to take advantage of the wide range of assessment opportunities now available.

There may also be useful theoretical and empirical work to be done to distinguish between construct-related disability (e.g. deafness in the case of a listening test) and disability that risks affecting performance in other aspects of a test, since greater knowledge and understanding of these can inform sound policy and appropriate practice. Further research is also merited into the use of video-based input for listening tests, especially as this might help to achieve a more standardised approach as well as align certain modified listening test formats more closely with a standard listening test.

A final area of potential research investigation for the future relates to the testing of second language listening ability among younger learners, which is a key area of interest in light of the growth in English language teaching and learning within primary education systems worldwide. Given the important role played in second language listening by factors such as memory, concentration, cognitive style and level of cognitive development, it would seem critical that more research is undertaken to determine how these factors develop with age and what implications this may have for listening test design. From the Cambridge ESOL perspective, this will be particularly relevant in respect of the for Schools and the Young Learners English tests.

Cognitive validity

As Weir and Taylor (2011:299) assert in the companion volume on assessing second language speaking ability:

> It is hard to see how one can build a convincing validity argument for any assessment practice without assigning cognitive processing a central place within that argument. Given our desire to extrapolate from test tasks to real world behaviour, it is essential to carry out research to establish with greater certainty that the test tasks we employ do indeed activate the types of mental operations that are viewed in the cognitive psychology literature as essential elements of the speaking process which are relevant to the contexts and purposes of test use. To the extent that this is not the case, extrapolation from the test data to speaking in the wider world is clearly under threat.

The view expressed by Weir and Taylor above regarding speaking assessment is equally true for the testing of second language listening. In fact, from a primarily cognitive perspective, the processes involved in second language listening are perhaps the least well described and analysed in the currently available literature on language assessment. For this reason, John Field's chapter on cognitive validity in listening represents a significant and timely contribution to the wider field of language testing because it assembles the latest theoretical and empirical findings from cognitive psychology and discusses their direct relevance for the design and analysis of listening tests.

A major goal of Chapter 3 was to outline a process model of the listening construct which can serve as a framework for judging the cognitive validity of any test of skilled listening performance. A secondary goal was to identify aspects of test design which impose additional cognitive demands upon the candidate and have the potential to divert the candidate from the processes which might normally be employed during a real-life listening situation. Adding to previous conceptualisations as to what cognitive validity entails, Field highlighted three key considerations in the cognitive validation of listening tests:

- *Similarity of processing*, i.e. are the processes adopted during a test sufficiently similar to those which would be employed in the target context, or do candidates adopt additional processes that are a product of facets of the test (e.g. procedure, test method, item) rather than part of the normal operations associated with the construct being tested?
- *comprehensiveness*, i.e. do the items in the test elicit only a small subset of the cognitive processes that a language user would employ in a natural context, or do they tap into a sufficiently broad range of such processes, at various levels, for the test to be deemed representative of real-world behaviour?
- *calibration*, i.e. across a suite of level-based tests, are the cognitive demands imposed upon test takers at each level appropriately calibrated in relation to the performance features that might be expected of a listener at these levels?

Drawing upon the available theoretical and empirical literature, Field proposed a comprehensive processing model for listening with five levels as follows:

- *input decoding*: when the listener transforms acoustic cues into groups of syllables, some marked for stress and others not
- *lexical search*: when the listener identifies the best word-level matches for what has been heard, based on a combination of perceptual information and word boundary cues
- *parsing*: when the lexical material is related to the co-text in which it occurs in order to a) specify lexical sense more precisely, and b) impose a syntactic pattern
- *meaning construction*: when world knowledge and inference are employed to add to the bare meaning of the message
- *discourse construction*: when the listener makes decisions on the relevance of the new information and how congruent it is with what has gone before; and, if appropriate, integrates it into a representation of the larger listening event.

The first three of these can be perceived as *lower-level* listening processes that take place when a message is being encoded into language, and the remaining two are *higher-level processes* associated with meaning building.

Chapter 3 applied this five-level cognitive model to analyse Cambridge ESOL's suite of General English tests, i.e. the five levels of listening represented by the KET–CPE exams (spanning CEFR Levels A2–C2). The analysis paid particular attention to three essential components of any listening test: *the recording, the test method* and *the test items*. The goal was to determine how representative the three components are of the types of input and processing implicated in general listening events, how comprehensive they are in representing the range of processes and how well graded is the cognitive load placed upon test takers in relation to the levels of the suite. Findings from this validation exercise raise a number of interesting issues for Cambridge ESOL's current policy and practice and they also throw up some potential research avenues for the wider language testing field.

One fundamental issue is the extent to which listening test input can be said to resemble normal everyday speech and thus to demand decoding processes resembling those of a real-world listening event. Since the input for the Cambridge Listening tests is scripted and studio-recorded, genuine questions can be raised over exactly how far the nature of the scripted, recorded material makes decoding easier or more difficult than it would be in real-world conditions, e.g. due to studio actors marking punctuation and sentence boundaries more clearly (thus aiding syntactic parsing) and using greater rhythmicity (which assists with lexical search). There are clearly constraints on what large-scale test producers need to do to guarantee test standardisation and recording quality; tape-scripting and studio-recording the listening input brings certain advantages in this regard. Nevertheless, according to Field (personal communication), some of the current weaknesses in tapescripts could be relatively easily addressed:

> If Cambridge ESOL continues to use re-recording, one way of achieving a greater approximation to natural speech might be to more accurately represent some of the features of the original source in the transcript. The instructions to item writers on how to transcribe a piece of authentic speech are noticeably light of touch: "Normal contractions should be used . . . There is no need however, to include non-standard contractions (e.g. 'cos', 'dunno' etc) or 'umms' and 'errs' as the actors will introduce these naturally when developing the character appropriate to the text type and content" (IWG: PET:7). There is, in fact, little evidence of this improvisation in the sample test recordings; and one can understand actors proceeding with caution given that the items have already been set. The helpful suggestion that "Transcripts do not have to conform to all the conventions of written punctuation as natural spoken discourse will have a different structure" (IWG: PET:7) is rather undermined by the lack of any recommended transcription system more suited to representing natural speech.

Field's comments would argue for developing a comprehensive set of standard transcript conventions which more faithfully reflect spoken language (both monologue and dialogue) as well as training test writers to adopt these conventions when generating their written transcripts for future studio-recording. A further recommendation is that instructions for item writers might usefully specify some of the mismatches between recording, script and items that can occur – not least, the possibility that variations in speech rate or in an actor's interpretation of the script can downgrade the perceptibility of an information point targeted by the item writer. There would also be value in submitting the audio recording to the original item writer for a final review. As Field points out, such measures would counterbalance the degree of attention accorded to task and item in the present test development process.

A related issue is the relative lack of listening input based upon authentic spoken (as opposed to written) sources, especially at the higher levels of the suite. Following Field's analysis, it is possible that this state of affairs is due to some inconsistency of messaging across the item writer guidelines (IWGs) for the various tests. This merits closer scrutiny from within Cambridge ESOL to ensure that the IWGs are systematic in encouraging the use of authentic spoken language as source material, with written sources treated as a last resort rather than endorsed as a comparable option. Furthermore, now that good-quality audio material is more readily available and accessible to item-writers via the internet, the examination board may wish to explore how this could be better exploited for testing purposes.

A further consideration raised in the chapter, once again linked to the input authenticity of an audio-based test, is the absence of the sorts of visual support that would typically be available in a real-life context. There is considerable scope for Cambridge ESOL to explore the potential for integrating more visual input into its listening tests in the future, especially in computer-based tests. As technology improves, and as test takers themselves become more accustomed to taking tests on computer as well as to encountering audio-visual contact with the target language through internet sources, examination boards will need to give careful consideration to the practicality of video-based testing of listening. This would also have relevance for some of the modified test formats suitable for use with lip-reading candidates, as mentioned earlier.

Despite the concerns touched upon above, the analysis of the Cambridge suite of Listening tests generated some positive findings on the balance of monologue/dialogue in the input across the levels and also on the management of speaker variation, including accent. Having said that, at the lower levels of the suite it might be helpful to introduce an explicit policy on the proportion of dialogue to monologue material, incorporating guidance on this issue into the IWGs rather than leaving it to the instinct of the test writer.

The issue of accent consistency clearly needs to be carefully monitored where studio actors are involved and the Cambridge ESOL board may wish to draw up more explicit guidance regarding the number of accents featured in any version of a test. Field comments that some standardisation would help particularly at the lower levels, where variations in the number of accents used may result in inconsistencies between the processing demands made by different versions of a test. In general, content across the levels of the Cambridge ESOL suite is shown to be finely graded in terms of the parsing of information units and the syntactic complexity of the links between units. Some caution is expressed at the danger of an over-reliance on information density and abstractness of argumentation as the means of raising the level of difficulty, given that this risks measuring candidate characteristics (memory capacity and abstract reasoning), which function independently of the listening construct. This is another area that may benefit from further investigation.

Chapter 3 examined various aspects of listening test methods, including the rubrics, the pre-presentation of test items, the number of times the recorded material was played, and features of the five main test formats adopted in the listening tests. Once again, the analysis highlighted a number of issues meriting further consideration or research investigation.

First of all, given the potential for expectations raised by the pre-set items (i.e. read prior to listening) in a listening test to prove stronger than information provided by the actual auditory input, research could usefully be undertaken to explore whether question preview affects comprehension positively (by focusing the attention or supplying information about the text) or negatively (by interfering with subjective comprehension processes). The alternative approach, i.e. post-setting test items, is also worthy of further investigation. The post-setting of items for the short passages is an option that might perhaps be considered in future by Cambridge ESOL, especially as it is an approach that is being increasingly explored in some other large-scale listening tests in the market. Computer-based test delivery naturally makes this approach much easier to implement since the test items can remain hidden until the test designer wishes to present them. Field suggests another approach which is particularly well suited to a CBT context and where the listening input is played twice, which is standard practice in the Cambridge exams: the test items become available between the two hearings of the recording, thus potentially reducing both the cognitive demands associated with reading the items out of context and the danger of predictive guessing. Cambridge ESOL is well placed to undertake useful experimental research studies in all of these areas.

Overall, the validation exercise undertaken in Chapter 3 suggested that the different item formats (multiple choice, visual multiple choice, gap filling, multiple matching and true/false) complemented one another quite well and that the use of several formats in each test ensures that a range of levels of processing are covered. However, Field notes one level of processing that appears to be significantly under-represented across the suite. The conventional test item formats used in the Cambridge Listening tests provide little opportunity to assess *discourse construction*, which covers identifying the relative importance of utterances that have been processed, linking idea units, integrating incoming idea units into a developing discourse representation and building a hierarchical structure representing the speaker's line of argument. Testing this high-level processing is a major challenge for test designers since objectively scored test items, such as MCQ or gap-filling, invariably tend to target discrete points of information which have been pre-selected as worthy of attention by the test writer, rather than by the test taker. It may be that the high-level *discourse construction* type of processing (which is likely to be especially relevant for the high-proficiency, C levels, i.e. for tests used for university education or professional employment) is best provoked through the use of integrated listening-into-speaking or listening-into-writing tasks. Further research is required.

In general, the cognitive validation exercise demonstrated that the use made of the five formats across the five levels of the suite is appropriately sensitive to the cognitive load imposed by the various tasks. Exceptions were noted at the CAE level, where some of the sections appear to rely heavily upon the nature of the task to create difficulty rather than upon the interaction between test taker and recording. In terms of the processing demands upon the test taker across formats and across levels, these were shown to be sufficiently varied and well graded. A progressive increase in item length and complexity can be seen as another way of grading difficulty; interestingly, the analysis showed a sharp increase in reading load from FCE level upwards, with some parts of the tests diverging considerably in amount of reading according to the format employed (particularly in the extended MCQ task). Once again, this phenomenon may be worthy of further investigation. Field makes the point that, in relation to cognitive validity, it raises the concern that difficulty is being manipulated by means of the written input that the test taker has to master rather than by means of the demands of the auditory input which is the object of the exercise. He is right to point out that it should be the nature of the construct to be tested, rather than the test format, that drives the thinking of test designers and item writers.

Context validity

Chapter 4 extensively examined the context validity of Cambridge ESOL Listening tests with reference to the detailed taxonomy of contextual task parameters developed and refined from the Weir 2005a socio-cognitive framework. Elliott and Wilson explored a wide range of essential task characteristics in listening tests, both within and across proficiency levels; in

doing so, they demonstrated that careful consideration is given to the gradation of difficulty throughout Cambridge ESOL's suite of levels on most of the
contextual parameters. Issues highlighted here relate to selected contextual
parameters that may need remedial attention for specific tests, and potential
avenues for further research are outlined that could help to inform future test
development and revision.

A dominant theme in this volume has been how best to test second language listening in light of the test formats available to test designers in the
past and which have conventionally been used in listening tests over many
decades, i.e. MCQ, true/false, gap filling. Several of the issues raised in
Chapter 3 concerning task purpose and rubric, response method and the
testing of high-level processing (e.g. pre/post-setting of test items, reading
demands, testing discourse construction) overlap to some degree with the
earlier discussion on cognitive validity so these will not be repeated here. One
aspect which is worth noting, however, is the apparent variation in terminology used to describe *focus* in test specification documentation (such as
the handbooks), which is not always standardised across levels. It is easy for
such anomalies to occur because tests often start out relatively independently
and later develop along their own trajectory, adopting their own terminology and traditions over time. However, since the Cambridge ESOL tests
are supposed to form a coherent suite and since variation in terminology
risks causing misunderstanding and confusion among item writers as well
as teachers and learners, it would be advisable to revisit this area in order to
ensure a more standardised approach to communicating test features in key
documentation, something that would benefit both internal and external test
stakeholders.

There is undoubtedly considerable scope for further research into the
testing of second language listening ability using computer-based technology. Hopefully, more of the research in this area will focus in future on the
added value of testing listening via computer and internet, rather than just
the feasibility of converting conventional paper-based listening tests to a
computerised platform. Though this inevitably raises questions concerning
the comparability of test scores between paper-based and computer-based
tests, innovations in managing the channel (or channels) of presentation in
a listening test should help to approximate the assessment of listening more
closely to the real-world listening experience.

As mentioned in the previous section, one particular advantage of testing
listening via computer could be that it enables a more sophisticated and integrated approach to language assessment, bringing together listening-into-
speaking/writing skills, and even combining an element of reading. This, in
turn, may make it easier to elicit and evaluate the higher-level processing that
is needed to discriminate key utterances, integrate idea units into the developing meaning construction and build a hierarchical discourse structure. If

Cambridge ESOL continues to position itself as a quality provider of valid and useful tests at the C levels (i.e. CAE and CPE), for university and professional purposes, then this is an area where further attention and research investigation may need to be targeted on the associated parameters, both cognitive and contextual. Studies involving verbal protocol analysis, questionnaire instruments and even eye-tracking technology could be helpful in better understanding cognitive load issues such as discourse construction, or in exploring the relative merits of using shorter versus longer stretches of listening input.

Chapter 4 echoes the issue raised in Chapter 3 of the nature of the listening test input in terms of its closer proximity to written rather than spoken language. Clearly, in fully authentic, spontaneous recordings it is difficult to ensure that there are sufficient testable points in the text to sustain the desired task length with reasonable spacing between items. As a result, listening texts tend to be heavily scripted and are sometimes manipulated to ensure that items perform satisfactorily. Further research may be helpful in identifying whether greater use of semi-scripted (rather than re-recorded) material would redress the balance, or whether more speech-like recordings could be achieved through enhanced approaches to transcription.

In terms of analysing the functional, grammatical and lexical resources as they pertain to spoken language, there remains considerable scope for further investigative work in all these areas, both in relation to what differentiates one proficiency level from another and specifically with regard to the higher C levels. The latter are levels for which functional, grammatical and lexical inventories typically do not exist, often for good reason; they are also levels which are noticeably underspecified in the CEFR. Given the use of CAE and CPE for academic and professional contexts, it is worth considering whether listening input at the C levels should include more academic and/or professional contexts, with a corresponding increase in the percentage of related functions, grammar and vocabulary. The findings of the English Profile Programme are undoubtedly beginning to bear fruit in the areas of functions, grammar and lexis, but the research agenda remains a substantial and long-term endeavour.

Scoring validity

Chapter 5 focused upon the scoring process associated with listening tests while acknowledging the interconnectedness of this dimension to other aspects of validity within the socio-cognitive framework. Although the various elements of the socio-cognitive framework are presented separately in this volume for convenience and ease of access, the chapter stressed the 'symbiotic' relationship (often referred to as construct validity) that exists between context validity, cognitive validity and scoring validity. The importance of the replicability of test scores under various conditions was highlighted and it was argued that developing valid tasks in terms of both cognitive and contextual parameters matters little if it cannot be demonstrated that student responses are reported consistently.

Improving score users' confidence in using test scores for making important decisions about test takers is an important aspect of scoring validity. The chapter focused not only on factors influencing the suitability of test material for listening tests from a scoring validity perspective such as *test difficulty* and *internal consistency* but also on statistical procedures which can help mitigate any potentially negative effects resulting from the influence of unwanted variables such as *item bias*. Different parameters that influence the scoring validity of a listening test were discussed: test difficulty, item bias, internal consistency, error of measurement and grading and awarding.

One of the main challenges in scoring validity is the way in which scores are reported to stakeholders in the testing process. Chapter 5 gave the example of score reporting from the FCE exam to show how it is possible to report a total standardised score, a total grade, an overall CEFR level and relative performance in each skill component. The aim is to provide meaningful information to test users so that they can use this effectively in their decision making. The discussion in Chapter 5 highlighted the challenge to examination providers to constantly improve upon their score reporting procedures in order to maximise the usefulness of their tests and to meet the growing expectations of test score users. No matter what explanation is provided around the meaning of scores on a certificate, test users increasingly want additional information from the score extending well beyond the context of a single exam. For example, they may want to compare scores in one exam (FCE) with scores on another (CAE). A legitimate question in this area may be over the value of the CEFR statement provided on the certificates of exams at adjacent levels, e.g. a C1 statement in CAE compared with a C1 statement from FCE. Do these statements have the same meaning? How can one explain or bring forward evidence for the relative alignment of different listening tests? How can alignment to external reference frameworks such as the CEFR be demonstrated? If exams were developed to meet different needs, how can the overlap between their scores be justified? Most important of all, how can clearer evidence of component performance (e.g. for listening) be provided in addition to providing results for overall language proficiency, as is done in IELTS? These are all questions that merit further consideration, and associated research investigation, right across the Cambridge exams and not just for the listening tests.

To address such challenges a new initiative in score reporting has recently started within the Cambridge English suite of examinations. The long-term aim is to build on the Cambridge English Common Scale which has evolved over many years through item banking and ongoing anchoring techniques and which covers all proficiency levels from pre-beginners to high-proficiency users. Although the Cambridge scale is the backbone of the Cambridge ESOL exams from which all the criterion ability levels are derived, it has never been used directly in reporting test scores to test users. The proposal for the future is to use a single scale linked to this common scale using current cut scores to various CEFR levels.

A further challenge for test providers in the future, and also an area where more research could perhaps be undertaken within and beyond Cambridge ESOL, might be the task of attaching more meaningful verbal descriptors to the listening test scores or grades that are reported. Generating user-oriented performance descriptors to accompany scores or grades from objectively scored tests of second language listening and reading ability has never been a straightforward enterprise. Attempts in the early 1990s to construct verbal descriptors as well as numeric band scores for the IELTS Reading and Listening components proved impossible to achieve with any degree of confidence or integrity (see Taylor 2012b:14–15). It is difficult to convert a number on a listening test to a plausible and useful statement that characterises the nature of a test taker's listening ability. Over-ambitious and generalised claims about what someone 'can do' on the basis of their test score are potentially risky given the limited sampling that is possible within the content and length constraints of an actual listening test. Unfortunately, the indirect testing of listening produces no visible 'performance' that can be described in a comparable manner to the descriptions of directly assessed speaking or writing performances. Though the proposed enhancements to score reporting procedures described above (i.e. the move to the Cambridge English scale) will undoubtedly aid score interpretation for test score users, there is still scope for exploring further what an individual score actually means in terms of listening performance and how this lines up with the broader Can Do descriptors which are articulated through communicative frameworks such as the CEFR. Advances in this area might also enable the test developers to move away from the current dependence on a loosely defined 'testing focus' for tasks and across levels, which tends to be a miscellaneous mix of listening depth (e.g. gist, detail), 'listening for' (e.g. attitude, opinion) and listening process (e.g. interpreting content).

Consequential validity

Chapter 6 re-visited the background and definitions of test washback and impact, attempting to establish where these phenomena belong in the complex process of validating examinations, particularly high-stakes tests, such as those offered internationally by Cambridge ESOL. The chapter proposed a modified interpretation of the original Weir (2005a) consequential validity concept, refined in the light of Cambridge ESOL's theoretical and practical experience in the validation of its own exams. It went on to survey and exemplify Cambridge ESOL research initiatives and studies that analyse and adjust positively the consequential validity of the suite's listening tests taking account of the many complex variables involved.

The socio-cognitive framework is perceived as offering a transparent and plausible system that can help test developers and validators to link the assessment validity and assessment use arguments which are nowadays generally expected in the field of professional language testing. Current Cambridge ESOL policy and practice on the validation of its exams emphasises the notion of 'impact by design' as the underpinning feature of its model for conceptualising and investigating impact. This perspective is articulated through Cambridge's own VRIPQ framework, via a variety of publications produced and disseminated by the exam board.

It is clear that Cambridge ESOL has developed for itself a well-considered and well-articulated theoretical position as far test impact and test consequences are concerned, a position that is faithful to Messick's (1989) original view of validity as an integrated evaluative judgement of the extent to which empirical evidence and theoretical rationales support the adequacy and appropriateness of inferences and actions based on assessment outcomes. Cambridge ESOL's commitment over a number of years to undertaking a wide range of empirical washback and impact studies is also consistent with modern conceptions of validity encompassing the use and consequences of test results (Bachman and Palmer 2010, Cizek 2011). Current thinking sees test consequences as a crucial element of validity and recognises that an assessment may be valid if it has the intended positive impact and does not have unintended negative impacts. A key issue here for listening tests is what effect they have on language teaching and learning. Chapter 6 noted the typically negative effect of listening assessment upon classroom practice in the form of: a) the use in teaching materials of standardised formats which ensure reliability in tests but provide highly artificial ways of eliciting information in a class; b) the tendency when preparing for high-stakes listening tests to spend too much time on intensive test taking practice; and c) the teaching in crammers of test-wise strategies which undermine the validity of the test and divert teaching from the development of relevant listening processes.

A significant amount of impact-related research has been conducted by Cambridge ESOL in recent years to confirm the attainability of listening test tasks, ensuring they are criterion-referenced and appropriate for test takers; other studies have checked that test takers, teachers and test score users are familiar with the tests and the meaning of test scores. It would perhaps be good to see more exploration of the relationship between Cambridge ESOL's Listening tests and classroom practice in the teaching and learning of listening skills, in the hope of confirming positive rather than negative washback in this area.

Cambridge ESOL recognises that test providers have a moral and ethical responsibility to strive for positive impact and to work proactively and collaboratively with their stakeholder constituencies. Given the considerable attention and resources the board invests nowadays in teacher support for its tests (e.g. seminars, online materials), it might be interesting to see the outcomes reported of more specific investigations into the effectiveness of this provision. Examination boards play a key role in the promotion and development of assessment literacy among test stakeholders. The research literature on how assessment literacy among teachers and other constituencies is best promoted remains relatively limited and Cambridge could have a useful role to play in enhancing our understanding of how assessment literacy levels can be improved.

Chapter 6 suggests that in the past IELTS has been the prime target for much of the impact-related research conducted by Cambridge ESOL and this is unsurprising given the high-stakes nature of the test and its international reach and reputation. Though some impact-related studies have been conducted with other tests in the Cambridge ESOL portfolio (e.g. CPE, PET), it would be good to see more of these in the future, both in light of the growing range of assessment products offered by the examination board and specifically in relation to the testing of listening, which is a somewhat neglected dimension. The Listening test components of the recently introduced KET and PET for Schools tests would seem to be a prime candidate for investigation given their potential role and status within a specified pedagogical framework. Another area of potentially fruitful research might be to investigate the consequences associated with the listening components of Cambridge assessments designed for teacher education, such as TKT and CELTA, or with the board's domain-related tests, such as ILEC and ICFE. Here, studies exploring issues of consequential validity have the potential to expand our understanding of how assessment processes interact with and shape the worlds of education and employment, at a national, regional and international level. It might also be interesting to see greater exploitation in future of the rich data resource contained in the Cambridge ESOL Impact Video Database referred to in Chapter 6. Video recording potentially provides very useful data enabling the investigation of speaker–listener interaction, back channelling by the listener, breakdowns of understanding and why such breakdowns occur (including whether they are the results of lack of clarity by the teacher or examiner). The Impact Video Database could thus support research into listening-into-speaking.

Findings collected from test washback and impact studies should inform, in an iterative manner, subsequent cycles of change designed to improve the test and its related systems. On the whole, this does seem to be the practice at Cambridge ESOL and several of the volumes published in the *Studies in Language Testing* series over recent years chronicle ways in which this has happened. As far as the assessment of listening is concerned, there remain some interesting research questions to be explored, the answers to which will help to shape the next generation of listening tests. One question concerns why so many test takers perceive the listening test as the most difficult of the skills on which they are being assessed – even if test scores do not bear this out. Other questions relate to the washback, impact and consequential validity implications of the different choices that can be made when testing listening, e.g. the comparative perceptions and merits of single play as opposed to double play; the issues surrounding listening via the computer/internet; the nature of listening with or without the support of visuals (and whether the latter are still or moving images); the relative merits of integrating listening with reading, writing and speaking assessment tasks. Though some work is already under way, there remains plenty of scope for research in these areas, especially as they concern large-scale, standardised assessment measures rather than just small-scale experimental tests.

Criterion-related validity

Chapter 7 examined issues of *criterion-related validity*. Evidence of criterion-related validity for listening tests is routinely generated by Cambridge ESOL through comparison with different forms of the same test, through cross-test comparability and through comparability with external standards and frameworks.

Well-established and documented procedures for generating examination materials in the form of item writer guidelines (see Appendix C) contribute to ensuring the production of comparable listening forms for the different proficiency levels. The importance of controlling cognitive and contextual variables that can affect test difficulty was emphasised in Chapters 3 and 4. The comparability of test forms is further supported by routine statistical analysis through the item banking system which uses a common measurement model – the Cambridge Common Scale – as discussed in Chapter 5. Chapter 7 demonstrated how each listening test is constructed to a pre-defined target difficulty in order to be suitable for its target audience (i.e. matched to their ability). Evidence was presented to demonstrate how consistently the target difficulty/ability has been applied to all Listening tests across the Cambridge English exams. Consistency in producing similar test difficulties for various listening tests testifies to the criterion-referenced approach to test construction and interpretation of test results. While considerable progress has been made in recent years to develop user-friendly and effective checklists for establishing the comparability of contextual factors across test versions, there remains a great deal of work to be done to investigate and demonstrate cognitive comparability across test forms. To enable this, further development of the checklists themselves will be needed to include additional contextual variables that may have an effect on the difficulty of listening items within and across levels, e.g. speech rate, discourse structure, as well as more cognitive parameters. Experimental, one-off research designs are time-consuming and labour-intensive and may well not be entirely practical for large-scale test producers to implement, but it is clearly important that further systematic investigation is undertaken into the cognitive validity elements identified in Chapter 3 so that an examination board can provide adequate evidence for claims of cross-task or cross-test cognitive comparability. Cambridge ESOL could have a significant role in developing new types of instrumentation to assist in this endeavour.

Chapter 7 reported various studies where performance on an exam at one level is related to performance on another exam at an adjacent level. This creates a picture of the coherent relationship between different Cambridge ESOL exams and hence provides evidence of cross-test comparability. More cross-test studies are needed in future to confirm whether what candidates supposedly can do at a particular level on one exam matches what they can do at the same level on another exam. The discussion on score reporting procedures in the earlier scoring validity section highlights the extent to which Cambridge ESOL has worked steadily in recent years to integrate its examinations into a coherent system or interpretative framework, developing, among other things, a common assessment scale on which listening ability and the other skills can be measured and test scores reported.

Some historical evidence of the link of Cambridge ESOL Listening tests to the external framework of the CEFR was provided and Chapter 7 reported on how Cambridge ESOL has over the years embedded the CEFR into its test development and validation practices. Again, the earlier scoring validity section discusses at some length the nature of the alignment with the interpretative frame of reference currently offered by the CEFR so will not be repeated here. It is important to note, perhaps, that the role and status of the CEFR remains somewhat controversial; significant reservations have been expressed both within Cambridge ESOL and more widely in the language testing profession about the process of aligning tests and the meaningfulness of test alignment claims. The contemporary reality, nonetheless, is that public and governmental demands for statements about the nature of the relationship between a given test and the CEFR cannot easily be ignored by examination providers. As Weir and Taylor (2011:311–312) astutely observe: 'All examination boards should be encouraged to consider carefully how they approach the process of linking their tests to external frameworks of reference in a valid and systematic manner.'

Though the descriptive levels of the CEFR remain underspecified for testing purposes (see Milanovic and Weir 2010, Weir 2005a), particularly as regards the testing of listening, work by Cambridge ESOL and other partners on the English Profile Programme of research over recent years and into the future should prove valuable in fleshing out our understanding of the nature and development of second language listening ability in terms of key test taker characteristics and contextual parameters.

This may help to resolve some of the differences that can be detected between the way Cambridge ESOL criteria for listening are formulated (often based upon goals in the form of 'listening for' descriptors) and the illustrative CEFR listening descriptors (which tend to relate more to listening context and the nature of listening input).

Conclusion

Chapter 1 of this volume argued that the credibility of a language test depends to a large extent upon a coherent understanding and articulation of the underlying latent abilities or construct(s) which the test seeks to represent. If these are not well defined or understood, then it becomes difficult to support claims test producers may wish to make about the usefulness of their test, including claims that a test does not suffer from factors such as construct under-representation or construct-irrelevant variance.

The issues of what a language construct is and whether it is possible to identify and measure developmental stages leading towards its mastery are critical for all aspects of language learning, teaching and assessment. Exam boards and other testing institutions need to demonstrate evidence of the context, cognitive and scoring validity of the test tasks they create to represent the underlying real-life construct. They also need to be explicit as to how they operationalise criterial distinctions between proficiency levels in their tests in terms of the various validity parameters discussed above. Using a socio-cognitive validation framework can help to clarify, both theoretically and practically, the various constituent parts of the testing endeavour as far as validity is concerned; it can offer a valuable means of revisiting many of our traditional terms and concepts, to redefine them more clearly and to enhance our understanding.

This volume demonstrates how Cambridge ESOL has found a socio-cognitive framework to fit particularly well with its way of thinking about the test development and validation questions that arise for the kinds of tests that the board offers. Following *Examining Writing* (Shaw and Weir 2007), *Examining Reading* (Khalifa and Weir 2009) and *Examining Speaking* (Taylor (Ed.) 2011), *Examining Listening* marks the fourth comprehensive attempt to expose the totality of Cambridge ESOL practice in a particular domain to scrutiny in the public arena. As this volume shows, much has already been achieved by Cambridge and other researchers towards a better understanding of the nature of second language listening proficiency and how it can be assessed; perhaps not surprisingly, it also becomes clear that there are many questions still to be answered and a great deal of work still to be done. Future research needs to investigate whether further work on refining the parameters identified in this volume, either singly or in configuration, can help to better ground the distinctions in proficiency in listening represented by levels in Cambridge ESOL examinations and its external referent the CEFR, as well as in the level-based tests produced by other language examination boards.

The editors' aim has been that the explication of theory and practice presented in this volume will lead to a broader and deeper understanding of some complex issues in language assessment. Hopefully, readers will have found the detailed description and discussion of Cambridge ESOL's operational language testing practices particularly useful. It would be good if the sharing of one examination board's expertise and experience in this way encourages and enables other institutions and test providers to review and reflect upon their own testing theory and practice, and thus engage in a similar exercise in public accountability for their own assessment products.

Appendix A

Sample Listening tasks at five levels

KET

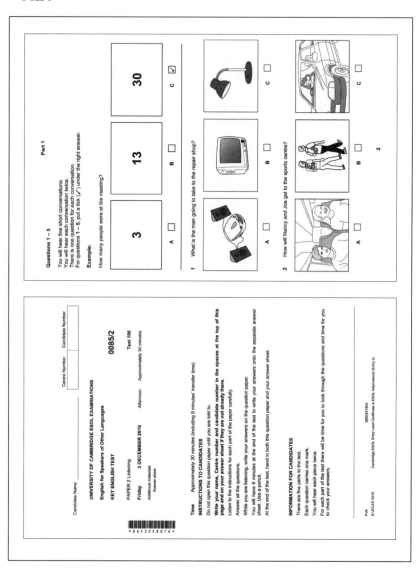

Appendix A

KET

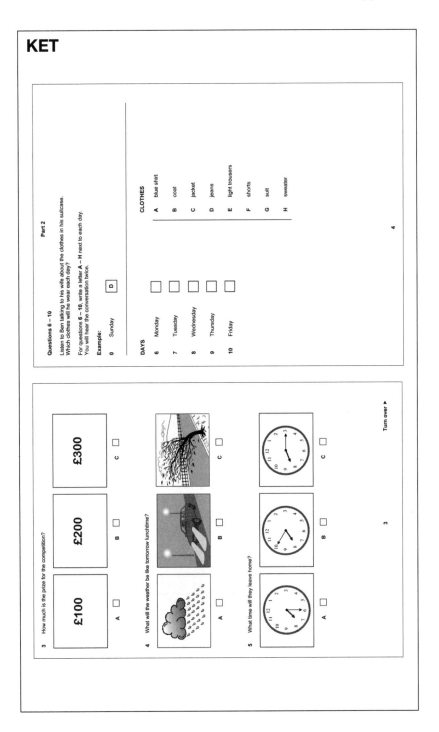

Part 2

Questions 6 – 10

Listen to Ben talking to his wife about the clothes in his suitcase.
Which clothes will he wear each day?

For questions **6 – 10**, write a letter **A – H** next to each day.
You will hear the conversation twice.

Example:

| 0 | Sunday | D |

DAYS

6 Monday ☐
7 Tuesday ☐
8 Wednesday ☐
9 Thursday ☐
10 Friday ☐

CLOTHES

A blue shirt
B coat
C jacket
D jeans
E light trousers
F shorts
G suit
H sweater

4

3 How much is the prize for the competition?

£100   £200   £300

A ☐   B ☐   C ☐

4 What will the weather be like tomorrow lunchtime?

A ☐   B ☐   C ☐

5 What time will they leave home?

A ☐   B ☐   C ☐

3

Turn over ▶

343

KET

Part 3

Questions 11 – 15

Listen to Duncan talking to a friend about a tennis course.

For questions **11 – 15**, tick (✓) **A**, **B** or **C**.
You will hear the conversation twice.

Example:

0 How long was the tennis course?

A one day
B two days ☐
C five days ✓

11 Duncan stayed in a hotel

A in a town. ☐
B near the sea. ☐
C in the mountains. ☐

12 Duncan's teacher comes from

A England. ☐
B France. ☐
C Canada. ☐

13 How much did Duncan pay for the course?

A £185 ☐
B £205 ☐
C £265 ☐

14 Before the course, Duncan bought himself some tennis

A shoes. ☐
B clothes. ☐
C balls. ☐

15 On the last evening, there was

A a party. ☐
B a film show. ☐
C a tennis match. ☐

Turn over ▶

5

Part 4

Questions 16 – 20

You will hear a woman phoning for information about a boat trip.

Listen and complete questions **16 – 20**.
You will hear the conversation twice.

Boat Trip on the River Dee

Days of boat trip:	Friday and Sunday
Get on boat at the:	**16**
Time boat leaves:	**17** .... p.m.
Boat goes to:	**18**
On boat, you can buy:	**19** drinks and ....
Cost of adult ticket:	**20** £

6

KET

BLANK PAGE

8

Questions 21 – 25

Part 5

You will hear a woman giving information on the radio about a theatre school.

Listen and complete questions **21 – 25**.
You will hear the information twice.

Children's Theatre School

Name of school: Silver Star

Cost for children over 14:   **21** £ .... per week

Children must take their own: **22**

There is a show every: **23**

The first summer course starts on: **24** 21st ....

Phone number: **25**

You now have 8 minutes to write your answers on the answer sheet.

7

345

KET

31/03/2011 16:57:18

Answer Key Report

Query Run from Bank: KETLL

Run against Test 12_0085_02_106, Year 2010

Order	Item Id	Description	Key	Item Order	Grouping
1	KL101087	What is the man going to take to the repair shop?	A		
2	KL100805	How will Nancy and Joe get to the sports centre?	B		
3	KL100725	How much is the prize for the competition?	B		
4	KL100977	What will the weather be like tomorrow lunchtime?	C		
5	KL100477	What time will they leave home?	B		
6	KL202215	Ben's clothes	G	1	
7			E	2	
8			B	3	
9			F	4	
10			A	5	
11	KL300151	Tennis course	C	1	
12			C	2	
13			B	3	
14			A	4	
15			A	5	
16	KL400113	Boat trip on River Dee	(at the)(next to) bridge / brige	1	
17			12.15 / twelve fifteen / (a)quarter past twelve (p.m.)	2	
18			ALDFORD, NFV	3	
19			(drinks &) (ice) cream(s)	4	
20			(£13.95 / three pounds (and) ninety-five (pence))	5	
21	KL500172	Children's Theatre School	(only) (£) 89(.00)(£00) / eighty('nine (pounds)s)) (for a week)	1	
22			(bring) (your/their) (the) lunch(es)	2	
23			(on) (every) Fri(day) (afternoon)/week.	3	
24			(on) (the) (21st) (of) July) (the) (21st) (21)(00)7;	4	
25			8447 6963	5	

Page 1 of 1

UNIVERSITY of CAMBRIDGE
ESOL Examinations

KET Paper 2 Listening Candidate Answer Sheet

Candidate Name
Candidate Signature
Examination Title
Centre

Supervisor:
If the candidate is ABSENT or has WITHDRAWN shade here

Centre No.
Candidate No.
Examination Details

Instructions

Use a PENCIL (B or HB).

Rub out any answer you want to change with an eraser.

For Parts 1, 2 and 3:
Mark ONE letter for each question.
For example, if you think C is the right answer to the question, mark your answer sheet like this:

0 A B C

Part 1

1	A B C
2	A B C
3	A B C
4	A B C
5	A B C

Part 2

6	A B C D E F G H
7	A B C D E F G H
8	A B C D E F G H
9	A B C D E F G H
10	A B C D E F G H

Part 3

11	A B C
12	A B C
13	A B C
14	A B C
15	A B C

For Parts 4 and 5:
Write your answers in the spaces next to the numbers (16 to 25) like this:

0 example

Part 4

16	
17	
18	
19	
20	

Part 5

21	
22	
23	
24	
25	

KETL

DP314066

KET

KEY ENGLISH TEST

LISTENING TEST 106
TAPESCRIPT

This is the Cambridge Key English Test Listening Test 106.
There are five parts to the test. Parts One, Two, Three, Four and Five.

We will now stop for a moment before we start the test.
Please ask any questions now because you must NOT speak during the test.

Pause 05"

Now, look at the instructions for Part One.

Pause 05"

You will hear five short conversations.
You will hear each conversation twice.
There is one question for each conversation.
For questions 1 – 5, put a tick under the right answer.
Here is an example:

How many people were at the meeting?

F1   Were there many people at the meeting?
M1   About thirty.
F   That's not many.
M   No, but more than last time.

Pause 05"

The answer is 30, so there is a tick in box C.
Now we are ready to start.
Look at question one.

Pause 05"

1   **What is the man going to take to the repair shop?**

F2   What are you doing today, Pete?
M2   I'm going into town to get a better lamp for my desk.   Then I'm going to the repair shop, my CD player is broken.
F   Do you think they'll be able to make it work?
M   Yes. I took my old television there. It's as good as new now!

Pause 05"
Now listen again.
Repeat
Pause 05"

2   **How will Nancy and Joe get to the sports centre?**

M1   Nancy, shall we go to the sports centre by car or by bus?
F1   I think we should walk, Joe. The traffic will be bad, and the walk will be good for us.
M   I suppose you're right. It's not that far. Can we get the bus back?
F   Let's see how tired we are when we've finished.

Pause 05"
Now listen again.
Repeat
Pause 05"

3   **How much is the prize for the competition?**

F1   What are you writing, Marco?
M2   It's a story. I want to win a competition. I need three hundred pounds for my holiday.
F   How much can you win?
M   Two hundred pounds. I've already got a hundred pounds, so if I win, I can go.

Pause 05"
Now listen again.
Repeat
Pause 05"

KET

Now look at Part Two.

Pause 05"

Listen to Ben talking to his wife about the clothes in his suitcase.
Which clothes will he wear each day?
For questions 6 – 10, write a letter A – H next to each day.
You will hear the conversation twice.

Pause 15"

F2   You've packed so many clothes, Ben.
M2   Well, it is a business trip – and the weather will be different everywhere I go.
F   I suppose on Sunday you'll travel in your jeans.
M   Yes. Then on Monday I'm going to meet the company boss, so I'll need my suit then. I can't wear jeans.
F   What's happening on Tuesday?
M   I'm visiting a factory in the south, so I've packed these grey trousers. They're light and I won't need a jacket – it'll be thirty-five degrees!
F   Then you're in the mountains on Wednesday.
M   Yes. A jacket won't be warm enough. I've got my coat for that day.
F   Are you taking a sweater as well?
M   There isn't room in the suitcase. On Thursday I'll be by the sea so I'm taking my swimming shorts.
F   And what about Friday?
M   I'm having lunch with some colleagues. I'll wear that blue shirt you gave me.
F   Look, here it is, under the suit.
M   Oh, good.

Pause 05"
Now listen again.
Repeat
Pause 05"

That is the end of Part Two.

Pause 10"

---

4   **What will the weather be like tomorrow lunchtime?**

M2   Have you got the newspaper there? Can you read me the weather forecast for tomorrow? I hope it isn't going to rain for our picnic lunch.
F2   *(reading)* There'll be fog early in the day but it will go by the middle of the morning with winds from the east.
M   Great!
F   Yes, but the wind will get stronger through the day!

Pause 05"
Now listen again.
Repeat
Pause 05"

5   **What time will they leave home?**
(female 30s, male teens)

F1   Paul, when do you want to go? It's seven thirty already.
M1   Be ready at ten to eight – we should leave then.
F   You booked the table for eight fifteen, didn't you?
M   Yes, and we mustn't be late.

Pause 05"
Now listen again.
Repeat
Pause 05"

That is the end of Part One.

Pause 10"

KET

Now look at Part Three.

Pause 05"

Listen to Duncan talking to a friend about a tennis course.
For questions 11 – 15, tick A, B or C.
You will hear the conversation twice.

Look at questions 11 – 15 now. You have twenty seconds.

Pause 20"

Now listen to the conversation.

F1 Hi, Duncan. How was your tennis course at the weekend?
M1 Well, I was actually there for five days – not two.
F Oh. Was the hotel nice?
M Beautiful. We were high up in the mountains. We looked down on the lake, where we swam every morning, and across to the town on the other side.
F Was the teacher good?
M Excellent. He's worked here in England for ages but he was born in Canada, so he speaks French and English.
F I'd like to do the course. Was it very expensive?
M The full price in the summer is two hundred and sixty-five pounds, but it only cost me two hundred and five pounds because I'm a student. In the autumn it's less, a hundred and eighty-five pounds.
F Hmm. Did you have to buy anything special?
M I already had tennis clothes, and the hotel had racquets and balls. But I got some new shoes because my old tennis ones were too small.
F What did you do in the evenings?
M Sometimes we watched videos of tennis matches, but on the last night we danced and sang songs in the hotel garden. That was great!

Pause 05"
Now listen again.
Repeat
Pause 05"

That is the end of Part Three.

Pause 10"

Now look at Part Four.

Pause 05"

You will hear a woman phoning for information about a boat trip.
Listen and complete questions 16 – 20.
You will hear the conversation twice.

Pause 10"

[FX: F2 on distort]

M2 Hello, Tourist Information.
F2 Hello, I'm phoning about the boat trips on the River Dee. Can you tell me which days they are?
M Every Friday and Sunday.
F And where does the boat leave from?
M You'll find it next to the bridge. It's ten minutes' walk from North Street car park.
F Are there several trips a day?
M Just one. It starts at twelve fifteen. It takes about an hour and forty-five minutes, so you'll be back by two.
F How far up the river will the boat take us?
M All the way to Aldford. That's A L D F O R D. You get off there and come back through the mountains on a bus.
F It sounds nice. Can I get any food on the boat?
M Not much, they only sell ice cream and cold drinks. But there are lots of cafés in Aldford.
F Can we get tickets on the boat?
M Yes. They're three pounds ninety-five for adults and two pounds seventy-five for children. Come early and get a good seat.
F OK. Thank you for your help.

Pause 05"
Now listen again.
Repeat
Pause 05"

That is the end of Part Four.

Pause 10"

KET

Now look at Part Five

Pause 05"

**You will hear a woman giving information on the radio about a theatre school.
Listen and complete questions 21 – 25.
You will hear the information twice.**

Pause 10"

F1   Do you love singing, dancing and acting?   Then come to Silver Star Theatre School.   We have courses every week during the school holidays for children between nine and sixteen years old.

If you are fourteen, fifteen or sixteen, the price is only eighty-nine pounds for a week.   If you are under fourteen, it costs ninety-five pounds per week.   You'll find we are cheaper than other theatre schools, but much better!

The only thing you should bring with you is your lunch.   We will give you any special clothes you need.

From Monday to Thursday you will work really hard.   Then, family and friends can come and watch you in a special show on Friday afternoon.   For many people, this is the best day of the week.

The first summer course begins on July the twenty-first and you must book by the twelfth.   If you want to join the Silver Star School, call Mary and ask for a booking form today.   The phone number is eight double four seven - six nine five three and you can call between nine a.m. and five p.m. every day

Pause 05"
Now listen again.
Repeat
Pause 05"

That is the end of Part Five.

You now have eight minutes to write your answers on the answer sheet.

Pause 07"
"Ping"

You have one more minute.

Pause 01"
"Ping"

That is the end of the test.

PET

Candidate Name _____

Centre Number | Candidate Number

UNIVERSITY OF CAMBRIDGE ESOL EXAMINATIONS

English for Speakers of Other Languages

PRELIMINARY ENGLISH TEST

0090/2

PAPER 2 Listening

Test 106

Friday   3 DECEMBER 2010   Morning   Approximately 35 minutes

Additional materials:
Answer sheet

2689549008

Time   Approximately 35 minutes (including 6 minutes' transfer time)

INSTRUCTIONS TO CANDIDATES

Do not open this question paper until you are told to do so.

Write your name, Centre number and candidate number in the spaces at the top of this page and on your answer sheet if they are not already there.

Listen to the instructions for each part of the paper carefully.

Answer all the questions.

While you are listening, write your answers on the question paper.

You will have 6 minutes at the end of the test to copy your answers onto the separate answer sheet. Use a pencil.

At the end of the test, hand in both this question paper and your answer sheet.

INFORMATION FOR CANDIDATES

There are four parts to the test.

Each question carries one mark.

You will hear each part twice.

For each part of the test there will be time for you to look through the questions and time for you to check your answers.

PV3
© UCLES 2010

500/2414/0
Cambridge ESOL Entry Level Certificate in ESOL International (Entry 3)

Part 1

Questions 1 – 7

There are seven questions in this part.
For each question there are three pictures and a short recording.
Choose the correct picture and put a tick (✓) in the box below it.

Example: Where did the man leave his camera?

A ☑   B ☐   C ☐

1 Which prize has the man just won?

A ☐   B ☐   C ☐

2 What was the man's first job?

A ☐   B ☐   C ☐

2

351

PET

6 What can you see on the television programme?

A □ B □ C □

7 Where will the man sit on the plane?

A □ B □ C □

4

3 Where will they have something to eat?

A □ B □ C □

4 What does the woman's house look like now?

A □ B □ C □

5 Which sport will they do tomorrow?

A □ B □ C □

3

Turn over ▶

PET

Part 2

Questions 8 – 13

You will hear an interview with a woman called Lucy Rainbow, who is talking about her job as a painter.
For each question, put a tick (✓) in the correct box.

8 What does Lucy usually paint?
- A scenery for stage plays
- B pictures of pop stars
- C the walls in people's homes

9 Lucy chose her present job because
- A she enjoys working by herself.
- B she couldn't get a job in advertising.
- C she thought it would be interesting.

10 What does Lucy find difficult about her work?
- A She sometimes misses lunch.
- B Some days are too busy.
- C She always has too much work to do.

11 How many hours a day does Lucy usually work?
- A seven
- B eight
- C eleven

12 How does Lucy travel to work?
- A on foot
- B by car
- C by public transport

13 What does Lucy do in her free time nowadays?
- A She studies.
- B She visits an art gallery.
- C She plays tennis.

5 Turn over ▶

Part 3

Questions 14 – 19

You will hear a radio announcement about a new magazine.
For each question, fill in the missing information in the numbered space.

NEW MAGAZINE

The name of the magazine is (14) ....

First issue of magazine
- healthy recipes using (15) ....
- a DVD about making (16) .... for summer

Second issue of magazine
- recipes using (17) .... for children
- special recipes to use for (18) .... for adults

The first issue of the magazine costs (19) £ ....

6

353

PET

8

Part 4

Questions 20 – 25

Look at the six sentences for this part.

You will hear a man called Karl, and his wife Jenny, talking about the holiday they have just had.

Decide if each sentence is correct or incorrect.

If it is correct, put a tick (✓) in the box under **A** for **YES**. If it is not correct, put a tick (✓) in the box under **B** for **NO**.

		A YES	B NO
20	Jenny and Karl are both pleased to be home after their holiday.	☐	☐
21	Jenny thinks the weather forecast they heard for their holiday week was correct.	☐	☐
22	Jenny and Karl both liked the way their hotel served meals.	☐	☐
23	Jenny thinks they had a better room on this holiday than last year.	☐	☐
24	Karl was angry about the state of the hotel sports equipment.	☐	☐
25	Jenny and Karl are both keen to plan another holiday immediately.	☐	☐

7

354

PET

Answer Key Report
Query Run from Bank: PETLL

Run against Test 12_0090_02_106, Year 2010

31/03/2011 11:42:53

Order	Item Id	Description	Key	Item Order	Grouping
1	P2101223	Tennis prize	B		
2	P2100807	What was the man's first job?	B		
3	P2101875	Can't stop	C		
4	P2100813	What does the woman's house look like now?	A		
5	P2100927	Which sport will they do tomorrow?	A		
6	OP2100294	Planet earth documentary	B		
7	OP2100297	Sit on the plane	C		
8	P22T0126	Scenic Painter	A	1	
9			C	2	
10			B	3	
11			C	4	
12			C	5	
13			A	6	
14	OP23T0039	New magazine	see markscheme	1	
15			see markscheme	3	
16			see markscheme	3	
17			see markscheme	4	
18			see markscheme	5	
19			see markscheme	6	
20	P24T0181	Holidays	B	1	
21			A	2	
22			A	3	
23			B	4	
24			B	5	
25			B	6	

Page 1 of 1

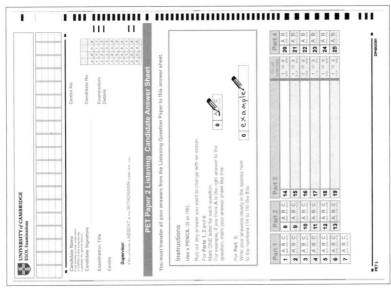

PET

PRELIMINARY ENGLISH TEST
LISTENING TEST 106 - TAPESCRIPT

Rubric: This is the Cambridge Preliminary English Test, Number 106.

There are four parts to the test. You will hear each part twice. For each part of the test there will be time for you to look through the questions and time for you to check your answers.

Write your answers on the question paper. You will have six minutes at the end of the test to copy your answers onto the answer sheet.

The recording will now be stopped.

Please ask any questions now, because you must not speak during the test.

PAUSE 00'05"

Rubric: Now open your question paper and look at part 1.

PAUSE 00'02"

Rubric: There are seven questions in this part. For each question there are three pictures and a short recording. Choose the correct picture and put a tick in the box below it.

Rubric: Before we start, here is an example.

Where did the man leave his camera?

M: Oh no! I haven't got my camera!

F: But you used it just now to take a photograph of the fountain.

M: Oh I remember, I put it down on the steps while I put my coat on.

F: Well, let's drive back quickly – it might still be there.

PAUSE 00'05"

Rubric: The first picture is correct so there is a tick in box A.

Look at the three pictures for question 1 now.

PAUSE 00'05"

Rubric: Now we are ready to start. Listen carefully. You will hear each recording twice.

Exam: PET Paper: Listening Syllabus/ Component: 0090/02 Session/date/test version: December 2010 (106) Mark Scheme version/date: Final 03/12/10

Mark Scheme

UNIVERSITY of CAMBRIDGE
ESOL Examinations
English for Speakers of Other Languages

PET Listening

PART 3

	KEY	ALTERNATIVE SPELLING	ACCEPTABLE MISSPELLING
14	(it's called) (a/an/the) good living(s)		liveing(s)
15	(for/a/an/the/some) fish/fishes		fishs
16	(a/an/the/some) salad(s)		Sallad(s)
17	(with/a/an/the/some) rice(s)		
18	(a/an/the/some) parties/party		partys partie
19	(on sale at)(£)2.49/two (pound(s)) (and) forty(-)nine (p/pence)		2.49£ poundes pense

CONFIDENTIAL   Page 1 of 1   DO NOT REMOVE

PET

Rubric: 1: Which prize has the man just won?

Part 1

Pretest No.: 153   Question No.: 3

Int: And in second place Tim Davidson. Tim, would you like to say a few words?

Tim: Well, I want to thank everyone who has helped me to do so well today, because it's not just about me the player, there's my trainer, my manager, and my wife Jane. I know she'll love this beautiful glass bowl, so it won't be up on a dusty shelf with the cups I've won in the past. We'll enjoy looking at it every day. And I'll be back next year to win that silver plate! Thank you.

92 words

PAUSE 00'05"

R: Now listen again.

REPEAT

PAUSE 00'05"

Rubric: 2: What was the man's first job?

Live Test 032

M: I know you think being a postman's not a very good job – long hours and not a lot of money – but I enjoy it. Better than some things I've done. When I first left school I spent a month or two cleaning windows, and then I got a job building houses. Now that was hard! Of course, when I was at school, I dreamed of becoming a pilot, but I failed to get on a training course.

77 words

PAUSE 00'05"

Rubric: Now listen again.

REPEAT

PAUSE 00'05"

3

Rubric: 3 – Where will they have something to eat?

Part 1

Pretest No.: 229   Question No.: 1

F: I'm really hungry. Can we stop for something to eat before we get to the airport?

M: Sorry, there isn't enough time to stop at a café. Your mother's flight gets in at ten o'clock, and we've still got quite a long way to go. We don't want to keep her waiting, so I think we'll go straight to the airport. We'll need petrol on the way home, so we can stop for a snack at a service station.

78 words

PAUSE 00'05"

Rubric: Now listen again.

REPEAT

PAUSE 00'05"

Rubric: 4: What does the woman's house look like now?

Live Test 034

F: It was really strange going back to Redmond, where I used to live. Everything has changed so much. I went to see my old house. It used to have trees in the garden and a hedge in the front. Well, the people who own it now have built another bedroom over the top of the garage, and removed the trees and hedge so they have more room to park their cars. It made me feel really sad, because it looked so different.

PAUSE 00'05"

Rubric: Now listen again.

REPEAT

PAUSE 00'05"

Rubric: 5: Which sport will they do tomorrow?

Part 1

Pretest No.: 185   Question No.: 2

M: It's great here. I've just been horse-riding for the first time in my life, and tomorrow I'm going to learn how to dive off the high board in the swimming

PET

pool. I had no idea there were so many things available.

F: No, I came for the cycling mainly, so I haven't tried all the other things. To be honest, I don't think the pool is for me really, although I'd like to try the riding. Would you be interested in doing that again tomorrow with me, instead of the diving?

M: Yeah, I suppose so.

94 words

PAUSE 00'05"

R: Now listen again.

REPEAT

PAUSE 00'05"

Rubric: 6 – What can you see on the television programme?

Part 1

Pretest No.: 232 Question No.: 3

Coming up next on The Science Channel is the latest documentary produced and presented by photographer Daniel Hamilton, who made the prize-winning series about African animals which you may have seen last year. His latest series is simply called Earth, and viewers can enjoy some amazing photography, with pictures of the planet shot from cameras in space using the latest satellite technology. So sit back, relax and enjoy!

68 words

PAUSE 00'05"

Rubric: Now listen again.

REPEAT

PAUSE 00'05"

Rubric: 7 – Where will the man sit on the plane?

Part 1

Pretest No.: Question No.:

M: On the plane at last! Now – our seats are in Row 12… over there!

F: Yes, A and B. Seat A is next to the window. Do you want that one? Or do

5

you prefer to sit in the middle?

M: Well, they said the seat on the end seems to be empty too, so I'll take that one instead. I love looking at the clouds, so I'll sit near the window. We'll put our newspapers in the middle. OK?

86 words

PAUSE 00'05"

Rubric: Now listen again.

REPEAT

PAUSE 00'05"

Rubric: That is the end of part 1.

PAUSE 00'10"

Rubric: Now turn to part 2, questions 8 to 13.

You will hear an interview with a woman called Lucy Rainbow, who is talking about her job as a painter.

For each question, put a tick in the correct box.

You now have 45 seconds to look at the questions for Part 2.

PAUSE 00'45"

R: Now we are ready to start. Listen carefully. You will hear the recording twice.

Pretest No.: 139 Part No.: 2 Question Nos.: 8-13

Radio programme

M: Today we have with us in the studio Lucy Rainbow, who earns her living as a painter. Good morning Lucy. Can you tell us about your job?

F: Well, I don't paint pretty pictures you can hang on your walls at home. Mainly, I work in a theatre, painting the background scenery for plays. I've also done a couple of CD covers. That was great, because I got to meet my favourite pop stars.

PET

Rubric: Now turn to part 3, questions 14 to 19.

Rubric: You will hear a radio announcement about a new magazine.

For each question, fill in the missing information in the numbered space.

You now have 20 seconds to look at part 3.

PAUSE 00'20"

Rubric: Now we are ready to start. Listen carefully. You will hear the recording twice.

Part 3

Pretest No.: Question Nos.: 14-19

[radio announcement.]

Today we begin the programme with some information about an exciting magazine that will be on sale in the shops next week. It's called 'Good Living' and the aim of the magazine is to show you how to eat well, and in a healthy way. So every month there will be information about which fruit and vegetables are in season as well as lots of recipes by top chefs for you to make. In the first issue of the magazine, there will be recipes for fish, which is a good choice if you want to eat healthily. In addition, you'll also find a special free gift. This is a DVD showing how to prepare summer salads, using a wide variety of different ingredients, some of them quite unusual.

The second issue will have an interesting article about the history of tea and the many kinds you can buy in different countries. It also has a special collection of recipes for children, which will show them some interesting things to make with rice. Of course, there'll be some good things for adults in this second magazine too. There are some wonderful recipes designed especially for parties. The recipes are quick to prepare and very colourful, and some can also be made ahead of time and frozen, which is always useful.

Now the price of the magazine will normally be £3.99, but the first issue will be on sale at £2.49, so that's a good offer, a reduction of £1.50. It will be on sale in supermarkets and newsagents on Monday. So make sure you buy it – the ideas and photos in it are great!

Moving on, next on the programme......

PAUSE 00'05"

279 words

M: So how did this start?

F: Well, I always intended to become a proper artist. But I couldn't sell any of my paintings, and anyway I got bored working alone! I was offered a job in an advertising agency, but the idea of working in a theatre attracted me more. I get the chance to paint something different every day, I get paid reasonably well, and I work with a team of wonderful people.

M: So you enjoy your work, but doesn't it have any disadvantages?

F: Mostly, I love it. The only thing that causes me stress is that often I have too many things to do at the same time, while at other times I have nothing to do. It's difficult to organise my time, but I always make sure I stop for lunch.

M: How many hours do you work on an average day?

F: There's no such thing as an average day! But generally, I start work at 8 in the morning, and go through until 7. That makes it an eleven-hour day, which is much longer than the 8 hours that most people work.

M: Is your journey to work difficult?

F: Not really. My dream job would be one where I could walk to work, but that hasn't happened yet. I could drive to the theatre, but that makes me tired and I get a lot of my best ideas when I'm on my way to work, on the bus or train.

M: Do you have time for any hobbies?

F: Not as much as I'd like. I used to play a lot of tennis until I hurt my ankle, and I was a regular visitor to an art gallery near my home until it closed down. In the little spare time I have, I'm doing a course in computer graphics. I hope what I learn will help me in my job.

M: Well, thank you, Lucy. It's been interesting talking to you.

393 words

PAUSE 00'05"

R: Now listen again.

REPEAT

Rubric: That is the end of part 2.

PAUSE 00'10"

6

PET

Rubric: Now listen again.

REPEAT

PAUSE 00'05"

Rubric: That is the end of part 3.

PAUSE 00'10"

Rubric: Now turn to part 4, questions 20 to 25.

Rubric: Look at the six sentences for this part. You will hear a man called Karl, and his wife Jenny, talking about the holiday they have just had.

Decide if each sentence is correct or incorrect. If it is correct, put a tick in the box under A for YES. If it is not correct, put a tick in the box under B for NO.

You now have 20 seconds to look at the questions for part 4.

PAUSE 00'20"

Rubric: Now we are ready to start. Listen carefully. You will hear the recording twice.

Pretest No.: 39A	Part No.: 4	Question Nos.: 20-25

Karl: Phew! Home at last! That journey seemed to last forever. I'm glad to be back, aren't you?

Jenny: [Sighs] Not really. I'm sorry our holiday's over. I'll miss the beach. We had a great time, didn't we?

Karl: Mmm... it was OK. The weather wasn't as good as I'd hoped. I thought the forecast was for bright sunshine the whole week!

Jenny: Well, most of the week was like that. We only had a little bit of rain, didn't we? And they did mention that on the forecast.

Karl: Yes, the day after it rained! Anyway, the food in the hotel was delicious, wasn't it?

Jenny: It was, yeah...

Karl: And it was good to be able to help ourselves to what we wanted.

Jenny: Mmm... it saved delays, and it meant we could get out quickly in the mornings, too. The waiters were very helpful, I must say.

Karl: Mmm... that was good.

Jenny: The only thing I wasn't happy about was the temperature in the room. It was so hot!

Karl: It certainly was. It didn't help when we opened the windows, either. It didn't cool it down at all, did it?

Jenny: No. Still, it was just the same when we went to that other hotel last year, so I wasn't surprised. I don't know why the air conditioning didn't work, though.

Karl: Well, that wasn't the only thing that wasn't working properly. One of the machines in the gym was broken too. But I suppose it was a very busy time, so the staff were probably just too busy to check it properly. These things happen, don't they? It didn't matter to me!

Jenny: Right...

Karl: So... what should we do for our next holiday then? We could go somewhere completely different.

Jenny: I'm not sure. I was hoping we could go to the coast again, but with all the work I've got at the moment, we'll have to wait and see.

Karl: OK, then...

312 words

Rubric: PAUSE 00'05"

Now listen again.

REPEAT

PAUSE 00'05"

PET

Rubric:	That is the end of part 4.
	PAUSE 00'10"
Rubric:	You now have six minutes to check and copy your answers on to the answer sheet.
	PAUSE 5'00"
	[Ping]
Rubric:	You have one more minute.
	PAUSE 1'00"
	[Ping]
Rubric:	That is the end of the test.

FCE

Candidate Name

UNIVERSITY OF CAMBRIDGE ESOL EXAMINATIONS

English for Speakers of Other Languages

FIRST CERTIFICATE IN ENGLISH

0101/4

PAPER 4 Listening

Test A

MAY 2010

Approximately 40 minutes

Additional materials:
Answer sheet

Time Approximately 40 minutes (including 5 minutes' transfer time)

INSTRUCTIONS TO CANDIDATES

Do not open this question paper until you are told to do so.

Write your name, Centre number and candidate number in the spaces at the top of this page and on your answer sheet if they are not already there.

Listen to the instructions for each part of the paper carefully.

Answer all the questions.

While you are listening, write your answers on the question paper.

You will have 5 minutes at the end of the test to copy your answers onto the separate answer sheet. Use a pencil.

At the end of the test, hand in both this question paper and your answer sheet.

INFORMATION FOR CANDIDATES

There are four parts to the test.

Each question carries one mark.

You will hear each piece twice.

For each part of the test there will be time for you to look through the questions and time for you to check your answers.

PV1

© UCLES 2010

500Z70045

Cambridge ESOL Level 1 Certificate in ESOL, International

5840045537

2

Part 1

You will hear people talking in eight different situations. For questions **1 – 8**, choose the best answer (**A, B** or **C**).

1   You hear a woman leaving a message on an answerphone.

What does she want to do?

A   postpone a meeting

B   cancel a meeting

C   change the location of a meeting

2   You overhear a woman talking about a meal she had in a restaurant.

What does she say about her meal?

A   The food looked unappetising.

B   She did not finish the main dish.

C   It was not good value for money.

3   You hear a man remembering something that once happened to him.

What is he talking about?

A   a meeting that led to his becoming a famous model

B   the part that he played in the development of a toy

C   the opportunity to take up a new profession

4   You overhear a conversation at a reception desk in a sports club.

What is the woman trying to do?

A   clarify some information

B   obtain some literature

C   correct a mistake

FCE

3

5 On the radio, you hear a man talking about new research into the human body.

According to the man, when is the best time to take exercise?

A in the morning

B in the afternoon

C in the evening

6 You hear a man and a woman talking about their daughter's school ski trip being cancelled.

Which view is expressed?

A The school should have been able to solve any problems.

B The teachers concerned should go ahead with the trip.

C It may be possible to arrange an alternative trip.

7 You hear a man who designs websites, talking about his work.

Which client is he designing a website for at the moment?

A a football club

B an artist

C a hotel

8 You overhear a woman talking on the phone.

Why didn't she catch her usual train?

A She had the wrong ticket.

B She was standing on the wrong platform.

C She was waiting at the wrong time.

Turn over ▶

4

Part 2

You will hear a radio interview in which a man called Charlie Lee talks about being a film extra.
For questions **9 – 18**, complete the sentences.

BEING A FILM EXTRA

Charlie's audition took place in a central London [9]

Charlie has a job as a [10] on a full-time basis.

Charlie was told he had to wear [11] clothes suitable for summer.

Charlie compares the outside of the film studio to an enormous [12]

Charlie says the inside of film studio was made to look like part of a [13] in Hong Kong.

Charlie was filmed standing next to some [14] which was near the main doors.

Charlie says the film extras had to take off their [15] during filming.

Charlie spent the afternoon in the [16] away from the action.

Charlie's [17] didn't permit him to talk to or to photograph the stars of the film.

Charlie had to wait [18] before he was paid.

363

FCE

5

Part 3

You will hear five different history teachers talking about how they make their classes interesting. For questions **19 – 23**, choose from the list (A – F) what each speaker says. Use the letters only once. There is one extra letter which you do not need to use.

A I encourage students to do research that has a personal significance for them.

B I use my students' interest in the media to liven up the class.

C I have the latest computer technology to involve my students.

D I show appreciation for the students' contributions in class.

E I set difficult tasks for all my students to do.

F I prepare different activities for weak and strong students.

Speaker 1	19
Speaker 2	20
Speaker 3	21
Speaker 4	22
Speaker 5	23

6

Part 4

You will hear a radio interview with a woman called Sandra Morelle, who is a champion in the sport of pole vaulting. For questions **24 – 30**, choose the best answer (A, B or C).

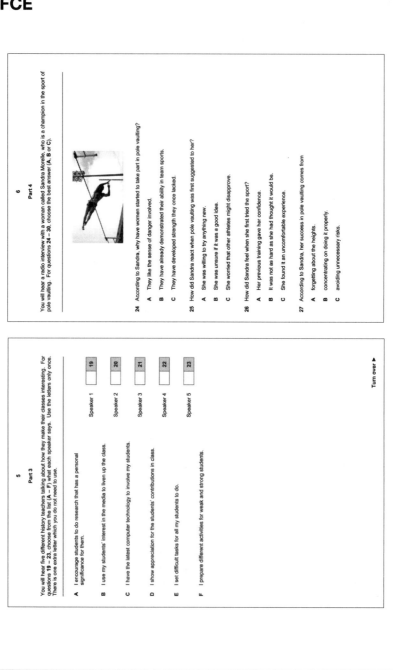

24 According to Sandra, why have women started to take part in pole vaulting?

   A They like the sense of danger involved.

   B They have already demonstrated their ability in team sports.

   C They have developed strength they once lacked.

25 How did Sandra react when pole vaulting was first suggested to her?

   A She was willing to try anything new.

   B She was unsure if it was a good idea.

   C She worried that other athletes might disapprove.

26 How did Sandra feel when she first tried the sport?

   A Her previous training gave her confidence.

   B It was not as hard as she had thought it would be.

   C She found it an uncomfortable experience.

27 According to Sandra, her success in pole vaulting comes from

   A forgetting about the heights.

   B concentrating on doing it properly.

   C avoiding unnecessary risks.

Turn over ►

364

FCE

7

28 How does Sandra account for her rapid progress as a pole vaulter?

A She has done well because it is a new sport.

B She trains with people who are better than her.

C She is motivated by the competition.

29 According to Sandra, why have so many good gymnasts taken up pole vaulting?

A It is not as physically demanding.

B It is better paid than many other sports.

C It is an easier sport to do as you get older.

30 How does Sandra regard her rival, Olga Karinova?

A She doubts if Olga is ready to challenge her.

B She has respect for Olga's ability in the sport.

C She accepts that Olga is likely to beat her eventually.

8
BLANK PAGE

FCE

FCE

FCE PAPER 4: LISTENING TEST - TAPESCRIPT

Part One

1.

Hi, it's Marta. I'm stuck in the office – I should have left by now to get to you for midday as arranged. I hope you haven't left already to meet me at the hotel. Anyway, there's no way I can leave 'til after lunch because I have to have a meeting with the manager here in 10 minutes. And even if I leave at 2.00 I won't get to you until at least 3.00 traffic permitting! I assume we'll still meet at the hotel. Ring me back and let me know if that's going to be okay with you – otherwise we'll have to cancel it altogether. I'll ring your mobile as well.

2.

I was very hungry, so I decided to have a starter before my main course. I had a vast dish of Chinese spring rolls with a lovely filling. There must have been a dozen spring rolls, enough to satisfy most appetites. I couldn't help wondering whether this was really good for business. I mean, if people feel a starter is enough, the customer may leave early and so the restaurant makes less money. Other people see them leaving and might wonder why they've decided to go so soon. I only had a few mouthfuls of my main course, which was a shame, as it was my favourite dish.

3.

Back in those days I was a soldier in the army, and I was simply sitting in a restaurant minding my own business, when a guy in a suit from a big toy company approached me and said, 'I can use your face, it's got character.' Well, a few weeks later, my commanding officer summoned me and told me to get changed and prepare for a rather unusual photoshoot. And you know what? They used my face as the model for a plastic soldier – a very well-known one – that boys used to play with... still do, in fact. It was just a bit of fun, and I didn't receive a penny for it.

4.

M: How can I help you?

F: Hello. You sent me a brochure last week and I was wondering if you could explain something to me?

M: Certainly Madam.

F: Well it says that we can have one free session with a sports coach. Is that right, because I'd like to have a tennis lesson?

M: Ah, there's a mistake in our literature. I'm afraid you can have one free session in the gym only.

F: Oh, what a shame. Never mind, I'm sure it'll do me good. Can I arrange that now?

M: Certainly, when would you like to come in?

5.

According to recent research, our body's systems are controlled by a twenty-four hour clock. This means we can time our behaviour to ensure our body is ready to deal with what we're asking of it – whether it's eating, working or taking exercise. Research so far indicates that early on in the day is best for work because our short-term memory and concentration are at their best then. Interestingly, contrary to popular belief, working out is probably best left to a couple of hours after a

---

Listening Answer Key

Part 1		Part 2	
1	A	9	school
2	B	10	waiter
3	B	11	casual (summer)
4	A	12	(huge) sport(s) centre/center
5	B	13	hotel
6	A	14	luggage/baggage
7	B	15	shoes/footwear
8	C	16	canteen
		17	contract
		18	(for) six/6 months

Part 3		Part 4	
19	D	24	A
20	B	25	B
21	F	26	C
22	A	27	B
23	E	28	C
		29	A
		30	B

Each question carries one mark. The total score is then adjusted to give a mark out of 40.

FCE

Part Two

Presenter: In the studio today I have Charlie Lee who was lucky enough to be a film extra in a recent film. Charlie, had you worked as an extra before?

Charlie: No, not at all. One day I got an email from a friend. He said an agency he knew was looking for Chinese people who lived in London to be extras in a film. Rather than having to go to the agency for the audition, I had to go to a school right in the heart of the city. It was in October and when I got there, there were hundreds of Chinese people queuing up outside, hoping to be extras.

Presenter: Did they tell you immediately if you'd got the part?

Charlie: Not for about a month and then I got a phone call to say I'd been selected. They wanted me to play the part of a tourist who is having an argument with a taxi driver. But I'm not unemployed like many extras. I actually work eight hours a day, five days a week as a waiter. My boss wouldn't give me the time off, so I thought that that would be the end of my film career.

Presenter: But it wasn't the end, was it?

Charlie: No. About a month later the agency rang to check if I was still available, but for a different part. This time I said 'yes', and decided that I would just take a day off sick. I was told that I would need to go in casual summer clothes, even though it was raincoat weather, and I had to be at the studio for 7 am.

Presenter: So, what happened when you got there?

Charlie: Well, when I got to the studio I was amazed. The exterior looked like a really huge sports centre. All around it were lots of offices and small storage buildings. Once I'd registered at reception I went to have my hair and make up done.

Presenter: So the moment had come. What was it like when you went inside the studio?

Charlie: Really weird. I literally walked from a cold winter's day outside into a studio which was very warm – it was supposed to be a hotel. Everything was there – the lifts, the reception area, the main doors with taxis outside and, as it was supposed to be Hong Kong, even the taxis were Chinese ones.

Presenter: Did you have to do very much?

Charlie: Not really. Apparently, my clothes weren't quite right, so instead of walking across the lobby with some beautiful women, I was asked to hang around beside the main doors by some luggage.

Presenter: And how long were you on the set?

Charlie: Well, the filming lasted about four hours. The extras had to be very quiet and we were told not to wear shoes as they made too much noise – we still had socks on though and the cameras weren't filming our feet! By lunchtime we were all hungry and tired of doing the same scene.

Presenter: Then, what happened after lunch?

Charlie: Nothing very much. They got different people on the set so I went off to the canteen, which was quite a distance from the main studio. I just stayed there for the rest of the day and then went home.

light lunch rather than first thing in the morning – our bodies are more flexible at that time of day and we should leave our main meal until later in the evening.

6.
Woman: Oh well, it can't be helped, I suppose. It's disappointing – I mean it would have been a really good experience for her, especially after all the practice she's done here.
Man: What a shame – you'd have thought the school would have some plans in reserve.
Woman: Such a pity – both teachers going down with flu at the last minute!
Man: Well, I suppose if I was in their shoes I wouldn't want to take a big group of teenagers abroad if I had flu.
Woman: True. It's just so unsatisfactory that no one else can step in and do it.

7.
I've been doing website design for ten years, and the profession has improved a lot since I began. There are still bad websites where it's difficult for people to access the information they need – like one famous hotel, where the website was so terrible they were losing customers. They called me in and I had to wipe out the old stuff and change everything. I'm half way through a contract with a sculptor. That's a challenge because it's difficult to show three-dimensional objects to best advantage on a flat screen. I'd love to get work with the football club I support. I can't imagine anything better than that.

8.
So there I was, in the freezing cold, standing on platform 3, waiting for the 8.30 train to Cardiff. It's my regular train – the one I've been catching for ages. But what I hadn't realised was that the timetable had changed the day before. My train had been rescheduled for 20 minutes earlier and they'd changed the platform, too – not that that made any difference as it happens, because it had obviously left by then. My ticket was one of those that's only valid for a certain train, so you can imagine how cross I was.

FCE

Presenter: Did you get to meet any of the stars?

Charlie: Well, the main characters only came on for the last take. They looked very glamorous. But we weren't allowed to talk to the stars or take photos or anything like that as we'd signed a contract to that effect. Pity, because my family and friends would've loved a photo.

Presenter: What a shame. But were you paid well for the day?

Charlie: Actually I was quite surprised by how much I had made – £195. But I didn't get it until six months later, which I thought was a bit long. However, friends who've been extras say that even nine months isn't unusual. But I saw the film when it came out and yes, there I am in the lobby right at the back.

Part Three

Speaker 1

My lessons are a mixture of fun and practicality, which starts with arranging the desks in a gentle curve round the whiteboard. I want students to think of History as more than just a lot of names – I hope I make it come alive for them. I often borrow my students' ideas – I pick up on a good point they are making and I thank them for it. It's a habit with me – I think it goes back to the encouragement that my sister and I got from our parents... If you do that, they'll want to give you something in return by being involved.

Speaker 2

Most teachers say that young people spend too much time in front of a screen, and don't read enough at home, which is true. But in my classroom, you can often hear well-known tunes precisely from things that they all watch at home. For my students, those things mean a lot and can really add a spark – for example, I use the tune of a well-known detective series to signal to the students that they should open their books and start reading, and another piece means that they should write down their answer to a question. It's not difficult and you don't need lots of computers or hi-tech equipment!

Speaker 3

I work with students of varying abilities, and I know that not everyone is crazy about history. Each student needs something from me, so that means each lesson has to have a variety of approaches. For example, I may need to help a student who is struggling to understand an article they found on the internet... Or, once, I had a student who was really keen on the history of art, so I got hold of some beautifully illustrated history books which really sparked his imagination and prevented him from getting bored.

Speaker 4

Learning history is not all about remembering hundreds of facts and dates, because you soon forget all that. I try to find ways to relate the history lesson I'm teaching to something interesting in the local area, so my students will go to museums or libraries and find bits of information, and write reports on them. Sometimes they will use the net at home, or they will interview their grandparents or other people they know well. My students tell me they never do anything boring in my lessons, and they often discover talents they never knew they had.

Speaker 5

Some teachers make everything sound easy, and they believe students will like history that way. I'm of a different opinion. If, for example, a student comes to me with an extract from a book they cannot understand, I encourage them to look at it again. I don't immediately give them my interpretation or try to make it simple for them. And I treat weak and strong students in the same manner. I know that if I don't make activities challenging, they won't learn. And my students are always keen to take part – even when they are tired they participate with enthusiasm.

FCE

Part Four

Int.: My guest today, Sandra Morelle, has made her name in a sport that's only recently been open to women, the pole vault. Sandra, why didn't women do the sport in the past?

Sandra: Well, it was tried thirty, perhaps forty, years ago, but it didn't catch on. I think a lot of people made the mistake of thinking that women simply didn't have the upper-body strength it requires. But women's sport has come a long way since then. For a start, they're now playing more so-called men's sports like basketball and soccer. But with the pole vault, I reckon the attraction's probably that it's slightly risky, so it appeals in the same way as other so-called extreme sports, you know, where there's some fear factor.

Int.: What made you take it up personally?

Sandra: Well, I'd always regarded it as one of those sports that women just didn't do. I was a heptathlete, doing a range of track and field sports – and my coach came to me and said, 'Hey, why don't you try the pole vault?' and I just looked at him in amazement and said, 'What me?' and he just said, 'Well why not?'

Int.: What was it like when you first did it?

Sandra: Well, I knew how to run, how to throw things; jump off the ground. But when I had to carry this long pole in my hand, running very fast, it was really awkward for me. Then when you jump and you try to get upside down, it needs a lot of gymnastic technique that I didn't have at first. I was very frightened to go upside down because it didn't come easy, it took me years to feel I was going to land safely on the mat. But I think it was the challenge that kept me involved in it.

Int.: And it's high up.

Sandra: It is, you know, sometimes I don't realise how high it is unless I actually go and stand underneath the bar and look up. But, you know, over the years, I've done well because I've perfected my technique and I've got a good coach who helps me every day when I train. And it's like anything else, it progresses and you have to be daring enough to keep putting the bar up a little bit higher each time and keep perfecting the jumps.

Int.: But you seem to have progressed incredibly quickly. Why is that?

Sandra: Well, I know that the sport's so new still and there are a lot of women who are taking it up, especially women who've been high-level gymnasts in the past, and could be Olympic-level gymnasts if they wanted. So I know that there are a lot of talented girls wanting to beat me, but I feel that if I'm fresh and that my technique is right, then I'm going to put the bar up as high as I can in each competition.

Int.: But what attracts those gymnasts to the pole vault?

Sandra: Well, as I say, their training is relevant and, of course, women gymnasts do tend to reach their best at a pretty early age. But I don't feel those are the main reasons. I reckon they just feel that this is a sport where you can make the same sort of money, but it's not so stressful on your body and it has a pretty fun and carefree atmosphere by comparison.

Int.: So, you're up against your great rival Olga Karinova at this weekend's event. She says she's going to beat you this time round. What do you think?

Sandra: Well, I'm glad she's confident because we had a great battle last season, and that really helps if, like me, you're keen to put the bar up and break records. She's got gymnastic training and she's come on the scene very fast, within the last two years, so I'd be a fool not to see her as a serious challenge, but I reckon I can handle it.

Int.: Sandra Morelle, thanks for joining us. We wish you the best of luck.

Sandra: Thank you.

CAE

Candidate Name

Centre Number | Candidate Number

UNIVERSITY OF CAMBRIDGE ESOL EXAMINATIONS

English for Speakers of Other Languages

CERTIFICATE IN ADVANCED ENGLISH

PAPER 4 Listening

Test A

DECEMBER 2009

Approximately 40 minutes

Additional materials:
Answer sheet

0151/4

Time Approximately 40 minutes (including 5 minutes' transfer time)

INSTRUCTIONS TO CANDIDATES

Do not open this question paper until you are told to do so.

Write your name, Centre number and candidate number in the spaces at the top of this page and on your answer sheet if they are not already there.

Listen to the instructions for each part of the paper carefully.

Answer all the questions.

While you are listening, write your answers on the question paper.

You will have 5 minutes at the end of the test to copy your answers onto the separate answer sheet. Use a pencil.

At the end of the test, hand in both this question paper and your answer sheet.

INFORMATION FOR CANDIDATES

There are four parts to the test.

Each question carries one mark.

You will hear each piece twice.

For each part of the test there will be time for you to look through the questions and time for you to check your answers.

PV5   500226983

© UCLES 2009   Cambridge ESOL, Level 2 Certificate in ESOL, International

|||||||||||||| *2 4 4 9 5 9 6 2 8 6 *

2

Part 1

You will hear three different extracts. For questions 1 – 6, choose the answer (A, B or C) which fits best according to what you hear. There are two questions for each extract.

Extract One

You overhear a sportsman called Alex talking to his coach.

1 What does the coach say about motivation?

A Sports people have different forms of motivation.

B All successful sports people understand what motivates them.

C It is important for coaches to study the psychology of motivation.

2 Alex says he is resolved to

A recover his winning form.

B find out why he gives up so easily.

C focus on performing to the best of his ability.

Extract Two

You hear part of a radio programme in which a reporter called Toby Beesley is talking about a museum located in a castle.

3 Toby thinks that the people running the museum have not installed modern technology because

A they are unwilling to do so.

B they lack the means to do so.

C they've not been allowed to do so.

4 He recommends this museum to people who appreciate

A an uncomplicated display.

B a traditional approach.

C comfortable facilities.

CAE

4

Part 2

You will hear part of a programme in which an Australian sheep farmer called Keith Reid is talking about a local event known as the Morongla Sheepdog Trials. For questions **7 – 14**, complete the sentences.

THE MORONGLA SHEEPDOG TRIALS

The new Sheepdog Trials aim to raise funds to improve the [7] used for the annual country show.

Keith is very happy that a total of [8] dogs participated in the event.

In the Sheepdog Trials, teams lose points for the offence known as [9]

When the [10] is closed, with the sheep inside the enclosure, the trial is over.

Handlers may ask to begin the course again if a sheep is [11]

The highest level in the Trials is called [12] level.

The winning dogs will each be given a [13] and some dog food.

Keith describes sheep as both [14] and stubborn.

3

Extract Three

You hear part of an interview with Adam Harrabin, who uses a metal detector, a hand-held machine which can discover metal buried in the ground.

5 When he answers the presenter's first question, Adam is

A describing how the machine works.

B estimating the value of objects he's found.

C justifying action taken during his investigation.

6 What does Adam most enjoy about using his metal detector?

A the thrill of finding something very old

B the variety of places to be explored

C the need to keep a location secret

Turn over▶

CAE

Part 4

You will hear five short extracts in which students on art courses are talking about their experiences.

TASK ONE

For questions 21 – 25, choose from the list (A – H) the difficulties each speaker has had to overcome.

TASK TWO

For questions 26 – 30, choose from the list (A – H) what each speaker enjoys most about the process of creating art.

While you listen you must complete both tasks.

A	the demands of a family	
B	a lack of work space	Speaker 1 [21]
C	financial pressures	Speaker 2 [22]
D	feelings of isolation	Speaker 3 [23]
E	peer group pressure	Speaker 4 [24]
F	poor job prospects	Speaker 5 [25]
G	an urban environment	
H	a lack of time	

A	visualising the finished piece	
B	doing background reading	Speaker 1 [26]
C	looking at something in detail	Speaker 2 [27]
D	recording ideas in words	Speaker 3 [28]
E	taking photographs	Speaker 4 [29]
F	copying the work of other artists	Speaker 5 [30]
G	combining different styles	
H	experimenting with colour	

6

5

Part 3

You will hear part of an interview with an actor called Peter Jameson, who is talking about his career. For questions 15 – 20, choose the answer (A, B, C or D) which fits best according to what you hear.

15 What type of roles did Peter want to play when he was younger?

A He was keen to specialise in famous Shakespearean parts.
B He thought working in television would be more rewarding.
C He wanted the freedom to explore a wide range of characters.
D He felt that classical plays would suit his personality best.

16 What do we learn about Peter's voice?

A He needs a microphone in order to be heard in a large venue.
B He makes use of the latest technology to enhance it.
C He finds it difficult to relax his voice when he's acting.
D He's learnt to get over problems through voice training.

17 According to Peter, when he took on the role of Prospero he was

A relieved to be playing a challenging character for a change.
B apprehensive at having to portray so much anger on stage.
C amused by the audience's reaction to his performance.
D doubtful as to whether he would enjoy the experience.

18 What does Peter say about learning the words in a play?

A He relies on the natural abilities he was born with.
B He's grateful for the training he received as a student.
C He finds it easier to remember them scene-by-scene.
D He accepts that memorising long parts is impossible now.

19 How does Peter feel about watching his past performances on television?

A He appreciates the support of friends when doing it.
B It's something he would rather avoid doing.
C There's little time for it when he's working.
D Being forced to do it makes him angry.

20 What particularly impressed Peter about *The Romans*?

A its relevance to modern times
B the accuracy of the historical details
C its original use of language
D the strength of the acting

Turn over ▸

373

CAE

BLANK PAGE

8

BLANK PAGE

7

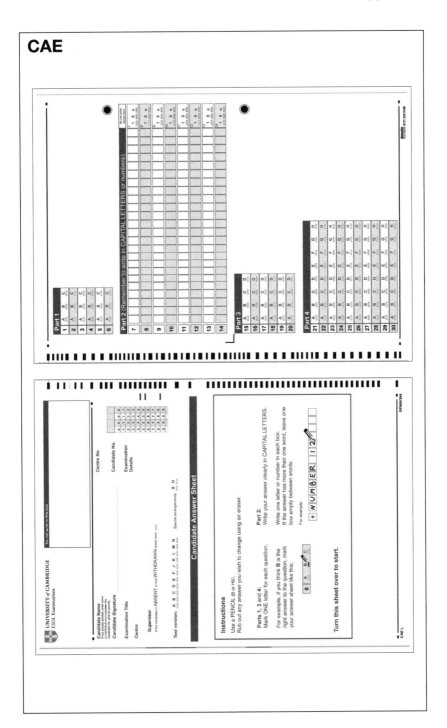

CAE

Answer Key Report
Query Run from Bank: CAE4L

Run against Test 12_0151_04_A, Year 2009

15/12/2009 16:32:48

Order	Item Id	Description	Key	Item Order	Grouping
1	E4100124	Motivation	A	1	
2			C	2	
3	E4100148	No Gadgets (Repurposed was E4100561)	A	1	
4			B	2	
5	E4100168	Metal Detector	C	1	
6			C	2	
7	E4AT0132	The Moonglis Sheepdog arena Track 83		1	
8			224 (two hundred (and) twenty-four	2	
9			turning fail	3	
10			gate	4	
11			hurt / injured (in competition) / (during theta competition)	5	
12			(the) open	6	
13			ribbon	7	
14			unpredictable		
15	E43T0001	An Actor recalls (Repurposed was E43T0168)	C	1	
16			D	2	
17			A	3	
18			A	4	
19			B	5	
20			A	6	
21	E44T0009	Art Students	G	1	
22			C	2	
23			E	3	
24			E	4	
25			A	5	
26			D	6	
27			C	7	
28			B	8	
29			E	9	
30			H	10	

Page 1 of 1

1

A1 This is the Cambridge Certificate in Advanced English Listening test. DECEMBER 2009 TEST A.

I'm going to give you the instructions for this test.

I'll introduce each part of the test and give you time to look at the questions.

At the start of each piece you'll hear this sound:

FX *****

A2 You'll hear each piece twice.

Remember, while you're listening, write your answers on the question paper.

You'll have 5 minutes at the end of the test to copy your answers onto the separate answer sheet.

There'll now be a pause. Please ask any questions now, because you must not speak during the test.

PAUSE 5 SECONDS

A3 Now open your question paper and look at Part 1.

PAUSE 5 SECONDS

A4 You'll hear three different extracts. For questions 1–6, choose the answer (A, B, or C) which fits best according to what you hear. There are two questions for each extract.

A5 Extract one.

You overhear a sportsman called Alex talking to his coach.

Now look at questions one and two.

PAUSE 15 SECONDS

FX *****

[Uses recording from PT273, track 7]

M: I can't seem to motivate myself any more. I know I've still got it in me to improve my fitness and my ability in sport but I can't seem to get there. What can I do?

F: At least you recognise the need to get motivated, Alex. That's a good start.
Any coach will tell you that being psychologically motivated is crucial to being the best in sport. Not everyone experiences the same kind of motivation and I think there are at least two main kinds. There's ego orientation – playing sport because you want to be the winner, or task orientation – continually trying to improve your own personal best performances.

M: I know my problem. When I'm winning, everything's fine. I'm totally motivated.

CAE

2

But when things aren't working out, like now, I give up too easily. So I've got to push myself. I'll have to aim as high as I possibly can and even if I fall short of my targets, hopefully I'll still achieve something. It sounds easy to say, but it's going to take hard work.

[176 words]

PAUSE 5 SECONDS
FX**
REPEAT EXTRACT 1
PAUSE 3 SECONDS

A6 Extract two.
You hear part of a radio programme in which a reporter called Toby Beesley is talking about a museum located in a castle.

Now look at questions three and four.

PAUSE 15 SECONDS
FX**
[Use recording from PT269, track 6]

F: In this city we're all very proud of our castle, but how many of us can say, hand on heart, we've been round its museum? Well, yesterday we sent our reporter Toby Beesley to the Castle Museum to see what it's like.

M: At the entrance you're greeted by a notice describing it as the largest, most comprehensive city museum in the world. But many of its galleries are still very traditional with exhibits in glass cases. They quite deliberately avoid technological gadgetry in terms of CD ROMS and holograms, etc. because, we're told, that wouldn't fit the dignity of the castle. Apparently, no one's saying that those things are in themselves undignified, but rather that they don't sit very comfortably in what's also a historical building. So this is a must for people who love the rather dusty quiet of a conventional exhibition with plenty of notices in a range of small print to peer at.

F: Thanks to Toby for that. And now here's Sophie, to tell us about the weekly farmers' market...

[173 words]

PAUSE 5 SECONDS
FX**
REPEAT EXTRACT 2
PAUSE 3 SECONDS

A7 Extract three.
You hear part of an interview with Adam Harrabin, who uses a metal detector, a

3

hand-held machine which can discover metal buried in the ground.

Now look at questions five and six.

PAUSE 15 SECONDS
FX**
[Use Pretest 278 recording, track 3]

Presenter: So, Adam, can you tell us a bit about your metal-detecting?

AH: Well, of course, the metal detector only does the easy bit, then I have to pick my spade up and get down to work! So far I've retrieved a couple of watches and a gold ring – hard to say how much they're worth. But my main find has been this ancient Roman coin, and what's important about it is that it was found on a beach where historians didn't think the Romans had ever been. So if people complain about all these holes in the sand, well, we're rewriting history.

Presenter: Using a metal detector's quite popular now, isn't it?

AH: Yes, it is. In theory you could go all over the country with a metal detector, but I find it easier, transport-wise, staying close to home. I never let on to anybody exactly where I'm searching, though – that's the fun of it for me, really – looking for clues that only I know about. And people find it exciting, of course – you can turn up really quite valuable things that someone might have dropped yesterday or a thousand years ago.

[199 words]

PAUSE 5 SECONDS
FX**
REPEAT EXTRACT 3
PAUSE 3 SECONDS

A8 That's the end of Part 1.

A9 Now turn to Part 2.
PAUSE 5 SECONDS

A10 You'll hear part of a programme in which an Australian sheep farmer called Keith Reid is talking about a local event known as the Morongla Sheepdog Trials. For questions 7–14, complete the sentences.

You now have 45 seconds to look at Part 2.

PAUSE 45 SECONDS
FX**
[Uses recording from J07B]

Int: How many of us see dogs as working animals? But there's one dog – a

CAE

sheepdog – that really does work hard for a living, controlling herds of sheep in absolute co-operation with a farmer. In Australia, as far back as the 1870s, the skill of these working dogs has been tested in competitions, known as trials. I joined Keith Reid, a sheep farmer in the small farming community of Morongla, for a very special occasion.

Keith: We host a country show here every year, but we needed to raise money to modernise the arena we use for the show, so in August we held our first-ever Sheepdog Trials. I'm very pleased it turned out as well as it did. About 400 sheepdogs regularly take part in trials all over Australia and we got 224 dogs. Not a bad turnout for our first event. We didn't expect more than 175.

The basics of trialling haven't changed much over the years. Each team – that's the sheepdog handler, the dog and three sheep – has fifteen minutes to complete the course. The team starts with 100 points and moves around the course, losing points for various offences. For instance, points are lost if the dog moves its head away from the sheep at any time – we call this 'turning tail'. There are two offences that result in automatic disqualification. The first is when the dog bites a sheep. Fortunately, that doesn't happen often. The second is known as 'crossing', which is when the dog passes between the sheep and the handler. The aim of the whole thing is to bring the sheep to you, not drive them away!

Our course begins with three sheep at one end of the field and the dog and handler at the other. The trial concludes when the sheep have entered the enclosure and the handler has secured the gate. The dog must bring the sheep to the handler in a straight line; we call this stage 'the draw'. Once they set off they can only stop at fixed points – generally near the obstacles. There's only one situation where the handler can ask for a re-run – and that's if a sheep is hurt during the competition.

We've got four levels in our trials: beginning with what's called 'encourage', then we have 'novice', then 'improver' and finally the top one which goes by the name of 'open'. Once a dog wins at one level, it moves up to the next. The whole event lasts for three days and then the top three dogs will

get a ribbon and a 20-kilo bag of dog biscuits for their efforts! And the handlers walk off with a trophy.

It all sounds easy, but believe me, it isn't. The great levellers in any sheepdog trial are the sheep. They can be incredibly stubborn and unpredictable, but anyone who thinks sheep are silly has got a lot to learn.
[482 words]

PAUSE 10 SECONDS
A11 Now you'll hear Part 2 again.
FX*****
REPEAT PART 2
PAUSE 5 SECONDS
A12 That's the end of Part 2.

A13 Now turn to Part 3.
PAUSE 5 SECONDS
A14 You'll hear part of an interview with an actor called Peter Jameson, who is talking about his career. For questions 15–20, choose the answer (A, B, C or D) which fits best according to what you hear.
You now have 1 minute to look at Part 3.
PAUSE 1 MINUTE
FX*****
[Uses PT265 recording, track 6]
Int: In the studio with me tonight is the famous actor, Peter Jameson, who is known above all for his classical roles on stage, particularly in Shakespeare plays. Peter, was it your choice to appear so often in this type of play or the prejudice of casting directors?

PJ: That's an interesting question. Let me answer by giving you an example. Years ago, I wanted to play a rather unusual detective in a series on a new TV channel, and when my agent put my name up for it they said 'No, no, no, he's too posh for commercial television.' At which my agent hit the roof, quite rightly so. I've always seen myself as an actor, a jobbing actor doing whatever comes along, rather than exclusively classical roles, Shakespeare and so on, although of course I do find those fascinating.

Int: And your voice is, perhaps to your irritation, what people often pick up on

CAE

6

because its range is unusual ... and its quality. Were you born with it or did you develop it over time?

PJ: Um. It was I suppose a gift originally, but I've had coaching – several people here in the UK. And then when I went to America on tour microphones were barred in the Gershwin Theatre. And I then said 'Look I can't get through this. You've got to get me a voice coach.' And he came three days a week and he allied voice production with the Alexander Relaxation Technique, and he, more than anybody I think, put a kind of microphone in my throat so that I could ... even when I had a cold, I could speak above it

Int: In your recent role of Prospero in the play The Tempest, it seemed to me that you brought out the darker edges of your voice sometimes. You also brought out his anger particularly. This is slightly against type for you, isn't it?

PJ: It's something that has dogged me throughout my career. I do have a reputation for being rather gentle and likeable – a totally unearned reputation, I have to say. But that's I suppose what comes across to the audience. That's why I relish the chance to play more demanding and complex roles like Prospero.

Int: I remember seeing you playing four big parts in close succession, and I don't generally ask actors but, about um... line learning, because it is part of the trade, but it did astonish me that you must've had thousands of lines in your head at that point.

PJ: I don't know whether I could do it so easily now, twenty years on, but I've always been blessed with a sort of photographic memory, right from my earliest childhood. My subject at university was history actually, for which a memory is essential. Um... and as the years have gone by, the photographs have got a bit blurred round the edges, but they're still visible, I think. (laugh).

Int: Most of your theatre performances have vanished – only a few, sadly, have been recorded on tape but TV does of course survive. Have you watched your most famous series on TV – The Romans?

PJ: When it first went out, we were still filming episode seven, out of thirteen episodes, and episode one started going out on air. So it wouldn't have been

7

a good idea to watch it then. I've always loathed watching myself anyway, but then about ten years later I was... some friends kind of locked me into a house in California and over the weekend, made me see the whole thing. Since then I check into hotels all over the world and switch the telly on and .... they're showing reruns of it. There's no escape.

Int: And when you finally got to watch The Romans, you were impressed by it presumably?

PJ: I was and the great thing about it was the script. It was funny and it was violent. In a curious way it was totally contemporary – while being set in ancient Rome, which is what at the end of the book it purports to be, when my character says 'I'll speak to you in all those years hence, I'll speak to you in a language you'll understand.' And the writer got that absolutely right.

Int: And those kind of television parts don't come along very often. [fade]
START CUT [But you had another one, it's a smaller role but it's one that made a big impact in The Long Night – George, the corrupt politician. Now how did that come about?

PJ: I don't know how these things work out, but I do know I found myself at a launch party, just went along with a friend who was invited. It was for John Lucas' new book. He wrote the book of The Long Night, as you know. Anyway, somebody from the company must have chatted to me briefly there and later thought 'Oh he'd be good as Sir George'. and rang my agent. That's how these things happen.

Int: Now what plans have you got for the future... (fade)] END CUT
[700 words with cut]

PAUSE 10 SECONDS
A15 Now you'll hear Part 3 again.
FX*****
REPEAT PART 3
PAUSE 5 SECONDS
A16 That's the end of Part 3.
PAUSE 5 SECONDS
A17 Now turn to Part 4.
PAUSE 5 SECONDS

CAE

8

A18 Part 4 consists of two tasks. You'll hear five short extracts in which students on art courses are talking about their experiences. Look at Task 1. For questions 21-25, choose from the list (A–H) the difficulties each speaker has had to overcome. Now look at Task 2. For questions 26-30, choose from the list (A–H) what each speaker enjoys most about the process of creating art. While you listen you must complete both tasks.

You now have 45 seconds to look at Part 4.

PAUSE 45 SECONDS

FX*****

[Use Pretest 275 recording with one cut]

Speaker 1 [Male 20s]

PAUSE 2 SECONDS

I find the lifestyle of a big city very stimulating. It's multicultural, full of activity – but I'd be the first to admit that there are frustrations, for me as an artist, living there. Unfortunately the grey surroundings affect the way my work ends up looking, particularly the colour scheme, so I've had to concentrate my efforts on counteracting that. I tend to shy away from imagining the outcome to a piece of work. Instead I'll sit alone in my bedroom, which is a vast loft space and so doubles as a workroom, scribbling notes on a scrap of paper. That's the real buzz for me – START CUT

[seeing where this takes me.] END CUT

[105 words with cut]

PAUSE 3 SECONDS

Speaker 2 [Female 30s]

PAUSE 2 SECONDS

After several years spent working, I've returned to art school full-time. There are no funds available for students taking a second degree, so it's hard to come up with the rent for my tiny flat but I just about manage it. But luckily my mother's converted part of her house into an art studio, so that helps. As an artist I'm fascinated by the human form. My paintings are self-portraits, so before I start painting I can literally spend hours making observational studies of myself. Sometimes I get so absorbed, the final piece never happens! I also use family photos as the work develops, working in colours similar to artists like Modigliani and Matisse.

[114 words]

PAUSE 3 SECONDS

Speaker 3 [Male 20s]

PAUSE 2 SECONDS

I picked up pen and paper at an early age – I used to draw characters from my favourite books. But at college I have to show I can handle different media, so I

9

spend hours there grappling with painting, to keep up with the other students, who are very competitive, and I think I hold my own. When I'm alone, though, I'll always return to pen and ink. Strangely, once I've found a subject, I actually get a lot out of just going to written accounts of what other artists have done – it sparks off original ideas of my own. I'd like to have a career illustrating children's books one day, although I don't imagine I'll make much money from it.

[121 words]

PAUSE 3 SECONDS

Speaker 4 [Female 50s]

PAUSE 2 SECONDS

I work as a part-time landscape architect in the city, only part-time but it provides money and free time for my art studies, which I work on for the rest of the week. I live in a cottage, and my studio is actually the main room, so it's tricky when anyone comes round, so I have to be very well organised. I like experimenting with different media, but what truly gets the creativity flowing is being out taking shots of the countryside, whatever the weather, and then printing them off on my computer. They can develop into anything, even townscapes or portraits, but somehow they'll always echo my passion for the landscape.

[112 words]

PAUSE 3 SECONDS

Speaker 5 [Male 30s]

PAUSE 2 SECONDS

My response to art and other artists' work used to be a matter of writing copious notes – but that got me nowhere. My own work really took off when I discovered oil paints. For me there's nothing that compares with dabbling with a rainbow of paints and seeing what comes. And achieving the right combination can evoke so much emotion in the viewer. I've got three young sons to bring up, which could take time away from my art, so I have to make sure I've got adequate childcare arrangements in place. But I've got a scholarship to study in Los Angeles soon, so we're all moving there, although they're not keen on big cities.

[115 words]

PAUSE 10 SECONDS

A19 Now you'll hear Part 4 again.

FX*****

REPEAT PART 4

PAUSE 5 SECONDS

A20 That's the end of Part 4.

CAE

10

There'll now be a pause of 5 minutes for you to copy your answers onto the separate answer sheet. Be sure to follow the numbering of all the questions. I'll remind you when there's 1 minute left, so that you're sure to finish in time.

PAUSE 4 MINUTES

A21 You have 1 more minute left.

PAUSE 1 MINUTE

A22 That's the end of the test. Please stop now. Your supervisor will now collect all the question papers and answer sheets.

CPE

UNIVERSITY OF CAMBRIDGE ESOL EXAMINATIONS

English for Speakers of Other Languages

CERTIFICATE OF PROFICIENCY IN ENGLISH   0301/4

PAPER 4 Listening   Test A

2010

Additional materials:
Answer sheet

Time   Approximately 40 minutes (including 5 minutes' transfer time)

INSTRUCTIONS TO CANDIDATES

Do not open this question paper until you are told to do so.

Write your name, Centre number and candidate number on your answer sheet if they are not already there.

Listen to the instructions for each part of the paper carefully.

Answer all the questions.

While you are listening, write your answers on the question paper.

You will have 5 minutes at the end of the test to copy your answers onto the separate answer sheet. Use a pencil.

At the end of the test, hand in both this question paper and your answer sheet.

INFORMATION FOR CANDIDATES

There are four parts to the test.

Each question carries one mark.

You will hear each piece twice.

For each part of the test there will be time for you to look through the questions and time for you to check your answers.

PV7   5092/24292

© UCLES 2010   Cambridge ESOL Level 3 Certificate in ESOL International

*6 1 0 3 0 2 3 5 6 4 *

2

Part 1

You will hear four different extracts.
For questions 1 – 8, choose the answer (A, B or C) which fits best according to what you hear.
There are two questions for each extract.

Extract One

You hear the beginning of a radio interview with designer Tom Hartest.

1   What is going to be discussed on the programme?

   A   the history of design

   B   what represents good design

   C   why design is becoming less original

2   What is Tom's view of the Design Museum?

   A   It's a rather old-fashioned place.

   B   It's unclear what it's trying to achieve.

   C   It's a strange name to give such a place.

Extract Two

You hear part of a radio interview in which a woman called Helen is talking about the sport of
Fencing – a form of sword fighting.

3   Helen compares fencing to the game of chess in order to emphasise

   A   what a long tradition the sport comes from.

   B   how rigid the various rules of the sport are.

   C   the demands the sport places on the player.

4   What unexpected benefit has Helen gained from fencing?

   A   acquiring a strategy for dealing with life's challenges

   B   finding an elegant way to keep physically fit

   C   learning how to avoid injury when exercising

CPE

4

Part 2

You will hear part of a talk in which a scientist, Dr Engle, is describing a project designed to improve water quality.
For questions 9 – 17, complete the sentences with a word or short phrase.

Dr Engle is working on a project currently named [9]

Chemicals from [10] sources are river pollutants which can remain undetected.

According to Dr Engle, a commitment to the [11] motivates everyone on the project.

The funding for this particular project has come from a local [12] company.

River water goes into what Dr Engle refers to as a [13] for the first stage of the process.

The pumps which control the level of the water use [14] as a source of power.

In order to ensure the public's safety, a [15] has been installed under the water.

Dr Engle says that [16] are used to control the flow of water, especially in spring.

The exhibition shows the role water has played in skilled occupations such as the cleaning of [17] since early times.

3

Extract Three

You hear part of a radio interview with a British farmer, Peter Rowland, who has recently started processing, packaging and selling his own vegetables.

5 What does Peter say farmers should do?

A find a new way of selling their produce

B grow the kind of food which supermarkets want to buy

C make sure they have a friendly approach to their customers

6 How does Peter feel about his current project?

A conscious of the risk he has taken in setting it up

B reluctant to put more time or effort into it

C confident that it will be successful eventually

Extract Four

You hear a writer, Simone, and a radio presenter, Leo, discussing memory and imagination.

7 Simone says memory and imagination are similar, because they involve

A an instinctive understanding of when something is right.

B making something from small pieces of information.

C the creation of something that can never be complete.

8 Leo says the three stages of memory distortion are defined by

A the accuracy of what is remembered.

B the stage of development of the brain.

C the different situations that the individual is in.

Turn over ▶

CPE

5

Part 3

You will hear an author, Ray Sweeney, being interviewed about the late Dorothy L. Sayers, a detective-story writer.

For questions **18 – 22**, choose the answer (**A, B, C** or **D**) which fits best according to what you hear.

18 According to Ray Sweeney, Dorothy L. Sayers thought that writers of 'The Golden Age'

- **A** produced works of literary merit.
- **B** ought to have reduced their output.
- **C** had too much influence on her work.
- **D** should have shared their ideas.

19 What aspect of Sayers' writing does Ray particularly praise?

- **A** the complexity of her storylines
- **B** the originality of the situations she invents
- **C** the fact that her characters are so realistic
- **D** the way in which she includes diverse viewpoints

20 In her hero, Lord Peter Wimsey, Sayers created a character

- **A** who would help to make her books more marketable.
- **B** whom she herself became emotionally attached to.
- **C** who would represent a lesser-known section of society.
- **D** whom she was prepared to replace if necessary.

21 What does Ray most admire about Sayers as a person?

- **A** her self-confidence when giving advice to other people
- **B** her modesty when talking about her achievements
- **C** her pragmatic attitude towards her relationships
- **D** her conscientious approach to her commitments

22 What does Ray's fictional hero have in common with Sayers' hero?

- **A** They both prefer not to talk about their private lives.
- **B** They both have a complex family tree, created by the author.
- **C** They are both easily irritated, and have no time for fools.
- **D** They are both in tune with contemporary trends.

Turn over ▶

6

Part 4

You will hear part of a discussion in which two friends, Claire and Mike, are discussing television. For questions **23 – 28**, decide whether the opinions are expressed by only one of the speakers, or whether the speakers agree.

Write: **C**   for Claire,
          M   for Mike,
or   **B**   for Both, where they agree.

23 Television provides people with a valuable chance to unwind. ☐ 23

24 Television encourages people to be lazy. ☐ 24

25 Watching television can stimulate genuine social interaction. ☐ 25

26 Television can distort people's perception of the world around them. ☐ 26

27 Nowadays, there seem to be fewer programmes which are intellectually challenging. ☐ 27

28 Television-viewing can lower people's self-esteem. ☐ 28

CPE

8

BLANK PAGE

7

BLANK PAGE

CPE

Part 1

	A	B	C
1	A	B	C
2	A	B	C
3	A	B	C
4	A	B	C
5	A	B	C
6	A	B	C
7	A	B	C
8	A	B	C

Part 2 (Remember to write in CAPITAL LETTERS or numbers)

9
10
11
12
13
14
15
16
17

Part 3

	A	B	C	D
18	A	B	C	D
19	A	B	C	D
20	A	B	C	D
21	A	B	C	D
22	A	B	C	D

Part 4

23
24
25
26
27
28

UNIVERSITY of CAMBRIDGE
ESOL Examinations

Do not write in this box

Candidate Name
If not already printed, write name
in CAPITALS and complete the
Candidate No. grid (in pencil).

Candidate Signature

Centre No.

Examination Title

Candidate No.

Centre

Examination
Details

Supervisor:
If the candidate is ABSENT or has WITHDRAWN shade here

Test version: A B C D E F J K L M N   Special arrangements: S H

Candidate Answer Sheet

Instructions

Use a PENCIL (B or HB).
Rub out any answer you wish to change using an eraser.

Parts 1 and 3:
Mark ONE letter for each question.

For example, if you think B is the
right answer to the question, mark
your answer sheet like this:

0 A B C

Part 2:
Write your answer clearly in CAPITAL LETTERS.

Write one letter or number in each box.
If the answer has more than one word, leave one
box empty between words.

For example:

0 N U M B E R   1 2

Part 4:
Write ONE letter only, like this:

0 A

Turn this sheet over to start.

DP622310

CPEL

CPE

Listening Paper Answer Key

(One mark for each correct answer)

Part 1

1	B
2	C
3	C
4	A
5	A
6	A
7	B
8	A

Part 2

9	Life Force
10	industrial / industry
11	(sense of) community
12	insurance
13	treatment pond
14	(the power of (the)) wind
15	(metal) grid
16	flood barriers
17	silk

Part 3

18	A
19	C
20	B
21	D
22	A

Part 4

23	M
24	B
25	M
26	B
27	M
28	C

In Part 2, bracketed words do not have to appear in the answer. Maximum mark for Paper 4 is 28.
The total score is then adjusted to give a mark out of 40.

CPE PAPER 4 LISTENING TEST - TAPESCRIPT

Part One

DESIGN MUSEUM

Myra: Good evening. Tonight's programme comes from London's Design Museum. In recent times, design has become increasingly important to the consumer. From the 1960s, which saw groundbreaking design brought to everyday objects like that car, the Mini, and the Trimphone, manufacturers have constantly tried to tempt us with more imaginative designs. But does this emphasis on design bring real benefits, or does a basic product, which does the job at a basic price, serve just as well? In other words, is something like the humble paperclip the ultimate in design? That's something we'll be discussing in a moment. But first of all, designer Tom Hartest is with me. Tom, you wanted to say something.

Tom: Well, yes. Everyone's thinking that design is something that's modern; it's about innovation – we think of this as framing the nation's view about itself and about the world; and yet the idea of a museum is something that's of the past and of our background and, if you like, of our cultural history and somehow one feels that 'Design Museum' is something of a misnomer for such a vibrant place.

FENCING

Presenter: Helen, why did you decide to take up fencing a couple of years ago?

Helen: Well, after my son was born I thought it would be good to learn something new and complex, prove to myself that I could, and particularly something that'd be extremely taxing both physically and mentally – you know, like playing chess with your whole body – in split seconds.

Presenter: And that thing was fencing?

Helen: Well, yes, and I'd always been interested in fencing in a casual sense, to the degree that I was keen on the old black and white movies with the Hollywood screen idols of the thirties and, you know, all the old terminology for the various moves has a certain romantic appeal.

Presenter: So, what has fencing given you?

Helen: Well, I knew it'd be an excellent workout and one that's relatively free from injury, fortunately. Strangely, though, the skills one needs to fence somehow

CPE

seem applicable to the rest of one's life. It's the greatest example of having to learn to be graceful, and stay focused when you're up against it, something which we desperately need in this frenetic world.

ROOT VEGETABLES

Presenter: I often talk to farmers on this programme who are farming very well, but don't have that much connection with the people who eat their food. How important is that for you, now that you're involved in every aspect, from the field to the dinner table?

Peter: Since I've embarked on this new project, it's really opened my eyes. I've seen there's so much potential for farmers to make a better living. They need to get hold of the results of research into what the general public want, rather than just listening and doing what the supermarkets tell them. Then they ought to be able to make the right sort of food available direct to the consumer.

Presenter: Are you making any money on this new venture yet?

Peter: It'll take at least a couple of years to break even. It's only just coming home to me what a leap into the unknown it all was – buying the machinery, getting it up and running. Sometimes I wake at four o'clock in the morning and wonder what I've done! But I've got to keep at it.

Presenter: So, was it all worth it?

Peter: I hope so, but selling food's always an unreliable business. Ask me again this time next year!

MEMORY AND IMAGINATION

Simone: As a writer, I find it very exciting that memory and imagination are part of the same process. When we imagine, we create the future out of fragments from the past. And when we remember, we construct pathways in our brains to remake the experience and, at a certain moment, it's as if the jigsaw comes together, and we'll accept that as the truth. But then, if your memories are acts of creativity, it does cast a terrible doubt on....

Leo: ....on all decision-making.

Simone: Exactly.

Leo: So, memories are distorted to create a new reality. Good for writers. Maybe not so good for the rest of us. And from what we've heard, there seem to be three stages. First, because the brain's a living thing, it's changing and developing all the time, so everything it registers is immediately slightly transformed. The past it takes us to never really happened quite in the way we think. At the next level, we

CPE

unconsciously refashion our memories further in our minds, to suit our self-image, nurse our myths, justify our agenda. And then, at a third level, the original information is totally lost.

Part Two

WATER GARDEN

Presenter: This evening we're pleased to welcome Dr Ruth Engle, a consultant on an innovative environmental project – a city water park. This project combines a water purification process, a leisure facility and an educational exhibition. Dr Engle...

Dr Engle: Thank you. Before I go into the details of the project, which we originally called *Green Zone* and then retitled *Life Force*, perhaps I should sketch in a bit of the background, and explain why clean water is so important in maintaining the balance of nature.

We want our rivers to be clean enough for fishing and even swimming. It's easy enough to see if domestic rubbish has been thrown into a river, and many agricultural pollutants discolour the water and can be traced back to source, but industrial chemicals in the water are more often invisible to the naked eye, and can severely pollute rivers.

That's where I come in and get involved with projects like this. This particular project focuses on a 500-metre-long garden – part of a city park – and this water garden will actually clean the river water. Naturally, there are all sorts of people working on the project – some are passionate about the environment, some are into the arts, some want to get the schools involved, but the thing that inspires them all is a sense of community and wanting to do their very best for it. They even have to chase up financial backing. In this particular case, pleas to the local authority fell on deaf ears and the investment companies weren't interested, but then an insurance firm in the area heard about the project and came up with the necessary cash.

But, getting back to the garden, at the beginning of the 500-metre stretch, the water's diverted from the river into what we call a treatment pond – not quite as thorough as a filtration plant, but we do have some filters, which make sure that dead or decaying vegetation, which releases poisonous gases, doesn't build up in the water. Micro-organisms are injected into the water, but that's not enough. A pump is needed to top up the water level automatically when sun and moonlight cause evaporation. To provide electricity for the pump – because of the nature of the project – we opted not to rely on oil or on electricity provided by other fossil fuels, but to harness the power of the wind instead.

CPE

CPE December 2007
(0300)

Part Three

THRILLER WRITER

Int.: Hello. The revered mystery writer Dorothy L. Sayers, who died in 1957, turned her hand to fiction after a career in publishing and advertising, and wrote 15 novels and short story collections. One of her biggest fans, New Zealander Ray Sweeney, himself no mean detective-story writer, is here to tell me about her – Ray.

Ray: She's one of the women writers of 'The Golden Age' – that usually refers to the period between 1918 and 1939, when there was a huge amount of fiction being written, which had a lot of influence on later writers' ideas. We know from Dorothy L. Sayers' correspondence that, although she didn't think much of trends or groups, she did recognise it as a time when writers were prolific and high-quality writing was being published.

Int.: And you think she was a good writer?

Ray: She was, although she wrote very much within the conventions of the time, especially in terms of background and setting. She nevertheless raised this very popular genre from being just a puzzle to a work which had some claim to being taken seriously as a novel. And that was because of her imagination – the way the people she writes about come alive for us. She also maintains control over the different sub-plots, so that we don't get distracted by conflicting ideas.

Int.: How do you feel about her hero, Lord Peter Wimsey? Is he an elitist, as critics have argued?

Ray: Well, I think by today's standards he probably was. She wanted him to be an aristocrat, not to make any kind of social point, but because she thought he'd be more fun to write about than writing about someone who hadn't got his privileges. She actually wrote somewhere that she was very poor at the time, so she enjoyed spending his money, when she hadn't got her own to spend! [laughing]

Int.: Do you think there are any parallels between the author and Harriet Vane, the character who falls in love with Wimsey?

Ray: Oh, undoubtedly, Harriet Vane is Dorothy L. Sayers. Sadly, she had a very unhappy life when it came to relationships with men, and I think Wimsey helped to make up for all that. I don't think she could have polished him off in the later books, even if sales had been going down.

CPE December 2007
(0300)

For several hours the water goes through the process, absorbing more beneficial substances, so that eventually the water will be able to sustain more plant and animal life. So, after the last stage, you can see an area where there are frogs, fish and water lilies; a water park where children can sail boats, paddle and play other water games. There's a metal grid a couple of centimetres below the water level in case anyone falls in! You can stroll along tree-shaded paths, over bridges, and for those interested in the project there are, in keeping with the natural feel of the area, stones with useful information displayed on them. Did you know, for example, that ninety-nine per cent of all chemical transformations on earth require water?

The amount of water passing through the water garden has to be regulated by flood barriers, because in this region, although the rainfall is fairly constant, seasonal water levels can vary enormously. This is mainly because of the snow in the mountains to the north, which melts in the spring. People ask about irrigation channels, but farmers in the area already have an adequate supply. There are all sorts of activities in the water park, and an exhibition which everyone can contribute to with photos, information, reviews and so on. Another area traces the history of our relationship with water, illustrating how water has played a vital role in the establishment of settlements. You can see ancient skills such as boat building, waterwheels, the washing of silk, dyeing and irrigation systems.

I'm really pleased with the way this project has turned out. Every time I go there, people seem to be having so much fun and... [fade]

CPE

Int.: What about the character of Sayers herself? What is it about her that you most admire?

Ray: She had in many ways an unhappy life – for various reasons, she was largely separated from her only child, and she never came to terms with that. I admire her hugely, both for achieving so much, which I think she was justifiably proud of, and the fact she was so industrious. Having a streak of indolence in me, I'm in awe of that. It was extraordinary – people would write to her about some obscure point, and they'd get pages back, telling them what they ought to think and do, when most of us would just shrug and say, 'Oh dear, another boring letter from so-and-so'. She saw it as part and parcel of the job.

Int.: Would you say your hero, Mackenzie, and Sayers' hero, Wimsey, have anything in common?

Ray: They're both supposed to be highly intelligent, and, I think, reserved – they divulge little about their thoughts and relationships. It's particularly fashionable at the moment to have a detective hero who isn't well-educated, but I wanted one who was, as did Sayers, and so we both have one. Obviously, I like Mackenzie because I'd be foolish to create a character I didn't admire – if I got bored or annoyed with him, or despised him, so would my readers – but Sayers was more involved with Wimsey. I mean, she had a whole background for him, with a list of eccentric relations, and I haven't done that for Mackenzie.

Int.: Thank you very much, Ray Sweeney.

Part Four

TV

Claire: Mike, did you know that the average person spends four hours watching TV every day? You're probably guilty of that, aren't you?

Mike: You make it sound like an accusation. I only watch the decent programmes, you know, Claire.

Claire: I know, but this article says it's an encroachment on our waking hours. They're right, aren't they? If you work for eight hours, and sleep for eight, and watch TV for four, that only leaves four hours for you to do all the important things in life!

Mike: Well, of course, it's bad for kids to watch too many hours.

Claire: Yes, apparently many children spend ten times more time with a television than with their parents! That's going to make them more passive and interfere with basic parent-child bonding. Obvious, isn't it?

Mike: Well, OK, but you have to remember even kids need a little relaxation at the end of the day, if they're anything like me. When I get home I'm fed up with talking and thinking, I want to clear my head with something undemanding.

Claire: *[Laughing]* It just goes past your eyes like animated wallpaper, doesn't it? But I don't subscribe to this idea that relaxation has to be passive. What strikes me about this kind of TV is that it isn't at all stimulating. It just tempts people to take the easy way out, slump in front of it and indulge in complete idleness!

Mike: You may have a point there, but you know, there's another kind of bonding that TV actually produces – the 'what did you see last night' thing. In the office, over the neighbour's fence, wherever: you're hearing it all the time. It's what makes the world go round.

Claire: It's only small talk, though, and what you're talking about is fictional characters in soap operas and TV plays, which is hardly the real world. No, I see that as more of a surrogate sociability – it fills a gap. I mean, haven't you heard of 'mean-world syndrome'? All this crime and horror on TV affecting the way a lot of parents see the world outside, so they think it's too dangerous to even let their children play in the park.

Mike: There's something in that, I guess. And there's patently a lot of dumbing-down these days. Programmers do seem to think that providing viewers with mindless

CPE

CPE December 2007
(0300)

stuff is somehow democratic, while giving them thought-provoking material is elitist. You have to be a very sad individual to accept that.

Claire: But I don't think it's the programmes; it's the watching that makes people feel bad. You see all these glamorous, wonderful people on TV and if you constantly compare yourself to them, it must chip away at your confidence.

Mike: I think most people can take all the glamour and razzmatazz with a pinch of salt; actually, it's mostly fairly tawdry anyway. Of course, one thing TV's great at is raising awareness of things.... *[fade]*

Appendix B

Candidate Information Sheet (CIS)

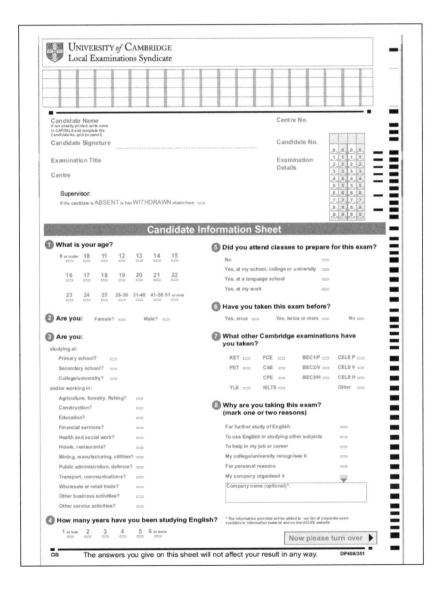

9 Where do you come from?
If it is not listed, please complete the box 'other'.

001 Afghanistan	075 Guinea	149 Portugal
002 Albania	076 Guinea-Bissau	150 Puerto Rico
003 Algeria	077 Guyana	151 Qatar
004 American Samoa	078 Haiti	152 Reunion
005 Andorra	079 Honduras	153 Romania
006 Angola	080 Hong Kong	154 Russia
007 Antigua	081 Hungary	155 Rwanda
008 Argentina	082 Iceland	156 San Marino
009 Armenia	083 India	157 Sao Tome and Principe
010 Australia	084 Indonesia	158 Saudi Arabia
011 Austria	085 Iran	159 Senegal
012 Bahamas	086 Iraq	160 Seychelles
013 Bahrain	087 Ireland	161 Sierra Leone
014 Bangladesh	088 Israel	162 Singapore
015 Barbados	089 Italy	163 Slovakia
016 Belarus	090 Ivory Coast	164 Slovenia
017 Belgium	091 Jamaica	165 Solomon Islands
018 Belize	092 Japan	166 Somalia
019 Benin	093 Jordan	167 South Africa
020 Bermuda	094 Kampuchea (Cambodia)	168 Spain
021 Bhutan	095 Kazakhstan	169 Sri Lanka
022 Bolivia	096 Kenya	170 St.Helena
023 Bosnia-Herzegovina	097 Korea, North	171 St. Kitts-Nevis-Anguilla
024 Botswana	098 Korea, South	172 St.Lucia
025 Brazil	099 Kuwait	173 St.Pierre and Miquelon
026 British Virgin Islands	100 Laos	174 St.Vincent and the Grenadines
027 Brunei	101 Latvia	175 Sudan
028 Bulgaria	102 Lebanon	176 Surinam
029 Burkina Faso	103 Lesotho	177 Swaziland
030 Burundi	104 Liberia	178 Sweden
031 Cameroon	105 Libya	179 Switzerland
032 Canada	106 Liechtenstein	180 Syria
033 Cape Verde	107 Lithuania	181 Tahiti
034 Cayman Islands	108 Luxembourg	182 Taiwan
035 Central African Republic	109 Macao	183 Tanzania
036 Chad	110 Madagascar	184 Thailand
037 Chile	111 Malawi	185 Togo
038 China (People's Republic)	112 Malaysia	186 Tokelau
039 Colombia	113 Maldives	187 Tonga
040 Comoros	114 Mali	188 Trinidad and Tobago
041 Congo	115 Malta	189 Tunisia
042 Costa Rica	116 Marshall Islands	190 Turkey
043 Croatia	117 Martinique	191 Turks and Caicos Islands
044 Cuba	118 Mauritania	192 Tuvalu
045 Cyprus	119 Mauritius	193 Uganda
046 Czech Republic	120 Mexico	194 United Arab Emirates
047 Denmark	121 Moldova	195 Ukraine
048 Djibouti	122 Monaco	196 United Kingdom
049 Dominica	123 Mongolia	197 Uruguay
050 Dominican Republic	124 Montserrat	198 US Virgin Islands
051 Ecuador	125 Morocco	199 USA
052 Egypt	126 Mozambique	200 Uzbekistan
053 El Salvador	127 Myanmar	201 Vanuatu
054 Equatorial Guinea	128 Namibia	202 Vatican
055 Estonia	129 Nauru	203 Venezuela
056 Ethiopia	130 Nepal	204 Vietnam
057 Faeroe Islands	131 Netherlands	205 Wallis and Futuna Islands
058 Fiji	132 Netherlands Antilles	206 Western Samoa
059 Finland	133 New Caledonia	207 Yemen, North
060 France	134 New Zealand	208 Yemen, South
061 French Guiana	135 Nicaragua	209 Yugoslavia
062 French Polynesia	136 Niger	210 Zaire
063 Gabon	137 Nigeria	211 Zambia
064 Gambia	138 Niue (Cook Island)	212 Zimbabwe
065 Georgia	139 Norway	
066 Germany	140 Oman	009 Other (please write below)
067 Ghana	141 Pakistan	
068 Gibraltar	142 Palestine	
069 Greece	143 Panama	
070 Greenland	144 Papua New Guinea	
071 Grenada	145 Paraguay	
072 Guadaloupe	146 Peru	
073 Guam	147 Philippines	
074 Guatemala	148 Poland	

10 Which is your first language?
(i.e. your mother tongue).
If it is not listed, please complete the box 'other'.

001 Afrikaans	075 Mongolian
002 Akan	076 Nepali
003 Albanian	077 Norwegian
004 Amharic	078 Oriya
005 Arabic	079 Palauan
006 Armenian	080 Panjabi
007 Assamese	081 Pashto
008 Aymara	082 Polish
009 Azerbaijani	083 Ponapean
010 Baluchi	084 Portuguese
011 Bambara	085 Quechua
012 Basque	086 Rajasthani
013 Bemba	087 Riff
014 Bengali	088 Romanian
015 Bihari	089 Romansch
016 Breton	090 Russian
017 Bulgarian	091 Samoan
018 Burmese	092 Serbian
019 Byelorussian	093 Shona
020 Catalan	094 Sindhi
021 Chinese	095 Singhalese
022 Croatian	096 Slovak
023 Czech	097 Slovene
024 Danish	098 Somali
025 Dutch	099 Spanish
026 Efik	100 Swahili
027 Estonian	101 Swazi
028 Ewe	102 Swedish
029 Faeroese	103 Swiss German
030 Farsi	104 Tagalog
031 Fijian	105 Tahitian
032 Finnish	106 Tamil
033 Flemish	107 Tatar
034 French	108 Telugu
035 Fulani	109 Thai
036 Ga	110 Tibetan
037 Georgian	111 Tigrinya
038 German	112 Tongan
039 Gilbertese	113 Trukese
040 Greek	114 Tulu
041 Gujarati	115 Tupi/Guarani
042 Haitian Creole	116 Turkish
043 Hausa	117 Uighur
044 Hebrew	118 Ukrainian
045 Hindi	119 Ulithian
046 Hungarian	120 Urdu
047 Ibo/Igbo	121 Uzbek
048 Icelandic	122 Vietnamese
049 Igala	123 Wolof
050 Indonesian	124 Xhosa
051 Italian	125 Yao
052 Japanese	126 Yapese
053 Javanese	127 Yiddish
054 Kannada	128 Yoruba
055 Kashmiri	129 Zulu
056 Kazakh	
057 Khmer	006 Other (please write below)
058 Korean	
059 Lao	
060 Latvian	
061 Lithuanian	
062 Luba	
063 Luo	
064 Luxemburgish	
065 Malagasy	
066 Malay	
067 Malayalam	
068 Malinka	
069 Maltese	
070 Maori	
071 Marathi	
072 Marshallese	
073 Masai	
074 Mende	

This listing of places implies no view regarding questions of sovereignty or status.

Appendix C

Standard procedures for the production of Listening test materials

Cambridge ESOL employs a set of standardised systems, processes and procedures for designing, developing and delivering all of the examinations offered by the board, Listening test papers included. This appendix provides a brief description of the standard procedures for the production of Listening test materials. They are reported in greater detail in the *Work Instructions for Routine Test Production,* a reference document for Assessment Managers, Chairs and Outsourcing Coordinators, and they are included in item writer guidelines as appropriate.

This appendix focuses on the process of question paper production (QPP) and the standard procedures employed during this process. The procedures and processes are certified as meeting the internationally recognised ISO 9001:2000 standard for quality management.

The key objectives of the QPP process are:

- production of valid, reliable and fair tests to a defined timescale
- production of items, tasks and test papers that are of a consistently high quality and appropriate difficulty
- ensuring task and item banks contain the appropriate number of test items and tasks
- co-ordinating test production schedules to the appropriate time scales
- keeping an accurate record of items/tasks and test usage.

The production of examination material for any given paper is the responsibility of the Assessment Manager for that paper, who is a Cambridge ESOL staff member, and the Chair of the Item Writing team, who is an external consultant. An Assessment Group Manager, who is also a staff member, has overall responsibility for all the papers in their suite of examinations.

The role of the Chair of the Item Writing team is principally concerned with the technical aspects of writing the examination materials and ensuring that the item writers on the team are fully trained and equipped to produce material to the best of their ability. In conjunction with the Assessment Manager and other members of the team, the Chair ensures that tasks for their paper are appropriate in terms of topic, content and level and that they comply fully with the Specifications for the paper and item writer guidelines. The Assessment Manager is responsible for managing the production of the examination material through the various stages, ensuring that sufficient material is produced to the agreed schedule and that test papers are produced to schedule and of appropriate quality. Both the Chair and the Assessment Manager bring expertise to the partnership from their personal experience of teaching and assessment.

Stages in QPP process

There are several stages in the production of a Listening test: commissioning, pre-editing, editing, pretesting, pretest review and test construction. Below is a brief description of these stages as they relate to the production of Listening test materials. Figure 1 provides a visual representation of the QPP process.

Commissioning

Commissioning of item writers is the first stage of the QPP process and is a task that has been centralised for Cambridge ESOL exams. The aims of centralised commissioning are:

- to co-ordinate the timing of commissions
- to plan well in advance across all Cambridge ESOL examinations
- to co-ordinate and utilise effectively the item writer resource
- to standardise commissioning procedures across examinations
- to ensure item banks have adequate levels of material.

The Assessment Manager for each paper, in consultation with the Assessment Group Manager, determines the number of commissions and the amount of material required for the forthcoming year in accordance with current banks of material and future requirements.

Pre-editing

Pre-editing takes place when commissioned tasks are received by Cambridge ESOL for the first time. The pre-editing stage is intended to select material which will progress in the production process and to improve the quality and maximise the quantity of material available for editing. The aims of pre-editing are:

- to suggest appropriate changes to material requiring amendments or re-writing
- by reference to the item writer guidelines, to reject unsuitable, problematic or weak material
- to comment on the item writer's proposed exploitation of a text or a visual prompt and to suggest possible alternatives (where appropriate).

Figure 1 Question paper production process

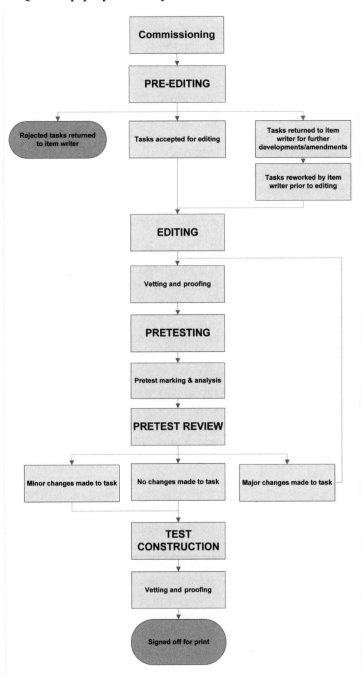

However, it is not intended that material is edited or rewritten by the pre-editing team, as this is not a function of this stage, which is:

- to carry out an initial check on the descriptive system information provided on the Task Description form
- to check that keys are comprehensive and accurate
- to speed up the editing process (i.e. the editing team will not have to spend time working on unsuitable material)
- to develop the skills of item writers in order to improve the quality of materials submitted
- to increase the efficiency of editing.

Participants in pre-editing include the Chair, the Assessment Manager, and an experienced item writer who is not currently on the team but has experience of working on the paper or on a similar paper at the same level. The pre-editing meeting attendees consider material, decide on the outcome, and prepare feedback for the item writers. Decisions are made on the basis of the quality of the material and conformity to the item writer guidelines. All decisions are based on or justified by reference to the item writer guidelines. Feedback to item writers is communicated on a form and/or notes on the submitted task at the pre-editing meeting. The following are possible outcomes of the pre-editing stage:

- material passes straight to the editing stage
- material is returned to the item writer for fine-tuning and, if necessary, request for additional stimuli
- material requiring extensive re-writing may be re-submitted for pre-editing as part of a future commission
- the material may be rejected; in this case it may be used for item writer training, item writer guidelines (as an example of possible pitfalls) or offered to another suitable exam.

Editing

Materials which successfully pass the pre-editing stage are re-submitted for editing. The editing stage ensures that, as far as possible, material is of an acceptable standard for inclusion in pretests. The aims of editing are:

- to re-check the quality of material against specifications and item writer guidelines
- to make any changes necessary to submitted materials so that they are of an acceptable standard for pretesting
- to ensure that the key, rubrics and any visual stimuli are accurate and comprehensive

- to fine tune specifications to artwork that needs to be commissioned from an external agency
- to further develop the skills of item writers in order to improve the quality of materials submitted and the input of item writers to future editing sessions.

Each editing group meeting consists of the Chair, the Assessment Manager and members of the item writing team who have written the particular pieces. Before the meeting Chairs check the material, as appropriate, to make sure all materials are ready for editing, and these are then sent to each meeting participant in preparation for the meeting. The expectation at the meeting is that material should require minimal changes only. However, re-writing of material and/or replacement of visual stimuli will sometimes be necessary, and may be an important part of training. Material is not usually rejected at editing on the grounds that it is of unacceptable quality or does not correspond with current guidelines relating to quality, length, subject matter, level, etc. These aspects have been dealt with at the pre-editing stage. The final decisions on acceptability of material rest with the Assessment Manager and Chair.

Edited material is entered into the appropriate bank in LIBS (Local Item Banking System), i.e. the edited bank. Attributes, such as task type, are added to LIBS according to the information on the Task Description form. The tasks are then sent to the Chair, who checks them against the editing meeting copy for both content and typographical errors and makes any necessary amendments. Meeting participants check that tapescripts for Listening tests have appropriate punctuation to assist the actors in their delivery. Pronunciation, e.g. of place names, is checked. Participants also check that the tapescript represents natural spoken discourse. At the studio, the Assessment Manager and Chair monitor the recording for factors such as speed and clarity of delivery, and make relevant changes to the tapescripts and question papers as appropriate.

Pretesting

After the editing meeting the edited materials are checked by the Chair in readiness for pretesting, which takes place at selected centres/schools around the world. Pretesting is intended to confirm that material is of a suitable quality to be used in a live Listening examination. The aims of pretesting are:

- to check that all acceptable answers are included in keys
- to establish the measurement characteristics of items (difficulty, discrimination and distractor analysis where appropriate)
- to enable tests of comparable difficulty to be constructed.

Pretest review

After pretesting, a meeting is held to review the performance of materials. Its aims are:

- to review the results of the pretests and evaluate the measurement characteristics of tasks and items
- to review pretested material in the light of candidate performance and feedback from examiners and candidates, as appropriate
- to finalise the material ensuring that it is acceptable for use in test paper construction
- to make decisions on whether to bank the material for test paper construction, revise and re-pretest it, or reject it
- to expand and finalise the marking key where appropriate
- to make essential adjustments to rubrics and visual stimuli so that, as far as possible, no further amendments will need to be made at the paper construction stage.

The pretest review meeting takes place as soon as possible after the pre-testing session. The Chair, the Assessment Manager, and an item writer on the team participate in the meeting. Systematic feedback to item writers is provided either in writing after pretest review or as part of a separate item writer training/feedback day.

Test construction

Test construction aims to construct sufficient examination papers to meet ongoing requirements and to ensure that all papers meet required standards in terms of level, coverage, content and comparability. Depending on the nature of the paper concerned, the Chair may make a proposal for test content in advance of the test construction meeting.

This meeting usually consists of the Assessment Manager, the Chair, an experienced item writer and a Research and Validation Manager (as required). The Chair firstly and subsequently the team at the meeting check that:

- a range of topics/tasks is maintained within each Listening test, bearing in mind the range of cultural perspectives desirable
- there is no obvious overlap in content either within a test, across papers or historically
- the tests are at the right level
- the rubrics are correct and the visual stimuli are clear and uncontroversial
- there is an appropriate mix of accents

- there is no overlap of actors
- the keys are accurate and comprehensive.

The draft materials are circulated to those attending in advance of the test construction meeting for preliminary consideration of content, and range of tasks. After the meeting, draft papers are amended by the Assessment Administrator, any necessary amendments are made on LIBS and the Assessment Manager checks all the material.

The material is then ready for the QPP process, whereby the constructed test is prepared for printing, printed and stored ready for use. The question paper, tapescript, key and CD go to the Chair, two content vetters and two proof readers before being approved for print by the Assessment Manager.

Appendix D

Administrative setting and management of Listening tests

It is well recognised that the circumstances under which an examination takes place can have a significant effect upon candidate performance. The socio-cognitive framework for test validation acknowledges this important dimension of the administrative and environmental conditions under which any test is taken. The model shown in Figure 1.1 (see Chapter 1, p.28) locates this dimension under the heading of context validity as part of the setting for the task. It is important to remember, however, that locating a test's administrative setting as an aspect of context validity is to some degree an oversimplification for the sake of convenience, since administrative and environmental conditions can also impact on both cognitive validity (i.e. mental processing) and on scoring validity (i.e. approaches to marking). As far as possible, test taking and test marking conditions need to be equivalent across administration sites and occasions; if not, the processing involved in completing test tasks or in applying marking criteria may well differ in important respects, potentially leading to invalid or unreliable results.

In light of this, examination boards need to set in place clear procedures to ensure that, as far as is possible, a test is administered in the same way whoever is in charge or wherever it takes place. This means that examination staff need to be provided with precise instructions on what they must do and should be familiar and comfortable with all aspects of the test before administering it. Test settings should be of equivalent standards with appropriate facilities (chairs, desks, clock); test equipment, e.g. playback equipment, should be carefully checked for any problems before the test is administered; procedures for dealing with any candidates caught cheating should have been sorted out in advance; all administrative details should have been clearly worked out prior to the exam, in particular ground rules for late arrivals, the giving of test instructions by supervisors or invigilators, procedures for confirming candidates' identity and all other necessary details (see Rose (2008) and Saville (2010, forthcoming), as well as Wild and Ramaswamy (2008) for a comprehensive discussion of the practical aspects of test management.)

As a large-scale, international examination board, Cambridge ESOL has in place an array of documentation dealing with the general requirements for the standardised administration of its English language examinations:

- *Regulations* for the relevant year (available on www.CambridgeESOL. org) specify, for the benefit of schools and candidates, the terms and conditions under which Cambridge ESOL examinations are offered
- the *Centre Registration Booklet* (available on CentreNet, a website restricted to Centre Exams Managers and their support staff) gives an outline of the responsibilities of test centres in regard to the administration of Cambridge ESOL exams, particularly with new applicants in mind
- the *Handbook for Centres* provides detailed general information on the running of a centre and guidelines on the administration of the examinations
- the *Exam Day Booklet* and *Timings and Instructions Booklets* provide detailed instructions and guidelines to supervisors and invigilators on the conduct of each examination.

All documentation for test centres is regularly updated by the Cambridge ESOL Centre Support Unit and the Assessment and Operations unit. The publications listed above are issued to Centre Exams Managers and are supplemented by promotional materials for specific examinations, e.g. exam-specific handbooks or leaflets (available on www.CambridgeESOL.org).

The administrative elements of the assessment, which may be centralised (i.e. Cambridge ESOL) or local (i.e. centre-based), include: ensuring that the candidates have information on what to expect when they are examined (the experiential dimension discussed in Chapter 2); making all necessary arrangements for the administration of tests under secure, standardised or special conditions (see Chapter 2 also for full discussion of Special Arrangements); providing the candidates with their results, with the means to interpret them and, if there are grounds, to have their results checked; and – to those candidates who have gained appropriate grades – issuing their certificates (see more on this in Chapter 5). Responsibility for these elements of carrying out assessment is shared between Cambridge ESOL administrative staff based in Cambridge and staff in the test centres where examinations take place (Centre Exams Managers, their supervisors and invigilators).

For those candidates with special requirements which make it difficult for them to demonstrate their ability in English (e.g. those with a permanent disability or with short-term difficulties), applications can be made to Cambridge ESOL for Special Arrangements to be set in place so that, insofar as possible, they are then able to take the examination on an equal footing with other candidates. The Scheduled Processing Unit (Special Circumstances) at Cambridge is able to give advice on the most appropriate arrangements for any given candidate. There is also a *Special Circumstances Booklet* available on CentreNet to assist test centre staff with any administrative support arrangements, and an *Access Technology Guide* for help involving specialist equipment. Documentation for test centres stresses the importance of ensuring that candidates with genuine needs receive the assistance they require, as to do otherwise would be discriminatory. Special Arrangements fall into two main categories: those involving the provision of modified material (often in conjunction with administrative arrangements), and those involving administrative arrangements only. (See Chapter 2 on test taker characteristics in relation to Special Arrangements made before the candidate sits the examination and during the examination.)

Uniformity of administration

There are some general administrative requirements that relate to the conduct of all examination papers, irrespective of which skill is being tested. These cover aspects such as: timetabling, supervision of candidates, checking IDs, completing the attendance register, late arrival of candidates, irregular conduct, emergency procedures, Special Consideration (for candidates who have been disadvantaged, e.g. due to sudden interruptions or excessive noise), collation of mark sheets and secure storage of test materials. These will be outlined briefly below in the following section.

In addition, detailed instructions for individual papers are provided in the examination-specific instructions. Every Supervisor in each centre is required to follow specific procedures for each of the respective examination papers and those that apply for the Listening tests are described later in this Appendix.

General examination requirements and arrangements

In Cambridge ESOL examinations the selection of venues takes into account a number of key factors including general ambience, accessibility of location and suitability of rooms (see below).

All candidates (except for the YLE tests) are informed that they are required to provide evidence of identity at each separate paper, by passport or national identity card. Ensuring that candidates' identities are checked against photographic evidence – a key responsibility for Centre Exams Managers – provides confidence regarding a candidate's true identity and is especially important for tests that carry high stakes. Methods are currently being explored that would enable photos of test takers on the day of their test to be uploaded for future checking by prospective test score users as part of enhanced security measures.

Cambridge ESOL has clear rulings on examination supervision. The purpose of supervision and invigilation is to ensure that all candidates are under surveillance for every moment of each examination period. Supervision and invigilation arrangements for the examinations are entrusted to the

Centre Exams Manager, who ensures that these tasks are carried out by suitably qualified people. Relatives of candidates in the examination room are specifically not eligible to serve as a supervisor or invigilator.

The supervisor is the person appointed at each centre or venue to be responsible for overseeing the general conduct of the examination sessions. The invigilator is the person in the examination room responsible for the conduct of a particular paper.

Centres must ensure that supervisors and invigilators are trained at least once a year, preferably before a major exam session. Training includes: checking IDs, detecting imposters and preventing fraud; being vigilant about the inappropriate use of electronic devices; being familiar with the exam regulations as contained in the *Exam Day Booklet*. Centres must keep brief records of this training, including details of when and how this training was conducted. Supervisors and invigilators are expected to abide by Cambridge ESOL requirements and must preserve the confidentiality and integrity of test materials before and after the examination.

Supervisor and invigilator familiarity with the relevant procedures and requirements is assured through the *Handbook for Centres*, the *Exam Day Booklet* and the *Timings and Instructions Booklet* – copies of which are kept in the venue's administrative area on the day of the exam. Venue supervisors must also be able to quickly access information and support if needed. For example, they should be able to contact their centre for advice. Centres keep signed records of the invigilation arrangements for each examination paper, which are made available to Cambridge ESOL on request.

Cambridge ESOL reserves the right to visit centres unannounced during the period of the examinations to inspect the arrangements made for the security of confidential examination material (see more on this below) and for the conduct of examinations. Inspections are intended to ensure that arrangements are in order, but can also offer an opportunity to capture first-hand knowledge of any problems from the centre's point of view. Centre Exams Managers are expected to point out the security facilities and examination rooms to visiting Inspectors. A copy of the Inspector's report is left with the centre and any shortcomings identified in the report are rectified. In the case of an adverse report which indicates cause for concern, the Cambridge ESOL Centre Inspections Officer will send the centre an Action Plan to complete, including details of how and when faults will be rectified.

Physical conditions

Cambridge ESOL seeks to ensure that any room in which an examination is conducted, whether on centre premises or in an external venue, provides candidates with appropriate conditions in which to take the examination. Matters such as room size, general cleanliness, air temperature, lighting, ventilation and the level of external noise must be taken into careful consideration. The overall aim is to conduct the test in a location and an atmosphere which are conducive to candidates performing their best.

Clear direction signs are important and a copy of the *Notice to candidates* must be displayed outside the examination rooms and visible to all. Disabled access to an examination room and to PCs may be necessary, e.g. on the ground floor. Any posters and other material that might be helpful to candidates (e.g. a classroom display) need to be removed or covered. A designated area needs to be provided where candidates can place their belongings during the test. If this is inside the exam room, all electronic devices, including mobile phones, must be switched off and stored securely. Mobile phones may have to be put into a metal box to block signals.

Seating arrangements for all the written examinations (i.e. Reading, Writing, Listening and Use of English) are carefully specified by the examination board in order to prevent candidates from overlooking, intentionally or otherwise, the work of others. Candidates must be seated at a desk or table. At least 1.25 metres is left between the centre of the working area assigned to any candidate and the centre of the working area assigned to the next candidate in any direction. If some candidates are seated higher than others (e.g. in a tiered lecture hall), then the distance between candidates is increased accordingly. Shared desks are discouraged but are permitted as long as the minimum distance between candidates is strictly observed. Chairs with side flaps are to be avoided and only permitted if the side flaps are large enough to allow candidates to work with question papers and answer sheets side by side. Candidates must all face in the same directions and be seated in column layout in candidate number order. Candidate numbers are securely attached to each desk throughout the examination and are clearly visible to invigilators from a distance.

During the test, candidates must be able to see a board showing the centre number, the time that each test component will start and the time it will finish. There must also be a reliable clock visible to all candidates. A simple sketch plan is completed for each room and this document accompanies the answer sheets and/or question papers being returned to Cambridge ESOL. This seating plan indicates the position of each candidate by candidate number, the direction in which candidates are facing, and the distance between the rows of candidates and between the candidates in each row. The room plan also indicates the number and base position of invigilators and it is signed by the supervisor. This seating plan can provide valuable information in cases of suspected malpractice.

Specific requirements for Listening test venues

For running the Listening tests there are some further specific requirements concerning suitable rooms and equipment, details of which are outlined below.

All candidates must be able to hear the test properly. The room and the equipment must be checked in advance and also on the day of the test. In assessing the suitability of a room and in preparation for holding a Listening test the following points need to be taken into account:

- The potential for reverberation caused by large rooms, unoccupied space or high ceilings. Room acoustics can vary, depending on whether a room is empty or full. It is advisable to try out the sound system with people in the room, rather than only when it is empty.
- Attention needs to be paid to the sound direction and the distance between speakers and candidates.
- If multiple speakers are available, the best positioning for these in each room should be determined to ensure even distribution of sound throughout the room.
- If a language laboratory is used, the supervisor needs to ensure that the invigilator's view of candidates is unobstructed; if necessary, extra invigilators may be needed.
- If headphones are used, they must be infra-red, not FM wireless.
- All sets of headphones to be used in Listening tests administered in language laboratories must be tested before the day of the examination.
- Awareness is needed of the potential for extraneous noise, no matter how faint, and how the direction of this sound and its proximity may impact on candidates' hearing.
- If possible, a practice test should be held in the room(s) to allow a more accurate assessment of the most appropriate tone and volume settings to use under examination conditions. (Sound reproduction can often be improved when bass is reduced, treble is boosted and volume is kept as low as is reasonable for the CD to be heard clearly in all parts of the room.)
- If playback facilities are equipped with a Dolby noise reduction system, it should be switched to the off position.

The checks listed above are extremely important and they can often help to avoid subsequent requests for Special Consideration from candidates unable to hear the test properly.

The conduct of the Listening tests

The *Timings and Instructions Booklet* for each examination gives details on the sequence and timing of Listening test papers, as well as on how to run the Listening test on the day. Cambridge ESOL Listening tests are taken on the same day as the other written components and are administered simultaneously to as many groups of candidates as possible. Only one form of a

Listening test and one CD player should be in use in any one room at any time irrespective of whether headphones are used.

If it is not possible to test all candidates simultaneously, the same Listening test form can be run 'back-to-back', so that candidates in the second group wait under supervision and have no contact with candidates who have completed the test. In such cases, the gap between test administrations is kept as short as possible. For some examinations, a different Listening test form can be offered if centres have received this from Cambridge ESOL.

On the day of the test, it is helpful to have a person available who is experienced in the technical aspects of sound equipment and reproduction, in addition to supervisory staff who have previously been familiarised with its usage.

Security

Test security is a high priority if the scores from a test are to maintain their integrity and be useful to stakeholders. Security is especially important in tests used for high-stakes decision-making purposes.

Security measures are intended to restrict access to test content and associated materials to those who need to know it for test development, test delivery, test scoring and test validation purposes. If test security is compromised then there is a risk that some candidates will be able to prepare their answers in advance and thus unfairly enhance their performance, potentially gaining scores that are not a valid and reliable indication of their actual ability.

The *Handbook for Centres* notes that, in the light of increasingly compact and sophisticated technology, it is important to be aware of the potential risks to the security of the examinations. Nowadays there exist a number of technological innovations such as digital sound recorders, mp3 players, scanning pens and mobile phones with cameras that would enable candidates to copy examination materials or make sound recordings and take them out of the examination room with the intention of publicising or circulating them. Supervisors and invigilators are encouraged to be fully aware of such threats and to be watchful for anything unusual. If they have strong suspicions about any candidate's behaviour, they are required to report it to Cambridge ESOL by using a Suspected Malpractice form (see above).

Listening test materials

The test centre and its staff, especially the Centre Exams Manager, are responsible at all times for ensuring the utmost security of examination materials, whether these materials are stored on centre premises or are in transit between venues. Materials must be transported in sealed packets and must never be left unattended during transfer. Any breach of question paper security (before, during or after an examination) is taken extremely seriously and may lead to a centre's authorisation being terminated.

Confidential test materials, both before and after an examination, must be locked away in a place of high security, ideally a strong safe. If a safe is not available or is of insufficient capacity, then a non-portable, lockable, reinforced steel or metal cabinet or other similar container can be used. The safe or container must be in a securely locked room with access ideally restricted to no more than two or three key holders. The room should preferably be windowless and on an upper floor; all windows, whether internal or external, should be fitted with security devices. In addition, the door to the room should be of solid construction (i.e. not hollow), have secure hinges and be fitted with a secure lock. Following their removal from the storage container, materials must be kept under constant and close supervision until they are ready to be used, during use and afterwards until they are returned to storage and subsequently securely destroyed.

Materials for the Cambridge ESOL Listening tests (question papers and CDs) are despatched with the test papers for the other components by secure consignment. For some high-volume examinations more than one Listening form is provided for each administration. On receipt of the materials the Centre Exams Manager is required to check that question papers and CDs match up (without opening the question paper envelope), and that the CDs and playback equipment in the test centre are compatible. They must also check the quality of CDs for each test well before the examination day itself by playing the Introduction and by random sampling. Centre staff are required to carry out the checking of CDs for each test in secure conditions. This means in a locked room, sufficiently far from the risk of candidates overhearing, and ideally using headphones. Any CD found to be faulty will be replaced by Cambridge ESOL as a matter of urgency. The CD package is then resealed and stored securely until required.

In addition, checks must be made of the recording quality and playback equipment in any premises where the Listening tests are to be taken, including speakers, to ensure that all technical specifications required for the test can be met (e.g. inbuilt pause facility, playback speed, sound reproduction/quality, volume capacity). Where these do not meet requirements, remedial action must be taken before the first test session. The Centre Exams Manager is responsible for ensuring that audio equipment is kept in good working order. Hardware including headphones should be regularly maintained and checked to minimise the risk of equipment failure.

Within three calendar days of a test being taken, all Listening test materials, both question papers and CDs, must either be returned to Cambridge ESOL by secure means or be securely destroyed locally.

If the security of the question papers or confidential ancillary materials is put at risk by fire, theft, loss, damage, unauthorised disclosure, or any other circumstances, Cambridge ESOL must be informed immediately.

Best practice principles and legal matters

As a responsible test provider, Cambridge ESOL is explicitly committed to operating according to ethical testing principles. As well as putting in place the standardised administrative procedures which have been described above, this commitment means adopting policies and practices which take account of data protection, individual privacy and protection, and equal opportunities that are consistent with the latest laws and regulations (e.g. UK Data Protection Act, UK Disability Discrimination Act, UK Child Protection and Safeguarding legislation, international legislation relating to copyright and intellectual property). As key partners in the delivery of Cambridge ESOL examinations, test centres worldwide are expected to adopt similar principles where possible, and to comply with all local laws and regulations.

Appendix E

Cambridge ESOL staff induction worksheet on the CEFR

Topic: The Common European Framework of Reference (CEFR)

Time req'd: 45-50 mins approx (accessing, reading, answering inc.)

Materials (all needed):
1. Council of Europe's (CoE) website on the CEFR
2. CEFR, 2001, Council of Europe
3. CoE's Publications List website
4. Materials illustrating the CEFR levels

Where to find materials:
1. http://www.coe.int/t/dg4/linguistic/CADRE_EN.asp
2. http://www.coe.int/t/dg4/linguistic/Source/Framework_EN.pdf
   or the CEFR hard copy ('blue book') in the ESOL library:
   Council of Europe (2001) *Common European Framework of Reference for Languages: Learning, teaching, assessment,* Cambridge: Cambridge University Press
3. http://www.coe.int/t/dg4/linguistic/Publications_EN.asp
4. http://www.coe.int/T/DG4/Portfolio/?L=E&M=/main_pages/illustrationse.html

Aims: - To understand the aims, uses and nature of the CEFR;
      - To learn about the CEFR 'toolkit'.

induction worksheet

CODE: R&V/009/1/11.03.08

The Common European Framework of Reference for Languages (CEFR)

Name ....

Unit ....

Location ....

CEFR: Its aims, uses and nature

Please consult the CoE's website on the CEFR [No 1 in the Materials list above] and answer the following questions.

1. In your own words what is the CEFR and what are its main aims?
....
....

2. To whom and why may the CEFR be of interest?
....
....

3. How many language versions of the CEFR currently exist?
....

Now please read pp. 1-2, 5-8 of the CEFR [2 in the Materials list], and answer the following questions.

4. Name two practical uses of the CEFR.
....
....

5. Why is the CEFR of interest for an assessment board such as Cambridge ESOL?
....
....

Please browse through the contents of the CEFR, and answer the following questions.

6. Which chapter of the CEFR discusses assessment issues? What are the main themes/topics in the chapter?
....
....

7. Two common misconceptions about the CEFR are that it provides a general guide on how to construct good language tests and prescribes a specific approach to test construction. Why do you think these two statements are not true?
....
....
....

UNIVERSITY *of* CAMBRIDGE
ESOL Examinations

English for Speakers of Other Languages

The CEFR 'toolkit'

The CEFR is accompanied by a number of supporting publications and documents.
1. Consult the CoE's Publications List website [3 in the Materials list] and match the following publications with their purpose.

	Publications		Purpose
1.	*Relating Examinations to the Common European Framework of Reference for Languages: A Manual*, January 2009	A.	detailed accounts of the use of the CEFR across Europe for language learning, teaching and assessment purposes
2.	*Illustrations of levels of language proficiency*	B.	a record of the language and cultural skills and experiences of language learners measured against the CEFR levels
3.	*Case studies concerning the use of the Common European Framework of Reference for Languages: Learning, Teaching, Assessment*, 2002	C.	guidelines for examination providers to situate their tests to the CEFR scale in a principled and transparent way
4.	*European Language Portfolio* (ELP)	D.	sample performances exemplifying the CEFR levels

....

2. Which of these 4 publications has the most relevance for your current job? Why?
....

3. What are the five stages suggested by the *Manual for Relating Examinations to the CEFR* (2009) for aligning language examinations to the CEFR levels? Consult Chapter 2 (pp. 7-9 & 10-11) of the Manual (or pp. 19-21 & 22-23 in the Adobe Reader Page numbering if you are viewing a pdf version of it). (You can access the Manual from the CoE's website on the CEFR [1 in the Materials list].)
....

4. Which of the above stages are you engaging in by filling in this induction worksheet?
....

5. What types of sample performances and materials has Cambridge ESOL published for illustrating the CEFR levels? Look at the 'Illustrations of levels of language proficiency' web page [4 in the Materials list].
....
....
....

Please contact Research & Validation if you have any questions about this worksheet.

References

Adeboye, K and Culwin, F (2003) *Validation of the Effectiveness of a Confidence Based Multiple Choice Examination System*, Proceedings of the 4th Annual LTSN-ICS Conference, NUI Galway.

Adolphs, S and Schmitt, N (2003) Lexical Coverage of Spoken Discourse, *Applied Linguistics* 24 (4), 425–438.

AERA/APA/NCME (1999) *Standards for Educational and Psychological Testing*, Washington, DC: American Educational and Research Association/ American Psychological Association/National Council for Measurement in Education.

Alderson, J C (1995) *Ideas for research into impact, washback and IELTS*, internal paper for the University of Cambridge Local Examinations Syndicate (UCLES).

Alderson, J C (2000) *Assessing Reading*, Cambridge: Cambridge University Press.

Alderson, J C (2004) Foreword, in Cheng, L, Watanabe, Y and Curtis, A (Eds) *Washback in Language Testing: Research Contexts and Methods*, London: Lawrence Erlbaum Associates, ix–xii.

Alderson, J C and Wall, D (1993) Does washback exist? *Applied Linguistics* 14, 115–129.

Alderson, J C and Wall, D (1996) Editorial for Special issue on washback, *Language Testing* 13 (3), 239–240.

Alderson, J C, Clapham, C and Wall, D (1995) *Language Test Construction and Evaluation*, Cambridge: Cambridge University Press.

Alderson, J C, Figueras, N, Kuijper, H, Nold, G, Takala, S and Tardieu, C (2006) Analysing tests of reading and listening in relation to the Common European Framework of Reference: The experience of the Dutch CEFR Construct Project, *Language Assessment Quarterly* 3 (1), 3–30.

Allen, M J and Yen, W M (1979) *Introduction to Measurement Theory,* Long Grove, Illinois: Waveland Press.

American Council for the Teaching of Foreign Languages (1985) *ACTFL Proficiency Guidelines*, Hastings-on-Hudson, NY: ACTFL Materials Center.

Anastasi, A (1988) *Psychological Testing*, New York: Macmillan, 6th edn.

Anderson, A, Brown, G, Shillcock, R and Yule, G (1984) *Teaching Talk: Strategies for Production and Assessment*, Cambridge: Cambridge University Press.

Anderson, J R (1983) *The Architecture of Cognition*, Cambridge, MA: Harvard University Press.

Anderson, A and Lynch, T (1988) *Listening*, Cambridge: Cambridge University Press.

Anderson, J R (2000) *Cognitive Psychology and its Implications*, New York: W H Freeman, 5th edn.

Anderson, R C (1974) Concretization and sentence learning, *Journal of Educational Psychology* 66 (2), 179–183.

Examining Listening

Angoff, W H (1971) Scales, norms, and equivalent scores in Thorndike, R L (Ed.)
    Educational Measurement, Washington, DC: American Council on Education,
    2nd edn, 508–560.
Association of Language Testers in Europe (ALTE) (1994) *Code of Practice,*
    available online: www.alte.org/cop/index.php
Association of Language Testers in Europe (ALTE) (1998) *Multilingual
    Glossary of Language Testing Terms,* Studies in Language Testing volume 6,
    Cambridge: UCLES/Cambridge University Press.
Association of Language Testers in Europe (ALTE) (2011) *Manual for Language
    Test Development and Examining: For Use with the CEFR,* Strasbourg:
    Council of Europe.
Association of Language Testers in Europe (ALTE) (n.d.) *Individual component
    checklist: Listening.* Available at: http://www.alte.org/checklists/listening_
    check.pdf
Austin, J L (1975) *How to Do Things With Words,* Oxford: Oxford University
    Press, 2nd edn.
Baars, B J (1980) The competing plans hypothesis: An heuristic viewpoint on the
    causes of errors in speech, in Dechert, H W and Raupach, M (Eds) *Temporal
    Variables in Speech: Studies in Honour of Frieda Goldman-Eisler,* The Hague:
    Moulton, 39–50.
Bachman, L F (1990) *Fundamental Considerations in Language Testing,* Oxford:
    Oxford University Press.
Bachman, L F (1991) What does language testing have to offer?, *TESOL
    Quarterly* 25 (4), 671–704.
Bachman, L F (2000) Modern language testing at the turn of the century:
    assuring that what we count counts, *Language Testing* 17 (1), 1–42.
Bachman, L F (2004) *Statistical Analyses for Language Assessment,* Cambridge:
    Cambridge University Press.
Bachman, L F (2005) Building and supporting a case for test use, *Language
    Assessment Quarterly* 2 (1), 1–34.
Bachman, L F and Palmer, A S (1989) The construct validation of self-ratings of
    communicative language ability, *Language Testing* 6 (1), 14–29.
Bachman, L F and Palmer, A S (1996) *Language Testing in Practice,* Oxford:
    Oxford University Press.
Bachman, L F and Palmer, A S (2010) *Language Assessment in Practice,* Oxford:
    Oxford University Press.
Bachman, L F, Davidson, F, Ryan, K, and Choi, I-C (1995) *An Investigation
    into the Comparability of Two tests of English as a Foreign Language,* Studies
    in Language Testing volume 1, Cambridge: UCLES/Cambridge University
    Press.
Baddeley, A (1986) *Working Memory,* Hove: Psychology Press.
Badger, R and Yan, X (2009) The use of tactics and strategies by Chinese
    students in the Listening component of IELTS, in Thompson, P (Ed.) *IELTS
    Research Reports Volume 9,* British Council/IELTS Australia, 67–96.
Bailey, K (1996) Working for washback: a review of the washback concept in
    language testing, *Language Testing,* 13 (3), 257–279.
Baltova, I (1994) The impact of video on the comprehension skills of core French
    students, *The Canadian Modern Language Review* 50, 507–532.
Bartlett, F C (1932) *Remembering,* Cambridge: Cambridge University Press.
Bates, E and MacWhinney, B (1989) Functionalism and the competition model,
    in MacWhinney, B and Bates, E (Eds) *The Cross-Linguistic Study of Sentence
    Processing,* New York: Cambridge University Press, 3–73.

Bauer, L and Nation, P (1993) Word Families, *International Journal of Lexicography* 6 (4), 253–279.

Baxter, G P and Glaser, R (1998) Investigating the cognitive complexity of science assessments, *Educational Measurement: Issues and Practice*, 17 (3), 37–45.

Beeston, S (2001) The UCLES EFL Item Banking System, *Research Notes* 2, 8–9.

Bejar, I, Douglas, D, Jamieson, J, Nissan, S and Turner, J (2000) *TOEFL 2000 Listening Framework: A Working Paper*, Princeton, NJ: Educational Testing Service.

Ben-Shakhar, G and Sinai, Y (1991) Gender differences in multiple-choice tests: The role of differential guessing tendencies, *Journal of Educational Measurement* 28 (1), 23–35.

Berne, J E (1995) How Does Varying Pre-Listening Activities Affect Second Language Listening Comprehension?, *Hispania* 78 (2), 316–329.

Binder, J R, Westbury, C F, McKiernan, K A, Possing, E T and Medler, D A (2005) Distinct brain systems for processing concrete and abstract concepts, *Journal of Cognitive Neuroscience* 17 (6), 905–917.

Blackhurst, A (2005) Listening, Reading and Writing on computer-based and paper-based versions of IELTS, *Research Notes* 21, 14–17.

Blackhurst, A (2007) Computer-based and Paper-based versions of IELTS, in Alexander, O (Ed.), *New Approaches to Materials Development for Language Learning*, Bern: Peter Lang AG, 265–274.

Blau, E (1990) The effect of syntax, speed and pauses on listening comprehension, *TESOL Quarterly* 24, 746–53.

Bloomfield, A N, Wayland, S C, Blodgett, A and Linck, J (2011) Factors related to passage length: Implications for second language listening comprehension, *CogSci 2011 Proceedings*, 2317–2322, available online: csjarchive.cogsci.rpi. edu/Proceedings/2011/papers/0553/paper0553.pdf

Boroughs, R (2002) Redeveloping Part 1 of the CPE Listening paper, *Research Notes* 10, 5–8.

Boroughs, R (2003) *The change process at paper level. Paper 4, Listening*, in Weir, C J and Milanovic, M (Eds) *Continuity and Innovation: Revising the Cambridge Proficiency in English Examination 1913–2002*, Cambridge: UCLES/Cambridge University Press, 315–366.

Bostrom, R (1996) Memory, cognitive processing, and the process of "listening" a reply to Thomas and Levine, *Human Communicative Research* 23, 298–305.

Braham, C G (Ed. In Chief) (1996) *Random House Webster's Dictionary*, New York: Ballantine Books.

Bransford, J D and Johnson, M K (1973) Consideration of some problems of comprehension, in Chase, W G (Ed.) *Visual Information Processing*, New York: Academic Press.

Bransford, J D, Barclay, J R and Franks, J J (1972) Sentence memory: a constructive versus interpretive approach, *Cognitive Psychology*, 3, 193–209.

Breeze, R and Miller, P (2009) Predictive validity of the IELTS Listening Test as an indicator of student coping ability in English-medium undergraduate courses in Spain, *IELTS Research Reports Volume 9,* 201–234.

Breuer, A and Geluykens, R (2007) Variation in British and American English requests: A contrastive analysis, in Kraft, B and Geluykens, R (Eds) *Cross-Cultural Pragmatics and Interlanguage English*, Munich: LINCOM.

Brindley, G (1998) Assessing listening abilities, *Annual Review of Applied Linguistics* 18, 171–91.

Brindley, G and Slatyer, H (2002) Exploring task difficulty in ESL listening assessment, *Language Testing* 19, 369–394.

Browman, CP and Goldstein, L (1991) Tiers in articulatory phonology, with some implications for casual speech, in Kingston, J and Beckham, M E (Eds), *Papers in Laboratory Phonology Volume 1: Between the Grammar and Physics of Speech*, Cambridge: Cambridge University Press, 341–376.

Brown, G (1986) Investigating listening comprehension in context, *Applied Linguistics* 7 (3), 284–302

Brown, G (1990) *Listening to Spoken English*, Harlow: Longman, 2nd edn.

Brown, G and Yule, G (1983a) *Discourse analysis*, Cambridge: Cambridge University Press.

Brown, G and Yule, G (1983b) *Teaching the Spoken Language*, Cambridge: Cambridge University Press.

Brown, J D (1996) *Testing in Language Programs*, Upper Saddle River, NJ: Prentice Hall Regents.

Brown, J D and Hudson, T (1998) *The Alternatives in Language Assessment*, TESOL Quarterly 32 (4), 653–675.

Buck, G (1988) Testing Listening comprehension in Japanese university entrance examinations, *JALT Journal* 10 (1), 15–42.

Buck, G (1990) *The testing of second language listening comprehension*, unpublished PhD thesis, University of Lancaster.

Buck, G (1994) The appropriacy of psychometric measurement models for testing second language listening comprehension, *Language Testing* 11 (2), 145–170.

Buck, G (2001) *Assessing Listening*, Cambridge: Cambridge University Press.

Buck, G (2011) *Testing Listening Comprehension*, North Fork, CA: Lidget Green Publishing.

Buck, G and Tatsuoka, K (1998) Application of the rule-space procedure to language testing: examining attributes of a free response listening test, *Language Testing* 15 (2), 119–157.

Burger, S and Doherty, J (1992) Testing receptive skills within a comprehension-based approach, in Courchene, R J, Glidden, J I, St John, J and Thérien, C (Eds) *Comprehension-based Second Language Teaching*, Ottawa: University of Ottawa Press, 299–318.

Burgoon, J K (1994) Nonverbal signals, in Knapp, M L and Miller, G R (Eds) *Handbook of Interpersonal Communication*, Thousand Oaks, CA: SAGE Publications, 2nd edn, 229–285.

Bush, M (2001) A Multiple choice test that rewards partial knowledge, *Journal of Further and Higher Education* 25 (2), 157–163.

Bybee, J (2001) *Phonology and Language Use,* Cambridge: Cambridge University Press.

Calvert, D R (1986) *Descriptive Phonetics*, New York: Thieme, 2nd edn.

Cambridge ESOL (2006a) *Item Writer Guidelines: Information Common to All Papers, FCE, CAE and CPE*, Cambridge: UCLES.

Cambridge ESOL (2006b) *KET: Information for Candidates*, available online: www.candidates.cambridgesol.org/cs/digitalAssets/105327_3812_6Y05_KET_IforC_w.pdf

Cambridge ESOL (2007a) *CPE: Information for Candidates*, available online: www.candidates.cambridgeesol.org/cs/digitalAssets/113322_cpe_infoforcand.pdf

Cambridge ESOL (2007b) *Handbooks for Teachers for the Cambridge Main Suite Examinations*, Cambridge: UCLES.

Cambridge ESOL (2007c) *Item Writer Guidelines: CAE Listening*, Cambridge: UCLES.

Cambridge ESOL (2007d) *Item Writer Guidelines for the Cambridge Main Suite Examinations*, Cambridge: UCLES.

Cambridge ESOL (2008a) *Certificate in Advanced English 2*, Cambridge: Cambridge University Press.

Cambridge ESOL (2008b) *Certificate of Proficiency in English Handbook for Teachers*, Cambridge: UCLES.

Cambridge ESOL (2008c) *Handbooks for Teachers for the Cambridge Main Suite Examinations*, Cambridge: UCLES.

Cambridge ESOL (2008d) *Item Writer Guidelines for the Cambridge Main Suite Examinations*, Cambridge: UCLES.

Cambridge ESOL (2008e) *Item Writer Guidelines: PET and PETfS Listening*, Cambridge: UCLES.

Cambridge ESOL (2009a) *Certificate in Advanced English 3*, Cambridge: Cambridge University Press.

Cambridge ESOL (2009b) *Handbooks for Teachers for the Cambridge Business English Certificates*, Cambridge: UCLES.

Cambridge ESOL (2009c) *Handbooks for Teachers for the Cambridge Main Suite Examinations*, Cambridge: UCLES.

Cambridge ESOL (2009d) *Item Writer Guidelines: CPE Listening*, Cambridge: UCLES.

Cambridge ESOL (2009e) *Item Writer Guidelines for the Cambridge Main Suite Examinations*, Cambridge: UCLES.

Cambridge ESOL (2009f) *Vocabulary List: KET and KETfS*, Cambridge: UCLES.

Cambridge ESOL (2009g) *Vocabulary List: PET and PETfS*, Cambridge: UCLES.

Cambridge ESOL (2010a) *Certificate in Advanced English 4*, Cambridge: Cambridge University Press.

Cambridge ESOL (2010b) *LIBS dictionary – guidelines for accepting misspellings*, Cambridge ESOL internal document.

Cambridge ESOL (2010c) *Special Circumstances Booklet*, Cambridge: UCLES.

Cambridge ESOL (2010d) *UMS Item Writer Guidelines: Information Common to All papers*, Cambridge: UCLES.

Cambridge ESOL (2011a) *Principles of Good Practice: Quality management and validation in language assessment*, Cambridge: UCLES.

Cambridge ESOL (2011b) *Using the CEFR: Principles of Good Practice*, available online: research.cambridgeesol.org/fitness-purpose

Cambridge ESOL (2011c) *Cambridge English: Advanced- Information for Candidates*, available online: cambridge-english-advanced.cambridgeesol. org/_guides/8182_1y10_ce_advanced_informationforcandidates_w.pdf

Cambridge ESOL (2012a) *Cambridge English: Advanced Handbook for Teachers*, Cambridge: UCLES.

Cambridge ESOL (2012b) *Cambridge English: First Handbook for Teachers*, Cambridge: UCLES.

Cambridge ESOL (2012c) *Cambridge English: Key Handbook for Teachers*, Cambridge: UCLES.

Cambridge ESOL (2012d) *Cambridge English: Preliminary Handbook for Teachers*, Cambridge: UCLES.

Cambridge ESOL (2012e) *Handbook for Centres*, Cambridge: UCLES.

Camilli, G, and Shepard, L (1994) *Methods for Identifying Biased Test Items*, Thousand Oaks, CA: Sage.

Canale, M and Swain, M (1980) Theoretical bases of communicative approaches to second language teaching and testing, *Applied Linguistics* 1 (1), 1–47.

Capel, A (2010) A1–B2 vocabulary: Insights and issues arising from the English Profile Wordlists project, *English Profile Journal* 1 (1), e3.

Carrell, P L (2007) *Notetaking strategies and their relationship to performance on listening comprehension and communicative assessment tasks*, TOEFL Monograph Series 35, Princeton, NJ: Educational Testing Service.

Carrell, P L, Dunkell, P A and Molhaun, P (2004) The effects of notetaking, lecture length and topic on a computer-based test of ESL listening comprehension, *Applied Language Learning* 14 (1), 83–105.

Carroll, D W (1994) *Psychology of Language*, Pacific Grove, CA: Brooks/Cole, 2nd edn.

Carter, R A and McCarthy, M J (2006) *Cambridge Grammar of English*, Cambridge: Cambridge University Press.

Cauldwell, R (2003) *Report on 'Motormouth' analysis of CPE, PET & IELTS recordings, and comparison with spontaneous speech data*, UCLES internal report.

Chafe, W (1979) The flow of thought and the flow of language, in Givon, T (Ed.) *Syntax and Semantics, 12: Discourse and Syntax,* New York: Academic Press, 159–181.

Chafe, W and Tannen, D (1986) The relation between written and spoken language, *Annual Review of Anthropology* 16, 383–407.

Chalhoub-Deville, M (2009) Standards-based assessment in the US: social and educational impact, in Taylor, L and Weir, C (Eds) *Language Testing Matters: investigating the wider social and educational impact of assessment – Proceedings of the ALTE Cambridge Conference, April 2008,* Studies in Language Testing volume 31, Cambridge: UCLES/Cambridge University Press, 281–300.

Chalhoub-Deville, M and Deville, C (1999) Computer adaptive testing in second language contexts, *Annual Review of Applied Linguistics* 19, 273–299.

Chalhoub-Deville, M and Deville, C (2008) Nationally mandated testing for accountability: English language learners in the US, in Spolsky, B and Hult, F (Eds), *The Handbook of Educational Linguistics*, London: Blackwell, 510–522.

Chapelle, C A, Enwright, M K and Jamieson, J (2008) *Building a Validity Argument for the Test of English as a Foreign Language*, New York: Routledge.

Chaudron, C, Loschky, L and Cook, J (1994) Second language listening comprehension and lecture notetaking, in Flowerdew, J (Ed.) *Academic Listening: Research Perspectives*, Cambridge: Cambridge University Press, 75–92.

Cheng, L (2005) *Changing Language Teaching through Language Testing: A Washback Study*, Studies in Language Testing volume 21, Cambridge: UCLES/Cambridge University Press.

Cheng, L and Curtis, A (2004) Washback or backwash: a review of the impact of testing on teaching and learning, in Cheng, L, Watanabe, Y and Curtis, A (Eds) (2004) *Washback in Language Testing: Research Contexts and Methods*, London: Lawrence Erlbaum Associates, 3–17.

Cheng, L, Watanabe, Y and Curtis, A (Eds) (2004) *Washback in Language Testing: Research Contexts and Methods*, London: Lawrence Erlbaum.

Chi, Y (2011) *Validation of an academic listening test: effects of "breakdown" tests and test takers' cognitive awareness of listening processes*, unpublished PhD thesis, University of Illinois at Urbana-Champaign, USA.

Choi, I-C, Kim, K S and Boo, J (2003) Comparability of a paper-based language test and a computer-based language test, *Language Testing* 20 (3), 295–320.

Cizek, G (2011) *Reconceptualizing validity and the place of consequences*, paper presented at the Annual Meeting of the National Council on Measurement in Education, New Orleans, LA, April.

Clapham, C (1996) *The Development of IELTS: A study of the effect of background knowledge on reading comprehension*, Studies in Language Testing volume 4, Cambridge: UCLES/Cambridge University Press.

Clark, H H and Clark, E V (1977) *Psychology and Language: An Introduction to Psycholinguistics*, New York: Harcourt, Brace.

Code of Fair Testing Practices in Education (2004) Washington, DC: Joint Committee on Testing Practices.

Cohen, A (1998) *Strategies of Language Learning and Language Use*, Harlow: Longman.

Coleman, D, Starfield, S and Hagan, A (2003) The attitudes of IELTS stakeholders: student and staff perceptions of IELTS in Australian, UK and Chinese universities, *IELTS Research Reports Volume 5*, 159–235.

Coniam, D (2006) Evaluating computer-based and paper-based versions of an English-language listening test, *ReCALL* 18 (2), 193–211.

Conrad, L (1985) Semantic versus syntactic cues in listening comprehension, *Studies in Second Language Acquisition* 7 (1), 59–72.

Coombe, C, Davidson, P, O'Sullivan, B and Stoynoff, S (Eds) (2012) *The Cambridge Guide to Second Language Assessment*, Cambridge: Cambridge University Press.

Cope, L (2009) CB BULATS: Examining the reliability of a computer-based test, *Research Notes* 38, 31–34.

Council of Europe (2001) *Common European Framework of Reference for Languages: Learning, Teaching, Assessment*, Cambridge: Cambridge University Press.

Council of Europe (2003) *Relating Language Examinations to the Common European Framework of Reference for Languages: Learning, Teaching, Assessment (CEF), Manual: Preliminary Pilot Version*, DGIV/EDU/LANG 2003, 5, Strasbourg: Language Policy Division.

Council of Europe (2004) *Reference Supplement to the Preliminary Pilot Version of the Manual for Relating Language Examinations to the CEFR*, Strasbourg: Council of Europe.

Council of Europe (2009) *Relating Language Examinations to the Common European Framework of Reference for Languages: Learning, teaching, assessment (CEFR)*, Strasbourg, France: Council of Europe. Available online: www.coe.int/t/dg4/linguistic/Source/ManualRevision-proofread-FINAL_en.pdf

Coxhead, A (1998) *An academic wordlist, English Language Institute Occasional Publication* 18, Wellington, New Zealand: Victoria University of Wellington.

Coxhead, A (2000) A new academic wordlist, *TESOL Quarterly* 34 (2), 213–238.

Cronbach, L J (1942) Studies of acquiescence as a factor in the true-false test, *Journal of Educational Psychology* 23 (6), 401–415.

Cutler, A (1990) Exploiting prosodic possibilities, in Altmann, G (Ed.) *Cognitive Models of Speech Processing: Psycholinguistic and Computational Perspectives*, Cambridge, MA: MIT Press, 105–121.

Cutler, A (1994) Segmentation problems, rhythmic solutions, *Lingua* 92, 81–104.

Cutler, A (1997) The comparative perspective on spoken-language processing, *Speech Communication* 21, 3–15.

Cutler, A and Clifton, C (1999) Comprehending spoken language: a blueprint of the listener, in Brown, C M and Hagoort, P (Eds) *The Neurocognition of Language*, Oxford: Oxford University Press, 123–166.

Dąbrowska, E (2003) *Language, Mind and Brain,* Edinburgh: Edinburgh University Press.

Davies, A (2001) The logic of testing languages for specific purposes, *Language Testing* 18 (2), 133–147.

Davies, A (2005) 40 Years in applied linguistics: an interview with Alan Davies, by Antony Kunnan, *Language Assessment Quarterly* 2 (1), 35–50.

Davies, A (2008) *Assessing Academic English: Testing English Proficiency 1950–1989 – the IELTS Solution*, Studies in Language Testing volume 23, Cambridge: UCLES/Cambridge University Press.

Davies, A, Brown, A, Elder, C, Hill, K, Lumley, T and McNamara, T (1999) *Dictionary of Language Testing*, Studies in Language Testing volume 7, Cambridge: UCLES/Cambridge University Press.

Davies, P (2002) *There's no Confidence in Multiple-Choice Testing, ...,* Proceedings of 6th CAA Conference, Loughborough.

Derwing, T M (1990) Speech rate is no simple matter: Rate adjustment and NS-NNS communicative success, *Studies in Second Language Acquisition* 12 (3), 303–313.

Dooey, P (2008) Language testing and technology: problems of transition to a new era, *ReCALL* 20 (1), 21–34.

Dorans, N J and Kulick, E (1986) Demonstrating the utility of the standardization approach to assessing unexpected differential item performance on the Scholastic Aptitude Test, *Journal of Educational Measurement* 23, 355–368.

Douglas, D (2000) *Assessing Language for Specific Purposes: Theory and Practice*, Cambridge: Cambridge University Press.

Douglas, D (2007) *Technology and the construct of language for specific purposes*, paper presented at the 40th annual meeting of the British Association for Applied Linguistics, Edinburgh.

Douglas, D and Hegelheimer, V (2007) Assessing language using computer technology, *Annual Review of Applied Linguistics* 27, 115–132.

Douglas, D and Nissan, S (2001) *Developing listening prototypes using a corpus of spoken academic English*, paper presented at the Language Testing Research Colloquium, St. Louis.

Dunkel, P A (1999) Considerations in developing or using second/foreign language proficiency computer-adaptive tests, *Language Learning and Technology* 2 (2), 77–93.

Ebel, R L (1972) *Essentials of Educational Measurement*, Englewood Cliffs, NJ: Prentice Hall.

Educational Testing Service (2002) *Standards for Quality and Fairness*, Princeton, NJ: Educational Testing Service.

Educational Testing Service (2010) *Linking TOEFL iBT scores to IELTS scores: A Research Report*, Princeton, NJ: Educational Testing Service.

Elder, C (2001) Assessing the language proficiency of teachers: are there any border controls?, *Language Testing* 18 (2), 149–170.

Elliott, M W (2008) *The expression of affect in spoken English: A case study*, unpublished MA thesis, King's College London.

Ellis, A W and Young, A W (1988) *Human Cognitive Neuropsychology*, Hove, UK: Erlbaum.

Ericsson K A and Simon H A (1993) *Protocol Analysis: Verbal Reports as Data*, Massachusetts Institute of Technology Press, Cambridge, MA.

Ericsson, K A and Smith, J (Eds) (1991) *Toward a General Theory of Expertise: Prospects and Limits,* Cambridge: Cambridge University Press.

European Association for Language Testing and Assessment (EALTA) (2006) *Guidelines for Good Practice in Language Testing and Assessment*, available online: www.ealta.eu.org/guidelines/English.pdf

Eurydice (2008) *Key Data on Teaching Languages at School in Europe*, Brussels: EACEA.

Farr, R, Prichard, R and Smitten, B (1990) A description of what happens when an examinee takes a multiple-choice reading-comprehension test, *Journal of Educational Measurement* 27, 209–26.

Feldt, L S and Brennan, R L (1989) Reliability, in Linn, R (Ed.) *Educational Measurement*, American Council on Education, Macmillan, 3rd edn, 105–146.

Feltovich, P J, Prietula, M J and Ericsson, K A (2006) Studies of expertise from psychological perspectives, in Ericsson, K A, Charness, N, Feltovich, P J, Hoffman, R R (Eds) *The Cambridge Handbook of Expertise and Expert Performance,* Cambridge: Cambridge University Press, 41–67.

ffrench, A and Gutch, A (2006) *FCE/CAE Modifications: building the validity argument: application of Weir's socio-cognitive framework to FCE and CAE*, internal report, Cambridge ESOL.

Field, J (1993) *An evaluation of listening comprehension material used in FCE testing*, unpublished MPhil dissertation, University of Cambridge.

Field, J (1999a) Key concept: bottom-up and top-down, *ELT Journal* 53 (4), 338–9.

Field, J (1999b) *Revision of Certificate of Proficiency in English: Listening paper*, unpublished internal report, Cambridge ESOL.

Field, J (2000) *Report on the revision of the Certificate of Proficiency in English Listening paper*, UCLES internal report.

Field, J (2001) *Lexical segmentation in first and foreign language listening*, unpublished PhD thesis, University of Cambridge.

Field, J (2003) Promoting perception: lexical segmentation in L2 listening, *ELT Journal* 57 (4), 325–334.

Field, J (2004) An insight into listeners' problems: too much bottom-up or too much top-down?, *System* 32, 363–77.

Field, J (2008) Revising segmentation hypotheses in first and second language listening, *System* 36, 35–51.

Field, J (2009a) *Listening in the Language Classroom,* Cambridge: Cambridge University Press.

Field, J (2009b) *Two bites of the cherry: the effects of reply on the listener*, paper presented at BAAL Annual Meeting, Newcastle.

Field, J (2011a) Cognitive validity, in Taylor, L (Ed.) *Examining Speaking: Research and Practice in Assessing Second Language Speaking*, Studies in Language Testing volume 30, Cambridge: UCLES/Cambridge University Press, 65–111.

Field, J (2011b) The elusive skill: how can we teach L2 listening validly?, in Powell-Davies, P (Ed.) *New directions: assessment and evaluation*, London: British Council, 139–145.

Field, J (2011c) Into the mind of the academic listener, *Journal of English for Academic Purposes* 10 (2), 102–112.

Field, J (2012) The cognitive validity of the lecture-based question in the IELTS Listening paper, in Taylor, L and Weir, C J (Eds) *IELTS Collected Papers 2: Research in Reading and Listening Assessment,* Studies in Language

Testing volume 34, Cambridge: UCLES/Cambridge University Press, 391–453.

Field, J (forthcoming) *The cognitive validity of the CAE listening test as a predictor of academic performance*, Cambridge ESOL internal research report.

Fortune, A J (2004) *Testing listening comprehension in a foreign language – does the number of times a text is heard affect performance?*, unpublished MA dissertation, University of Bristol (UK).

Foulke, E (1968) Listening comprehension as a function of word rate, *Journal of Communication* 18 (3), 198-206.

Fraser, H, Stevenson, B and Marks, A (2011) Interpretation of a crisis call: persistence of a primed perception of a disputed utterance, *International Journal of Speech Language and the Law*, 18 (2), available online: www.equinoxpub.com/IJSLL/article/view/11212

Frazier, L and Rayner, K (1982) Making and correcting errors during sentence comprehension: Eye movements in the analysis of structurally ambiguous sentences, *Cognitive Psychology* 14, 178–21.

Frederiksen, J and Collins, A (1989) A systems approach to educational testing, *Educational Researcher*, 18 (9), 27–32.

Freedle, R O and Kostin, I (1996) *The Prediction of TOEFL Listening Comprehension Item Difficulty for Minitalk Passages: Implications for Construct Validity*, Princeton, NJ: Educational Testing Service.

Freedle, R and Kostin, I (1999) Does the text matter in a multiple-choice test of comprehension? The case for the construct validity of TOEFL's minitalks, *Language Testing* 16, 2–32.

Fried-Booth, D (2007) Reviewing Part 1 of the FCE Listening test, *Research Notes* 30, 23–24.

Fulcher, G (2004) Deluded by artifices? The common European framework and harmonization, *Language Assessment Quarterly* 1 (4), 253–266.

Fulcher, G and Davidson, F (2007) *Language Testing and Assessment*, London and New York: Routledge.

Fulcher, G and Davidson, F (2009) Test architecture, test retrofit, *Language Testing* 26 (1), 123–144.

Gagnon, R, Charlin, B, Roy, L, St-Martin, M, Sauvé, E, Boshuizen, H P and van der Vleuten, C (2006) The cognitive validity of the script concordance test: a processing time study, *Teaching and Learning in Medicine*, 18 (1) 22–27.

Galaczi, E and ffrench, A (2011) Context validity, in Taylor, L (Ed.) *Examining Speaking: Research and Practice in Assessing Second Language Speaking*, Studies in Language Testing volume 30, Cambridge: UCLES/Cambridge University Press, 112–170.

Galaczi, E D and Khalifa, H (2009a) Cambridge ESOL's CEFR DVD of speaking performances: what's the story?, *Research Notes* 37, 23–29.

Galaczi, E D and Khalifa, H (2009b) *Project overview: examples of speaking performances at CEFR levels A2 to C2*, available online: research.cambridgeesol.org/fitness-purpose/examples-speaking-tests

Galaczi, E D, ffrench, A, Hubbard, C and Green, A (2011) Developing assessment scales for large-scale speaking tests: A multiple method approach, *Assessment in Education: Principles, Policy & Practice* 18 (3), 217–237.

Gallois, C and Markel, N N (1975) Turn Taking: Social Personality and Conversational Style, *Journal of Personality and Social Psychology* 31 (6), 1,134–1,140.

Ganong, W F (1980) Phonetic characterisation in auditory perception, *Journal of Experimental Psychology: Human Perception and Performance* 6, 110–125.

Gaskell, M G and Marslen-Wilson, W D (1995) Integrating form and meaning: a distributed model of speech perception, *Language and Cognitive Processes* 12, 613–656.

Gates, S (1995) Exploiting washback from standardized tests, in Brown, J and Yamashita, S (Eds) *Language testing in Japan*, Tokyo: Japan Association for Language Teaching, 101–106.

Gathercole, S E and Baddeley, A (1993) *Working Memory and Language*, Hove: Erlbaum

Geluykens, R and Kraft, B (2007) Gender variation in native and interlanguage complaints, in Kraft, B and Geluykens, R (Eds) *Cross-Cultural Pragmatics and Interlanguage English*, Munich: LINCOM, 143–158.

Geranpayeh, A (2005a) *Building the construct model for the CAE examination*, Cambridge ESOL internal report.

Geranpayeh, A (2005b) *Language proficiency revisited: Demystifying the CAE construct*, paper presented at the 12th Language Testing Forum, Cambridge, England.

Geranpayeh, A (2007) Using Structural Equation Modelling to facilitate the revision of high stakes testing: the case of CAE, *Research Notes* 30, 8–12.

Geranpayeh, A (2008) Using DIF to explore item difficulty in CAE Listening, *Research Notes* 32, 16–23.

Geranpayeh, A and Kunnan, A (2007) Differential item functioning in terms of age in the Certificate in Advanced English Examination, *Language Assessment Quarterly* 4 (2), 190–222.

Geranpayeh, A and Taylor, L (2008) Examining listening: developments and issues in assessing second language listening, *Research Notes* 32, 2–5.

Gernsbacher, M (1990) *Language Comprehension as Structure Building*, Hillsdale, NJ: Erlbaum.

Gibbs, R (1994) Figurative thought and language, in Gernsbacher, M (Ed.) *Handbook of Psycholinguistics*, San Diego: Academic Press, 411–446.

Gibbs, R and Colston, H (2004) Figurative language, in Traxler, M and Gernsbacher, M, (Eds) *Handbook of Psycholinguistics*, London: Elsevier, 835–862.

Gimson, A C (1989) *An Introduction to the Pronunciation of English*, London: Edward Arnold, 4th edn.

Ginther, A (2002) Context and content visuals and performance on listening comprehension stimuli, *Language Testing* 19 (2), 133–167.

Glaser, R (1991) Expertise and assessment, in Wittrock, M C and Baker, E L (Eds) *Testing and Cognition*, Englewood Cliffs, Prentice Hall, 17–30.

Goh, C C M (1998) How ESL learners with different listening abilities use comprehension strategies and tactics, *Language Teaching Research* 2, 124–47.

Goldinger, S D (1997) Words and voices: perception and production in an episodic lexicon, in Johnson, K and Mullennix, J W (Eds) *Talker Variability in Speech Processing*, San Diego: Academic Press, 33–66.

Goldman-Eisler, F (1954) On the variability of the speed of talking and on its relation to the length of utterances in conversation, *British Journal of Psychology* 45 (2), 94–107.

Goldman-Eisler, F (1961) The significance of changes in the rate of articulation, *Language and Speech* 4 (3), 171–174.

Goldman-Eisler, F (1968) *Psycholinguistics: Experiments in Spontaneous Speech*, London: Academic Press.

Goulden, R, Nation, I S P and Read, J (1990) How large can a receptive vocabulary be?, *Applied Linguistics* 11 (4), 341–363.

Grabe, E and Low, E L (2002) *Durational variability in speech and the rhythm class hypothesis*, in Gussenhoven, C and Warner, N (Eds) *Laboratory Phonology*, Berlin: Mouton de Gruyter, 515–546.

Graddol, D (2004) The Future of Language, *Science* 27, 1,329–1,331.

Graddol, D (2006) *English Next: Why Global English May Mean the End of English as a Foreign Language*, The British Council.

Graham, S (2011) Self efficacy and academic listening, *Journal of English for Academic Purposes* 10, 113–117.

Graham, S, Santos, D and Vanderplank, R (2008) Listening comprehension and strategy use: a longitudinal exploration, *System* 36 (1), 52–68.

Granström, B, House, D and Karlsson, I (Eds) (2002) *Multimodality in Language and Speech*, Berlin: Springer.

Green, A (2007) *IELTS Washback in Context: Preparation for Academic Writing in Higher Education*, Studies in Language Testing volume 25, Cambridge: UCLES/Cambridge University Press.

Green, A (2012) *Language Functions Revisited: Theoretical and Empirical bases for Language Construct Definition Across the Ability Range*, English Profile Studies volume 2, Cambridge: UCLES/Cambridge University Press.

Green, A and Hawkey, R (2004) Test Washback and Impact: What do they mean and why do they matter?, *Modern English Teacher* 13, 66–72.

Green, A and Maycock, L (2004) Computer-based IELTS and paper-based versions of IELTS, *Research Notes* 18, 3–6.

Green, K P (1998) The use of auditory and visual information during phonetic processing: implications for theories of speech perception, in Campbell, R and Dodd, B (Eds) *Hearing by Eye II: Advances in the Psychology of Speechreading and Audiovisual Speech*, Hove: Psychology Press, 3–25.

Griffiths, R (1992) Speech rate and listening comprehension: Further evidence of the relationship, *TESOL Quarterly* 26 (2), 385–390.

Grosjean, F (1985) The recognition of words after their acoustic offsets: Evidence and implications, *Perception and Psychophysics* 38, 299–310.

Grosjean, F and Gee, J (1987) Prosody structure and spoken word recognition, *Cognition* 25, 135–155.

Gruba, P A (1999) *The role of digital video media in second language listening comprehension*, unpublished PhD thesis, University of Melbourne.

Gude, K and Duckworth, M (2002) *Proficiency Masterclass: Students Book*, Oxford: Oxford University Press.

Gulliksen, H (1950) *Theory of Mental Tests*, New York: Wiley.

Gutteridge, M (2010) *Review of Cambridge ESOL hearing-impaired versions*, internal Cambridge ESOL report.

Haberlandt, K and Graesser, A C (1985) Component processes in text comprehension and some of their interactions, *Journal of Experimental Psychology: General* 114, 357–374

Hackett, E (2005) The development of a computer-based version of PET, *Research Notes* 22, 9–13.

Hackett, E (2008) Adapting listening tests for on-screen use, *Research Notes* 32, 23–25.

Hackett, E, Geranpayeh, A and Somers, A (2006) *Listening skills group spelling project: Investigating the impact of the revision of an FCE 4 productive task mark scheme based on the recommendations of four external consultants*, Cambridge ESOL internal report.

Haertel, E H (2006) Reliability, in Brennan, R L (Ed.) *Educational Measurement*, Westport, CT: American Council on Education/Praeger Publishers, 4th edn, 65–110.

Hale, G A and Courtney, R (1994) The effects of note-taking on listening comprehension in the Test of English as a Foreign Language, *Language Testing* 11 (1), 29–47.

Halliday, M A K (1994) *An Introduction to Functional Grammar*, London: Edward Arnold, 2nd edn.

Hambleton, R K and Kanjee, A (1995) Increasing the validity of cross-cultural assessments: use of improved methods for test adaptations, *European Journal of Psychological Assessment* 11 (3), 147–157.

Hambleton, R K and Pitoniak, M J (2006) Setting performance standards, in *Educational Measurement 4th edition*, USA: American Council on Education & Praeger Publishers, 433–470.

Hamp-Lyons, L (1987) Cambridge First Certificate in English, in Alderson, J C, Krahnke, K and Stansfield, C W (Eds), *Reviews of English Language Proficiency Tests*, Washington, DC: TESOL, 18-19.

Hamp-Lyons, L (1997) Washback, impact and validity: ethical concerns, *Language Testing* 14 (3), 295–303.

Hamp-Lyons, L (1998) Ethical test preparation practice: the case of the TOEFL, *TESOL Quarterly* 32 (2), 329–337.

Hamp-Lyons, L (2000) Social, professional and individual responsibility testing, *System* 28, 579–591.

Hansen, C and Jensen, C (1994) Evaluating lecture comprehension, in Flowerdew, J (Ed.), *Academic Listening: Research Perspectives*, Cambridge: Cambridge University Press.

Harding, L (2011) *The Use of Speakers with L2 Accents in Academic English Learning Listening Assessment: A Validation Study*, Frankfurt: Peter Lang.

Hawkey, R (2002) *The Cambridge ESOL Progetto Lingue 2000 Impact Study*, full report to The Ministry of Education, Italy and Cambridge ESOL.

Hawkey, R (2004) *A Modular Approach to Testing English Language Skills: The Development of the Certificates in English Language Skills (CELS) Examinations*, Studies in Language Testing volume 16, Cambridge: UCLES/ Cambridge University Press.

Hawkey, R (2006) *Impact Theory and Practice: Studies of the IELTS test and Progetto Lingue 2000*, Studies in Language Testing volume 24, Cambridge: UCLES/Cambridge University Press.

Hawkey, R (2007) The 2004–2008 FCE and CAE Review Project: historical context and perennial themes, *Cambridge ESOL Research Reports* 30, 2–8.

Hawkey, R (2009) *Examining FCE and CAE: Key Issues and Recurring Themes in Developing the First Certificate in English and Certificate in Advanced English Examinations*, Studies in Language Testing volume 28, Cambridge: UCLES/ Cambridge University Press.

Hawkey, R, Thompson, S and Turner, R (2007) The development of a video database for language educational research projects, *Learning, Media and Technology* 32 (1), 83–97.

Hawkey, R and Milanovic, M (2013) *Cambridge English Exams- The First Hundred Years: A History of English Language Assessment from the University of Cambridge, 1913-2013*, Studies in Language Testing volume 38, Cambridge: UCLES/Cambridge University Press.

Hawkins, J A and Buttery, P (2010) Criterial features in learner corpora: Theory and illustrations, *English Profile Journal* 1 (1), available online: // journals.cambridge.org/action/displayAbstract?fromPage=online&a id=7908278

Hawkins, J A and Filipović, L (2012) *Criterial Features in L2 English: Specifying the Reference Levels of the Common European Framework*, English Profile Studies Volume 1, Cambridge: UCLES/Cambridge University Press.

Henning, G (1991) *A Study of the Effects of Variation of Short-term Memory Load, Reading Response Length, and Processing Hierarchy on TOEFL Listening Comprehension Item Performance*, Princeton, NJ: Educational Testing Service.

Hindmarsh, R (1980) *Cambridge English Lexicon*, Cambridge: Cambridge University Press.

Holland, P W and Thayer, D T (1988) Differential item performance and the Mantel-Haenzel procedure, in Wainer, H and Braun, H (Eds) *Test Validity*, Hillsdale, NJ: Lawrence Erlbaum Associates, 129–145.

Holland, P W and Wainer, H (Eds) (1993) *Differential Item Functioning*, Hillsdale, NJ: Lawrence Erlbaum, 67–113.

Hudson, R A (1996) *Sociolinguistics*, Cambridge: Cambridge University Press, 2nd edition.

Huff, K L and Sireci, S G (2005) Validity issues in computer-based testing, *Educational Measurement: Issues and Practice* 20 (3), 16–25.

Hughes, A (2003) *Testing for Language Teachers*, Cambridge: Cambridge University Press, 2nd edition.

Hyland, K and Tse, P (2007) Is There an "Academic Vocabulary"?, *TESOL Quarterly* 41 (2), 235–253.

Hymes, D L (1972) On communicative competence, in Pride, J and Holmes, J (Eds) *Sociolinguistics*, Harmondsworth: Penguin.

Ingham, K (2008) The Cambridge ESOL approach to item writer training: the case of ICFE Listening, *Research Notes* 32, 5–9.

In'nami, Y and Koizumi, R (2009) A meta-analysis of test format effects on reading and listening test performance: focus on multiple-choice and open-ended formats, *Language Testing* 26, 219–244.

Interagency Language Roundtable (1985) *Interagency Language Roundtable Language Skill Level Descriptions*, available online: www.govtilr.org/Skills/ILRscale1.htm

International Language Testing Association (2000) *Code of Ethics*, available online: www.iltaonline.com/images/pdfs/ILTA_Code.pdf

International Language Testing Association (2007) *Guidelines for Practice*, available online: www.iltaonline.com/images/pdfs/ILTA_Guidelines.pdf

Jakobson, R (1960) Closing statement: Linguistics and poetics, in Sebeok, T A (Ed.) *Style in Language*, Cambridge, MA: MIT Press, 350–377.

Jenkins, J (2000) *The Phonology of English as an International Language: New Models, New Norms, New Goals*, Oxford: Oxford University Press.

Jenkins, J (2002) A sociolinguistically based, empirically researched pronunciation syllabus for English as an international language, *Applied Linguistics* 23 (1), 83–103.

Jenkins, J (2006) The spread of EIL: a testing time for testers, *ELT Journal* 60 (1), 42–50.

Jennings, S and Bush, M (2006) A comparison of conventional and liberal (free-choice) multiple-choice tests, *Practical Assessment, Research & Evaluation* 11 (8), 1–5.

Jensen, C and Hansen, C (1995) The effect of prior knowledge on EAP listening-test performance, *Language Testing* 12 (1), 99–119.

Johnson, K (2005) The 'general' study of expertise, in Johnson, K (Ed.) *Expertise in Second Language Learning and Teaching*, Basingstoke: Palgrave Macmillan.

Johnson, M K, Bransford, J D and Solomon, S K (1973) Memory for tacit implications of sentences, *Journal of Experimental Psychology* 98, 203–205.

Johnson-Laird, P (1983) *Mental Models*, Cambridge, MA: Harvard University Press.

Joint Council for Qualifications (2011) *Regulations and Guidance – Access Arrangements, Reasonable Adjustments and Special Consideration: General and vocational qualifications*, available online: www.jcq.org.uk/attachments/published/538/AA%20regs%202011-2012%20edited%2011102011.pdf

Jones, N (2000a) Background to the validation of the ALTE can do project and the revised common European framework, *Research Notes* 2, 11–13.

Jones, N (2000b) *Reliability estimates and item weighting: The effect of calculating reliability indices on weighted data*, UCLES internal report.

Jones, N (2001) The ALTE can do project and the role of measurement in constructing a proficiency framework, *Research Notes* 3, 5–8.

Jones, N (2002a) *Cassettes vs CDs for listening, performance of FCE 0101 candidates June–December 2001*, Cambridge ESOL internal report.

Jones, N (2002b) Relating the ALTE Framework to the Common European Framework of Reference, in Alderson, J C (Ed.) *Case Studies in the Use of the Common European Framework*, Strasbourg: Council of Europe, 167–183.

Jones, N and Maycock, L (2007) The comparability of computer-based and paper-based tests: goals, approaches, and a review of research, *Research Notes* 27, 11–14.

Jones, N and Saville, N (2009) European language policy: Assessment, learning and the CEFR, *Annual Review of Applied Linguistics* 29, 51–63.

Jones, N and Saville, N (2010) *Cambridge ESOL and e-assessment*, presentation at the 3rd Cambridge Assessment Conference.

Kachru, B B (1992) *The Other Tongue: English Across Cultures*, Urbana: University of Illinois Press, 2nd edn.

Kane, M T (1992) An argument-based approach to validity, *Psychological Bulletin* 112 (3), 527–535.

Kane, M T (2011) The errors of our ways, *Journal of Educational Measurement* 48 (1), 12–30.

Kane, M T, Crooks, T and Cohen, A (1999) Validating measures of performance, *Educational Measurement: Issues and Practice*, 18 (2), 5–17.

Keddle, J S (2004) The CEF and the secondary school syllabus, in Morrow, K (Ed.) *Insights from the Common European Framework*, Oxford: Oxford University Press, 43–54.

Khalifa, H (2005) *CAE Paper 4 Part 4 Modifications*, Cambridge ESOL internal research and validation report No. 724.

Khalifa, H and Weir, C J (2009) *Examining Reading: Research and Practice in Assessing Second Language Reading*, Studies in Language Testing volume 29, Cambridge: UCLES/Cambridge University Press.

Khalifa, H, ffrench, A and Salamoura, A (2010) Maintaining alignment to the CEFR: The FCE case study in Martyniuk, W (Ed.) *Aligning tests with the CEFR: Reflections on Using the Council of Europe's Draft Manual,* Studies in Language Testing volume 33, Cambridge: UCLES/Cambridge University Press, 80–101.

Kinneavy, J E (1969) The basic aims of discourse, *College Composition and Discourse* 20 (5), 297–304.

Kintsch, W (1998) *Comprehension: A Paradigm for Cognition*, Cambridge: Cambridge University Press.

Kintsch, W and van Dijk, T (1983) Towards a model of text comprehension and production, *Psychological Review* 85, 363–94.

Kintsch, W and Yarborough, J C (1982) Role of rhetorical structure in text comprehension, *Journal of Educational Psychology* 74 (6), 828–834.

Klatt, D H (1979) Speech perception: a model of acoustic-phonetic analysis and lexical access, *Journal of Phonetics* 7, 279–312.

Kobeleva, P P (2008) *The impact of unfamiliar proper names on ESL learners' listening comprehension*, unpublished PhD thesis, Victoria University of Wellington, New Zealand.

Kolen, M J and Brennan, R L (2004) *Test Equating, Scaling and Linking: Methods and Practices*, NY: Springer.

Kormos, J (2006) *Speech Production and Second Language Acquisition*, Mahwah, New Jersey: Lawrence Erlbaum Associates.

Koskey, K L, Karabenick, S A, Woolley, M E, Bonney, C R and Dever, B V (2010) Cognitive validity of students' self-reports of classroom mastery goal structure: What students are thinking and why it matters, *Contemporary Educational Psychology* 35 (4), 254–263.

Kounios, J and Holcomb, P J (1994) Concreteness effects in semantic processing: ERP evidence supporting dual-encoding theory, *Journal of Experimental Psychology: Learning, Memory and Cognition* 20 (4), 804–823.

Kunnan, A J (1995) *Test Taker Characteristics and Test Performance: a Structural Modelling Approach*, Studies in Language Testing volume 2, Cambridge: UCLES/Cambridge University Press.

Kunnan, A J (2000) Fairness and justice for all, in Kunnan, A J (Ed.), *Fairness and Validation in Language Assessment, Selected Papers from the 19th LTRC, Orlando, Florida*, Studies in Language Testing volume 9, Cambridge: UCLES/ Cambridge University Press, 1–14.

Kunnan, A (2003) The art of nonconversation by M Johnson, *The Modern Language Journal* 87, 338–340.

Kunnan, A J (2004) Test fairness, in Milanovic, M and Weir, C J (Eds), *European Language Testing in a Global Context*, Studies in Language Testing volume 18, Cambridge: UCLES/Cambridge University Press, 27–48.

Kunnan, A J (2008) Towards a model of test evaluation: using the Test Fairness and Test Context Frameworks, in Taylor, L and Weir, C J (Eds), *Multilingualism and Assessment: Achieving Transparency, Assuring Quality Sustaining Diversity – Proceedings of the ALTE Berlin Conference May 2005*, Studies in Language Testing volume 27, Cambridge: UCLES/Cambridge University Press, 229–251.

Larichev, O I (1992) Cognitive validity in design of decision-aiding techniques, *Journal of Multi-Criteria Decision Analysis* 1, 127–138.

Larkin, J H and Simon, H A (1987) Why a diagram is (sometimes) worth ten thousand words, *Cognitive Science* 11 (1), 65–100.

Laufer, B (1997) What's in a word that makes it hard or easy: some intra-lexical factors that affect the learning of words, in Schmitt, N and McCarthy, M (Eds) *Vocabulary: Description, Acquisition and Pedagogy*, Cambridge: Cambridge University Press, 140–155.

Laufer, B and Ravenhorst-Kalovski, G C (2010) Lexical threshold revisited:

Lexical text coverage, learners' vocabulary size and reading comprehension, *Reading in a Foreign Language* 22 (1), 15–30.

Lee, D Y W (2001) Defining core vocabulary and tracking its distribution across spoken and written genres, *Journal of English Linguistics* 29 (3), 250–278.

Leung, C and Lewkowicz, J (2006) Expanding horizons and unsolved conundrums: Language testing and assessment, *TESOL Quarterly* 40 (1), 211–234.

Levelt, W J M (1987) *Speaking*, Cambridge MA: MIT Press

Levinson, S C (1983) *Pragmatics*, Cambridge: Cambridge University Press.

Lewkowicz, J (2000) Authenticity in language testing: some outstanding questions, *Language Testing* 17 (1), 43–64.

Lewkowicz, J (2007) *Should authenticity continue to trouble language testers (and teachers)?*, paper presented at the TESOL Symposium on English Language Assessment, Kyiv, Ukraine.

Liddicoat, A J (2007) *An Introduction to Conversation Analysis*, London: Continuum.

Lim, G S (2012) Developing and validating a mark scheme for writing, *Research Notes* 49, 6–10.

Lim, G S (forthcoming) Assessing ESL in Europe, in Kunnan, A J (Ed.) *The Companion to Language Assessment*, volume 4, Malden, MA: Wiley-Blackwell.

Lim, G S, Geranpayeh, A, Khalifa, H and Buckendahl, C (forthcoming) Standard setting to an international language framework: Implications for theory and practice, *International Journal of Testing*.

Linacre, J M (2000) Computer-adaptive testing: a methodology whose time has come, MESA Memorandum No. 69, in Chae, S, Kang, U, Jeon, E and Linacre, J M (Eds), *Development of Computerised Middle school Achievement Test*, Seoul, South Korea: Komesa Press.

Linn, R L, Baker, E L and Dunbar, S B (1991) Complex performance-based assessment: Expectations and validation criteria, *Educational Researcher* 20 (8), 5–21.

Little, D (2007) The Common European Framework of Reference for languages: Perspectives on the making of supranational language education policy, *The Modern Language Journal* 91(4), 645–655.

Londe, Z C (2009) The effects of video media in English as a second language listening comprehension tests, *Issues in Applied Linguistics* 17 (1), 41–50.

Long, M (1990) Maturational constraints on language development, *Studies in Second Language Acquisition* 3 (12), 251-285.

Lord, F M (1977) A study of item bias, using item characteristic curve theory, in Poortinga, Y H (Ed.) *Basic Problems in Cross-cultural Psychology*, Amsterdam: Swets & Zeitlinger, 19–29.

Lord, F M (1980) *Applications of Item Response Theory to Practical Testing Problems*, Hillsdale NJ: Erlbaum.

Lord, F M and Novick, M R (1968) *Statistical Theories of Mental Test Scores*, Reading, MA: Addison-Wesley.

Lund, R J (1991) A comparison of second language listening and reading comprehension, *Modern Language Journal* 75 (2), 196–204.

Lynch, T (2009) *Teaching Second Language Listening*, Oxford: Oxford University Press.

Lynch, T (2011) Academic listening in the 21st century: Reviewing a decade of research, *Journal of English for Academic Purposes* 10 (2), 79–88.

Lyons, J (1977) *Semantics: Vol.1*, Cambridge: Cambridge University Press.

Macaro, E, Graham, S and Vanderplank, R (2007) A review of listening strategies: focus on sources of knowledge and on success, in Cohen, A D and Macaro, E (Eds) *Language Learner Strategies*, Oxford: Oxford University Press.

MacWhinney, B and Bates, E (Eds) (1989) *The Crosslinguistic Study of Sentence Processing*, New York: Cambridge University Press.

Marsen, S (2006) How to mean without saying: Presupposition and implication revisited, *Semiotica* 160, 243–263.

Marshall, H (2006) The Cambridge ESOL item banking system, *Research Notes* 23, 3–5.

Marslen-Wilson, W (1973) Linguistic structure and speech shadowing at very short latencies, *Nature* 244, 522–523.

Marslen-Wilson, W (1989) Access and integration: projecting sound on to meaning, in Marslen-Wilson, W (Ed.) *Lexical Representation and Process*, Cambridge, MA: MIT Press.

Martinez, R and Schmitt, N (2011) *Assessing L2 knowledge of multiword expressions*, paper presented at AAAL, Chicago, 26 March 2011, available online: nottingham.academia.edu/RonMartinez/Talks/38238/Assessing_L2_knowledge_of_multiword_expressions

Martyniuk, W (Ed.) (2010) *Aligning Tests with the CEFR: Reflections on Using the Council of Europe's Draft Manual*, Studies in Language Testing volume 33, Cambridge: UCLES/Cambridge University Press.

Maycock, L (2005) *Investigating the comparability of paper-based and computer-based versions of PET: Findings of the February 2005 equivalence trial*, Cambridge ESOL internal report.

Maycock, L and Green, A B (2004) *An investigation into the effects of computer familiarity and attitudes towards CB IELTS on candidate performance*, Cambridge ESOL internal report.

Maycock, L and Green, A B (2005) The effects on performance of computer familiarity and attitudes towards CB IELTS, *Research Notes* 20, 3–8.

McCarthy, M J and Carter, R A (1995) Spoken language: What is it and how can we teach it?, *ELT Journal* 49 (3), 207–218.

McCarthy, M J and Carter, R A (1997) Grammar, tails, and affect: Constructing expressive choices in discourse, *Interdisciplinary Journal for the Study of Discourse* 17 (3), 405–429.

McCarthy, M J and Carter, R A (2001) Ten criteria for a spoken grammar, in Hinkel, E and Fotos, S (Eds) *New Perspectives on Grammar Teaching in Second Language Classrooms*, Mahwah, NJ: Lawrence Erlbaum, 51–75.

McClelland, J L and Elman, J L (1986) The TRACE model of speech perception, *Cognitive Psychology* 18, 1–86.

McDonald, R P (1999) *Test Theory: A Unified Treatment*, Mahwah, NJ: Lawrence Erlbaum Associates.

McDowell, C and Merrylees, B (1998) Survey of receiving institutions' use and attitude to IELTS, *IELTS Research Reports* 1, 6–139.

McGurk, H and MacDonald, J (1976) Hearing lips and seeing voices, *Nature* 264, 746–748.

McLaughlin, M and Shepard, L (1995) *Improving Education Through Standards-based Reform. A Report By the National Academy of Education Panel on Standards-based Education Reform*, Stanford, CA: National Academy of Education.

McNamara, T (1996) *Measuring Second Language Performance*, London: Longman.

McNamara, T (2000) *Language Testing*, Oxford: Oxford University Press.

McNamara, T (2006) Validity in language testing: The challenge of Sam Messick's legacy, *Language Assessment Quarterly* 3 (1), 31–51.

McNamara, T and Lumley, T (1997) The effect of interlocutor and assessment mode variables in overseas assessments of speaking skills in occupational settings, *Language Testing* 14 (2), 140–156.

McNamara, T and Roever, C (2006) *Language Testing: The Social Dimension*, Malden, MA and Oxford: Blackwell.

McQueen, J (2007) Eight questions about spoken word recognition, in Gaskell, G, *The Oxford Handbook of Psycholinguistics*, Oxford: Oxford University Press, 37–54

Meara, P (1997) Toward a new approach to modelling vocabulary acquisition, in Schmitt, N and McCarthy, M (Eds) *Vocabulary: Description, Acquisition and Pedagogy*, Cambridge: Cambridge University Press, 109–121

Mehrens, W (1998) Consequences of assessment: what is the evidence?, *Evaluation Policy Analysis Archives* 6 (13).

Mehrpour, S and Rahimi, M (2010) The impact of general and specific vocabulary knowledge on reading and listening comprehension: A case of Iranian EFL learners, *System* 38 (2), 292–300.

Merrylees, B (2003) An impact study of two IELTS user groups: candidates who sit the test for immigration purposes and candidates who sit the test for secondary education purposes, *IELTS Research Reports* 4, 1–58.

Messick, S (1989) Validity, in Linn, R L (Ed.), *Educational Measurement*, Washington DC: The American Council on Education and the National Council on Measurement in Education, 3rd edn, 13–103.

Messick, S (1995) Validity of psychological assessment: Validation of inferences from persons' responses and performance as scientific inquiry into scoring meaning, *American Psychologist* 9, 741–749.

Messick, S (1996) Validity and washback in language testing, *Language Testing* 13 (4), 241–256.

Meunier, L E (1994) Computer adaptive language tests (CALT) offer potential for functional testing. Yet, why don't they?, *CALICO Journal* 11 (4), 23–39.

Milanovic, M (2003) Series Editors' note, in Weir, C J and Milanovic, M (Eds) (2003) *Continuity and Innovation: Revising the Cambridge Proficiency in English Examination 1913–2002,* Studies in Language Testing volume 15, Cambridge: UCLES/Cambridge University Press, xv–xx.

Milanovic, M (2009) Cambridge ESOL and the CEFR, *Research Notes* 37, 2–5.

Milanovic, M and Saville, N (1996) *Considering the impact of Cambridge EFL examinations – Principles of Good Practice*, internal UCLES EFL paper.

Milanovic, M and Weir, C J (2010) Series Editors' note, in Martyniuk, W (Ed.) *Aligning Tests with the CEFR: Reflections on Using the Council of Europe's Draft Manual,* Studies in Language Testing volume 33, Cambridge: UCLES/Cambridge University Press, viii–xx.

Miller, G (1956) The magical number seven, plus or minus two: some limits on our capacity for processing information, *Psychological Review* 63 (2) 81–97.

Ministry of Education (Italy) (1999) *Progetto Lingue in Communicazionedi Servizio,* September 1999 *[www.istruzione.it/argomenti/autonomia/documenti.]*

Mislevy, R J, Almond, R G and Lukas, J F (2003) *A Brief Introduction to Evidence – Centred Design*, Research Report RR-03-16, Princeton, NJ: Educational Testing Service.

Mislevy, R J, Steinberg, L S and Almond, R G (2002) Design and analysis in task-based language assessment (TBLA), *Language Testing* 19 (4), 477–496.

Mislevy, R J, Steinberg, L S and Almond, R G (2003) On the structure of educational assessment, *Measurement: Interdisciplinary Research and Perspective* 1 (1), 3–62.

Moon, R (1997) Vocabulary connections: multi-word items in English, in Schmitt, N and McCarthy, M (Eds) *Vocabulary: Description, Acquisition and Pedagogy*, Cambridge: Cambridge University Press, 40–63.

Moreno, R, Martínez, R J and Muñiz, J (2004) Directrices para la construcción de ítems de elección multiple [Guidelines for the construction of multiple-choice items], *Psicothema* 16 (3), 490–497.

Moreno, R, Martínez, R J and Muñiz, J (2006) New guidelines for developing multiple-choice items, *Methodology* 2 (2), 65–72.

Morrow, K (1979) Communicative language testing: revolution or evolution?, in Brumfit, C and Johnson, K (Eds) *The Communicative Approach to Language Teaching*, Oxford: Oxford University Press, 143–157.

Munby, J L (1978) *Communicative Syllabus Design*, Cambridge: Cambridge University Press.

Murray, S (2007) Reviewing the CAE Listening test, *Cambridge ESOL Research Reports* 30, 1–28.

Nakatsuhara, F (2011) The relationship between test-takers' listening proficiency and their performance on the IELTS Speaking Test, *IELTS Jointly Funded and Published Research Volume 12*, available online: www.ielts.org/pdf/Vol12_Report4.pdf

Nassaji, H (2006) The relationship between depth of vocabulary knowledge and L2 learners' lexical inferencing strategy use and success, *Modern Language Journal* 90 (3), 387–401.

Nation, I S P (1990) *Teaching and Learning Vocabulary*, New York: Newbury House.

Nation, I S P (2001) *Learning Vocabulary in Another Language*, Cambridge: Cambridge University Press.

National Commission on Excellence in Education (1983) *A Nation at Risk: The Imperative For Educational Reform*, Washington DC: United States Government Printing.

National Governors Association Center for Best Practices and Council of Chief State School Officers (2011) *Common Core State Standards Initiative*, available online: www.corestandards.org

Nevo, N (1989) Test-taking strategies on a multiple-choice test of reading comprehension, *Language Testing* 6 (2), 199–215.

Ng, A W Y and Chan, A H S (2009) Different methods of Multiple-choice test: implications and design for further research, *Proceedings of the International MultiConference of Engineers and Computer Scientists*, available online: www.iaeng.org/publication/IMECS2009/IMECS2009_pp1958–1963.pdf

Nitko, A J (1996) *Educational Assessment of Students,* New Jersey: Prentice Hall.

Norris, D, McQueen, J, Cutler, A and Butterfield, S (1997). The possible word constraint in the segmentation of continuous speech, *Cognitive Psychology* 34, 191–243.

North, B (2004) Europe's framework promotes discussion, not directives, *Guardian Weekly*, 15 April, available online: www.guardian.co.uk/education/2004/apr/15/tefl6

North, B (2006) *The Common European Framework of Reference: development, theoretical and practical issues*, paper presented at the symposium 'A New Direction in Foreign Language Education: The Potential of the Common

European Framework of Reference for Languages', Osaka University of Foreign Studies, Japan, March 2006.

North, B (2008) The CEFR levels and descriptor scales, in Taylor, L and Weir, C J (Eds) *Multilingualism and Assessment: Achieving Transparency, Assuring Quality, Sustaining Diversity – Proceedings of the ALTE Berlin Conference, May 2005*, Studies in Language Testing volume 27, Cambridge: UCLES/ Cambridge University Press, 21–66.

North, B (2009) The educational and social impact of the CEFR, in Taylor, L and Weir, C J (Eds) *Language Testing Matters: Investigating the Wider Social and Educational Impact of Assessment – Proceedings of the ALTE Cambridge Conference, April 2008*, Studies in Language Testing volume 31, Cambridge: UCLES/Cambridge University Press, 357–377.

Nygaard, L C and Pisoni, D B (1995) Speech perception: new directions in research and theory, in Miller, J L and Eimas, P D (Eds) *Speech, Language and Communication*, San Diego, CA: Academic Press, 63–96.

Oakhill, J and Garnham, M (1988) *Becoming a Skilled Reader*, London: Blackwell.

Ockey, G J (2007) Construct implications of including still image or video in computer-based listening tests, *Language Testing* 24 (4), 517–537.

Ockey, G J (2009) Developments and challenges in the use of computer-based testing for assessing second language ability, *Modern Language Journal* 93 (1), 836–847.

O'Donnell, K (1990) Difference and dominance: how labor and management talk conflict, in Grimshaw, A D (Ed.) *Conflict Talk*, Cambridge: Cambridge University Press, 210–240.

Ogiermann, E (2007) Gender-based differences in English apology realisations, in Kraft, B and Geluykens, R (Eds) *Cross-Cultural Pragmatics and Interlanguage English*, Munich: LINCOM.

O'Sullivan, B (2000) *Towards a model of performance in oral language testing*, unpublished PhD thesis, University of Reading.

O'Sullivan, B (2006) *Issues in Testing Business English: The Revision of the Cambridge Business English Certificates*, Studies in Language Testing volume 17, Cambridge: UCLES/Cambridge University Press.

O'Sullivan, B (2011) Introduction, in O'Sullivan (Ed.), *Language Testing: Theories and Practices*, Basingstoke: Palgrave Macmillan, 1–12.

O'Sullivan, B and Green, A (2011) Test taker characteristics, in Taylor, L (Ed.) *Examining Speaking: Research and Practice in Assessing Second Language Speaking*, Studies in Language Testing volume 30, Cambridge: UCLES/ Cambridge University Press, 36–64.

O'Sullivan, B, Weir, C J and Saville, N (2002) Using observation checklists to validate speaking test tasks, *Language Testing* 19 (1), 33–56.

Paivio, A, Walsh, M and Bons, T (1994) Concreteness effects on memory: when and why?, *Journal of Experimental Psychology: Learning, Memory and Cognition* 20, 1,196–1,204.

Papp, S and Rixon, S (forthcoming) *Assessing Younger Language Learners*, Cambridge: UCLES/Cambridge University Press.

Pashler, H and Johnston, J C (1998) Attentional limitations in dual task performance, in Pashler, H (Ed.) *Attention*, Hove: Psychology Press, 155–189.

Peterson, E R, Rayner, S G and Armstrong, S J (2009) Researching the psychology of cognitive style and learning style: Is there really a future?, *Learning and Individual Differences* 19 (4), 518–523.

Pisoni, D B (1997) Some thoughts on "normalization" in speech perception, in Johnson, K and Mullennix, J W (Eds) *Talker Variability in Speech Processing*, San Diego: Academic Press, 33–66.

Pollack, I and Pickett, J M (1963) The intelligibility of excerpts from conversation, *Language and Speech* 6, 165–71.

Progosh, D (1996) Using video for listening assessment: opinions of test-takers, *TESL Canada Journal* 14 (1), 34–44.

Proudfoot S (2010) *A productive use of testing time? An analysis of listening test responses and how they relate to the construct being measured*, unpublished MA thesis, University of Leicester, UK.

Raju, N S (1988) The area between two item characteristic curves, *Psychometrika* 53, 495–502.

Ramsaran, S (1978) *Phonetic and phonological correlates of style in English: a preliminary investigation*, unpublished PhD thesis, University of London.

Rea-Dickins, P, Kiely, R and Yu, G (2007) Student identity, learning and progression: The affective and academic impact of IELTS on 'successful' candidates, *IELTS Research Reports Volume 7*, 5–136.

Riding, R J (1997) On the nature of cognitive style, *Educational Psychology: An International Journal of Experimental Educational Psychology* 17 (1–2), 29–49.

Roach, J O (1944) *The Cambridge Examinations in English: a survey of their history*, personal papers of J O Roach.

Rodriguez, M C (2005) Three options are optimal for multiple-choice items: a meta-analysis of 80 years of research, *Educational Measurement: Issues and Practice* 24 (2), 3–12.

Rogers, J and Swaminathan, H (1989) *A logistic regression procedure for detecting item bias*, paper presented at the annual meeting of the American Educational Research Association, San Francisco, 1989.

Rose, D (2008) Vocabulary use in the FCE Listening test, *Research Notes 32*, 9–16.

Rost, M (1990) *Listening in Language Learning*, London: Longman.

Rost, M (2002) *Teaching and Researching Listening*, Harlow: Pearson Education.

Ruiz-Primo, M A and Shavelson, R J (1996) Rhetoric and reality in science performance assessments: An update, *Journal of Research in Science Teaching* 33 (10), 1,045–1,063.

Ruiz-Primo, M A, Schultz, S E, Li, M and Shavelson, R J (2001) On the validity of cognitive interpretations of scores from alternative concept-mapping techniques, *Educational Assessment* 7 (2), 9–141.

Rupp, A A, Ferne, T and Choi, H (2006) How assessing reading comprehension with multiple-choice questions shapes the construct: a cognitive processing perspective, *Language Testing* 23 (4), 441–474.

Sadler-Smith, E (2011) The intuitive style: Relationships with local/global and verbal/visual styles, gender, and superstitious reasoning, *Learning and Individual Differences* 21 (3), 263–270.

Salisbury, K (2005) *The edge of expertise: towards an understanding of listening test item writing as professional practice*, unpublished doctoral thesis, King's College London.

Sanford, A J and Garrod, S C (1981) *Understanding Written Language: Explanations of Comprehension beyond the Sentence*, Chichester: John Wiley.

Saville, N (2003) The process of test development and revision within UCLES EFL, in Weir, C J and Milanovic, M (Eds) *Continuity and innovation: Revising the Cambridge Proficiency in English examination 1913–2002*, Studies in

Language Testing volume 15, Cambridge: UCLES/Cambridge University Press, 57 – 120.

Saville, N (2009) *Developing a model for investigating the impact of language assessment within educational contexts by a public exam provider*, unpublished PhD thesis, University of Bedfordshire.

Saville, N (2010) Auditing the quality profile: From code of practice to standards, *Research Notes* 39, 24-28.

Saville, N and Hawkey, R (2004) The IELTS Impact Study: investigating washback on teaching materials, in Cheng, L, Watanabe, Y and Curtis, A (Eds), *Washback in Language Testing: Research Contexts and Methods*, London: Lawrence Erlbaum Associates, 73–96.

Schank, R C and Abelson, R (1977) *Scripts, Plans, Goals and Understanding*, Hillsdale, NJ: Erlbaum.

Schmidt-Rinehart (1994) The Effects of Topic Familiarity on Second Language Listening Comprehension, *Modern Language Journal* 78 (2), 179–189.

Schwanenflugel, P J and Stowe, R W (1989) Context availability and the processing of abstract-concrete words in sentences, *Reading Research Quarterly* 24 (1), 114–126.

Seidelhofer, B, Breiteneder, A and Pitzl, M (2006) English as a lingua franca in Europe: Challenges for applied linguistics, *Annual Review of Applied Linguistics* 26, 3–34.

Shaw, S D and Weir, C J (2007) *Examining Writing: Research and Practice in Assessing Second Language Writing*, Studies in Language Testing volume 26, Cambridge: UCLES/Cambridge University Press.

Sheerin, S (1987) Listening comprehension: teaching or testing?, *ELT Journal* 41 (2), 126–31.

Shepard, L, Camilli, G and Williams, D M (1984) Accounting for statistical artifacts in item bias research, *Journal of Educational and Behavioral Statistics* 9 (2), 93–128.

Sherman, J (1997) *The effect of question preview in listening comprehension tests*, Language Testing 14 (2), 185–213.

Shohamy, E (1997) Testing methods, testing consequences: are they ethical? Are they fair?, *Language Testing* 14 (3), 340–349.

Shohamy, E (2001) *The Power of Tests: A Critical Perspective on the Uses of Language Tests*, Harlow: Pearson Education.

Shohamy, E (2008) Introduction to Volume 7: Language Testing and Assessment, in Shohamy, E and Hornberger, N (Eds), *Encyclopedia of Language and Education*, Language Testing and Assessment, Volume 7, New York: Springer Science+Business Media LLC, 2nd edn, xiii–xxii.

Shohamy, E and Inbar, O (1991) Validation of listening comprehension tests: the effect of text and question type, *Language Testing* 8 (1), 23–40.

Shohamy, E, Donitsa-Schmidt S and Ferman, I (1996) Test impact revisited: Washback effect over time, *Language Testing* 13 (3), 298–317.

Simpson-Vlach, R and Ellis, N C (2010) An academic formulas list: New methods in phraseology research, *Applied Linguistics* 31 (4), 487–512.

Singer, M (2007) Inference processing in discourse comprehension, in Gaskell, G (Ed.) *The Oxford Handbook of Psycholinguistics*, Oxford: Oxford University Press, 343–359.

Small, M Y (1990) *Cognitive Development*, Orlando, FL: Harcourt Brace Jovanovich.

Smith, H and Haslett, S (2007) Attitudes of tertiary key decision-makers towards English language tests in Aotearoa New Zealand: Report on the results of a national provider survey, *IELTS Research Reports Volume 7*, 2–44.

Snow, R E, Corno, L and Jackson, D (1996) Individual differences in affective and conative functions, in Berliner, D C and Calfee, R C (Eds) *Handbook of Educational Psychology*, New York: Macmillan, 243–310.

Somers, A (2007) *Headphones vs loudspeakers for listening*, Cambridge ESOL internal report.

Spearman, C (1904) 'General intelligence,' objectively determined and measured, *The American Journal of Psychology* 15 (2), 201–292.

Spolsky, B (1981) Some ethical questions about language testing, in Klein-Braley, C and Stevenson, D (Eds) *Practice and Problems in Language Testing*, Frankfurt am Main: Verlag Peter D Lang, 5–30.

Spolsky, B (1985) The limits of authenticity in language testing, *Language Testing* 2 (1), 31–40.

Spolsky, B (1989) Communicative competence, language proficiency, and beyond, *Applied Linguistics* 10 (2), 138–156.

Spolsky, B (1995) *Measured Words*, Oxford: Oxford University Press.

Spolsky, B (2008) Introduction – Language Testing at 25: Maturity and responsibility?, *Language Testing* 25 (3), 297–305.

Spratt, M (2005) Washback and the classroom: the implications for teaching and learning of studies of washback from exams, *Language Teaching Research* 9 (1), 5–29.

Stæhr, L S (2008) Vocabulary size and the skills of listening, reading and writing, *Language Learning Journal* 36 (2), 139–152.

Stæhr, L S (2009) Vocabulary knowledge and advanced listening comprehension in English as a Foreign Language, *Studies in Second Language Acquisition* 31, 577–607.

Stanovich, K E (1980) Toward an interactive-compensatory model of individual differences in the development of reading fluency, *Reading Research Quarterly* 16, 32–71.

Stevens, B (2004) A common solution to a common European challenge, *Research Notes* 17, 2–6.

Suvurov, R (2011) The effects of context visuals on L2 listening comprehension, *Research Notes* 45, 2–8.

Sweet, H (1899) *The Practical Study of Languages*, London: Dent.

Swinney, D (1979) Lexical access during sentence comprehension: (Re-) consideration of context effects, *Journal of Verbal Learning and Verbal Behavior* 5, 219–227.

Tannen, D (1982a) The oral/literate continuum in discourse, in Tannen, D (Ed.) *Spoken and Written Language: Exploring Orality and Literacy*, Norwood, NJ: Ablex, 1–16.

Tannen, D (1982b) Oral and literate strategies in spoken and written narratives, *Language* 58 (1), 1–21.

Tauroza, S and Allison, D (1990) Speech rates in British English, *Applied Linguistics* 11 (1), 90–105.

Taylor, L (1999) *Constituency matters: responsibilities and relationships in our testing community*, paper delivered to the Language Testing Forum, University of Edinburgh, 19–21 November 1999.

Taylor, L (2000) Stakeholders in language testing, *Research Notes* 2, 2–4.

Taylor, L (2001) Revising the IELTS Speaking test, *Research Notes* 6, 9–11.

Taylor, L (2002) Assessing learners' English: But whose/which English(es)?, *Research Notes* 10, 18–20.

Taylor, L (2004) Issues of test comparability, *Research Notes* 15, 2–5.

Taylor, L (2006) The changing landscape of English: implications for language assessment, *ELT Journal* 60 (1), 51–60.

Taylor, L (2008) Language varieties and their implications for testing and assessment, in Taylor, L and Weir, C J (Eds) *Multilingualism and Assessment: Achieving Transparency, Assuring Quality, Sustaining Diversity*, Studies in Language Testing volume 27, Cambridge: UCLES/Cambridge University Press, 276–295

Taylor, L (2009a) Developing assessment literacy, *Annual Review of Applied Linguistics* 29 (1), 21–36.

Taylor, L (2009b) Setting language standards for teaching and assessment: a matter of principle, politics or prejudice?, in Taylor, L and Weir, C J (Eds) *Language Testing Matters: Investigating the Wider Social and Educational Impact of Assessment – Proceedings of the ALTE Cambridge Conference, April 2008*, Studies in Language Testing 31, Cambridge: UCLES/Cambridge University Press, 139–157.

Taylor, L (2011) (Ed.) *Examining Speaking: Research and Practice in Assessing Second Language Speaking*, Studies in Language Testing volume 30, Cambridge: UCLES/Cambridge University Press.

Taylor, L (2012a) Accommodation in language testing, in Coombe, C, Davidson, P, O'Sullivan, B and Stoynoff, S (Eds) *The Cambridge Guide to Second Language Assessment*, Cambridge: Cambridge University Press, 307–315.

Taylor, L (2012b) Introduction, in Taylor, L and Weir, C J (Eds) *IELTS Collected Papers 2: Research in Reading and Listening Assessment*, Studies in Language Testing volume 34, Cambridge: UCLES/ Cambridge University Press, 1–33.

Taylor, L and Falvey, P (Eds) (2007) *IELTS Collected Papers: Research in Speaking and Writing Assessment,* Studies in Language Testing volume 19, Cambridge: UCLES/Cambridge University Press.

Taylor, L and Geranpayeh, A (2011) Assessing listening for academic purposes: defining and operationalising the test construct, *Journal of English for Academic Purposes* 10 (2), 89–101.

Taylor, L, and Jones, N (2006) Cambridge ESOL exams and the common European framework of reference (CEFR), *Research Notes* 24, 2–5.

Taylor, L and Weir, C J (2012) Introduction, in Taylor, L and Weir, C J (Eds) *IELTS Collected Papers 2: Research in Reading and Listening Assessment*, Studies in Language Testing volume 34, Cambridge: UCLES/Cambridge University Press, 1–33.

Thelk, A D and Hoole, E R (2006) What are you thinking? Postsecondary student think-alouds of scientific and quantitative reasoning items, *Journal of General Education* 55 (1), 17–39.

Thighe, D, Jones, N and Geranpayeh, A (2001) *IELTS PB and CB equivalence: A comparison of equated versions of the reading and listening components of paper-based IELTS in relation to CB IELTS*, Cambridge ESOL internal report.

Thissen, D, Steinberg, L and Wainer, H (1993) Detection of differential item functioning using the parameters of item response models, in Holland, P W and Wainer, H (Eds) *Differential Item Functioning*, Hillsdale, NJ: Lawrence Erlbaum, 67–113.

Thomas, P R and McKay, J B (2010) Cognitive styles and instructional design in university learning, *Learning and Individual Differences* 20 (3), 197–202.

Thompson, B and Levitov, J E (1985) Using microcomputers to score and evaluate test items, *Collegiate Microcomputer* 3, 163–168.

Thompson, B and Vacha-Haase, T (2000) Psychometrics *is* datametrics: The test is not reliable, *Educational and Psychological Measurement* 60 (2), 174–195.

Toulmin, S E (2003) *The Uses of Argument*, Cambridge: Cambridge University Press.

Tyler, M D (2001) Resource consumption as a function of topic knowledge in nonnative and native comprehension, *Language Learning* 51 (2), 257–280.

Urquhart, A H and Weir, C (1998) *Reading in a Second Language: Process, Product and Practice*, New York: Longman.

Vähäpassi, A (1982) On the specification of the domain of school writing, *Evaluation in Education* 5 (3), 265–289.

Van Dijk, T A and Kintsch, W (1983) *Strategies of Discourse Comprehension*, New York: Academic Press.

van Ek, J A and Trim, J L M (1998a) *Threshold 1990*, Cambridge: Cambridge University Press.

van Ek, J A and Trim, J L M (1998b) *Waystage 1990*, Cambridge: Cambridge University Press.

van Ek, J A and Trim, J L M (2001) *Vantage*, Cambridge: Cambridge University Press.

van Gompel, R P G and Pickering, M J (2007) Syntactic parsing, in Gaskell, G (Ed.) *The Oxford Handbook of Psycholinguistics*, Oxford: Oxford University Press, 289–308.

van Zeeland, H and Schmitt, N (2011) *Lexical coverage and L1 and L2 listening comprehension: The same or different from reading comprehension?*, unpublished manuscript, University of Nottingham, UK.

Vandergrift, L (1997) The Cinderella of communication strategies; Receptive strategies in interactive listening, *Modern Language Journal* 8, 494–505.

Vandergrift, L (2003) Orchestrating strategy use: Toward a model of the skilled second language listener, *Language Learning* 53 (3), 463–96.

Vandergrift, L (2004) Listening to learn or learning to listen?, *Annual Review of Applied Linguistics* 24, 3–25.

Wagner, E (2007) Are they watching? Test-taker viewing behaviour during an L2 video listening test, *Language Learning & Technology* 11 (1), 67–86.

Wagner, E (2010) The effect of the use of video texts on ESL listening test-taker performance, *Language Testing* 27 (4), 493–513.

Wainer, H, Dorans, N J, Eignor, D, Flaugher, R, Green, B F, Mislevy, R J, Steinberg, L and Thissen, D (2000) *Computerized Adaptive Testing: A Primer*, Mahwah, NJ: Laurence Erlbaum Associates, 2nd edn.

Wall, D (2005) *The Impact of High-stakes Examinations on Classroom Teaching: A Case Study using Insights from Testing and Innovation Theory*, Studies in Language Testing volume 22, Cambridge: UCLES/Cambridge University Press.

Wall, D and Horak, T (2006) *The Impact of Changes in the TOEFL® Examination on Teaching and Learning in Central and Eastern Europe: Phase 1, The Baseline Study*, RR-06-18 TOEFL-MS-34, Princeton, NJ: Educational Testing Service.

Wall, D and Horak, T (2008) *The Impact of Changes in the TOEFL Examination on Teaching and Learning in Central and Eastern Europe: Phase 2. Coping with Change*, TOEFL iBT Research Series Report No. TOEFL iBT-05, Princeton, NJ: Educational Testing Service.

Watanabe, Y (2004) Methodology in washback studies, in Cheng, L, Watanabe, Y and Curtis, A (Eds) (2004) *Washback in Language Testing: Research Contexts and Methods*, London: Lawrence Erlbaum, 19–36.

Webb, S and Rodgers, M P H (2009) The lexical coverage of movies, *Applied Linguistics* 30 (3), 407–427.

Weir, C J (1983) *Identifying the Language Problems of Overseas Students in Tertiary Education in the United Kingdom*, unpublished PhD thesis, University of London.

Weir, C J (1990) *Communicative Language Testing*, New York: Prentice Hall.

Weir, C J (1993) *Understanding and Developing Language Tests*, New York: Prentice Hall.

Weir, C J (2003) A survey of the history of the Certificate of Proficiency in English (CPE) in the twentieth century, in Weir, C J and Milanovic, M (Eds) *Continuity and Innovation: Revising the Cambridge Proficiency in English Examination 1913–2002*, Studies in Language Testing volume 15, Cambridge: UCLES/Cambridge University Press, 1–56.

Weir, C J (2005a) *Language Testing and Validation: An Evidence-based Approach*, Basingstoke: Palgrave Macmillan.

Weir, C J (2005b) Limitations of the Council of Europe's framework of reference in developing comparable examinations and tests, *Language Testing* 22 (3), 281–300.

Weir, C J (forthcoming 2013a) An overview of the influences on English language testing in the United Kingdom 1913–2012, in Weir, C J, Vidaković, I and Galaczi, E, *Measured Constructs: A History of Cambridge English Language Examinations 1913–2012*, Studies in Language Testing volume 37, Cambridge: UCLES/Cambridge University Press.

Weir, C J (forthcoming 2013b) The testing of listening comprehension, in Weir, C J, Vidaković, I and Galaczi, E, *Measured Constructs: A History of Cambridge English language examinations 1913–2012*, Studies in Language Testing volume 37, Cambridge: UCLES/Cambridge University Press.

Weir, C J and Milanovic, M (2003) (Eds) *Continuity and Innovation: Revising the Cambridge Proficiency in English Examination 1913–2002*, Studies in Language Testing volume 15, Cambridge: UCLES/Cambridge University Press.

Weir, C J and O'Sullivan, B (2011) Language testing = validation, in O'Sullivan, B (Ed.) *Language Testing: Theories and Practices,* Basingstoke: Palgrave, 13–32.

Weir, C J and Taylor, L (2011) Conclusions and recommendations, in Taylor, L (2011) (Ed.) *Examining Speaking: Research and Practice in Assessing Second Language Speaking*, Studies in Language Testing volume 30, Cambridge: UCLES/Cambridge University Press, 293–313.

Weir, C J and Wu, J (2006) Establishing test form and individual task comparability: A case study of a semi-direct speaking test, *Language Testing* 23 (2), 167–197.

Weir, C J, O'Sullivan, B and Horai, T (2006) Exploring difficulty in speaking tasks: an intra-task perspective, *IELTS Research Reports Volume 6*, British Council/IELTS Australia, 119–160.

Weir, C J, O'Sullivan, B, Yan J and Bax, S (2007) Does the computer make a difference? The reaction of candidates to a computer-based versus a traditional hand-written form of the IELTS Writing component: effects and impact, *IELTS Research Reports, Volume 7*, British Council/IELTS Australia, 311–347.

Weir, C J, Hawkey, R, Green, A and Devi, S (2009) The cognitive processes underlying the academic construct as measured by IELTS, *IELTS Research Reports, Volume 9*, British Council/IELTS Australia, 157– 189.

Weir, C J, Vidaković, I and Galaczi, E (forthcoming 2013) *Measured Constructs: A History of Cambridge English language examinations 1913–2012*, Studies in Language Testing volume 37, Cambridge: UCLES/Cambridge University Press.

Wells, J C (1982) *Accents of English 3: Beyond the British Isles*, Cambridge: Cambridge University Press.

Wickens, C D (1984) Processing resources in attention, in Parasuraman, R and Davies, D R (Eds) *Varieties of Attention*, New York: Academic Press, 63–101.

Widdowson, H G (1978) *Teaching Language as Communication*, Oxford: Oxford University Press.

Wild, C and Ramaswamy, R (2008) (Eds) *Improving Testing: Applying Quality Tools and Techniques*, New York: Lawrence Erlbaum Associates.

Wilkins, D A (1976) *Notional Syllabuses: A Taxonomy and its Relevance to Foreign Language Curriculum*, Oxford: Oxford University Press.

Wilson, J (2009) *Multiple matching and matching listening tasks in CAE, BEC Higher, BULATS and IELTS*, Cambridge ESOL internal report.

World-class Instructional Design and Assessment (2004) *The WIDA Model*, available online: www.wida.us

Wray, A (2001) *Formulaic Language and the Lexicon*, Cambridge: Cambridge University Press.

Wright, B D (1977) Solving measurement problems with the Rasch model, *Journal of Educational Measurement* 14 (2), 97–116.

Wright, B D and Stone, M H (1979) *Best Test Design*, Chicago: Mesa Press.

Wu, Y (1998) What do tests of listening comprehension test? – A retrospection study of EFL test takers performing a multiple-choice task, *Language Testing* 15 (1), 21–44.

Wyatt, T S and Roach, J O (1947) The examinations in English of the Cambridge University Local Syndicate, *ELT Journal* 1 (5), 125–130.

Zumbo, B D (1999) *A Handbook on the theory and methods of differential item functioning: logistic regression modelling as a unitary framework for binary and Likert-Type (ordinal) item scores*, Ottawa: Directorate of Human Resources Research and Evaluation, Department of National Defence.

Zumbo, B D and Rupp, A A (2004) Responsible modelling of measurement data for appropriate inferences: Important advances in reliability and validity theory, in *The Sage Handbook of Quantitative Methodology for the Social Sciences*, Thousand Oaks, CA: Sage Press, 73–92.

Author Index

A

Abelson, R 100
Adeboye, K 165
Adolphs, S 216
Alderson, J C 7, 24, 161, 164, 166, 167, 174, 183, 204, 213, 275, 276, 279, 281, 287, 289, 298
Almond, R G 2, 35, 282
Allen, M J 243
Allison, D 229
American Council for the Teaching of Foreign Languages (ACTFL) vi, 199
American Educational Research Association (AERA) vi, 6, 17, 18, 19, 62, 254, 257, 258, 304, 310
American Psychological Association (APA) vi, 6, 17, 18, 19, 62, 254, 257, 258, 304, 310
Anastasi, A 31, 256, 260
Anderson, A 151, 235, 236
Anderson, J R 82, 94, 95, 151
Anderson, R C 151, 224
Angoff, W H 318
Armstrong, S J 39
Association of Language Testers in Europe (ALTE) vi, xv, xxi, 6, 10, 11, 12, 19, 62, 80, 81, 185, 225, 276, 285, 304, 305, 306, 316
Austin, J L 208

B

Baars, B J 211
Bachman, L F xii, xiii, 2, 8, 17, 24, 35, 41, 122, 123, 153, 154, 256, 278, 279, 280, 281, 282, 283, 286, 311, 336
Baddeley, A 38, 82
Badger, R 297
Bailey, K M 287
Baker, E L 78
Baltova, I 115

Barclay, J R 92
Bartlett, F C 92
Bates, E 105, 299
Bauer, L 216
Bax, S 306
Baxter, G P 78
Beeston, S 247
Bejar, I 238
Ben-Shakhar, G 40, 54
Berne, J E 198, 199, 227
Binder, J R 224
Blackhurst, A 190, 294, 295
Blau, E 119
Blodgett, A 194
Bonney, C R 78
Bons, T 124
Boo, J 190
Boroughs, R xvii, 165, 179, 182, 200, 202, 291, 294, 295
Boshuizen, H P 79
Bostrom, R 288
Braham, C J 256
Bransford, J D 92
Breeze, R 297
Breiteneder, A 234
Brennan, R L 259, 266, 313, 319
Breuer, A 208, 236
Brindley, G 134, 145, 162, 166, 167, 181, 231
Browman, C P 204
Brown, A 16, 280
Brown, G 87, 92, 101, 102, 115, 116, 151, 186, 204, 205, 235, 236
Brown, J D 36, 161, 166
Buck, G xvii, 81, 104, 127, 130, 131, 134, 149, 163, 164, 181, 185, 187, 188, 189, 195, 198, 199, 201, 207, 208, 229 280, 290, 301
Buckendahl, C 313
Burger, S 166
Burgoon, J K 189
Bush, M 165

Buttery, P 212
Bybee, J 88

C
Calfee, R C
Calvert, D R 119
Camilli, G 254
Capel, A 217, 218
Carrell, P L 162
Carroll, D W 38
Carter, R A 211, 212
Cauldwell, R 207
Chafe, W 121, 204
Chalhoub-Deville, M 191, 192, 283
Chapelle, C A 2
Charlin, B 79
Chaudron, C 162
Chan, A H S 165
Cheng, L 7, 276, 277, 282, 287, 413
    418, 434
Chi, Y 185, 226
Choi, H 164
Choi, I C 190, 311
Clapham, C 43, 161
Clark, E V 94
Clark, H H 94
Clifton, C 94, 95, 96
Cohen, A D 107, 150, 282, 419,
    427
Collins, A 279
Coleman, D 297
Colston, H 91
Coniam, D 191
Conrad, L 213
Cook, J 162
Cope, L 194, 265
Corno, L 79, 435
Council of Europe vi, xii, xiii, 1, 8, 10,
    12, 13, 14, 31, 39, 58, 80, 166, 169,
    195, 197, 205, 206, 219, 220, 224,
    227, 228, 230, 236, 237, 300, 303,
    304, 314, 316, 317, 319
Courtney, R 162
Coxhead, A 217, 221
Cronbach, L J 166, 258, 262, 263,
    265
Crooks, T 282
Culwin, F 165
Curtis, A 7, 276, 287, 413, 418
Cutler, A 89, 94, 95, 96, 97, 98
Cizek, G J 276, 336

D
Dąbrowska, E 88
Davidson, F 17, 21, 311
Davies, A 13, 16, 18, 280, 285
Davies, P 165
Dechert, H W
Derwing, T M 230
Dever, B V 78
Devi, S 306
Deville, C 191, 192, 283
Doherty, K 166
Dooey, P 191
Donitsa-Schmidt, S 279
Dorans, N J 191, 254
Douglas, D 17, 23, 188, 199, 226, 238,
    415
Duckworth, M 164
Dunbar, S B 78
Dunkel, P A 162, 192, 418

E
Ebel, R L 132, 183
Educational Testing Service (ETS) vii,
    x, 184, 290, 311, 312
Eignor, D 191
Elder, C 16, 18, 280
Elliott, M W v, xiv, xv, xvii, xviii, xx, 32,
    36, 152, 236, 331
Ellis, A W 94
Ellis, N C 218, 221
Elman, J L 86, 94
Ericsson, K A 82
European Association for Language
    Testing and Assessment (EALTA)
    vii, 6, 62
Eurydice 314

F
Falvey, P 277
Farr, R 129, 145, 164
Feldt, L S 259
Feltovich, P J 82
Ferman, I 279
Ferne, T 164
Figueras, N 204
Field, J xiv, xvii, xviii, xx, 32, 68, 77, 80,
    82, 84, 87, 90, 95, 97, 104, 107, 108,
    109, 126, 127, 128, 129, 131, 133,
    145, 148, 149, 155, 156, 161, 164,
    167, 170, 171, 186, 190, 199, 200,
    201, 204, 212, 216, 231, 232, 239,

280, 290, 297, 301, 326, 327, 328, 329, 330, 331 315
Flaugher, R 191
Fortune, A J 200
Foulke, E 229
Franks, J J 92
Fraser, H 126
Frazier, L 91
Frederiksen, J 279
Freedle, R 129, 130, 145, 149, 181
Fried-Booth, D 117, 294, 295
Fulcher, G 17, 21, 315

G
Gagnon, R 79
Galaczi, E xviii, 2, 21, 40 205, 210, 231, 305, 316
Gallois, C 236
Ganong, W F 90
Garnham, M 102
Garrod, S C 92
Gaskell, M G 94
Gates, S 279
Gathercole, S E 82
Gee, J 98, 424
Geranpayeh, A xv, xix, xx, 33, 36, 127, 129, 153, 158, 167, 168, 170, 184, 186, 190, 197, 198, 199, 200, 201, 202, 203, 242, 254, 255, 256, 294, 295, 313, 322
Gernsbacher, M A 93, 102, 103
Gibbs, R 91
Gimson, A C 119
Ginther, A 188
Glaser, R 78
Goh, C C M 107
Goldinger, S D 87
Goldman-Eisler, F 118, 229
Goldstein, L 204
Grabe, E 233
Graddol, D 22, 233
Graesser, A C 124
Graham, S 107, 280
Green, A B 7, 36, 190, 206, 277, 279, 282, 286, 289, 295, 306, 315, 316
Green, B F 191, 315
Green, K P 115, 315
Griffiths, R 119, 229, 230
Grosjean, F 89, 98
Gruba, P A 115, 190
Gude, K 164

Gulliksen, H 244
Gutch, A 292
Gutteridge, M xvii, 69

H
Haberlandt, K 124
Hackett, E 168, 170, 190 - 194, 294, 295
Haertel, E H 244, 256, 257
Hagan, A 297
Hale, G A 162
Halliday, M A K 155
Hambleton, R K 162, 266
Hamp-Lyons, L 277, 279, 289
Hansen, C 204, 224, 226
Harding, L 117
Haslett, S 297
Hawkey, R ii, v, xii, xv, xvii, xxi, 7, 22, 24, 33, 128, 202, 267, 273, 277, 279, 284–287, 289–293, 296, 298, 301, 306, 312
Hawkins, J 212, 315
Hegelheimer, V 188
Henning, G 163
Hill, K ii, 16, 280
Hindmarsh, R 217
Holcomb, P J 224
Holland, P W 254
Hoole, E R 78
Horai, T 306
Horak, T 7, 290
Hubbard, C xviii, 316
Hudson, R A 235
Hudson, T 161, 166
Huff, K L 191
Hughes, A 164, 166, 186, 279, 280, 282
Hyland, K 217
Hymes, D L 236

I
Inbar, O 204
Ingham, K xvii, xviii, 294
In'nami, Y 145
Interagency Language Roundtable (ILR) vii, 199
International English Language Testing System (IELTS) ii, vii, xxi, xxii, 7, 12, 13, 16, 17, 126, 131, 277, 179, 182, 193, 203, 233, 262, 263, 277, 286, 290, 294–300, 310, 312, 313, 318–320, 334, 335, 337

International Language Testing
    Association (ILTA) vii, xxi, 6, 62,
    285

J
Jackson, D 79
Jamieson, J 2, 238
Jakobson, R 203
Jenkins, J 26, 116, 233, 234
Jennings, S 165
Jensen, C 204, 224, 226
Johnson, K 82
Johnson, M K 92, 102
Johnson-Laird, P 92, 102
Johnston, J C 129, 131
Joint Committee on Testing Practices
    6
Jones, N xviii, 10, 183, 187, 190, 191,
    285, 313, 315, 316

K
Kachru, B B 233
Kane, M T 17, 63, 282
Kanjee, A 162
Karabenick, K L 78
Kay, P 39
Keddle, J S 212
Khalifa, H ii, v, ix, xiv, xv, xvii, xxi, 1,
    27, 31, 33, 77, 84, 85, 136, 146, 148,
    152, 161–164, 166, 185, 209, 211,
    213, 218, 242, 274, 279, 303, 313,
    314, 316, 317, 340
Kiely, R 296, 297
Kim, K S 190
Kinneavy, J E 203,205
Kintsch, W 92, 102, 161, 185
Klatt, D H 150
Koizumi, R 145
Kolen, M J 266, 313, 319
Kormos, J 82
Koskey, K L 78
Kostin, I 129, 130, 145, 149, 181
Kounios, J 224
Kraft, B 236
Kuijper, H 204
Kulick, E 254
Kunnan, A J 6, 7, 37, 81, 129, 254, 255,
    283

L
Larichev, O L 79

Larkin, J H 188
Laufer, B 215, 216, 218, 224
Lee, D Y W 217
Levitov, J E 245
Lewkowicz, J 154, 233
Liddicoat, A J 215
Lim, G S v, xv, xvii, xxi, 33, 303,
    313–316, 319
Linacre, J M 191,253
Linck, J 194
Linn, R L 78
Little, D 40
Londe, Z C 189
Long, M 227
Lord, F M 244, 254, 260
Loschky, L 162
Lukas, J F 2
Lumley, T ii, 16, 280
Lund, R J 155
Lynch, T 107, 151, 190
Lyons, J 100

M
Macaro, E 107
MacDonald, J 190
MacWhinney, B 105
Markel, N N 236
Marks, A 126
Marsen, S 227
Marshall, H 247
Marslen-Wilson, W D 89, 94
Martinez, R 218
Martinez, R J 165
Martyniuk, W ii, 314
Maycock, L 190, 191, 294, 295
McCarthy, M J 211, 212
McClelland, J L 86, 94
McDonald, R P 244
McDowell, C 297
McGurk, H 190
McKay, J B 39
McKiernan, K A 224
McLaughlin, M 314
McNamara, T ii, 7, 16, 20, 35, 275, 279,
    280
McQueen, J 89, 90
Meara, P 105
Medler, D A 224
Mehrens, W 289
Mehrpour, S 218
Merrylees, B 297

Messick, S A 6, 30, 31, 80, 275, 276, 279, 281, 286
Meunier, L E 191
Milanovic, M ii, ix, xi, xvi, xix, 8, 21, 31, 2772, 78, 284, 291, 295, 315, 339
Miller, G 129
Miller, P 297
Mislevy, R J 2, 35, 191, 282
Molhaun, P 162
Moon, R 218
Moreno, R 165
Morrow, K 24
Munby, J L 174, 288
Muniz, J 16
Murray, S 127, 136, 165, 167, 176, 178, 293–295

N
Nakatsuhara, F 205
Nassaji, H 218
Nation, P 216
Nation, I S P 216–218
National Commission on Excellence in Education 314
National Council on Measurement in Education (NCME) viii, xx, 6, 17–19, 62, 254, 257, 258, 304, 310
Nevo, N 161
Ng, A W Y 165
Nissan, S 199, 238
Nitko, A J 260
Nold, G 204
Norris, D 89
North, B xxi, 8, 10, 26, 27, 236, 316
Novick, M R 244
Nygaard, L C 86

O
Oakhill, J 102
Ockey, G J 115, 188, 192
O'Donnell, K 236
Ogiermann, E 236
O'Sullivan, B ii, xii, 9, 13, 17–19, 36, 37, 55, 81, 275, 306

P
Paivio, A 124
Palmer, A S 2, 8, 17, 35, 41, 153, 154, 278–280, 282, 286, 336
Papp, S xviii, 39, 40, 54, 162

Pashler, H 129, 131
Peterson, E R 39
Pickering, M J 91
Pickett, J M 89
Pisoni, D B 86, 97
Pitoniak, M J 266
Pitzl, M L 234
Pollack, I 89
Possing, E T 224
Prietula, M J 82
Progosh, D 189
Proudfoot, S 179, 182

R
Rahimi, M 218
Raju, N S 254
Ramsaran, S 119
Ramaswany, R 402
Ravenhorst-Kalovski, G C 216, 218, 224
Rayner, K 91
Rayner, S G 39
Rea-Dickins, P 296–298
Riding, R J 39
Rixon, S 39, 40, 54
Roach, J O 19–21
Rodgers, M P H 216
Rodriguez, M C 164
Roever, C 7
Rogers, J 254
Rose, D 294, 402
Rost, M 107, 189, 212
Roy, L 79
Ruiz-Primo, M A 78, 164, 256, 262
Ryan, K xii, 311

S
Sadler-Smith, E 39
Salamoura, A 317
Salisbury, K xviii, 112
Sanford, A J 92
Santos, D 107
Saville, N ix, 8, 267, 282, 284, 285, 291, 298, 304, 308, 311, 315, 402
Sauvé, E 79
Schank, R C 100
Schmidt-Rinehart, 226
Schmitt, N xviii, 216, 218, 221
Schultz, S 78

Shavelson, R J 78
Shaw, S D ii, ix, xiv, 1, 27, 77, 84, 148, 279, 325, 340
Sheerin, S 280
Sherman, J 126, 127
Shillcock, R 235, 236
Shiotsu, T ii
Shohamy, E 7, 161, 204, 279, 283
Simon, H A 82, 188
Simpson-Vlach, R 218, 221
Sinai, Y 40, 54
Singer, M 92
Sireci, S G 191
Slatyer, H 145, 181, 231
Small, M Y 39
Smith, H 297
Smitten, B 129, 164
Snow, R E 79
Solomon, S K 92
Somers, A xviii, 168, 170, 187
Spearman, C 244
Spolsky, B 7, 20, 35, 154
Spratt, M 287
Stæhr, L S 215, 216
Steinberg, L S 2, 35, 191, 254, 282
Stevens, B 306
Stevenson, B 126
St-Martin, M 79
Stone, M H 272
Stowe, R W 124
Suvorov, R 189
Swaminathan, H 254
Swinney, D 90

T
Takala, S 204
Tannen, D 204
Tardieu, C 204
Tatsuoka, K 181, 229
Tauroza, S 229
Taylor, L ii, iii, v, ix, xiv, xv, xix, xxi, 1, 5, 26, 27, 33, 63, 77, 116, 117, 127, 134, 153, 158, 168, 184, 186, 197–199, 201–203, 232–235, 273, 274, 277, 279, 284, 285, 288, 294–296, 307, 313, 316, 322, 326, 335, 339, 340
Thayer, D T 254
Thelk, A D 78
Thighe, D 190
Thissen, D 191, 254
Thomas, P R 39

Thompson, B 245, 259
Thompson, S 296
Toulmin, S E 17, 282
Trim, J 208, 209, 220, 316
Tse, P 217
Turner, J 238
Turner, R 296
Tyler, M D 226

U
Urquhart, A H 81, 149, 155

V
Van der Vleuten, C 79
Van Dijk, T A 93, 102
Van Ek, J 208, 209, 220, 316
Van Zeeland, H 216
Vähäpassi, A 204
Vandergrift, L 107, 188, 280
Vanderplank, R 107
Vidakovic, I 2, 21, 305

W
Wagner, E 189
Wainer, H 191, 254
Wall, D ii, 7, 161, 279, 280, 282, 287, 289, 290
Walsh, M 124
Watanabe, Y 7, 276, 287
Wayland, S C 194
Webb, S 216
Weir, C J ii, ix–xiv, xvi, xviii, 1, 2, 5, 8, 9, 19–22, 24–31, 35, 77, 79, 81, 82, 84, 85, 90, 130, 138, 146, 148, 149, 152, 153, 155, 156, 161–164, 166, 183–185, 209, 213, 218, 239, 242, 273, 274–277, 279, 282, 288, 291, 292, 295, 303–306, 311, 314–316, 322, 325, 326, 331, 335, 339, 340
Westbury, C F 224
Wickens, C D 54, 167, 178, 187
Widdowson, H G 24
Wild, C 402
Wilkins, D A 208
Williams, D M 254
Wilson, J v, xv, xvii, xxii, 32, 89, 94, 152, 167, 331
Woolley, M E 78
World Class Instructional Design and assessment (WIDA) viii, 314

Wray, A 88
Wright, B D 266, 272
Wu, J 304
Wu, Y 130, 149, 164
Wyatt, T S 21

Y
Yan, J ii, 306
Yan, X 297

Yarborough, J C 161
Yen, W M 243
Young, A W 94
Yu, G 296, 297
Yule, G 92, 101, 102, 115, 116, 151, 205, 235, 236

Z
Zumbo, B D 254, 256, 262

Subject Index

A

Academic listening 12, 42

Academic word list 217–218, 221

Accent 13–14, 15, 16, 28, 34, 43, 60, 87–89, 116–118, 142, 151, 186, 195, 202, 216, 226, 231–235, 237, 288, 301, 307, 329, 330, 400

Accommodations xiv, 62, 63, 324, 325
Test takers with disabilities xiv, 63, 64, 66, 324, 325

Accountability 3, 6, 7, 314

Accuracy xviii, 103, 107, 154, 168, 169, 246, 253, 258, 264, 265
grammatical 42, 83, 91, 99, 106, 170–171, 174, 179, 195, 211–215
of pronunciation 169

ACTFL scale vi, 199

Acoustic 187, 192, 407
cue 86, 95, 96, 97, 327
input 23, 25, 28, 94–97, 104, 290
signal 150

Administrative setting 23, 30, 41, 152, 153, 402

Analytic
criteria 7, 79–82, 150
rating scales 258

Anchor items 249, 308

Appropriacy xiv, 198, 200, 204, 208

Assessment criteria 3, 284, 285

Assessment Use Argument (AUA) vi, 2, 17, 282, 336

Assimilation 87, 216

Attention 39, 40, 54, 64, 69, 76, 82, 83, 85, 106, 111, 114, 117, 119, 122, 126, 130–133, 135, 137, 139, 145, 147, 149, 155–157, 171, 178, 188, 241–243, 329

Audio-recordings 10, 23, 26, 65, 70, 75, 114–115, 119, 215–126, 142, 157, 158, 188–192, 198, 207, 230, 239, 306, 318, 329, 409

Authenticity 26, 110, 113, 114, 154, 163, 188, 261, 278, 291, 292, 329

interactional 24, 154, 261

situational 24, 154, 170, 171, 197, 198, 261

Automaticity
in speaking 81, 82
in processing 106, 137, 195, 199, 213

Avoidance strategies 30, 173, 255, 274

B

Background knowledge 226, 227, 292

Backwash 279, 289

Band descriptors 10, 40, 58, 158, 166, 194, 212, 219–220, 225, 227–228, 230, 236, 258, 316–318, 335, 340

Basic User 271, 313

BEC (Business English Certificates) 12, 13, 17, 265
Higher 16, 263, 313
Intermediate 16, 263, 312, 313
Preliminary 16, 194, 263, 313

Benchmarking 118–119, 221, 229, 285

Bias 30, 36, 37, 39, 41–45, 52, 53, 68, 76, 232, 283, 296

Braille 65, 67–69, 71, 73, 74

Breakdown of understanding 45, 50

BULATS (Business Language Testing System) vi, 7, 17, 194, 253, 265, 313

Business English Certificates *see* BEC

Business Language Testing System *see* BULATS

C

CAE (Certificate in Advanced English *or* Cambridge Advanced) vi, viii, x, 7, 15, 18, 46, 50, 52–55, 57, 59, 60, 61, 70, 76, 81, 108, 113, 117, 120, 121, 123, 124, 126, 127, 131, 134–136, 138–140, 144–146, 148, 150–152, 159, 171–173, 176, 178, 180 184, 186, 187, 195, 196, 201,

202, 206, 209, 210, 213, 220–223, 225, 226, 228, 231, 240, 251, 255, 256, 263, 267, 277, 291–295, 301, 310, 313, 319, 333, 334

Calibrated items 248, 305

Candidate information sheet (CIS) v, vi, 45, 49, 50, 56, 60–62, 323, 324, 393

Can Do
  descriptors 335
  scales 10, 80, 169, 231, 258, 315–318, 395
  statements 10–12, 80, 241

Case study 277, 298, 300, 317, 318, 325

CEFR (Common European Framework of Reference) xiii, 1, 8, 31, 80, 247, 271, 300, 303, 304, 313
  criteria 12, 169
  levels 169
  listening scales 10, 58, 81, 166, 231, 247, 314–318

Certificate in Advanced English *see* CAE

Certificate of Proficiency in English *see* CPE

Channel of presentation 153, 187, 192, 200

Classical test theory 243, 257, 259

CLA model (communicative language ability) 261, 264, 311

Code complexity 82, 88–89, 94–96, 102, 107, 134, 212, 236, 327

Codes of practice 62, 285, 302

Cognitive
  load xv, 78, 120, 122, 136, 149, 167, 169, 199, 328, 331, 333
  parameters 10
  processing xv, 9, 25, 27–30, 32, 38, 64, 76, 78–82, 85, 107, 182, 184, 185, 199, 204, 210, 260

Coherence 8, 70

Common European Framework of Reference *see* CEFR

Common reference levels 13, 14

Communication 8, 34, 65, 68, 100, 107, 115, 150, 155, 156, 158, 189, 193, 205, 220, 281, 288, 292, 299, 300, 324, 328

Communicative
  competence 35, 296

language ability (CLA) 153, 189, 226, 261, 264, 311

language teaching xii, 24

language testing 24
  use 280

Comparable forms 304, 307–309

Competence
  interactional 13, 205
  language competence 18

Comprehension, factors in
  accent 13, 25–26, 43, 60, 87–89, 116–118, 142, 151, 186, 195, 202, 216, 226, 231–235, 237, 288, 307, 329–330
  hesitation 143, 215
  phonological modification 84, 94–98, 105–106, 109, 117, 128, 137–138, 147, 204
  prosody 91, 97, 98
  speech rate 25, 26, 28, 81, 87, 88, 108, 109, 118, 147, 153, 186, 194, 229–231, 239, 288

Comprehension questions 4, 22, 287

Computer-based (testing) 74, 163, 165, 188, 190, 244, 330

Consequences 6, 7, 17, 30, 61, 144, 199, 266, 274–277, 282, 283, 286, 289, 302, 336, 337

Construct ix–xi
  definition xiii
  irrelevant variance 34, 161–164, 167, 168, 180, 190, 197, 219, 224, 226, 233, 242, 340
  representation 28–29, 34, 93
  under-representation 34, 80, 161, 173, 192, 281, 340

Content
  coverage 30
  knowledge 25, 28, 39, 44, 153, 226, 227

Context
  of language use x, 17–19, 25, 42, 153, 154, 235, 236
  of listening 94–99, 101–105

Contextual parameters 78, 152, 153, 242, 304–306, 310, 312, 320, 332, 340

Conversation 10–12, 15, 20, 102, 109, 115, 119, 127, 142, 143, 156, 160, 188, 204–207, 212, 216, 228, 229, 231, 293

Examining Listening

Criteria
for assessment 284, 303–305, 307,
314, 317, 322, 326
scoring 28, 242–249, 272–278, 333,
334
Criterion-referenced approach 266, 338
Cross-test comparability 304, 310, 311,
313, 339
Cultural context 30
Curriculum 4, 10, 22, 286–289, 314
Cut scores 4, 10, 22, 286, 287, 289, 301,
314

D
Decoding 28, 94–98, 107–110, 119,
1307, 146, 290, 327
Delivery 4, 14, 74, 109, 193, 231, 295
Descriptors, *see* Band descriptors
Dialect 14, 236
Dictation 22, 24, 181, 305
Differential item functioning 27, 30, 37,
243–255, 295
Difficulty 28
Dimensionality 260–261
Direct tests xii, 19, 20, 59, 144, 213,
282
Disabilities, test takers with 37, 63, 64,
66, 324, 325
Discourse
analysis 82, 85
management 236
mode 28, 153, 203–207, 229
representation 28, 38, 92, 93,
101–104, 120, 121, 123, 127, 132,
133, 146–148, 195, 290, 331
type 111–112, 216, 223, 328, 399
Discrete point tests 123, 128, 132, 133,
146, 148, 176, 191, 261, 310, 331
Discussion 13, 15, 16, 172, 225, 228,
237, 240, 296–297, 299, 301
test specifications xiii, 84, 247, 292,
332
Double play 26, 56, 127, 142, 197, 202,
203, 295, 338

E
Educational contexts 18, 19
Educational Testing Service *see* ETS
Elision 87, 181, 216, 264
ELTS (English Language Testing
Service) 233

Empirical validation 31, 318–320
Environment 19, 42, 51, 74, 205, 214,
265, 324
Equipment 23, 73, 75, 143, 192, 402,
406–409
Equivalent forms 304, 305, 307
Errors 179, 180, 233, 237, 244, 245, 257,
259, 399
ETS (Educational Testing Service) 184,
290, 311, 312
Ethics 6, 66, 285
Evaluation 2, 8, 27, 62, 82, 153, 225,
257, 289, 306, 307, 310, 317, 318,
322
Evidence-centered design (ECD) vii,
2
Examination
conduct 403–405, 407–408
materials 227, 305, 338, 395, 408
requirements 404
Expert judgement 62, 165, 180, 181,
241, 266
Exposure 26, 42, 43, 60, 105, 106, 144,
198, 232–235, 248

F
Factor analysis 79, 129, 311
Fairness 42, 43, 66, 161, 165, 168, 184,
201, 202, 234, 283, 295, 307
Familiarity
topic 11–14, 25, 42, 43, 58, 68, 107,
219, 226–227, 299
FCE (First Certificate in English or
Cambridge First) vii, x
Feedback 51, 180, 193, 202, 221, 228,
231, 235, 240, 271, 291, 293, 301,
318, 398, 400
First Certificate in English *see* FCE
Foreign Service Institute *see* FSI
Foregrounding 87, 113
Framework
socio-cognitive xiv–xviii, 2, 8, 25–29,
32, 35, 79, 153, 240, 242, 260–261,
272, 273–277, 282, 290, 292, 294,
301, 302, 304, 311, 312, 320, 323,
331, 333, 336, 340, 402
Functional
resources 28, 153, 208, 209, 236
Functions 25, 39, 42, 81, 100, 189, 203,
206, 208–210, 212, 218, 228, 236,
237, 293, 311, 312, 333

450

G

Gap-filling 127, 128, 130, 131, 133, 138, 144, 147, 151, 193, 331
Gapped text 145, 181, 288
Gatekeeping 296
Gender 45–48, 52, 53, 87, 141, 235, 239, 240, 253, 255, 292
General proficiency 313
Generalisability 31, 155, 195, 257, 259
Genre 15, 81, 134, 150, 159, 161, 177, 207, 288
Gist 12, 15, 16, 81, 136, 139, 159, 160, 176–178, 186, 288, 293, 301, 335
Goal
  setting 156
Grading and awarding 28, 242, 243, 266, 267, 334
Grammar
  spoken 25, 184, 211–213
Grammatical
  complexity 213–215
  knowledge 91, 106
  resources 28, 153, 207, 211, 213
  structures 179, 211, 212, 214, 215
Group
  discussion 58, 237

H

Hesitation 110, 111, 143, 208, 215, 229, 230
High-stakes tests xxi, 60, 149, 280, 297, 335
Holistic
  criteria 88
Human judgement 262

I

Idea units 121–123, 132, 133, 146–148, 150, 331, 332
IELTS (International English Language Testing System) 7, 12–14, 16, 17, 126, 131, 179, 182, 193, 203, 233, 262, 263, 277, 286, 290, 294–300, 310, 312, 313, 318–320, 334, 335, 337
Illustrative descriptors 166, 316
ILR (Interagency Language Roundtable) vii, 199
Immigration 5, 79, 296, 297, 314
Impact xiii, 7–8, 30, 33, 60, 273–275, 277–302, 325, 335–338
Independent User 11, 271, 313

Inference 17, 25, 39, 82–83, 92, 95, 100, 101, 107, 108, 133, 136, 137, 138, 146, 147, 158, 159, 163, 188, 190, 199, 208, 218, 290, 327
Inferencing 39, 199
  visual 10, 28, 114, 125, 187, 188, 190, 192, 329
Information
  transfer 86, 191–193, 195, 197, 201, 202, 207
Input
  characteristics of 12, 23, 26, 28, 50, 77, 81
Integrated
  listening into speaking 338
  reading into writing 1
Integrating information 103, 133
Integrative tests 131
Intelligibility 234
Intended consequences 7, 30, 268, 276–279, 282, 283, 286, 289, 302, 336
Interactionalist 9
Interagency Language Roundtable see ILR
Interlocutor 26, 66, 69–71, 152, 275
  status 297
Internal consistency 28, 233, 242, 243, 256–259, 261–263, 334
International English Language Testing System see IELTS
Internet 24, 112, 143, 312, 329, 323, 338
Interpretation 30, 56, 63, 56, 91, 100, 105, 109, 114, 119, 124
Interpretive argument 17
Interview
  task 15, 16, 70, 112, 156, 158–161, 172, 173, 174, 176, 177, 196–197, 206, 240, 252, 301
Intonation 87, 97–99, 110, 198, 211
Item
  analysis 245, 248
  banking 247, 263, 303, 307, 308, 312, 320, 334, 338, 399
  bias 28, 243, 245, 253–255, 334
  calibration 80, 147, 312, 327
  difficulty 28
  discrimination 28, 170, 200, 243, 245, 246, 249
  facility 28, 243–245, 249
  writing 180, 395, 399

Item response theory (IRT) 28, 70, 243, 244, 248, 250, 253, 257, 260, 265, 267, 312

J
Judgements 37, 53, 258, 281
  expert 78
  human 262

K
KET (Key English Test or Cambridge Key)
Key English Test *see* KET
Knowledge of criteria 28, 153, 184
Knowledge of the world 37, 44, 61

L
Language
  for specific purposes (LSP) 43
Language acquisition 10
  second vii, 83
Lectures 14, 16, 111, 162, 179, 197–200, 204, 224, 229, 296, 299, 231, 301, 318
Lexical
  resources 28, 87, 153, 215–224, 333
Lexico-grammatical 58, 219
Lexicon 88, 90, 98, 217
Lexis 1, 22, 25, 59, 88, 93, 105, 111, 130, 162, 169, 177, 211, 215–224, 333
Linguistic
  demands 18, 28, 30, 152, 153, 157, 203–205, 275,

M
Main Suite vii, viii
Malpractice 406, 408
Marker
  judgements 168, 244
  reliability 28, 170, 243, 258, 264
Marking 128
Matching 52, 59, 106, 113, 120–123, 127–129
Meaning
  building 38, 81, 85–86, 92–95, 98, 100–103, 108, 115, 120, 122, 123, 125, 128, 159, 180, 185, 195, 197, 208, 218–219, 221, 327, 332
  enrichment 82, 182, 212
  negotiation of 239
  representation 28, 104, 138, 146, 147

Measurement scale 308
Memory
  long-term 88, 288
  short-term 163, 288
  working 37, 38–39, 54, 82, 87, 100, 106–107, 111, 119, 123, 129, 136, 146, 149, 184, 188
Metacognitive strategies 41, 58, 154, 156
Monitoring 25, 27, 45, 50–53, 103, 104, 156, 310
Monologue/s 15, 16, 70, 109, 115, 118, 119, 132, 133, 141, 158, 159, 172, 176, 178, 238, 293, 329
Motivation 6, 29, 83, 111, 226, 256, 289, 311, 313
Multi-faceted Rasch (MRFM) 247–253, 265–266, 272, 303, 308–309, 320
Multiple-choice question 59, 128, 163, 164, 173, 174
Multiple matching vii, 113, 128, 131, 135, 137, 147, 166, 167, 172, 178, 293, 330

N
Native speaker 10, 26, 58, 119, 142, 151, 206, 232–237
Nature of information 28, 153, 224, 225
Non-native speaker 119, 142, 151, 229, 232, 234
Non-verbal 175, 188, 189, 192, 207
Normalisation 87, 8, 116, 142, 186, 195
Note completion 170, 171–173, 182
Number of speakers 26, 28, 153, 171, 205, 238–240

O
Oral tests xi
Order of items 28, 153, 185, 186, 200, 238

P
Parallel forms 257, 258, 304, 307
Paraphrase 59, 131, 144, 145, 147, 177, 256
Parsing 28, 38, 91–97, 99, 100, 105, 122–124, 127, 132 ,133, 137, 146, 212, 327, 328, 330
Pauses 13, 67–69, 89, 110, 118, 143, 192, 201, 202, 216, 230, 231

Pausing 22, 68, 100, 197
Pedagogy 22, 280, 295
Perceptions 80, 290, 291, 297–300, 338
Performance
  conditions 30
  testing 199
PET (Preliminary English Test or Cambridge Preliminary) 300, 316
Phonology 20, 21
Physical conditions xv, 28, 405
Point-biserial correlation 246
Post-exam analysis 50, 310
Practicality 8, 115, 197, 278, 286, 329
Pragmatic
  competence 208
  knowledge 100–102, 105, 128
Preliminary English Test see PET
Presentation 11, 28, 65, 119, 125, 127, 144, 153, 187, 190, 192, 200, 330, 332
Pretesting 51, 180, 202, 220, 221, 228, 231, 235, 240, 241, 248, 255, 292, 293, 305, 306, 308, 396–400
Propositional meaning 28, 390
Pronunciation 26, 208, 216, 232, 234, 399
Purpose 5, 8, 15–18, 20–22, 81, 115, 153, 154–159, 177–179, 203–207, 224, 232, 261, 272, 288, 293

Q
Qualitative analysis 180, 293, 300, 305, 310
Quality
  assurance xiii, xviii, 13, 67, 73, 245, 315
  management xiii, 277, 278, 285, 395
Quantitative analysis 30–31, 180, 221, 300, 305, 310
Quantitative research methods
  correlation 130, 245–246, 249–259, 296, 313
Question paper production viii, 241, 395, 397
Questionnaires 291, 298, 300, 306, 307

R
Rasch model see multi-faceted Rasch analysis
Rating scales, see scales

Reading aloud xi, 19, 22, 23, 100, 141, 143
Real life 24, 77, 78, 84, 114, 127, 131, 143, 154, 155, 170, 188, 197, 200, 205, 233, 307, 327, 329, 340
Real world 80, 82, 108, 110, 115, 124, 126, 127, 133, 139, 141, 142, 144, 148, 151 152, 179, 199, 239, 271, 288, 315, 326–328
Reliability
  estimates 258, 261, 262, 265
  inter-rater 171, 257, 258, 264, 265
  intra-rater 258
Repetition 102, 120, 196–199, 207, 214
Response
  expected 306
  format 43, 54, 59, 156, 157, 162, 163, 167, 170–173, 178, 178, 179, 182, 187, 191, 202, 241
  method 28, 30, 153, 156, 161–165, 171, 173, 174, 190, 219, 332
Results
  reporting 28, 184, 242, 243, 268–271, 334–335, 339
  statement of 269–270
Rubrics 4, 28, 54, 58–60, 68, 69, 115, 125, 135, 142, 151, 153, 154, 156–162, 166, 190, 192, 197, 201, 223, 224, 238, 247, 306, 330, 332, 398, 400

S
Sampling 30, 197, 232, 255, 335, 409
Scales
  ACTFL 199
Schemata 37–39, 41, 44, 55, 56, 154, 188
Scoring
  dichotomous 260
Scripted 109–113, 143, 163, 204, 207, 215, 231, 307, 328, 333
Selected response 162, 163, 167, 173, 187, 200, 202, 253
Semi-scripted 113, 207, 215, 333
Sentence
  length 111, 175, 211, 213–216
  stress 216
Short answer question 167
Single play 197, 202, 203, 291, 295, 338
Socio-cognitive approach 8

Socio-cultural
    awareness 236–238
    competence 236–238
Sociolinguistic 28, 153, 235–237, 240
    competence 236
Sound
    Quality 71, 192
Speech
    acts 208
    rate 25, 26, 28, 81, 87, 88, 108, 109,
        114, 118–119, 122, 147, 153, 186,
        194, 229–231, 239, 288, 306, 312,
        329, 339
    variability in 90
Spelling
    Correct 167–170, 179–181, 184, 194,
        264–265
Stakeholders 274, 277, 284, 285,
    287–289, 291, 292, 297, 300, 316,
    318, 324, 323, 324, 337, 408
Standard error of measurement 257,
    259, 260, 262, 263
Standard setting 318–320
Status
    interlocutor status and familiarity
        297
    socio-economic 235, 324
Strategic competence 108, 311
Strategies
    compensatory 139, 280
    for listening 107
Stress 17, 19, 56, 78, 95–99, 102, 110,
    169, 204, 211, 216, 233, 256, 327
Structural equation modelling viii, 167,
    178

Structured tasks 171
Support
    interlocutor 26, 69, 70, 152, 231, 275,
        297
Syntactic
    knowledge 97, 182
    parsing 28, 91, 97, 182, 212, 328
Syntax 17, 22, 91, 111, 176, 182,
    212

T
Target language 42, 43, 50, 119, 121,
    237, 280, 329
    domain 25, 60, 152
    use 65, 97, 98, 106, 115, 154, 198

Task
    attributes 399
    banks 192
    collaborative 210, 231
    description 398, 399
    design 113, 78, 85
    focus 158–159, 177
    purpose 153–158, 204
    rhetorical 214
    type 39, 41, 54, 56, 58, 155, 172–173,
        193, 195, 200, 205, 291, 292, 293,
        306, 307, 312, 399
Test
    bias 26, 30, 37, 53, 165, 254, 255,
        274
    conditions 84, 139, 199, 284
    purpose 15, 16, 17, 20, 21, 22, 169,
        197, 232
    usefulness 278, 286
Test taker characteristics
    experiential 36, 37, 41–44, 56–62
    physical/physiological 36–38, 50–53,
        62, 66, 72
    psychological 36, 37, 38, 54–56
Test taker profile
    age 46–52
    educational level 42, 56–58
    exam preparation 42–43
    gender 52–53
    L1 50
Text
    length 28, 147, 153, 194–197, 200,
        201, 202, 222–223
    purpose 153, 203, 205, 206, 261
    structure 299
Threshold level vii, 316
Timing 4, 122, 169, 184, 197, 201, 287,
    295, 396, 407
Time constraints 25, 28, 153, 197, 201,
    227, 241, 261
TOEFL viii, x, xii, xiii, 26, 126, 129,
    188, 290, 310–312
Topic familiarity 226
Topical knowledge 154
Training
    examiners 405
Trialling 193, 194, 202, 248
True/False items 126, 132, 165, 166,
    173, 177
Turn-taking 236
Type-token ratio 221

U
Uniformity of administration 28, 404
Unintended consequences 7, 286, 291, 336
Unscripted 216, 231

V
Validity
a posteriori validity 27, 30, 241, 284, 285, 294
a priori validity 27, 29, 37, 85, 241, 284, 285, 294
cognitive 26–30, 77–152, 154, 161, 198, 200, 242, 273, 275, 283, 290, 326–331, 332, 333, 332, 402
consequential 26–30, 33, 273, 335–338
context 25–32, 78, 152–242, 273, 275, 331–333, 402
criterion-related 26–31, 33, 258, 275, 303–321, 338
model 276
scoring 13, 25–31, 33, 75, 152, 241, 242–272, 273, 274, 275, 333–335, 339, 340, 402

Vantage level 11, 16, 194, 208, 209, 263, 312, 313, 316
Variability
interlocutor 70–71, 152, 195, 275, 296–297
Verbal protocol analysis 164, 333
Video 25, 65, 66, 71, 74, 115, 143, 187–193, 207, 239, 196, 306, 326, 329, 337
Visuals 69, 130, 131, 139, 175, 187, 188, 338
Vocabulary
lists 185, 220, 224
VRIP (Validity, Reliability, Impact, Practicality) viii, 8, 9, 278, 279
VRIPQ viii, xiii, 278, 282, 336

W
Washback
positive 76, 297, 281, 289, 295
Waystage level 12, 209, 213, 220, 308, 316
Weighting 28, 153, 172, 182–184, 241, 262
Word recognition 86, 90, 97, 135, 212